ACADEMIC PATRONAGE IN THE SCOTTISH ENLIGHTENMENT

Academic Patronage in the Scottish Enlightenment

Glasgow, Edinburgh and St Andrews Universities

Roger L. Emerson

Edinburgh University Press

For
Fred Dreyer
Old friend, critic and remarkable man

© Roger L. Emerson, 2008

Edinburgh University Press Ltd
22 George Square, Edinburgh

Typeset in Adobe Sabon by
printed and bound by CPI Group (UK) Ltd,
Croydon, CR0 4YY

A CIP record for this book is available from the British Library

ISBN 978 0 7486 2596 3 (hardback)

The right of Roger L. Emerson to be identified as author of this work has been
asserted in accordance with the Copyright, Designs and Patents Act 1988.

Published with the financial support of The Strathmartine Trust.

CONTENTS

Preface   ix
A Note about the Text   xi
Abbreviations   xii

PART I   PRELIMINARIES

Chapter 1   Introduction   3
    1.   Patronage and The Enlightenment   3
    2.   The Data and Scope of the Study   4
    3.   Politics and University Patronage   5
    4.   The Processes of Appointment   11
    5.   Other Aims of this Book   13

PART II   GLASGOW UNIVERSITY

Chapter 2   Glasgow University to 1701   21
    1.   The Structures of Patronage at Glasgow
       University   21
    2.   The Purge of 1690 and the Revolution
       Settlement to 1692   26
    3.   Appointments, 1692–1701   34
Chapter 3   Principal Stirling's Regime: Family and Politics,
1701–1725   43
    1.   The Political Environment   43
    2.   John Stirling and the Expansion of the
       University, 1701–1714   49
    3.   The Decline of Principal Stirling,
       1714–1725   60
Chapter 4   Glasgow under the Campbells, 1725–1742   84
    1.   Ilay's Visitation and the End of the Stirling
       Regime, 1725–1727   84
    2.   The Regime of the Campbells, 1727–1742   89

Chapter 5   Squadrone Glasgow and the Return of the
             Duke of Argyll, 1742–1761   107
             1.   Squadrone Glasgow   107
             2.   Glasgow after the '45   115
             3.   Argyll's Return to Power   119
             4.   Argyll, Greatest of Patrons   140
Chapter 6   The Age of Bute and the Moderates   150
             1.   The Age of Merit?   150
             2.   Catch as Catch Can   156
             3.   Other Glasgow Appointments Made by the
                  Masters   160
Chapter 7   Glasgow University in the Age of Dundas   178
             1.   'Harry the Ninth'   178
             2.   Dundas's Glasgow Before the French
                  Revolution   181
             3.   Glasgow Appointments During the French
                  Revolution   186
             4.   Conclusion   201

PART III   EDINBURGH UNIVERSITY

Chapter 8   Edinburgh University to 1704   211
             1.   Introduction   211
             2.   The Revolution Settlement   213
Chapter 9   Edinburgh Appointments in the Faculty of
             Divinity   231
             1.   The Principals   231
             2.   Divinity Professors   236
             3.   Ecclesiastical History   239
             4.   Oriental Languages   243
Chapter 10   Chairs of Interest to Lawyers   252
             1.   Humanity   252
             2.   Universal and Civil History and Roman
                  Antiquities   255
             3.   The Law Chairs   260
             4.   Public Law   260
             5.   Civil Law   263
             6.   Scots Law   264
Chapter 11   Surgical and Medical Chairs   273
             1.   Introduction   273
             2.   Botany and *Materia Medica*   273

3.	Anatomy	279
4.	Surgery, Clinical Surgery and Military Surgery	286
5.	Chemistry to 1726	288
6.	The Founding of a Medical School	290
7.	Midwifery	298
8.	Chemistry after 1726	300
9.	The Institutes or Theory of Medicine	302
10.	The Practice of Medicine	304
11.	Natural History	306
12.	The Chair of Agriculture	309

Chapter 12 The Arts Chairs   325

1.	Mathematics	325
2.	Astronomy	334
3.	Greek	334
4.	The Regents, 1695–1707	336
5.	Logic and Metaphysics	338
6.	Moral Philosophy	339
7.	Natural Philosophy	346
8.	Rhetoric and *Belles Lettres*	349
9.	Conclusion	350

PART IV   ST ANDREWS UNIVERSITY

Chapter 13 The Arts Chairs, 1690–c. 1715   367

1.	The Uniqueness of the Place and Its Institutions	367
2.	The Purge of 1690 and the Revolution Settlement	374
3.	The First Principals	376
4.	Other Appointments at St Salvator's and St Leonard's Colleges, 1691–c. 1693	378
5.	College Appointments to 1716	381
6.	The Mathematics Professorship, 1690–1708	391
7.	So?	394

Chapter 14 St Mary's College and Other Appointments, 1713–1747   406

1.	St Mary's Appointments, 1693–1713	406
2.	The '15 and After	414

	3.	Appointments in the Arts Colleges, 1714–1739	419
	4.	St Mary's College, 1720–1747	421
Chapter 15		The Untold Story	441
	1.	Aspirations and Disappointments	441
	2.	Signs of Crisis	448
	3.	The Union of the Arts Colleges in 1747	450
Chapter 16		Thomas Tullideph's St Andrews, 1747–1777	459
	1.	The Making of a 'Usurping Tyrant'	459
	2.	The Tullideph Regime	466
Chapter 17		The Dundas Era at St Andrews, 1780–1806	491
	1.	Gaining Control	491
	2.	Dundas as Patron	495
	3.	A Summing Up	507

PART V   CONCLUSIONS

Chapter 18		Summaries and Results	523
	1.	Appointments: Politics, Processes and Constraints	523
	2.	The Managers	536
	3.	The People Appointed by the Patrons and What They Did	541
	4.	Scotland and Europe	547

Bibliography		555
Appendix 1:	Estimated Values of the Chairs in the Scottish Universities for the 1690s, 1725, 1760, 1795	591
Appendix 2:	Average Total Incomes of the Professors from All Sources by Faculty	615
Index of Names		619
Index of Subjects		633

PREFACE

Over many years, I have become indebted to a host of scholars for references and information which has enriched this book. Among the most notable contributors have been: Mr Jack Baldwin, Dr Michael Barfoot, Dr David Brown, Dr Iain Gordon Brown, Professor James H. Burns, Professor John Cairns, Dr Tristram Clarke, Dr Andrew Cunningham, Professor Gordon DesBrisay, Dr Michel Faure, Dr Vicenzo Merolle, Dr Esther Mijers, Mrs Helen Rawson, Professor David Raynor, Professor Ian S. Ross, Dr Anne Skoczylas, Professor Richard B. Sher, Professor M. A. Stewart, Professor David B. Wilson and Professor Paul Wood. I thank them all. I am also indebted to many librarians and archivists at: the Scottish National Archives, the National Library of Scotland, The Royal College of Physicians, Edinburgh, the Lothian Medical Archive, the Royal Botanic Garden, Edinburgh; the Universities of Aberdeen, St Andrews, Edinburgh, Glasgow, Strathclyde, Guelph University and the University of Western Ontario; the Aberdeen and Edinburgh City Archives; the Edinburgh Public Library; The Royal College of Physicians and Surgeons, Glasgow, The Faculty of Procurators of Glasgow, The Mitchell Library; the Aberdeen Town Council Archives. In England I am also indebted to the Librarians and Keepers of manuscripts at the British Library, Dr Williams's Library and Nottingham University Library. I thank them all for allowing me to quote from manuscripts in their keeping.

I also thank for allowing me the privilege of working with their papers the present and last Marquises of Bute, the Marquis of Linlithgow, the representatives of the Earls of Seafield, the late Sir John and Sir Robert Clerk of Penicuik, Bts, and the Stirlings of Keir. Without their help and goodwill, this work could not have been produced. To all the holders of copyright materials, who have allowed me to quote from their manuscripts, I am deeply grateful.

I also am happy to acknowledge Oxford University Press's kind permission allowing me to reprint some of an article, 'The Founding of the Edinburgh Medical School: The Real Story', which appeared in the *Journal of the History of Medicine and Allied Science*, 59 (2004), pp. 183–218. Vincent Gray and Elizabeth Hill of the Social Science Computing Laboratory of the University of Western Ontario have been more than helpful. They dealt with many problems and salvaged a large portion of this text when computer problems seemed to have ruined it.

I am especially indebted and grateful to Michael Barfoot, David Brown, Frederick Dreyer, Anne Skoczylas, Mr Robert Smart, Mark Spencer and Paul Wood. They have all commented on drafts or sections of drafts of this book. Fred will not think I have taken much advice but I am grateful to him for his help on this and other projects. I know of no better person with whom to disagree.

Finally, without the generous subsidy towards the costs of publication awarded by the Strathmartine Trust, Sandeman Award Fund, this book would not have appeared. I was delighted to receive the award and will always be grateful to the Trustees for their support for this project.

A NOTE ABOUT THE TEXT

All spellings are as they appear in the manuscripts quoted. Some quotations have been given punctuation to replace spaces in the manuscript text. The citation of sources uses a short title with a full title given in the bibliography. Notes give the pages of the article cited and are often followed by a ', p –'. giving the particular pages of interest. Not all individual items in larger collections have been separately noticed with a title in the bibliography; neither have some single manuscripts which are given headings and titles in the notes. They are simply too numerous but all the manuscript numbers have been given in the text and bibliography. All the dates begin the year at 1 January, as the Scots had done since 1600, and otherwise conform to the calendars in use in Britain – the Julian to 1752 and the Gregorian thereafter.

ABBREVIATIONS

APS	Acts of the Parliament of Scotland
ATCA	Aberdeen Town Council Archive
AUL	Aberdeen University Library
DAB	*Dictionary of American Biography*
DSB	*Dictionary of Scientific Biography*
DSCHT	Dictionary of Scottish Church History and Theology
EUL	Edinburgh University Library
GUA	Glasgow University Archives
GUL	Glasgow University Library
HMC	Historical Manuscripts Commission
LRCPE	Library of the Royal College of Physicians, Edinburgh
LRCP&SG	Library of the Royal College of Physicians and Surgeons, Glasgow
LRCSE	Library of the Royal College of Surgeons, Edinburgh
NAS	National Archives of Scotland
NLS	National Library of Scotland
ODNB	*Oxford Dictionary of National Biography*
PCS	Principal Clerk of Session
RCSL	Royal College of Surgeons, London
RSE	Royal Society of Edinburgh
SAUL	St Andrews University Library
SCJ	Senator of the College of Justice
USA	University of Strathclyde Archives
USL	University of Strathclyde Library

Part I

Preliminaries

1

INTRODUCTION

❧

1. Patronage and The Enlightenment

Accounts of enlightenments deal too much with ideas while ignoring improvements and those who made them. We read about thinkers and artists who are said to have made or contributed to enlightenments but our accounts exclude too much of the social context and too many of those who shaped it. We particularly lack accounts of the patrons who made successful careers possible and who found it in their interests to further the work of improvers and the enlightened. One can read classic studies of the European Enlightenment, such as Ernst Cassirer's *The Philosophy of the Enlightenment* (1932), and find little context and no patrons at all. One would have thought the situation might have changed but mentions of patrons are almost equally absent from recent, trendy textbooks by Dorinda Outram and Roy Porter and not only because these are slight publications.[1] Outram's book covers fashionable topics – salons and the public sphere – but patronage is not on her list. Porter's larger book on the British Enlightenment is so lacking in a concern for context that it does not even see the need to treat Scotland as a separate place or the Scottish Enlightenment as a development with a character of its own. Even studies of the Scottish Enlightenment such as Nicholas Phillipson's now dated but still much quoted essay, 'Culture and Society in the 18th Century', pay little attention to academic patronage.[2] Few would today see the Scottish Enlightenment as almost wholly an Edinburgh creation and fewer should agree with Phillipson's view of it as the ideological creation of a local aristocracy and a dependent *literati* eager to find a way of asserting their importance in a kingdom becoming a province. He seldom asks who helped either group to make the changes it considered good or asks about the origins of ideas and practices in the period preceding the one which concerns him.

Surely, when dealing with any set of intellectuals, and especially those working in an aristocratically structured society, one ought to ask who put in their places the men and women who had expressed and institutionalised novel ideas in that society. Why were they patronised? Who made it possible for their ideas to be acted upon? This monograph tries to answer some of those questions with respect to Scotland during the period 1690 to 1806, from the settlement of the country in the aftermath of the 1688 revolution to the end of the reign of 'Harry IX' – Henry Dundas (1742–1811). Dundas lost power when he was impeached in 1806. It offers an account of the political context in which the Scottish Enlightenment developed, flourished and then began to wind down. Scottish politics in the period revolved around the management of Scottish society through patronage. This study focuses on patronage in one set of institutions essential to the articulation of the Scottish Enlightenment – the universities.

2. THE DATA AND SCOPE OF THE STUDY

There were 388 men appointed to teaching positions in the Scottish universities, of whom 108 held places in the Aberdeen universities. In an earlier book, I discussed those men.[3] Here I consider the 280 men who held university teaching positions in the three southern Scottish universities of Glasgow, Edinburgh and St Andrews after the purge of 1690.[4] Aberdeen had two universities: King's College and University and Marischal College and University, in the Old and New Towns respectively. The appointees of the five universities collectively held at least 494 places. Competing for university places were at least 212 other men – of whom the names of 130, often only surnames, are known. One should not think that 212 is the total number of other contenders. One commentator on a contest for an Edinburgh professorship noted there were 'numberless others' who also sought the job he wanted. That was particularly so after c. 1740 at Edinburgh and Glasgow but less often the case at other colleges. It is not clear how many would-be academics there were. Perhaps there were enough to make three contenders for every post which paid well and at least two for most others. Ultimately only 98 men, who are known to have sought places, were disappointed. Some of the latter may in the end have found teaching posts in other institutions.[5]

By looking in detail at placements and patrons, this study seeks to show how politics worked to shape the universities during this period. Politics pervaded life. In general, the patrons who filled university chairs filled most of the other livings in Scotland's public offices and semi-public corporations. Looking at the universities is a way of seeing who counted in the politics of Scotland and at what they sought to promote during a period in which the kingdom became one of the centres of European thought.

The data for this study have been assembled over many years in a somewhat random fashion with no comprehensive book-length study in mind. I was initially interested in the universities more for what individuals taught than for how they came to teach it. One result of that is that much of what follows was unsystematically researched and is, unfortunately, often incomplete. I have not worked systematically in the archives of the burgh of Edinburgh. That would certainly yield more materials useful for this account.[6] I have not worked in English archives. What I have done, for almost thirty years, is to note down items which concerned the Scottish professors, including the ways in which they came to hold their jobs. Unfortunately, many negotiations for positions were not put on paper but were the stuff of conversations and face-to-face meetings in Edinburgh, Glasgow, St Andrews, Aberdeen or London. Those dealings left little record but were a large part of the story, a part not now recoverable. Other things have been lost or exist in manuscripts deposited in places I have not visited. To list their likely locations is to point to other short-comings of this study. Some libraries in Scotland, such as The Mitchell Library in Glasgow, have not been much consulted. Access to the archive of the Campbells of Argyll, which might possibly have added something to this study and to every other topic in Scottish history during the period covered here, was denied. That archive has too long been closed to scholars; no one knows what it may contain – much, or nothing more than what has been published from it.[7]

Some conclusions from my researches have been previously published but in those publications there has been little attention given to the patronage of *all* the chairs during the period surveyed.[8] Here I have tried to do that for the three universities I have not previously discussed in print. Part of my intention is to show how different the three were and how their professoriates differed as a consequence. I hope others will find this work relevant to the study of enlightenments not only in Scotland but elsewhere.

3. POLITICS AND UNIVERSITY PATRONAGE

University patronage reflected the politics of parliamentary representation and the struggles among factions for control of government influence and power in Scotland. It consequently followed the shifts in parliamentary representation in Scotland and offers sure signs of who mattered when and who did not. University appointments can be used to chart the politics of eighteenth-century Scotland. Men in all the Scottish political factions, in both the state and Kirk, had interests in keeping the universities ideologically sound. For that reason alone, the colleges were intently watched by politicians in both Scotland and London. Scots managed the colleges partly through visitations, grants and favours but mostly through appointments. Since those appointments were for life and constituted a sort of property, they keenly interested politicians eager not to make choices which would impair their ability to control the corporations and some of the local patronage the masters exercised. The patronage of the universities almost always served particular local patrons connected with politicians who mattered nationally. The only exceptions were at the arts colleges at St Andrews and King's College which were sometimes controlled by academic families. Those places were also often not worth the bother of an important politician.[9] The major political patrons exercised the Crown's legal rights to fill regius chairs but their recommendations to the legal patrons of *all* chairs carried so much weight that, in effect, they negotiated over most appointments and helped to fill a majority of the college chairs during this period. One can follow the fortunes of the Scottish political factions by looking at the chief dispensers of university patronage and in that activity one can see the methods and goals they tended to pursue more generally.

Throughout the early part of this period, those seeking to control the country were organised into loose and changing political factions led initially by great magnates such as the Dukes of Queensberry, Hamilton, Argyll and Montrose. Religious and political principles mattered to those men but factional concerns probably counted for more. By the end of the century, a lawyer like Henry Dundas, who lacked the fortune and social standing of those whom he succeeded but who controlled a 'machine', came to dominate the processes of appointment in a period when religious and political orthodoxy had again become of urgent importance.

In the period 1690–1715, there was no dominant party but a shifting set of coalitions which led to many men being active in seeking and getting chairs for their friends and dependents. Between 1705 and 1714, John Erskine, 11th Earl of Mar (1675–1732), was for some of those years one of the Secretaries of State and served as the front man and broker for shifting coalitions. Mar counted for much from the accession of Anne in 1702 until her death in 1714, when he was ousted from power by George I. After that he headed a Jacobite Party which was always active but whose members had little chance of obtaining jobs for themselves or their followers.[10]

From c. 1705 to 1755, the most important of the competing factional groups were the Squadrone and the Argathelians.[11] After a sharp struggle in 1715–16, the Squadrone party was entrusted with the disposal of most government patronage in Scotland until c. 1723. That was reflected in the distribution of university chairs at Glasgow and St Andrews, and at the Aberdeen colleges which were purged after the '15. The principal rivals of the Squadrone were led by John Campbell, 2nd Duke of Argyll (1680–1743), and his brother, Archibald, Earl of Ilay, who in 1743 became the 3rd Duke of Argyll (1682–6 April 1761). The Argathelians held a prominent place in Scottish public life for a short time after the '15, in which the Campbell brothers had distinguished themselves. However, they quickly lost their edge and did not play great roles again until after the elections of 1722. What solidified their position, both in London and Scotland, were ministerial changes which gave the Campbell brothers the confidence of Charles, 2nd Viscount Townshend (1674–1738), and Sir Robert Walpole (1676–1745). For that to happen, Charles Spencer, 3rd Earl of Sunderland (1674–1722), and John Carteret, later 1st Earl of Granville (1690–1763), and their friend, John Ker, 1st Duke of Roxburghe (?–1741), had to leave the ministry. All three had done so by the end of 1725.[12] Argyll and his brother Ilay then came to dominate Scottish politics. By the end of that decade, Ilay, his faction's chief manager, was doling out many places, although he never gained exclusive control of all Crown patronage. That eluded him but his hold on Scotland was tight from c. 1725 until his death in 1761, with the exception of the years 1742 to 1747.[13]

Ilay's emergence as a trusted manager in 1725 depended on his ability to control the country in the aftermath of the Malt Tax Riots, disturbances which Sir Robert Walpole's government could not tolerate. In Ilay, Walpole found a Scot who could be relied upon to act sensibly and to use for the government his family's political weight in the Western and Highland areas. It mattered that Ilay, unlike the Squadrone men, generally got on with Jacobites and was sensitive to the reasons for their discontent. Although often accused of being a Jacobite, he probably never deviated much, or long, from his family's long-standing Whiggism.[14]

Both the Squadrone lords and Ilay constructed efficient political machines which sent information and nominations from Scotland to

London and then implemented the decisions taken by the principal managers and the ministry.[15] Ilay's principal Edinburgh assistant was his relative, Andrew Fletcher, Lord Milton, SCJ (1692–1766). Their machine was inherited by Ilay's nephew, John Stuart, 3rd Earl of Bute (1713–92) who, with his brother, James Stuart Mackenzie (c. 1719–1800), managed Scottish patronage for a few years – Bute from 1761 to 1763; Stuart Mackenzie, roughly from 1763 until 1765. The instability of governments in London after those years was reflected by the awarding of university jobs in Scotland to men backed by a variety of patrons who owed no fast allegiance to any particular faction among those who formed the kaleidoscopic ministries in London which ended only in the mid or late 1770s. Disorder in London allowed groups like the Scottish *literati* and their friends, the Moderate Party ministers in the Kirk, to exercise more influence on appointments than had been possible for comparable groups earlier in the century. That period ended c. 1778 when Henry Dundas put together another political machine which was more efficient and popular than had been the one run by the Argathelians.

From time to time, opponents of the government managers could and did successfully push their opposition in the universities. Men in the universities with family or local interests sometimes showed the politicians that they counted and were not ciphers. Politicians negotiated with professors but the former could usually determine appointments if they were set on doing so. Still, others were not always subservient to the interests of vote-seeking politicians with eyes only on Westminster. Among them were clerics and members of corporations who had clear ideas about who should be appointed. One should also not infer that the filling of chairs was done with only parliamentary political goals in mind.[16]

Appointments reflected the interests of patrons but those interests included many things about which Parliament and its leaders never cared a toss and which figured only marginally in local elections. Sometimes those were related private family interests. The Kennedys of Cassillis took care of old tutors by appointing them to the humanity or Latin chair which the Kennedys controlled at St Andrews. Appointments might also serve the particular interests of patrons quite directly, as did the establishment of the Edinburgh and Marischal College chairs of agriculture in 1790. Both were founded by enthusiasts for agricultural improvements. When Ilay appointed medical men, chemists or astronomers, he was looking after his own intellectual interests and seeing that they were served by men in Scotland who could work for him and his friends as well as teach subjects which excited him as an amateur medical man and 'scientist'. Many other appointments were made to support local interests in the university or the town in which it was situated. Some of those were religious in nature. Still, all who were appointed had to fit broad patterns of belief and behaviour which would not imperil the political position in Scotland of a legal or a *de facto* patron. That applied to other British institutions and was generally the case in other countries.

University appointments offer a glimpse of the *Scottish* political life which was possible in the Kingdom after the Union, a politics still controlled by Scots. It was not just about jobs but also about the direction to be taken by the culture which Scots supported and developed. Posts were given to particular people for reasons having to do with utility, politeness or a vision of what the country should become as it changed from a greatly depressed and backward agrarian region in 1690 to one which by 1806 was not only thriving but had an agricultural sector which in parts of the Lowlands was as good as any elsewhere. By then, Scots possessed two of the best medical schools in Europe and some of its most advanced factories. One could appoint a man to a medical chair but to favour those trained in Leiden, and not in England, was a decision which affected the development of Scottish culture and kept it distinct in a United Kingdom where distinctions were being rubbed smooth and institutions made more alike. That was also true of appointments made to scientific chairs. Favouring the Moderate Party in the Kirk with divinity appointments changed the nature of the Kirk and, in the long run, altered the social outlook of the country. Scots might be united with the English but they controlled their educational institutions and used them for purposes they defined. Those definitions depended on particular patrons and their personal interests. When Mar, Argyll or Bute appointed mathematicians or medical men, chemists or astronomers, they were looking after their own intellectual and, sometimes, material interests. They tended to appoint men who could work for them and teach well subjects about which they were enthusiastic. When Henry Dundas appointed his friends to chairs, he was giving a sanction to a certain kind of literary man and a particular view of Scotland which he shared and promoted by other appointments in the civil administration, the courts and the Kirk. University appointments, like others, constituted a species of patronage with important cultural dimensions. The long-run effects of the appointments conferred by the Scottish politicians made Scotland a distinctive place. The brilliance of the eighteenth-century universities was not wholly the unintended result of decisions made for political reasons. Eighteenth-century Scots were lucky in their patrons.

Those who dispensed patronage in the eighteenth century gave the country its medical schools, good science training and the moral and social philosophy which taught boys their duties in a world growing more complex and commercial. It fitted men to go out to govern an empire and even to speak or read some of its essential languages such as Persian and Arabic. Scots used their universities to make themselves more prosperous and exportable. Patrons, like James Graham, 1st Duke of Montrose (?– 1742), or John Hay, 4th Marquis of Tweeddale (?–1762), or their rival, the Earl of Ilay, were willing, sometimes eager, to make the colleges and universities serve such ends. Over the many years in which such men made appointments, the colleges came to be increasingly secular in outlook, committed to utilitarian ends and to the education of boys who could thrive both in and out of Scotland. That achievement was a Scottish one and little concerned Englishmen in London who only in the nineteenth century would seriously inter- fere in the Scottish universities.[17]

Scotland's history in this period was more influenced by these patrons than is often realised. Both Lord Ilay and Henry Dundas appointed many professors, and many more men to other bodies in the kingdom. One of Ilay's obituaries spoke of the 54,000 jobs he had handed out over a career of fifty-five years. One need not believe the figure but one must recognise that his appointments ran into the thou- sands and that his patronage was exercised over more than the forty- year period during which he had considerable power.[18] Ilay helped into the universities Frances Hutcheson, William Cullen, John Anderson, Joseph Black, Adam Smith, Adam Ferguson, Robert Watson, William Wilkie, George Campbell and many others. Through his appointments, Ilay had an impact on Scottish culture greater than that of any other single man between 1725 and the end of the period covered by this study. He did so without ever holding the positions which entitled men to exercise the influence he exerted.[19] His influence was in a sense pro- longed by his nephews, the 3rd Earl of Bute and his brother, James Stuart Mackenzie. They inherited his political machine and continued to make distinguished appointments until c. 1766. Their appointees included John Millar, Hugh Blair, William Robertson, John Hope and at least six other professors. Those members of the extended Campbell family all had an agenda of their own as well as a desire and need to serve the ministries in London to which they belonged. Their agenda can be seen in the extension of medical and scientific teaching, in the founding of a rhetoric chair at Edinburgh, and in the cultivation of Moderate clergymen which changed the Kirk and made Scotland a more tolerant place.

Henry Dundas so dominated Scottish politics c. 1780–1806 that he could remark in 1801, 'Every professor in the universities of St Andrews and Edinburgh has been appointed for more than 20 years either actually by myself or upon my recommendation, and I take the satisfaction to reflect that in not one instance have I been mistaken.'[20] He could have said the same thing of most appointments made at Glasgow after 1790 and about all appointments made from the late 1790s to 1805. By the 1790s, Dundas was using his university appointments to inculcate political conformity and loyalty to the Crown in an age of revolutions which he hated and feared. Dundas was not as enlightened a man as the 3rd Duke of Argyll, but his record was one which initially contributed to the development of the Enlightenment and then to its end in Scotland. Even as late as 1830, about a quarter of the sitting professors had been appointed by him and more by the members of his faction who continued in power beyond his time.

Patronage mattered. Looking at an extended example of it in the universities sheds light on all the areas in which those patrons were active. Their clerical, legal and other civil appointments were of men not so different from the professors. Appointments outside the universities usually had the same ends in view, often considered men from the same families or family interest groups, and were designed to institutionalise the same beliefs or values. In general, the men who filled the university chairs were like those who filled most of the other livings in Scottish public and semi-public offices and corporations.

4. THE PROCESSES OF APPOINTMENT

What was true of patronage patterns in one university cannot simply be generalised to all of the others. They all had unique structures which caused their patronage to be differently exercised and manipulated. King's College or the Colleges of St Leonard and St Salvator were often so dominated by professorial family groups or the protégés of private patrons that contests for their chairs were not numerous. At St Mary's College, where all the livings were Crown creations, and were controlled by politicians, competitions depended much on who was in power and the importance of the chair. Divinity chairs were usually contested but the chairs of ecclesiastical history and Hebrew, the first a virtual sinecure for some periods and the second generally poorly paid, were not so actively sought. At Glasgow, where the masters were in charge – but usually deferred to their betters – chairs were contested at least half the time. Despite Edinburgh's attractiveness as a place to live, its places seem not to have been so sought after as were those in Glasgow. Edinburgh's rate of contestation (43 per cent) was lower than Glasgow's.[21] There eligible local men probably had fewer opportunities to use their educations while in the capital more major politicians were involved with appointments. That acted as a discouragement to those with few political friends among the great.

In each university, the professors almost always came to office after two sets of men had been consulted. The first were the legal patrons who held the right to appoint to the chair. They varied from place to place. At Glasgow, most of the chairs were in the gift of the College masters or the members of the University – the masters and professors afforced by the rector and the dean of faculty – who had the right to make appointments. The positions which they did not fill were filled by the Crown, the only other patron with legal appointment rights in the University. From time to time the Town Council used its political weight or its legal interests in bursaries and the College library to try to get its way but it was not a serious factor in university placements at Glasgow. Chairs were generally filled by men who had no legal rights to appoint but who had national influence. Their recommendations to the masters were almost invariably taken. At St Mary's College in St Andrews, all the livings were regius chairs filled by the Crown; college men and locals had little influence on appointments there. The Crown installed men who would be useful to the politicians then in power while paying a decent regard to orthodoxy, merit and to the interests of those who acted for the King. In the St Andrews arts colleges, two chairs were filled by private patrons while the masters appointed to the rest, save for mathematics which was a regius chair. Because the masters tended to promote men already on the staff, that often left the private patrons to fill again the poorest paid of the chairs. In the end, many of the teachers at St Andrews, until after the union of the colleges in 1747, were men whom the private patrons at each of the arts colleges had initially appointed. The private patrons rewarded old tutors and clerics just as they sometimes looked after those of their friends. Merit was not consistently high on their list of qualities needed by appointees. The other chairs in that University were filled by the masters, who tended to look after their own families and friends.

At Edinburgh the situation was much more complex. The Town Council was the legal patron to most chairs, with the Crown naming to others. At the end of the period there was one chair which had been privately endowed and specially filled. However, bodies such as the Incorporation of Surgeons, the Royal College of Physicians, the lawyers, acting collectively in the Faculty of Advocates, the Society of Writers to the Signet or as the judges of the sovereign courts, also influenced many decisions. So too did clerics who everywhere asserted rights to pass on the orthodoxy of the men appointed. A legal right to appoint was never a guarantee that the legal patron would in fact choose the person appointed, only that he would in the end sign the necessary appointment papers. The 'men of power' called most of the shots.

5. Other Aims of this Book

In an earlier study of the Aberdeen universities, I set out a description of the Scottish professoriate up to 1800. The statistics given in my earlier book are not substantially changed by extending the time through 1806.[22] I have not revised the figures given in that volume but I have added information about the professors. Each is listed with birth and death dates in the text when first mentioned. There is also more information about incomes which, in the past, have been underestimated.

The incomes of the professors have been re-calculated, as have actual minimum incomes for salaries in selected years. Some salaries varied from year to year because the price of meal fluctuated. It constituted a component of many salaries. Over time salaries rose. Minimal incomes depended on one's salary but total incomes were generally enhanced by fees, the possession of offices, income from land or rental properties and often by the boarding of students. It was total incomes which defined the prospects of a professor as much as did the salary he received. Total incomes have often been ignored and they have always been underestimated by those who have studied these universities. When it is said that the Scottish university men were poorly paid, one should quickly note that most made at least two or three times what clerics in the surrounding towns were paid and often, by the end of the period, as much as four or five times as much, even though average clerical stipends had risen a bit. In the case of some Edinburgh professors, the figure was over twenty times the average clerical salary in Scotland. Incomes were respectable but garnered from salaries and perquisites, from pensions and writing, from the keeping of students and from rents, consulting fees or the practice of law or medicine.

I have calculated incomes for the professors for given years using whatever I could find to do so. Those estimates may not be quite accurate but they cannot be far off the true figures. Sometimes they come from one or two years before or after the dates given. The kinds of education offered over the course of the century were partly determined by the incomes which the professors could expect. Well-paid men worked harder because they had to. While all of them received more than is sometimes realised, the hierarchy of total incomes placed the men at Edinburgh on top with Glasgow, Marischal College, St Andrews (after 1747) and King's College following in that order.[23] The best incomes attracted the best men and promotions or translations to other chairs are often partly explained by the differing salaries and the opportunities offered by the chairs to which men were translated.

This work also offers not only some account of the motives for the expansion of the colleges but a new account of the founding of the medical school at Edinburgh, one of the most important educational achievements of the period.[24]

While the book has miscellaneous information about the Scottish professors, it does not seek to say about them all that is known. There is much more information in the sources for university histories which are listed in the notes and bibliography and in many more which are not because they have nothing in particular to say about patronage. What I principally have tried to do is to study the patronage of the chairs, and to make the account of that as complete as I could make it. If that has been successful, it will serve as a guide to future university histories in Scotland, histories which need to be written since only Glasgow and Aberdeen have histories which are at all adequate.[25] It should also help us to see the origins of and the pressures to maintain the Scottish Enlightenment. Hierarchical, aristocratic societies, with scarcities and needs as great as those of eighteenth-century Europe, made patronage politics pervasive, but only exceptional patrons, such as Scotland had, made enlightenments not only possible but brilliant.

Notes

1 Outram, *The Enlightenment*, 1995; Porter, *The Enlightenment*, 1990. In Porter's *The Creation of the Modern World*, 2000 [The British edition is entitled *Enlightenment: Britain and the Creation of the Modern World*,

2000], patronage gets a few pages with much of the space being devoted to Dr Johnson and Lord Chesterfield. In Daniel Roche's account of the background to the French Enlightenment, *France in the Enlightenment*, 1998 [*La France des Lumières*, 1993], the Enlightenment is swamped in a hotchpotch of social analyses and factual details almost none of which deal with patronage, a subject not even warranting an entry in the index.

2 This is to be found in *The University in Society*, ed. Stone, 1974, II, 407–48. Phillipson's most recent pronouncement on the Scottish Enlightenment is 'Scottish Enlightenment', in *Encyclopedia of the Enlightenment*, 2 vols, ed. Michel Delon and translated by Fitzroy Dearborn et al. (Chicago and London, 2001); 2:1196–1200. There Phillipson tends to see the Scottish Enlightenment as rooted in responses to social changes and in university reforms designed principally by and for the clergy.

3 Emerson, *Professors, Patronage and Politics*, 1992. That study stopped in 1800; this one goes slightly longer.

4 There were sixteen men who taught at two places.

5 Among the disappointed were men who taught at the extramural medical school in Edinburgh (1), in London hospitals (3), at the Royal Military School at Woolwich (1) and at private academies (2).

6 Where the Edinburgh Town Council Minutes are cited, they are cited without a source from extracts which appear in the D. B. Horn Papers, EUL, Gen 1824 or from the appropriate volumes of *Extracts from the Records of the Burgh of Edinburgh*, ed. Armet, 1967.

7 That little of relevance exists in Inveraray is made likely by remarks in the *Fourth Report of the Royal Commission on Historical Manuscripts*, 1874, p. 442f. There the editors commented that the manuscripts had been carelessly kept and much hurt by damp, particularly those dating from c. 1740. The papers of Lord Ilay, the 3rd Duke of Argyll, were probably never there. He had no legitimate children and his papers seem to have gone to his natural son, General William Williams Campbell. The manuscripts seem to have been last used by William Coxe, the biographer of Sir Robert Walpole, in the 1790s.

8 For a list of those publications see the bibliography.

9 The chairs at Marischal College before 1715, with the exception of the divinity and mathematics chairs, were controlled by the Lord Marischal. In 1716 his interest was confiscated by the Crown and appointments were made by the leading Scottish managers for the ministry in London. King's College was purged at the same time and new men imposed by Squadrone politicians.

10 The best recent account of the Jacobites is Szechi, *1715 The Great Jacobite Rebellion*, 2006.

11 The Squadrone were led by the Dukes of Montrose and Roxburghe from c. 1713 to 1730 and by the Marquis of Tweeddale from 1740 to 1746,

but others among their numerous aristocratic relatives and dependants also played roles. The Argathelians were the party of the 2nd and 3rd Campbell Dukes of Argyll (c. 1704–61). For the best short accounts of them see: Shaw, *The Political History of Eighteenth-Century Scotland*, 1999 and his *The Management of Scottish Society 1707–1764*, 1983; Murdoch, *'The People Above'*, 1980; Scott, 'The Politics and Administration of Scotland 1725–1748', unpublished PhD dissertation, 1982; Wehrli, 'Scottish Politics in the Age of Walpole', unpublished PhD. dissertation, 1983; Sunter, *Patronage and Politics*, 1986; more useful information about patronage and related matters is contained in Whetstone, *Scottish County Government*, 1981.

12   Plumb, *Sir Robert Walpole*, 1960, p. 105ff.

13   This has been disputed by Andrew MacKillop in *'More Fruitful than the Soil'* (2000). MacKillop uses Ilay's military patronage as a gauge of his overall power in Scotland, which leads him to underestimate the degree of control over Scottish life which the Duke actually exercised. Military patronage was not essentially Scottish and interested more men in London. In Scotland, the Duke's power was buttressed by his personal patronage and by the years of placing men in offices and livings. It grew with time.

14   Ilay and his brother, the 2nd Duke of Argyll, showed Jacobite sympathies when they were disaffected with the government in c. 1716–19. See the many letters of Fanny Oglethorpe to Lords Mar and Ilay in Vols II–VII of *Calendar of Stuart Papers belonging to His Majesty*, 1904–23. It is clear that both Mar and George Lockhart of Carnwath thought the Campbell brothers' professions of devotion to the Pretender insincere and not to be relied upon. Lockhart had grown up with the Campbell boys and knew them well. Lockhart to Mar, 28 March 1718, *Stuart Papers*, VI: 272–8 and *Letters of George Lockhart, Scottish History Society*, ed. Szechi, 1989, p. 127–36. This letter comes from what seems to have been the period of Ilay's maximum interest in the Jacobites. See also Szechi's *George Lockhart of Carnwath*, 2002.

15   The Squadrone 'machine' of the period 1715–24 is described in a 1741/2 letter from James Erskine, Lord Grange to John Hay, 4th Marquis of Tweeddale (1695–1762), Yester Papers, NLS, 7044/45–6.

16   This is often said, e.g. Sunter's review of *Professors, Patronage and Politics* in *Scottish Tradition*, 1995, p. 95, and Sunter's *Patronage and Politics*, 1986.

17   For a somewhat tendentious account of that, see Davie, *The Democratic Intellect*, 1964.

18   The writer was clearly guessing that over a career of about fifty-five years, Ilay had appointed 1,000 people a year. It is given some plausibility by the sheer number of letters about appointments addressed to Andrew Fletcher, Lord Milton, SCJ, in the Saltoun Correspondence held

at NLS. There are roughly 250 boxes of letters with, on average, over 100 letters in each. If each letter dealt with one place, then there were 25,000 appointments which Ilay and his aide sought to influence. In addition to those, Ilay handled in London some appointments with which Lord Milton was unconcerned, and others of a military nature, with which Milton also had little or nothing to do. Milton became Ilay's manager in 1724, twenty years after the Earl's political career had begun. 54,000 begins to look like a plausible estimate.

19 This struck one of his opponents who in 1742 wrote to Henry Home that Ilay had had the authority of the Secretaries of State for Scotland but had 'governed . . . in some Measure behind the Curtain', which he could do because of his 'Capacity, joined with his Influence at Court'; James Ogilvie, Lord Deskford to Home, 18 February 1742, NAS, Abercairny MSS, GD24/1/552/6.

20 Quoted by Michael Fry in *The Dundas Despotism*, 1992, p. 184.

21 Masters in the Scottish colleges were those who held voting and management rights under the initial charters and under charters which had been amended by Visitation Commissions and by Parliament to give these rights to new members of the corporation. There were no masters at Edinburgh because the Town Council retained financial control and the rights of ultimate oversight in every area of academic affairs. The rise of the *senatus* in the 1720s obscured this but did not eliminate the Town Council from university affairs. The teachers were overseen by a standing committee of the Council and by a bailie who presided over it.

22 There are now a few more sons of small landowners, artisans and ministers, a few more eldest sons and more men who are known to have studied abroad and married. However, these changes come to less than 3 per cent in most of the categories of the earlier tables. That must be well within the margin of error for averages such as these which are based on often less than certain evidence and where years have been rounded off. The medians, too, are virtually unchanged by adding new data for the men who entered the universities between 1800 and the end of 1806.

23 Incomes at St Andrews were about the same as those at King's until after the union of the arts colleges at St Andrews in 1747. See Appendix 1.

24 An earlier version of this account appears in 'The Founding of the Edinburgh Medical School', Emerson, 2004, pp. 183–218.

25 *The University of Edinburgh*, by Anderson, Lynch and Phillipson, 2003, is a public relations book only important for sections dealing with the nineteenth and twentieth centuries.

Part II

Glasgow University

2

GLASGOW UNIVERSITY TO 1701

⌒

1. THE STRUCTURES OF PATRONAGE AT GLASGOW UNIVERSITY

A study of patronage in an eighteenth-century university should begin with the legal structures that defined the corporations in which patronage was awarded. Knowing those is knowing how they could be manipulated and managed.

At Glasgow there were two chartered corporations: the College and the University of Glasgow. The University had as its chief officers the chancellor, rector and dean. The first, in Episcopal times, usually had been the Archbishop of Glasgow, whose powers were those assigned to the chancellor at Bologna.[1] Under the Presbyterians, in 1692, a chancellor was elected by the rector and the masters who lacked a clear warrant for this election. It would later be claimed by the Argathelians that the right to appoint a chancellor vested in the Crown but this argument was not pushed and did not prevail in 1692. Chancellors generally did so little and had so few powers that it was perhaps not worth contesting the election of men usually belonging to the group in power in Scotland. The chancellor elected in 1692 was John Carmichael, 2nd Baron Carmichael and later the 1st Earl of Hyndford (1638–1710), a layman with political clout, as were the three Dukes of Montrose who succeeded him in the eighteenth century. The chancellor or his appointed vice-chancellor (usually the principal), admitted graduates to degrees, admitted new members to the University, and was the usual transmitter of letters from the University and College to the Crown and its ministers. In the eighteenth century, he often conveyed to them the professors' suggestions about who might be picked to serve in regius chairs. Chancellors had influence not because of their University place but because they were noblemen with large incomes and many friends. Men like Carmichael or the Montroses could and did get dependants placed in the University and College. They were useful but mainly ornamental.

The chancellors in this period were local noblemen such as the Dukes of Montrose. When their friends such as the Squadrone leaders or later Henry Dundas were in power, the chancellor could aid them. When they were out of power, they could be and often were obstructive in the interest of their faction. A chancellor might ignore the masters and their requests or refuse to transmit nominations to the Crown for regius chairs. He usually had friends in the College and might maintain a faction to frustrate those who backed his political opponents.

The rector, the University's chief magistrate, was, after 1727, elected annually in a complicated process which came to involve all the members of the University. In the early part of our period, he sat for years on end with the annual elections only a formality in which the masters or charter members of the University and College had a vote. Eventually the rector came to be elected with student votes, generally for two one-year terms. The rector and his assessors (usually the principal and professors of his faction) had judicial functions which mattered. The rectorial court had initial jurisdictions over all civil and criminal cases involving a member of the University, a point which the town sometimes disputed. The rector was the head of the main University disciplinary court for students and heard the cases of masters appealing from disciplinary procedures initiated in the College. The rector also sat as an elector of some professors and sometimes assumed some administrative functions. He was one of the three visitors of the College named in the charters. Four times a year, the visitors were to audit accounts and to see that affairs were conducted in accordance with the charter and the rules which had changed as the charter had been amended by Royal and Parliamentary Visitation Commissions. In a College in which factions were often closely divided, it was important to have him on one's side both because of the votes he cast but also because of his legal jurisdiction. In the absence of the principal or dean, the rector sometimes presided over College Meetings, although the right to do so probably belonged not to him but to the senior regent of the College. The sphere of the rector's jurisdiction was contested throughout the century, as were those of the principal and dean.

A second visitor of the College created by the charter was the dean of faculty (or faculties) who was elected annually. His function as a visitor was to audit the accounts and see that rules were followed. He also had the right to vote in some elections of new members of the

College and participated in College business, often keeping a record in the 'Faculty Minutes', a set of books whose titles varied over time. With the principal and rector, he managed the monies of the University. The third visitor was the minister of Glasgow, the principal preacher at the cathedral, who sometimes held a professorial position as well.

In addition to those officials, the University included all the matriculated students and all who held appointments to positions mentioned in the often amended charter. The University Senate was composed of the rector, dean, principal, professors and masters. The function of the Senate was the election of new professors but not the professors and lecturers established and funded from the College revenues. Those men were chosen in the College Meeting, a body which sat under the principal and controlled all the property held by the College. The University as such had little or no property and did little but grant degrees and allow the rectorial court to function. Sometimes when the principal was incapacitated, the Senate acted in place of the College Meeting. It doing so, it overstepped its limits, notably under professor Leechman who functioned for many years as Vice-Rector during the long illness of principal Campbell in the 1750s and up to Campbell's death in 1761. Leechman did business in the body he could best control.

Glasgow was a university of one college. The College did all the arts teaching and was the most important part of the University. The College was a self-governing corporation composed of the principal and masters who, until 1727, were regents and thereafter were referred to as professors, except in some legal documents where they retained their technical designation of regents.[2] Also on the foundation were bursars and other students and some of the servants, but not the lecturers appointed by the College, who had only precarious positions. The principal was the College's most important figure. Nominally a professor of divinity, he spent most of his time administering the College. His deputy was the senior master or, in some circumstances, the professor of divinity. The principal and professors constituted a court competent to punish both students and professors for infractions of rules but most of the College Meeting's business concerned the administration of funds.

The way in which the University and College were supposed to be governed was nicely described by Thomas Reid (26 April 1710–7 October 1796) in the account of the University published in *The Statistical Account of Scotland*, edited by Sir John Sinclair and published in 1799. Reid had been clerk to the faculty and knew how things should have been run, although they were not always run as he describes:

> In Glasgow, the whole property and revenue pertaining to the University, is vested in the college, and is administered by a meeting of the Principal and Professors, commonly called *the College Meeting*, very often, though perhaps with less propriety, *the Faculty Meeting*. The record of this meeting is visited and authenticated by the Rector, Dean of Faculty, and the Minister of the High Church of Glasgow. Other business of the University, besides matters of revenue, and the discipline of the students, [principally appointments] is managed in what is called *an University Meeting* or *Senate*; in which the Rector and Dean of Faculty sit, along with the Principal and Professors. Indeed, besides the College, all that remains of the University is a Chancellor, Rector, and Dean . . . The Rector and Dean are chosen annually . . . the Rector always names the Principal and Professors to be his Assessors; and with them, occasionally forms a court of law, for judging in pecuniary questions, and less atrocious crimes wherein any member of the University was party. The University has always maintained its exemption from all jurisdiction of the City Magistrates, but not of the Sheriff or Court of Session.[3]

The various higher officers of the University all had some role to play in the recruitment of new members of the University or College. Chancellors could refuse to admit men to office or try to obstruct their election. Rectors voted for new men and then might, in some circumstances, hear cases related to the elections of professors, deans and bursars. Deans were electors to some posts and had a right to make representations about the keeping of the rules specified in the charter or made by past Royal and Parliamentary Visitations. Distinctions between the College Meeting and Senate were not always observed, particularly when the principal was incapacitated and it was convenient to manage affairs through the University Meeting. This led to challenges of some actions by those who lost in the votes taken at meetings. Most professors of divinity were elected by the Senate but eventually the Court of Session found that the right to elect to this office belonged only to the College Meeting which excluded the rector and dean. The complexity of the structures offered many ways in which the disgruntled might try to question and frustrate the ambitions or choices of others. With the exception of Edinburgh, the other colleges and universities were equally complex and subject to the same sorts of disputes about the power and rights of officers as Glasgow had throughout the century.

The Crown – really its Scottish political managers – had a hand in many appointments. Over the century politicians here and elsewhere recommended the appointment of an increasing number of men to university chairs funded by the Crown. This gave it an added interest in the institutions.[4] The bases for that interest were the regius chairs. In 1690 the Crown at Glasgow appointed only the principal; by 1806 it named the principal and professors of ecclesiastical history, law, anatomy and botany, medicine and astronomy. If a manager stayed long in power, he could build up a professorial clientele which was likely to do his bidding for a while after he had lost power. Usually the professors expressed an opinion about those appointments but they belonged to the Crown and it was thought somewhat improper to try to determine the nomination, although the College expected its choice to be considered by the politicians.

Glaswegian clergymen, before whose Presbytery all the new professors had to subscribe the Westminster Confession, could and did sometimes object to a man's signing the Confession. They, or others, sometimes made it difficult for an appointee to be translated from his church living to the University or to a kirk in the town. When clerics made trouble, they did so as much as political partisans as men of the cloth pursuing religious ends.

Unlike the other universities in this period, there were no teaching posts at Glasgow controlled by private patrons other than the College meeting. There was, however, much meddling by genteel outsiders in the selection of professors. It occurred because so many desired to place dependants and to further their, or someone's, political or cultural agenda. Most of those who interfered came from families which had long been connected to the College and, like the Dukes of Hamilton or the Mures of Caldwell, had endowed bursaries to which they might name holders and over which they still had some oversight. Some interference presumed future benefactions.

Professors themselves wanted the support of the politicians and gentlemen for reasons of their own. The College was partially funded by the Crown. It farmed or collected teines [tithes] for the Crown on former Bishop's lands in the area and needed the subsidies provided by the profits of this operation to maintain or expand its facilities. Most of the professors at one time or another sought patronage for relatives or friends. Most had children who needed something. The university men who sought to determine the choices for regius chairs were required to pay attention to the needs of those from whom they had to beg favours. Politicians on their side sought voices and votes in church courts to support their policies. They were not averse to having the university men help in the management of local politics. The consequence was that local managers and noblemen were as active in the university politics of Glasgow as they were in the capital or elsewhere.

The University also had places for influential outsiders. The greater gentry could be chancellors and rectors. Local ministers often served as deans of faculty and one was always a visitor. Those offices institutionalised outside influence, which it was often impossible to do in the St Andrews colleges or at King's College. Outside influences at Edinburgh came through the Town Council but at Glasgow through chancellor, rector and dean of faculty. At St Andrews and King's, the chancellors were usually absent and represented by professors serving as vices. During many years, rectors at King's were not elected. Glasgow's always had a chancellor and rector who were often resident in the area and the dean and minister of Glasgow always were. The university men all fitted into the politics of the burgh and region and helped to make Glasgow appointments mirror the ups and downs of party factions and the strains of Kirk politics. When compared to St Andrews, King's and Marischal, Glasgow probably experienced greater involvement in its affairs by the local nobility, by government managers and alumni and donors. It also tended to involve in its affairs men of more influence and power than were concerned with the other universities except for Edinburgh. The main outside players – the government's managers and those who opposed them – were mostly the same or the same kind of men at all the Scottish universities.

Having looked at the structures we should now turn to the appointments, taking them in chronological order because that shows just how dependent on political influences the Scottish universities were. All the universities were politicised; that politicisation formed an important but often unnoticed context for the development of the Scottish Enlightenment. Factional politics affected who was selected for a place, how this was done, and the culture which Scotland came to possess as a result of such appointments. That is most obvious in the placements made in the wake of the Revolution of 1688–90.

2. The Purge of 1690 and the Revolution Settlement to 1692

Purges occurred after every change of regime and indicated the Crown's and the politicians' determination to ensure that the schooling of boys and young men accorded with new views and was in the hands of friends of the new rulers. In 1690, all the grammar schools and the five universities were purged by a Parliamentary Visitation Commission eager to ensure that Episcopalian teachers, professors and masters, who might oppose the new Whig regime, were extruded and replaced by a corps of loyal teachers whose morals, Whiggism and Presbyterian commitments were beyond question.[5] The Commission was struck by Parliament on 4 July 1690 when about sixty men were named to sit on it.[6] Its chairman was William Lindsay, 18th Earl of Crawford.[7] Most of the members served only on the committees which visited the university in the region from which they came or sat in the general sessions of the Commission held in Edinburgh. Among the West of Scotland noblemen who could have sat in Glasgow were the 4th Duke of Hamilton, 10th Earl of Argyll, 1st Viscount Stair, 3rd Baron Cardross and 2nd Baron Carmichael – men who might be taken to represent Lanarkshire, Argyllshire, Ayrshire, Dumbartonshire and Renfrewshire.[8] Those who did sit included Lord Carmichael, Sir John Maxwell of Pollock, W[illiam] Cunningham of Craigends, Alexander Spittal, the laird of Leuchat, James Smollet of Bonhill, John Anderson of Dowhill (Provost of Glasgow), and the ministers Gabriel Cunningham, George Campbell and John Oliphant – 'all of them personnes of great Honour and Justice, as also great Moderation and temper'.[9] Their judgement on the professors they outed was remarkably charitable.

The Revolution Settlement deprived Glasgow of its chancellor, James Paterson, the Archbishop of Glasgow. Until a chancellor was elected in 1692, the effective heads of the corporations would be the rector and principal. In 1690 there seems to have been no rector, at least none was outed although the principal was. To maintain orthodoxy, the Visitors ordained that new appointees were to fulfil several conditions.[10] They were to accept the Presbyterian establishment of the Kirk and worship in it, subscribe the Westminster Confession of Faith as their own personal beliefs, swear oaths of allegiance to the King and of faithful conduct in their offices, live blamelessly and peaceably with others, and, finally, show that they were fit for scholarly employment. The latter was to be shown by comparative trials or competitive tests for the new professors and regents who were to fill the vacated places.[11] Formally these tests remained in effect throughout the period, although they effectively lapsed everywhere by the early 1700s.

The Glasgow Commissioners met first at Edinburgh toward the end of July and then sat in the 'high Common hall' at Glasgow to interrogate the principal and all the masters who were asked to give written replies to the Commissioners' interrogatories. On 24 September 1690, the university men were summoned to Edinburgh to appear before the whole Commission and asked about their written replies, particularly about the requirement that they take oaths to uphold the new government and the new ecclesiastical settlement. After examining all the masters, the Commissioners on 27 September 1690 deposed the principal, professor of divinity and two regents who would not swear.[12] Thomas Gordon (?–1702\3), a Jacobite regent and professor of oriental language, had resigned earlier.[13] This purge was remarkable only because the outed principal and those who went with him were thanked for their careful administration of the College and for the improvements they had made to it.

The regents who survived, John Boyd (?–1699) and John Tran (?–1704), were willing to conform to Presbyterianism, just as earlier they had accommodated themselves to the Episcopalian regime. They seem to have been men of some flexibility as well as learning.[14] A third man, George Sinclair (?–1699), had replaced Gordon but had not yet been installed. He was eager to conform since he had been forced out of the College in 1666 and had returned with the Revolution of 1688. While little is known of Tran and Boyd, Sinclair is well known. After a teaching career of twelve years, he had spent some time in self-imposed exile in Holland but he also served George Seton, 4th Earl of Winton, to whom he dedicated a book. Winton was an Episcopalian commander of troops used against Covenanters in 1666 and again in the late 1670s.[15] That Sinclair should have been friendly with such a patron shows an ability to tolerate creedal differences which was needed in the 1690s. The book he dedicated to the Earl argued, on empirical grounds, for believing in the existence of witches. It is not irrelevant to note that some of Sinclair's relatives had discovered and prosecuted witches in the 1680s during the last great outbreak of witchery in Scotland. But Sinclair was a modern virtuoso like Joseph Glanvill and Henry More, who also wrote similar works trying to give empirical evidence for a spirit world. Sinclair was also an engineer, to give him an anachronistic title. In 1691, he became the first to hold the professorship in mathematics, a post created by the College.

The new men who replaced those whom the Visitors outed are an interesting lot. The new chancellor, John Carmichael, 2nd Baron Carmichael and 1st Earl of Hyndford (1638–1710), had been the chairman of the Visitation committee sent to Glasgow. In 1690, he served as HM Commissioner, Lord Privy Seal and a member of the

Council. Carmichael was active in the Kirk but not bloody-minded. In the General Assembly of 1690, he famously read, to an Assembly bent on revenge, the royal agenda set out in a message with which he seems to have agreed:

> We expect that your management shall be such as we shall have no reason to repent of what we have done. A calm and peaceable procedure will be no less pleasing to us than it becometh you. We never could be of the mind that violence was suited to advancing of true religion; nor do we intend that our authority shall ever be a tool to the irregular passions of any party. Moderation is what religion enjoins, neighbouring Churches expect from, and we recommend to you.[16]

Carmichael continued to hold high office as Secretary of State from 1696 to 1702 and his services were rewarded with promotion to his earldom in 1701. He became an active advocate of the Union of the Kingdoms. He was probably responsible for bringing Gershom Carmichael to Glasgow. In 1694, he enabled another regent, James Knibloe, to leave his office by providing the money for the College (or Carmichael, Knibloe's successor) to buy him out.[17] Lord Carmichael intervened with London politicians in 1709 to establish the regius chair of oriental languages.[18]

Like unto the chancellor was the new rector, David Boyle of Kelburn, after 1703 1st Earl of Glasgow (1666–1733). Boyle had spent time in Dutch exile and was a friend of William Carstares, later principal of Edinburgh University. Like Lord Carmichael, he was an active politician important in Glasgow and in the West of Scotland. His politicking was carried on under the wing of the Duke of Queensberry and was rewarded with a place on the Council in 1698 and with his peerage. In 1707, his political and religious interests were acknowledged by his being made HM Commissioner to the General Assembly, a temporary but lucrative post. Rector for only one year, Boyle aided in the creation of a chair of humanity and endorsed the principal's efforts to improve the College.[19] Under such men as Carmichael and Boyle, the reformed university received aid and protection but also supervision.

The new principal, the reverend William Dunlop (1654–8 March 1700), was the son of a minister who had married the daughter of Mure of Glanderston, a family which had old ties to the university and one which would be involved in its affairs throughout the eighteenth century. Dunlop himself had wed the sister of the reverend Mr William Carstares (11 February 1649–28 December 1715), then Chaplain to

William III and already probably interested in reforming the universities.[20] Principal Dunlop, like Carstares, had been a sufferer under Episcopacy. Unable to preach legally, he had become a tutor to Lord Cochrane but also one of those who incited the rebellion which led Covenanters to Bothwell Bridge. By the early 1680s, Dunlop had emigrated to Carolina where he functioned both as a cleric and militia officer.[21] Like Carstares, also a revolutionary in his youth, Dunlop became a moderate man and one having wide interests. He wrote an antiquarian 'Account of Renfrewshire', supplied Sir Robert Sibbald with miscellaneous historical materials and bits on natural history, and sought the improvement of the kingdom. In the last endeavour he was not always successful; he invested some College funds in the Darien Company, of which he was a director.[22]

Dunlop, like Carstares, was a politician but of a more militant sort. His politics had been played out on the field, in exile, and more recently in the delation to Carstares of the Montgomery or 'The Club Plot', a 1690 scheme by Jacobites and others to extract more power for the Parliament and to hurt the Presbyterian interest in the Kirk.[23] His actions made him acceptable to the men brought to power by William III. Lord Crawford asked in a letter of 1 November 1690 to the Earl of Melville, HM Commissioner to Parliament, that Dunlop be appointed.[24] Henry Erskine, 3rd Baron Cardross (1650–1725), another returned exile who had been in Carolina, wrote to Melville on the same day making a similar request. Dunlop's reward for his constancy in their cause was the principalship of the University. This paid off a loyal supporter and gave the government assurance that the University would be in reliable hands. At the same time, men more rigid than himself saw the place going to one who had supported and suffered in their cause. His tenure was marked by an expansion of the College and by the improvement of its finances owing to his and William Carstares' success in agitating for increased subsidies.[25] Dunlop was influential in attempting to have the curriculum reformed and standardised texts printed and introduced in all the colleges – a plan which sounds sensible until one realises that it would have saddled the country with texts which would have been slow to change just when the novel ideas of Locke, Pufendorf and Newton were being introduced into the schools. Dunlop busied himself with church affairs and found his further reward in the office of Historiographer Royal of Scotland (1693).

Dunlop's new colleague as professor of divinity was James Wodrow (2 January 1637–25 September 1707). A strict Presbyterian from a genteel land-owning family, he had served as tutor to Alexander Stuart, Lord Blantyre and to the Duke of Hamilton. He also had ties to the Montgomerys, the family of the Earls of Eglinton. During the 1670s he had taught in grammar schools, during which time he too had suffered.[26] A conventicle preacher in 1679, he had been hunted. In 1688 he was teaching theology privately in Glasgow. By marriage, he was related to the Dunlops of Dunlop, the Maxwells of Pollock, various Stirlings and to the Stewarts of Blackhall, local landed families of influence who had intermarried.[27] Sir John Maxwell of Pollock was to be rector from 1691 to 1717. Wodrow married twice, both times to women from Glasgow merchant families. The principal and the politicians could trust him even though they might have found his teaching about when revolt against established authority was justified coming rather too close to them as well as hitting at the Jacobites.[28] His broader message was the primacy of the conscience rightly guided, a message that later men would use against subscriptions to creeds, for legal reforms and on behalf of other enlightened causes. He was also, like the principal, interested in natural history and had studied medicine and botany. Not surprisingly, he raised two sons who followed him in these interests – Robert, the well-known historian and virtuoso, and John, an MD who taught botany at his Glasgow botanical garden and was a candidate for Glasgow medical chairs.[29]

The other appointments that the Visitation Commission made were to regencies and to the chair of oriental languages which the College had founded and funded. The latter was filled by regent John Tran, who replaced Thomas Gordon as both regent and professor.[30] Tran got a slightly higher salary, perhaps as much as £64 (sterling) a year.[31] The new regents were chosen according the rule which mandated comparative trials for those who sought to fill vacancies. The first of those trials in Glasgow was a more or less public event with the Provost of Glasgow, the burgh's ministers, Maxwell of Pollock and other gentlemen invited to the disputations which were held over a fourteen-day period in late 1690.[32] The winner was installed at the beginning of 1691. John Law of Ballarnock (c. 1666–1718) was the successful candidate but about him nothing of substance has been found.[33]

Two others who were tried were appointed a bit later to new foundations. James Knibloe (?–?) became the humanist or regent of humanity and William Jameson (c. 1660–20 October 1720) became the first lecturer in civil and ecclesiastical history in 1692. Those were new positions with small salaries supplied by the College. Knibloe later accepted an arts regency but stayed at Glasgow only a short time. As noted above, he seems to have 'sold' his place and then disappeared.[34] William Jameson replaced him as a teacher of humanity and history. Combining the two was common in the Dutch universities of the time.[35] 'Blind' Jameson (he had been blind since childhood) was eventually subsidised by the Crown with a grant of £400 Scots [about £33 sterling]. This was a precarious gift which principal Stirling asked to be continued. It was not just charity to a worthy blind man. Jameson was a learned and relatively prolific writer against Catholics, Episcopalians, Quakers and Deists. He too belonged to the circle of antiquaries gathered in Edinburgh about Sir Robert Sibbald and in Glasgow about principal Dunlop and Robert Wodrow.[36] With those appointments, Glasgow's Revolution Settlement was effected.

Although the College and University were poor, the masters had found money to allow Sinclair, Tran, Knibloe and Jameson to become respectively specialist teachers of mathematics, Hebrew, humanity and history. They tried in 1702 to fund a Greek chair, as the Kirk wished them to do, but nothing immediately came of solicitations of 'His Grace'.[37] Still, the College had appointed reasonable men who were mostly in their forties and generally had interests beyond what they taught. The oldest of them, Sinclair, was among the most modern in his interests. The College had also done well to specialise the teaching of Latin and mathematics and to introduce or revive the teaching of history. Those were all steps which brought it into line with what William Carstares and others, who had spent time in Holland, hoped to see the universities do as they became more modern. They were also steps taken by an institution in competition with the University of Edinburgh which already had a regent of humanity but which would get an ecclesiastical historian only in 1702 and a civil one in 1719, about the time the Glasgow chair was endowed by the Crown. The appointment of a mathematician brought Glasgow level with Marischal College, St Andrews and Edinburgh. Its planned second professorship in divinity would have given it a more impressive set of theology teachers than Edinburgh possessed. The second theology post failed to materialise. George Meldrum, for whom it was designed, was appointed at Edinburgh.[38]

The men appointed did not modernise the curriculum, which remained rather scholastic, but they included three or four virtuosi who intended to see Scotland improved in diverse ways. Three of the men might once have been revolutionaries willing to suffer for their beliefs, but their beliefs were generally Whiggish in nature and led them to respect due process and to oppose torture, which lasted in Scotland well into the eighteenth century.[39] Such men did not usually find the political ideas of John Locke strange. Personally, some had got on with Episcopalians like Lord Winton or Sir Robert Sibbald, MD, although not with a government run by Episcopalians with views more extreme than Sibbald's. They constituted something of a clique related by kinship, outlook and other ties. That was not a good omen for future appointments. The next ones extended the family connections.

The rector appointed after the installation of the new principal in 1691 was Sir John Maxwell (January 1648–4 July 1732). He was related to Dunlop and Wodrow and after 1692 would find in the chancellor, Lord Carmichael, another distant relative. Another relative by marriage was Sir James Steuart (1635–1 May 1713), a long-serving Lord Advocate, whose opposition to Episcopacy and the Stuarts, Maxwell had shared. Both had suffered before 1688. Maxwell had been imprisoned, fined, forfeited and then made a Privy Councillor by William III. From 1696 until 1702 he would serve as one of the Lords of Treasury and a judge of the Court of Session (1699–d). Later he was a Commissioner of Union.[40] Maxwell and Steuart defended the College's interests for a generation. Other ties ran to friends who were not relatives. Principal William Dunlop had come from Renfrew, which in 1690 supplied the dean of the faculty, Patrick Simson (1628–1715).[41] Simson was minister of the town and a man well connected to the Presbyterian nobility of the West of Scotland. He remained dean until 1695. His son, John, became professor of divinity. The well-connected James Wodrow found at least one of his old teachers in the College. That man, John Tran, was married to a woman named Law – but this may not have been a relative of the regent bearing that name.[42] George Sinclair's brother had kept a school attended by principal Dunlop's brother-in-law, William Carstares. The latter gave George's cousin, Patrick Sinclair, a berth on the Edinburgh faculty. It looks as if half a dozen of the men in 1691 – there were only ten in both the College and University – were related by ties of kinship or close association. Most of them also had easy relations with many of the nobility and greater gentry of the area. James Wodrow's father had been chamberlain to the Earl of Eglinton and Patrick Simson, as a young man, had been a functionary in the household of the Marquis of Argyll. Dunlop's ties to the great ran partly through William's Chaplain, William Carstares, but Dunlop had known other aristocrats in Carolina and tutored Lord Cochrane in his younger days. Glasgow professors throughout the century generally had more ties to the greater gentry of their region than the professors teaching elsewhere.

The Parliamentary Visitation Commission continued to exist, but with a changing membership, and continued to make new rules. It issued reports and recommendations in 1690, 1695 and 1699 which agitated the colleges for years. Its proposals included having a common school year and producing a standard set of printed teaching texts for all the colleges in Scotland.[43] It wanted fixed Greek chairs and said all regents should teach some mathematics to their charges. It mandated the teaching of Aristotle but also of more modern thinkers in natural philosophy. It encouraged experiments and the purchases of instruments with which to make them. It set a minimum age for faculty members – twenty-one – and paid attention to the discipline of both regents and students. The latter were to wear distinctive gowns, be godly and moral, come to college prepared in Latin and take degrees only after rigorous examinations in which they would be ranked by their performance.[44] It discussed the desirability of adding chairs in law and medicine and for the better funding of the institutions. Divinity students were admonished to study Hebrew. Those recommendations were somewhat unsettling because they tended to set colleges in competition for scarce resources and because they envisioned a common curriculum when the masters were unlikely to agree on one. Most of the recommendations were not immediately effective. Common texts could not be agreed upon and the project was abandoned when the manuscripts of the texts were lost when the papers and effects of the recently deceased principal Gilbert Rule of Edinburgh were misplaced or burned around 1701. Greek was not required everywhere until c. 1702 and thereafter was a subject often evaded. Quite a few young men were appointed to teach before they were twenty-one and graduations were not conducted as they should have been.

3. APPOINTMENTS, 1692–1701

Between 1692 and 1704, only four academic appointments were made. The first of those appointed was Gershom Carmichael (1672–25 November 1729), who came recommended by the Duke of Hamilton and was probably placed through the influence of his distant relative, Lord Carmichael, then the King's Commissioner to the General Assembly.[45] Like some of the men appointed earlier, he too came from a family which had suffered during 'the killing times'. His father had been exiled to London where he preached to a congregation of Scots Dissenters and where he died. Gershom Carmichael probably grew up there. He and his mother had very likely returned to Scotland by 1687. By that time she had probably married Sir James Fraser of Brea, another sufferer and the author of famous books. They justified the Glorious Revolution and the sacking of bad kings and taught that all men were naturally called to live a moral life, although only the elect were to be saved. Carmichael attended Edinburgh University, taking his MA there in 1691. The following year he spent at Leyden where he may have picked up the Cartesianism he taught at Glasgow until c. 1700. In March 1693, he obtained a regency at St Andrews which was in the gift of the Earl of Cassillis. The Earl had also suffered outlawry in the Restoration period. Carmichael resigned his living in September 1693 in order to study further at Glasgow, where he took a second MA in 1694. When James Knibloe resigned in October of that year, he succeeded him. By then he was a believer in the righteousness of the revolutionary cause of 1688 and had some knowledge of natural law theory. He remained at the University until his death.[46]

John Loudoun (?–1 November 1750), Carmichael's equally well-connected friend, was appointed in 1699 to replace John Boyd. Loudoun had tutored the children of the Earls of Rothes and Haddington.[47] He had been one of the candidates for a regency at Glasgow in 1690[48] and in 1695 he had been appointed a regent at St Andrews through the influence of his noble patrons.[49] In Glasgow, Loudoun also seems to have found backing from the Duke of Hamilton. He would have been known to the masters because he had taught privately in the burgh c 1689.[50] He served the College until his death in 1750.[51]

In 1699, Dr Robert Sinclair (by 1665–after 1717), probably a son of George, was made professor of mathematics. The younger Sinclair was a virtuoso physician trained in Utrecht who was in touch with the circle of Sir Robert Sibbald. He possibly had made a trip to Italy and, like George Sinclair, was an inventor – in his case, of a lamp.[52] He was also enough of a linguist so that, in 1704, he added to his mathematics teaching instruction in Hebrew. He replaced the deceased John Tran.[53] In 1703, Sinclair was made extraordinary professor of medicine and, with two assessors, examined and then granted a degree to a candidate for the MD For him to be a plausible examiner, he must have been reputable as a physician as well.[54] Like the other two men, Sinclair was no backward-looking bigot but a man who had seen a bit of the world and had ties to modern men in Edinburgh, London and Holland. He had at least a local reputation as a virtuoso.

The most important appointment of these years was that of John Stirling (August 1654–28 September 1727), who succeeded William Dunlop as principal in 1701. Principal Dunlop's death in March 1700 set off a scramble for his office with 'many trying at the Catch'.[55] Stirling, the minster of Greenock, was the one chosen. He was then a vigorous man of forty-six whose mother was a Dunlop, which also related him by marriage to William Carstares, soon to become the Principal at Edinburgh.[56] Another relative was Sir James Steuart, then the Lord Advocate. Stirling was a thoroughly reliable man. He had been recommended to the Crown, the patron to the principalship, by his cousin, Sir John Maxwell, then the rector. Sir John would long support the arbitrary rule that the principal was to introduce along with plans for expansion which were largely realised. Stirling's place had been procured by Lord Carmichael in May 1701 but the minister could not bring himself immediately to say 'yes'.[57] Professor James Wodrow urged him to do so, telling him that it was God's will that he become principal. Wodrow wrote again to Stirling on 12 June 1701 saying that, should Stirling refuse the place, his decision would irk the government, especially Sir James Steuart and William Hamilton of Whitelaw, SCJ.[58] Professors Tran, Law and Carmichael urged him to take up the post, which he finally agreed to do.[59] Robert Sinclair too was later said to have been 'Active in the Interest of the Principal when his Election to that Post was coming on.'[60] Those professors helped to select a man few on the faculty would consistently like in years to come.

Why did so many want this man? Some probably realised that he would be a firm manager and would find support for his requests in Edinburgh among his relatives and powerful friends. Those men wanted to expand the universities to include the teaching of law and medicine and they sought to fund the College more adequately. Stirling later shared those aims and might have done so when he was appointed. He would have looked good to the masters who needed a well-connected man to speak for them. Others saw in him, as did Robert Wodrow, an earnest and powerful preacher of God's word who would hew to an orthodox line.[61] That voice would be heard in the local Presbytery, where he and the professor of divinity sat *ex officio*, and very often in the yearly General Assembly held in Edinburgh. There Stirling could be expected to follow the lead of Carstares and the moderate and *politique* clergy, which, in general, he did. One also suspects that his relatives and friends were taking care of one of their own who in turn would repay the favour – as he did when he appointed more relatives to University livings. Finally, the politicians who secured his appointment probably saw him as a man who would serve them as a loyal local lieutenant. None of his supporters were disappointed. Stirling's career provides a fine example of the political services expected of a college principal. He was active in the parliamentary elections in 1707/8, in a burgh election in 1709, and in preparations for the parliamentary elections of 1714 in the Glasgow burghs, in Lanarkshire, and possibly in Midlothian.[62] He supplied ringing endorsements of government actions and gave in political intelligence during the 1715 and at other times when political tensions rose.[63] He fulfilled similar tasks in the Kirk. Principal Stirling's tenure saw the faculty expand and the revenues put on a better footing. The University library he inherited was a scholastic one but the one he left possessed most of the modern classics, including the *Spectator Papers* and the works of Newton.[64] While he became unpopular with some of his colleagues within a very few years, and involved the University in turmoil and political infighting, some of that was forced on him by political opponents outside the College and by changed conditions in Scotland itself. Nevertheless, he was a willing political servant of the Duke on Montrose and the Squadrone interest throughout the period he served as principal.

Notes

1 Coutts, *History of the University*, 1909, pp. 8, 12f.
2 Regents took an entering class of students through the whole curriculum, teaching them philosophy, mathematics, and whatever else they might learn except for Latin and Greek in the universities where there were chairs in those subjects. They attended church with their boys and gave them some religious instruction. Regents often looked after the boys' finances and generally supervised them while they attended college. Regenting ended at Edinburgh in 1708, at Marischal College in 1753, at St Andrews in 1747 but at King's College only in 1800. On the changing composition of the Senate and Faculty, see Murray, *Memories of the Old College*, 1927, pp. 63–7.
3 Reid, *The Statistical Account of Scotland*, I:198–247, ed. Withrington and Grant; this piece is also reprinted in Reid, *Philosophical Works*, ed.

Hamilton and Mansell, 1967, II:729f. This is not quite how the operation of the University was understood by others. Coutts says that after 1772 the rector's powers were diminished by the Court of Session and those of the principal enhanced; Coutts, *History*, 1909, pp. 75–8.

4 In 1690 the Crown appointed to six of about forty-eight professorships in Scotland (13 per cent). By 1806 it appointed twenty-six men to about eighty-eight chairs (28 per cent) and paid salaries to three more.

5 Its remit is given in A. G. Stewart, *The Academic Gregories*, 1901, pp. 55–7 and in GUA, 47393. Other Visitation papers can be found in GUA, 47328–47395.

6 APS, 1908, IX:163f.

7 In 1690, Crawford was President of the Convention Parliament, President of the Council and a Commissioner of Treasury. Personally pious, he prized orthodoxy but was not a man given to extreme measures. To his credit, he was made sick by witnessing the torture of prisoners, which seems not to have bothered other members of the Commission. *Leven and Melville Papers*, 1843, p. 583.

8 *An Account of the Proceedings of the Estates*, ed. Balfour-Melville, 1954, I:227.

9 Undated entry [1690] in the 'Principals Memorandum Book', GUA, 26630/10. Principal Fall listed others whose names do not appear here (Sir George Campbell, Sir Robert St Clare and the ministers George Meldrum and William Violant). He omitted Cardross. See also: Monro, *Presbyterian Inquisition*, p. 19 and *Munimenta* II, 1854, pp. 493–512. Of the Glasgow University Visitors, at least five continued to be involved with universities: Lord Carmichael, Sir John Maxwell of Pollock, George Campbell, Meldrum and Violant. That was everywhere the pattern.

10 Excepted were 'the principalls, professors of divinity and other professors', in 1690 mostly holders of regius chairs. AUL, K.257/23/15/2.

11 *Fortuna Domus*, ed. J. B. Neilson, 1952, p. 8.

12 GUA, 26630/11.

13 Gordon had been prosecuted for scandal in 1689 but had been assoiled by the Court of Session. Although he resigned as regent, he claimed he still held his professorship of Hebrew. He was, in effect, bought out by the Visitors, another sign of their leniency. His place was given to George Sinclair. GUA, 26630/5; Mackie, *The University of Glasgow*, 1954, p. 134.

14 Tran was selected to write the *Ethics* for the projected new printed university course which the Visitors wished to see adopted. He did but it was then found wanting, as was the *Physicks* text which had been produced by William Black of King's College. That remains in manuscript at AUL and is discussed by Christine Shepherd in 'Newtonianism in Scottish Universities', *The Origins and Nature of the Scottish Enlightenment*, ed. Campbell and Skinner, 1982, pp. 65–85, 78–80; two

other texts were published, see below, pp. 379 and 400, n. 44. Robert Wodrow, 'An Essay to recover some Accompt of the Life of the Reverend Mr James Wodrow', EUL, La. II.690/147.

15 Sinclair, *Satan's Invisible World Discovered*, ed. Parsons, 1969, p. x.

16 Quoted by Fawcett from *The Acts of the General Assembly* in *The Cambuslang Revival*, 1996, p. 10.

17 To 'sell' a chair was to give it up to another who, with the permission of the legal patron, paid a sum to the holder. The rate was often five year's purchase based on either the total income or the salary of the place. The retiring incumbent often retained the salary, house and other perquisites for life, while the purchaser got the students' fees. It was a common retirement arrangement. 'Minute Book of the Facultie of the University of Glasgow from Decr 18 1702', GUA, 26631/61. The purchase price of the regency was only one year's purchase – 500 marks Scots, about £25 sterling. Over the course of the period here surveyed at least sixty-three of 470 placements (13 per cent) seem to have involved payments that amounted to a sale.

18 GUA, 26631/75.

19 GUA, 1915.

20 Blaikie and Lloyd, 'William Dunlop' in ODNB, 17:317f; E. Mijers, 'Scotland and the United Provinces', unpublished PhD dissertation, Chapter IV.

21 He would have been known to Lord Crawford who at one time planned to emigrate to Carolina. Jackson, *Restoration Scotland*, 2003, p. 154.

22 Facts about his life can be gleaned from Scott, *Fasti Ecclesaie Scoticanae*, VII:405, III:164 and Story, *William Carstares*, 1874. The Scottish virtuoso community to which Dunlop belonged is described in Emerson, 'Natural philosophy', *Studies on Voltaire*, 1986, pp. 243–91 and in 'Sir Robert Sibbald', *Annals of Science*, 1988, pp. 41–72. See also D. Hay, 'The Historiographers Royal in England and Scotland', *Scottish Historical Review*, 1951, pp. 15–29.

23 Dunlop, *William Carstares*, 1964, pp. 70–5.

24 *Leven and Melville Papers*, ed. Melville, 1843, p. 561. Crawford in this letter deplores a man in the running for a St Andrews post because of his 'warm temper'.

25 Story, *Carstares*, 1874, p. 227f.

26 Reid, *The Divinity Professors*, 1923, pp. 172–7.

27 'Essay to recover some Accompt of the life of the Reverend Mr. James Wodrow', EUL, La. II.690.

28 His teaching programme is outlined in Skoczylas, *Mr Simson's Knotty Case*, 2001, pp. 55–7. They also trusted the colleague they had proposed to give him in theology, George Meldrum, who went to Edinburgh instead. John Tran had earlier been in line for the chair but was passed over. *Munimenta*, 1854, II:347f.

29 Geyer-Kordesch and Macdonald, *Physicians and Surgeons*, 1999, pp. 159, 199.
30 Gordon, when outed at Glasgow, went to King's College, Aberdeen, whence he had come; Emerson, *Professors, Patronage and Politics*, 1991, p. 20; Reid, *Divinity Professors*, 1923, p. 72.
31 *Fortuna Domus*, ed. Neilson, 1952, p. 142f; Coutts, *History*, 1909, p. 168f; 'State of the University when Mr Stirling came in Sepr 1701', GUA, 47410.
32 The invitations were issued in the name of Patrick Simson, dean of faculty; GUA, 46718.
33 He was nephew and heir to (?William) Stirling, Clerk of Glasgow. GUA, 13495/S/I; *Fasti*, III:356; Coutts, *History*, 1909, p. 169; Murray MSS, GUL, 650, 23 May 1704. Law resigned in 1714; Glasgow Minutes, GUA, 26631/194.
34 Coutts, *History*, 1909, p. 170. The names of the other candidates are given in GUA, 46761. Knibloe may have been related to the Edinburgh printers having that surname.
35 See Mijers, 'Scotland and the United Provinces', Chapter 3.
36 John Stirling to John Erskine, Earl of Mar, 17 January 1709, Mar and Kellie Papers, NAS, GD124/15/948/1.
37 It is not clear which duke the masters approached but it was probably Queensberry since he was HM Commissioner in that year. The plan to force the teaching of Greek in the first or 'bejun' year was a Kirk plan.
38 Coutts, *History*, 1909, p. 172.
39 Magistrates in Dumfries were still applying the boot to extract confessions as late as 1709; M. M. Stewart, 'Crime and Punishment in 17th and 18th Century Records', *Dumfries and Galloway Natural History and Antiquarian Society*, 1997, pp. 69–78.
40 His political career and the careers of some of his friends are conveniently summarised in Kelsall, *Scottish Lifestyle*, 1993, pp. 95–8.
41 Simson had been deprived of his living at the restoration but was reponed in 1690; Skoczylas, *Mr Simson's Knotty Case*, 2001, p. 30.
42 An ambiguous letter by John Law to Principal John Stirling can be read to make Tran, Law's brother-in-law; John Law to Principal Stirling, 23 May 1704, GUL, Murray 650/I.
43 The logic and metaphysics texts were published in London in 1701.
44 Glasgow Visitation records covering the period 1690–1702 are partially preserved in *Munimenta*; ed. Innes, II:493–559. This source has the rules issued by the Commissioners and many discussions of the texts which the colleges were mandated to produce. The Commission seems to have ceased to function in 1702.
45 Wodrow, *Analecta*, ed. Leishman, 1853, IV:95; Hamilton to Principal Stirling, 11 March 1704, GUL, Stirling Letters, Gen. 204/2/51. Lord Carmichael claimed also to have been the patron of John Loudoun.

Professor Carmichael later dedicated publications to Lord Carmichael and to his son and to sons of the 3rd Duke of Hamilton. See Carmichael, *Natural Rights*, ed. Moore and Silverthorne, 2002, pp. x–xi.

46 For more on his career, see ibid., pp. ix–xvi and the studies noted in the bibliography.

47 Wodrow, *Analecta*, 1853, IV:41. These earls would later be members of the Squadrone faction of Whigs.

48 GUA, 46761.

49 See below, p. 385f; Francis Pringle, 'Common Place Book', SAUL, LF1111:P8C99, p. 245.

50 He was one of the 'young men [who] had presumed to take upon them to Teach philosophie privately in the Town of Glasgow', against whom Principal Fall complained to Lord Melville in c. 1688/9. Fall described their actions as 'being a manifest breach of the priviledges of the University, Against all law, or president in former times and they withdrawing students from the Colledge.' GUA, 26630/7f.

51 For details on his life and teaching, see Emily Michael, 'Francis Hutcheson's *Logicae compendium*', in *Logic and the Workings of the Mind*, ed. P. Easton, 1997, pp. 83–96.

52 Emerson, 'Sir Robert Sibbald', pp. 41–72, 71; and the Sibbald MSS in the NLS, Advocates MS 33.5.19/110,330. Other Sibbald MSS are held at the Royal College of Physicians, Edinburgh.

53 Coutts, *History*, 1909, p. 190.

54 Ibid., p. 482.

55 [?] to John Stirling, 11 March 1701, and James Wodrow to Stirling, 3 June 1701, GUL Murray 650/1. Others seeking the post included N. Gillis, Patrick Cuming, Mr Robert Trail (then a minister in London), David Blair, David Williamson, J. Bannatyne, John Tran and Robert Wylie.

56 Carstares sometimes referred to Stirling's wife as 'my Cousin his spouse', Carstares to Stirling, 9 March 1710, Stirling Letters, GUL, Gen 204/2/105.

57 Stirling to Sir John Maxwell, Lord Pollock, SCJ, 30 May 1701, GUL, Murray 650/1; Stirling asked that his patent not be released.

58 James Wodrow to Stirling, 3 June 1701, GUL, Murray 650/1.

59 James Wodrow et al. to Stirling, 12 June 1701, GUL, Murray 650/1.

60 Henry Newman to William Carstares, 18 June 1709, Carstares MSS, EUL, DK.1.1[2].

61 Skoczylas, *Mr Simson's Knotty Case*, 2001, p. 42f.

62 Montrose Papers, NAS, GD220/5/171/1, 171/6, 171/11; 198; 227; 323; 324; 339; 341; 351/5, 351/6; 382/7; 416; 620/9–10; 628/3; 220/5/1918/4. These citations and those in the following note are mainly to letters from Stirling to Montrose c. 1712–16. There was no diminution in the correspondence until near the end of the principal's life. Charles Morthland,

professors William Anderson and John Loudoun also left extensive cor-
respondences with Montrose. Both Stirling and Morthland tried to get
men chosen to municipal positions and as MPs; both were rewarded for
that work. Morthland was particularly active in the elections of 1727
when Ilay's victories confirmed the ouster from power of the Squadrone
men.

63 NAS, GD220/5/30/36–40; GD220/5/351/14, 382/12; 472/3; 472/4;
472/30/1–2, 30–8; 472/48; 529/3; 554/3; Stirling to [?], 18 August 1715,
State Papers, Scotland, Public Record Office SP 54/7/53; Stirling to [?],
7 October 1715, Stirling to Lord Ilay, 7 October 1715, SP 54/19 and 20.
[All of the SP references, unless otherwise noted, are from photostats at
the National Archives of Scotland.]

64 See the manuscript catalogue of the library during the years 1691–
c. 1723. It is misleadingly titled 'Catalogus Librorum Bibliothecae
Universitatis Glasguensis anno 1691', GUL, Gen 1312. In the future this
catalogue will be available online. Principal Stirling left his books and
£166 13s 4d to the library.

3

PRINCIPAL STIRLING'S REGIME: FAMILY AND POLITICS, 1701–1725

∾

1. The Political Environment

The Scottish political environment of Stirling's early years as principal was much like that of the 1690s – no Scottish political faction was dominant and the kaleidoscope of politics changed almost yearly as magnates struggled against one another to make the most of the pickings in their poor kingdom.[1] The great issues of these years centred on what to do to make the Scottish state viable and how to improve it. This required men to take stands on the relations that Scots should have with the English. Scots could maintain a sovereign state ruled by a King not the King of England or a sovereign state with a King shared with the English. Either option entailed great costs, perhaps war. Or, they might join in a federal or an incorporating union with the English. Ending the sovereignty of the Scottish state had implications for the Kirk and the Scottish legal system. When Oliver Cromwell had occupied the country and joined it to England during the mid-seventeenth century, the Scots experienced an incorporating union meant to assimilate them to English ways. Choices had to be made because the state could neither defend itself nor survive economically in a mercantilist world in which it tended to be excluded by English policies both from continental trade and from English markets.

One upshot of those commotions was the formation of somewhat more stable political groupings in the Scottish Parliament. These came about partly because of the positions taken by the magnates and their family connections with respect to the Revolution of 1688 and the matter of union with England. They also owed something to the conflicts that came in the aftermath of the 1707 Union and culminated in the Rebellion of 1715. Jacobites were defined by their beliefs in divine right kingship and legitimacy, tenets which led them to oppose the 1690 Revolution Settlement. For them, the Revolution had unnaturally and impiously imposed on Scots an illegitimate ruler. They opted out of the legal and ordinary politics of the time. Scottish Tories resembled them but included some men with purely pragmatic interests in order, hierarchy and the continuity of old forms. Those who were not legitimists tended to have few (and flexible) principles. Somewhere between the Jacobites and the Tories was the Duke of Hamilton, a man with a distant claim to the throne who did not want to see union with England because that would effectively end his claim. Scottish Whigs wanted to preserve the Revolution Settlement and to administer the kingdom for the government in London and for themselves. They were generally opportunistic in outlook but divided into family factions. The Argathelians, led by the 2nd Duke of Argyll and his brother, the Earl of Ilay, were as much Tory as Whig. Another group not unlike theirs, based not in the West and North but in the Borders and Southwest, was led by James Douglas, 2nd Duke of Queensberry (1662–1711). A third family connection came in time to be called 'the Squadrone *volante*' or simply 'the Squadrone'. The name came from the period of the Union debates and referred to this group's willingness to change stands as a matter of strategy and tactics. There were of course many other men and small groups whose politics was purely opportunistic. The absence of ideological unity, the opportunism of poor noblemen, the discontents of the populace and the fears of the pious were all exacerbated by government instability in London to which the malaise of Scots contributed. Between 1690 and 1715, Scotland was a very unstable and uncertain political scene.

Prior to 1707 there had been almost yearly shuffles of ministers as one set of loosely linked politicians followed another. The Court Party was usually led by Queensberry, Argyll or lesser men. It vied for power with the Squadrone faction led by Tweeddale, Montrose and Marchmont. Both groups were criticised – or joined – by a considerable opposition formed of Jacobites on the right and others excluded from power but generally willing to be bought. In the years leading up to the Union, the factions of Argyll, Queensberry, Hamilton and the Squadrone had gained and tried to regain control of the government. From the Glasgow perspective, those struggles pitted against one another Hamilton, Argyll and Montrose – the three local magnates who could hope to dominate the city and its electoral hinterland. When Stirling assumed the principalship, the men who would form the Squadrone were more or less in power and remained so until 1702 when Queensberry became the leader of the Court Party and government. By 1704, the future Squadrone men were back for a short time, after which Queensberry and the young 2nd Duke of

Argyll took control. By 1705, Argyll was head of the government as HM Commissioner, while his brother served as Lord Treasurer. They more or less arranged the terms of the Union and carried crucial votes on the Treaty which was finally passed by a Court Party led by Queensberry, Seafield and the Squadrone, among whom Montrose was a prominent leader. Argyll and Ilay both voted for the Union as members of the Court Party. Their rewards came principally in honours and power and not in the monies distributed by the Crown to overcome the reluctance of some of the voters. In 1705, Archibald Campbell became the Earl of Ilay and his brother, the Duke, became Earl of Greenwich in the peerage of England. By 1709, he was a Lieutenant General and second in command of the British troops in Europe.[2]

After 1707 most Scots nobles aligned themselves with English factions and connections but changed their allegiances as ministries changed and hopes altered. Only the Jacobites and some of the Squadrone chose more or less permanent English political allies for ideological reasons. Most magnates did so too because the ministries began to nominate, or at least control, the election of the sixteen Scottish peers who, according to the Act of Union, could sit in the House of Lords. Seeking to hold and retain power became more difficult and the lesser men tended to be relegated to positions determined for them by the magnates who found they counted for far less in a British system than in a Scottish one. They might ally themselves with the men in power in London but they were not allowed a free hand to exercise power in Scotland. This was partly because English politicians wanted control, but also because men like Robert Harley would not trust Scots to manage Scotland in the interest of a United Kingdom. The Squadrone faction, which had helped pass the Act of Union, felt aggrieved at their treatment by governments which had not given them the powers they sought. Its leaders tended to be defenders of the Kirk and of what remained of national liberties, even while they advertised their interest in British unity. Argyll and his brother also came to feel that they had not been given their due. They too posed as defenders of the Kirk. Most Scottish MPs and Representative Peers went with those who they thought would secure for them the greatest rewards. They had few qualms about leaving factions which did little for them. Throughout the reign of Queen Anne (1702–14), Scottish dissatisfaction grew. Anne gradually displaced Whigs, replacing them with English Tory ministers and favourites who had little love for the Kirk and not much more for Scots.

The Act of Union was negotiated and voted for by both the Scottish and English parliaments in this tense atmosphere. From the perspective of clerics like Principal Stirling, what counted as much as anything was the position of the Kirk. This he and his friends tried to keep as independent of the state as they could while recognising, as a political necessity, that their Kirk was one established by law and supported by the state. All that had been hard enough to do under a sympathetic King nominally a Calvinist, but after William's death in 1702 it became much more difficult. Anne's personal sympathies were with High Church Anglicans, little better than papists to many Scots. The Union of 1707 clipped the wings of the magnates and shocked Presbyterians. They soon found that the Union had made the final court of appeal for Scots the House of Lords, which would apply English legal principles in Scottish cases. Tory ministers in London were not averse to changing Scottish taxes, treason laws, the functioning of government agencies or even the rules of who might sit in the House of Lords. They were not disposed to do much to promote economic development in the North. In a world where parliament ruled, the Treaty of Union offered no guarantees whatsoever – a fact with which Scots still live. All this became clear in the years 1707–12 and was productive of great discontent in Scotland. Worse yet, Scots found that the doctrine of parliamentary sovereignty meant that the Treaty of Union was subject to wilful amendment by the English majorities in the House of Commons and the Lords. The English were quite willing to use this court to force upon Scots the sort of toleration enjoyed by Dissenters in England and to restore the rights of patronage to heritors. Those were both regarded by many Scots as clear impositions upon the Kirk, which, it was believed, the Union treaty had protected. Strict Calvinists thought the Kirk should be separated from the state, which should not meddle with it.

Equally clear was the ambiguous record of Scots politicians. Argathelians had to defend themselves for joining the Tories on the eve of the Sacheverall affair (1709–10), for not supporting more vigorously the intolerance of those who opposed the toleration forced on Scots in 1712, and for not being more vehemently against the restoration of patronage in the same year. In 1713, Scottish frustrations led men in all of the Scottish political factions to unite in an attempt to repeal the Union. When a bill to repeal the Union was introduced in the House of Lords, it failed by only four proxy votes. After the parliamentary elections of 1713, Robert Harley, whose Tory party was anything but united, could not count on more than a handful of

Scottish votes in the House of Commons and became gradually weaker. Tory weakness was made worse by the failing health of the Queen and then by her death in 1714. The Tories were replaced by a more Whiggish ministry serving a new Hanoverian King helped to the throne by the Duke of Argyll.

By 1715 Scots' hopes of prosperity under the Union had come to little. Many had reasons to be unhappy and the Jacobites among them were driven to desperation by the Hanoverian succession. The effect of all that was to polarise Scottish politics. The factions had almost coalesced into three Scottish groups: Jacobites, led in 1715 by John Erskine, Earl of Mar; the Squadrone, led by James Graham, 1st Duke of Montrose; and the Argathelians, led by Argyll and his brother Ilay. The last two groups were nominally unionists but all Scots wanted more from the union.

George I came to the throne in 1714. In the elections of 1715 following his accession the Argathelians did better than others in Scotland, which was not a good omen for Montrose and his friends. The Squadrone had support in Fife and the counties around Edinburgh and in the Borders but they lacked support elsewhere. They also were not efficient during the uprising in 1715, which brought renewed prominence to Argyll and his brother whose reputations were enhanced by the '15. Argyll, the Commander-in-Chief of government forces in Scotland, had beaten Mar at Sheriffmuir despite being outnumbered by the Jacobites. Ilay defended Inveraray and was wounded at Sheriffmuir. The brothers and their followers did much to suppress the rising in the North of Scotland but they did it with a minimum of bloodshed. The Squadrone would have been more repressive and harder on Jacobites. In the long run this mattered because it gave the Argathelians a grip on much more of the country, including the regions most difficult to control. They were able to recruit to the Argathelian faction men in the North who then voted for and with them. The Argathelians extended their power base from the West and mid-regions of Scotland to the North and Northeast. In West of Scotland terms, this meant an increase in power of the Campbells of Argyll and an intensification of their rivalry with the Dukes of Montrose and the House of Hamilton, led after 1712 by the formidable Dowager Duchess who held the title in her own right.[3] Glasgow was contested ground in which those families had interests involving the College and its business.

Argyll's popularity with the King and Englishmen did not last through 1716 because leniency to Highlanders did not seem right to a German King more eager to coerce and punish than to pacify by graceful means. Argyll and his brother fell into disgrace in London and compounded this by making up to the Prince of Wales. By 1718, Ilay was writing letters to Mar which were meant to reach the Pretender. It is not certain how seriously he meant the approaches he made but it is significant which he made them and that some among the Jacobites knew that he had done so.

Squadrone prospects revived but their success did not last. Montrose had had to resign in 1715 because of his failure to handle the rebellion well. His replacement in 1716 was the Duke of Roxburghe, a personal friend of the new King. The Squadrone did not lose most of the offices held by their supporters and they continued to make minor appointments in the universities. But they continued to lose elections. They had been weakened in elections held in 1715 and by 1716 they could not elect the provosts of Edinburgh and Glasgow. There were numerous reasons for this. Glasgow had seen a long party struggle which also involved church affairs. There was conflict over the building and staffing of St David's Church, often called the Ramshorn Kirk. The Squadrone clerics had opposed those whom the Campbells wished to install in the church they had helped to found. In 1712, John Anderson, a former tutor of the 2nd Duke of Argyll, was translated to the parish. The Squadrone men did not appear as forceful in the defence of Scottish liberties as the Argathelians after the '15 and they did not seem zealous enough in the parliamentary debates over religious issues that affected the status of Presbyterian Dissenters in England. Those debates were closely followed by Scots and particularly in Glasgow.[4] The Argathelians scored better on those counts and went on to further successes in the general election of 1722. They seemed to English politicians like Townshend, Sutherland and Walpole the most reliable men to act for them in Scotland. By 1723 the Squadrone had been marginalised. Roxburghe held onto his office as Secretary of State for Scotland but he would have to go, and did, in 1725. After that the Argathelians held power in Scotland until 1742.

Men at the Scottish universities had to work with all the factions since it was important to them to increase their funds – both institutional and personal – and to see that their Kirk remained as independent as possible. That meant they were generally supporters of government – any government – but that they tended to prefer the programme of the Squadrone to the opportunism tinged with sympathy to the Jacobites and to 'high-flying' Calvinists that marked the outlook of the Campbell brothers until the 1720s.[5] By c. 1726, the brothers had learned that they could not work with high-flyers who were ultimately resistant to erastianism and thus to management. Ilay could not stomach men who would not allow him to include the Kirk in his manipulation of all the important corporations in the kingdom. This put him at odds with Principal Stirling and his supporters who were mostly Squadrone men and, in religious terms, were for a more independent Kirk.

At Glasgow, the university men generally supported the government. They backed the Union in 1707 and helped to put down rebellions in 1708 and 1715.[6] As the nobles and gentry of the Glasgow area, and other men, like William Carstares, drifted into the camp of the Squadrone, so too did those at Glasgow University. This became fairly clear when Glasgow elected the 1st Duke of Montrose as its Chancellor in 1714. When it did so, it chose a side in the factional conflicts. The choice was a natural one. In the recent past the Squadrone lords had seemed more supportive of the policies urged by the Kirk than had been the Argathelians. At the University, the rector, Sir John Pollock, was both a relative of Montrose and a Squadrone man.[7] Montrose's estates were but a short distance from the College.[8] All that formed the backdrop to Principal Stirling's administration.

2. JOHN STIRLING AND THE EXPANSION OF THE UNIVERSITY, 1701–1714

Principal Stirling had the ability to get things done. The first twenty years of his administration saw the College grow and respond to numerous challenges as the principal negotiated his way through the political chaos of the times. The arts chairs were augmented by a chair of Greek and adequate funding was found for teaching oriental languages and history. Medical and legal education was begun. All of the chairs were better paid by 1721 than they had been when he became principal. At the same time, he packed the College with relatives and friends initially recruited from one political party. He divided the University by his heavy-handed administration which brooked little opposition even from his relatives. His reign was in many ways glorious but by its end he was seen by many as a tyrant, not as a benevolent despot.

The expansion began in 1704 with the College's decision to create a physic garden and to appoint a keeper for it. This was a year after the University had granted its first MD to Samuel Benion.[9] As Stirling told the Secretary of State, Lord Mar, in 1705, this was a step toward the teaching of medicine in the University.[10] The keeper appointed was John Marshall (by 1660–1719), a Glasgow surgeon who was a friend of both Principal Stirling and David Brown, dean of the faculty.[11] John Marshall came from a polite and well-heeled family that may have had royalist leanings. His elder brother had married a woman linked to the Earls of Wigton and Perth. Marshall had been able to study botany abroad, in Paris in 1677.[12] He held this post until his death.

The other appointee of 1704 was a professor of Greek. When regent John Tran died some time in the Spring of 1704, the College meeting decided to fulfil the demands made by the Visitors and created a chair of Greek. Word of Tran's death had spread rapidly and nominations soon began to come in. The Earl of Seafield, the Lord Chancellor, wrote to the principal on 6 May 1704 asking that William Black, his son's tutor, be considered.[13] Seafield solicited others to support Black. William Carstares was lobbied by him as late as the third week in June.[14] On 17 May, the Lord Advocate, Sir James Steuart, wrote to say that he and Principal Carstares thought that Alexander Dunlop (1684–April 1747), the son of the former principal, might teach both Greek and Hebrew. Carstares was nominating his nephew but Steuart was also distantly related to Dunlop, whose father he had admired. The University's chancellor, Lord Carmichael, now the 1st Earl of Hyndford, wrote on 28 May:

> If I can make any interest in the disposall of it I wold earnestly recommend to you a near friend of my own who is son to the laird of Gleneghies [Gleneagles].[15] He is a very well accomplished youth and willing to Undergoe a tryall; My near concern in him Makes me intreat of you that you Would let me know who stands fairest for it at present and how friends may be made for him for I would not have his name exposed unless there be good probabilitie of his carying it, not questioning my interest with your self or your assistance to take off others, If not positively pre-determined.[16]

On 23 June, Carstares wrote to Stirling that Black had withdrawn and Seafield would now support the candidacy of Dunlop.[17] Others may have sought the post but by 4 July 1704, with the rector in attendance (a lawyer and judge who might sit on any appeal of this ruling), it was established that the foundation allowed this chair to be filled without a comparative trial.[18] At some point the masters backed away from this position because on 14 September the Lord Advocate wrote to the principal that 'both you and Mr Dunlop may take your hazard Nay even tho a competitor should compear and offerr, Yet the hazard is not great.' He recommended that the masters 'settle this office and place without dispute', that is, without a public disputation and trial.[19] This they did – thus ending comparative trials at Glasgow.[20] Formal, often only nominal, trials of the competence of men selected for office continued but open competitions for jobs had ended because in that age it was unnatural. It was also, as the Lord Advocate had noted, unlikely to produce the best person to serve in an institution where social, political and administrative skills might in the long run count as much as learning and teaching ability. Comparative trials were not to prevail over influence and the reliable recommendations of the great. This helped to ensure that the tutors of noblemen found places and that the College would have its share of the fashionable and clever as well as learned men. The College would remain a predictable and sound institution from the point of view of those concerned with order in the state and Kirk. That may have been part of the motivation for giving to Robert Sinclair the lectureship in Hebrew or oriental languages which went to him in 1704 also as a consequence of Tran's death.

The settling of the Greek chair had brought letters of recommendation from politicians of national importance who long had been concerned with the management of the Kirk. That they should have been active in the appointment of a language teacher at Glasgow, a position whose salary and fees were worth at best £70 a year, is both an indicator of how scarce were suitable positions for well-educated men and of the desire of politicians to control places and to display their influence. The Chancellor of the kingdom, the Lord Advocate, a former Commissioner to the General Assembly, one of the chief Scottish advisors to the recent King and the most responsible leader of the Kirk were all involved in this appointment. That sort of interference would remain typical of university appointments at Glasgow and elsewhere throughout the period here surveyed.

In October 1705, the University realised its hope of adding a second professor of divinity. He was James Wodrow's son, Alexander (1674–6 March 1706), a former librarian of the College, but then a minister in Glasgow preaching at the North West Church – which opposed his translation.[21] He was to assist his father not by lecturing but by training the theologues in practical theology – sermon writing, casuistry and counselling. His salary was complexly funded, coming in part from a grant from the Crown, in part from the College, and from his father, whose salary was reduced to help make up the £1000 Scots (£83 6s 6d) that the younger Wodrow was to be paid. This brought into the College another man related to Maxwells, Stirlings and Steuarts but he was not there long; Alexander Wodrow died about five months later and was not replaced.

In the same month in which the younger Wodrow joined the College, the masters 'resolved that the said Profession of Humanity be again set up In this University against Oct: 1706.'[22] This was a resolution to create a post distinct from an ordinary regency and to separate that from the history taught by Jameson, which included much more. Stirling wrote to the Earl of Mar, the Secretary of State, on 3 December 1705, asking for a royal grant for chairs of humanity and medicine.[23] In the meantime, the masters were found the funds to maintain the humanity chair, which they saw not as a place in which grammar was to be taught – that was the town grammar school – but one which would resemble the continental chairs of humanity which prepared men to take Roman law courses. As they put it in their minute, the new master 'shall be obliged to teach Humanity, and the Roman Antiquities, In such manner and with such Restrictions with respect to the Grammar School as the faculty shall find Necessary both for the flourishing of the Profession and the good of the said School.'[24] A few days after their resolution had been passed, they had a nominee, Andrew Ross (c. 1682–1751). He came from their own circle. His mother was the daughter of James Brown, minister of the High Church of Glasgow and thus a visitor and in 1704 also the dean of the faculty.[25] Ross within a few days offered the masters testimonials from the ministers of the Edinburgh Presbytery and from all the professors of the University of Edinburgh, where he had studied after leaving Glasgow as an arts student and where he seems recently to have been studying divinity and tutoring boys.[26] Four days after receiving these recommendations, and after a trial of his ability, Ross was chosen as the new humanist. The head of his clan, Lord Ross, thanked the principal for the 'great friendship ye have shoen him on my account'. He asked that Ross be installed 'befor the colledge rise' as a favour to himself and to Andrew Ross, who would then get a bit more money.[27] Lord Ross had sat in the General Assembly with Principal Stirling, and in 1704 had served as Lord Commissioner. He had been a member of the government since 1705 and knew Carstares and the Edinburgh clergy very well. His son would be a rector at Glasgow. There seems to have been no others who sought the job; perhaps they lacked the timely notice which Ross clearly had had.

The next man picked to serve the College was not dissimilar. John Simson (13 July 1667–2 February 1740) became professor of divinity on 10 November 1708. Some of the time between his appointment and James Wodrow's death had been used trying to persuade James Hadow, the St Andrews professor of divinity, to accept the post.[28] Hadow in September 1707 had been made principal of St Mary's College, St Andrews, but he was willing by March 1708 to move to Glasgow if the invitation were unanimous. He wrote that he was tired of 'wrestling in ys place'. The strife and contention of the St Andrews colleges had become too great.[29] Hadow was a leading light in the Kirk and a man of strong character who proved to be more useful in St Andrews. These were ticklish times and divinity professors were to be chosen with care. Simson turned out to have been a poor choice from the point of view of the institution but one which helped to make Scotland more enlightened.

Hadow's invitation had been extended by Stirling but it was probably not unanimous since, in letters to Stirling about his own nomination, John Simson spoke of Lachlan Campbell as 'fitter than I [,] as are all the others proposed to you'.[30] Simson, unlike Campbell, was a man from the inner circle.[31] Simson's father, Patrick, minister of Renfrew, had served as dean of faculty from 1690 to 1701 and had been Moderator of the General Assembly in 1695 when Lord Hyndford had been its Commissioner.[32] John Simson had studied at Glasgow and had held the post of College librarian which was in the gift of the town. He later went to Leiden University where he studied divinity under Jan Marck [or Joannes Marckius], whose textbook on theology he used in his own courses. He seems also to have gone to Utrecht in 1698 as a tutor to John Montgomerie, son to the Earl of Eglinton, a man who had also patronised the Wodrows. Simson was a polite man who corresponded with antiquarians such as Sir John Clerk of Penicuik.[33] During his later career, when he nearly sank under legal troubles, he developed an increasing commitment to radical Whiggish politics. In 1708, he seemed a perfectly orthodox man against whom none found fault even though by that time he had been a minister for about ten years. Two years after coming to Glasgow, he married Jean Stirling, the principal's niece.

Every appointee since Stirling came to the principalship with some tie to a noble family which, of course, meant some political connections. After Simson's appointment, most appointments made during the remainder of Stirling's tenure seem politically motivated. The sponsors of those placed were generally of the Squadrone party and allied with the Duke of Montrose and his friends. Stirling had chosen his side – that of his friends in Edinburgh who had worked easily with

Mar but more easily with the men in the Squadrone connection. The next additions to the University's staff showed the continuance of that trend.

Robert Sinclair seems to have desired to retire from the professorship of oriental languages c. 1708. He may have wanted to retire but the way in which he was retired irked him. Before he resigned, the principal had found an unqualified candidate for his post and was prepared, or seemed prepared, to pay him more than Sinclair had received for his teaching. The latter felt he had been mistreated. He was probably correct. In 1708, Stirling had been in London raising money from the Crown for a general augmentation of salaries. The grant secured from the Crown stipulated that the professor of mathematics, Sinclair's other chair, was to have a salary of £40 a year, an increase of only about £7. The humanist, in the same schedule, got an increase of almost £30, a circumstance which galled Sinclair. What he thought of it is reported in a letter of (? James) Hodges to William Carstares dated 6 August 1709:

> the Dean of the Faculty's [James Brown] son in Law [Andrew Ross] hath his salary Augmented from 20lb to 55 lb per ann. Whils the Doctor [Sinclair] hath only about 6 lb added to his former salary, as professor of mathematics. For which Addition the principal demanded of him 30lb as his part of the charges in procuring the said grant which 30lb he pay'd.[34]

Stirling had travelled to London at some cost to secure the grant. There were also fees to pay various clerks who passed the documents required to warrant the expenditure of Crown funds. All that he was getting back.[35] Still, what he charged does seem rather an extortionate amount, especially when one considers that in 1709, when Sinclair resigned, only £15 was returned to him. The same letter notes that the Glasgow ministers had been preaching against 'Mathematics, as a sinful science' and that Sinclair had not been defended by the principal, although such preaching might inhibit his getting a decent retirement settlement from the College. Hodges, and probably Sinclair, held that mathematics, as he taught it, was more useful 'than that of school philosophy' which he saw being taught by others.[36] In the end Sinclair was censured by the faculty and resigned his chair of mathematics in December 1710.[37]

Sinclair's place does not seem to have been sought by more than one person, which suggests that, as in the case of Ross, events moved rapidly and there was an insider with an edge. The insider was another friend and relative of the principal but also a protégé of the

Duke of Montrose – Charles Morthland (?–4 September 1744).[38] He came from a Glasgow merchant family and had attended both Glasgow and Edinburgh as he prepared for the ministry. Morthland had served as a tutor to the children of Ker of Moriston and had kept school for a short time. In 1707–8, he had been in London where he wrote *Account of the Government of the Church of Scotland as it was established by law* (London, 1707). This pamphlet he dedicated to the former rector, David Boyle, now the 1st Earl of Glasgow.[39] What he had not done was teach Hebrew. Indeed, it was surprising that he got the job – and a job it was. Writing to Stirling on 10 April 1708, Morthland confessed his lack of training for a post which even Principal Carstares did not expect him to seek:

> I did not in my last answer a passage of your last to me concerning ye pro-fession of ye Or: Lang: which you wrote I wou'd not be for: Its very true that I have not studied ye Hebrew as I might have done, yet after advice of some friends and persons very well seen in that language, I am resolved to fitt myself for yt profession and they tell me in 6 or 7 months at most I may be very capable to teach ye hebrew, I am now very closely applying myself to it and have read several psalms already and against next winter I doubt not by ye blessing of god be capable to teach it and I hope you'll not doubt that I'll soon improve after I have begun to teach it . . . so that I expect you'll do me the favour as to procure me the profession of Hebrew and let Mr Sinclair confine himself to the Mathematicks. If you couldn't do this let me know that I may spend my time some other way.[40]

Knowledge of his inadequacies did not stop others from second-ing his candidacy. Some time in 1708, the chancellor, the Earl of Hyndford, supported him.[41] By 17 December 1708, the rector, Maxwell of Pollock, had consented to the appointment, having had 'a good report . . . from persons of good Credit'.[42] Among those who probably gave him information was William Carstares, who in January 1709 wrote that 'when that post was first spoken about to me I was for it, though the first suggestion came not from me.' He now worried because Morthland had not taken up his living. The Earl of Sunderland, the Secretary who would issue the crown warrant for the payments to Morthland, had not been told why this was the case. Carstares thought Morthland might lose the place through dither-ing.[43] This seemed to be a worry still later in the year when Alexander Dunlop wrote about it.[44]

The chief reason for the delay was that Morthland had gone to Utrecht to study Hebrew.[45] A secondary reason was that the College was making sure that it had the legal right to fill this chair. Its funding came from the Crown which had not made of it a regius chair. To establish the College's right to appoint, professor Alexander Dunlop searched the records of the University.[46] On 12 January 1709, Morthland was elected to the office, for which he gave the principal his thanks on 22 January, noting that Stirling had been a 'Martyr' for him.[47] He was admitted on 12 October 1709, after his trial and after producing testimonials from his Utrecht teacher, Henri Reland. Morthland's inaugural lecture was attended by the Duke of Montrose, the Lord Advocate, Sir David Dalrymple of Hailes, the Lord Justices, then on circuit in the West, and a large crowd of others. In the end, he taught not only Hebrew but Aramaic, Syriac, Chaldee and Arabic. It may have been a standing joke to some that Scots had appointed a professor who then went to Holland to learn his trade but Morthland must have been one of the first in Scotland to train men in Arabic. Arabic was useful to traders in the East India Company, which suggests that the Glasgow trading community, as well as Dutch example, had led to its inclusion in his teaching routines. In the end, he justified the good opinion of him that his sponsors held.[48] For the rest of his life, he was also a faithful supporter of the politics of the Duke of Montrose in the University and burgh. He published nothing more but a short introductory text to Hebrew and Aramaic grammar.[49]

On 3 March 1710, Robert Sinclair finally resigned his professorship of mathematics and the College chose as his successor Robert Simson (14 October 1687–1 October 1768), a nephew of the divinity professor who was now by marriage related to the principal.[50] Robert Simson was then a divinity student at Glasgow. When it became clear he was to be the new professor, he went to London to study mathematics for a year at Christ's Hospital. Like Morthland, he came back with testimonials to his abilities from men in London and Oxford and was admitted to office on 20 November 1711. He occupied this post until 1761.[51] Simson was not only a man interested in mathematics and its uses but a very good classicist and botanist. While he belonged to the family connection which Stirling was building, he came to disagree with many of the policies followed by the principal and his supporters and in time vigorously opposed them. Later in his life, he helped to establish the Foulis Press and wrote books on classical mathematics that were published by the Foulis brothers. He became a friend and advisor to Lord Ilay who shared most of Simson's intellectual interests, including mathematics and its applications in astronomy and insurance. Simson turned out to be a brilliant appointee.

In 1714, the University added professors in law and medicine and the College replaced John Law with a new regent, Robert Dick (?–24 December 1763). Those professors were needed if Glasgow were to compete with Edinburgh, which already had men teaching law and had been seeking to appoint anatomists and medical teachers. In each case, aristocratic sponsors were involved but in the first two cases questions of competence may have counted for more. All the men probably had Squadrone backers.

The decision to appoint law and medical professors had been taken in 1712 by Principal Stirling and the rector, John Maxwell of Pollock. They also decided to seek funds from the Crown for the new chairs. On 3 August 1713, their proposal was supported by the faculty. Morthland solicited funds in London. Those were granted by 16 December 1713 and allowed the lawyer a salary of £90; the physician got £40. The difference in the value of the chairs shows that the College expected both men to practise but that the physician's practice would return the larger income. Alexander Dunlop was sent to Edinburgh to discuss possible professors with lawyers whom the College men trusted.[52] The College men were interested in two advocates, William Forbes (c. 1669–27 October 1745) and James Craig, the recently appointed Edinburgh professor of civil law. Dunlop consulted the rector, Sir John Maxwell of Pollock, John Carnegie of Boysack, MP and soon to be Solicitor General, Sir Walter Pringle of Newhall, Robert Alexander, PCS, Walter Stewart of Pardovan, Clerk of the General Assembly and Stirling's brother-in-law, Sir William Calderwood of Polton and Lord P – ne [? James Hamilton of Pencaitland, SCJ], and one other who remains unidentified but seems to have had the initials 'B– K– ge'.[53] The known men were probably not all of one party – Carnegie was a Jacobite in 1715 – but they all had a common tie to the government. They all thought well of William Forbes, who was admitted to his chair on 18 February 1714.[54]

Forbes had attended classes at Leyden, had sought a regency at Edinburgh in 1690 and served as Clerk of the Faculty of Advocates. He had been made Joint Clerk and Keeper of the Advocates' Library. He published a good deal, with most of his works being dedicated to men in office who were likely to be able to help him. Forbes had been a supporter of the Union, a good Presbyterian and a polite man with antiquarian interests and some historical learning. He did not train many students at Glasgow but he continued to lengthen his publication list while often opposing the principal and his friends. He was from outside the area and the family and connections of the majority of his colleagues.[55] In this case, the need to appoint a man of widely recognised merit to a new chair had been clear even to the usual nepotists. As in Edinburgh, the teaching of law and medicine could not be made wholly a party matter or one to be determined by blood relations to sitting professors.

The medical chair was the next one filled. As early as 1705, Principal Stirling had assured the Earl of Mar that there was a market in Glasgow for medical teaching. The Earl remained unconvinced and willing to fund only a humanity chair.[56] By 1712, the time had come to do more. A regius chair of medicine was sought and granted in 1713.[57] At about the same time, the College allowed the Glasgow surgeon John Gordon (c. 1695–1770) to teach anatomy within its walls. He taught from 1714 to 1720.[58] The medical chair complemented this innovation but there was little competition to fill it. Advertised in 1713, it seems to have attracted no applicants other than Dr James Crawford, the new Edinburgh professor of chemistry and medicine. He probably wanted it because it carried a salary, unlike his own chair which gave him only fees. If he was eager to teach for its £40 salary, then he probably had taught fewer than twenty students in Edinburgh where they would have paid him about 2 guineas each. He sought it with the permission of his Edinburgh colleagues. By the latter part of January 1714, Crawford had decided not to pursue the Glasgow post or he had been refused it.[59] By early February 1714, 'no Person being proposed The Faculty recommend it to their several Members to consider who may be fit to be proposed.' Letters came surprisingly quickly from Stirling's friend Thomas Blackwell, an influential clerical politician from Glasgow who had been sent north in 1711 to become professor of divinity at Marischal College. He wrote on 15 February 1714 and again on 3 March asking for the chair for his brother-in-law, John Johnstoun, MD (1685/6–30 January 1762). Blackwell assured the principal that the doctor was no Jacobite but well satisfied with the present church settlement.[60] Shortly thereafter, he was recommended to the Crown by the Earl of Mar and admitted on 1 June 1714.

Johnstoun was the son of a Paisley physician.[61] Like Forbes, he had studied in Holland at Leyden and Utrecht. Like Forbes, he found few students and in 1719 the Visitors would try to force him to teach even small numbers. He had scientific, antiquarian and historical interests like those of the virtuosi of 1700. Glasgow in this case got more than they bargained for since Johnstoun had a rather profane wit and was a man whom John Ramsay of Ochtertyre called the 'Pitcairn of

Table 1. The University and College Staffs in 1714

R = blood relation of; RM = related by marriage to		R	RM
1. Principal	John Stirling	6	
2. Professor of Divinity	John Simson	10	1, 9
3. Professor of Oriental Languages	Charles Morthland		
4. Lecturer in Ecclesiastical and Civil History	William Jameson		
5. Regent of Humanity	Andrew Ross		17
6. Professor of Greek	Alexander Dunlop		1
7. Regent	Gershom Carmichael		
8. "	John Loudoun		
9. "	Robert Dick		1, 2
10. Professor of Mathematics	Robert Simson	2	1, 2
11. Professor of Law	William Forbes		
12. Lecturer in Botany	John Marshall		
13. Professor of Medicine	John Johnstoun		
14. Chancellor	Duke of Montrose	16	
15. Rector	John Maxwell		1, 6
16. Vice Rector	Mungo Graham	14	15
17. Dean	John Brown	5	

Glasgow'.[62] By 1722, Johnstoun and Forbes had become *persona non grata* whom the chancellor, the Duke of Montrose, was hoping to sack so that better teachers and more loyal men might be appointed.[63]

The third appointee of the year was Robert Dick, who had recently been tutor to the Master of Belhaven but about whose antecedents next to nothing is known. He was later said to have been related to Stirling but that relationship was probably created by a marriage not yet made. Like the others, he was a bright man and later in life an innovating teacher who taught general education classes in experimental natural philosophy in the College to Glaswegian artisans after he was 'fixed' to the specialised chair of natural philosophy in 1727.

The College and University by 1714 had expanded to nearly the full extent of what it would be in Stirling's time. Only the professorship of anatomy was yet to be added to the lectureship in botany. Every chair was now more adequately funded thanks to the principal's efforts. Six of them had been funded by the government, which had not extended its control over the appointments of men in all those which it helped to establish. That was an achievement in itself. The corporations had a rather familial look, as can be seen in Table 1, which notes the ten related members in an institution which had altogether only seventeen important members.

3. THE DECLINE OF PRINCIPAL STIRLING, 1714–1725

Despite the increased salaries and the better facilities that Stirling had provided, Glasgow University and its College were not homes to a happy family. Over the years Stirling had annoyed almost all of the professors. As early as 1704, regents Carmichael and Loudoun objected to his autocratic management of the institution.[64] They questioned the faculty minutes because Stirling presided over the meetings, acted as clerk and took the minutes, and then signed them as principal. For their criticisms, both men were suspended and forced to apologise. As we have seen, Dr Robert Sinclair felt aggrieved by his treatment c. 1708–11. At least four of Stirling's twelve-man staff in 1714 had gripes from the past, while only John Simson, Charles Morthland and Andrew Ross were unswervingly loyal. Two others, Mr John Marshall and William Jameson, were loyal but had no votes since they were not members of the College or University but held posts at the sufferance of the masters. Stirling had a slim majority in the meetings if the rector and dean voted with him. If the votes were tied, he could cast a tie-breaking vote, but the divisions in the College were closer than is sometimes thought, which would only have intensified the frustration of those whom he controlled by a vote or two. Still, he ran the College as he saw fit.

Stirling's power was buttressed by his good relations with his betters. His letters show that Hyndford and Montrose, but also Mar, Robert Harley, Argyll, Ilay and important Edinburgh functionaries, dealt easily with him most of the time up to 1715. His success lay partly in his ability to help them in church affairs, partly in his willingness to place or help their protégés, and in his displays of loyalty to the government, notably in 1708 and 1715. He usually enjoyed the support of men in other colleges. Some were his relatives by blood and marriage, such as Principals William Carstares at Edinburgh[65] and Joseph Drew at St Andrews. He was another of Carstares' brothers-in-law. Others were allies in Kirk politics, such as Thomas Blackwell of Marischal College. Those easy relationships were disrupted by rising factional feelings in Scotland. An early symptom of this was the election of a new chancellor in 1714.

The Duke of Montrose was unanimously chosen chancellor by the masters on 1 October 1715 after the post had been vacant for four and a half years.[66] The Duke was bound to be a contentious choice. Grahams had been opposing Campbells since at least the mid-seventeenth century. Both dukes had property in Glasgow, where

Montrose was 'principall Baillie of the Regalitie Lordship and Baronie of Glasgow'.[67] The major portion of Montrose's estate lay in nearby Stirlingshire. Argyll's lands were further away, lying mostly in the county bearing the name of his dukedom. Both dukes had electoral interests in Glasgow which Argyll could often dominate. In 1714, the Duke of Montrose seemed launched on the more promising career. Argyll had been abroad fighting for some time in the wars against France in which he became a hero. His brother, Ilay, was not yet a really important political player in either England or Scotland and he too had been out of the country off and on for some time. Montrose had been President of Council (1706), a Representative Peer (1707–10, 1715–34) and Lord of Regency. He was now a leading member of the Squadrone and in 1714 became Secretary of State for Scotland. He expected to manage Scottish political life to the advantage of his friends. That meant he would be opposed with increasing vigour by Lord Ilay and his brother the Duke, especially after the Squadrone had proven ineffective in suppressing the '15. Montrose had failed and had to resign. Argyll and Ilay had distinguished themselves in the defence of the King's government. The Glasgow professors' choice of Montrose had been ill-timed.[68]

The election of Montrose provoked students who had been excluded from the election. The man chosen was not to their liking and they rioted. In the disturbances, a boy who insulted the principal had been confined to the bell tower but was freed by his friends. The boys were forced to apologise and fined, but young gentlemen such as they would know where to turn for the redress of their grievances and some of them, namely the theologues, would be around long enough to do so with determination. So too would some of the professors. This gave the Argathelians groups within the University with which they could work.

In the Winter and Spring of 1715–16 the Campbell brothers celebrated their victories. In January 1716 they were in Glasgow, where they were feted in the town hall and made freemen of the burgh. But it was noted that of the College men, only the principal came to see them. Ilay was rumoured to have the gift of the estate of Orr of Barrowfield, a Jacobite friend of Montrose whose son would eventually serve as a rector of the University.[69] In 1716, the Argathelian candidate for MP from the Glasgow burghs, Daniel Campbell, won election replacing a man loyal to Montrose. By September of that year there were said to be no Squadrone men left on the Town Council.[70] As factional fights heated up, the Campbells had an interest in making life difficult for Montrose and could find allies in the College and burgh corporations if they proved able to protect them. All that must have been apparent to those in the College who resented the principal's high-handed ways – ways which continued and got worse. Those men soon found support from Argyll and Ilay.

Stirling continued to preside and serve as clerk of the faculty meetings. He transacted business at meetings when no quorum was present and during vacations when many were absent. Sometimes he did not consult the masters. He vetoed measures that had majority support. He retained custody of the records and papers of the corporations, even threatening at one point to prevent a rector from being installed by keeping him from signing the book that showed he had taken the requisite oaths.[71] Stirling more or less named the rectors and deans of faculty who upheld his power. He could do this because in 1692 the method of choosing the rector had been changed so that the student members of the corporation were excluded from the electoral process and the right of nomination was given to the principal. He presented a leet of three to his faculty colleagues who, with him, voted for one of them. Naming men who would not serve ensured that the principal could pick the rector and thus pretty much control the University court.[72] Here was an issue that could be politicised to the disadvantage of the Squadrone party, the new chancellor and the old rector, who was still Sir John Maxwell of Pollock. College fights between Stirling and his friends and the students and professors who disliked him soon became factional fights mirroring the politics of Scotland at the time.

In 1716, student and perhaps faculty dissatisfaction with Stirling's regime led to students breaking in upon a College meeting and accusing the masters of injustice.[73] Three students were rusticated for this. The students and the masters who confronted Stirling, and who opposed him in rectorial elections, now began to further politicise their protests.[74] Professor Forbes had had a long rancorous dispute about his first year's salary and then about whether he should teach when he had very few students, an issue he now shared with Dr Johnstoun.[75] By 1717 Forbes was writing letters asking for help to prevent the principal from engrossing all the College business.[76] Carmichael had his grudges and in the past had protested the way the rector was chosen because he thought it was not sanctioned by law and led to an abuse of power by the principal. He had not yet made it a 'party business' but the grounds for political interference by Argathelians had been laid.[77] Students had gripes other than the manner of choosing the rector. Stirling's entries in the 'Minute Book of the Facultie of the Universitie of Glasgow' record many student fines for swearing and blasphemy,[78] fighting, riots, charges of threatened arson, noise, drunkenness, whoring and one case of rape, card playing and libelling of masters, tradesmen and ministers.[79] Stirling cannot have been a popular man on his own ground, however well he got on with the politicians.

The dissident professors joined with students on 1 March 1717 to choose a rector according to the old way, a way that allowed the students to have some voice in the process.[80] This was principled opposition of a serious sort, since the professors involved believed they were defending their own and their students' rights and liberties against the infringements of an unjust principal. They also recognised that this embarrassed the Duke of Montrose and they went even further by choosing as their rector a man said to be an Argathelian. How shocking this was to Stirling and his friends can be seen in the account of the affair received by Mungo Graham of Gorthy, Montrose's local manager:

> . . . a very surprising affair has happened here with relation to the Rector of the College who at present is [Sir John Maxwell] Lord Pollock, but by a majority of the faculty is to be discontinued the year to come. [I]t was a great surprise upon the principal to be so disappointed in a matter of such Consequence both to the College & himself and as I think to my Lord Duke . . . [Professors Forbes, Johnstoun, Carmichael, Loudoun, Dick and Robert Simson] have not only affronted my Lord Pollock by having him out without ever speaking to him or letting any body concerned in him know of it, but have putt the highest Contempt upon the poor principal who is Martyr enough already for us, they have chosen Mr William Mure who in the shire of Renfrew promoted the Address in favour of the D. of Argyle; by the Assistance of the Boys but neither the principal [,] Dean of Faculty, professor of divinity [,] Mr Ross nor Mr Morthland concerned . . . I look upon it as a stroak to our Interest [,] all our Ennemies rejoyce att it.[81]

The writer urged his recipient to persuade Montrose to react vigorously to this insult. Sir John himself was certainly annoyed, saying that he would have satisfied the masters had he known of their grievances. He was upset at the dishonour which they seemed to have brought on him and the University he had long served with obvious affection. He also hoped that 'the Government will think fitt to protect you [Principal Stirling]'.[82] Stirling's own letter to Montrose referred to 'Seven mutinous members' who had insulted him, the rector and chancellor because 'of my attachment to a party as they speak'. For him the worst of the lot seemed to be Loudoun, who wanted a Visitation; but he also said Dunlop 'has been a great contriver & promoter of this mutiny' and had been abetted by Johnstoun. He called him an Argathelian and Jacobite. Johnstoun had influenced Forbes and Dick. Stirling also listed some of the particular grievances the masters had. Among them were that Stirling had favoured some, such as Morthland, in the division of monies granted by the Crown and that he had unfairly given out the Snell Exhibitions. Some time later, he reported that men outside the College were calling it an Argathelian plot.[83] He was sure it would be used by his and Montrose's local opponents for political advantage.[84] Stirling now called for a Royal Visitation Commission to discipline the professors, and for 'discontinuing the Rector of the University [chosen by the boys and the masters] and in Chusing a new one.'[85] The rector chosen by the students and professors had refused to serve so a new election was necessary. Thus began an uproar which would continue for more than ten years.

The mutineers were not penitent even though they had been chastised or written to by Stirling, Gorthy and Montrose.[86] That may have been because they consulted an Edinburgh lawyer, Sir Walter Pringle, before they acted. They certainly believed the University charter was on their side. It distinguished the University, College and Faculty from one another, something which Stirling had ceased to do when he did business in a single meeting and called himself 'principal of the University'. One of them perhaps drafted the memorandum which called for a College of Arts separate from those of Divinity, Law and Medicine.[87] They wrote to Montrose that they believed past elections had been illegal and that they had determined to remedy that. They meant no disrespect to Lord Pollock but someone other than he had to be named. They denied William Mure was an Argathelian, calling him a man of 'capacitie and great affection to Your Graces interests and family'. A later letter denied this was a party business; they were only defending their and the students' rights. And they ended resoundingly:

> ... the true motives of our acting, besides the recovering of the Constitution, were the sence we had of the evil of carrying on our affairs in a cabal, an open affectation of power which did not rightly belong to the pretenders to it [,] an artificial way of hindering applications to be made to the Masters that it might appear things were done by one, a Suppressing of some and Supporting of others, ways of bringing in business upon a Surprise & and voting them suddenly.[88]

They had had enough of Stirling's management. Forbes, the lawyer among them, described Stirling as 'an absolute man who would be thought infallible' and believed that only a new rector would rein him in.[89]

What Stirling hoped from a Visitation is made clear in a draft proposal for the Visitation which may be the one he sent to Montrose. His draft called for disciplining the professors of medicine and law by regulating their teaching and seeing that there was 'due subordination to the Superior officers of the Society'. He asked that precedence and administrative policies be made clear and that current disputes be settled. He included on his call a list of those who might serve as rector.[90] Stirling's nominees for the Visitation Commission were the chancellor, the Duke of Montrose, the Earls of Rothes and Hyndford, Lord Orkney; Adam Cockburn of Ormiston, Lord Justice Clerk; the rector, Sir John Maxwell, Lord Pollock; Mr Francis Montgomerie, Sir Robert Pollock, Sir Hugh Montgomery of Hartfield, John Maxwell of Blawerthill, Mungo Graham of Gorthy, John Graham of Dugalston, the reverend Mr William Mitchell, Professor William Hamilton of Edinburgh University, and James Ramsay, minister of Kelso, Mr John Gray, minister at Glasgow and Mr James Smith, minister of Cramond. All were friends of Stirling and at least six of the men were related by blood or marriage. Most are known to have supported the Squadrone interest. With such members, it was clear that he intended this to be a partisan body. To drive the point home, he advised the recipient of his memorandum that the quorum should be 'but 5 [,] at most'. That meant that it would be dominated by local men, all of whom belonged to the Squadrone faction.

Montrose acted quickly to secure a Royal Commission and, as was customary, packed it with his supporters who would uphold the principal.[91] But this time things would be more complicated because some on this Visitation Commission, and in the one appointed in the following year, favoured compromises with the students and masters. They seem to have become unhappy with the principal and his ways which made trouble rather than ended it.

The political nature of this body was clear to those who were to be disciplined. William Dunlop, probably writing in the late Autumn of 1717 from Edinburgh to his brother, Alexander, in Glasgow, said that Lord Hyndford had told him that the Visitation Commissioners 'owned that their procedure hitherto flowed from a belief that the change of your Rector was owing to the same spring with the difference in the town and took its rise from the intrigues of the state party.'[92] This was a continuation of the struggles for the political control of the burgh and kingdom now being carried on by other means. It would be contested outside Glasgow and Edinburgh. Alexander Dunlop on 1 November 1717 noted that, 'the enemies to our Scots ministry [the Argathelians] will not fail to take any handle in the Parliament for exclaiming even against the Commission itself, and more agst its actings.'[93] The Dunlops had some sort of financial involvement with the Duke of Argyll and were not disposed to think well of the Squadrone.[94] By 1718 Ilay was writing to Newcastle about the affairs of the University.[95]

The Visitors of 1717 met quickly and did what they were meant to do.[96] They mandated that the electors of the rector be the chancellor, rector, principal and dean of faculty, or their deputies, and the masters, but not the students. The first four were all to send in leets naming different people, none of whom were to be ministers or University officers. The newly chosen rector was to name two of the assessors in his court, while the University meeting was to name two more. Those looked like concessions to the dissidents but they did not see them as concessions. The protesters also had been admonished about their duties. According to the new rules, the rector and his assessors were still to be chosen by a body which excluded the students. The masters' reaction was not to vote for the rector when the new election was held on 11 November. Professors Forbes, Johnstoun, Carmichael, Loudon, Dick, Dunlop, Robert Simson and Ross absented themselves. The professorial rump then re-elected Sir John Maxwell and named Mungo Graham of Gorthy as his vice rector. Maxwell's name seems to have been the only one then given in.[97] Loudoun believed this would not restore peace and that the Argathelians would use the affair to their advantage.[98]

Later, in January 1718, much the same minority elected professor Morthland and the Glasgow minister George Campbell as University assessors to the rector. Stirling was displeased that the Visitation Commissioners had criticised his regime.[99] Dissatisfied students, including Francis Hutcheson, who would later be appointed a professor in the University, took their case to the Court of Session. They argued that the rectorial court, in the hands of Stirling's friends, would give them no justice. By June, there was another reason to think that the Visitors had failed to bring peace. The dissident masters, now back at meetings, tested their strength by electing John Millar, minister of Neilston, as dean of faculty. This had been opposed by the principal who wanted returned the old dean, the reverend

James Hamilton. Millar would not serve but this business took from June to October to sort out. A new Visitation Commission was appointed in September 1718 as the court cases were being prepared but it would not function until later in the Autumn.[100] The old Visitors voided the dean's election, suspended the troublesome professors who had elected Millar and ordered a new election. The old rump chose as the new dean John Scott, another Glasgow minister.[101] The scene then shifted to Edinburgh, where Argathelian politicians were involved.

The legal proceedings in the Court of Session quickly became an openly partisan matter. The Argathelian advocate, Duncan Forbes, argued for the students and Stirling's brother-in-law, Walter Stewart of Pardovan, and Sir Walter Pringle, who would shortly be made a SCJ by the Squadrone, acted for the rector and the masters who had elected him. That group now included professor Ross. William Millar, their law agent, writing to Stirling on 28 November 1718, described it as 'a party business which is pretty palpable from the concern certain people begin to show in it and those employed as advocates to witt, Mr Duncan fforbes, Mr Thomas Kennedy and Mr Hugh Dalrymple [all Argathelians later made judges by the Duke of Argyll's influence] and they already begin to compt the Binch on the affair.'[102] Millar informed someone, almost certainly Stirling, that Pringle 'will serve you on every occasion and particularly in that intended Process'. Millar said that Montrose knew all about this arrangement and had instructed his kinsman, Mungo Graham of Gorthy, on how to act in the case. The Solicitor General, Robert Dundas of Arniston, was also to be apprised 'as soon as ever they move in it'. This case was to be one involving government men and the Squadrone leaders.[103]

Pamphlets were written and two of the student leaders were rusticated by John Simson, the professor of divinity, because of absence from his classes while they attended the trial in Edinburgh. That led to actions by Duncan Forbes for their reinstatement and to counter moves by Stirling and his friends in court and in Glasgow. The students were reinstated.

While the masters wrangled and the students employed willing Argathelian lawyers and threatened more disturbances and legal actions, the rectorial election was postponed due to a flaw in the regulations given by the Visitors of the first Commission who by early November 1718 had been superseded by the new set of Visitors.[104] Meeting early in December, the new Visitors established other rules for the election of the rector, rules which still did not give the students a role in the election. Those Visitors realised that they had to offer some redress and that Stirling was part of the problem. J. D. Mackie well sums up what the Commission did:

> It bluntly asserted that the statutes made by its predecessors in 1717 were not in proper form, promised, at least by implication, to consider the claims of the students, made it plain that the arrangements made for the 1718 election were purely of a temporary nature; the Principal was made President of the electoral meeting (from which the students were still excluded), but the abolition of the 'leet' obviously left the decision with 'the plurality of the voices' of the governing body. The recalcitrant Professors, under the impression that a reform would speedily be made, withdrew their opposition, were duly reinstated and agreed to the election of Mungo Graham of Gorthie.[105]

There were no further reforms until a new Commission packed with Argathelians in 1726 forced a change of procedure. Stirling went on pretty much as before. The court cases petered out but student discontent did not subside and some of the masters remained eager for further change. The commotions had other results as well.

In 1720/1, students, adopting the libertarian rhetoric of the professors, tried to put on plays advocating liberty. Joseph Addison's *Cato* was one; James Arbuckle's *Tamerlane* was another. Its 'Prologue' mocked the principal and his party. The Trinamphorian and Sophocardian Clubs, founded by the students at about this time, seem to have addressed similar themes.[106] The latter was named for William Wishart II, an Argathelian minister in Edinburgh whom Ilay and his friends would make dean of faculty in 1728 and would help into the principalship at Edinburgh University in 1736.[107]

From 1720 to 1725, the students annually protested the rectorial election against a backdrop of local and national politics which saw the fortunes of the Argathelians markedly improve. The latter secured patronage for their friends and were successful in the peerage elections held in 1721 and 1722 but not in 1723.[108] In 1721, a student named William Morrison was sent down for insulting or even threatening professor John Simson. About the same time, students petitioned to have professor Brisbane teach anatomy as he was supposed to do. This was hassling a negligent man loyal to Stirling and the Squadrone interest.[109] Students also decided to petition Parliament for redress of their grievances. Montrose complained to Stirling, saying the masters had failed to obtain a copy of the petition and that he did not know which boys were involved. He wondered if 'any body will be so foolish as to take upon them to present such a ridiculous Address as this might be.'[110] By 18 February 1722, Montrose had the information he wanted and had spoken to the Lord Advocate.[111] The students continued to look for, and in the following year they found, MPs to present a petition on their behalf to the House of Commons, but the dissolution of Parliament prevented its presentation. One such MP was Robert, Lord Molesworth, an Irish peer who sat in the English House of Commons. When the news came of Molesworth's re-election (it turned out to be false), the students celebrated, on 25 April 1722, with a bonfire at the University gate. They went on to break some of the principal's windows.[112] The bonfire was put out by professor Carmichael, whose loyalty had been bought by the principal with gifts to his sons Frederick and Alexander.[113] The Glasgow magistrates, loyal to Argyll, refused to aid Carmichael in suppressing this outrage to law and order. This affair resulted in the rustication of John Smith, a student whose sentence of expulsion was reversed after the Argathelians took over the College in 1726.[114] On 22 December 1722, the chancellor wrote to Gorthy enclosing letters to professor Loudoun and Principal Stirling which said that there would be 'no end of it if the Masters allow themselves once to be Led in a matter of this sort by the Scholars.'[115] Montrose must also have known that, so long as Argyll struggled for the control of Scotland, there would be political support for the scholars.

In 1723, the students seem again to have petitioned or addressed someone since there is discussion of 'ye Students address' in a letter from Montrose to Stirling written on 1 July of that year.[116] In 1724 nothing much seems to have happened save that the talk of liberty had spread among the divinity students and now embraced confessions and subscription to them. It had thus taken a serious turn which involved the Kirk. This issue begins to appear in Wodrow's *Analecta* and is increasingly associated with the liberal and, from his point of view, disreputable, views of the Trinamphorians and those who in Edinburgh belonged to the Rankenian Club.[117]

In the following year, protests began again over the selection of the rector. William Robertson and William Campbell, son to Colonel Campbell of Marmore, a first cousin to the Duke of Argyll and Ilay's eventual heir of line, tried to give the principal a petition signed by sixty or so of the students, but this was refused. They then 'took instruments', i.e. had their protests notarised, and proceeded to the home of the rector, Hugh Montgomerie of Hartfield. Finding his house locked, they stormed it and protested his election. Stirling very diplomatically wrote to Campbell's father saying that his son had led the disturbances because he was 'imposed on by bad counsel and unwarily led into it because of his age'. Still, he had to be punished:

> . . . had it been a simple protest for yt which they fancy to be their privilege and had they not published and dispersed it and sent it to England and Ireland as they confess and had they not tummultously entered Hartfield's house to make the Protest, it had been wholly overlooked but it contains such injurious reflections on the Rector, as you'll see by ye inclosed copy, yt the Faculty were unanimously of opinion it could not be pass'd wtout censure.[118]

Stirling wanted Colonel Campbell to make his son publicly apologise but the Colonel did not do that and the boy would not do so. 'Liberty and virtue' were at stake. Robertson, after a trial lasting several days, was extruded.[119] He went off to London to lay his grievances before the Duke of Argyll who sent him to his brother, Lord Ilay, who began to think about a Commission of Visitation to sort out the affairs of the University.

Those events gave rise to rumours of a new visitation but who was to direct it was unclear. Stirling urged Montrose to approach the King because 'this affair goes so deep' that it required a remedy which only a visitation commission could provide. Montrose, misjudging the situation, thought he might not interfere since he had had only 'a good dale of muddle in requittal of my good wishes and offices to ye Society.' It was clear the boys were winning. The chancellor could not and his legal advisors in Edinburgh were not going to punish the boys severely, a sure sign that Stirling's power was coming to an end, as was the power of his political faction which was increasingly ineffective in Scotland.[120]

The imposition of a malt tax on Scots led to serious rioting in the Summer of 1725 which diverted everyone's attention, but by the end of November 1725 Ilay had determined 'that there may be methods fallen upon to put the Government of Glasgow into good Hands.' One was to control the University.[121] By the end of October, he had asked Newcastle to end the still-sitting Commission's mandate and to plan for a new one.[122] By the end of the year, he had done his research on previous visitations and was ready to move.[123]

While those commotions had been going on, the University added two new chairs. The first had been many years in the works. As early as 1711, William Carstares tried to establish at Glasgow a regius chair of ecclesiastical history which would have been held by his nephew, Alexander Dunlop. That plan came to nothing because of clerical opposition to the appointment of a layman. It would have been a divinity chair not in the control of the Kirk and one not necessarily held by a clergyman.[124] Since William Jameson was then very much alive and teaching the subject, that may have scuppered the plan. Jameson was receiving from the Crown a life grant of £400 Scots (£33 sterling) a year given in 1709, which would have meant that the Crown would have been paying two salaries for what ought to have been the work of one man.[125] By 1715, Jameson, then likely to have been in at least his late fifties, was probably in failing health and had not long to live. The University sought funds for a chair of church history in 1716 and was given £100 a year from the Crown but allowed to choose the new professor itself. No move to appoint a professor was made until 1719, the year before Jameson's death in the Autumn of 1720. One reason for this was the fact that the College was so divided by faction that it was difficult for the masters to do anything which required cooperation.

In 1718, the principal had had a candidate, a Mr Smith,[126] but a majority of the masters wanted professor Alexander Dunlop who by then looked like the leader of an Argathelian faction in the College. Montrose, at first, did not interfere but let the masters choose, expecting them to choose the principal's candidate or their own if it was not a regius chair as some argued it was because the Crown had funded it.[127] Most of the same men who opposed the principal in the rectorial elections now opposed his choice for the new chair. They decided that the new chair would not be styled a professorship in divinity and would not be filled by a cleric. Dunlop, however, doubted he was qualified for this office. He was also working harder but making more money teaching Greek than he could expect in the new chair were he to take it.[128] Some time in 1718, the principal and masters agreed that 'each of the two parties in the College should have a negative on the other in the choice of the new professor.'[129] By June of that year, Dunlop was willing that someone unnamed should be elected.[130] By October, Montrose had decided that the contest was another trial of political strength and treated it as such. He hoped it would turn out to be a regius chair in the gift of his friends, as indeed it did. But the College had not resolved the matter of a nomination to the Crown, which was unlikely to pick the candidate of a majority in a divided College. Early in February 1719, Mungo Graham, the rector, responded to Stirling's desire that the new professor agreed on by Graham and his friends be named by the King 'even tho they think that otherways it is to be avoyed'.[131] Once again Stirling and his friends had their way.[132] James Dick (?–4 May 1737), another relative by marriage of the principal and the professor of divinity and brother to regent Robert Dick, was named as the new professor of ecclesiastical history about January 1720. He submitted his commission in March. Against this appointment, professors Forbes, Carmichael, Dunlop and Robert Simson immediately protested. They fought his translation from the parish of Carluke (the Earl of Hyndford's parish) which, in the end, the General Assembly of 1721 did not allow.[133]

When Dick's nomination fell through, a new warrant was secured for William Anderson (c. 1690–22 April 1752) who came from Drymen, a parish close to Montrose's home and one in which the Duke and other Grahams were the principal heritors. Anderson was a Glasgow graduate who had been licensed to preach but had acted as a travelling tutor and was in Italy at the time of his appointment. He was almost certainly the choice of the chancellor, who may well have given up on the masters choosing a man by themselves. Anderson's appointment was probably opposed by Stirling, who had not helped him to secure the place.[134] When Anderson came to be admitted, the masters made no problems but, as the Town Council of Edinburgh did in similar circumstances, they reserved to themselves the right to create a chair of 'Church History in this University in time coming' which might compete with the new regius chair should they not like a future Crown's nominee and wish to harass him or, indeed, the first incumbent.[135] Anderson soon proved his worth to his faction. In 1727 he matriculated all manner of men in the city so that they could vote in the rectorial elections of that year to unseat the Argathelian candidate, the Master of Ross.[136] Anderson was not only a politician but, despite his tendency toward an evangelical outlook, a somewhat worldly man very different from the blind polemicist who previously had held the chair. Jameson seems not to have served a faction but Anderson throughout his career was a good partisan for the Squadrone. Unlike Jameson, he had a vote in meetings.

The other professorship created at this time was that of anatomy and botany, which was given in March 1720 to Dr Thomas Brisbane (1684–March 1742). Brisbane was a former Glasgow student who graduated MD at Leiden in 1707.[137] His family had had a long connection with the College. He was brother-in-law of professor Charles Morthland and could be expected to bolster the principal's party with another vote in the College Meeting. Brisbane seems to have been picked in 1719 because the University could not get rid of Dr Johnstoun and could not force him to teach as the principal and some masters believed he should.[138] Principal Stirling, the rector and members of the Visitation Commission of 1718 seem to have agreed that the creation of a second medical chair for Brisbane was a way to solve those problems and to get a funded anatomist to replace John Gordon, their teacher since c. 1714.[139] Getting the Crown to name Brisbane to a new chair provided a salary for the anatomist, one slightly larger than had been allowed to John Marshall (£20) who had died in 1719.[140] Professor Johnstoun claimed that the chair had been promised to him because his own salary was so small.[141] He was ignored but the College did not improve its medical teaching. Brisbane could not stand the sight of blood and did not teach anatomy, although he does seem to have taught botany. From some time in the 1720s until his death, John Paisley (1698–1740), a distinguished local surgeon, taught anatomy.[142]

The principal may have thought in 1720 that he had increased his security with the new rules given by the Visitors and the appointments of two new men who would vote with him, but this was not the case. Disturbances continued and his patrons weakened. In 1721 a friend wrote to Robert Wodrow that the Argathelians 'hath caried all befor them' in the burgh elections.[143] The parliamentary elections of 1722 returned more Argathelians to Parliament. In 1723, John Maclaurin, another Campbell protégé, was settled at the Ramshorn Kirk. He came from Argyllshire and had been opposed by Stirling's party. There was also a lengthy case in church courts against an Argathelian merchant named Thomas Harvey [or Harvie] which ended in a virtual draw.[144] Then, in 1724, Lord Carteret was driven from office, to be followed by the Earl of Sunderland and the Duke of Roxburghe, the Squadrone's leader in London. The Squadrone men in Scotland also chose not to help Walpole suppress the Malt Tax Riots of 1725. That was the culminating event which now swept the Argathelians into power. They were not to be removed for another seventeen years when the fall of Walpole ended, for a time, Lord Ilay's management of Scottish patronage. As Ilay's power grew, Stirling's ebbed, reaching a low in 1727 when he and the chancellor were threatened with removal by Ilay's Visitation Commission.

Notes

1 What follows is largely dependent on Riley's *King William*, 1979, and his *The Union of England and Scotland*, 1978.
2 Riley, *Union*, 1978, p. 336f; Whatley, *Bought and Sold for English Gold?*, 2001, pp. 95, 50.
3 Marshall, *The Days of Duchess Anne*, 1973, passim.

4 Between 1716 and 1720 these discussions concerned the Test Acts, the status of Dissenters and the Bangorian Controversy about the nature of the church. How this looked to Stirling can be seen in *An historical Account of My Own Life* . . . by his friend Edmund Calamy, 2 vols, ed. J. T. Rutt, London, 1829, I:344–436.

5 'High flyers' tended to be rigid Calvinists who held to the scholastic Calvinism of the seventeenth-century theologians. They were not tolerant or believers in anything which seemed to give a role to reason at the expense of grace or which placed works above faith. The Westminster Confession had for them almost biblical authority and rebellion was not a dirty word so long as it was for 'King Jesus'. They hated state interference in the Kirk and believed in emotional, evangelical preaching to save souls, not to reform the morals of sinners. They also believed in a limited atonement and did not generally dwell on the love of God or the virtue of charity.

6 Chancellor Seafield had thanked them in 1708; Seafield to Stirling, 27 March 1708, GUL, Murray 650/2. In 1715 the College raised a company for service against the rebels.

7 The leading clerics of this time are discussed by Lachman, *The Marrow Controversy*, 1988, pp. 157–80.

8 He was followed in that post by later Dukes of Montrose until 1875.

9 Coutts, *History*, 1909, p. 482.

10 Stirling to Mar, 3 and 26 December 1705, in *HMC Manuscripts of the Earl of Mar and Kellie*, ed. Melville, London, 1904, I:240f.

11 Glasgow Minutes, GUA, 26631; 7 September 1709, [?James] Hodges to Carstares, 6 August 1708, EUL, DK1.1.2. James Hodges is noticed in the biographical materials contained in *Anglo-Scottish Tracts, 1701–1714*, ed. MacLeod and MacLeod, 1979, p. 178f. What this source omits is that he was paid for some of his pamphleteering by the Scottish Parliament; APS, 1703, p. 244; 1705, App. 81.

12 *Memorials of the Faculty of Physicians and Surgeons of Glasgow*, ed. Duncan, 1896, pp. 246, 248; Geyer-Kordesch and Macdonald, *Physicians and Surgeons*, 1999, pp. 197–99, 296f; Boney, *The Lost Gardens of Glasgow University*, 1988, p. 48f. Boney thought he had been only an overseer of the garden but he is listed by Stirling as a professor in a salary schedule prepared for the Visitors in 1717; 'State of the University when Mr. Stirling came in Sepr 1701', GUA, 47410. Since his chair had been created by the corporation, it did not carry a vote in Senate until it was re-established by the Crown in 1720.

13 GUL, Gen 204, II/56.

14 Black withdrew out of deference to the principal of Edinburgh. GUL, Gen 204, II/63.

15 This was probably Patrick Haldane of Gleneagles who later held chairs at St Andrews.

16 Hyndford to Principal Stirling, 28 May 1704, GUL, Gen 204, II/62.
17 GUL, Gen 204, II/62.
18 Glasgow Minutes, 4 July 1704, GUA, 26631.
19 Sir James Stewart to Stirling, 14 September 1704, GUL, Murray 650/I.
20 Glasgow Minutes, 19, 21, 26 September 1704, GUA, 26632.
21 'Reasons for Transportation etc.', GUA, 45234–7; see also Laing Manuscripts held at EUL and *HMC Report of the Laing Manuscripts*, 2 vols, ed. Paton, London, 1914 and 1925, I:469. Alexander's parishioners thought Principal Stirling himself should supply the needed teaching because the foundation required the principal to teach divinity.
22 Glasgow Minutes, October 1705, GUA, 26631.
23 *HMCR Manuscripts of the Earl of Mar and Kellie*, ed. Melville, London, 1904, I:240.
24 *Munimenta*, ed. Innes, 1854, II:388f; Glasgow Minutes, 29 October 1705, GUA, 26631. Brown had secured his Glasgow living through the influence of the Duke of Montrose. Loudoun to John Stirling, 16 September 1714, Stirling Letters, GUL, Gen 204/3/7.
25 *Extracts of the Records of the Burgh of Glasgow, A.D. 1691–1717*, ed. Renwick, 1908, p. 645. Ross married the daughter of John Brown, a Glasgow minister.
26 Glasgow Minutes, 26 October 1705, GUA, 26631. Ross was described by Robert Wodrow to Dr James Fraser in 1725 as a diligent and polite man who went often to London in vacations 'to converse with learned men and to observe what may be of use to his country.' *The Correspondence of Robert Wodrow*, ed. M'Crie, 1843, III:215.
27 Ross to Principal Stirling, 2 May 1706, GUL, Murray 650/I. The Ross family had old ties to the College in which it had established bursaries in 1678.
28 Skoczylas, *Mr Simson's Knotty Case*, 2001, p. 36.
29 Hadow to Stirling, 16 March 1708, GUL, Gen 204/295. See below, pp. 408–11.
30 John Simson to Stirling, 19 April 1708, GUL, Murray 650/I. Campbell was a Dutch-educated minister from Argyllshire who had by then more celebrity than Simson. Being from Argathelian territory may have been no recommendation to Stirling.
31 What follows depends on Skoczylas, *Mr Simson's Knotty Case*, 2001. Simson's call to his chair can be found in GUA, 45238.
32 GUA, 26630/14.
33 There are letters by him to Clerk, Clerk of Penicuik MSS, NAS, GD18/5019 and 5212; 5041/3; 5047/3.
34 EUL, DK.1.1^2.
35 The bills are detailed by Murray, *Memories of the Old College*, 1927, p. 214f.

36 EUL, DK.1.1²; Coutts, *History*, 1909, p. 189f. The salary of the professor of oriental languages was set at £40 but Sinclair's rises were all taken by the principal for his expenses. Sinclair's alleged comment refers to the teaching of his fellow regents, Carmichael, Loudoun and Law, and seem unfair to Carmichael: see Carmichael, *Natural Rights*, ed. Moore and Silverthorne, 2002, pp. 357–87.

37 Coutts, *History*, 1909, p. 194.

38 He is identified in [?James] Hodges' letter to Carstares, EUL, DK.1.1². This says that Stirling had appointed other friends who were not qualified, such as the botanist John Marshall. He, however, had studied botany abroad and seems to have been respected by Edinburgh's professor James Sutherland. The latter is alleged to have helped him set up the new garden, but that claim is likely to be false. GUA, 30638.

39 GUA, 30638; I thank Esther Mijers for this information.

40 GUA, 30638.

41 *Munimenta*, ed. Innes, 1854, II:395.

42 Stirling Letters, GUL, Gen 204/2/99.

43 Stirling Letters, GUL, Gen 204/2/100.

44 Alexander Dunlop to Carstares, [?1708], EUL, La. II.407/13.

45 Ibid.

46 Sunderland told Stirling on 27 November 1708 that the Crown could have named the professor; Sunderland to Stirling, 27 November 1708, GUA, 30638.

47 GUL, Murray 651/3.

48 Coutts, *History*, 1909, p. 190. Arabic was probably not taught at Edinburgh until after the mid-century and elsewhere not before the 1790s.

49 *Brevis introductio ad grammaticum Hebraicam et Chaldaicam in usum Academiorum Glasguensium* (Glasgow, 1721). This was based on the text of his teacher at Utrecht, Henry Reland.

50 John Maxwell of Pollock allowed the masters a free choice in filling this chair. NAS, Montrose Papers, GD220/6/1746/13.

51 Trail, *Life and Writings of Robert Simson*, 1812; Coutts, *History*, 1909, p. 194f; 'Robert Simson', Sneddan, *DSB*, 12: 445–7.

52 Cairns, 'The Origins of the Glasgow Law School', in *The Life of the Law*, ed. Birks, 1993, pp. 151–94, 154–7; Coutts, *History*, 1909, p. 193; Faculty Minutes, 4 August 1713, 21 and 28 January 1714. GUA, 26632.

53 Robert Alexander to Stirling, 12 January 1714; John Maxwell to Stirling, 16 January 1714, GUL, Murray 650/I. The missing name may perhaps be Sir Andrew Hume, Lord Kimerghame, SCJ.

54 This is the date given in Charles Mackie's 'Index Funereus' which is very accurate; the date usually given is 23 October 1745; Mackie MSS, EUL, Dc.1.47 and SAUL, 36987.

55 On Forbes, see Walker, *The Scottish Jurists*, pp. 185–94; Cairns, 'The Origins of the Glasgow Law School', in *The Life of the Law*, ed. Birks, 1993, pp. 151–94, especially pp. 152–83.

56 *HMCR Mar and Kellie Manuscripts*, ed. Melville, 1904, I:240.

57 Coutts, *University*, 1909, p. 193.

58 Geyer-Kordesch and Macdonald, *Physicians and Surgeons*, 1999, pp. 172, 196, 296.

59 '. . . we were all very unwilling to part with Dr Crauford, but yet did not desire to stand in the way of any thing that he might think would be for his advantage . . . and told him . . . [we] left it to his own determination; but he answered that he was so sensible of the civilities he had met with from us that he did preferr staying with us to going any where else, so in my opinion it will be fitt you have your eye on another.' Carstares to Stirling, 21 January 1714, GUL, Gen 204/2/135.

60 Thomas Blackwell to Principal Stirling, 15 February and 1 March 1714, Stirling Letters, GUL, Gen 204/2/139–41.

61 Geyer-Kordesch and Macdonald, *Physicians and Surgeons*, 1999, p. 194f.

62 Ramsay, *Scotland and Scotsmen*, ed. Allardyce, 1888, I:277. The original manuscript used in the preparation of these volumes is at NLS [MS 1635] and has materials not included in the published volumes – mostly variant repetitions and notices of scandalous things such as drunkenness and insanity. Archibald Pitcairne, MD, was a witty and bibulous physician noted for his Jacobitism, deism, and dislike of Presbyterians whom he ridiculed in poems and plays.

63 Sunter, *Patronage and Politics*, 1986, p. 73.

64 The complaints of professors were often noted and sometimes found support among their sponsors (the Duke of Hamilton, Sir James Stewart, the Lord Advocate, and the rector, Sir John Maxwell). Hamilton to Stirling, 24 March 1704, Stirling Letters, GUL, Gen 204/2/51, 58–60; Montrose to Stirling, 11 March 1704, GUL Murray 650/1; Carmichael, Forbes, Dunlop, Robert Simson, Johnstoun and Robert Dick summarised for the Visitation Commission of 1717 complaints going back to 1704. Coutts, *History*, 1909, pp. 197, 199; see also 'Grievances Relating to proceedings in ffaculty and other Business Relating to the University', March 1717, GUA, 47414–25.

65 Carstares and Stirling had a falling out in 1709 over the right of Edinburgh to grant honorary degrees – really about the university's efforts to attract English dissenting students. Dunlop, *William Carstares*, 1964, pp. 124ff.

66 *Munimenta*, ed. Innes, 1854, III:310f.

67 NAS, GD 220/5/1927.

68 Coutts, *History*, 1909, p. 191f.

69 Unsigned but in the hand of Charles Morthland to [?Montrose], 9 January 1716, NAS, GD220/5/1918/2.
70 Grant of Grant to Duncan Forbes of Culloden, 29 September 1716, in *More Culloden Papers*, ed. Warrand, 1924, II:147.
71 Alexander to William Dunlop, n.d. [probably October 1718], GUL Gen 83. I have here used the typescript transcriptions of these letters which run from 1714 (not 1715 as the title to them says) to 1720. See also University Minutes, GUA, 26631/266.
72 *Munimenta*, 1854, 'Prefatio et Indices', I:lxv.
73 This has recently been seen as the result of the masters' dissatisfaction but a wider view of this matter should be taken owing to the political situation in the burgh and the students' previous discontents. See M. A. Stewart, 'Principal Wishart', *Records of the Scottish Church History Society*, 2000, pp. 60–102, p. 67.
74 Also complicating this was the attempt to select in the years 1711–21 a professor of history. Stirling's choice, in 1716, was another relation and a protégé of Montrose, the reverend James Dick.
75 See, Cairns, *Legal Education in Edinburgh*, forthcoming.
76 Forbes to John Pollock, 4 March 1717, Stirling Letters, GUL, Gen 204/1/17. One wonders how this letter came to Principal Stirling.
77 Montrose to Mungo Graham of Gorthy, 12 March 1717, NAS, GD220/5/802/12a-b. Montrose seems not to have thought the upset in 1717 was politically motivated, but he threatened the masters with a visitation; 11 April 1717, NAS, GD220/5/16b.
78 In March 1713, William Campbell was extruded for heresy and blasphemy, having denied the doctrine of predestination. That, he claimed, made God the author of sin. He had also railed against presbyteries and ministers, whom he called 'bloody minded Villains' who had 'sold the Nation for Thousands'. And he allegedly favoured the Pretender. Perhaps his greatest sin was calling the principal 'a greeting hypocrite'. GUA, 26631/153.
79 Some of these and other charges are mentioned in Mackie, for whom these issues were related to increasing Tory sentiment and the reaction to it toward the end of Anne's reign; others 'were due to domestic and not to national politics'. They blend into later cases which were political and involved the election of the rector and Ilay's struggle to dominate the University, a task he had accomplished by 1727. Mackie, *The University of Glasgow*, 1954, pp. 172–6.
80 Carmichael's letter to Montrose of 19 April 1717 says that he had 'on all occasions formerly expressed my Dissatisfaction at that way of continuing a Rector by ye Faculty (for which I never saw any sufficient Warrant)' which he believed to be a violation of charter rights and liberties of both the students and the masters. NAS, GD220/5/727.
81 [?] to Graham of Gorthy, 1 March 1717, NAS, GD220/5/1932/1.

82 Pollock to Stirling, 4 March 1717, copied in NAS, GD220/5/1932/2.
83 Stirling to Montrose, n.d. and 14 March 1717, NAS, GD220/5/1933/1 and 4.
84 Loudoun tried to smooth things over with his political friends but would not concede that the professors had done wrong or that the imposition of Sir John Maxwell of Pollock as rector was an action good for the University: Loudoun to [?], 27 November 1717, Loudoun to [?Gorthy], 2 December 1717, Loudoun to [?Gorthy], n.d. [1718], NAS, GD220/5/978/1–3, 982/1.
85 William Mure refused to serve as rector, Stirling to Montrose, 8 March 1717, NAS, GD220/5/1933/5.
86 See n.125.
87 Anon., n.d., NAS, GD220/5/1936/13.
88 The seven masters to Montrose, 1 and 4 March 1717, NAS, GD220/5/1933/6 and 1934/2.
89 Forbes to Montrose, 11 March 1717, NAS, GD220/5/1936/3.
90 Undated but almost certainly 1717, GUA, 47328.
91 Its members in 1717 included: the Earls of Hyndford and Torphichen, Mungo Graham of Gorthy, Hugh Montgomerie of Hartfield, James Lockhart of Lee, James Hamilton of Aikenhead, Major George Monro of Auchenbowie, and the Glasgow ministers John Gray, John Hamilton and John Orr. In 1718 the commissioners included Montrose, Hyndford, Torphichen, Lord Advocate Sir David Dalrymple of Hailes, Adam Cockburn, LJC, Solicitor General Robert Dundas, Sir John Maxwell of Pollock, SCJ, James Lockhart of Lee, James Hamilton of Aikenhead, Francis Montgomery of Giffan, Hugh Montgomery of Hartfield, Mungo Graham of Gorthy, the ministers John Grey, John Hamilton and John Orr, William Hamilton, professor of divinity at Edinburgh, Principal James Hadow of St Mary's College, James Ramsay, James Gray and James Smith. NAS, SP 54/16/118 and *Munimenta*, ed. Innes, II:562f. In the following year it consisted of at least Torphichen, James Lockhart of Lee, James Hamilton of Aikenhead, Major George Monro of Auchinbowie, advocates Walter Stewart, Charles Cockburn and John Sinclair, and ministers John Hamilton and Robert Horsburgh and John Orr. NAS, SP 54/16/118. The same document says that the 1717 commission was poorly attended and did little. Of the aforementioned men, eight held or would hold office in the University and two of the lawyers were employed by it.
92 William to Alexander Dunlop, n.d. but probably late autumn of 1717, GUL, Gen 83.
93 GUL, Gen 83.
94 The financial transactions are mentioned in William to Alexander Dunlop, 27 March 1718 and Alexander to William Dunlop, 7 June 1718, GUL, Gen 83.

 95 NAS, SP 54/16/119.
 96 They may have discussed fixing the philosophy chairs since there exists
     a memorandum saying that the 'last intrant Professor of Philosophy'
     asked for this. If the paper was for this set of Visitors, then the profes-
     sor was Robert Dick. The same piece goes on to describe the bachelor
     class in ways that could have applied to the Edinburgh course taught
     by Robert Steuart. The class was held to have been much improved in
     recent years. It began, as did Steuart's, with pneumatics and moral phi-
     losophy and then went on to natural theology. The Boyle lecturers seem
     to have been either read or used as the basis of lectures. Another frag-
     ment in the hand of John Loudoun praised the former regent, John Law,
     for teaching more and better mathematics than the boys had formerly
     been taught. NAS, GD220/61746/6. A third fragment, dated October
     1712, says that the bachelor or third-year class already was confined to
     pneumatics and moral philosophy while the magistrands got 'a
     Complete System of Natural Philosophy'.
 97 The decree is printed in *Munimenta*, ed. Innes, 1854, II:559ff. See also
     Mackie, *University of Glasgow*, 1954, pp. 174–7; GUA, 47386.
 98 Loudoun to Sir [?Mungo Graham of Gorthy], 27 November 1717,
     NAS, GD220/5/978/1.
 99 Montrose to Gorthy, 26 December 1717 and 30 February 1718, NAS,
     GD220/5/10–11a.
100 Skoczylas, *Mr Simson's Knotty Case*, 2001, pp. 184–9.
101 Mackie, *University of Glasgow*, 1954, p. 175.
102 Millar to Stirling, GUA, 27146, 27147.
103 William Millar to [?Stirling], n.d., GUA, 27145.
104 *Munimenta*, ed. Innes, 1854, III:338–41. The members of this body
     included: Earls Lauderdale, Hyndford and Torphichen; the Vice-
     Rector, Mungo Graham of Gorthy; Adam Cockburn, LJC, James
     Hamilton of Pencaitland, SCJ, and Charles Cockburn, Advocate and
     son to the LJC; Robert Dundas, Solicitor General; Hugh Montgomerie
     of Hartfield, James Lockhart of Lee, Major George Monro of
     Auchinbowie and the ministers William Mitchell, James Hadow,
     William Hamilton, Robert Horsburgh, James Ramsay, John Sinclair
     and John Orr.
105 Mackie, *History of the University*, 1954, p. 176. Graham was an agent
     of Montrose and a friend and colleague of Sir John Maxwell.
106 M. A. Stewart, 'Principal Wishart', *Records of the Scottish Church
     History Society*, 2000, pp. 60–102; pp. 67, 70; see also Stewart's
     account of Arbuckle in ODNB, 2:316f.
107 Stewart notes that the students were 'aided and abetted' by Wishart and
     George Turnbull. Those men belonged to the Edinburgh Rankenian
     Club and corresponded with Robert, Viscount Molesworth. Stewart,
     'Principal Wishart', ibid., p. 68.

108 Morthland to Gorthy, 7 July 1721, NAS, GD220/5/982/4; Morthland to Gorthy, 19 July 1721, NAS, GD220/5/989/4; Robertson, *Proceedings Relating to the Peerage*, 1790, pp. 71–104. After 1727, Ilay's men seem not to have been defeated, except in rectorial elections, until 1740.

109 Robert Dundas to Principal Stirling, 28 November 1721, GUL, Gen 204/I/95.

110 Montrose to Stirling, 21 November 1721, GUL, Gen 204/93.

111 Montrose to Gorthy, 18 February 1722, NAS, GD220/5/841/16a.

112 Murray, *The Old College*, 1927, pp. 490f.

113 Frederick Carmichael had sought a chair at St Andrews with the help of the principal and Lord Hyndford but it had gone to a man supported by the Earl of Rothes, another Squadrone lord; Hyndford to Stirling, 31 March 1720, Stirling Letters, GUL Gen 204/1/69. In 1726 and 1727, Frederick taught for Andrew Ross; Coutts, *History*, p. 215. Alexander Carmichael became Collector of Teinds for the College in March 1720; Alexander to William Dunlop, 18 March 1720, GUL Gen 83; Skoczylas, *Mr Simson's Knotty Case*, 2001, p. 193.

114 Mackie, *University of Glasgow*, 1954, p. 177; an account of Smith and his problems is given by M. A. Stewart, 'John Smith and the Molesworth Circle', *Eighteenth-Century Ireland*, 1987, pp. 89–102.

115 NAS, GD220/5/841/17.

116 GUL, Gen 204/1/104.

117 Wodrow, *Analecta*, ed. Leishman, 1853, III:155–81, passim. There is no adequate account of the Rankenian Club, but see M. A. Stewart, 'Berkeley and the Rankenian Club', *Hermanthena*,1985, pp. 25–45. Stewart's essay does not list all those thought to have been Club members. There is no account of the Trinamphorians other than M. A. Stewart, 'Principal Wishart', *Records of the Scottish Church History Society*, 2000, pp. 60–102.

118 Stirling to John Campbell of Mamore, 11 March 1725, GUL, Gen 204/1/126.

119 'Memoires of Dr Robertson', *Gentleman's Magazine*, 1783, pp. 745–50, 747f; M. A. Stewart, 'William Robertson', ODNB, 47:269–72.

120 Montrose to Gorthy, 29 February and 18 March 1725, 1 January 1726, NAS, GD220/5/841/19a; 852/10 and Montrose to Stirling, 18 March 1725; 12 April 1725, GUL, Gen 204/1/125, 128.

121 Ilay to the Duke of Newcastle, 5 October 1725, NAS, SP 54/16/38.

122 Ilay to Newcastle, 21 October 1725, NAS, SP 54/16/53.

123 Even though busy with the Malt Tax Riots and the legal proceedings and municipal elections which followed those, Ilay examined the records of all the visitation commissions since 1690. This confirmed his opinion that the Crown possessed all of the rights in the colleges and universities formerly held by the Archbishops of St Andrews and Glasgow and the Bishop of Aberdeen: Memorandum sent to Charles

Delafaye, 10 December 1725, NAS, SP 54/16/118. This useful document also lists the commissioners for the earlier visitations.

124 Carstares to Stirling, 24 October 1711, GUL, Gen 204/3/113; Wodrow, *Analecta*, I:370f. Dunlop was a layman.

125 Stirling to Mar, 17 January 1709, Mar and Kellie Papers, NAS, GD124/15/966/1–2; *Munimenta*, I:lxviii.

126 He was probably James Smith, one-time tutor to Dundas of Arniston and, after he switched political allegiance c. 1727, one of Ilay's managers of clerical affairs.

127 Johnstoun to Montrose, n.d. but after Marshall's death in 1719, NAS, GD220/5/830/9; Professors Rosse, Simson, Carmichael, Dunlop, Johnstoun and Dick to Montrose, 2 December 1719, NAS, GD220/5/830/9 and 15a.

128 Alexander to William Dunlop, 11 February 1717, GUL, Gen 83.

129 William Dunlop to Alexander Dunlop, n.d. but possibly early in 1718, GUL, Gen 83.

130 Alexander to William Dunlop, 7 June 1718, GUL, Gen 83.

131 Graham of Gorthy to Stirling, 3 and 7 February 1719, Stirling Letters, GUL, Gen 204/1/57.It is possible, but unlikely, that the professorship in question was the medical chair since the principal was trying, with the aid of some of the Visitors, to sack John Johnstoun and to reduce opposition in the Faculty.

132 NAS, GD220/5/830/18b, 19a, 20.

133 GUA, 45243–6; 47456.

134 Morthland to Gorthy, 19 July 1721, NAS, GD220/5/989/4. Scattered comments in the Montrose Papers suggest that Anderson was initially not much liked by his new colleagues.

135 Coutts, *History*, 1909, p. 193; Glasgow Minutes, 29 August 1721, GUL, 26634.

136 Mackie, *University of Glasgow*, 1954, p. 197f.

137 More information on Brisbane's career is given in Geyer-Kordesch and Macdonald, *Physicians and Surgeons*, 1999, pp. 194–6.

138 Another candidate for the chair may have been Dr John Wodrow, a Leyden student who graduated at Reims in 1718 and later taught botany extramurally in the city. Montrose in 1721 was considering some scheme involving him and Brisbane, probably a sharing of the duties of the chair. Montrose to Gorthy, 12 December 1721, NAS, GD220/5/837/18a.

139 Geyer-Kordesch and Macdonald, *Physicians and Surgeons in Glasgow*, 1999, p. 215.

140 Mungo Graham to Stirling, 3 and 7 February 1719, GUL, Murray 650/II.

141 John Johnstoun to Montrose, n.d. but after Brisbane's death in 1719, NAS, GD220/5/828/13.

142 Geyer-Kordesch and Macdonald, *Physicians and Surgeons*, pp. 214–20. They argue that the teaching of anatomy within the College had been continuous from 1715 but this is tenuously supported by their evidence, as is their claim that it followed an Edinburgh pattern. In 1722, when there seems to have been discussion of the removal of professors Forbes and Johnstoun, there was talk about a new commission for Brisbane, one which would make him a professor of medicine. The rector, Lord Pollock, was to advise on a suitable replacement for Johnstoun; Montrose to Gorthy, 6 February 1722, NAS, GD220/5/838/15.

143 Mr Dougal to Robert Wodrow, 5 October 1721, NLS, Wodrow Quarto Letters XV/93. Montrose despaired of success in the election, saying that Argyll wanted to pick the candidates with him but would not then honour any power-sharing agreements. It was, as he termed it, 'an ugly situation'. Montrose to Gorthy, 21 November 1721, NAS, GD220/5/837/8a.

144 Skoczylas, *Mr Simson's Knotty Case*, 2001, pp. 195–200. Harvie went bankrupt but the Argathelians tried to provide him with a University job in 1729; Wodrow, *Analecta*, 1853, IV:28.

4

GLASGOW UNDER THE CAMPBELLS, 1725–1742

ᐒ

1. Ilay's Visitation and the End of the Stirling Regime, 1725–1727

The Visitation of 1726–7 was the last important event of Stirling's years as principal and one which marked the end of his effective power and that of his party. A Visitation may have been requested by the Squadrone politicians in January of 1726. They were thinking about one which would finally settle the manner of the election of the rector and try to bring peace to the troubled College.[1] When the Commission was struck, on 31 August 1726, it was Ilay who chose its members and it was his aims which were fulfilled. The Visitors were not Stirling's friends but his enemies, men who were even willing to remove a principal for serious offences.

The members of this Commission showed the changes that had swept Scotland as a consequence of the shuffles in London which gave power to Ilay and his friends. Chief among the Commissioners was Ilay himself, abetted by two noblemen in his connection, the Earl of Findlatter and Seafield and George Ross, the Master of Ross. Duncan Forbes, the new Argathelian Lord Advocate and Charles Erskine, HM Solicitor, sat on the body, as did Andrew Fletcher of Saltoun, SCJ (Ilay's chief Scottish deputy) and another Argathelian judge, James Erskine of Grange, SCJ. A judge-to-be, Patrick Grant of Elchies, was also included. So was John Campbell, brother to Campbell of Shawfield, the Glasgow MP whose house had been destroyed by rioters in 1725. The reverends William Wishart I, principal of Edinburgh University, William Millar from Edinburgh and James Alston from Dirletoun completed the membership. This was a small group, most of whom were close to or dependent upon Ilay and his brother. It included Ilay's managers of church and secular patronage, a former Edinburgh lord provost who had served Ilay when in office and others who had close ties to Glasgow, and clerics whom he could expect to follow his lead with little questioning because they were

ambitious men.[2] The group did not include, as had the earlier
Commissions, either the chancellor or former rectors and deans. It
had no Glasgow clerics and was lacking in local lairds, although Ross
and Ilay could claim to be from the region and both were alumni of
the College. It had only one man, Millar, who may not have been an
Argathelian. Robert Wodrow lamented that there was only one gentleman from Glasgow and that the members were 'all Campbells
almost'.[3] It was a body that could make a thorough revision of things
and settle many problems. That it intended to do so was clear even in
January 1726 when Duncan Forbes was saying in Edinburgh that the
students should have a vote in the choice of the rector and that there
should be many other changes. Ilay had disciplined the cities of
Edinburgh and Glasgow after the 1725 riots; he would now subject
Glasgow University to his control, as he was doing with the other
institutions in the kingdom. The threat was seen. Principal Stirling
told Montrose it would be a reproach to the Commissioners of the
previous Visitation and harmful to the University.[4]

When the Glasgow students had appealed to Argyll, they showed
that they thought their libertarian rhetoric accorded better with the
views of the Argathelians than with the opinions of the 'tyrannical'
Squadrone men who would not give them justice. Justice was now
done and with justice came punishment and humiliation. Ilay wanted
to make sure that those who opposed him and his friends would suffer
for past deeds and be deterred from making mischief in the future.
The Visitors ordered William Robertson's expulsion to be erased.
This was a triumph for those masters who had supported the boys,
especially for Loudoun and Dunlop who had written to Robertson's
father to say that his son was, in his son's own words, 'suffering in the
cause of what he thought justice and right'.[5] The Argathelian Visitors
satisfied the students' demands about the election of the rector. They
set a day for the matriculation of students. Matriculated students
were allowed to vote in rectorial elections which they also decreed
should be held on a fixed date. The nomination of the rector could no
longer be manipulated by the principal but would be made by
members of the electing body. The arbitrary decisions of the past, even
the past decisions upheld by legal officials in the other faction, were
found to be erroneous and proclaimed to be so.

The Visitors regulated the conduct of meetings and the keeping of
records, thus putting an end to Stirling's abuse of those processes.
They set fixed quarterly meeting dates for the faculty and restricted
the jaunting and expenses of those who served the University. They

provided rules for the administration of the monies and assets of the corporations and had Thomas Harvey prepare an account of the finances of the College and University. The Visitors set out rules for the faculty, the most interesting of which was the abolition of regenting and the fixing of the chairs to specialist professors. The Commission even stipulated that the professor of natural philosophy was to 'teach and go through a course of Physics and Experimental Philosophy', a rule in which we may see reflected Ilay's own interests as much as those of Robert Dick who now became the first professor of natural philosophy. It decreed that the professors of medicine and law were to teach whenever five or more scholars applied to them for instruction and, in an implicit threat to his place, it ordered Brisbane to 'teach Anatomy as well as Botany'. The Commissioners set the duration of the teaching year. Rules of precedence were uttered which put the principal first followed by the professor of divinity but ranking all the rest by seniority of appointment. It made degree requirements but only *recommended* the 'regulations of former Visitations, for inculcating upon the students the principles of the Christian religion', a provision in which we should see a measure of toleration and perhaps countenance for those who had opposed subscription to confessions. Argathelian lawyers were a more competent group of constitution makers than those who served the competing interest. They voided all of the old rules and statutes that conflicted with the new regulations. Their decree was issued on 19 September 1727 and signed by all eleven of the members of the Commission. Ilay could do all this because he had been successful in the elections of 1722, had sorted out the mess created by the Malt Tax Riots in 1725 and because he was increasingly useful to Sir Robert Walpole.

The chancellor and Principal Stirling, who had been threatened with deprivation for embezzlement,[6] were left in place but Stirling, like the non-teaching professors, had been warned that his ways were to change.[7] His ordeal had impaired his health and affected his spirits. Montrose noted that he was 'not the same man he was through age', which was perhaps partly the reason why the principal refused any longer to try to direct the granting of Snell Exhibitions which went almost invariably to political friends.[8] Lasting change had come; Snells would now go to boys with Argathelian support.

The results of the Visitation exhibited Ilay's interest in controlling significant Scottish corporations and the ruthlessness with which he would do so when he could. He was willing to impose rules mandating things that he himself prized. A lawyer by training, he held an honorary MD given to him by King's College in 1708 in recognition of his interest in and knowledge of medicine. He wanted teaching of natural philosophy by experiments and the diligent teaching of law and medicine. While he had little real commitment to the Whiggism asserted by the students, he was certainly closer to their views than any of the Squadrone men who tended to have more elitist views than did the Earl. Ilay happily dined with men far beneath him in status and listened to their advice. He was more pragmatic in his approach to politics but he was also less interested in maintaining a Kirk independent of the state than they were or said they were. In those years, Ilay was finding the attitudes of clerics – he often called them 'Levites' – troublesome and in need of careful management. He cowed the officers of the University and packed the College with right-thinking men so that his control would be secured for a long time to come. A more thorough man than Montrose, Ilay meant to establish a system by which all Scottish institutions might be controlled.[9] Glasgow University was added to his list by the Visitors. Robert Wodrow, who distrusted Ilay and disliked his attitudes toward the Kirk, saw the Visitation as a political triumph for the anti-Squadrone men. He predicted that its results would lay 'the foundation of unhappy divisions and constant broyles in that society'. He was not far off the mark.[10]

The most obvious sign of the triumph of the new party came with the election of a new rector under the new rules given by the Commissioners.[11] George Ross, the Master of Ross, was chosen by the students and masters and accepted on 2 December 1726. This was resented by half the masters and not even a conciliatory visit by the Master of Ross in March 1727 could do much to sweeten tempers. They were only temporarily improved by the traditional supper which a rector offered the masters. All were merry except for Charles Morthland; he stayed away. For some the merriment was, as the Master wrote, predicated on their assumption that Walpole would soon go out of power and the Earl of Ilay with him.[12] It happened – but only in 1742.

Resentment surfaced again in the rectorial election held on 15 November 1727. This event pitted Montrose against the Argathelians advised by Lord Milton.[13] Dunlop mounted something of an insurrection in the College where his faction lacked a majority:

> Mr Dunlop Immediately after prayers made a very mutinous speech and Immediately after finishing it cryd out to the boys come all with me that are for the Master of Ross and then went off and without our notice carried of[f] ye Mace & one of our books but missed the principal one[.]

We could have hindered them from doing either but was affraid of a dis-
sorder for our party was by far the strongest.[14]

The boys and masters who followed Dunlop again elected the Master
of Ross.[15]

Ilay's opponents, led by professor Anderson, had matriculated
young men from the town who were now qualified to vote although
they were not really students. Their numbers were more than the
Argathelian side could muster. In the absence of a principal (Stirling
had died on 28 September 1727) and the defection of professor Ross
from the Argathelians, the Squadrone men chose James Hamilton of
Aikenhead as their the rector.[16] He had served earlier as a Squadrone
rector.[17]

When three days later notices of the impending admission of the
Master of Ross on 24 November were put up by Dunlop's side, they
were torn down by professor Carmichael's order [he was senior regent
and temporary head of the College] and the rector's robe and the
mace and books were secured by him. Carmichael had the porter nail
up and lock the hall where the ceremony was to take place. The
Master of Ross was admitted by his friends, instruments were taken
by his opponents and the case was referred to the courts. Everyone
sought legal opinions, the Master from Lord Milton, Lord Advocate
Duncan Forbes and HM Solicitor, Charles Erskine, the usual lawyers
for the Argathelians.[18] In late November, Lord Milton sent the Master
back to Glasgow to show the flag, a move Ilay approved.[19]

The case was decided on 16 December and went against Ilay's
friends. The trick of the Squadrone men had worked; they had done
nothing legally wrong. The defeat prompted the Argathelians to think
about more visitations because they had lost control of the Faculty
meeting. Instead, their response was to obstruct it. The Squadrone
men had a majority but they could not exercise it if they lacked a
quorum which the absence of Ilay's friends ensured they would not
have.[20] Montrose had given a commission to a local man to be his vice
chancellor and to vote in meetings in which it was not clear the chancellor had a vote. If he did have a vote, a quorum could be formed.[21]
Fights continued about this and other issues. Those questions too
ended in the Court of Session, which eventually suspended the rector,
vice chancellor, dean and professors Forbes, Brisbane, Loudoun,
Carmichael, Anderson and Morthland. Now the roles were reversed;
the Squadrone men could not vote but a quorum was possible because
of their suspension.[22] The Argathelian rump then elected William

Wishart II as the new dean in 1728. Because Morthland attended the meeting as clerk, he was not deprived of this office, but he forfeited the goodwill of his political friends. After the installation of the new principal, there would be few such upsets because the votes were now with the Argathelians.

Ilay was determined to undercut the position of the chancellor whom he wished to reduce to a nullity, something he had accomplished by 1732. That process had begun earlier, as can be seen in a scrape of 1727. Just prior to the issuing of the Visitors' decree on 19 September 1727, Stirling's friends (the principal was thought to be dying) tried to block a letter of thanks to the King for the Visitation Commission but, in the end, they were forced into sending it when the Master of Ross managed to get two men to stay away from the meeting and then himself cast a deciding vote to send up the letter – but without the names of the chancellor and principal. Stirling had requested they be left out, which was something of an insult to the government that had reduced his power and thrown his friends out of office. The embarrassing letter was, by the same vote, sent to Ilay for presentation to the King and not to the chancellor who would normally have handed in such a missive. In July, after some grants had lapsed with the death of George I, Montrose signified his intention to present the address to the new King and to get the University's grants renewed.[23] He was not allowed to meddle with the grants dependent on the King's favour and was peevishly reduced to refusing to present the College's address to the new King.[24] The power of his faction was constantly sapped and his men believed themselves ill used.

2. THE REGIME OF THE CAMPBELLS, 1727–1742

After the Visitation of 1726–7, it was clear that Principal Stirling had not long to live. Glasgow was the second city of the kingdom and the place to which men in the West looked for leadership and the training of their ministers. It had a reputation for being a more pious city than Edinburgh and it was the meeting place not only of a Presbytery but of a Synod. Its University principal, professors and ministers were important figures in those judicatories and in the annual meetings of the General Assembly. The appointment of the right sort of man as Glasgow's principal was of great importance both to the politicians and to men in the Kirk.

Long before Stirling died, a pack of Argathelian divines was in full cry seeking his chair. The Argathelian victory had been so complete that there seems to have been no Squadrone candidate to succeed Stirling. This did not mean that once a man was chosen, there would be no opposition within the College to his translation from his church living to the principalship. To create delays, embarrassments and turmoil were all aspects of the political game. There was, however, no doubt about the outcome – a man chosen by Ilay or his brother the Duke would be the next principal of Glasgow. The Duke of Newcastle made that clear to Montrose in London on 26 October 1727, long before the new man was installed, possibly before he was known. Montrose noted, 'this nomination of a Princll. Is a stroak that can't be recover'd.' He determined that he would meddle no more in the College affairs because he could do nothing to protect and help his friends.[25] It was not a resolution to which he stuck but one he made more than once.

The choice for principal lay between several of Ilay's clerical aids and helpers and one layman – an unprecedented turn which again shows that Ilay was willing to contemplate awarding the post, nominally a divinity chair, to a layman. The layman was the redoubtable Alexander Dunlop, who seems to have been Ilay's personal choice. Dunlop thought he had been promised the post as the reward for his long opposition to Stirling.[26] Giving him the principality would have gratified landed families in the area: the Dunlops of Dunlop and the Mures of Glanderston and Caldwell into whose family Dunlop had married.[27] Dunlop seems also to have been the choice of the majority of the masters but the Kirk would oppose him since it was a post never held by a layman.[28] To give it to Dunlop was to make it easy for the Squadrone men to fight his nomination. The Duke of Argyll favoured Neil Campbell (1678–22 June 1761). In the end a compromise was arranged. Neil Campbell, who 'had a great oppinion of Dunlop and thinks he ought to be continued where he now is', was willing to 'hold a chaplains place in trust for him . . . [so] by this My Lord Ilay provides for Dunlop and fixes another good hand in Glasgow who will be very Active in promoting his interest both in the Town and Colledge.'[29] This arrangement settled Dunlop's pretensions for about £25 a year, that being the value of half of the chaplaincy which seems to be what in the end he got.[30] Dunlop's usefulness and loyalty came cheap. Lord Milton's correspondence contains numerous letters from him reporting on the state of the College and on appointments. The letters sometimes include other matters: '. . . I have talked with the Principal about what persons might be proper to be proposed to be brought into the Town Council.' He remained a man politically useful and offered Ilay another set of eyes with which to watch Glaswegians.[31]

Aside from Campbell, who probably had been the Argathelian choice since 26 March 1726,[32] the clerics in contention for the principality were: William Hamilton, James Hart, James Alston, William Gusthart (or Gusthard), William Wishart II and James Smith, all of whom in the end got something. In the spring of 1727, Robert Wodrow thought that the order of likelihood of appointment to the principalship was Dunlop, Alston, Campbell and William Wishart II.

James Smith, minister of Cramond, had been a protégé of Montrose and this may have been too soon after Ilay's accession to power to help such a turncoat.[33] William Wishart II was also an unlikely choice. His selection would, for a time, have given two principalities – Edinburgh and Glasgow – to a single family. Ilay throughout his career was opposed to such appointments; it did not pay to buy twice a family's loyalty. By the autumn, Gusthart and Hart had dropped off the list. Both were put forward for royal chaplaincies. The first had had the support of Ilay's relative, the Marquis of Lothian, who had spoken to the Earl on Gusthart's behalf, but he was not a likely candidate since later in his career he supported the 'Cambuslang Wark', an open-air revival of the early 1740s. He probably was already known as an evangelical. Some time later, Ilay was prepared to give the place to Mr Hart[34] but he had undoubtedly found out that Hart had refused the Abjuration Oath in 1717. Neither would be a good Erastian.[35]

Hamilton's case was more complex. He had served on an earlier Visitation Commission and he had not always voted in the General Assembly as the Argathelians wished. In May 1726, well over a year before Stirling died, Ilay had decided to punish Hamilton for his 'late impertinance'.[36]

That left only Neil Campbell. By the autumn of 1727, he had the endorsement of a Colonel Campbell, who wrote to Ilay for him. This was almost certainly Ilay's cousin and eventual heir of line, the father of the boy whom Principal Stirling had fined. After delays occasioned by political opponents,[37] Neil Campbell was installed in January 1728, where for some years he buttressed Ilay's power in the University, the town and in the local courts of the Kirk.[38] Principal Campbell's tenure was slightly longer than that of his kinsman the Earl. His long regime was, unsurprisingly, marked by his lordly cousins' interference in the affairs of the University and College, which flourished partly as a consequence of their attentions.

With the rectorship and the principality now secured, Ilay could count on a near majority of the members of the faculty meeting. Others quickly saw where their bread was to be buttered. Ilay's first convert was probably John Simson, the professor of divinity. He had troubles with church courts and needed Ilay's protection, which he got after 1727.[39] Each needed the other's help. Professor Morthland's comment on this was, 'both [Lords] Grange and Milton now softened with respect to our professor[;] you see what conversion will do.' The professor of medicine, John Johnstoun, once threatened with deprivation, was now on Ilay's side, as were Dunlop, Robert Simson and usually Alexander Ross. Ross, however, was going mad and by some time in 1727 was crazy and ceased to vote in meetings.[40] Ranged against Ilay's friends were Montrose's dependants, Charles Morthland and William Anderson, William Forbes, the law professor, and the professor of anatomy and botany, Thomas Brisbane, who was now lecturing weekly.[41] The former regents, John Loudoun, Gershom Carmichael and Robert Dick, also opposed the new principal. The numbers were usually seven to six on party matters, with rector's and dean's votes being of critical importance in the choice of new members. Robert Dick soon changed sides and in 1728 Forbes was bought by the Argathelians, for whom he voted after November 1728. They made his son, Thomas, the College law agent on 14 October, just before the Court of Session met to decide if the chancellor had a right to appoint a vice chancellor.[42] Those changes ensured that after a year or so the rectors and deans would be men who, for some years, would not question the leadership of the Argathelians. The Squadrone contested the rectorship in 1728 but their candidate, Maxwell of Pollock, was beaten by 'all the power & might of the Government'.[43] Still, dominance was not complete or absolutely sure. Even Robert Simson could write on 14 October 1728 to Lord Milton that he was sorry that he could not vote for the bursars whom Milton and Ilay wished to be chosen because he had already promised his votes for other boys. At the same time he asked for a larger salary and Ilay's help in obtaining a new Exchequer grant for the College.[44] Other signs that political victory had not ended the war were to be found in the fact that intramural fights continued between the professorial partisans.[45]

Some of those involved the chancellor whose claims to power were shaky. In 1716 the Visitation Commissioners at Aberdeen had found that the masters at King's College had chosen a chancellor although the charter gave them no right to do so. The Visitors' belief seems to have been based on the opinion, voiced by Charles Erskine c. 1726 with respect to Marischal College, that the right to appoint a chancellor, a right once belonging to the Bishop of Aberdeen, had devolved to the Crown. At Marischal College the right to appoint a chancellor had fallen to the Crown with the attainder of the Earl Marischal in 1716.[46] At the universities in Aberdeen, Glasgow and St Andrews the right to appoint chancellors should have come to the Crown after the abolition of episcopacy.[47] Ilay may have believed all that in 1716 when he refused the chancellorship at King's. That opinion had been supported by the 1727 Visitation Commissioners who found that there was only a customary right for the Glaswegian masters to elect a chancellor, a right confirmed by later visitations but which under Scots law might be found to be highly doubtful.[48] They also held the chancellor had no right to appoint a vice chancellor, although the masters might elect one so that degrees could be granted. Ilay certainly believed in 1728 that the right to elect a chancellor in a university established under a bishop belonged 'in ye K[in]gs person' since it was a right which devolved to the Crown at the Reformation.[49] At Glasgow, the chancellorship ought to be an office in the gift of the Crown. If this were so, then chancellor Montrose could be largely ignored in the running of the College because he had been illegally chosen. Ilay rejected the Aberdeen masters' claim that 'constant practice, past prescription and man's memory' gave them the right to elect.[50]

As we have seen, Montrose and the masters in 1727 made a man vice chancellor with 'all the power wch the Chancellor or we can give him'.[51] That act was challenged. Professor Carmichael, who was acting vice chancellor, was served with a suspension secured from the Court of Session at the insistence of the Master of Ross and those who had elected him rector.[52] Montrose's reaction to that was to say: 'Its certain I will not remain upon the foot I am on in the College[.] If I am Ch[ancellor]: of ye University my right must be asserted, If I am not I must have ane Empty name or If a Judge lay down anything out of ye way Let all his brethren judge of the part he has acted.'

Montrose expected his friends to appeal the decision of a Lord Ordinary to the 'whole '15'.[53] The immediate result was a process ending in a judgement in favour of the Argathelians but one which left the other side some hopes.[54] By 1730 Montrose was fed up with this business and was insisting that the College build the Chandos library, whose funds he held, so that 'I may have so much the less to do wt that Society'.[55] In 1731–2, Ilay warned the Squadrone men that the law was not on their side and that if his party lost in the Scottish courts he would take the matter to the House of Lords.[56] The problems concerning the chancellor and vice chancellor were finally resolved in 1731.[57] The case seems to have been abandoned because of Ilay's threats to take the matter to the House of Lords, where the rights of two other universities would have been imperilled had there been an adverse decision. At St Andrews, the Squadrone had people to protect; they seemed unwilling to risk a decision.[58]

Others beside the chancellor were to be made to pay. By the time Neil Campbell was chosen as principal in the autumn of 1727, Charles Morthland was worrying about his position in the University which he served as clerk. He had a basic salary of £40 a year, to which had been added £16 13s 4d more as his share of an extraordinary grant. That was topped up with an additional £10 for being clerk to the Faculty. For some time he was also factor at £28 per annum, which gave him a yearly income of about £95 plus what he made in fees from non-theological students and what derived from his occasional boarding of boys at the College.[59] His total income was probably in excess of £120. By 3 November 1727, he was pleading with Montrose to protect him.[60] He was worried about his share of the royal grant, which had to be renewed because of the death of King George I. The renewed grant would be distributed in the new warrant. Ilay had indicated that he would look at the distribution of money to professors with an eye to the unfairness of the distributions which Stirling had authorised – in short, Morthland would get less. The new principal and Colonel Campbell objected to punishing Morthland and Ilay relented for the moment, alluding to their intercessions.[61] Morthland believed he was being strung along and that Ilay would hurt him in the end, since the Earl had also noted that few men appreciated the favours done them. In the spring of 1729, Morthland learned that he was to lose his clerkship or factory or both. Morthland lost his clerkship in March 1729. The factory went in June. The principal chose the day of the election of a new dean to discuss Morthland's finances with him.[62] Two days later, the professor wrote to Gorthy that he had been asked to be absent from the election and 'promised many good things beside'.[63] He was not the only one to suffer. In 1730, the old law agent for the College, William Millar, was replaced by a son of Campbell of Succoth whom the professors chose at Ilay's urging.[64] Professor Brisbane was forced to lecture and did so partly because it was rumoured that a 'Dr Paton had gott a patent for to be prof. of anatomy' which would greatly reduce Brisbane's salary or lead to his ouster.[65] As it turned out, the new lecturer on anatomy was John Paisley, the foremost teacher in the area, who lectured in the College but was not of it.

By 1732 Ilay had taken power from the chancellor and could elect the other officers in meetings which bent to his or his friends' wishes. From 1729 on, the deans were friendly and often picked not from the local clergymen, as had been the custom, but from the right-thinking professors themselves. Two of the three Ordinary Visitors would now be friendly to the Argathelians. In 1728, the reliable Master of Ross was again elected rector and from 1729 until 1738, with the exception of two years,[66] the rector was an Argathelian. Squadrone candidates may have run but they won only under exceptional circumstances and no important law cases arose from their efforts. But affairs in the University remained turbulent, as Robert Wodrow noted in February 1729:

> I hear ther are severall dicisions in the Colledge of Glasgou upon more subjects than one. The nominating a Factor is what the Principal's party are particularly divided about. The P[rincipal] and Doctor Johnstoun and some others are for Wood, factor to the Duke of Hamiltoun's part of Dundonald, with a reservation of somewhat for Mr Carmichael's son, as under-factor, or somewhat that way. Mr Dunlop, Mr Dick and R. Simson, are for Mr Thomas Harvey[67] but he is a bankrupt, and he cannot find caution. Hou that will end, time will try. Another thing like to divide them is a designe in the Pr[incip]le to setle Doctor [John] Campbell, in Paislay, Professor of Anatomy. He wants persons in the Faculty, to whom he can entirely trust, and when he spake to Doctor Brisbane and Doctor Johnstoun, they stormed furiously, and told him he must not take such steps to encrease persons to vote for him. They are divided, they say, as to the successor of Mr Simson, [professor of divinity] whom they begin nou to despair of carrying his point. The P[rincipal] and some feu they are for Mr Connell of Kilbride; Mr Dunlope, R. Simson, and Dick, are for Mr W. Wisheart; Mr Loudon, Carm[ichael,] and some others, for Mr Smith of Craumond. Houever, these are not yet come to any bearing, because the matter is not ripe.[68]

The place was factional but there were also the problems of keeping unity in one's faction when personal interests, loyalties and friendships played against policy and former appointments. Wodrow's account also suggests that Ilay was promoting better medical education in the University. If Principal Campbell meant to replace Brisbane, he could not have done so by himself or even with the help of his colleagues because Brisbane held a regius chair. Any alteration to that post would have required action by the Crown or its agents. To tamper with the chair of botany and anatomy would not have been discussed without Ilay's knowledge and approval. A new professorship would have demanded funding and a royal warrant. It was a political matter which would have needed the sanction of men in London. Appointing Paisley as a deputy or a lecturer in the College was a cheap way around such problems. It is interesting that the choice of a new divinity professor had already split the faculty along non-political lines. Matthew Connell, the minister of Kilbride, was a notable evangelical later involved with the 'Cambuslang Wark'.[69] Others on the list, such as James Smith of Cramond, were moderates and Erastians. Smith himself had become an Argathelian and by 1732 was professor of divinity at Edinburgh, where he succeeded to the principality in 1733.

The persistence of faction in 1729 also can be seen in the placement of the next professor, Francis Hutcheson (8 August 1694–8 August 1746), who, in 1729, succeeded Gershom Carmichael as professor of moral philosophy. Hutcheson had been one of the Irish divinity students who had been willing to take the matter of the rector's election to the Court of Session in 1717. In the interim he had become a successful Irish schoolmaster and notable philosophical writer, a man who, it was thought, might raise enrolments at Glasgow by attracting greater numbers of Irish students. His wife was professor Dunlop's first cousin.[70] That tied him to the rector chosen in the autumn of 1729 prior to his own election in December of that year. There were, however, other well-recommended candidates, including one unnamed who was favoured by the principal.

One candidate was Gershom Carmichael's son, Frederick, who had at some time the backing of several of his father's colleagues in the College, where he deputised for professor Ross in 1726–7.[71] Those associations and his father's dubious loyalty probably damned his chances here and elsewhere in Scotland.[72]

In November 1728, David Verner (or Warner), a regent at Marischal College from the Glasgow area and a nephew and cousin of the former divinity professors James and Alexander Wodrow, sought the post. He was a Glasgow graduate who had studied law for three years at Edinburgh and Glasgow but had opted for a teaching career. In 1717 he had been imposed on Marischal College by Squadrone men when orthodox Whigs were needed there. Verner would have been a good replacement for Carmichael, whose course dealt with natural law and contained references to the civil law.[73] Verner wrote to Robert Wodrow about the possibility of buying out Carmichael or exchanging places with his son should Frederick be given the living.[74] Nothing came of this overture.

A third contender for the place was Alexander Clarke, librarian of Glasgow University and son to a minister in Glasgow. He too was a relative of the Dunlops, a distant relative of Ilay and an intimate of the Mures of Caldwell. Among his sponsors was Magdalen Kinloch, who wrote to her relative, Lord Milton, asking for Ilay's support if it were not already committed.[75] By then Milton and Ilay had almost certainly decided to support Hutcheson.

At the election, the masters split, with the principal and others committed to 'Old Light' views voting against Hutcheson.[76] The influence of Ilay was decisive in Hutcheson's appointment:

. . . somebody had went up to Lord Ilay in favours of one ffran Hutcheson a relation of Mr Dunlops wife and who teaches philosophy at Dublin So the Congé d Elire having come down[,] the faculty was called on fryday and Hutcheson was chosen by a majority of two votes viz Wisheart, Dr Johnstoun[,] professor of Divinity[,] Mr Dunlop, Mr Rob: Simson, Mr Ross, Mr Dick, five of us voted for Mr Carmichael's son ffrederick a very pretty lad.[77]

It would have been known in advance that there was a clear majority for Hutcheson. That makes understandable the rector's decision not to come up for the meeting to which he sent a message saying that he hoped it would make 'a happy choice for the good of the University'. The well-informed Wodrow thought the rector had helped Hutcheson to obtain the post. Ilay's support may also explain why the masters decided unanimously not to resort to a comparative trial but to elect a man to the chair. That decision allowed full scope for political influences, something on which they might all agree while differing about whom they thought should exercise it. This election set a precedent by picking the first of the new specialised philosophy professors by a majority vote, but without a trial.[78]

There were no other professorial appointments until 1735 when the humanist, Andrew Ross, was permanently succeeded by his son George (c. 1716–26 August 1754), the first appointee in this period to be born in the eighteenth century. Andrew Ross had been unwell for many years and had been unable to teach between 1726 and 1729. Frederick Carmichael had taught for him in the first two years but in 1728–9 he was ignored and replaced by Alexander Campbell, son of Robert Campbell of Stockholm.[79] He was permanently replaced by Ross's son, whose trial of qualification was to translate into Latin 'the Duke of Argyll's speech for a standing army'. This appointment was not of the sort favoured by Ilay, who disliked seeing sons follow their fathers in office, but to the Carmichaels Ilay owed less than to the Rosses.[80] There may have been no other way to get Alexander Ross to relinquish his classroom. He did not fully resign until 1747.[81] Alexander Campbell was taken care of in other ways, which shows that he had been a serious candidate to whom the Argathelians owed something. In 1740, the election of a new professor of divinity would be more difficult.

Professor of divinity John Simson had had many problems with members of the Kirk who thought his teaching heretical. His problems culminated in a series of clerical court actions leading to his suspension from teaching in May 1727. The court cases and agitation lasted into the early 1730s as Simson and his defenders tried to gain his reinstatement.[82] After 1726–7, he relied upon the Argathelians for support in his efforts to escape conviction for heresy. In 1740, he finally died and a new man had to be chosen. There was a good deal of concern in the Kirk that the new professor be an orthodox divine. From the point of view of the political managers, he needed also to be reliable, someone who would be helpful to them in the management of the Kirk and someone from the Glasgow region. From the standpoint of the political opposition, which included now not only the Squadrone men but Ilay's brother, the 2nd Duke of Argyll, who had broken with the ministry in 1738, what was needed was someone who was not Ilay's candidate and not unorthodox. That man was found in an obscure country cleric, Michael Potter (1670–29 November 1743), minister of Kippen.

Political disorder afflicted the Argathelians both in and outside the University. In 1735, the reliable Francis Dunlop was again persuaded to be rector after Lord Milton had declined running. The following year the place went to a Squadrone man.[83] The largely student electorate chose rectors from Squadrone families until 1753, after which time the office was again occupied by Ilay's friends. All that is more explicable when one remembers the up-and-down fate of the Argathelians in those years. When the masters petitioned the House of Commons for money out of the ale duties levied in 1736, it was to Ilay that they turned for help and it was he whom they asked to congratulate the King on the marriage of the Prince of Wales in June of that year.[84] Later that autumn, when sentiment in Scotland began to favour the opponents of Ilay and Walpole, John Orr of Barrowfield was chosen as rector and served for two years. Ilay's supporters also lost the Glasgow burgh elections of that year.[85] In 1737, when the Duke of Argyll had asked for a Glasgow church to be given to Principal Neil

Campbell, the principal failed to get it.[86] Ilay was thanked in 1738 for 'obtaining a new Tack [lease] of the Archbishoprick of Glasgow to the University' but the masters also waited upon their chancellor, the 2nd Duke of Montrose, which they seem not to have done for a long time.[87] Two years later, the University men waited upon Montrose and again upon Argyll when he visited the city to canvass votes for the coming election of 1741.

The rectorial elections can be taken as a sign of the changes that were partly rooted in politics but partly in the increasing distaste felt for the regime of Principal Campbell.[88] The rector chosen in 1738 was George Bogle of Daldowie, a Squadrone man popular enough in later years to attract even the votes of men like Alexander Dunlop, Robert Simson, Robert Dick and Francis Hutcheson. After the visits of Montrose and Argyll, the rector chosen in the autumn of 1740 was John Graham of Dougalston.[89] He was succeeded by Orr of Barrowfield and then by Bogle of Daldowie. Until 1752, when William Mure of Caldwell became rector, the office was held by relatives of Montrose – Sir John Maxwell of Pollock II, John Graham of Dougalston – or by either Orr or Bogle. The opposition, entrenched in the rector's office, reflected student and faculty opposition to the regime of Neil Campbell, who was seen as something of a new Stirling.[90] The principal's opponents saw some point in electing as the University's chief magistrate a man who might oppose his acts. They were replaying the old opposition scenario that had once benefited Ilay but now helped his opponents. Politics had shifted and power in 1740 was moving out of Ilay's hands. Still, the deans of faculty and the professors were generally loyal to him until 1742, when the Squadrone regained power in Scotland. Ilay's control of the professors at the University and College was firm even though it was tried and contested by opponents in most years. But the Earl's wishes did not dictate the next appointment.

Michael Potter, who succeeded Simson as professor of divinity, had had Squadrone supporters but also help from Argathelians loyal to the Duke and less worried about Potter's political allegiances than about the religious outlook and evangelical temper of his opponent. Potter's family also had long been tied to the Erskines of Cardross, a family noted for its evangelical leanings, and earlier in his career he had found a patron in James Erskine, Lord Grange, now in opposition and no longer friendly with Ilay.[91] It helped Potter that Ilay's friends did not control the rectorship; Bogle's election in 1739 gave Potter an extra vote in the College meeting. The Argathelians split along religious and political lines. Ilay's candidate for the chair of divinity seems to have been John Maclaurin, the minister of the Ramshorn Church in Glasgow. The Earl could not have liked his theology and his support probably reflected loyalty to a family long connected to his own – and mischief-making since he knew the Squadrone leaders would not want to install a stiff-necked divine. John Maclaurin was not likely to preach or teach modern, tolerant and rationalistic divinity but the grace of God rooted in the sacrifice of Christ upon the Cross and mercifully dispensed to undeserving sinners as He decreed and predestinated from all eternity. Principal Campbell liked that theology and wanted Maclaurin to be professor of divinity but he knew the Squadrone rector would oppose him. With Campbell in support of Maclaurin were professors Johnstoun, Dick and Ross. Loudoun and Anderson might vote for him too. That would have left in clear opposition Morthland, Dunlop, Hutcheson, Simson, Forbes and Brisbane – a tie vote which the rector could break. He also believed he could call an election meeting at any time. Neil Campbell asked Milton to press professor Forbes to vote for Maclaurin in what was partly a factional fight and partly a struggle over whether to seat a theological moderate or a 'high flyer' and a vigorous evangelical.[92]

Maclaurin's brother, Colin, the distinguished Edinburgh professor of mathematics, made a bid for Squadrone support when he wrote to Gorthy on 15 March 1740 saying that he would have approached Montrose in London had there been more time. He wanted to '[clear] my brother from an imputation, that is particularly odious in a minister, namely that he would vote and act for political motives' and not as his conscience dictated. He would be no toady for the principal. Colin claimed that, like himself, John Maclaurin did not meddle with politics.[93]

In the end, Michael Potter was elected, with the rector voting for him along with Anderson, Morthland, Loudoun and Brisbane (Squadrone men) and Simson and Hutcheson (Argathelians). He was loosed from his parish and installed.[94] The College majority had shifted against Ilay and his friends and had done so partly because of the long-continued disarray in the Argathelian camp caused by the principal's behaviour and the Duke of Argyll's defection from Walpole's ministry. After the 1741 parliamentary elections, in which Ilay did well but not well enough, his support slipped even further. By the time the next professor was chosen, Squadrone men were again in power in Scotland and in the University.

Notes

1 Morthland to Gorthy, 11, 14, 23 and n.d. [but January] 1726, Montrose Papers, NAS, GD220/5/1030/2, 4, 6 and 8.
2 *Munimenta*, ed. Innes, II:569.
3 Quoted in *The Argyll Papers*, ed. Stevenson, 1834, p. 18.
4 Principal Stirling to Montrose, 21 January 1726, NAS, GD220/5/1031/2.
5 'Memoires of Dr Robertson', *Gentleman's Magazine*, 1783, p. 747f.
6 Walter Stewart to Robert Wodrow, 10 September 1726, ADV MSS, NLS Wodrow Letters Quarto XVII/131; see also Wodrow's account of the Visitation in *Analecta*, III:329–33. The embezzlement charge originated in the ' "Grievances" presented by the professors' in 1717 and rested on the fact that the principal had custody of most of the College's valuables but had no adequate inventory of them.
7 'I am preparing some measures to make uneasie some of the foe at Glasgow Colledge. There are (among other matters) two of them Law & Medicine who have been elected, & I think the Exchequer has made some memorandum upon the payment of their money containing its reservations of the right of the Crown; the medicine Dr Johnstoun is for us, the law, Forbes agt. Us, pray send me the name of A proper person in case I should happen to molest Knave Forbes.' Ilay to Lord Milton, 2 December 1727, Saltoun Correspondence, NLS, 16535/133.
8 Montrose to Gorthy, 3 August 1726, 1 September 1726; Montrose to? [Gorthy], 11 August 1726, NAS, GD220/5/856/1, 856/8, 856/5.
9 This paragraph draws on three articles on the Duke: Emerson, 'Catalogus Librorum A.C.D.A.', 2000, pp. 12–39; ——, 'The Scientific Interests of Archibald Campbell', 2002, pp. 21–56; and ——, 'Archibald Campbell, Terzo Duca di Argyll', *Filosofia, Scienza e Politica nel Settecento Britannico*, ed. Turco, Padua, 2003, pp. 127–61.
10 Wodrow, *Analecta*, ed. Leishman, 1854, III:440f.
11 *Munimenta*, ed. Innes, 1854, III:345.
12 George, Master of Ross to Lord Milton, 31 March 1727, NLS, 16537/152f.
13 Alexander Dunlop to Milton, 24 November 1727, NLS, 16536/86f.
14 Morthland to Gorthy, 16 November 1727, NAS, GD220/5/1066/3.
15 Robert Simson, Robert Dick, Alexander Dunlop, Andrew Ross to Lord Milton, 15 November 1727, NLS, 16535/84.
16 Ross, who was going mad, defected from the Argathelians. Within a year he was 'tyd hand and foot' and was thereafter periodically restrained until his death in 1751. Neil Campbell, 7 November 1727, NLS, 16535/210; Alexander Dunlop to [?Lord Milton], 24 November 1727, NLS, 16536/86.
17 Ilay described the events on 24 November 1727 in a letter to Lord Milton: 'The Malice of the ye Enemy has I am affraid turned Profr Ross's

head. Mr Anderson Ano[the]r & prof of Ecclesiastick History [*sic.*] gave rise to all yse discords by leting into his Class several of ye tradesmen Apprentices Supercargoes preachers & c.' NLS, 16535/131.

18 Dunlop to Milton, NLS, 16536/86–7.

19 'I am glad to find you sent the Master of Rosse to Glasgow, for otherwise the Enemy would have thought we gave it up.' Ilay to Milton, 2 December 1727, NLS, 16535/133; Alexander Dunlop to Lord Milton, 24 November 1727, NLS, 16536/86.

20 Alexander Dunlop to Lord Milton, 15 November 1727, NLS, 16535/82. This is one of a series of letters which Dunlop wrote that autumn to keep Milton abreast of developments in Glasgow.

21 Coutts, *History*, 1909, p. 204.

22 Morthland to Gorthy, 26 June and 3 July 1728, NAS, GD220/5/1081/23, 24.

23 Montrose to Gorthy, 17 July 1727, NAS, GD220/5/860/8.

24 Montrose to Gorthy, 4 and 6 April 1728, NAS, GD220/5/863/1b.

25 Montrose to Gorthy, 26 July and 28 October 1727, NAS, GD220/5/861/6 and 9a.

26 Charles Morthland to Gorthy, 9 November 1727, NAS, GD220/5/1066/2.

27 The professor even acted for some time as a factor to the Glanderston estate. Col. John Campbell to [?Lord Milton], 2 October 1727, NLS, 16539/180.

28 Wodrow, *Analecta*, ed. Leishman, 1853, III:444.

29 Col. John Campbell to [?Milton], [?] October 1727, NLS 16539/182. 1727 was an election year and the control of the Glasgow burghs was important to Ilay's friends. Campbell of Shawfield lost the poll but was seated by the House of Commons on a technicality. *The History of Parliament*, ed. Sedgwick, 1970, I:520.

30 It was valued at £50 a year but by c. 1745 had risen to £67. Neil Campbell agreed to this arrangement in a letter to Milton but also asked Milton to keep looking for something else for Dunlop. Neil Campbell to Milton, 13 November 1727, NLS, 16535/182, 208. This deal may have made easier the translation of Neil Campbell from his living in Renfrew, which could not take place without active support in the College to prosecute his case and the willingness of his Presbytery to let him go. The Squadrone opposed his translation, which was seen as a party matter, both within the Presbytery and in the College. George Gordon to Principal George Chalmers, 26 December 1727, AUL, K255, Crown Tower* Box 43.

31 Alexander Dunlop to [?Lord Milton], 8 September 1729, NLS, 16540/161.

32 Charles Erskine to Charles Delafaye, 26 March 1726, NAS, SP 54/17/20.

33 Wodrow, *Analecta*, ed. Leishman, 1853, II:332.

34 Robert Hepburn to Milton, 9 October 1727, NLS, 16537/37; Fawcett, *The Cambuslang Revival*, 1996, p. 220. Gusthart became Dean of the

Chapel Royal but by 1756 Milton's friends were telling him that Gusthart should not meddle in the plans of the Argathelian divines; William Alston to Lord Milton, 8 August 1756, NLS, 16694/6.

35 Lachman, *The Marrow Controversy*, 1988, p. 169.

36 Ilay to Milton, 14 May 1726, NLS, 16533/80

37 The opposition, at the urging of Montrose, intended to examine Campbell's fitness as a professor and then to find him unfit. Alexander Dunlop to [?Lord Milton], 24 November 1727, NLS, 16536/86.

38 Lord Milton suggested to Ilay that another Visitation might still be necessary to quash political opposition at Glasgow: Milton to Ilay, 1 December 1727, NLS, 16535/157.

39 See Skoczylas, *Mr Simson's Knotty Case*, 2001, passim. Morthland to Gorthy, 16 March 1728, NAS, GD220/5/1081/9.

40 He had been in Edinburgh where he was confined; he later sued his colleagues for 'wrongous Imprisonment'. Charles Morthland to Gorthy, 5 February 1729, NAS, GD220/5/1106/1.

41 Morthland to Montrose, 27 March 1727, NAS, GD220/5/1081/23, 24.

42 Robert Simson to Lord Milton, 14 October 1728, NLS, 16539/174 and Morthland to Gorthy, 6 November 1728, NAS, GD220/5/1081/30. Ilay's plans to harass 'knave Forbes' involved withholding his salary which was paid by the Exchequer; Ilay to Milton, 2 December 1727, NLS, 16535/133.

43 The voting was witnessed by Col. Campbell of Mamore, later the 4th Duke of Argyll. Charles Morthland to Gorthy, 15 November 1728, NAS, GD220/5/1081/32.

44 Simson to Lord Milton, 14 October 1728 NLS, 16539/174; Wodrow, *Analecta*, ed. Leishman, 1853, IV:28.

45 Charles Morthland to Gorthy, 26 June and 3 July 1728, NAS, GD220/5/1081/23, 24.

46 Collections Regarding Kings College [made by professor Thomas Gordon], AUL, K 34, pp. 5–6.

47 Emerson, *Professors, Patronage and Politics*, 1991, p. 35; *Fasti Academiae Mariscallanae Aberdonensis*, ed. P. J. Anderson, 1889, II:6.

48 Erskine and Ilay believed this to have been the opinion of the Lord Advocate of 1716 when he was a Visitor of the Aberdeen Universities. Ilay stated his belief to Newcastle in a letter of 28 June 1728, NAS, SP 54/19/36. See also Charles Erskine to Newcastle, 26 March 1726, NAS, SP 54/17/20. This contains a 'Memorial Anent the Interest of the Crown . . .' The Argathelians were trying to impose on Marischal College a mathematician named Campbell – probably George Campbell, an extramural teacher in Edinburgh. That failed because by its foundation the chair was to be granted only after a comparative trial which in this case was won by the son of the Provost of Aberdeen, John Stewart. He became a distinguished mathematician and teacher.

49 Alexander Dunlop to [?Andrew Fletcher, Lord Milton], 24 November 1727, NLS, 16536/87; Morthland to Gorthy, 29 November 1727, 1 [or 8] December 1727, and Morthland's undated memorandum, NAS, GD220/5/1066/6, 8 and 10.

50 Charles Morthland to Gorthy, 16 March 1728, NAS, GD220/5/1081/9.

51 Morthland to Gorthy, 19 January 1728, NAS, GD220/5/1095/2.

52 John Hamilton to Montrose, 26 June 1728, NAS, GD220/5/864/2.

53 Montrose to Gorthy, 9 July 1728, NAS, GD220/5/864/3.

54 John Hamilton to [?Gorthy], 26 February and 22 July 1728, NAS, GD220/5/1095/1 and 2.

55 Montrose to Gorthy, 5 July 1730, NAS, GD220/5/872/1b.

56 Charles Morthland to Montrose, 26 February 1728, NAS, GD220/5/1081/5; Morthland to Gorthy, 26 June 1728, NAS, GD220/5/1081/5; 1081/23. Morthland to Gorthy, 11 December 1728, NAS, GD220/5/1081/34. Ilay had in 1716 refused the offer of the chancellorship of King's College, as did the Duke of Roxburghe. It is very unlikely that Ilay was chancellor of Marischal College and University as is sometimes claimed, e.g. P. J. Anderson, *Fasti Academiae Mariscallanae*, 1889, II:8.

57 Mackie, *University of Glasgow*, 1954, pp. 196–201.

58 Charles Morthland to Gorthy, 11 December 1728, NAS, GD220/5/1081/34.

59 'The Case of Mr Morthland', NAS, GD220/5/1918/7.

60 Morthland to Montrose, 3 November 1727, NAS, GD220/5/861/13.

61 Charles Morthland to Gorthy, 26 January–15 April 1728, NAS, GD220/5/1081/2–14.

62 Charles Morthland to Gorthy, 26 March 1729, NAS, GD220/5/1106/2.

63 Charles Morthland to Gorthy, 19 and 21 June 1728, NAS, GD220/5/1081/20, 23.

64 Motherland to Montrose, 26 June 1730, NAS, GD220/5/872/2.

65 Charles Morthland to Gorthy, 21 September 1728, NAS, GD220/5/1081/28.

66 In 1731 the professors elected as rector John Orr of Barrowfield, a man from a Jacobite family, who was referred to as a Squadrone man in a letter of Morthland to Gorthy, 19 January 1732, NAS, GD220/51214/1. Orr was friendly with professors of both factions. Several lent him money to establish himself in business after nearly failing. He gave £500 to the library in 1730. The interest on this was to be used initially to buy classical works and then, once the collection was complete, for books in other fields. Coutts, *History*, 1909, p. 255.

67 Hervie was the man set upon by the Squadrone in 1719; see Skoczylas, *Mr Simson's Knotty Case*, 2001, p. 195. He became an accountant to the Visitation of 1726–7 and was well paid for his work; see Coutts, *History*, 1909, p. 207.

68 Wodrow, *Analecta*, ed. Leishman, 1853, IV:28.

69 Fawcett, *The Cambuslang Revival*, 1996, p. 215.

70 Wodrow, *Analecta*, ed. Leishman, IV:99; Jones, 'The Scottish professoriate and the polite academy, 1720–46', *Wealth and Virtue*, ed. Hont and Ignatieff, 1985, pp. 89–117; p. 103.

71 Wodrow says five men supported him; *Analecta*, IV:99. Loudoun named as his supporters Forbes, Brisbane, Anderson, Morthland and himself. Loudoun to Graham of Gorthy, 25 November 1729, NAS, GD220/5/1106/7.

72 Frederick Carmichael failed to secure posts in Aberdeen, St Andrews and Edinburgh.

73 Verner's teaching is described in Wood, *The Aberdeen Enlightenment*, 1993, pp. 3, 24, 26, 27, 36, 39, 40, 49, 55, 60, 72, 162. See also Cairns, 'Lawyers, Law Professors and Localities', *Northern Ireland Legal Quarterly*, 46 (1995), pp. 304–31; Emerson, *Professors, Patronage and Politcs*, 1991, p. 36.

74 Wodrow, *Analecta*, ed. Leishman, IV:99; NLS, Wodrow Letters Quarto, XVIII:190.

75 Magdalen Kinloch to Andrew Fletcher, Lord Milton, 29 November 1729, NLS, 16540/169; see also Jones, 'The Scottish professoriate and the polite academy, 1720–46', *Wealth and Virtue*, ed. Hont and Ignatieff, 1985, pp. 89–117; p. 103.

76 Scott, *Francis Hutcheson*, 1966, pp. 54–5. Warner is likely to have been the candidate of the evangelicals.

77 Charles Morthland to Gorthy, 22 December 1729, NAS, GD220/5/1106/7.

78 Minutes, 12 December 1729, GUA, 26635.

79 Coutts, *History*, 1909, p. 215; Minutes, 11 October, 13 October, 5 November 1728, GUA, 26635. Those who opposed the appointment of Campbell seem to have included Carmichael and Loudoun, Anderson and Morthland. The first two were old and close friends; all were Squadrone loyalists.

80 Ross later voted with the College's evangelicals.

81 Glasgow Minutes, 11 February 1747, GUA, 26639.

82 Those are discussed in Skoczylas, *Mr Simson's Knotty Case*, 2001.

83 Neil Campbell to Milton 10, and 31 October and 7 November 1735, NLS, 16559/306ff.

84 'Minutes of the University Meeting', 20 February and 4 June 1736, GUA, 26639.

85 Morthland to Gorthy, 9 November 1736, NAS, GD220/5/1388/3.

86 Milton to Ilay, February or March 1737, NLS, 16569/62.

87 'Minutes of the University Meeting', GUA, 26639, 7 April 1738.

88 The Master of Ross to Lord Milton, 21 November 1735, NLS, 16563/62.

89 'Minutes of the University Meeting', GUA, 26639, 26 June 1740.

90 As early as 1732 Ilay noted that it might be a good thing to bring Campbell to an Edinburgh church and replace him with a more popular man. Ilay to Milton, 28 April 1732, NLS, 16548/119.

91 [?James Erskine, Lord Grange] to James Erskine, 20 January 1708, Mar and Kellie Papers, NAS, GD124/15/771/2. I thank Anne Skoczylas for this information.

92 Men like John Maclaurin believed in preaching the Word not to all but to those who professed to be Christians and came to church or to revival meetings. They hoped those people would respond even though they thought that most of their hearers were damned. Men like them opposed the soul-saving efforts of men like George Whitefield who was quite willing to preach to all the wayward and to those whose hearts were not prepared by presbyterian discipline to receive the Word. The High-flyers liked their gospel 'hot', and wanted no interference in the Kirk by the government – which should nonetheless support it. They opposed patronage, disliked the toleration which they had to extend to others, and tended to think that moralising sermons did not serve the Lord so well as preaching 'Christ and him crucified'. At the same time, many of them were, like Maclaurin, good Lockean Whigs, readers of polite literature and interested in science and improvements.

93 Colin Maclaurin to Gorthy, 15 March 1740, NAS, GD220/5/1500. Maclaurin went on to say that he had only intervened in two appointments in Edinburgh, those of John Stevenson and John Pringle, both men with Squadrone backing. Maclaurin, had he acted from political and family loyalty, would have supported men backed by the Argathelians and not those whom he had supported.

94 Hutcheson's own preference for the post was William Leechman; 'Letters of Francis Hutcheson', GUL, Gen 1018/12; details of the business of releasing or 'loosing' him from his parish are contained in GUA, 45268–700.

5

SQUADRONE GLASGOW AND THE RETURN OF THE DUKE OF ARGYLL, 1742–1761

℘

1. Squadrone Glasgow

The decline of Ilay's faction was quick in coming and occurred even before Walpole resigned in February 1742. John Graham reported to Mungo Graham of Gorthy early in 1741, long before the spring parliamentary elections of MPs, that only two or three professors were firm Argathelians. He was sure that the election of a new chancellor, which he expected soon, would be 'an affront upon them'. It came later than he had hoped but it was an affront: the 2nd Duke of Montrose was installed in 1743, which ensured that tensions in the corporations would continue for years to come.[1] Also galling was the election of a professor of anatomy and botany to replace Brisbane in 1742.

Thomas Brisbane died on 27 March 1742 after a lingering illness and the University soon got a new professor of anatomy and botany. He was Robert Hamilton (11 July 1714–15 May 1756), who for some time had taught anatomy (but not botany) for Brisbane. It was not just his professional skills that led to his appointment by the Crown. William Anderson had been asked by the Squadrone managers to recommend a successor for Brisbane. In a letter to the Marquis of Tweeddale, now the leader of the Squadrone faction, Anderson wrote, '. . . our Rector[,] Dean of Faculty and four other friends Joyn on the 29th in recommending to our Chancellor the D. of Montrose[,] Dr Robert Hamilton Younger of Airdrie as a fit person on all account to Supplie that Vacancie'.[2] Outside the University, Hamilton was supported by Sir John Inglis, who offered to send in testimonials of Hamilton's qualifications for the place. Other Squadrone men backed a Mr McLean.[3]

Two other candidates were mentioned in a letter from Robert Dundas which is interesting for showing the state of the College political factions at this time:

I find the case among the Colledge folks is, they are still in a sort of divi-sion into two partys, one led by principal Campbell[,] the other opposers[,] the remains of what was formerly the D. of Montroses interest, the last favours Doctor Hamilton, the principal and his set favour one Doctor Clerk or one Widrow[.][4] I know none of them. [B]y what I hear the physi-cians in Edr give it for Hamilton in point of knowledge, and if I give an opinion, it is with submission this, that I think neither p. Campbell nor his set, are to be favoured by your Lo in point of politick[,] and I also think a man so nearly concerned in the late professor Hamilton and his sons,[5] who behave very well[,] may deserve some regard in competition with the other two, who I doubt have other merit than P[rincipal] Campbells favour.[6]

Hamilton was chosen and William Anderson thanked Tweeddale for an election which 'is most agreeable to the greater number of Masters in our Societie'. He went on to say, 'Thanks have been return'd our Chancellor by the Rector in name of these Masters for his good offices in that affair'.[7] The new professor gave in his presen-tation to the regius chair on 18 May 1742 and the Squadrone inter-est in the corporations increased by one. There is no correspondence in the Saltoun papers about this appointment which Ilay was unable to stop or influence. He had lost the right to name to regius chairs. Hamilton's vote ensured that the next University professor chosen would not be from Ilay's faction.

When Ilay was deprived of the right to administer government patronage in Scotland by the fall of Walpole, in February 1742, he did not cease to be a power in Scotland. On 4 October 1743, he became the 3rd Duke of Argyll and inherited with his title the influence which his brother had formerly exercised over a vast area of the country. He owned or was the feudal superior of lands which covered between 3,000 and 4,000 square miles. About this time he also began the con-struction of Inveraray Castle, a project which increased his personal influence in the West of Scotland because of the purchases and the work it brought into the area. His building costs often exceeded £4,000 in a year, a sum not far below the reputed landed income of the Dukes of Montrose. Argyll may have been out of power but in the West of Scotland he was still a man to reckon with. He could and did contest the next professorship when again he backed John Maclaurin but many of his friends did not. Ilay's motives were likely mischievous and not ones which on principle really favoured the man he supported.

Professor Potter died on 23 November 1743. Within hours there was an open competition to succeed him in the divinity chair. This contest again pitted John Maclaurin against a moderate man. Francis

Hutcheson and others had been planning for this election for some time. As early as 5 August 1743, Hutcheson had given a friend character of William Leechman (1706–3 December 1785), one which listed all the virtues that moderate men sought in candidates for such positions:

> You never knew a better sweeter man, of excellent literature, & except his air, and a litle roughness of voice, the best preacher imaginable. You could not get a greater blessing among you of that kind . . . Leechman is well as he is and happy, tho preaching to a pack of horsecopers & smugglers of the rudest sort . . . He was the man I wished in the first place to be our Professor of Theology.[8]

He could have added that Leechman was descended from a Covenanting family which was dependent on Baillie of Jarviswood whose political ties ran to the Squadrone.[9]

On the day Potter died, Hutcheson wrote to William Mure of Caldwell asking him to write letters on behalf of Leechman, his old tutor.[10] Hutcheson writes as if he and Mure were of the chancellor's party. He hoped Montrose would write letters to professor Morthland who might then convince professors Loudoun, Anderson and Forbes to vote for Leechman. From the letter, it is clear that Hutcheson saw Leechman as a man 'universally approved for literature and eloquence'. He made no comment on his doctrinal beliefs. Maclaurin, like William Anderson, had been involved in the open-air religious revival at Cambuslang which all sensible moderate men and clerics had opposed and regarded as a frightful manifestation of enthusiasm. Hutcheson wanted this known, particularly to Andrew (later Sir Andrew) Mitchell, the under-manager for the Squadrone in London, and to the latter's boss, John Hay, 4th Marquis of Tweeddale. Hutcheson thought that the right-thinking might carry the election of Leechman without some of the evangelical-leaning masters – Anderson, Forbes, Loudoun or Principal Campbell. Relying on their votes 'might be thought a disagreeable obligation'. He would rather have Leechman clearly, and only, indebted for his post to the Duke of Montrose and his friends. Hutcheson listed the sure votes for Leechman as his own and those of Dunlop, Simson, Hamilton, Ross and Morthland; Dick was leaning their way. That left Anderson, Loudoun and Forbes opposed. The principal and Johnstoun were unlisted but they had opposed him earlier.[11]

Others were writing letters too. Minds had been made up by the time Potter died. The issues that had swayed men were party loyalty and a liking for, or dislike of, enthusiastic religion. It did not matter that Maclaurin was also a learned and clever man and a better and more orthodox theologian than Leechman who was known only as a preacher.

Principal Campbell had been counting votes as long as Francis Hutcheson. His count was probably the one given by Colin Maclaurin to Mitchell in a letter of 22 November, one in which he regretted that he could not decently ask for help for his brother because of the latter's role at the Cambuslang revival which most of the Squadrone men would have resented, feared or despised. Colin guessed the votes for his brother to be those of Anderson, Loudoun, Johnstoun, Forbes, Dick and Principal Campbell. The principal hoped that Lord Ross would be able to persuade professor Ross to vote for Maclaurin.[12] All the voters were committed but one he thought approachable – professor Hamilton, who was, unfortunately, distantly related by marriage to Leechman. Colin Maclaurin expected his brother would lose. Dunlop, Morthland, Hutcheson, Simson, Hamilton and Ross would vote against him, as would the rector. His count proved correct.[13]

Others besides the professors had been working on the election. William Craig, the minister of Cambusnethan, had had his eye on the place but soon withdrew his candidacy in favour of his friend Leechman. The votes of the moderate men would not be split.[14] Three days after Potter's death, his office was being sought by men outside the University who had no doubt already made their plans knowing that the elderly Potter had not long to live. On 26 November, Thomas Hay, the Edinburgh manager for his faction, wrote to the Marquis of Tweeddale, the leader of the Squadrone, that

> [?Houston of] Clerkington told me that the professor of Divinity in the University of Glasgow was dead and desired earnestly that I would write to your Lordship in behalf of Mr Stedman the second Minister of Haddington for the office who he said he was sure would be most accept-able and taken as a great honour by Sir Robert Sinclair [of Stevenson] and all his family. He spoke likewise of the Earl of Hopetowns being disposed to assist Stedman – which is very probable and he said he believed that Mr Charles Hope [Lord Hopetoun's son who later adopted the name Hope-Weir] intended to write to Lord George [?Hay] upon it and that Mr Hope would have spoke to me but supposed I might be engadged I said I did not pretend to have a voice in disposing of anything and thought it my duty to make a ffair representation of all recommendations imparted to me and would have done so by Mr Hopes if he had desired me.

After noting that the post was not a regius chair, he suggested that Tweeddale should write to William Anderson about Stedman, if this seemed feasible, but he supposed that Anderson had already written to his Lordship with some opinion in the matter.[15]

Lord George did write on behalf of Lord Napier to both Tweeddale and professor Anderson but by then the faculty had split into two groups engaged to others – six for Maclaurin and six for Leechman. In his letter of 29 November, Hay mentioned that Bailie Hamilton and Robert Dundas, another Squadrone man, had been active in this matter.[16] On that same day, the faculty meeting voted to select the new professor on 13 December. Such notices of elections were signs of a divided meeting and allowed time for each side to muster all its forces before a decisive vote. The outcome is reported in a letter from John Graham to Graham of Gorthy in which he says that the division favoured Leechman. Dunlop, Morthland, Hutcheson, Simson, Hamilton, Ross and the rector were for him. Against him were Loudoun, Anderson and Principal Campbell, 'so Leechman will Carry to be professor'. Ten days later he wrote to say the election went to Leechman but the vote was closer than he had expected. Anderson protested the rector's vote.[17] Argyll's friends had split: Simson, Dunlop and Ross voted for Leechman, along with the rector, Morthland, Hutcheson and Hamilton, who belonged then to the Squadrone faction. For Maclaurin were Anderson and Dick, who sometimes voted with the Squadrone, and Principal Campbell, Loudoun, Forbes and Johnstoun.[18] Neither political faction had held together in the face of conflicts over theological issues which had divided masters in unusual ways. Neither of the new factions, if they can be called that, was content to drop the dispute.

All of the losing voters requested that their names be noted in the minutes as having voted for Maclaurin. Anderson then challenged Bogle's right to vote because he believed the right resided only with the masters acting in the College meeting presided over by the principal and not in the senatus which met at the rector's call and in which the rector voted. Anderson's reason was the source of funding for the divinity chair. His protest was in turn protested by the winning voters and another protest was lodged by the rector who claimed his 'undoubted right to call and preside at any meeting for Electing a Professor'.[19] The cases then went to the courts. More politicking took place to prevent Leechman from being 'loosed' or translated from his living. If this were prevented, then he could not take up his new chair. Obstructing his translation now became an objective. If it could be accomplished, the Squadrone men who had backed Leechman outside the College would suffer humiliation.

Colin Maclaurin shortly after the decision was in touch with Argathelians concerning the strategy which might be pursued. Preventing Leechman's translation would occasion a new election, one in which professor Ross had promised his vote for Maclaurin. Lady Eglinton, the person of highest status in Leechman's parish and a friend of Argyll, was to be written to, as were other local notables, in the hope that they could organise a protest in the Presbytery of Irvine and defeat the plan to translate Leechman to the University. There was some prospect of the case getting into the Synod where, it was thought, Leechman would lose.[20] Maclaurin also wrote to Andrew Mitchell reporting that the case was now in the courts and that some, including Mungo Graham of Gorthy, Montrose's factor and agent, thought the chancellor had not been duly regarded in a hurried process. This was a bid for aid from the Squadrone although Colin Maclaurin recognised that it was difficult to ask for help for his brother because of his involvement in the 'Cambuslang Wark'. Still, as he concluded, 'My friend is really over Orthodox, but is not honesty and sincerity some ballance for this, considering how much that College suffered formerly by a Profr of D-y'.[21] Despite the efforts to prevent it, Leechman was loosed from his parish on the application of the rector and a committee was appointed by the College to wait on his Presbytery.[22] On 4 January 1744, Leechman appeared before the Presbytery of Glasgow to sign the Confession of Faith but was denied the right to do so by John Maclaurin's Glasgow colleagues. The next day, Leechman accepted the place to which he had been elected but those masters who voted against him did not attend the faculty meeting.[23] On 11 January, he was admitted, with the minority who voted against him still protesting. The processes dragged on until the next meeting of the General Assembly in the following May when Leechman's election was found good.

The election of Leechman is an interesting case. It involved a large number of Squadrone politicians who saw it in factional terms. The Argathelians were seen as not only defending Maclaurin as one of their own but creating trouble for rivals newly come to the exercise of power after many years in the wilderness. Ilay himself had no sympathy with the views which Maclaurin held. Indeed, he regularly deplored 'the hot brethren' and never supported for university office in Glasgow another man like Maclaurin. Neither did his opponents. Despite its political cast, this election turned on the religious opinions of the candidates and those who voted for them. It installed a divine with good connections to the moderate men in the church, to literati, such as Hume and his friends, and to politicians who were not going to have an 'overly Orthodox' divine breeding up more like himself to preach to them of their sins. Leechman was a smooth man not bent on the saving of souls. He preferred to make men moral, a much lower, if more useful, calling. Glasgow University was changed by this appointment.

Leechman's election ended the control of any Scottish university seminary by orthodox high flyers and evangelicals until the nineteenth century. It also installed a heretic worse than Simson. Even though Hutcheson might describe Leechman to Thomas Drennan as 'a Right Professor of Theology, the only thorough right one in Scotland', all that showed was that Hutcheson himself was less a Calvinist than a Christian Stoic.[24] With the appointment of Leechman, less attention was given at Glasgow to areas of traditional religious concern. The chairs of oriental language and ecclesiastical history for much of the rest of the century were filled by men who seem barely competent to teach their subjects but who were willing to take the places and then move on to other chairs. Moderatism might be 'polite' but it tended to slight the linguistic and historical training which had allowed Calvinists to defend their beliefs against the errors of Catholics, Anglicans and others. Men like William Robertson and Robert Watson wrote secular, not ecclesiastical history; and they tended to write about the modern period, not the primitive, medieval or reformation churches in which doctrines held by their Kirk were shaped and set. Those trends were reinforced when Leechman became principal in 1761. Another part of the legacy of the Leechman election was short-term bitterness, which led most of the masters who had opposed his election to the chair of divinity to oppose his quick election as dean of faculty. However, in the following year he was unanimously elected dean of faculty, a tribute to his winning ways. Faction of the usual sort, however, emerged again in the selection of a replacement for Charles Morthland who died in 1744 and was replaced by Alexander Dunlop II (c. 1717–4 September 1750).

Dunlop was son of professor Alexander Dunlop and the father of yet another Alexander who became a prominent surgeon in the city and dean of faculty from 1778 to 1780. Alexander II had served the College as librarian from 1739 to 1742. He then left to become a travelling tutor to the son of Sir James Campbell of Ardkinglass. Like his father, he adhered to the Campbells. Squadrone men opposed

Dunlop's election which in the end was unanimous but for Loudoun.[25] They did so partly for party reasons but partly because he was not a fit man for the place but one whom they wished to keep in the College.

The party reasons are made clear in a letter William Anderson wrote to Tweeddale after Morthland died on 4 September 1744. There he suggested that the Crown had the right to present to the chair and that doing so would give their faction 'one half of the members named above' which, with the rector's vote, would be decisive on many issues. Anderson also had a candidate for the oriental languages chair but surmised that 'the other candidate [Dunlop] who will surely be chosen by us soon after the 10th of Octr when the College sits down, unless you prevent it, is I believe a very good youth but being designed for a better post amongst us will neither study to fit himself for this nor continue longer in it than a better falls vacant'. In short, Dunlop was unqualified and uninterested in learning or teaching oriental languages but he was a man who could do other things.[26] Competence and politics were against him but the Squadrone managers overreached in their efforts to bolster their management of the College and lost the place.

Others had written to Montrose as well. On 4 October 1744, Andrew Mitchell reported to Tweeddale that 'the Masters were greatly divided, one part being for Mr Dunlop's son, and the other for one Mr Dick, and that it was reported there that the minority woud apply to the Crown to present, tho' the Masters had formerly elected to the professorship'. This was followed by an account of earlier elections and of the funding of the chair by the Crown.[27] That news was shortly after followed by a letter from Robert Craigie, then the Lord Advocate, to the College saying that because the Crown funded the chair of oriental languages, it retained the right of appointment. The University men should not elect a new professor before the Lord Advocate had considered the matter further. The masters and rector George Bogle replied on or about 15 October that this was not their understanding of the matter. They believed this professor was elected by them in the same manner as the professor of divinity. They might be divided in political loyalties but they united to defend their University's privileges. The masters and rector sent Craigie a record of elections and of the funding grants which showed no royal right to appoint.[28] The Lord Advocate eventually conceded the point but only after Dunlop was unanimously elected on 22 October 1745 before Craigie had replied.[29] Dunlop served in this post until his death in 1750, but did not take it up until the spring of 1746.

2. GLASGOW AFTER THE '45

If partisan politics was evident in the previous appointments, things changed somewhat after 1745. The '45 had absorbed the energies and attention of the managers of the two principal Scottish factions but it left each uncertain of their positions. When the '45 came, Argyll and his friends, even though out of power, were again more effective agents for the government than were their political opponents who lacked significant Highland connections and were generally not very active in opposing the rebels. Argyll was unsure of returning to power but Tweeddale and his friends were equally uncertain of their position. The consequence was that no one could dominate the appointment process; all had to make some compromises. The absence of strong management meant that men outside the parties might snag an appointment for their friends. There are no indications that the Squadrone had a hand in the first of the three appointments made in 1746 but in only one did the Argathelians exercise much influence.

James Moor (22 June 1712–17 September 1779) succeeded the elder Dunlop in the chair of Greek after a contest with an unknown opponent. Moor had been a Glasgow schoolmaster and tutor to three lords – the Earls of Selkirk and Errol and Baron Kilmarnock.[30] When Moor was elected, he was librarian of the College and remained so until 1747. The College men were looking after one of their own. He was a good Grecian, an amateur mathematician of considerable ability and a polite and clubbable man also known to be somewhat irascible. Moor was a useful man who had been active as an editor for the Foulis Press. Later he was a particular friend of Robert Simson and on good terms with the 3rd Duke of Argyll, with whom he shared interests in numismatics and mathematics. Francis Hutcheson was especially helpful to Moor but the money to buy the chair from its incumbent came from the 4th Earl of Selkirk, who seems to have put up the £600 which enabled Dunlop to retire. Dunlop kept his house and salary until his death in 1747. This appointment does not seem to have involved much more than accommodating a nobleman and appointing a man who was known to the masters as bright, capable and already within the College. Such appointments were made when outsiders did not intervene. A great importance was given to it by Hutcheson and his biographer who thought it involved 'the Soul of the College . . . and all may be ruined by one vote'.[31] Moor's vote made the moderates' interest in the College unbeatable. Other men appointed soon after seem not to have had any interest in high-flying religion, which was Hutcheson's chief concern. They may not even have been good Christians. Indeed, William Cullen hung in his house an engraving of the noted deist, Matthew Tindal.[32]

The second appointee of 1746 was William Cross (25 June 1711–22 May 1775), who became the new regius professor of law. Many people wanted Cross to get this post but for different reasons. It appears that Argyll was the one who in the end secured it for him. But Cross was not the only one who wanted it. Cross thought that the man whose chances were best in November 1745 was Charles Hamilton Gordon. Gordon had seemingly been elected to the sinecure position of civilist at King's College in 1743 but the seeming loser of that chair, James Catanach, appealed to the Court of Session and then to the House of Lords. In 1745 the House of Lords found that Catanach was the duly elected man and Gordon was extruded.[33] In Aberdeen, Gordon was supported by some but not all of the local Squadrone men. In Glasgow he was expected to have the support of another man prominent in that connection, Robert Dundas, now Lord Arniston, SCJ.[34]

Among the other men who wanted the place was Hew Dalrymple's son, David Dalrymple of Westhall (or Westerhall). His family were Argathelians and Principal Campbell and Lord Milton actively supported him.[35] By April 1746, Argyll himself was said to be 'in favour of Mr Erskine' but it is not clear which Mr Erskine this might be.[36] Another who sought the place was Hercules Lindsay. Professor William Anderson had written to the Marquis of Tweeddale in 1744 saying that Lindsay

> has been about us gaping for [Professor of Law, William] Forbes death these four years past, And he and his friends gave it out that the present D. of Argyll stood engaged to procure that post for him: And considering his patron[,] I never once doubted but he would have your Lop's interest also.[37]

The patron Anderson had in mind is unknown but it was probably Duncan Forbes of Culloden, then the much-respected Lord President of the Court of Session who was not particularly friendly with the 3rd Duke of Argyll. Lindsay had other backers too. He had been teaching in Glasgow as a deputy since 1740 and the professors thought he would make a good professor of law, although he had only recently become an advocate.[38] Argyll's friends in the College wanted no part of Cross but favoured Lindsay. By November 1745, Montrose had been told that by eight of the professors and by the rector.[39] The same professors had written to Argyll on 17 March 1746 over the opposition of Robert Dick and William Anderson, who had been appointed by the Squadrone and were still loyal to it. By then Argyll thought he could do nothing about this appointment and had written to the principal to say so.[40] Lindsay had also met determined opposition from Robert Dundas, who saw him as the friend of the Jacobite lawyer, Sir James Steuart, who had humiliated Dundas with a lawsuit brought in the court on which Dundas sat as a judge.[41] To overcome that animus, Lindsay had made up to Squadrone men and may have changed his political allegiance. It also helped him that the chancellor voiced some discontent with William Cross, whom some professors thought would become a sinecurist and an absentee. Despite Lindsay's political waverings, the professors favoured him, probably recognising that his Squadrone sentiments were not deeply rooted and that trimming was in fashion. Argyll or his party had been involved with all of the above-named candidates; they would try to have a say in this appointment and show Ilay's power and claims to office and the exercise of patronage. This was not an unrealistic stance since the fourth candidate, William Cross, had approached Principal Campbell in October 1745 and by the winter of 1745/6 had the backing of old Argathelians. Those men included Duncan Forbes of Culloden and some on the Glasgow Town Council, of whom Andrew Cochrane, Provost of Glasgow, was the most important.

Provost Cochrane was a man much harried in 1745. With the rebellion, business in Glasgow had come to a halt. The city was not defended by the government but was told to arm and defend itself. It was not given arms but was criticised for not doing more than it did. That was hard enough, but the rebels occupied the burgh and took away many thousands of pounds in 'fines', 'cess', and plunder which made the bad situation worse. In London, the burgh leaders looked culpable and needed help in the defence of their reputations. They turned to Argyll, to whom they wrote for arms, men, direction, relief and the defence of their integrity and to whom they also sent intelligence.[42] Cochrane also wrote rather similar letters to Lord Milton, LJC, and to Lord President Duncan Forbes.[43] Cross had been helpful and well placed to be so since his father was a Glasgow merchant who rose to be Dean of Guild. Cross also helped to organise the defence against the rebels and volunteered in the Glasgow battalion which marched to Stirling in the late autumn of 1745. He had carried dispatches and intelligence to keep the provost informed of troop movements. Earlier, in December 1745, the provost had written that 'the magistrates and most of our principal

inhabitants' wanted Cross to be given the professorship. Duncan
Forbes of Culloden seconded those recommendations. When called
upon to do so, he had in 1746 and again in 1747 written memoranda
justifying the conduct of the city officials.[44] In September 1746, the
burgh sent Cross to London to convey, in a gold box, the freedom of
the city to the Duke of Cumberland.[45] They expected Cross to visit
Argyll, to whom Cochrane wrote a letter of introduction that would
allow him 'the opportunity of acknowledging your favour of procur-
ing him the professorship of law in our university'.[46] Forbes had
appealed not only to Argyll but to Tweeddale in November 1745. The
Marquis said it would have been churlish to refuse the Lord President
because of his service in the '45. He would also have remembered that
the Lord President was not of the 3rd Duke's party but had been closer
to the 2nd Duke of Argyll. Indeed, Forbes had broken with the 3rd
Duke years before.[47] Tweeddale was willing to support a man whom
Argyll now backed. Did he know Argyll had already secured the
promise of the chair from Henry Pelham? Cross was appointed because
of his services in the '45 and because the town wanted him appointed.
Cross's case was not unique; John Chalmers of King's College seems to
have owed his elevation to the principal's chair there to similar services.
Unlike Cross, he was a satisfactory placeman. Cross taught by
deputies, including Lindsay, who in 1750 succeeded him, to the relief
of his colleagues.[48]

John Cairns has seen this appointment as evidence that the Scottish
managers in London had little control over appointments during a
time of crisis when power was being lost by one faction but was not
yet firmly in the hands of another.[49] They were, he thought, too
dependent on their agents and were manipulated by them. This may
be true of Tweeddale but not of Argyll. Robert Dundas and the
Squadrone men saw the appointment as evidence that Tweeddale had
lost power; he resigned shortly after the appointment was made.
From Argyll's perspective, it was his recommendation that secured
Forbes' job – thus demonstrating his superiority over the Squadrone
lords who did not manage a prompt nomination or even efficient
negotiations for the place sought by several men. As for manipulation, Argyll could not in 1746 have given a job to a man like Lindsay
who was rumoured, albeit falsely, to be a Jacobite. Argyll had faced
the same allegations for many years. To give the place to Charles
Hamilton Gordon, Dundas's friend, would have been helping the
enemy, while giving it to Dalrymple would not have gratified many
outside a family not always loyal to the Argathelians. Argyll chose the

man who was most likely to maximise his influence in Scotland. That decision does not seem one he was manipulated into but one of the kind he was accustomed to make. If Cross was a sinecurist, the town and the University could deal with that problem, as the University did. Argyll supported the appointment of Lindsay in 1750.

The third appointment in 1746 replaced Francis Hutcheson who had died. It went to Thomas Craigie (1708–27 November 1751), then teaching at St Andrews. Craigie was a nephew of the Squadrone Lord Advocate, Robert Craigie, and had recently been recommended by Hutcheson for the Edinburgh chairs of moral philosophy[50] and mathematics.[51] Patrick Cuming, Argyll's manager for the Kirk, noted of him, after Robert Craigie had gone out of power with the Squadrone in 1746, that Thomas Craigie 'is a relation of the late Advocates And therefore will have a partie to Support his Merit' – merit which Cuming clearly thought he had as a mathematician.[52] Although the choice of him by the masters was unanimous, the minutes note that they took several meetings to make their selection, usually a sign that the masters had been divided over an appointment.[53]

The three appointments of 1746 show that in a time of great uncertainty about who had power, university men might make appointments with little apparent outside intervention and that the city could succeed in getting a man of its choosing. Argyll would no doubt have stopped the appointment of Craigie had he been able to do so but the votes were not there in the College meeting to overturn arrangements which almost certainly had been made before Hutcheson died and before Argyll had again come into power. If votes had been promised, politicians tended to respect the promises. Professors fancied themselves to be gentlemen and expected to be treated as men whose word could not be lightly broken. When the next appointment came in 1747, it was of more concern to Argyll and it was one he was then strong enough to arrange. This was the appointment that gave a place in the University to William Cullen (15 April 1710–5 February 1790).

3. Argyll's Return to Power

Cullen's father had been factor to the Duke of Hamilton and he himself had been physician to the 5th Duke of Hamilton who had died in 1744, relieving Cullen of his obligation to attend the family. Cullen had served as a Hamilton magistrate and had a local reputation as an improver. He moved to Glasgow in 1744 and in that year had begun to lecture extramurally on medicine, which he continued to do until the summer of 1746.[54] His teaching of medicine reflected a rising demand in the city for more teaching of medical subjects to the city's surgeon-apothecaries and physicians. This now required more attention from the University, which had never had a lively or, sometimes, even a functioning professor of medicine.[55] All this now changed as a real medical faculty took shape.

Like Alexander Monro I in Edinburgh, Glaswegian anatomists, when they began to teach more anatomy, had had problems, ones that caused riots over alleged 'resurrections' in the city.[56] Despite problems, anatomising was carried on at the new Infirmary at the town's Hospital built in the early 1730s. Clinical instruction was also offered there after 1733.[57] The professor of botany and anatomy was dealing with anatomy while *materia medica* was probably being taught by a local botanist. Glasgow had no one teaching chemistry and no regular teacher of medicine, although Dr George Montgomery (?–1778) seems to have taught the theory and practice of medicine in 1744–5.[58] Cullen taught for a year or two extramurally before he and Montgomery worked out a deal with professor Johnstoun to lecture in the University as Johnstoun's deputies in the winter of 1746–7.[59] By January 1747, Cullen added to his medical lectures a course on chemistry for which the College provided him £52 for equipping a laboratory. The masters also made him lecturer in chemistry, a lecturer who was to be assisted by John Carrick (1724–50), a recently qualified surgeon who also assisted the professor of anatomy, Robert Hamilton. By 1748, Carrick held an appointment in the Town's Hospital as a surgeon.[60] Carrick soon fell ill and did not long lecture. By the end of school year 1746–7, Cullen had become the sole lecturer on chemistry as well as an ad hoc teacher of medicine. Carrick returned in 1748 to lecture in summer courses on botany which he gave until his death in 1750. Montgomery disappeared as a teacher by 1748, although he lived in Glasgow until 1778.[61] Cullen's arrangement with Johnstoun continued; so too did his connection with the chemistry lectureship which was funded on an annual basis by the College. The University now offered anatomy with professor Hamilton, medicine and chemistry with Dr Cullen, pharmacy and botany with Messrs Carrick and Hamilton, and clinical instruction in the Town's Hospital, which had been rebuilt in 1739–40.[62] Those arrangements allowed the University, for the first time, to compete more or less equally with Edinburgh in the teaching of medicine.

By 1748, Scotland had settled down and the country was returning to normalcy, even in the Highlands. Argyll had more or less returned

to power as the manager of most civil patronage. He had had five years
to settle his personal affairs as the new Duke of Argyll and his building schemes at Inveraray had increased his hold over Glasgow and the
West of Scotland because of the size of his annual expenditures. Letters
concerning patronage in the universities again appear regularly in the
papers of Lord Milton. The effects of those changes began to be
increasingly felt in Glasgow. Cullen's appointment to the regius chair
of medicine in 1750 was evidence of the Duke's growing strength. Why
Argyll should have been interested in him is not far to seek.

The Duke and various of his friends through the 1740s had been
much involved with chemical experiments related to farming, the
making of pottery and to finding alkalis for Scottish industries. They
had been trying to foster the linen trade through better capitalising
and by organising the trade through the British Linen Company.[63]
They had sought better ways of bleaching the fabrics with chemical
bleaches. In 1749–50, the Philosophical Society of Edinburgh revived
after a period of near failure. The animating figure in that revival was
Henry Home. Home, in 1748, wrote a paper on evaporation, a
subject of interest to Cullen, and in the following year he wrote
another paper on lime. He was involved in agricultural experiments,
activities which would have recommended him to Argyll whom he
already knew from other contexts.[64] Home and Cullen had been
introduced by 1748 when both of them were dealing with Arthur
Martine, the owner of a brick factory in Fife.[65] Home and Martine
followed Cullen's 1749 experiments and his writings on agriculture
which formed part of his chemistry course – a course addressed to a
general audience and not specifically to physicians and surgeons.[66]
The manuscript lectures on agriculture were read by Martine in
January 1750.[67] In 1751, Cullen sent to Argyll, who was an amateur
chemist whose properties included salt pans, a memorial on the
making of salt.[68] Home, now a lawyer for the British Linen Company,
Argyll made a Court of Session judge in 1752 where he sat as Lord
Kames. Argyll promoted the careers of such men.

By the summer of 1749, Cullen was sounding out the Glasgow
medical professor, Dr Johnstoun, about retirement and the possibility of succeeding him. In August 1749, Cullen met with Argyll to
discuss this. The Duke agreed to help him to secure the grant of the
regius chair of medicine. In October 1749, Cullen and Johnstoun
came to some arrangement and in the following month the professor
agreed to resign if he were allowed to keep his house for life.[69] To this
the masters assented but Cullen's warrant was not secured for over a

year.[70] Argyll was generally prompt about getting warrants for those whom he favoured but his efforts to hasten the process in this case were frustrated owing to a 'jumble in the ministry'.[71] Cullen's patent came late and involved him in a dispute over precedence with the appointee to the oriental language chair, William Rouet (c. 1720–4 June 1785). Before that matter was settled, Cullen had pointedly told his new colleagues that 'His Grace might possibly think . . . [that their actions] were designedly to disappoint his intention and it is presumed the Society will think it prudent to avoid any such suspicions'.[72] Argyll's intercession had brought about his appointment; Cullen would make the most of it and insisted on his seniority to Rouet, another man whom Argyll seems to have liked. Rouet was a man with many connections to the University. His father was minister of Dunlop where the principal heritors were Dunlops, to whom he was related. He was also a cousin and Glasgow classmate of William Mure of Caldwell, who in 1753 became rector. Glasgow professors had taught him.[73] Rouet had tutored the son of Sir John Maxwell of Pollock, who was serving as the University rector when Rouet was installed.[74] Perhaps of equal interest is the fact that Rouet's grandfather and the then Duke of Argyll had been in some way connected. His ties thus ran to both political factions. He had probably studied divinity for some time although he seems never to have been licensed to preach. Instead, from c. 1740 until his appointment at Glasgow, he acted as a travelling tutor to boys studying in Holland or on the grand tour. He was said to have got his first Glasgow chair through the influence of the Earl of Hyndford who obtained the support of Argyll while on a visit to Inveraray in 1750.[75] This is not unlikely since Hyndford continued to patronise Rouet, who became something of a favourite of the 3rd Duke of Argyll as well. When Rouet was in London, as he often was on College business, he was a frequent visitor at Argyll's London home, but he does not seem to have been often, perhaps ever, invited to Whitton, a privilege Argyll tended to reserve for botanists and others more interested in science. Like Robert Simson, James Moor and Robert Dick, whom the Duke especially liked, Rouet was something of a mathematician and a man who knew a bit about antiquities and art. Appointees at Glasgow and elsewhere often shared the interests of the man who facilitated their placements.

After 1750, Argyll continued to be the final determiner of Glasgow appointments but he seems usually to have acted only after consulting with men at the College. A 1752 letter from Cullen to Robert Simson shows his typical method of proceeding: 'The folkes here [in

Edinburgh] who have sollicited the D. of Argyle about our new professorship have as yet received no other answer but that he must
consult the College before he gives opinion'.[76] The Duke had his way
but he consulted first. His influence at Glasgow was augmented in
1751 by the appointments of Hercules Lindsay (?–2 June 1761), Adam
Smith (1723–17 July 1790) and Robert Dick II, MD (c. 1722–26 May
1757).

Lindsay had been at Leiden in 1737 as travelling tutor to Lord
Garlies, Alexander Stewart, later the 6th Earl of Galloway. He had
also taught in Glasgow as a professorial deputy for many years, which
would have given him the support of several of the masters. Because
the chair of law, which he sought and got, was a regius chair, he
needed political backing to obtain the Crown's warrant. This came
most likely from Garlies' relative the Duke of Montrose, and from
Argyll, to whom Lindsay had been looking for support since the early
1740s. Argyll had probably favoured him for that post in the summer
of 1745; he almost certainly did so in 1750.[77] Like his successor, John
Millar (22 June 1735–30 May 1801), Lindsay is said to have been a
protégé of Lord Kames, which would have been a plus in the Duke's
mind.

The chair Adam Smith obtained also came from Argyll. Correspondence relating to that post includes the following letter from professor John Stevenson of Edinburgh whose own choice for the post
was George Muirhead whom he described:

> He [Muirhead] is not only a Man cut out for a blessing to a Society of that
> kind; but of Universal Learning, particularly in all the Branches of
> Philosophy, as well as the best Greek Scholar any where. As the Greek and
> Latin Impressions of Glasgow [the books printed by the Foulis Press]
> exceed all the World at present; that branch of the business wou'd full rise
> to a greater height by his Assistance to the Fouliss, with whom he is in
> Connection . . . My knowledge of most of the Masters of that University
> enables me to say that, if any body who is thought to be in Confidence
> with the Duke of Argyle, would intimate, in the most private way never
> to be heard of; to Principal Campbell and Mr Simson, that his Grace
> would not be offended if Mr Muirhead were elected; the affair would be
> done immediately.[78]

This is interesting for saying openly what most held to be the case:
whomever Argyll favoured would be chosen and no one would be
chosen to whom he objected. Muirhead, we should note, pursued two
of the Duke's particular interests – philosophy 'in all the Branches'
and classics. Muirhead did not get this place but one can confidently

assume that Smith had Argyll's countenance since the election of the new professor was unanimous. However, that unanimity was reached only after some discussion. Those who voted for Smith, but who seemed reluctant to do so, included William Leechman and Thomas Craigie, who appear to have cast their votes only after pressure was brought to bear on them by Argyll and Lord Hyndford. Cullen, from one of whose letters this information comes, seems to suggest that Smith had written to London to the 3rd Duke of Argyll and to his cousin and guardian, William Smith, the 2nd Duke's secretary, about his election, and that this had been taken amiss in Glasgow.[79] The cause of the resentment may have been residual party animosities (neither Leechman nor Craigie were initially Argathelians) or the fact that some of the professors were making a dictated choice and not one they saw as based on any merit they had discerned. The issue would arise again in the election of Muirhead to the professorship of oriental languages.

The third professor chosen in 1751, Robert Dick II, was the son and successor of the first professor of natural philosophy. As early as 1746, there had been discussions in the College about the younger man succeeding his father. The masters had unanimously agreed to this in a year in which they were subject to very little outside pressure.[80] The younger Dick had by that time almost certainly completed his medical training at Leiden, to which he had gone in 1744. He had not qualified for practice in Glasgow and would not do so until 1751, when he took his MD at Glasgow University. In the interim, he aided his father in teaching but he may not have done so continuously. In April 1751, professor Dick resigned in favour of his son, who was admitted as conjoint professor and successor on 5 June 1751. There seem to have been no other candidates and no controversy over the arrangements which added to the College a respected man whose principal contribution to science may have been his encouragement of James Watt and his teaching of many other men of distinction.

In 1752, the regius chair of ecclesiastical history was vacated by the death of William Anderson. This post was sought by a number of men. Robert Gillon wrote to Lord Milton the day after Anderson died that 'tho' I can neither be profitable to yor Lop or any other great man, yet I am sure not one of the Many your Lop's goodness and Influence have made happy shall ever exceed me in a grateful sense of favour or a care according to my best ability, to answer as a member of that College all the ends of your Lops Recommendation'. Such a promise of fealty was a promise to help manage the College as Anderson had done for the rival set of politicians. Gillon went on to say that, 'Next to Merit, I believe Indigence and a Modest dependence is the object of your Lop's regard'. He wrote a week later to offer to take the place 'with as much abatement of the Sallary in favours of another, as should be thought equall' and was willing to do so even for Dr [John] Wodrow. Argyll seldom favoured grovellers. It is doubtful that he or Milton had any idea of recommending Dr Wodrow to a sinecure chair for which he was not an obvious candidate and which he was unlikely to fill for long.[81] On 9 June, Gillon wrote to thank Milton for recommending him to the Duke and to ask for the chair of oriental languages which William Rouet, who had secured the ecclesiastical history chair, was now vacating.[82] Once again his letter made clear how matters went in these years: 'Principal Campbell told me yesterday that Mr Rowat by L. Hyndfords Recommendation to the D. of Argyll had succeeded Mr Anderson – And this day by a very Sympathising letter from [Argyll's cousin, Campbell of] Boquhan I was informed of it'. No one doubted that Argyll's word was binding on the corporation where his friends now had an unassailable majority. Indeed, Gillon said that Argyll two years before, when he applied for the same chair, had sent him a nice letter and so he was sure that if he recommended him now 'to the faculty in whose gift this place is and who Im Sure would unanimously make the compliment', he would get the place.[83] The Duke's polite letters were often not quite sincere. Another who was disappointed in this competition was Richard Betham, a recent alumnus of the College who later married a daughter of Principal Campbell.[84] He had written to Cullen that he had got 'a very warm letter of Recommendation in my favour from the Town of Glasgow to his Grace of Argyle' but he feared the post would be filled by 'Millar's Interest' or that Argyll would leave the 'contest to be decided betwixt my Lord Hopetoun & the College'.[85] He also noted that four unnamed professors and Leechman were against him. Betham in the end had better luck; he ended up as a Collector of Customs in the Isle of Man, a position worth more money than the professorship.

Rouet's move from the oriental languages chair to that of ecclesi-astical history set off a frenzy as others tried to secure the post he vacated. Robert Gillon wrote to Lord Milton that the job should be his since Argyll had been gracious to him when he had previously applied for it. Also listed as competitors were both 'Mr Cleland A minister, & once Chaplain to Sir John Maxwell' and 'Mr [Thomas] Melvil who is said to have Baron Maule's Interest'. Gillon wanted Milton to write to Argyll on his behalf and noted that 'The Principal told me he had been solicited already but neither he or any of the masters will engage till they know the D— of A—ll's mind'.[86] Argyll, however, seems not to have known his own mind. He was willing that the College men should choose the best of the candidates he approved but he gave them no precise guidance. What followed from this freedom is related by William Cullen:

The Principal and several others had written his Grace asking him to approve their choice of George Muirhead for this chair. They thought he had done so in the answer he returned to them. But, when Argyll visited Glasgow in November on his annual trip to Scotland, he met with the University men and was pleased to blame some part of the principals conduct in that affair & to say that he did not intend his approbation of G. Muirhead Should be exclusive of Mr Robert Dick Minr of Lanark if the Society should now incline to choose him. The effect of this declaration has been to alter the Sentiments of many of our masters so that Dick who was never intended by any one but his own Cousin [professor Robert Dick] is now likely to be the choice of a majority[.] It is neither proper nor agreeable to enter into the detail of our politics it is enough to say that this accident is likely to deliver us toss to furious discord & to do us an infinite deal of mischief[.] As this is likely to be always the case when we are left to ourselves[.] It had been my endeavour ever since I came into the Society to unite us under one Leader but my Schemes are blown in the Air[.] I was not the proposer of George Muirhead & if Cleland had been on the field as I hinted to you before[,] I must have been against Muirhead but as now I cannot help being concerned for him as upon good grounds he had got assurance of the place & hath taken measures that must make him appear very silly if he is disappointed[.] I cannot help being concerned for the College whose changes of measures must render them very contemptible[.] In such circumstances it is to be expected that Muirheads friends will show the keenest acharnement[87] & indeed I shall leave no stone unturned to assist them[.] I write to your Lordship in hopes you will do the same in what manner you may I cannot presume to say. The D. of Argyle did me the honour to speak to me on this subject & I begged to have his particular directions but he refused to give me any[.] He spoke favourably of Muirhead but concluded If we chose Muirheid he would say we had made a very good choice[.] If we chose Dick he —— would be very well pleased[.] After this I think His Grace is not to be spoken to but at the same time I think every body is at liberty to take their own measures at least it can never be expected that G. Muirheids friends can desert him.[88]

Robert Simson at about the same time wrote to Lord Milton asking him to intervene on Muirhead's behalf. The poll on 10 November stood at five for the reverend Mr Dick and five for Mr Muirhead. Principal Campbell was certainly for Muirhead but he was too sick to vote. Others for Muirhead probably included William Leechman, Robert Simson and Cullen. Among Dick's supporters were his cousin, Robert, the recent rector, Sir John Maxwell of Pollock, and possibly Rouet, who would have been likely to follow Maxwell who once had been his patron.[89] Simson asked for letters pressing Robert Hamilton to switch his vote. Hamilton was got to by 'Mr Fletcher' [almost certainly Milton's son] and switched his vote to Muirhead. Simson expected that the final vote would be unanimous for Muirhead, as it was in most cases.[90] The vote was held a month later – a sign that others were still campaigning. Argyll took care of the worthy Mr Dick by finding him an Edinburgh church as compensation for losing this post.[91]

Argyll's role in these last two appointments was decisive but in quite different ways. About Rouet's appointment, he made a clear choice and intimated it. The election was then held with a minimum of fuss. In the case of Muirhead, he narrowed the field to two acceptable men and let the masters pick the one they thought the best or best recommended by others. This created a contest, which turned into a rancorous dispute among the masters which left ill will between men feeling humiliated and betrayed. The Duke was seldom tempted to act as he had done in this case because he knew what was likely to happen. Giving direction minimised conflicts not only in the universities but among his own supporters. Patronage and management kept order in a world ever on the brink of chaos.

Before Muirhead was finally appointed in the late autumn and winter of 1752, two other men had received chairs. James Clow (c. 1715–9 July 1788) replaced Adam Smith in the chair of logic when Smith moved to the moral philosophy chair which had been vacated by the death of Thomas Craigie. Adam Smith was translated from the logic to the morals chair with no difficulties but not without competitors. Hercules Lindsay seems to have hoped to get this chair, as did George Muirhead. The former had the backing of the Principal.[92] Muirhead had other men on the faculty who were for him.[93] Smith was again probably helped by Argyll.[94] All that was fairly routine but Clow's appointment was more interesting.

Clow's father had been a functionary of the Dukes of Montrose and he had tutored aristocratic boys including those of Alexander Stewart, the Earl of Galloway, who was no friend to Argyll. Clow would have had backing from chancellor Montrose and rector Sir

John Maxwell in 1751. That this chair went to a man connected to Montrose suggests a diminishing of factional struggles and a willingness on the part of Argyll to give a living to old enemies despite his seeming position of dominance in the town and College. He could afford to be generous and to appoint a polite gentleman who was a good teacher well known to his new colleagues. What he could not afford was a donnybrook over a sceptic and unbeliever who also wanted the chair. That man was David Hume. Hume thought he could have obtained the chair had Argyll given him the backing he deserved.[95]

Hume wrote to his friend Dr John Clephane, 'You have probably heard that my friends in Glasgow, contrary to my opinion and advice, undertook to get me elected into that College; and they had succeeded, in spite of the violent and solemn remonstrances of the clergy, if the Duke of Argyle had had courage to give me the least countenance.'[96] The ministers' stand is made clear in a letter of James Wodrow:

> . . . the Clergy of Glasgow [went] in a body to the Faculty to express their desire that Hume might not be the person elected into the vacant Office[,] The Prin[l] received them with a hauty Air & tossing his head asked them if they were come to Dictate to the Faculty or come as his brethren[.] The minr[s] got no answer. Every body seems to imagine he will not be the man. I have good reason to think it will go betwixt Tom Melvil & Clow altho' it is said that Hume himself has recommended Mr George Muirhead as the fittest person in Scotland & that if H. be out of the play, all his friends will vote for the person recommended by him.[97]

That Argyll was unwilling to fight for Hume is borne out by a letter from Lord Milton's son to his father in which he discussed the Duke's reaction to letters recommending Hume: 'I laid before His Grace the Letters &c concerning the Affair pendant at Glasgow: His Grace desires me to acquaint you that Mr David Hume cannot be recommended to a professorship there and that for many reasons which must easily occur to you.'[98] Had Hume been appointed, those irritated clerics would have refused to let him sign the Confession and the case would then have gone to the ecclesiastical courts. Litigation might have gone on for months, which would have damaged Argyll's political interests in the burgh at a time when he was a bit insecure. The failure of Hume to secure a chair shows the degree to which the clerics could still affect the outcome of a contest in which they felt the Kirk had a real stake. Hume's belief that the Duke lacked courage is but another sign of his own political naivety. Such contests were not good for politicians, for the College or, in the long run, for men like Hume, who would have been more deeply scarred by the ensuing legal battles than he realised. While the process of appointment at Glasgow was usually one dominated by professors and politicians, it could still be swayed by determined ministers.

The third candidate, Thomas Melvil (1726–53), was a brilliant Glasgow theological student and mathematician with a bent for natural philosophy who had not secured the oriental languages chair in 1750. Had he lived, he would undoubtedly have been remembered as a first-rate Scottish scientist and perhaps as an inventor. He became a travelling tutor and died in Geneva in 1753 after making a reputation as a physicist with papers read at the Glasgow Literary Society and the Edinburgh Philosophical Society and later published in the *Philosophical Transactions of the Royal Society of London*.[99] His was a brief but distinguished career but in 1752 he was a little-known theology student whose interests were mainly scientific.

These appointments show how little specialised the requirements of office were deemed to be. Almost anyone with a good education could have taught the classics courses. Expectations of special competence in moral philosophy and logic were not overly high and it is a tribute to Scots philosophers like Carmichael, Hutcheson, Smith and Reid that their courses were as sophisticated as they became. Only in Hebrew, third year of mathematics or in the private classes in natural philosophy were teachers likely to be stretched by teaching things which were not familiar to them or which required determined study. But about half of the academics had had theological training and thus had some Hebrew. That included men like Rouet and John Anderson, who made their careers in quite different disciplines. The search for posts by the unspecialised continued with the appointment of the successor of George Ross, the humanist.

Professor Ross died on 26 August 1754.[100] His chair went to George Muirhead (24 June 1715–3 August 1773) but there were complications for what should have been a fairly normal promotion from the oriental languages chair to better things. Humanity was a better thing. Enrolments in that subject were higher and the work was less onerous than teaching Hebrew. One would have expected Muirhead's promotion to be easily made because he was a popular man, but his appointment was opposed by those who supported the candidacy of John Anderson (1726–3 January 1796). In the end Anderson failed to obtain the chair but replaced Muirhead in the oriental languages chair.

Anderson was in contention from soon after Ross's death. As he wrote to a friend in January 1755:

> Not long after the Death of poor Mr Ross, the Rector, the Principal, Dr Hamilton, Messers Simson, Leechman, Closs [Clow], and Ruat, joined in writing to the Duke of Argyle that they thought me the properest Person to fill up the Vacancy. The Duke upon this recommends me to the Faculty with these Words among others. 'Mr A. has received the highest Character from a Man who to my Knowledge is one of the best Latin Scholars in England'. After this Recommendation, my Friends thought all was safe. But Doctor Cullen and Mr Smith, in a manner that I need not relate, jockied me out of it; and I learned by the last Post that I was on the 17th of December elected Prof: of Orient Languages. Mr Muirhead is a worthy Man, and will be a very faithful laborious Teacher.[101]

The jockeying probably involved the advertisements of the vacancy which appeared in the Edinburgh and Glasgow newspapers in the autumn of 1754. It is not known if other candidates appeared; perhaps Muirhead was one. By November, the faculty had met twice on this matter, finally deciding to elect early in December. Muirhead was elected on 3 December and a week later the faculty informed the rector, the Earl of Glasgow, that Muirhead had been translated. Someone, perhaps Cullen who was then as close to Argyll as any of the masters,[102] had secured the Duke's consent to Muirhead's election and of that of John Anderson to Muirhead's vacated chair. He was elected to that two weeks after Muirhead had secured his post.

Anderson, the most colourful of the eighteenth-century Glasgow professors, was the grandson of the reverend John Anderson who had been imposed on Glaswegians by the 2nd Duke of Argyll when the Ramshorn Church had been opened early in the century. His grandson was a polymath who had inherited his grandfather's books and many of his theological attitudes, including his intolerance of Roman Catholics. When he was appointed, he was abroad in France and Switzerland as a travelling tutor to Sir James Campbell of Ardkinglass, an important Campbell tacksman. Anderson was probably just able to teach Hebrew but some of the time he begged to be allowed before assuming his chair went not just on the completion of his tour in France but on the study of that language. He had a rather light-hearted attitude toward all this, knowing that he would not stay long in that professorship. In the letter cited above he wrote to his friend Gilbert Lang:

> . . . pray fervently for me as a Teacher or rather Learner of the sacred Tongue. I should be quite melancholy did not the following Circumstance

make me hope that I shall not perhaps be altogether unworthy of the Office which the College has conferred upon me. It is observed that I never see a Jew but I look at him as if he were my Kinsman; and that I am apt to cry Selah when I feel any Emotion. I am grave, I assure you, as a Rabbi. I would not eat Pork yesterday to my Dinner, and my Landlady asked me with a blushing Leer, whether I intended to go thro all the rites of Jewish Religion.

The teaching of Hebrew did not have a high priority among those who now dominated the Scottish universities. That too reflected the attitude of Argyll toward ancient and modern 'Levites'.

Those appointments have an added interest because they portended the end of the Squadrone as a political faction. In 1754, in the aftermath of the death of Henry Pelham, Argyll was being pressed by the Duke of Newcastle to surrender some of his power. Newcastle, Pelham's brother, who succeeded him as chief minister, neither liked nor trusted Argyll. He would happily have managed Scotland without any Scottish manager. If he had to have a Scottish manager, he would have had someone other than Argyll. A number of letters in the correspondence of Lord Milton concern a projected 'new Scotch Ministry' to which Tweeddale and other Squadrone men might be added.[103] By 19 December 1754, Argyll wrote to Milton that 'the Scheme of a new Scotch Ministry is strongly disclaimed', a view he modified the following day.[104] In the end Argyll prevailed. The effort to weaken his authority did not substantially lessen his ability to manage Scottish appointments. By the spring of 1755, a correspondent reported the Marquis of Tweeddale apologising for being unable to help an old supporter, saying that 'as he was not employed in the Service of the Government, he cou'd give small assistance for he medled little in publick affaires[;] that such favours were only to be obtain'd by application to the Duke of Argyle . . .'.[105] This failure to end or alter the Duke's regime proclaimed Argyll's control of university posts and of Scotland more generally, a control he would relinquish only with his death seven years later.[106] Argyll's success in his conflict with Newcastle marked the end of the old Squadrone–Argathelian quarrels and the effective end of the Squadrone. Not until c. 1760 would Argyll again be seriously challenged. When he was, the opposition arose in and was centred on London, not Scotland. It found its focus in Argyll's nephew, the 3rd Earl of Bute, the tutor of the Prince of Wales. Since it was court-centred, this was potentially serious but it did not prevail in the Duke's lifetime.

There were no further Glasgow appointments until 1756, although a lot of energy in 1754–55 went into the filling of the not-yet-vacant Glasgow principal's chair. Principal Neil Campbell had had a stroke but he refused to die. The efforts were wasted.

In 1755, Cullen's translation to the chemistry chair in Edinburgh opened the chair of medicine and in fact created a vacancy in the Glasgow chair of anatomy and botany as well. Cullen's successor was Dr Robert Hamilton, who held the other medical professorship, but his placement was not a foregone conclusion. There were other candidates. One was Dr John Moore, later famous as a novelist but then the partner of Robert Hamilton's brother, Thomas.[107] Tobias Smollett, on 11 December 1755, penned a rather jaundiced account of Moore's hopes:

> I am heartily sorry to find your Cause is so slenderly supported with the Duke of Argyle because, without his Concurrence or rather his creative Word, I believe no Professorship can be filled up. Merit is altogether out of the Question. Every thing here as well as in your Country is carried by Cabal; and in Scotland, the Cabal of the Campbells will always preponderate. The Time is fast approaching when all the Lands, all the Places of Honour, Power and Profit will be in the possession of that worthy Clan. Then you can exclaim *non Numinis sed Cambellorum omnia plena!*[108]

That is the comment of a man who did not know the achievements of Black or the skills of the Hamiltons.

Another candidate appears only as 'C—ke'. He was almost certainly Dr David Clerk, an Edinburgh physician and chemist who was friendly with Cullen. Clerk came from medical families, being the third son of Dr John Clerk, a man whom Cullen revered. His mother was the daughter of Thomas Rattray of Craighall to whose surgeon son, John, David Clerk had been apprenticed. Clerk was educated at Edinburgh University and took his MD there in 1746. He then spent some time at Leiden. When he returned, he entered the RCPE (FRCPE, 1749). He seems also to have taught medicine or chemistry extramurally in Edinburgh but after 1756. Clerk was an ideal candidate for the anatomy chair but, like most of the medical chairs, it went to a local man who held a Glasgow degree.[109]

The appointment was complicated by the fact that Robert Hamilton's brother, Thomas, who had once been Cullen's partner in medical practice, wanted to fill the chair of anatomy and botany while Cullen wished it to go to Joseph Black (1728–13 January 1796). Argyll had some personal knowledge of the abilities and skills of the competitors. How things stood in January 1756 is made clear in a letter of William Rouet to Robert Simson:

I acquainted you in my last that ye D. of A. was positive against the two Brothers [Robert and Thomas Hamilton] being members of ye University, & had express'd himself warmly on that Subject first to Ld Hyndford, & then to myself, I urged ye Character of both ye Brothers, as no way tending to faction & division &c but his Grace said, though you all at present Live in harmony & Unanimity, Nobody can tell how long this may continue &c. And in short I found it too delicate a point to push for fear of not succeeding in our main point, getting our good friend ye Doctor [Robert Hamilton] to succeed Cullen, against a very strong Combine'd recommendation sent up in favours of Dr Black– My last letter to Leechman, & Dr Hamilton wt a copy of ye memorial I putt into ye D. of A. hands & which he was to give to ye Duke of Newcastle, will have I hope satisfy'd all my friends in ye College that I have done all in my power to obtain Their wishes as far as we could reasonably expect to be comply'd with & I found we must have gott C—ke If I had not drawn ye Memorial for these Gentlemen [presumably Robert Hamilton and Black] in ye Manner I did, for Ld H—d [Hyndford] was vastly keen in his Interests, as I found ye Duke of H—n [Hamilton] had also been & upon discovering ye least footing amongst ye masters I verily believe ye D. of A. would have come into him, so that I thought no time was to be lost to prevent This step being taken.[110]

From this letter, despite its syntax, we can see that the unanimous faculty of the Duke's imagination did not agree on the candidates for the chairs. Cullen and others had urged the appointment of Black as Cullen's successor with, perhaps, Dr David Clerk coming into the chair of anatomy and botany. Most of the masters wanted Hamilton to have Cullen's post but Rouet and his friends also seem to have wanted Thomas Hamilton in the second chair. The Duke, always a realist in his assessment of likely behaviour, was true to his usual rule banning the appointments of close relatives in the same corporation, but he knew enough about medicine and Robert Hamilton to see that a good anatomist would be teaching medicine. Argyll would also have known that Black, already possessed of a fine reputation as a chemist, was contesting the Edinburgh chair with Cullen.[111] Keeping him in Glasgow would put good chemists and teachers in both universities. Unfortunately, the arrangements made were not to last because Robert Hamilton died within three months of being appointed.

When professor Hamilton perished, the appointment processes started over again. Milton quickly reported to Argyll that new applications by Black (for the chair of medicine) and Thomas Hamilton (for anatomy and botany) were occasioned by the death of professor Hamilton about which he thought Argyll might not have heard.[112] Both Black and Thomas Hamilton were quickly approved since the only other known candidate, John Wodrow, who sought the chair of medicine, was elderly and supported partly by the city council. Hamilton's appointment was the more important since it kept in the College his brother's collections of anatomical preparations which were useful for teaching purposes and would in 1781 help to secure the same post for his son, William Hamilton. Cultural property mattered here just as it did in Edinburgh, where the three professors Monro succeeded one another in the anatomy chair partly because they owned a very valuable collection of anatomical preparations necessary for successful teaching.

Two other postings at the College were made in 1757. John Anderson left the chair of oriental languages for one which he was truly fitted to hold – natural philosophy – and was in turn replaced by James Buchanan (c. 1727–21 June 1761). The first appointment deeply concerned Argyll, whose efforts to find the College a distinguished natural philosopher took too long and led the masters to fill the place by themselves. This angered the Duke, who was not happy to have his efforts for the College slighted.

The professor of natural philosophy, Robert Dick II, died on 27 May 1757. On 8 June 1757, William Rouet, who was then in London on College business, waited upon Argyll to tell him of this:

> I found his Grace had already got various applications. He proposed speaking to Ld Macclesfield to enquire if any young man of Genius & who had already acquired some reputation for Astronomy could be found in This Country . . .[113]

Argyll was a keen amateur astronomer and clearly wanted someone who could profitably use the astronomical equipment which had recently been left to the College by Alexander MacFarlane of Jamaica, equipment which James Watt had been putting in order. He sought the best advice he could get. Among others, he consulted George Parker, 2nd Earl of Macclesfield. Macclesfield was a notable amateur mathematician and an astronomer with a fine observatory set up by Ilay's old friend, James Bradley, the Savilian professor of astronomy at Oxford. His lordship had been instrumental in getting England to change to the Gregorian calendar a few years earlier when he was the President of the Royal Society, to whose *Philosophical Transactions* he had contributed papers. He may have recommended the talented Englishman Argyll wanted to appoint.

The College would build an observatory but Rouet thought it could not pay the professor enough to attract the best English talent. That was because the elder Dick had resigned in favour of his son but had kept the house and salary which could not now be given to a new professor. The elder Dick still lived and was still the holder of the chair that had been granted to him and his son with the right of survivancy to the one who lived longest.[114] The talented man the Duke had in mind was not young but was certainly distinguished and would have expected a place worth more than the professorship could pay. He was John Bevis, a physician who had done significant work as an astronomer and had written on a variety of other natural philosophical topics. The Duke asked him if he would take the post. Rouet believed Bevis 'most unfitt and improper for that office', perhaps because he had not taught and was already in his sixties. Bevis seems to have refused to take the required religious oath and dropped out of competition.

By the end of June, Argyll was considering the candidacy of Alexander Wilson (1714–16 October 1786), a man whom he had long patronised. Wilson had come to his attention as a clever young surgeon-apothecary finishing his education in London in the 1730s. He proved to be a good chemist and a better instrument maker. The Duke received from him thermometers, barometers, and hydrostatic balls used to measure the specific gravity of fluids.[115] He had assisted Wilson in setting up his type foundry in Glasgow, where it came to be situated in the University precincts, conveniently close to the Foulis Press which it supplied with fonts. Wilson was a published astronomer who around this time had thoughts of moving to London for business reasons. His appointment would keep an accomplished, versatile man and his flourishing business in Glasgow, something the Duke was eager to do. On 30 June, Rouet reported that the Duke was 'well disposed to befriend Mr Wilson and family . . . he offered to provide his Son in a Commission in ye Army, & twice putt it to me what way he could serve ye University in giving Mr Wilson some inducement to stay at Glasgow & give his assistance in ye using the Astronomical Instruments.'[116] Argyll wrote to Robert Simson that he should 'aquaint Mr Wilson that Mr Ruat & I have had some conversation about him & I am forming a Scheme to mend his situation'. He was not to think of going to London. Wilson might be an assistant or an astronomer but no one else seems yet to have thought of him as *the* professor of natural philosophy. The Duke continued to seek a professor.

By then the masters too had a candidate for the natural philosophy chair, James Buchanan, a young Glaswegian mathematician who in 1759–61 would teach mathematics for Robert Simson. He was a protégé of William Leechman who had secured for him the tutorship of David Steuart Erskine, later 11th Earl of Buchan, who became an amateur astronomer and scientist and praised Buchanan's teaching. Rouet lobbied the Duke for Buchanan's appointment: 'Mr Buchanan is the most Universally agreeable to my Colleagues, I therefore yesterday waited on ye D. of Argyl and recommended him – I find his Grace had been strongly Solicited in favours of various Candidates but agreed that ye person best qualified according to all information was Mr Buchanan.'[117]Argyll seems to have been relying principally upon reports of the masters which Rouet had presented. He was willing that Buchanan should be installed in the professorship but he seems now to have had in mind some sort of sharing of the responsibilities of the office. That arrangement would have given Wilson part of the salary and the use and charge of the instruments. Rouet concluded, 'So I hope you will immediately unite in electing Mr Buchanan, giving some charge of ye Instruments to Mr Wilson'.[118] Those who would have done so included Clow and Simson but perhaps not Anderson, who may not yet have become a candidate for this place. Outside the University, Buchanan had the backing of the family of the Earl of Buchan.[119] Providing in this way for their son's tutor was cheaper than paying him an annuity. It looked from London as if Buchanan would get the post. However, the masters were too divided to proceed to an election.

Among others recommended to the Duke was James Williamson (?–3 June 1795) who eventually became the successor to professor Simson. His sponsors were Matthew Stewart, the Edinburgh professor of mathematics, also a protégé of Argyll, and Sir Thomas Kirkpatrick, who had formerly employed Williamson as a tutor and chaplain.[120] Still others favoured the reverend David Wark, a chemist-improver who had worked on lime, various improving schemes, and would later invent a primitive seismograph.[121] Finally, there was an Edinburgh student named Erskine who had been studying in London. Rouet wrote to say that he knew nothing of his abilities because he had attended Edinburgh and not Glasgow University but that he had 'talents for Mechanicks &c' but that 'his age (being only 23) is a great objection against him'.[122] His candidacy did not go so far as to reveal his full name. Amid these applications and the delays in London, John Anderson became a real candidate by the summer of 1757.

Matters then dragged on until the autumn, with the election for the professor being postponed while Argyll looked for a fit man and a way to provide for Wilson. The professors returned from summer vacations eager to elect someone. Pressure increased because the school year was about to commence and a teacher was needed for the course. The masters felt they had to act or lose fee-paying students. The recalcitrant were now urged to vote for professor John Anderson, which of course meant that another complicated matter, the choosing of a successor to Anderson, had been added to the mix. While nothing happened, another candidate appeared for either the natural philosophy or oriental languages chair. This was the poet and scientist the reverend Mr William Wilkie.

Most assumed the chair of oriental languages would go to Buchanan should Anderson be elected to the natural philosophy chair. John Home, writing on behalf of the Edinburgh literati to Milton some time in September, said that Anderson would win but asked that 'Wilkie get the vacancy' in oriental languages created by his victory. He went on:

> Mr Wilkie is extremly well qualified to fill it . . . I am pretty certain that those professors who in the present election unluckily oppose the person whom the Duke protects will not continue in opposition but very readily concur in electing Mr Wilkie . . . [who] is not the aptest man in the world to speak or act for himself.[123]

The election had become a near thing, with Anderson determined to vote for himself as he believed he had a right to do and as he did on a procedural matter. On 6 September, in a heated Faculty meeting attended by the rector, Patrick Boyle, Lord Shewalton, SCJ (Argyll had made him a SCJ), the date of the election was postponed for several reasons. Some wanted to schedule the election after the rectorial election in October. A new rector might favour their candidate. Others may have thought it would help to ensure the election of Buchanan. Delay allowed Argyll more time to try to find funds for a stipend to pay Wilson. The masters next met on 30 September when nothing was done because there was no quorum; the diet had been deliberately deserted by those who favoured delay. The majority of the professors sent a letter to Argyll remonstrating with him for his delays and saying that the College would have to choose a professor soon since the course needed be taught. On 2 October, Robert Simson sent Milton a report on how things stood. Anderson's supporters included Simson,

Thomas Hamilton, the rector, Patrick Boyle, Rouet (he had been recalled from London to vote) and the very ill Principal who could be carried to a meeting where his mere presence would make a quorum even though physically he might not be able to cast his vote. Simson concluded his letter saying, 'This Sir is the present Situation of the affair, and we shall be greatly obliged to His Graces condescension if he will be pleased to desire you to give us his Opinion and direction in what may be proper further to do'.[124]

The other side was also active. On 4 October, Moor, Muirhead, Black and Smith wrote express to Milton asking that Wilkie be added to their number and ordering the courier to wait for an answer that 'no crass accidents may longer interrupt that union among ourselves which we are so uneasy to think has ever been broken & wish so earnestly to see restored by his Graces wanted goodness'.[125] They clearly saw the elections as a way of taking care of two worthy friends. Milton seems to have ambiguously recommended Wilkie. Some masters thought, or pretended to think, that he had merely given Wilkie leave to be a candidate and that they were free to vote for him or not vote for him as they chose. The day before the election, Moor, Smith, Black and Muirhead again wrote to Milton asking for 'an express recommendation of Mr Wilkie' and a quick reply. They thought the election would be hurried on in a few days and Buchanan elected while Milton and Argyll delayed writing.[126]

On 20 October, after the rectorial election had returned the same rector, the masters recorded that the session had started and they must have a professor who would be chosen the following day. This signalled the victory of Anderson and Buchanan, a slim one upheld by the casting vote of the rector and the willingness of Anderson to vote for himself. Smith, Moor, Black and Muirhead all protested against Anderson's voting in matters which concerned himself but they had a candidate for the vacancy his election would create, a candidate they wanted Argyll and Milton to support. Buchanan was chosen to fill the Hebrew chair on 31 October, Wilkie got the St Andrews chair of natural philosophy two years later, and in 1760 Alexander Wilson became regius professor of practical astronomy. Argyll and Milton took care of the men who had impressed them.

Wilson's appointment had involved a good deal of finagling. In 1757, at about the time the foundations of the new College observatory were laid, Argyll had spoken to the Duke of Newcastle about a fund to keep Wilson at the University.[127] Nothing had immediately come of this but the idea was not dropped. In 1758, a means of effecting it turned up in the Earl of Hopetoun's proposal to Rouet to go abroad as a travelling tutor to the Earl's two sons. John Anderson, writing from London, where he had been talking to Argyll, explained the deal to Milton in the following terms:

> [Hopetoun's] scheme is this, If the College can be prevailed upon to give Leave of Absence to Mr Ruat, the Duke of New[castl]e has agreed to accept of £400 & found a new Professorship in our University the Salary of which is to be £50 per An, that is to say the King will grant £30 a Year out of the Exchequer which joined to Lord H—n's £400 will make a Salary of £50 for a new Professor who is to be named by the Crown . . . & Mr Wilson is to be the Man so that Wilson will have a Seat among us.[128]

This, he also noted, would give an absolute majority to Argyll's party in the University, which he listed as composed of himself, Simson, Leechman, Clow, Buchanan, Hamilton, presumably Rouet and the ailing Principal Campbell who could not then attend meetings.[129] If the other professors did not agree to these terms, then the Duke seemed prepared to have the portions of professorial salaries which were dependent on previous Crown grants diverted to form a salary for Wilson. The Duke was determined to help Wilson and quite capable of doing things of this sort to get his way. To establish the fund without such a desperate measure was partly the purpose of Anderson's letter.[130] Nothing immediately came of this, perhaps because of the delicacy of negotiations over appointments. These had been complicated by Argyll's efforts to get Adam Ferguson appointed as the travelling tutor to Hopetoun's sons, a scheme not relished by the Earl or his friend and brother-in-law, Lord Deskford. They were not Argathelians and had been fed stories by William Leechman, who seems not to have liked this plan.[131] Hopetoun wanted and eventually got Rouet whom, in the end, he found unsatisfactory.[132]

By 1759, the deal was accepted in principle, although most of the professors voted not to give Rouet his extended leave. His response, in September 1759, was to go anyway, a move which some, led by James Moor, disapproved. Eventually Rouet was deposed in a meeting at which Leechman, Simson, Clow and Anderson protested the decision. The case then went its way into the courts, where litigation continued until 1767.[133] The royal warrant establishing the regius chair of practical astronomy was issued on 11 January 1760 and named Wilson to the new chair of practical astronomy. It assured his staying in Glasgow, where his type foundry became of increasing importance to the city. Argyll's wishes had been fulfilled. The new chair was not primarily a teaching chair. Rather, it was one designed to promote observations and the teaching of practical astronomy. Wilson was to aim at making men better observers and navigators rather than making them learned about sunspots, comets and other theoretical topics on which he did lecture.[134] It was the sort of job he could hold while devoting most of his time to his type foundry.

The establishment of the chair of astronomy was Argyll's last act for the College. He died suddenly in April of the following year and there were no appointments in the meantime. The appointments which quickly followed his death changed dispositions which he had made or intended. What, then, can one make of his career as a patron in Glasgow?

4. ARGYLL, GREATEST OF PATRONS

The 3rd Duke of Argyll was an alumnus of the College and his enduring interest in its welfare must have owed something to his memories of time pleasantly spent there in his youth, when he was said to have displayed 'the brightness of his Genius'.[135] Certainly he looked after the College and was credited by others with a benevolent concern for the institution which transcended ordinary political calculations.[136] Much of what he did for the College seems not primarily motivated by political interests centred on parliamentary politics. While the men he appointed had patrons and families, they were picked as much for their merit in his eyes, or those of academics whom he trusted, as they were picked for the political advantage he and his friends might derive from their placements. While he had often struggled to place men who would be loyal to him and who would demonstrate his control in Scotland, his struggles after c. 1750 did not centre on votes to secure this or that seat in the House of Commons or to gratify a Representative Peer. Those things are simply not mentioned, although they figure in his other correspondence with Milton dealing with other kinds of patronage positions. Those to whom he denied jobs at Glasgow and elsewhere were men often as well or better recommended than were those who got them. Some who got them had little backing from anyone but the Duke. He occasionally said he was seeking the best man; we should believe him because the record bears that out.

A surprising number of the men he picked or helped into office in the last fifteen years of his career shared his personal interests. James Moor was a mathematician and numismatist. Cullen was a chemist and agricultural improver as well as a physician. Carrick resembled him. Rouet, well versed in history, had some mathematical skills, and knew a good deal about Europe. Adam Smith's first interest was mathematics and science, not morals or economics. Robert Dick I was an experimenter who taught science to apprentices and townsmen and was capable of practical works. His son, Robert II, was a Leiden-trained physician who shared his father's interests and work. Anderson was as much a virtuoso as the Duke who gave him bread. A chemist, an improver of ordnance, a meteorologist and instrument maker, an antiquarian and historian, Anderson was just the sort of man the Duke saw as useful. Black was a chemist who over the course of his working life did a lot of industrial consulting, some of it for Argyll's friends. Buchanan was a mathematician and not fit only for the language chair he got. Indeed, he probably would have succeeded Simson had he lived longer. Simson's successor, James Williamson, had already begun to dicker with Simson for his chair and had help from the Duke as he did so.[137] Finally, there was Wilson – surgeon-apothecary, chemist, astronomer, instrument maker and type founder – a man after Argyll's own heart and one whom he looked after for a generation. Most of those men, like the Duke, had a command of several languages and were quite secular in outlook. All of them felt at ease with the Duke. He himself preferred the company of men like them to that of most noblemen. Men like the professors visited the Duke for Sunday dinners at Whitton, his estate down the Thames, where he spent his happiest hours. Argyll invited few of his own rank unless they were visitors from Scotland (and those were often relatives) or were like the Duke of Richmond. He too was botanist, MD and amateur scientist.[138] Argyll favoured and appointed men at Glasgow and elsewhere who shared his outlook and concerns. In time, the nominations that came to him were almost certainly affected by his interests and were increasingly of men resembling himself. In the long run, this reshaped the colleges. The consistent and continued appointments of such men made Scotland a more secular country in which practical learning of a scientific or medical cast came to be more highly prized. The Duke was as much an originator and sustainer of the Scottish Enlightenment as any who wrote the books which make it memorable.

Notes

1 John Graham to Gorthy, 18 January 1741, Montrose Papers, NAS, GD220/5/1546/6.

2 Anderson to Tweeddale, 9 April 1742, Yester MSS, NLS, 7046/28.

3 This was almost certainly Hector McLean, later Surgeon at the Glasgow Town Hospital. For his career, see Geyer-Kordesch and Macdonald, *Physicians and Surgeons*, pp. 221, 304. Thomas Hay to Tweeddale, 14 April 1742, NLS, 7046/37ff.

4 Dr Clerk was probably Dr John Clerk of Listonshiels, an Edinburgh physician who had been principal editor of several editions of the *Edinburgh Pharmacopeia* and, with others, a founder of the Edinburgh Royal Infirmary. Wodrow was Dr John Wodrow, who maintained a botanical garden in Glasgow where he taught the subject to the town's medical apprentices. He probably had been a candidate when Brisbane was appointed. This time he had the backing of his cousin, John Graham of Dougalston, then the rector. John Graham to Gorthy, 3 April 1742, NAS, GD220/5/1546/17.

5 This refers to William Hamilton, formerly principal of Edinburgh University, and his son Gavin, who, as an Edinburgh town councillor, sometimes acted in the Squadrone interest but was also friendly with Ilay who haunted his bookstore when he was in Edinburgh.

6 Robert Dundas to Tweeddale, 15 April 1742, NLS, 7046/61. Bailie Hamilton was described as negotiating the appointment for his cousin and offered to get certificates of his abilities from Edinburgh medical men; NLS, 7047/4. Those were later supplied to Tweeddale by 'Doctors Stevenson and Cochran' but arrived after Hamilton had been chosen to be the professor; Thomas Hay to Tweeddale, 4 May 1742, NLS, 4707/8.

7 William Anderson to Tweeddale, 11 June 1742, NLS, 7047/127.

8 Letters of Francis Hutcheson, GUL, Gen 1018/12.

9 Reid, *The Divinity Professors*, 1923, pp. 243–63.

10 Coutts, *History*, 1909, p. 237.

11 Mure of Caldwell papers, 1883, I:53f.

12 Colin Maclaurin to Sir Andrew Mitchell, 22 November 1743. *The Collected Letters of Colin Maclaurin*, ed. Mills, 1982, p. 115. This date is incorrect. Hutcheson correctly gave the date of Potter's death as Wednesday the 23rd.

13 Ibid., p. 116.

14 Clark, 'Moderatism and the Moderate Party', unpublished PhD dissertation, p. 227; Jones, 'The Scottish professoriate and the polite academy', *Wealth and Virtue*, p. 103. There is more on this appointment in the letters of Francis Hutcheson to Thomas Drennan for 1740–3, GUL, Gen 1018.

15 Thomas Hay to Tweeddale, 26 November 1743, NLS, 7059/63.

16 Thomas Hay to Tweeddale, 29 November 1743, NLS, 7059/71.

17 John Graham to Mungo Graham of Gorthy, 7 and 17 December 1743, NAS, GD220/5/1570/9 and 10.

18 Faculty Minutes,13 December 1743, GUA, 26639; Coutts, *History*, 1909, p. 237.

19 A generation later Anderson was found by the Court of Session to be correct. Coutts, *History*, 1909, p. 238.

20 Archibald Campbell to Lord Milton, [?] December 1743, NLS, 16571.

21 Colin Maclaurin to Andrew Mitchell, 17 December 1743, Maclaurin, *Collected Letters*, p. 117f. The man he had in mind was professor John Simson.

22 The committee consisted of two from each political faction and the oldest and youngest members of the college. The rector's letter to the Presbytery of Irvine is in GUA, 45273. Leechman's brief letter of acceptance is in GUA, 45272. His protest at not being allowed to sign the Westminster Confession is in GUA, 45271. Normally the principal would have written the letter to the Presbytery, not the rector.

23 Leechman seems to have sent letters to the dissidents: GUA, 45272.

24 Hutcheson to Drennan, n.d., GUL, Gen 1018/17.

25 Tweeddale probably had a candidate for this office, a Mr Bartram, whom he pushed for other university jobs as well. Bartram never landed one. Thomas Hay to Tweeddale, 23 April 1743, and William Anderson to Tweeddale, 22 September 1744, NLS, 7051/148 and 7063/135. An earlier candidate had been Robert Dalgleish who died before he could be elected. Francis Hutcheson to Thomas Drennan, n.d., GUL, Gen 1018/21; see also *The Origins of the Scottish Enlightenment*, ed. Jane Rendall, 1978, p. 57f.

26 Anderson to Tweeddale, 26 September 1744, NLS, 7063/135f.

27 Mitchell to Tweeddale, 4 October 1744, NLS, 7064/12–14. Mr Dick was probably the same man who had failed to gain the ecclesiastical history chair in 1721.

28 George Bogle to the Lord Advocate, Robert Craigie, n.d. (14 October 1744), GUA, 47462 and 47463; Coutts, *History*, 1909, p. 239.

29 Alexander Dunlop to Charles Mackie, 22 October 1744, printed in *The Origins of the Scottish Enlightenment*, ed. Rendall, 1978, p. 57f.

30 See R. B. Sher, 'James Moor', ODNB, 38:901–3. Lord Kilmarnock was executed in 1746 for his participation in the '45. Moor journeyed to London to testify at his treason trial. Moor was distantly related to the Mures of Caldwell and, later, by marriage, to Robert and Andrew Foulis. Sher says that Ilay had something to do with his appointment but I no longer believe that.

31 Scott, *Francis Hutcheson*, 1966, p. 95.

32 Cullen to John Allen [1754], Thomson/Cullen MSS, GUL, 2255/2/9.

33 This case is discussed in Emerson, *Professors, Patronage and Politics*, 1991, p. 66f.

34 William Cross to Andrew Cochrane, 13 November 1745, in *The Cochrane Correspondence*, ed. Smith, 1836, p. 33.

35 Hew Dalrymple, Lord Drummore to Lord Milton, 3 April 1746, NLS, 16619/31–2. This letter says that Principal Campbell 'does not see how he can not follow the Duke's [Argyll's] recommendation'. Argyll at that point was probably not for Dalrymple but for the man whom the local politicians wanted. Dalrymple was given Procuratorship for the Church in 1746.

36 John Erskine, the Edinburgh professor, would have had no reason to consider the position so Mr Erskine may well have been James Erskine, the son of Charles Erskine, Lord Tinwald, an old Argathelian always on the lookout for more for himself or his family.

37 Anderson to Tweeddale, 26 September 1744, NLS, 7063/135.

38 John Cairns believes the lord was Tweeddale. Another of Lindsay's patrons was the Earl of Galloway, whose son had been abroad at Leiden with him. Cairns, 'William Cross, Regius Professor', *History of Universities*, 1993, pp. 166, 168.

39 Ibid., pp. 159–96, 164.

40 Ibid., p. 165.

41 Ibid., p. 167.

42 Letters of Andrew Cochrane to Argyll, 28 September, 4 October and 1 December 1745 and [?] July 1746, *Cochrane Correspondence*, ed. Smith, 1836, pp. 21, 22f, 44, 93f.

43 William Corse [Cross] to Forbes of Culloden, 15 February 1746, *Culloden Papers*, ed. H. R. Duff, 1815, pp. 269–73.

44 Cochrane to Duncan Forbes, 31 May 1746, *Cochrane Correspondence*, ed. Smith, 1836, pp. 87, 80–5.

45 The College had raised a company of men for service against the rebels and later sent a delegation to congratulate Cumberland on the defeat of the Highlanders. Its later gift of a doctorate in law was a somewhat ironic honour. Coutts, *History*, 1909, p. 232f.

46 Cochrane to Argyll, n.d. [September 1746], *Cochrane Correspondence*, ed. Smith, 1836, pp. 95, 98.

47 Forbes to Tweeddale, 13 November 1745, NLS, 7070/22.

48 For more on his career as a professor and his ouster through the pressure of his colleagues, see Cairns, 'William Cross, Regius Professor of Civil Law in the University of Glasgow, 1746–1749: A Failure of Enlightened Patronage', *History of Universities*, XII (1993), pp. A.159–96.

49 Ibid., p. 182.

50 Hutcheson to Sir Gilbert Elliot, Lord Minto, 4 July 1744, Minto Papers, NLS, 11003/57.

51 He was said to be the candidate of Lord Cathcart, who seems to have belonged to no party; Shaw, *The Management of Scottish Society*, 1983, p. 81, and 'The Mathematics Chair', D. B. Horn Papers, EUL, Gen 1824.

52 Cuming to [?Charles Erskine], 13 August 1746, Mar and Kellie Papers, NAS, GD124/15/1565.

53 Glasgow Minutes, 22 September and 1 October 1746, GUA 26639.

54 This and what follows relies principally on Donovan, *Philosophical Chemistry in the Scottish Enlightenment*, 1975, pp. 49–76, and on Geyer-Kordesch and Macdonald, *Physicians and Surgeons*, 1999, passim.

55 Geyer-Kordesch and Macdonald dispute the claim that the professors did not teach but seem to suggest that, if they did, it was more by taking apprentices than in the lecture hall; *Physicians and Surgeons*, 1999, p. 195.

56 Ibid., p. 221f; Coutts, *History*, 1909, p. 486.

57 Macdonald, 'The Infirmary of the Glasgow Town's Hospital, 1733–1800', *Bulletin of the History of Medicine*, 1999, pp. 64–105.

58 Geyer-Kordesch and Macdonald, *Physicians and Surgeons*, 1999, pp. 306–8.

59 Macdonald, 'The Infirmary', 1999, pp. 64–105.

60 Geyer-Kordesch and Macdonald, *Physicians and Surgeons*, 1999, p. 222f.

61 For more on his interesting early career, see ibid., p. 306f.

62 Isabel Brown, 'A short Account of the Town's Hospital', *Bibliotheck*, 1958, pp. 37–41; Macdonald discusses teaching at the hospital where Cullen, Carrick and Montgomery held appointments between 1745 and 1749; 'The Infirmary', 1999, pp. 85–92, 104.

63 Emerson, 'The Scientific Interests of Archibald Campbell', *Annals of Science*, 2002, pp. 21–56, 44–8.

64 Donovan, *Philosophical Chemistry*, 1975, p. 68ff.

65 Martine was the brother of Dr George Martine, a distinguished, but now dead, physician and chemist who had tried to become a professor of medicine at Edinburgh. See below, pp. 291–5; Arthur Martine to William Cullen, 10 August 1749, GUL, 2255/2/65.

66 Martine to Cullen, 4 January 1750, Cullen Manuscripts, GUL, 2255/2/67.

67 Arthur Martine to Cullen, 4 January 1750, Cullen Manuscripts, GUL, 2255/2/67.

68 Cullen to Argyll, 1751, GUL, 2255/2/60.

69 'Memorial for Doctor Cullen', [1750], GUL, 2255/I/14–16.

70 On 17 November 1749, Home proposed Cullen as a member of the Edinburgh Philosophical Society because of his work in chemistry and on agriculture: Emerson, 'The Philosophical Society of Edinburgh', *British Journal for the History of Science*, 1981, pp. 134–76, 136–8.

71 Dr John Clerk to Cullen, 22 December 1750, GUL, 2255/69; 'Memorial', 2255/14–15; Cullen described the cause of the delay as 'a train of Accidents at the Secretary's Office'.

72 'Memorial for Doctor Cullen', [1750], GUL, 2255.
73 See the notes on his life by William Johnston, *Enlightenment in France and Scotland*, compact disk published by *Officina*, 2004.
74 Draft, 'Memorial for Doctor Cullen', [1750], GUL, 2255.
75 Robert Gillon to Lord Milton, 9 June 1752, NLS, 16679/12.
76 Cullen to Simson, 8 February 1752, GUA, 26223.
77 Cairns, 'The Origins of the Glasgow Law School', in *The Life of the Law*, ed. Birks, 1993, pp. 151–94, 184f.
78 John Stevenson to Lord Milton, 2 November 1750, NLS, 16672.
79 Ross, *The Life of Adam Smith*, 1995, p. 110; it is difficult to make complete sense of this letter which is undated; see also GUL, 2255/1.
80 Glasgow Minutes, December 1746, GUA, 26639.
81 Gillon to Milton, 24 April and 1 May 1752, NLS, 16679/9, 11; the only likely Dr Wodrow was John, the younger brother of Robert Wodrow. He was a Glasgow physician and botanical teacher of the town's medical apprentices. What Gillon may have had in mind was a retirement income for Wodrow. Gillon would lecture and hold the right of survivancy; Wodrow would get the salary. Since Wodrow was fifty-seven years old, Gillon might have thought he would have not long to wait; Wodrow died in 1769. Argyll's interest in helping Wodrow, if he had any, would have been in rewarding a man who had long taught a subject in which the Duke was keenly interested.
82 There is little in print about Rouet, but see Fleming, *Robert Adam and His Circle*, 1962. This has a portrait of him and an account of his tour of Italy with the sons of the Earl of Hopetoun; Gibson-Wood, 'George Turnbull and Art', *Revue d'art canadienne/Canadian Art Review*, 2001–3, pp. 7–18; Johnston, *Enlightenment in France and Scotland*, compact disk.
83 Gillon to Milton, 9 June 1752, NLS, 16679/12; four days earlier Principal Campbell had written to Robert Simson that Argyll had secured the warrant for Rouet's chair; GUA, 26233. See also Argyll to Campbell, 8 June 1752, GUA, 26233a.
84 I thank Dr David Raynor for this information for which he did not give me the source.
85 Richard Betham to Cullen, n.d. [1752], GUL, 2255/75. It is not clear what influence either Hopetoun or the unidentified Millar might have had. 'Millar' is probably the Glasgow Town Clerk of those years (1748–66), Thomas (later Sir Thomas) Millar, 1st Baronet of Barskimming, SCJ and LPCS. He was then handling the city's legal business in Edinburgh. The influence he could exert would have been that of the town, not a personal one. Rouet had been supported by Hopetoun as well as Hyndford.
86 Gillon to Milton, 9 June 1752, NLS, 16679/12. This was probably Thomas Clelland (1706–69), minister of Cambusnethan. He and

Cullen had attended Glasgow University at the same time. For an account of Thomas Melvil (Melvill or Melville), see above, p. 129 and J. D. North, 'Thomas Melvill', DSB, 9:266–7.

87 This archaic word means 'blood thirsty fury'.

88 Scroll letter from Cullen to [? Lord Milton], [?] November 1752, GUL, 2255/13. This is evidence that Milton sometimes played an independent role in appointments. His independence increased over time but he was always on a chain which Argyll could yank.

89 Simson to Milton, 10 November 1752, NLS, 16680/97.

90 Simson to Milton, 24 November 1752, NLS, 16680/98.

91 Argyll to Lord Milton, 18 December 1753, NLS, 16681/134. This information supplements the account of Dick's appointment given by Richard Sher in 'Moderates, Managers and Popular Politics' in *New Perspectives*, ed. Dwyer, Mason and Murdoch, 1982, pp. 179–209. By the time he had been appointed, Dick had ingratiated himself with the Duke by defending the right of John Home to write for the stage and not be punished for it. Argyll was a supporter of this play and defended its author.

92 William Cullen to [?Adam Smith] GUL, 2255/11.

93 Ross, *Life of Adam Smith*, 1995, p. 108; John Anderson to Gilbert Lang, Lang-Anderson Correspondence, USL, A2.

94 Ross, *Life of Adam Smith*, 1995, p. 113.

95 I. S. Ross lists Hume's sponsors for the chair as Cullen, Hercules Lindsay, Baron William Mure of Caldwell and possibly Gilbert Elliot of Minto, MP One should perhaps add Lord Milton, who seems at least to have forwarded the letters of others to the Duke and probably seconded them since he had not come to the conclusion, as he would in 1757, that Hume acted imprudently and was not to be governed by wiser heads. *Life of Adam Smith*, 1995, p. 113.

96 Hume to Dr John Clephane, 4 February 1752, *Letters of David*, ed. Grieg, 1969, I:164. See also Emerson, 'The "affair" at Edinburgh and the "project"at Glasgow', in *Hume and Hume's Connections*, ed. Stewart and Wright, 1994, pp. 1–22; Ross, *The Life of Adam Smith*, 1995, p. 113.

97 James Wodrow to Samuel Kenrick, 21 January 1752, 'Correspondence of Samuel Kenrick . . . and Dr James Wodrow . . .', Dr Williams Library, MS 24.157/16. I thank P. B. Wood for this information.

98 Ross, *Life of Adam Smith*, 1995, p. 113.

99 North, 'Thomas Melvill', DSB, IX:266–7.

100 He is said to have died a suicide, one of two professors in this period to die by their own hands. Others went mad, including Gilbert Cunningham, Alexander Rule, Alexander Ross and John Wylde. The serious drug addicts included perhaps two notable alcoholics – Verner and Moor – and John Robison, who was addicted to opium. Doubtless

there were others but those numbers, particularly the ones on insanity, compare favourably with those of the faculties in which I have served.

101 Typescript of the letter from Anderson to Gilbert Lang, 16 January 1755, given to me by Paul Wood; the original is in the USA, A2/2.

102 On 6 September 1755, Lord Kames wrote to Lord Milton saying, 'I know Cullen to be a fast adherent to the Duke of Argyle, and that his Grace has a good opinion of him'. NLS, 16692/101.

103 Shaw, *The Management of Scottish Society*, 1983, p. 48. See also Murdoch, *The People Above*, 1980, pp. 52–84 and NLS, 6685/183.

104 Argyll to Lord Milton, 19 and 20 December 1754, NLS, 16685/183 and 185.

105 John Hay to Milton, 22 March 1755, NLS, 16692/75.

106 Argyll, as Murdoch has shown, had other troubles with appointments and was even willing to nominate for a place on the Court of Session Tweeddale's old Edinburgh manager, Thomas Hay, who in February 1755 became a Senator of the College of Justice. Hay thanked Milton, saying, 'I will endeavour to do Justice to His Graces recommendation & to behave myself in every instance in such a manner as may be acceptable to His Grace'. Hay to Milton, 2 September 1754, NLS, 16688/27.

107 See the forthcoming biography of Moore by Henry Fulton.

108 *Letters of Tobias Smollett*, ed. Knapp, 1970, p. 42. The editor translates this as: 'all things are full, not of divine power, but of Campbells'.

109 Clerk was likely born c. 1722 and died in 1768. He was a prominent member of the Royal Medical Society, the Philosophical Society, the Select and Edinburgh Societies, the Edinburgh Musical Society and the Royal Company of Archers. He was appointed as Physician to the Royal Infirmary and Physician to Sick Soldiers.

110 William Rouet to Robert Simson, 4 January 1756, GUA, 30485. Both warrants passed the seals on 11 March 1756. Black was admitted on 22 March, Hamilton the following day. Scroll letter of Milton to Argyll, 9 December 1756, NLS, 16694/114.

111 See below, p. 300f.

112 Scroll letter of Milton to Argyll, 9 December 1756, NLS, 16694/114.

113 Rouet to [?Robert Simson], 9 June 1757, GUA, 17982.

114 I thank Professor David B. Wilson for bringing this to my attention. Faculty Minutes, 19 December 1750 and 24 December 1763, GUA, 26642.

115 Emerson, 'The Scientific Interests of Archibald Campbell', *Annals of Science*, 2002, p. 49.

116 Rouet to Simson, 30 June 1757, GUA, 17983.

117 Rouet to Simson, 30 June 1757, GUA, 17983A/GS.

118 Rouet to Simson, 30 June 1757, GUA, 17983A/GS.

119 Rouet to Simson, GUA, 30485.

120 Matthew Stewart to Sir Thomas Kirkpatrick, 4 June 1757, NLS, 16702/99.

121 Wark is noticed in Emerson, 'The Philosophical Society of Edinburgh, 1748–68', *British Journal of the History of Science*, 1981, pp. 134–76.

122 Rouet to Simson, 28 June 1757, GUA, 30525.

123 John Home to Milton, n.d. [September 1757], NLS, 16700/198; other letters for Wilkie came from Alexander Wedderburn, whom Adam Smith had put up to suggesting Adam Ferguson as well. NLS, 16702/210.

124 Robert Simson to Lord Milton, 2 October 1757, NLS, 16702/72.

125 Moor et al. to Milton, NLS, 16700/104.

126 NLS, 16700/106; as Wilkie noted in a letter to Milton on 10 October 1757, they wanted him to write to professor Clow who was still uncommitted. NLS, 16702/223.

127 Argyll to Robert Simson, 6 August 1757, GUA, 17986.

128 John Anderson to Milton, n.d. [1757], NLS, 16707/56.

129 Anderson clearly thought Argyll's opponents were Smith, Lindsay, Moor, Muirhead and Black; John Anderson to Robert Simson, [copy with no date but 1759 or 1760].

130 John Anderson to Milton, n.d. [1757], NLS, 16707/56, and Anderson to Robert Simson, [copy with no date but 1759 or 1760], Papers of Sir John Leslie, EUL, Dc.2.57/16.

131 I thank David Raynor for telling me that there is *somewhere* material about all this, perhaps at the NAS.

132 He is said to have given him a poor letter of recommendation to the Duke of Queensberry in 1766; Robert Liston to Sir Gilbert Elliiot, MP, 3 November 1766, Liston MSS, NLS, 5517/23.

133 Coutts has a long discussion of this (*History*, 1909, pp. 252–7); a shorter one is contained in Mackie, *University of Glasgow*, 1954, p. 192f.

134 Ibid., p. 22f.

135 Anon., *A Letter to the Author of the North Briton*, 1763, p. 41.

136 'Bred at Glasgow, he had a Strong Attachment to that University And by many instances of his Patronage and favour he promoted its interests during the whole of his life'. from 'A Character of His Grace Archibald Duke of Argyll 1761', NLS, 17612/218.

137 Thomas Kirkpatrick to Lord Milton, 16 June 1761, NLS, 16721/103.

138 The dinner guest lists survive for some of his career in the diaries of Andrew Fletcher, who served Argyll as a Secretary; NLS, 17745–50.

6

THE AGE OF BUTE AND THE MODERATES

⁂

1. THE AGE OF MERIT?

Archibald Campbell, the greatest of the Dukes of Argyll, died on 15 April 1761. Principal Neil Campbell, who had long been disabled by illness and ineffective as an administrator or teacher, died toward the end of the following June. Their deaths set off a wave of changes which transformed the University of Glasgow. Those changes were made with the guidance of a new set of outsiders, initially men associated with John Stuart, 3rd Earl of Bute (1713–10 March 1792).

Bute was Argyll's nephew and like him in some respects. He was a more notable amateur scientist whose specialities were botany, astronomy, mineralogy and chemistry, fields which his uncle had also pursued.[1] Priggish and pious, the Earl helped the Moderates in the Kirk not because it was expedient to do so but because he agreed with them.[2] Bute followed his uncle's system in the management of Scotland. He wanted an Edinburgh manager to whom supplicants would write and one in London who could do what the Duke had done himself or delegated to his secretaries. By the end of April 1761, Bute had made Gilbert Elliot, MP his London manager for Scotland. In Edinburgh, he continued Milton in his old capacity. By the end of that year, Bute's brother, James Stuart Mackenzie, would be handling much of Bute's Scottish business in London and Baron William Mure of Caldwell (long Bute's Scottish man of business) was being phased in as a replacement for Milton who still carried on in some activities until 1763 when Bute resigned. Not long after, Milton suffered a debilitating stroke and ceased to be involved with patronage. Of these men, Stuart Mackenzie was the most important because from 1761 until 1767 he was active in the administration of university patronage in Scotland. He helped Bute and then served the London ministries which succeeded Bute's. Not as learned as his uncle or brother, James Stuart Mackenzie (c. 1719–1800) shared Bute's intellectual interests and added agriculture to his list of avocations. Argyll's successors brought into the Universities of Scotland distinguished men of letters but not important scientists or doctors. At Glasgow their men were not, with the exception of Thomas Reid, notable figures. Reid, however, did not directly owe his post to Bute's support.

Bute was as lucky at Glasgow as he was at Edinburgh. In both places he put his stamp on the institutions very quickly because of vacancies which existed by the time he was fully in power or which came shortly thereafter. The most pressing appointments to be made at Glasgow were those of the principal and professor of oriental languages, both incumbents having died at about the same time. Robert Simson's chair also needed to be permanently filled since Simson was old and wished to retire. Because of the departure of Rouet on the grand tour with the Earl of Hopetoun's sons in 1762, and his later extrusion from the College, yet another place was empty. Bute had a hand in the filling of all four of these posts.

The principalship had obvious candidates who long had prepared for the demise of Principal Campbell but seemingly not for that of the Duke of Argyll. James Oswald of Methvan's candidacy went back to 1754, when he had been recommended by the Glasgow Town Council when Campbell showed signs of dying.[3] Another was William Rouet who, along with William Leechman, is very likely to have been recommended to Lord Bute shortly after Campbell's death by Baron Mure of Caldwell. Mure was a newly made Baron of Exchequer and a friend of the Moderate literati and of David Hume. Rouet was Mure's distant cousin; Leechman had been Mure's tutor. Bute's reply, on 2 July 1761, to the letter sent by Mure was the sort of reply one learns to expect from the Earl:

> I have received your letter with the double application. One of them seems made *manière d'acquit*, because he was your relation [Rouet]. You might save yourself trouble in such cases, by assuring the person at once, that tho' Ld Bute has the greatest friendship for you, he, in things of public concern, will neither regard your relation nor his own one minute, but turn his thoughts solely to a worthy subject. Luckily you have pitched on one of this kind in your second request; I mean Mr Leechman, whose character and simplicity of manners I am well acquainted with, and shall recommend to the King. I have directed [Gilbert] Elliot to write him accordingly. I repeat once more, and beseech you would attend to it: merit and efficiency will ever weigh with me for publick office before private consideration.[4]

Rouet and Leechman were not the only ones who were in the running. On 24 June 1761, Lord Milton wrote to Elliot that Alexander

Carlyle sought the principalship or the chair of Hebrew and had written to Charles Townshend in London asking him to recommend him to the King. Carlyle had the interest of the Duke of Buccleuch to whose mother Townshend was married. Carlyle also claimed that the Duke of Argyll had 'marked my name down in his private notebook for Principal of the College of Glasgow, a body in whose prosperity he was much interested, as he had been educated there, and he said to Andrew Fletcher junior [Milton's sons and Argyll's former secretary], to whom he showed the note, that it would be very hard if he and I between us could not manage that troublesome society.'[5] That sounds plausible until one remembers that Patrick Cuming had served Argyll well over many years. Milton's scroll letter to Elliot also says that the Duke had the intention

> to give upon Principal Campbell's Death his Principality & Chaplaincy to Mr [Patrick] Cuming one of the Ministers of Edr who, upon obtaining that place should give up his church & office of Professor of Church history[,] the Sallary of which is a Hundred pounds a year in the gift of the Crown and for life if the Crown does not dispose of the Principality in thirty days after the death it falls into the hands of the College[.] I know Mr Cuming was always a favourite of the Duke of Argyle and trusted by him and will be faithful to the Earl of Bute.[6]

Patrick Cuming certainly believed he had a claim on the post, one which he had already asserted but with the proviso that he keep a chaplaincy: 'Without which it would not be easy for my great family to live with decency Not to say dignity as Head of a College.'[7] Others were aware of this claim too. Leechman wrote to Mure on 23 June 1762, the day after Principal Campbell died, to say that it was thought that Argyll had promised the post to Cuming. He wrote again three days later saying that it ought to go only to a cleric. That excluded Rouet.[8] In the end, Cuming failed to get his principalship and stayed in his Edinburgh chair. Later he failed again to get the Edinburgh principalship which went to William Robertson. He was given, instead, the succession to his own chair for one son while another was taken care of in Glasgow University.

Leechman became the principal at Glasgow with Bute's blessing[9] and within a short time settled into the autocratic ways which seem to have marked all the eighteenth-century Glasgow principals and which evoked protests from those who suffered during their regimes.[10] He turned out to have far less 'character and simplicity of manners' than Bute had expected. Indeed, he showed himself to be a deviant Calvinist, a harsh and litigious administrator and a man with little of the 'sweetness' which Hutcheson had once discerned in him. Leechman's appointment, and the still-vacant chair left by Buchanan's death on 21 June 1761, meant that two more livings in the College were now open – the professorships of divinity and oriental languages. Manoeuvring for both had begun before the end of June 1761.

Buchanan's place was the first to be filled. The post went to the reverend Robert Trail (c. 1720–19 October 1775), once a tutor to a Ayrshire laird, Fergusson of Kilkerran, and then a minister in Banff. He had been presented to his living by the Earl of Seafield and Findlatter. The Earl's son, James Ogilvie, Lord Deskford, was one of Trail's sponsors in Glasgow. Deskford was an ally of Bute. Baron Mure also supported Trail, to whom he was distantly related. A third supporter may well have been the rector, the Earl of Erroll, who, like Trail, was a man from the North.[11] There seem to have been few problems about this appointment which was not unopposed. Patrick Cuming (11 October 1738–27 October 1820), the son of the Edinburgh professor, sought it.[12] So too did Alexander Carlyle, who, as we have seen, wanted either this or the principalship. Another candidate, James Crombie, still nominally a student in Glasgow but already a minister in Elgin, was nominated by the rector.[13] The rector doubtless thought his office should be worth something but his nomination went nowhere. Bute's friends lacked both his earnestness for merit and his self-righteousness.

Trail went to Glasgow where he was installed on 15 July 1761. Once there, he and his friends sensed that they might do better. By late July, the new professor was angling for appointment to the chair of divinity, a chair he had secured by the end of August. There were no other known candidates. He was elected on 1 September and admitted on 2 November 1761. David Hume, a nice judge of such matters, thought him as unorthodox a Calvinist as Leechman.[14]

Trail's election opened the Hebrew chair, which this time did go to Patrick Cuming. His appointment was a sop to his father, Patrick, but Cuming had some support on his own. David Hume wrote to Adam Smith recommending him but in terms which do not stress his knowledge of the subject he was to teach:

> . . . I have known Mr Cummin for some time, and have esteemed him a young Man of exceeding good Capacity, and of a Turn towards Literature. He tells me, that he has made the Oriental Tongues & particularly the Hebrew a Part of his Study and has made some Proficiency in them: But of this Fact, craving his Pardon, I must be allowd to entertain some Doubt:

For if Hebrew Roots, as Cowley says, thrive best in barren Soil, he has a small Chance of producing any great Crop of them. But as you commonly regard the Professorship of Hebrew as a Step towards other Professorships, in which a good Capacity can better display itself; you will permit me to give it as my Opinion, that you will find it difficult to pitch on a young Man, who is more likely to be a Credit to your College, by his knowledge & Industry.[15]

William Cullen also sent a letter from Edinburgh soliciting the post for Cuming.[16] Cuming was another undistinguished Hebraist who published nothing but was long known for his teaching of French and Italian. The precedent for teaching of this sort from this chair had been set by that eminent Hebraist, John Anderson.

The year 1761 saw two more appointments. One went to James Williamson (?–3 June 1795), who at some time that year came to a definite arrangement with professor Simson about the mathematics chair. Simson demitted office on 19 October 1761. Williamson was elected eight days later but the apparent simplicity of the transfer conceals the fact that they had dickered about this business since at least 1757 and would continue doing so until 1763.[17] Argyll had helped them to come to terms; Bute was encouraged to smooth Williamson's way as well.[18] Thomas Reid, in 1766, saw Williamson as a man with whom Lord Deskford's word would carry weight.[19] The real choice, by courtesy of the masters and the politicians, was certainly Simson's, as was the timing of the succession.

The other appointment of 1761 was that of John Millar to the chair of law; it was of more moment and a simpler business. Professor Hercules Lindsay died on 2 June 1761. The faculty met the following day and resolved to ask Bute to present John Millar's name to the King – clearly the masters had made up their minds about a successor long before that day and had made arrangements to secure the post for Millar. Their letter to Bute noted that he had 'upon former occasion[s] shown so great disposition to patronise the University of Glasgow' that they hoped he would again aid them in finding 'a proper person to fil this office'. They went on,

He [Millar] was educated at this University, he has been long known to many of us as a man of genius, abilities & application, he has already distinguished himself in his profession & is willing to accept of this office. We can assure your Lordship that a person who is both proper to fill this office & willing to accept of it, is not very easy to be found, so great are the emoluments of a well employed Lawyer, & so small those of a Proffessor in a College.[20]

Bute wrote to them a week later to assure them that they would have their way.[21] Behind this nomination was the support of Lord Kames, whose son Millar had tutored, 'the interest of the guardians of the Duke of Hamilton' and the recommendation of Adam Smith.[22] Still, the letter to Bute went express to London to beat out any other applicants' letters to men of power. Until a warrant was issued it was never a sure thing because many men had enough influence in London to secure a regius chair. Millar's was a brilliant appointment which brought into the College a useful, productive and increasingly independent man.

In the following year, Rouet was finally replaced for good. He had left the College to go abroad with the sons of Lord Hopetoun in late 1759 or early 1760 and did so without the permission of the masters. He had been deprived by the College on 2 February 1760, despite a warning by Principal Leechman that this was not likely to be legal and would disoblige Argyll.[23] That action was found to be illegal by lawyers employed by the College because Rouet had not been given an opportunity to defend himself and his conduct. Reinstated after the opinions of the College lawyers, Rouet was cited to appear on 26 November 1762 but justified his conduct by mail and resigned on 22 December.[24] Bute played some role in this. At the insistence of Bute, the former rector, Lord Erroll, on 27 October 1762 wrote to professor Adam Smith, who then conducted much of the College's business, saying:

> I am this moment come from Lord Bute, and he desires me to inform the University that the King's orders are that you immediately vacate Mr Rouets place de novo, and that every thing may be done in a legal way, as soon as that is done His Majesty will appoint a Successor. There is a Necessity of complying with this else it may be of the worst consequences to the University, I could do no more, I said all that was possible but to no effect. One thing Lord Bute told me is that he is engaged to no body, but that the man who is recommended as the fittest for filling the place properly will be his man.[25]

It was unusual for a sovereign to act in this manner, but then George, if it was him and not Bute, was young and Bute was there to guide him. The process of finding a new man was well under way.

One man in the running was Robert Spens, the brother of Henry Spens, a young man later recommended to posts by the Edinburgh Moderates. Henry Spens hoped that Baron Mure 'will be able to get something done for my brother' and sought Bute's permission to dedicate to him the first translation into English of Plato's *Republic* which he was just finishing.[26] Bute did not appoint Robert. By the spring of 1762, the masters had pitched on James Oswald, minister of Methven, but Bute seems not to have liked this nomination.[27] Instead, the lobbying of Alexander Carlyle for his cousin, William Wight (22 December 1730–29 July 1782), a Dublin minister of some learning and more charm, was effective. Wight, an urbane man of no distinction, used the chair to teach a western civilisation course which ended with a section on the interests of Great Britain. The course ran to 102 lectures (four a week), with the last section dealing with Britain. He later shaped this section to counteract what he thought the too liberal and wrong-headed teaching of John Millar.[28] Wight was professor of ecclesiastical history and lecturer on civil history but his course was one which had been nearly wholly secularised. If he also taught ecclesiastical history, the memory of that seems not to have endured.

Bute's period of importance in the management of things Scottish gave prominence to men like Carlyle who were associated with the Moderate Party in the Kirk, a party which Bute greatly strengthened by his appointment of Leechman and Wight and others at Edinburgh.

2. CATCH AS CATCH CAN

When the Earl of Bute's period of greatest influence in Scotland ended in 1763, there followed a time in which jobs tended to go to men supported by Scots with influence but who did not necessarily belong to a stable political faction such as that Argyll had run.[29] This somewhat chaotic situation began with the patronage administration of Bute's brother and continued for about fifteen years.[30] Some of the influential men were members of the Moderate Party in the Kirk. Others able to secure posts for friends were secular intellectuals and politicians, such as Lords Deskford and Kames, the Earl of Kinnoul, Sir Gilbert Elliot, MP and Baron Mure of Caldwell. While the lines of patronage to some degree reflected the politics of London, they also smacked of the interest in merit which Argyll and Bute had both professed and shown. Because of the appointments of Argyll and Bute, more leeway was now allowed for professors and their personal patrons to make choices not dictated by parliamentary politics. One beneficiary of this laxity in Glasgow was Thomas Reid (26 April 1710–7 October 1796), who succeeded Adam Smith in the chair of moral philosophy in 1764. In securing this post, Reid beat out William Wight, the candidate of the Edinburgh Moderates who were eager to see a clubbable man in a post for which he was not suited.[31]

When Smith resigned on 14 February 1764, Reid was not an obvious choice. He was neither a Glasgow alumnus nor from the region but had long held a regency at King's College, Aberdeen and was himself a graduate of Marischal College. His own dearest intellectual interests were not in morals but in epistemology, mathematics and science. Given the encouragement of the proper fixed chair – King's regents still taught everything – he might have done significant work in mathematics or the natural sciences.[32] He had competition for the Glasgow chair. It seems to have been offered to George Muirhead; he refused.[33] Another man who is said to have declined was Samuel Charteris, a bright Border minister with ties to Glasgow.[34] Adam Smith helped his assistant and deputy, Thomas Young, to secure the post and in that endeavour he had the aid of John Millar and Joseph Black.[35] They failed; Reid had influential supporters.

Reid's most important political backer was Lord Deskford, who had written to his protégé, Robert Trail, seeking his support in this election. Deskford also wrote to William Cullen, now at Edinburgh University, asking him to use his good offices for Reid.[36] Someone had probably engaged the 3rd Duke of Queensberry and Lord Hopetoun to ask Stuart Mackenzie to use his influence for Reid with the professors who would elect. The somebodies were most likely to have been Lord Kames and Deskford. Deskford was Hopetoun's brother-in-law by his first marriage to a now-deceased wife. Kames knew Hopetoun well through the Philosophical Society of Edinburgh and the various improving activities which interested them both. Queensberry had some interest in the latter and would have known Kames because His Grace held the sinecure office of Lord Justice General which made him the official head of the Justiciary Court, the criminal court to which Kames had been appointed in 1763. Kames was also able to certify Reid's abilities as a philosopher since Reid occasionally spent vacations with him discussing intellectual matters. There was a formidable array of influence led by men who knew what they were doing. Reid was admitted on 11 June 1764 and Glasgow received a distinguished amateur scientist, a sensible administrator and perhaps its greatest eighteenth-century philosopher.

Over the next few years, there were openings in the medical school. The first were occasioned by the departure of Joseph Black to teach in Edinburgh. Black left two vacancies – one in the chair of medicine, the other the lectureship of chemistry. His posts were split, enabling Glasgow to compete more effectively with Edinburgh where chemistry and *materia medica* were separated at about this time. Chemistry, especially in Glasgow, was becoming a subject more oriented toward industry than medicine so *materia medica* was made a separate lectureship. To compete with Edinburgh, and to meet the local demands for chemical knowledge, this change was necessary.[37]

The medical chair went to Alexander Stevenson (1725–29 May 1791), an improving Ayrshire laird who had belonged to fashionable Edinburgh clubs and who possessed a Glasgow MD. He had not long before moved to the city where he already had a large practice. Others were interested in the post and had some chance of obtaining it because it was a regius appointment. Among them may have been Dr David Skene of Aberdeen. Thomas Reid informed him of the vacancy as soon as it was clear that Black would leave. Reid noted, however: 'The recommendation of the College would probably have great weight, if unanimous; but I think there is no probability of an unanimous recommendation; so the Court interest must probably determine it.' He went on to say that he knew of three candidates: Stevenson, 'Dr Smith Carmichael' and a 'Dr Stork'.[38] Reid got two of the names wrong but he was correct about the lack of unanimity and the court interest.

The medical professorship was indeed sought by two young physicians who clearly thought that at Glasgow they had some chance of being appointed at a school which might not be as choosy as the one in Edinburgh. In this they were wrong, but it is interesting that they should have held such ideas. Dr William Stark (1740–70), was an Englishman from Manchester who had matriculated at Glasgow in 1753 and received his MA there in 1758. He seems then to have studied in Edinburgh and at Leiden, where he took his MD. By 1766, he may have practised briefly in Edinburgh and already had been in London at St George's Hospital, where he may have done some clinical teaching. He died in 1770, having written medical works published by his friend, the other contender for the post, James Carmichael Smythe (1741–1821).

Carmichael Smythe had been educated at Edinburgh, where he received his MD in 1764. At some time he had been abroad in France, Italy and Holland. In 1766 he was at loose ends and in need of a permanent place. Like his friend, he eventually went on to London, where he had a successful career. By the end of his life he was known as a notable hospital and prison sanitary reformer and as a medical chemist. It is not known who, if anyone, supported either man.[39] Either might have been more of an ornament to the University than Stevenson who published nothing and was notable only for improving his Ayrshire estate.

On 21 April, three days after Reid wrote his letter about this appointment, Dr Stevenson set out to gather the 'Court interest'. He contacted his Ayrshire neighbour, Lord Loudoun (a Campbell with improving and scientific interests), noting that 'the College in general seems inclined to befriend me and Baron Mure, who is the Rector, has had the goodness to act in my favour, & I flatter myself will still do it more effectually – the nomination belongs to the Crown – I am at a loss to find the proper Method of Application; but shall esteem myself happy if I have your Lordships good wishes.'[40] This was not a bad way to apply. It put him in touch with a principal manager of Crown patronage and with an important figure in his county who had a large cousinage. By 5 May, eight of the masters (including Reid) wrote to Baron Mure asking for Stevenson's appointment. He had by then secured the backing of the Royal College of Physicians of Edinburgh, a body to which he and his father had belonged.[41] Still, it seems not to have been a sure thing for him. Thomas Reid wrote to a friend in Aberdeen several days later that, 'We have had great canvassing here about a professor of the Theory and practice of Physic', canvassing which had resulted in Stevenson obtaining 'a recommendation from the majority of the College, not without much interest'. Sponsors had been active on his behalf. Stevenson had overcome the ground of objection to him – that he had too great a practice to give full attention to his academic duties.[42] He was appointed. Despite the canvassing, none of the doctors cited earlier shows up in known discussions of this chair, and, stranger yet, neither do any other applicants.

Black's chair of chemistry was sought by some of his students, among them William Irvine (1743–9 July 1787) and John Robison (1739–30 January 1805). The chemistry lectureship in 1766 went to John Robertson or Robison as he became. Robison had been one of Robert Dick II's and Robert Simson's best students. He studied divinity, tutored and was for several years a midshipman responsible for testing Harrison's chronometer for the Board of Longitude and for surveying portions of the St Lawrence River. When he returned to Glasgow he assisted Black, who recommended him as his successor.[43] He later became a most distinguished teacher of natural philosophy at Edinburgh University, the editor of Joseph Black's *Lectures on the Elements of Chemistry* (1803) and a notable contributor of science entries to the third edition the *Encyclopedia Britannica* (1788–97) and to its *Supplement* (1801). He was one of the most notable Scottish scientists of the period but most of his career was spent outside Glasgow.

Irvine was not forgotten. In 1765–6, he gave, while still a medical student, a course in *materia medica*. That was given with the permission of the College, but he seems not to have been made a lecturer. Perhaps worried about their reputation, the masters had refused to give a title to a mere student without an MD degree. In 1766, Irvine graduated MD at the University and his place was renewed as a lectureship. He repeated the course he had already given. He was annually appointed to give *materia medica* lectures from this chair until 1769, when he assumed the duties of the lecturer in chemistry as well.[44] In the end, Irvine became more of an industrial than a medical chemist. His career thus followed those of Cullen and Black. He wrote important papers on heat, the density of water and other chemical topics. In the chemistry and *materia medica* chairs, the masters had chosen well-qualified men who made considerable reputations.

3. OTHER GLASGOW APPOINTMENTS MADE BY THE MASTERS

During the years 1767–73 no new men came into the University. It was the longest barren period in this study of patronage at Glasgow. After that the masters enjoyed a relative independence until c. 1780. They picked men with little interference from the London ministers but with some deference to local gentlemen and noblemen. The tutors whom those gentlemen had employed to travel with and to educate their sons were desirable college teachers because of their abilities, known skills and experience of the world. The kind of struggles which ensued when competing interests engaged the Glasgow professors can be clearly seen in the efforts made by gentlemen in 1773 to place dependants in the chair of humanity.

George Muirhead died on 3 August 1773, after being 'cut for the stone'. His post seems to have been offered to professor William Wight but rejected by him for reasons of health.[45] No great matter, there were twelve or fifteen others who sought the place as well. The chances of most were slim and only the names of four have survived.[46] Those men were formidable candidates because they were well backed by gentlemen who could pull strings. Three of them had ties to the College or to influential men in it.

One was Charles Shaw, 9th Baron Cathcart, who in 1773, and 1774 was elected rector of the University. He had estates near Paisley and was an alumnus of the College. Rising in the army to be a Lieutenant-General and Commander-in-Chief in Scotland, he had recently been in Russia as the British Envoy (1768–71). He had taken with him William Richardson (1 October 1743–3 November 1814), who acted as his secretary and tutor to his sons. Richardson earlier had tutored his lordship's heirs both at home and at Eton. He needed to be taken care of; a university place would suit him well.

A second would-be patron was William Mure of Caldwell, another Glasgow alumnus. Mure had been an MP (1742–61), a Baron of the Exchequer since 1761 and a former manager of Scottish patronage for Bute and those who followed him. By the 1770s he was no longer much involved with government patronage but many owed him favours and he knew the College well. Mure had been rector of the University in 1752–4 and 1764–6, and was defeated for the place in 1776, the year in which he died. His sons had been tutored at home and in Paris by George Jardine (1742–28 January 1827). Like Richardson, Jardine had trained to be a cleric but had not fancied a clerical living. A university post would also suit him.

The third gentleman who aspired to place a dependant in the College was Sir Gilbert Elliot, MP. He had sat in Parliament since 1754 and had held office under various ministries. In 1773 he was Keeper of the Signet and Treasurer of the Navy. Elliot had served Bute as an advisor on Scottish politics and, like Mure, was a very good friend of David Hume and much associated with the Edinburgh literati and members of the Moderate Party in the Kirk. He was not in much favour in London in 1773 because he had quarrelled with his leader, Lord North, and was known to resent the failure of the King to give one of his sons seniority in a guards regiment in which the young man had held a commission since he was a toddler. His boys had been tutored in Paris by Robert (later Sir Robert) Liston. Like the other would-be professors, Liston had begun training for the ministry but had not persisted. In the late 1760s and early 1770s, he was still unplaced but likely tutoring boys at Glasgow and Edinburgh. For part of 1773 he was possibly off with Lord Aberdeen.[47] Liston needed a permanent berth but Glasgow was not exactly the place to look for one since neither he nor Elliot had important ties to the University. Despite that, Liston lived there during part of the year 1773 and Elliot knew many men on the faculty.

Finally, there was a fourth man named Robert Clason [Classon, Clason or Clawson].[48] Little is known of him and it may in fact have been his better-known brother, Patrick (c. 1740–1811), who was actually nominated. The latter by this time had been several times abroad as a tutor and had served and would serve many well-born families, including that of the 4th Earl of Dunmore, a Glasgow man

then Governor of New York. Patrick Clason came to know everyone who counted. He was friendly with Hume, dined with the
philosophes in Paris, and married a noble Swiss lady and settled in
Lausanne. When the French Revolution began, they moved to
London.[49] He had attended Glasgow in the 1750s and was himself
still at loose ends. His younger brother had also been at Glasgow in
the 1760s and might have found local sponsors among Patrick's
patrons, including Dunmore, Sir Thomas Wallace or John Glassford.
Dunmore and Glassford came from great merchant families and the
latter was a supporter of the Foulis Academy of Art. Patrick Clason
knew these men and had travelled with them or their sons.[50] Those
men had influence but none of them had been rector and none is
known to have been involved with university patronage. Clason's
backing seems the weakest and he suffered by not being on the scene.
Still, George Jardine regarded him as a strong candidate.[51] Unlike the
other three, no records have been found of Clason's efforts to secure
the chair.

Robert Liston was an impressive candidate. He had been in Paris
with the sons of Sir Gilbert Elliot, MP and, with the backing of David
Hume and Baron Turgot, he had hoped to secure the post of tutor to
the Prince of Parma in 1768.[52] Two or three years later, he was one of
those considered to become tutor to the heir of the Duke of Douglas.[53]
In 1772 he had sought the humanity chair at St Andrews, for which
Elliot wrote letters seeking support for his candidacy from General
Scot, brother to David Scot of Scatstarvit, the private patron with the
right to present to the chair.[54] Nothing had come of that and nothing
came of a later attempt to buy the Edinburgh humanity chair from
George Stuart in 1774–5.[55] Early in 1773, perhaps knowing that
Muirhead was ailing, Elliot had written letters to Glasgow introducing Liston to professors William Wight and James Williamson and to
Principal Leechman, three men whom Elliot would have known from
politicking with the Moderates. He told Liston to canvass others for
support should he decide to apply. Elliot's somewhat illegible letter
jauntily, but cynically, assessed the process by which the place would
be granted:

> . . . it will be Necessary for you while at Glasgow to be introduced to Him
> [Leechman] as a Stranger[.] Frend to each of them [that is the professors
> he would contact, who, Elliot assumed, would not belong to the same
> political connections] Because Like all Wise and Important Bodys of
> Society They are wretchedly keen on Political Division and[,] on a
> [?Promotion] [illegible in the text] to their High Station or Merit[,] Claim

a superior Degree of Devotion[.] I give you this hint Because if an Angell be Supported by one Party the other would Support a Devil rather than allow themselves to be defeated C Such is the Meritorious Virtue of our party Leaders In church and State . . . be Careful to Contrive Methods to Gain the Countenance and Support of Those Superior Beings – Baron Muir or [the then rector] Lord Frederick Campbell at whose Nodd the University itself trembles – Such is the glorious Independence which prevails In our Happy Land of Liberty and among free-born Brittains.[56]

If Elliot was correct, factional infighting continued in the College, with the factions now those of the Moderates and the literati opposed by the parliamentary politicos led by Lord Frederick Campbell, the MP for the Glasgow burghs. Campbell was the Duke of Argyll's man, while Mure was Bute's friend. Elliot did not think this place was going to be awarded to a man on his merits.

By September, Liston believed he had lost, even though 'the professors are now it is said to chuse without partiality a proper Successor to Mr Muirhead. No great man is expected to intermeddle . . . No Character; I am assured, is likely to go farther with them than one given by you.' Despite his pessimism, he had been studying ancient history and doing 'grammatical Studies' just in case he got elected.[57] Elliot replied that he had written to professor Alexander Wilson and had got an Edinburgh minister, John Drysdale, to write to professor John Anderson. He feared the contest had come down to one between Mure and Cathcart. They mattered more than the men they supported. The first, he said, 'took the field two hours after George [Muirhead] was defunct & Cathcart the day after'. He went on:

The Principal was his [Mure's] Tutor & owes the Principality to him. Ruat is his Couzin who was long a Profr in that College & has influence with some of the Professors. Since the demise of G. Muirhead I apprehend the J[ustice] Clerk [Thomas Millar] has no influence in that Society so we have nothing either to hope or fear from him. This brings to my mind that John Hills friends are somewhat anxious still about the St Andrews affair [the humanity chair there, vacated by Hill when he moved to the same chair at Edinburgh in 1775] . . .

Elliot quoted Joseph Black as saying the contest would be between Jardine and Richardson, Mure and Cathcart.[58] By 25 September, professor John Stevenson of Edinburgh wrote to Liston saying that professors Williamson and Patrick Cuming had been approached and that professor Alexander Stevenson would be. He advised Liston to 'take advantage of your former friendship with D. Hume in this affair'.[59] Three days later, Sir Gilbert Elliot wrote to ask if Liston's name had 'been stated' to Leechman, a curious comment after all this time.[60] On the last day of September, the Faculty set 9 October as election day, a sign that negotiations were still going on but that the issue had to be resolved by the beginning of term and that it would be settled before the rectorial election. Cathcart enjoyed a double victory: Richardson was elected professor and a bit later his lordship became rector. The tutor of the most important and influential politician had come first.

From the point of view of George Jardine, 1772–3 was hardly more satisfying than it was to Liston. In March 1772, while Jardine was tramping around Paris with Mure's sons, the Baron was thinking of finding Jardine a university job and expected it to be at Glasgow.[61] There was hope that William Wight, professor of history, might move to Edinburgh to replace professor Adam Ferguson but that did not happen. Had it happened, Jardine would have gone for the ecclesiastical history chair. In May, Mure was again focused on Glasgow, where he probably knew professor Muirhead might not long survive.[62] By 14 July 1772, Jardine had been advised 'to be on the field and making application like others – that in the shuffling of parties &c: some occasion may turn out favourable.' Jardine worried: 'I shall be sorry either to meet [John] Robison – or any of my friends in opposition and can assure you that in all such cases – shall most earnestly beg of all who may wish to serve me – not to make any appearance for me when it is likely to have no other effect than to [tear in the manuscript] the Interest of my friends.' If he was thinking of meeting Robison, he was thinking of a science chair as a possibility or Robison was willing to take one in the humanities. Nearly the last thing those who made the appointments had on their minds was a specialist professor. That was equally true of the would-be professors. Jardine had also been told that 'Interest had been making for . . . more than twelve month . . . for R[obert] C[la]-son' and William Richardson, who was said to be 'in a line that will have no interference with you'. This probably meant that Richardson wanted not the humanity chair but the Greek chair held by James Moor, now an alcoholic. Mure had written to Principal Leechman but Jardine did not think that relying upon the promises and votes of professors was the way to approach the problem: 'correspondence with Masters – is not the thing – I am promised & can depend upon a most hearty assistance from the Quarter you hint when it may be necessary.' That was political influence from outside the College. By 6 November, Jardine was willing that his friend and correspondent, Robert Hunter, should tell professor James Williamson of his eagerness to be elected a professor but he relied upon Baron Mure to push his candidacy. By the beginning of the following June, Jardine was back in Scotland and visited Caldwell, where he found 'them all very civil & Disposed to treat me like a Gentleman – and making some allowances – for the cold interested humour of the family – I hope I shall soon learn to make it tolerably agreeable.' Professors were forever deferential to those above them and knew whence their favours came, but they expected genteel treatment. Jardine's appraisal of Baron Mure would change.

Within a week of Muirhead's death, Jardine was confident that he and Richardson were the men to beat, but it was not a sure thing. Again, Jardine's description of the situation, written on 8 September, is of interest for giving the flavour of many contests for which we lack this sort of documentation.

> You may believe me Candidates are all on the wing – I have had neither peace nor rest for these days past – I wish to God it were over – for then in spite of fate and Disappointment I shall sleep soundly. I have not time to display all the Political manoeuvre that is at present exerting. As in many other cases – The Best Politicians will fail – My friend The B[aron]. God Bless him – with a Sagacity peculiar to himself plays Battery after Battery with great dexterity but a most diabolical combination has been forming for four or five years past is likely to render all attempts ineffectual – Some of these who ought naturally to be on our side cannot get free from engagements – Theres doubts even with respect to the P[rincipal]. J[ohn] A[nderson] my declared Foe – expressly acknowledging his engagement to Richardson. The B[aron] is resolved however to sweat him as much as possible. Clasons parts [?partisans] are yet uncertain what they are to do – they have not yet got his answer with his determination to stand or not. If he stands the affair will be somewhat complex – If not – the struggle will be purely betwixt R[ichardson] & me – with what party they will join in that case – is not yet certain – they'll certainly endeavour to make the best terms possible with the oyr party for their friend. The Professors are yet quite separate in every part of the Country – that no certain idea can be formed – except that pre-engagements to R[ichardson] appear in every quarter – Still however there is some chance – Perhaps the Jostling of partys & the well directed Policy of my friend may bring some good out of the present confusion . . . One good effect may probably arise from this competition – that we will tye them down neck & heel for the next vacancy & ye know [that] is always something . . .

All the jostling and stir point to more people being involved in these affairs by 1773 than had been true earlier. That was an indicator of the lack of management in Scottish politics generally, something seen at the same time in Edinburgh where the competition for the natural philosophy chair was equally open and intense. Securing a chair was now not a simple business of canvassing the political managers and the legal patrons. In the absence of real managers, it meant getting on your side as many of the electing professors' friends and associates as you could and hoping they would exert pressure on the electors. One needed letters such as that of the 5th Duke of Argyll to John Anderson asking him to vote for Jardine or the one which the Duke of Queensberry wrote to professor Wight asking that he vote for Richardson. Even those did not always work; neither duke was successful in his application. When election day came, Jardine moaned that he and Mure lost by 'the Rotten vote of James Moore who solemnly promised twice to the Baron and after drew back and voted against us.' The seven voters for Jardine were: Principal Leechman, Robert Trail, James Williamson, William Wight, John Millar, Patrick Cuming and Lord Frederick Campbell, the rector, who was days later replaced by Cathcart at the rectorial election. The eight voting against him were James Clow, John Anderson, Thomas Reid, James Moor, Thomas Hamilton, Robert Findlay, Alexander Stevenson and Alexander Wilson. Despite their previous engagements, the final tally suggests that the literary men had a candidate and the professors most interested in science and medicine had another.

That election is typical but curious. It pitted bright men with little specialised knowledge against one another. They were judged, by their backers and others, by their general competence rather than by special scholarship and accomplished work. The expectations were not that they would stay in the chair forever but would move on to other more suitable or lucrative fields. Anyone could teach Latin, but the recipient of the post would be eligible for other chairs which might well require different skills. Despite the 'great men' involved, most of the professors stood by their previous engagements and exercised a good deal of independence. Jardine did not manage to 'tye them neck and heel' since he did not get the next open position but the one after that and not because anyone was tied. Richardson, despite the jiggery-pokery which led to his win, was probably the best man for the post he received. He published interesting and ground-breaking critical studies, a great deal of poetry well thought of in its day and a book on his time in Russia. He wrote essays for the *Mirror* and *Lounger*, was a good teacher and, like his predecessor, was active in the Foulis Press. He also had the most far-sighted patron, one who began his campaign for the chair earlier than the others. Sir Gilbert

Elliot was the patron with the second greatest political importance but his candidate did not come by anything at Glasgow, St Andrews or Edinburgh. Liston's candidacy did not matter and is not even mentioned, although Liston was in Glasgow and canvassing for votes with powerful support. By the end of the year, one of Sir Gilbert's sons offered Liston the secretaryship of his diplomatic mission to Bavaria. Liston took it and embarked on a new career in diplomacy which in the end brought him a knighthood and great distinction. His experience may say more about his patron than himself. Jardine feared Clason not Liston but we never hear who backed Clason or if he decided to stand. In the end Clason's votes and those of Liston (if he had any) were almost certainly distributed when their friends saw their man would not stand or could not win. Patrick Clason, if it was he, may have been a serious candidate partly because of his book. Jardine would do one big book on education and be renowned as a teacher but he never published the historical account of the French *parlements* which he contemplated in November 1773 as he lived in Glasgow and accompanied the sons of Sir James Campbell to the lectures of William Wight and Thomas Reid.

No sooner was this election over than attention at Glasgow began to focus on two others. James Moor was ill, drunken, difficult and employing a deputy to teach for him. He could not hold out much longer and would have to be permanently replaced. James Clow, who had long held the logic chair, was thinking about retirement. Jardine, in the wake of his defeat, hoped to get Moor's Greek chair since he thought that would be the next on offer. Moor, while he might often have been in his cups, had not lived in this society so long and learned nothing about the ways men got jobs. By the spring of 1774 he had come to an arrangement with John Young (c. 1748–18 November 1820), who had taught classes for him since 1766. He would sell out but he needed the permission of his colleagues who wanted rid of him because his life was an embarrassment to them. In 1767 he had had his goods distrained for debt and five years later he beat a student who then took him to court and won a libel action against him. Professor Anderson brought an action against him and, when Moor said he was too ill to appear to answer it, his colleagues prepared to oust him. It became clear that his price for an easy and unlitigated resignation was naming his successor and keeping his salary and house.[63] Legally, he had no right to do either but his choice of Young was respected and he was graciously allowed his salary and house. Young agreed to teach for fees. Moor resigned on 5 May 1774 and died five years later.

Jardine had again been disappointed but he was not the only one. His friend John Robison had also sought the place,[64] as had John Gillies (1747–1836). The last had taught for Moor and had been a tutor to Lord Hopetoun's boys. Later he became a notable Greek historian and Historiographer Royal.[65]

The election of Young to the Greek chair had moved Clow, reputedly a wealthy man, to resign in favour of Jardine if his colleagues would appoint him.[66] He came to this resolution in May 1774. On 3 June, Jardine wrote to his friend Robert Hunter that 'this day the Faculty confirmed Mr Clows desire and chose me Assistant and Successor – so that the Class next winter falls into my hands with the perquisites – the house & Salarie reserved – But it is thought Mr Clow will not keep them long.' Clow was tougher than Jardine imagined; he did not relinquish the house and salary or his vote in the senate and College meeting until 1788, the year he died. There was in this appointment little or no outside interference; that had all come earlier. Those who elected Jardine well knew whom they would please.

In 1775, the University had to appoint a new professor of divinity owing to the death of professor Robert Trail. This led to a conflict between local men and outsiders. The Glaswegians, the Edinburgh Moderates and their friend David Hume were for the promotion of William Wight; other outsiders wanted the reverend James Baillie, a minister in Hamilton but not a person much connected with the College. Hume's letter to William Strahan soliciting support for Wight is interesting both because it is from an irreligious man, but also for stating what Hume took to be the requirements for such a post:

> The place is to be filled by a Vote of the Professors: You are understood to have great influence with Wilson, the Professor of Astronomy [Strahan bought type from him]: And I interest myself extremely in Dr Wight's success: These are my Reasons for writing to you. But I must also tell you my Reasons for interesting myself so much in Dr Wight's Behalf. He is a particular Friend of mine: He is very much connected with all mine and your particular Friends in the Church: He is a very gentleman-like agreeable Man: And above all, he is (without which I should not interest myself for him) a very sound and orthodox Divine . . . Now, I shall answer for Dr Wight, that his Pupils shall have all the Orthodoxy, without the bigotry, instill'd into them by his predecessor. I believe Dr [Principal William] Robertson will write you on the same Subject; and I beg you woud not lose any time in applying to Mr Wilson, in case he shoud take any other Engagements, tho we do not yet hear of any other Candidate.[67]

The next day Hume reiterated his support when he asked his old friend Baron Mure for a letter to Principal Leechman. He said again that Wight was 'a sensible, good humoured, Gentleman-like Fellow, and as sound and orthodox as you coud wish.'[68] Qualities of character weighed most with Hume but he knew that orthodoxy was requisite as well. While Hume and others tried to get this place for Wight, most of Wight's colleagues realised that his election would cost the University more than he was worth.

The reason for that was that William Hunter, the eminent London surgeon and medical teacher, had asked for this place for his brother-in-law, the reverend James Baillie. It was understood that in exchange for this office, Hunter, who had no children, would leave to the College some of his effects, what Jardine delicately called 'particular Expectations'.[69] These were anatomical teaching preparations and perhaps more. Baillie's claim went back to 1763, when Stuart Mackenzie wrote to Baron Mure saying that Bute and he had promised Baillie a Glasgow job.[70] Nothing had come of that promise in the intervening years but by 1775 William Hunter and his brother, John, had much more clout than they had possessed in 1763. William, FRS, had become a well-known male midwife and Physician Extraordinary to Queen Charlotte. He was also the proprietor of the best medical school in London. John, FRS, had won fame as an anatomist and was forming an important collection but one still dwarfed by William's larger one. John Hunter was Surgeon Extraordinary to George III and the most notable comparative anatomist in Britain. The promise to Baillie was honoured. The Hunters' brother-in-law was translated from the manse in Hamilton to the College. In the end the University received William Hunter's anatomical preparations, a great natural history collection and one of the best numismatic collections in Europe. Most of that is still housed in the University's Hunterian Museum. Hunter's priceless books, manuscripts and art works now adorn the University's library and art museum. Wight's pretensions weighed little next to the expectation of even some of that. Baillie, who is best known as the father of Joanna Baillie, the poetess, died after three years and another man had to be selected in 1778. This time the chair went to William Wight as the College men, without cost, looked after one of their own.

Wight's appointment was a sign of the growing ascendency of the Moderate Party in the Kirk, as was the interest shown in the position by professor George Hill of St Andrews and the reverend Mr Henry Grieve. Hill became the most notable Moderate theologian. He was said to have been asked by William Robertson to stand for the post but, in the end, he declined.[71] Henry Grieve later tried for the principality but this 'affair was virtually determined before any Application was made for Dr Grieve either by himself or his friend'.[72] A third man, now unknown, was supported by John Millar, Thomas Hamilton and others.[73] He was possibly the reverend Robert Findlay, the son of a Glasgow merchant, who would succeed Wight in 1783. He nearly beat him in 1778. During 1776–8 Findlay served as dean of faculty.

Wight's resignation and translation to the divinity chair in June 1778 created a vacancy in the ecclesiastical history chair which the Crown filled in August 1778 with Hugh MacLeod (27 December 1730–22 May 1809). This appointment seems to have had little input from the masters, although MacLeod had been librarian of the College in the 1750s and was well known to the professors. What undoubtedly won him the place was the fact that he had tutored the son of Lt Gen. Charles Fitzroy, a fashionable soldier who was created 1st Baron Southampton in 1780. MacLeod's appointment seems to have been arranged in London by a man with enough influence to secure the post but with few connections to the College. Neither the patron nor the new professor saw quite what was involved in the job. When he was appointed, MacLeod was still tutoring and in the following year asked for leave to attend his charge at Eton. He was forced to return to Glasgow to teach and found the College's demand 'quite beyond my Comprehension'.[74] The fact that he was forced to return shows that his colleagues were probably miffed by the manner of his appointment. They intended to make him earn his salt or leave. There was no hint of dissatisfaction when William Hamilton (1758–13 March 1790) replaced his father Thomas as professor of botany and anatomy.

Professor Thomas Hamilton became ill in 1777 and never fully recovered, even though he went with his son William to take the waters at Bath.[75] When he relapsed in 1780, his son was given permission to assist him in teaching. On 13 February 1781, professor Hamilton asked the College to seek from the Crown a joint appointment for himself and his son, who by then had been a medical student at Glasgow and Edinburgh and had studied in London with William Hunter. The unspoken assumption was that, should William not be appointed, the place would be poorly served because the extensive collection of teaching preparations which the Hamiltons had accumulated over two generations would be removed from the College at Thomas's death along with the 'leather ladies', dummies which he used in the teaching of obstetrics.[76] Thomas Hamilton died on 7 January 1782. By that time, the Crown had acceded to the requests of the family and the University.[77] William Hamilton was appointed and became a fine teacher, a clever anatomist and a man to whom professors Cullen and James Gregory referred cases and with whom they and Hamilton's former students consulted. It was a good appointment made on grounds of merit and the need to preserve a teaching collection in the University.

The last appointment before the coming of Henry Dundas's regime was that given to Thomas Reid's assistant and successor, Archibald Arthur (6 September 1744–14 June 1797). This too was one made by the College men with no outside interference. Arthur had been appointed College chaplain in 1767 and was librarian from 1774 to 1794. Before assisting Reid, he had at various times taught logic, botany and Latin. He began teaching for Reid c. 1779. At the end of that academic year, on 6 May 1780, Reid, now 70, requested that Arthur be chosen his assistant and successor. Like Moor, Reid kept his house, salary and position in the Faculty. Arthur taught for fees and fully succeeded only in 1796, after which he held office for less than a year.

Instability in the ministries in London from c. 1760 to c. 1770 led to uncertainty about whose direction should be followed in Scotland. As Michael Fry has written in an unequalled description of this period which was perhaps longer than he says, 'The plain fact was that for a decade or so nobody took charge of Scottish affairs, hardly even of the most routine patronage.'[78] That allowed the professors and the local gentlemen of influence to pick more college teachers than had been the case under Argyll's regime. The government established by Lord North was more stable and the situation changed as Henry Dundas (28 April 1742–2 May 1811) began in the mid-1770s to gather voters and influence into his connection. Dundas was a good politician who could make the most of opportunities. Still, at Glasgow, until the French Revolution made everyone jumpy – especially the chancellor, the 3rd Duke of Montrose – the masters were the chief pickers of professors as they were supposed to be. This allowed them to determine who was to succeed them and to secure places for relatives. In most cases in which this happened, the men chosen were candidates to whom no one could heartily object. Because some of them were also rather extreme Whigs, this meant that in the long run there were bound to be problems when political sensitivities increased, as they did after 1789.[79] Dundas, like most prominent Scots, moved to the right and became reactionary in his views. As he did so, he became more sensitive and assertive about political issues. His period in power did not start that way and in the beginning he himself looked fairly enlightened.

Notes

1 Bute wrote and privately printed much on botany but his true memorial in that field is Kew Gardens. He left manuscripts which dealt with minerals and chemistry and other fields of natural history which he thought about systematically. Professor John Walker thought him the most knowing of the Scots interested in fossils. David P. Millar, ' "My favorite studdys": Lord Bute as naturalist', in *Lord Bute*, ed. Schweizer, 1988, pp. 213–40; see also 'John Walker's Fossil Collection', EUL, Gen 1061/22.

2 After 1752 one can speak of a Moderate Party in the Kirk. Its programme was quite like that of James Smith and other earlier men: the enforcement of laws and rules, the preaching by a polite and more cultured clergy of uncontentious morality rather than doctrine which would be disputed. The Moderates were led from c. 1754 to 1780 by William Robertson and after him by a variety of men such as Alexander Carlyle, Joseph McCormick, and George Hill. After c. 1780 the Moderates took a good deal of guidance from the politicians of the Dundas connection. The best general account of the Moderates is by Sher, *Church and University*, 1985, but this needs to be supplemented by accounts which are less adulatory of this group of generally overrated men. See: McIntosh, *Church and Theology in Enlightenment Scotland*, 1998, and various essays by Landsman and others. Several of those are listed in, Emerson and Wood, 'Science and Enlightenment in Glasgow, 1690–1802', in *Science and Medicine*, ed. Withers and Wood, 2002, pp. 79–142; p. 112 n.3.

3 William Tod to Lord Milton, 6 April 1754, Saltoun Correspondence, NLS, 16690/172.

4 Bute to Mure, 2 July 1761, *Mure of Caldwell Papers*, 1883, Part 2: I:127f. The next, undated, letter from Gilbert Elliot to Mure says that Rouet had been recommended by Lord Hopetoun (I:128f). Had Hopetoun secured this post for Rouet, his lordship could have reduced his pension to Rouet by at least £100 and perhaps paid him no pension at all for throwing up his job and accompanying the Earl's sons to Europe. Rouet to Hopetoun, 26 September 1759, Mure of Caldwell MSS, NLS, 4941/298. Rouet's own estimate of his chances was given in a letter to Robert Simson, 10 July 1761. There he said he would stand, were he in Scotland, but that Patrick Cuming, professor of ecclesiastical history at Edinburgh, would probably get it, although 'our good & worthy friend Mr Leechman is still more deserving of that office & I

think wt proper application might be sure of success, I hertily wish it . . .'. Rouet to Simson, GUL, Murray 660.

5 *Autobiography of Dr Alexander Carlyle*, ed. Burton, 1910, p. 401; Carlyle had impressed the Duke on a visit to Inveraray in 1758; Alexander Carlyle, 'Notes for Autobiography', GUL, Murray MS 41/3.

6 Scroll, Milton to Sir Gilbert, 24 June 1761, NLS, 16720/69.

7 Ibid.; see also Cuming to Lord Milton, 24 June 1761, EUL, Laing II.152.

8 Rouet seems to have studied divinity but was never ordained. His career is most amply described by William T. Johnston in *Enlightenment in France and Scotland*, CD issued by Officina (Livingston, 2004). See also Leechman to Baron Mure, 23 and 26 June 1761, Mure of Caldwell Papers, NLS, 4942. I thank Richard Sher for giving me transcriptions of parts of these letters.

9 Gilbert Elliot to Milton, 2 July 1761, NLS, 16720/72.

10 Coutts, *History*, 1909, p. 269.

11 Deskford to Mure, 2 August 1761, *Mure of Caldwell Papers*, 1883, Part 2: I:129f. Erroll was chosen rector in 1761 and 1762.

12 Robert Cullen to Adam Smith, 24 June 1761, Bannerman MSS, GUL, Gen 1035/135–77.

13 Erroll to Adam Smith, 8 July 1761 [the letter is misdated 1762, by which time there would have been no need to write it], *Correspondence of Adam Smith*, ed. Mossner and Ross, 1987, p. 87.

14 Hume to Baron Mure, 27 October 1775, *Letters of David Hume*, ed. Grieg, 1969, II:303.

15 Hume to Smith, 29 June 1761, ibid., I:345f.

16 Robert Cullen to Adam Smith, 24 June 1761, GUL, 1035/135–77.

17 William Ruat to Robert Simson, 7 June 1757, GUA, 30522; Thomas Kirkpatrick to Milton, 27 June 1759 and 5 March 1760, NLS, 16711/18, 16713/74; Robert Simson to Baron Mure, 3 February 1763, *Mure of Caldwell Papers*, 1883, Part 2: I:169f; Simson to Mure, 4 July 1763, Watson Autographs, NLS, 582.

18 Matthew Stewart to Bute, 5 June 1766, Bute MSS, Mount Stuart House, Isle of Bute. I an grateful to the late Marquis of Bute for allowing me access to this collection and to the present Marquis for permission to quote this and other papers held there.

19 Reid to Dr David Skene, 18 April [1766], in Reid, *Philosophical Works*, 1967, II:46.

20 William Leechman to Bute, 3 June 1761, transcribed at Cardiff and given to me by Richard Sher. The manuscript is now at Mount Stuart House, Isle of Bute.

21 Bute to William Leechman, 10 June 1761, uncatalogued Bute Papers, Mount Stuart House.

22 John Craig, 'An Account of John Millar', in Millar's *The Origin of the Distinction of Ranks*, 1806, p. ix.

23 Principal Leechman and professors Simson, Clow and Anderson, 'protest against the Resolution to proceed immediately to determine mr Rouets Affair', GUA, 27026. The other masters answered in GUA, 27027.

24 There are accounts of these transactions in GUA, 45274–8, which includes his letters of justification and his resignation.

25 Erroll to Adam Smith, 27 October 1762, *Correspondence of Adam Smith*, ed. Mossner and Ross, 1987, p. 78f.

26 Hary Spens to Baron Mure, 22 January 1762, *Mure of Caldwell Papers*, 1883, Part 2: I:140.

27 Coutts, *History*, 1909, p. 324.

28 Carlyle, *Autobiography*, ed. Burton, 1910, p. 445; Wight, *Heads of a Course of Lectures*, [1767].

29 Bute's influence at Marischal College, where he was chancellor, persisted until c. 1790.

30 It was described in 1763 by William Strahan: 'Lord Bute's Brother Mr Stewart Mackenzie is Viceroy of Scotland, & is at present there: He is a weak timid Man, & Suffering the Affairs of [that] Kingdom to run into greatest Confusion, which the late Duke of Argyll used to manage with the greatest facility.' Strahan to[?], 18 August 1763, source not found.

31 Hugh Blair to David Hume, 6 April 1764, Hume Papers formerly at the RSE but now at the NLS. I thank Richard Sher for bringing this to my attention.

32 See the forthcoming volume devoted to Reid's scientific and mathematical papers edited by P. B. Wood for the *Edinburgh Edition of Thomas Reid* and Wood's life of Reid to be published by Edinburgh University Press.

33 Ross, *Lord Kames*, 1972, p. 100.

34 Scott, *Fasti*, II:143. He later became a member of the Glasgow Literary Society.

35 Millar to Smith, 2 February 1764, *Correspondence of Adam Smith*, ed. Mossner and Ross, 1987, p. 99f. The same letter lists the supporters for Reid.

36 Deskford to Cullen, 22 January 1764, GUL, 2255/78.

37 Geyer-Kordesch and Macdonald, *Physicians and Surgeons*, 1999, pp. 242–9; Emerson and Wood, 'Science and Enlightenment in Glasgow', in *Science and Medicine in the Scottish Enlightenment*, ed. C. W. J. Withers and P. B. Wood, 2002, pp. 79–142; 92–4, 109f.

38 Reid to Skene, 18 April 1766, in *Philosophical Works*, 1967, I:45f.

39 *The Roll of the College of Physicians of London*, compiled by Munk, 1878, 2:383–5; Peter and Ruth Wallis, *Eighteenth Century Medics*, 1988, p. 567. Their entry for Carmichael Smyth seems to conflate the careers of two men.

40 Loudoun MSS held at Mount Stuart House, Isle of Bute; cited with the permission of the Marquis of Bute.

41 William Leechman and the professors of Glasgow College to Baron Mure, 5 May 1766, *Mure of Caldwell Papers*, 1883, Part 2: II:83f.

42 Reid to Dr Andrew Skene, 8 May 1766, *Philosophical Works*, ed. Hamilton and Mansell, 1967, I:46f. Andrew was the father of David Skene.

43 Dorn, 'John Robison', DSB, 11:495–8; see also the introduction to P. B. Wood's recent reprint edition of Robison's *A System of Mechanical Philosophy*, 2004, and Wood's life in the ODNB, 47:432–4.

44 Coutts, *History*, 1909, p. 495; *Memorials of the Faculty of Physicians and Surgeons of Glasgow*, ed. Duncan, 1896, p. 261; Glasgow Faculty Minutes, 10 June 1769, GUA, 26643.

45 Robert Liston to Sir Gilbert Elliot, 1 September 1773, Liston MSS, NLS, 5514/198. This letter suggests that Liston may also have hankered after the ecclesiastical history chair which Wight would then have abandoned.

46 Robert Liston to Andrew Dalzel, 15 September 1773; Patrick Wilson to Robert Liston, 28 September 1773, NLS, 5517/55 and 5514/209.

47 Matthew to Robert Liston, n.d. [1773], NLS, 5514/147.

48 George Jardine to Robert Hunter, 14 January 1772, GUL, Gen 507/I. Jardine may well have mistaken the name.

49 Robert Clason (1746–1831) was the youngest son of James Clason, a farmer in Logie, Stirlingshire, where Robert settled as minister in 1801 [he was presented by Lord Dunmore] after having served the parish of Dalziel from 1786 to 1801. Patrick is the more probable candidate. He is mentioned in the *Correspondence of Adam Smith*, ed. Mossner and Ross, 1987, pp. 81, 161f. In 1769, he produced a volume of essays on education and other topics which he dedicated to Rousseau. He appears in Hume's letters as one seeking to become travelling tutor to Lord Chesterfield's son in 1772; *Letters of David Hume*, ed. Greig, 1969, II:262. Patrick Clason was later a member of the Philosophical Society of Edinburgh.

50 John Glassford to Adam Smith, 5 November 1764; David Hume to Adam Smith, 27 June 1772, *Correspondence of Adam Smith*, ed. Mossner and Ross, 1987, pp. 104, 161f. Patrick Clason was in Paris writing a book in 1772 and hoping for another well-paid governor's position; George Jardine to Robert Hunter, 14 July 1772, GUL, Gen 507/Box 1. Robert Clason seems also to have been absent.

51 *An Inquiry whether the study of the ancient languages be a necessary branch of modern education*, Glasgow, 1769.

52 Hume to Baron Turgot, 16 June 1768, *Letters of David Hume*, Grieg, 1969, II:179–82; Hume to Elliot, 24 May 1768; Hume to Robert Liston, 5 July 1768, *New Letters of David Hume*, ed. Mossner and Klibansky, 1954, pp. 182–4.

53 Ed. McCormick to Robert Liston, 2 February 1771, NLS, 5514/18.

54 Nicholas Vilant to Robert Dick, 30 December 1772; Sir Gilbert Elliot to Robert Liston, 2 January 1773, NLS, 5514/145; 154. The first letter says the chair will be awarded by the patron to the most qualified candidate.
55 Dalzel, *History of the University of Edinburgh*, 1862, I:9.
56 Gilbert Elliot to Robert Liston, 20 February 1773, NLS, 5514/154.
57 Liston to Elliot, 1 September 1773, NLS, 5514/198.
58 NLS, 5514/199.
59 John Stevenson to Robert Liston, 25 September 1773. Hume during the 1760s had some oversight of Elliot's boys who were in school in Paris. Hume befriended them and their tutor, whom he introduced to Rousseau.
60 Elliot to Liston, 28 September 1773, NLS, 5514/208.
61 The Jardine letters cited in the following can all be found at GUL, Gen 507/Box1 unless it is otherwise noticed.
62 Jardine to Robert Hunter, 28 January, 30 March and 25 May 1772.
63 Coutts, *History*, 1909, p. 311.
64 GUL, Murray 503/1–6.
65 *Roll of Graduates at the University of Glasgow . . . 1727 . . . 1898*, compiled by Addison, 1898, p. 221.
66 About this time Jardine had thought a place, very likely the Greek chair, would elude him because it would go to either Patrick Cuming or to William Wight. He did not expect to get the chair of the ailing Clow. He said he had 'neither character nor Interest enough' to secure that and he believed others were better qualified to teach logic. Jardine to Robert Hunter, n.d., GUL, 505/Box3.
67 Hume to Strahan, 26 October 1775, *Letters of David Hume*, 1969, II:299f.
68 Ibid., II:303. Another sign of the interest of Hume's friends in Glasgow University posts is seen in the attempt of others to secure William Wight's chair should Wight get the divinity position. Hume's friend, Colonel James Edmonstoune, approached his cousin, James Stuart Mackenzie, who wrote to Baron Mure asking for the disposal of Wight's chair should the latter be elevated to the divinity chair. He got the promise of a Crown appointment for his friend should that happen. Stuart Mackenzie to Mure, 1 November 1775, Mure MSS, NLS, 4946/237.
69 Jardine to Robert Hunter, 25 November 1775, GUL, 505.
70 *Mure of Caldwell Papers*, 1883, Part 2, I:171; H. M. B. Reid, in *The Divinity Professors*, 1923, p. 266, says that Baillie also had the interest of the Duke of Hamilton who had given him his pulpit at Hamilton.
71 *Chambers Biographical Dictionary*, ed. Chambers, 1856, III:54.
72 Millar to Alexander Carlyle, 7 September 1782, EUL, Dc.4.41.
73 The man may have been Robert Findlay.
74 MacLeod to John Young, 2 December 1779, GUA, 43163; Coutts, *History*, 1909, p. 325.

75 William Hamilton to his mother, 23 November 1777, GUL, Gen 1356. These are modern transcripts of seventy-eight letters by William Hamilton, made by Dr Louisa Hamilton. They were written between 1771 and 1787 to his father, Thomas, and others, including William Irvine, William Cullen, James Jaffray, John Hunter, James Gregory, William Stark, James Russell, Benjamin Bell and Matthew Baillie. The originals are in the RCSE and the RCSL.

76 For an account of the machinery, see Geyer-Kordesch and Macdonald, *Physicians and Surgeons*, pp. 261–9. When William Hamilton died in 1790, the collection was offered to the College which found the price (£298) too high and refused to purchase it. The heirs then sold it piece-meal. The new anatomist bought some of it but he had also to start for himself a new teaching collection. Coutts, *History*, 1909, p. 502; Boney, *Lost Gardens*, 1988, pp. 205–8.

77 The University's petition had been conveyed by the chancellor, Montrose, who seems to have also urged the appointment. Mackie, *The University of Glasgow*, 1954, p. 226.

78 Fry, *The Dundas Despotism*, 1992, p. 34.

79 'Whig', in this context, means one favourable to parliamentary and burgh reform in Scotland and a sympathiser with the French Revolutionaries at least up to 1792. Most were followers of Charles James Fox. 'Tories' refers to government supporters who thought any changes were at the time unfeasible and probably unneeded. They were unsympathetic to the revolutions in America and France and in Scotland followed the leadership of Henry Dundas.

7

GLASGOW UNIVERSITY IN THE AGE OF DUNDAS

❧

1. 'HARRY THE NINTH'

Henry Dundas had been a bright student at Edinburgh University
with many friends in the Belles Lettres Society and the Speculative
Society of which he was an early member.[1] Those friendships persisted
but the clubs changed into the Feast of the Tabernacles and then, in
the 1770s, into the Mirror Club. That produced the famous periodi-
cal called *The Mirror* (1779) and later *The Lounger* (1785–7). In
those groups, Henry Mackenzie, 'the Man of Feeling', led a passel of
other lawyers and literary men who formed for Dundas a bridge to
some of the literary intellectuals of his time. While he was no litera-
tus himself, Dundas was a man aware of and able to encourage literary trends such as the increasing sentimentalism of the times. He
was quite willing that his friends should write things which made
his growing party look enlightened and fashionable, things which
showed him to be an acceptable member of the Northern Athenian
culture.[2] At the same time, he was, like most of them, not a man of
sentiment when it came to politics or most other things.

Dundas's life began well. He passed advocate in 1763 and became
Solicitor General in 1766 at the age of twenty-four, a rapid promotion owing in part to his talents but also to family connections. His
family had been important in the Squadrone but, since that was a
largely spent force by the 1750s, he had to forge connections with
others outside that circle. This he did. He also became involved in the
Douglas, Heron and Co. Bank – the Ayr Bank as it was popularly
known. The bank failed spectacularly in 1772. Its failure cost Dundas
money but helping to sort out the mess created by its indebtedness
won him many friends and backers. Among the losers and among his
backers were the Dukes of Queensberry and Buccleuch, with whom
he became friendly. Buccleuch aided him financially and schemed with
him politically; he also acquainted with the Duke's old tutor, Adam
Smith. In 1774, Dundas became MP for Midlothian. He quickly came

to the notice of Lord North, whose American policy he supported in his maiden speech in the House of Commons. In the following year, Dundas was made Lord Advocate, a place he held until 1783. As a member of the government, he could aspire to manage affairs in Scotland which no one had done for some time. He was soon dispensing patronage, arranging elections and even hoping to become the government's chief advisor on things Scottish. Those hopes put him at odds with others who shared similar aspirations but possessed fewer abilities. The most important of those men was Sir Lawrence Dundas, the MP for Edinburgh from 1768 to 1780 and again, for a short time, in 1781 just prior to his death in that year.

Sir Lawrence, Henry's very distant cousin, had made a fortune as an army contractor in the 1740s and had been befriended by the Duke of Cumberland. By the 1750s, he was able to defend his Linlithgow Burghs seat against the machinations of Argyll, Newcastle and others. He came to dislike Argyll and opposed his interests and those of Campbells generally. Sir Lawrence was distrusted by most of the old Squadrone connection except for the Duke of Montrose. By the 1760s, Sir Lawrence was a supporter of Shelburne, who secured for him a baronetcy in 1762. Dundas subsequently followed Bute, Grenville and Rockingham. His daughter even married Lord Rockingham's son. By the mid-1760s, Sir Lawrence was building a parliamentary interest which he hoped would allow him to exercise in Scotland the sort of power which the 3rd Duke Argyll had possessed. Unlike Argyll, he alienated people; many believed he could not be trusted. No government would give him a peerage. He was disliked by Campbells, Douglases, Homes, and by gentleman who found him invading electoral territories they deemed their own. He could buy seats in the Scottish burghs but by the mid-1770s he was disliked even by many of his own constituents in Edinburgh, and his loyalty to the ministry by 1778 was questionable. All this made him a man whom Henry Dundas could oppose out of personal ambition and a sense of obligation to those whom he served. He hoped to beat him and he did.

By 1778, Henry Dundas's politicking had been well rewarded by the government. He was not only Lord Advocate but had been appointed Keeper of the Signet, a sinecure office which gave him a yearly income of over £2,000. Backed by the government and the funds of the Duke of Buccleuch, Henry Dundas proved an adroit man whose candidate for the Edinburgh seat in 1780, William Millar of Barskimming, defeated Sir Lawrence. Sir Lawrence was returned upon petition to the House of Commons but the election made Henry

Dundas popular in Scotland and showed that his electoral machine was better and more monopolistic than anything seen in Scotland for many years. From that time, until he went into opposition in 1782–3, he was the government's man in Scotland. When he returned to power after 1784, he was, after Pitt, the second most important member of the ministry in the House of Commons. He began to be known in Scotland as 'Harry the Ninth'. Until 1805, he continuously held high and lucrative office and managed Scotland for the ministries he served. Even after his impeachment in 1806, his machine survived him under the ostensible management of his nephew, Robert Dundas of Arniston, and his own son, Robert, later 2nd Viscount Melville, who followed him as chancellor at St Andrews University.

Like Ilay before him, Dundas set out to control all that he could and to place men loyal to him and his friends in as many institutions as he could. It is not surprising to find him being elected rector at Glasgow in 1781 and 1782. Dundas's election there shows that the Glasgow University men sensed a change in the wind. That they were not yet sure of its permanence is shown by the election the following year of the very Whiggish Earl of Lauderdale whom Dundas would consistently oppose in politics. The universities were places Dundas meant to dominate and by the end of his career he dominated them more thoroughly than Ilay ever did and had imposed on them an ideological uniformity which was both reactionary then and repellent now. As the 3rd Duke of Argyll had helped to make the Scottish Enlightenment, Henry Dundas helped to end it.

In the beginning, Marischal College eluded his grip because Bute was chancellor there. It would have been bad manners to interfere there. When Bute became ineffective and then died in 1792, Dundas did interfere. Bute was followed as chancellor by Dundas's friends the 2nd Earl of Mansfield and he a few years later by Dundas's ministerial colleague William Eden, Lord Auckland. King's College tended to be aloof from politics but even there, after the controversies stirred up in the 1780s over proposals to unite the two Aberdeen universities, Dundas had some power. It was rooted in gratitude for his having saved King's College from absorption into a university uniting both King's and Marischal Colleges and Universities. By 1793, Dundas and his friends could control King's, which had chosen as its chancellor his chief northern supporter, the Duke of Gordon. At St Andrews, Dundas became chancellor in 1788 in succession to the Earl of Kinnoul. He retained the post until 1811. Dundas had no trouble with Edinburgh appointments. There he could pull far more strings, particularly after

Principal Robertson retired from clerical politics c. 1780. There is no reason to disbelieve Dundas's 1801 claim that every professor appointed at St Andrews and Edinburgh from 1780 to 1801 had been his initial choice or had had his approval. That claim can be plausibly extended to the end of his political career in 1806 when this study ends. At Glasgow things were not that simple, but by the end of the period surveyed here they came very close to that mark because there he was aided by the 3rd Duke of Montrose and the 5th Duke of Argyll, dukes no longer at odds with one another. Dundas's career as a Glasgow manager began with an election he probably lost.

2. DUNDAS'S GLASGOW BEFORE THE FRENCH REVOLUTION

When Robert Findlay (25 May 1721–15 June 1814) succeeded professor William Wight in the divinity chair in 1782, it was not another victory for the Moderate Party, which has sometimes been called 'the Dundas interest at prayer'. Findlay was orthodox enough to write against Voltaire and Alexander Geddes (a liberal Catholic biblical scholar from Aberdeen) but he also wrote against pluralities and voted in faculty meetings against charging fees to divinity students.[3] Those were positions more likely to be supported by the high-flying Popular Party. Findlay was described to Alexander Carlyle in a letter from law professor John Millar as being considered a 'bigot' by some. Millar did not see him as one:

> He is a Man who thinks & Enquires for himself and fixes his own Articles of Creed & does by no <u>means</u> follow the Multitude – when we were all in a combustion here agt Repealing the Penal Statutes concerning the Roman Catholics, he would not join or give any support either to Clergy or Laity who were zealous on the Point[.] And in his Pulpit appearances, he is a distinct, habitual & zealous Preacher of Practical Religion, spending no time on high Points of mere Speculation – He has indeed Scruples about concurring in what are called violent settlements when you and I have none: And I am inclined to think that it is this circumstance that makes those who have no access to know him thoroughly to conceive of him as a high flying Bigot in all things.[4]

Dundas occasionally backed men who were not Moderates but it seems most unlikely that Findlay was one of them. Professor Millar in August 1782 told Alexander Carlyle, then a Moderate Party manager, that the College was closely divided over this appointment and that Dundas was expected to favour Henry Grieve if he came over to vote in the election, as he was entitled to do because he was still rector. After stating his own present preference for Grieve, whom he had been solicited to support, Millar went on:

> You will easily see that I cannot well be more explicit at present, as it is but fair to give some little time for the appearance of candidates. Besides in order to get a good man, we must take the person that is agreeable to the greater number of our friends. In the present State of our University I am of opinion that much will depend on the Lord Advocate [Henry Dundas]. I do not mean from his influence as Treasurer of the Navy, but if he can be persuaded to come personally and give his vote. My notion is that if he takes the part of a good man there is room for his making a majority.[5]

Dundas had supported Catholic relief in Scotland, as had the Moderates. Like them, he had few qualms about making 'violent settlements'. He is unlikely to have supported Findlay.

Findlay's principal opponent, Henry Grieve, was a Moderate. He had substituted for that hot Moderate, Adam Ferguson, the Edinburgh professor of moral philosophy, when he was on leave some years earlier. Grieve now tried hard for this post because he saw it as a step toward the principalship which he knew would soon be available and which he hoped to get.[6] He was opposed by a College faction, headed by Principal Leechman, which did not want him, although it is not clear that they were all for Findlay.[7] Principal Joseph McCormick of the United College at St Andrews, writing to Alexander Carlyle, whom he called 'the Father of the Moderate Interest or rather Leader at present', clearly stated a principal reason for Grieve's failure:

> I have heard that he has a very powerful Rival to whom it was promised some time ago by the same Ld N—th [North] on whom Harry [Grieve] relyes & as the Promise was made to Ld Frederick Campbell [MP for the Glasgow Burghs], it may be more for his Lordship to give the Go-bye to Bryden than to him.[8]

Findlay may have been the man to whom the chair had been promised but the reverend Mr Bryden also had an interest, one which would surface again when the principalship became vacant in 1785. Grieve failed to obtain the divinity chair but was rewarded for his failure by being made Moderator in 1783.[9] He may have thought this would strengthen his future claims on this chair or the principalship, particularly since Findlay was already verging on old age. Sixty-one when he was appointed, Findlay taught for thirty-one years to the disappointment of a great many. This election was the first one since

Dundas had extended his reach to Glasgow's College and University. It showed him that the independence of the place could be a problem for anyone bent on close management.

The next opening in the faculty was one created by Alexander Wilson's wish to resign in favour of his son Patrick (16 January 1743–31 December 1812). Patrick was not only a competent astronomer and scientist but had the management of the type foundry located in the University precincts. Around 1780, Alexander Wilson began to think of resignation and in 1782 asked that the Crown appoint his son as assistant and successor. This was refused as creating a bad precedent. Montrose and Dundas wanted a free hand. The College then hired Patrick to observe, care for the instruments and to teach his father's course.[10] In 1784, the College again approached the government on behalf of the Wilsons and this time it was successful. They were made joint professors with the right of survivorship vested in him who lived longest. Alexander died two years later, when his son became possessed of the emoluments and perquisites of the regius chair.

At the end of 1785, the College had to pick a new principal because William Leechman finally died, having for a long time made the University unpleasant for some of his colleagues. The choice of the College men was Dr William Taylor (1744–29 March 1823), minister of Glasgow, who for some years had sat with the professors in the Glasgow Literary Society.[11] He had very likely been a prospective candidate for some time since the University had given him a DD in 1783. That honour was often a sort of preliminary to a divinity professorship. Had Taylor been chosen by the Crown, he would have been expected to resign his living because the minister of Glasgow was, under the University charter, an *ex officio* visitor of the College. He did not get government backing. Neither did Henry Grieve, who also sought the place.

The third candidate is likely to have been Robert Brydone, the father of the well-known travel writer and electrician, Patrick Bryden, Principal Robertson's son-in-law. Robert Brydone held the living at Coldingham, Berwickshire.[12] In the end, the place went to Archibald Davidson (c. 1732–7 July 1803). He had held livings in the gift of Lord Dundonald and Col. John Campbell of Blytheswood, men with electoral interests in the Glasgow area who probably approved of Davidson's elevation. However, that was not the only probable reason why he got the living. He had an older brother, John, to whom the post seems to have been promised by Dundas but who had become too feeble to hold it. Dundas honoured his promise by giving it to the younger brother, who seems to have impressed him.[13] Dundas was, as George Jardine said when he related this to a correspondent, 'the great conductor of such jobs' – a comment which suggests that Jardine already held a dim view of Harry IX.[14] In 1788, the new principal was made Moderator by the Moderates with government help, and several years later he was given by Montrose and Dundas a lucrative sinecure, the Deanery of the Thistle.[15]

The next few appointments were of medical men or scientists. They seem to have been rather unpolitical contests decided mainly on merit, although the professors, in several cases, were also picking relatives. These appointments resembled others made at Edinburgh around this time and for the same reasons – the medical school was too important, both to the town and University, not to have the best men available teaching in it. Fathers with well-trained sons tended to get them appointed partly because they were so well trained. The first of these men was Thomas Charles Hope, who in 1787 was appointed lecturer in chemistry and *materia medica*. Hope was the son of Dr John Hope, the Edinburgh professor of botany, and had, in a sense, grown up with *materia medica*. He had won a chemistry prize while a student of professor Joseph Black at Edinburgh. His maternal grandfather was another Edinburgh doctor, the father of Alexander Stevenson, the Glasgow professor of medicine. Professor Stevenson was probably thinking of Hope as a possible successor when the latter came to the College in 1787, soon after taking his MD degree at Edinburgh. Hope is said to have defeated two other unknown contenders.

The chair of chemistry and *materia medica* was split in the next year with the lectureship in *materia medica* going to Dr Robert Cleghorn (1755–18 June 1821). One curiosity of this appointment was that the professor of botany, William Hamilton, 'declare[d] that though he heartily agrees to the appointment of Doctor Hope as lecturer in Materia Medica yet he thinks it necessary to enter a Protestation that this election shall in no shape prejudice any claims which he may have to teach that branch of Medical Knowledge in this University.'[16] Many teachers of botany still thought of themselves as essentially medical men and of botany as a medical speciality, not an autonomous science, which is what Hope's father had made it in Edinburgh and what it was becoming in Glasgow.

Dr Cleghorn, 'Dr Wormwood' as he was called by some, was not a man whom Dundas and his friends would have on any faculty. Later, they refused to advance him to a chair. He was a Whig who since 1783 had belonged to the Society of Scottish Antiquaries run by that eccentric Whig, the Earl of Buchan. Later in his career Cleghorn would find praiseworthy the philanthropies of David Dale of New Lanark. He was also a distinguished medical man whose student days had been marked by election to the Presidency of the Royal Medical Society of Edinburgh. He became a founder of the Glasgow Royal Infirmary and the Royal Asylum for Lunatics. A good chemist noted for his work in industrial chemistry, he was eventually associated with the Mackintoshes and Glassfords, businessmen who were among the city's largest and most innovative manufacturers.[17]

Another notable appointment of 1787 made by the masters was that of Mr LaGrange, who took over the Fencing School in the College.[18] The school seems to have been there since 1761 as a sort of gymnasium for the boys, one which may have started in emulation of the one promoted at Edinburgh University at about the same time. Like other such places, the Glasgow school taught fencing, riding and dancing. Such schools were modelled on Dutch institutions which had flourished by the end of the seventeenth century and sometimes taught drawing.[19] Not officially an academic post, this was still one of importance for the skills it taught and because such institutions attracted aristocratic boys and maintained the College's reputation for polite accomplishments.

The last appointments before the French Revolution sent jitters along the spines of the right-thinking were made in 1789. The first was a nepotistic appointment involving the placement of the son of professor John Millar in the mathematics chair. James Millar had trained as a cleric, worked as a tutor and at the time of his appointment (he was twenty-seven) was Cashier [chief operating officer] of the Greenock Banking Company. The company had been formed in 1785 to serve the needs of the port, of the Western Highlands and Islands, of some in Northern Ireland and it even had a few customers in America.[20] When the College decided on 12 February 1789 to sanction the arrangement to which Millar and professor James Williamson had come, and elected them conjoint professors, it was moving away from the view of mathematics as primarily useful to the physical sciences to a position which saw other uses for mathematics which might involve commercial subjects such as actuarial calculations. Millar is not known to have had competitors and his appointment was a tribute more to his father's than to his own brilliance. He became an eccentric and rather poor teacher.[21] In 1795, when Williamson died, James Millar got his salary, house and vote in the College meeting.

The other appointment of 1789 went to T. C. Hope, who succeeded his uncle in the chair of medicine. There seems to have been no competition for the place partly because no one, not even his colleagues, knew Stevenson was about to resign. Stevenson was ailing and toward the end of June 1789 approached his relative and friend, Sir Adam Fergusson of Kilkerran, MP, asking him to solicit from the government a joint appointment for him and his nephew, Thomas Charles Hope, who would hold the chair after Stevenson died or resigned. Fergusson wrote to Lord Advocate Ilay Campbell, who quickly arranged the matter even before Stevenson had asked the College to support his request – which the masters did after the fact.[22] By 3 July 1789, Stevenson could thank Sir Adam and eighteen days later he thanked the University chancellor, Lord Graham, who had told the Secretary of State that he approved of this regius appointment. By 21 July the business was done. Hope was installed on 27 October 1789, serving with his uncle until May 1791. Stevenson had an estate in Ayrshire and his connections with politicians were very good.[23] The masters were also quite satisfied with Hope, who by this time had done significant work as a chemical analyst.

3. GLASGOW APPOINTMENTS DURING THE FRENCH REVOLUTION

After Hope's appointment, much more attention was given to the political beliefs of applicants for positions. The first case in which that became apparent occurred in 1790. William Hamilton's health had been failing through the winter of 1789–90. On 13 March, he died from overwork at the age of thirty-two. A replacement for him in the chair of anatomy and botany had to be found. A scramble to succeed him began. Knowing this would happen, the College meeting had authorised the principal to write to the chancellor asking him not to recommend any person for appointment until the College had 'submitt[ed] our views to your Lordship on what may be conducive to the Interests of the Medical School here.' The answer they got back was that the College should not submit an institutional recommendation, as it had usually done in the past, because 'Government is always jealous of its Patronage. I would not recommend resolutions of the faculty on the subject.' The new Duke of Montrose added that he would be willing to consider the opinions of individual masters and that he had so far kept at bay many applicants.[24] This was the Duke's warning that the government would no longer have a regard principally for the interests of the University expressed in recommendations from the College meeting, but would appoint to the regius chairs as it saw fit. It was its right to do so but this also meant a decided change in course, one which probably owed more to Montrose than to Dundas.

One man who did not get the job was Robert Cleghorn. He was only one of the 'several candidates' who George Jardine said were seeking the post on 1 March, almost two weeks before Hamilton died.[25] Cleghorn vehemently opposed Tories later named to the College. The commission for the new professor of anatomy and botany, James Jeffrey (1759–28 January 1848), came down on 15 May 1790. He was tried and admitted three days later.[26] It is not known who recommended him to the Duke of Montrose or if some College men individually approached the Duke on Jeffrey's behalf. That is not implausible since Jeffrey had been one of Hamilton's better students and one who had kept in touch while he studied in Edinburgh, where he took his MD in 1786. There he had been a president of the Royal Medical Society. Even as a student Jeffrey had been interested in making a reputation as an anatomist and probably as an academician.[27] He is known today mainly as a Brunonian theorist and the inventor of a surgical chain saw but in his time he was an innovating teacher and the author of several anatomical works.[28]

On 24 March 1790, the College masters realised a long-desired change in the medical faculty when they appointed a lecturer in midwifery. He was James Towers (before 1770–1820), whose grant was annually renewed until 1815, when he became the first professor of midwifery.[29] A surgeon, he had been Hamilton's partner in obstetrical practice and had, in effect, been teaching students for some time alongside the professor. Later he opened a lying-in ward at the Royal Infirmary.

In 1791 the masters allowed Robert Cleghorn to swap his *materia medica* lectureship for the one in chemistry, which paid marginally more and much better fitted his interests which ran to heat, explosions, the manufacture of salts and alkalis, and to industrial processes. He was replaced in his lectureship by Richard Millar (by 1760–4 December 1833), a young physician who would hold the *materia medica* post until he resigned shortly before his death in 1833. He became the first regius professor of *materia medica* in 1831. Neither of these appointments seems to have attracted the notice of the politicians and the masters did not divide in any serious way over them. That was not true of the next one made in 1796, when professor Hope was replaced by Robert Freer (c. 1745–9 April 1827).

Between 1791 and 1796, the French Revolution stirred all too much excitement in Scotland. That made it impossible for a Whig like Cleghorn to be appointed to anything at all. Montrose could not have stomached him in a professorial chair. The Duke was then a Lord Lieutenant much taken up with keeping order in a world beset by mobs rioting with enthusiasm for the French but showing none for press gangs and forced enlistment in regiments to be sent out of Scotland. Montrose and other politicians were unwilling to give anything to those who opposed their Tory sense of the political requirements of the time.

When Hope left Glasgow for Edinburgh in the autumn of 1795 to become professor of chemistry there, someone had to take over his medical classes. There was a competition between Cleghorn and Jeffrey for this temporary post. It was settled by the masters, who gave the place to Cleghorn. It was the hope of those voting for Cleghorn that this would help ensure that he would get permanent tenure of the chair. What happened is described in a letter of George Jardine:

> Dr Cleghorn from a General Conviction of his fitness, could almost have had no Competitor even though it be in the Gift of the Crown – if it had not been his alledged attachment to Modern Politicks and his connexion with that party here. This at present seems likely to cast the balance against him – though not yet absolutely certain. No General Recommendation on the above account & others could be got from the College – A majority but not without great opposition, appointed him to teach the Class in the mean time. Though I disapprove of his Politicks, yet I was ready to support that point as the best recommendation we could give him, and some have no doubt blamed me for it. – but I do not care – I can never allow Politicks to get the better of every consideration: and I was piqued that Jeffy [sic.] with no other motive but to disappoint C. offered to Teach the Class. We have now heard that a Dr Freer from Edinr is likely to get it.[30]

Among those dissenting from the decision to allow Cleghorn to teach out Hope's year were Principal Davidson and professor Richardson, whose stated reasons for opposing Cleghorn were that, not being a professor, he was junior to Jeffrey.[31] The objections to Cleghorn were reported to Henry Dundas five days later by Lord Advocate Robert Dundas, who had received word of them from someone in Glasgow named Dunlop. Robert Dundas was less concerned with the abilities of the men teaching at Glasgow than with their politics. He thought Cleghorn's 'conduct and character has been such as I trust will prevent any application of his from succeeding'.[32] The chair went to Adam Freer (c. 1745–9 April 1827), a former army surgeon and ensign whose father had been an Edinburgh physician. Freer was still on half pay and would not fully retire from the army until 1816. He taught until well into his eighties, dying in office in 1827.[33] Indeed, the medical faculty would change little until about 1820 and the political tensions would continue and exacerbate differences over educational policies and commitments to differing medical theories.[34]

There were other appointments made in 1796 which involved political fights. The most protracted and interesting was that involving the replacement of John Anderson, who died in January 1796 but whose failing health and inability to teach full-time had long made the settlement of the succession to his chair of great interest. As early as 16 February 1790, John Millar, writing to Samuel Rose in London, expressed Anderson's approval of the 'revolution in France' and of reform generally. He also noted that Anderson 'has now thought of a resignation, upon a private transaction. But I question whether the person he has pitched upon will be accepted.'[35] Anderson, a radical Whig, sent a cannon of his own design to the Revolutionary Assembly in Paris in 1792.[36] The person pitched upon found no favour and nothing came of his plan to resign.

On 13 November 1794, Anderson again wrote to the Faculty asking that they appoint either a temporary or permanent assistant and successor to aid him in his teaching. A week later the College agreed to give him William McIlquham [later Meikleham] (1771–7 May 1846) as 'Occasional assistant during this Session of the College'.[37] Anderson's response to this was to tell the principal that he had no candidate and that he was prepared to employ McIlquham since his colleagues would not have either of the men he proposed as a successor in 1790, —— Meiklejohn and James Headrick.[38] He also wanted to employ 'my own Journeyman', by which he must have meant his demonstrator, and he demanded that the masters give him a 'Bond of Cautionary' which would cover breakage by any man they imposed on him. It was just the sort of irksome business for which he had long been notorious, the sort which had led him to sue, at one time or another, most of his colleagues and which had led them to remove him from voting in Faculty meetings. In the following December, his colleagues, some of whom had not been talking to him for years, agreed to McIlquham's helping him a second year.[39] He surely needed help since he was described by Jardine as

. . . almost carried out of [his class] a few days ago, but has returned to the Charge – He means, I really believe, if he can, to Die in his Class. In his vaunting ostentatious Language, He says, 'There are other Beds of Honour than there on the Banks of the Rhine.' He really has a Notable Spirit.[40]

Anderson finally died on 13 January 1796 and a week later the contest among his would-be successors, begun years earlier, became a public one. To quote Jardine again, 'The Spirit of Discord has arisen from Andersons Ashes and has set us all at variance about it.'[41] The people in contention for the chair were John (later Sir John) Leslie, James Brown, John Allan, James Headrick and Robert Cleghorn – four Whigs and a man willing to be a Tory.

John Leslie and Cleghorn had no chance because of their politics but that was not immediately apparent – at least to them. Leslie by 20 January 1795 had begun his 'canvass at Glasgow, with a pretty favourable prospect'. He noted, '. . . I would be pleased by the mortification which it would cause St Andrews people' were he to get the place.[42] The majority of the St Andrews professors earlier had refused to consider him for places because of his politics. Still, letters on Leslie's behalf were sent by John Hunter, a St Andrews professor, to John Young and by John Playfair in Edinburgh to Patrick Wilson. Wilson's reply said that there were then no other candidates in the field. Leslie noted that he would be supported by, among others, Dugald Stewart, then the Edinburgh professor of moral philosophy, who had earlier taught mathematics. Stewart had an informed judgement of Leslie's abilities since the latter had spent time in Edinburgh teaching briefly for John Robison.[43] Leslie thought he would be opposed by Cleghorn and the Millars and he knew that others on the faculty were being lobbied. He probably saw himself as one of four Whig candidates.

Robert Cleghorn was said to be the candidate of John Millar. This was hardly helpful, since from May to September 1796 Millar published anonymously in the *Scots Chronicle* of Edinburgh an extended attack upon the policies of Pitt's and Dundas's ministry. Dedicated to Charles James Fox, the work included opinions for which Millar was well known and which would have ensured that Cleghorn's candidacy would have gone nowhere if Millar supported it.[44] But Cleghorn may also have had Opposition backing from the Prince of Wales.[45] That would not have been much better given the current climate of opinion and Dundas's position in the government.

By April, Millar had switched his support to John Allan.[46] In the same letter, which Jardine gave to Robert Hunter, he gave a fuller account of the state of play:

Many candidates appeared particularly a Mr [James] Brown from St Andrews College – a Mr Leslie, Mr Allan both from Edinr[,] a Mr Hedrick of this place. Most unfortunately Millar and his old friends – Young & me – could not agree ab[out] the best Man – we were for Brown & He for Allan – and beyond every expectation – The Ministry have interfered in favour of Hedrick – who five or six years was supported by some of us when Anderson meant to thrust in a more disagreeable man – but whom we at that time told He was to have no dependence upon us when the place became open to Candidates of the first Literary Reputation. If Millar, who has greatly the advantage of us – by his Son & Hutchison at present Dean of Faculty[,] & and we had Joined – we could easily have carried it agt. Hedrick even with all the weight of the Ministry – But this is not yet done.[47]

The man with ministerial support was James Headrick, a chemist and later a minister who in 1788–9 had belonged to the first chemical society founded in Glasgow.[48] His supporters included some of the city's businessmen who would have found it useful to keep an industrial chemist at the University, and 'many respectable members of the Board of Agriculture'. Among the latter was the President of the Board, Sir John Sinclair.[49] Headrick was also supported in March 1796 by members of the faculty, including the divinity professor Robert Findlay, who wrote to Lord Advocate Robert Dundas asking for ministerial support for him. Robert Dundas did not forward the letter to Henry Dundas but told Findlay that he and the Duke of Montrose had 'hesitated about the propriety of supporting that Gentleman's Pretension'. Then the Duke changed his mind and Robert Dundas recommended Headrick to the masters in a letter to Findlay.[50] Montrose asked Henry Dundas to write as well. Ministerial support brought onto Headrick's side Principal Davidson, professor Richardson and 'other of their agents here'.[51] In early April the factions stood:

> *For Headrick*: Davidson, Findlay, Richardson, Jeffrey, Freer and the rector, William Macdowall of Garthland [6]
> *For Allan*: Millar, Millar, Hutchison [3]
> *For Brown*: Reid, Wilson, MacLeod, Jardine, Young [5]
> *Unknown*: Cuming [1]

With an absolute majority required, Millar's or Jardine's faction held the deciding votes if others did not rat. In early April, Jardine thought that Millar would join with the ministry and elect Headrick but he did not. In the end, the ministerial men divided. The principal at the request of the chancellor and Robert Dundas, Lord Advocate, sought the permission of Ilay Campbell, Lord President of the Court of Session and a former Glasgow MP, to change his vote from Headrick to Brown.[52] Since Macdowall, a Dundas politician, was among the men voting for Brown, all the government's support had probably swung to him. On 4 April, the Faculty voted to elect and on 13 April they chose Brown. The vote in the end was 'nem. con.', which sometimes meant that some abstained. Brown was admitted to office on 3 May 1796. Headrick believed he lost by the casting vote of Macdowall but he was almost certainly wrong in this belief, although not wrong in thinking that the ministry had abandoned him.[53] Men in St Andrews who had denied posts to both Brown and his friend John Leslie would have been amused.[54]

Brown was an impressive candidate who even came recommended by the eccentric philosopher, Lord Monboddo.[55] When he was appointed, he was minister at Denino, a place in the gift of St Andrews University. He had been tutor to the Earl of Home and a schoolmaster on a frigate. For about twelve years, he had substituted for the crippled St Andrews professor of mathematics, Nicholas Vilant. His correspondence with Leslie shows him to have been a knowing scientist. Brown turned out to be the worst sort of sinecurist. He did not teach after his first year and he would not resign. When he did resign, he made a pension of £163 a year his price. In 1801, Dundas would not give any countenance to proposals from William Meikleham, Brown's deputy, or the Duke of Montrose, to give Brown a St Andrews chair and allow Meikleham to replace him on the Glasgow faculty.[56]

Shortly after Anderson's chair was filled, so too was another but in a very different way. The professor of ecclesiastical history, Hugh MacLeod, who had taught for eighteen years and was sixty-seven, petitioned his colleagues in December 1796 for an assistant and successor. He asked that they appoint William M'Turk (or MacTurk, McTurk; c. 1745–10 March 1841), a man from a Glasgow merchant family who had trained as a minister. He had been librarian to the College in 1794–5 and became University chaplain in 1799. These are indications that he was acceptable to most of the members of the College when he was given his commission by the Crown in February 1797. There were other candidates but perhaps no serious ones, since their names remain unknown. M'Turk's political opinions can be inferred from a letter of the Duke of Montrose who was responding to an enquiry about this post by Henry Dundas. The Duke wrote:

It has been my system and my practice, not to interfere with the Elections in the College at Glasgow, except when I thought an attempt was making to introduce Men of wild principles; on the present occasion from the Candidates, I Think there is not any necessity for my taking a part, but better to allow them to determine uninfluenced, unsolicited.[57]

Men who were Tories could be elected without interference if the masters chose to vote for them. Montrose sent a letter of recommendation for M'Turk to the Home Secretary, the Duke of Portland, who issued the warrant.[58]

On 7 October 1796, Thomas Reid died and was replaced by his deputy, Archibald Arthur. When Arthur died on 14 June 1797, there were at least seven men who sought to replace him in this prestigious chair.[59] One was the recently appointed M'Turk, who seems not to have made much of a showing. Jardine had vetoed his own son's candidacy and opted for that of George Hamilton, minister of Gladsmuir. He was expected to have ministerial support and that of most of the faculty but he did not win. Government backing seems to have gone to William Taylor (1744–29 March 1823), the minister of Glasgow who had long been connected with the College.[60] He lost but was chosen Moderator in the following year. Lockhart (or Lochhead) Muirhead (1766–23 July 1829), nephew to the former professor George Muirhead, was also a strong candidate. He had replaced M'Turk as the College librarian and was then teaching French and Italian in the place of Patrick Cuming, who had taught those subjects for more than thirty years. Muirhead would have to wait until 1803 for a University place and until 1807 for a full professorship. Since he got a regius chair early in 1807, it is very likely that he too was a good Whig and would have had no government help in 1797. John and James Millar were for a Mr Allan, 'a young man of Extraordinary Talents at Edinr' who may have been the person who had sought Anderson's chair. Given his backers, he would have had no real chance, a point Jardine made by saying that Allan and James Mylne (1756–1839) 'lay under Suspicion of democracy & Democracy is the greatest recommendation in that quarter [i.e. Millar's].' Mylne was Millar's second choice – perhaps he was already interested in Millar's daughter whom he eventually married in 1798. He had previously been married to a woman named Davidson, which may also have brought him a vote. Mylne explained his political principles to the 'Ministerials' who then split, some voting for him and others for Hamilton. Mylne carried the vote by a majority of one. It may have helped him to have been Chaplain to the 83rd Foot. Jardine conceded that he was 'a man of considerable abilities – something in the style of Arthur . . . perhaps as much Genius – but inferior in application, Industry & General Knowledge'. That probably meant that he taught a version of Reid's moral philosophy but that he did little to develop it further and published little. Reid's philosophy was more compatible with radical Whiggism because it gave a greater place to rights and to 'the common good' seen as involving ordinary people. The other fashionable Scottish moral philosophy was more sentimental and looked back to Francis Hutcheson and Adam Smith. In the following year, Jardine noted that Mylne was 'favorable to the Novel Doctrines, He will therefore add considerably to that party in the College',[61] a party to which he was shortly linked by marriage. All that mattered in the 1799 contest for the chair of astronomy which pitted Thomas Jackson against William Meikleham.

Patrick Wilson now wanted to resign the astronomy chair for business reasons; he planned to move his type-founding business to London.[62] He also wanted to name the successor to his regius chair. When Wilson first signified his intentions of leaving office on 23 October 1798, he cited his declining health as his principal reason. At that time he promised to leave the College some instruments and to give £1,000 to the fund which supported the chair of astronomy.[63] The University requested him to think it over and to stay on but his period of reconsideration was just about the time taken to draft a reply to be sent by the next post from London to Glasgow. Dundas was willing for him to do as he wished but Montrose refused to allow it because the man whom Wilson named as a successor was not beyond political reproach. On 7 November, Wilson reiterated his desire to be gone but said he would wait until the College had picked his successor.[64] Three weeks later the Earl of Cassillis recommended Thomas Jackson to Henry Dundas.[65] Jackson had been teaching at the University for James Brown (1797–8) and was well known to the masters. He was a respectable scientist who a decade later would hold the comparable post at St Andrews. By the end of January, he had become the candidate of Wilson and his colleagues. It was generally known that Wilson's resignation was imminent. Jardine even referred to his resignation in the past tense. That was probably because Wilson had met with Dundas in London and told him of his plans.

Dundas responded by 'promis[ing] his aid in the appointment of your successor' and had asked for a recommendation.[66] Wilson, still in London, consulted Neville Maskelyne, the Astronomer Royal, who had turned up two men. They were Anglicans in orders. Neither was a Scot, neither was willing to sign the Westminster Confession.[67] Writing to Principal Davidson to tell him that, Wilson also wrote that Montrose had met his efforts and his willingness to give money and instruments to the University with 'Reserve . . . till he should know who the Candidate was to be.' Dundas, however, had assured him that the ministry entertained 'no jealousy whatever of the kind in question', in other words they were willing that Wilson and the University should find their own meritorious candidate.[68]

On 4 March, the University sent a memorial to Montrose containing Wilson's resignation and a recommendation of Jackson as the best person for the appointment.[69] Montrose construed the resignation as being dependent upon Jackson's succeeding. He refused to accept the resignation, which had also been copied to Dundas but which miscarried in the mails. On 18 March, Wilson sent Dundas a gracious letter referring to the missing memorial. He thanked him for past favours, gave his reason for resigning and named Jackson as the best person to succeed him.[70] On the same day the dean of the faculty added his support to that of Jackson's other friends.[71] Two days later the faculty meeting affirmed Jackson's 'firm Attachments to the constitution and Religion of the Country' and recommended him to the Crown. But the vote was not unanimous. The principal and professors Richardson, Jeffrey and Freer dissented. The rest voted to send Jackson's name on to the Secretary of State. They asked Montrose to transmit it on the 23rd but he refused, saying 'His Majesty's Ministers have always wisely opposed conditional resignations, as inconsistent with the dignity of the Royal patronage . . . I therefore cannot have the honour to obey the wishes of the Faculty, by transmitting the Memorial . . . ' He went on to say that he hoped the College was not 'attempting to bargain for the appointment of a Professor' – which was of course what they were doing and doing with Dundas's permission. Montrose added: 'I shall not think it my duty as Chancellor of the University of Glasgow, to concur with the Faculty, should the Majority of that respectable Body recommend Mr Jackson to the Chair of Practical Astronomy.' He returned to Wilson his resignation.[72] It was to Wilson's credit that he did not then withdraw his generous offer of instruments and funding after the obtuse nobleman had intervened in this way.

On 2 April, Principal Davidson and George Jardine, then Clerk of the Faculty, wrote to Dundas transmitting a memorial to be given to the Duke of Portland recommending Jackson as one who had been unanimously elected to take Brown's place in the natural philosophy chair and as one who was fit for this chair and politically untainted.[73] The principal who had dissented from the Faculty act obeyed it by writing a letter. The majority of the masters hoped Dundas would do for them what Montrose would not.[74] Those who favoured Jackson also wrote to the rector, George Oswald, asking him to send the minutes of the faculty meeting to Montrose and to tell him 'How sorry they are, and how unhappy they think themselves to have fallen under anything like the imputation or remotest Suspicion of proposing a "A conditional resignation"[,] attempting to Bargain, or doing any other thing inconsistent with the Dignity of the Royal Patronage.' They again testified to Jackson's loyalty to church and state and said that Wilson was proposing to double the funds in the astronomy chair's foundation. The following day, Principal Davidson wrote privately to Dundas saying that the vote to nominate Jackson had been seven to four and that he had himself voted against the man, although he was a good teacher and had Wilson's recommendation. Davidson was not prepared to cross the chancellor whose sense of decorum and political bias was clearly doing the University harm.[75] His opposition and that of others, and the fact that Montrose would not present the memorial to the Secretary of State, meant that Jackson's chances were now extremely slim.

Dundas replied on 10 April. He had sent the memorial nominating Jackson to the Secretary of State, but

> I think it right however to observe to you, that it appears to me impossible for his Grace [The Duke of Portland] to recommend any person to fill the Chair of the profession of Astronomy who has not the Concurrence and Support of the Chancellor of the University, more particularly as the other Members of that Society are not unanimous in their Support of the Gentleman named in the Memorial: – as far as My Influence goes I shall always feel extremely happy in promoting the advancement and prosperity of the University of Glasgow but on the present occasion I do not feel Myself at Liberty to recommend any Candidate for the Professor's Chair in opposition to the wishes of the Chancellor, and in the divided State in which the opinion of the other Members appear to be.[76]

Perhaps knowing this was coming, Wilson had approached Portland directly on 8 April, sending in his resignation and an account of his dealings with Montrose. Normally the resignation of the regius chair would have gone first to the principal or chancellor. He again recommended Jackson and said that he had given a similar account to Dundas. He was now officially done with the business but the business was not done.

On 5 May, Jardine wrote to his friend Robert Hunter that none at the University knew what was happening but that he supposed 'Some Creature of the Duke of M.' would get the place. Jackson, who had taught so well for the absent professor of natural philosophy, would not be permanently settled at the College. Two weeks later he knew who it would be:

> You would probably see a Dr Meikleham appointed Peter Wilson's Successor[.] We know him well – He was brought up with us – Many of us however wished for a Young man of much greater Genius & Fitness – But a disappointed party raised a Cursed & false insinuation about Politicks which so terrified the D. of Montrose, that he would not hear his name mentioned.[77]

Years later when, despite the Dundas interest, Jackson had secured a chair at St Andrews, he must have taken some satisfaction in finally beating a mediocre, but politically correct, government candidate.[78]

The appointment to the astronomy chair is interesting as a sign of the times. Wilson and the College were concerned to preserve the teaching and observations. Practical astronomy at Glasgow had become a serious scientific chair in a university giving good training to physicians, chemists and others in the natural sciences. The pressure to make it such a place came largely from the faculty, the Glasgow business community and patrons like Lord Ilay who had installed in the College men who had shown their usefulness. The professors looked earnestly in London and Scotland for an eminent astronomer. This contrasts very favourably with the way in which the Edinburgh chair was managed during these same years.[79] But their view of the function of the professors was no longer shared by the politicians who dispensed Crown appointments in the 1790s. That is made clear by other correspondence from the period. James Leslie in a letter to Lord Advocate Robert Dundas is worth quoting to show the degree to which men in Montrose's connection were willing to debase a chair whose first two incumbents had done good work as astronomers. Leslie wanted the ecclesiastical history chair, then held by Hugh MacLeod, whose assistant and successor was William M'Turk. Leslie proposed making an arrangement with MacLeod to take his chair when he retired. M'Turk could hold the astronomy chair which Leslie thought had long been 'a mere sinecure'. Or, if 'Dr Payten', the minister of the High Church, had made an arrangement with MacLeod, then perhaps other terms might be proposed.[80] That such a scheme could be proposed shows that some candidates thought the politicians cared little about learning and the integrity of appointees. Nothing came of Leslie's proposal, which would have been fought by the professors.

The affair of the astronomy chair points to the tensions in the College between Whigs and those who were becoming ever more conservative in their principles. It so soured some of the professors that Montrose thought the government might for a long time have lost its ability to place men in the College. Jardine was to say in mid-1801, 'Our chancellor now is an absolute Dictator – and I have no Connection with him.'[81] That state of things lasted until the end of the Napoleonic Wars.

Throughout the years at the end of the century, there was a nearly constant succession of Dundas men who came into the University as rectors. Edmund Burke in 1783–4 may have been the last man whose presence in that chair during this period was due primarily to his intellectual distinction. He was followed by a stream of minor, local politicians and Edinburgh lawyers whose common features were the fact that they were Glasgow alumni and were loyal to the Dundas machine. In this stream Adam Smith appears exceptional until one remembers that he too was a placeman connected to the Dundas interest through his ties to the Duke of Buccleuch. This did not even change when the ministry changed and Dundas was impeached. Indeed, until the election of Francis Jeffrey in 1820, the Dundas machine produced rectors and quite often deans of faculty who were more loyal to politicians than to the College where they had studied and which they should have better served. The professors they helped to elect were of diminished distinction and achievement because the body electing them had been reinforced by Tory voters more interested in the politics than in the merit of the candidates. In the long run, the College became a place sympathetic to reactionaries and dunderheads, which it had never been in the heyday of Anderson, Reid, Young, Jardine and Millar, men who were often supported by Findlay and Wilson. The deteriorating quality of the faculty can be seen in elections made up to the time of Dundas's impeachment. Few of the men installed in this period were of the slightest distinction. In most cases there seems to have been no competition for the posts. Worse yet, many of them lived long lives.

On 22 June 1801, John Millar suddenly died and on the same day Robert Davidson (29 March 1763–24 July 1842), with support from William Richardson and the Duke of Montrose, asked for his chair of law.[82] There was no contest for the post, which would not have attracted most bright lawyers because they could expect to make much more money practising in the courts in Edinburgh which were now much busier than when Millar took the post in 1761.[83] Glasgow did not have courts attracting a lot of high-paying legal business and one could not just walk into the sort of local practice that Millar had had. That was mostly acting as an arbitrator of disputes among merchants. As Jardine wrote, 'None who like the Bar and have any prospect of rising there could be tempted by it.' He refused to let his own son apply for the post and discouraged others.[84] Principal Davidson's son had been a collector of decisions for the Faculty of Advocates in Edinburgh, a post usually given to a clever man with no practice or to one well-connected who might not do, or had not done well, in prac-tice.[85] The issue in this appointment was really the political reliability of the new professor, a point made very plain by the Duke of Portland to Robert Dundas.[86] The chair went from the hands of a brilliant teacher, writer and polemicist to a non-entity, but one who, like his father, was perfectly 'safe'. Robert Davidson abandoned the teaching of Roman law for lack of students. He kept his place until 1842 but Glasgow ceased to be a centre for the study of the law and a resort for English boys who wished to study jurisprudence and its history.

In 1803, Principal Davidson died and was replaced by William Taylor who had earlier been passed over for professorships, although the faculty had wanted him for principal in 1785 when Davidson was appointed. In the intervening years, Taylor had been an informant for the government on Glasgow affairs and is probably the author of an interesting listing of the political sympathies of the professors sent to Ilay Campbell c. 1800.[87] By 1801, he was discussing this place with William Richardson, whom he feared might seek it, and with the Duke of Montrose, whom he thought might favour professors Richardson or even James Brown. He put his worries to Lord Advocate Charles Hope, to Lord Chief Baron Robert Dundas, and to Lord President Ilay Campbell.[88] When Davidson died, Taylor's worries proved well founded. His opponents were Richardson and a Dr Ritchie. Richardson was elderly and not a cleric but he had the rec-ommendation of George Jardine and other colleagues, not all of whom had been friends to Montrose. Montrose in the end did not support him. Dr Ritchie was certainly David Ritchie, a notable Moderate and later professor of logic at Edinburgh University best known for his attacks on John Leslie in 1805 and for a life of Hume. According to Richardson, his backers included Richard Oswald, Lord Methven, the Duke of Atholl, Lords Eglinton and Montgomery and 'all the Northern interest of the Earl of Kintore'. They were not

Glasgow men but men whom Montrose would see as poaching on his territory.[89] Ritchie's candidacy went nowhere.

Taylor's loyalty was rewarded when he was appointed. He thanked Montrose and the Lord President for making him principal.[90] This posting much resembled the appointments which the Dundas men engineered in Edinburgh and Aberdeen in these years. Taylor was a time-serving party man who had been made Moderator in 1798 and whose published works bore titles such as *French Irreligion and Impiety alarming to Christians* (1794) and 'The love of our country Explained . . . a sermon' (1807). No one of importance in government could have failed to note the eagerness and obsequiousness with which he pursued his quest. As minister of Glasgow he had a stipend of £400 and was a visitor of the College. When he was made principal, he did not resign his kirk and so became a potential visitor of his own actions, although he seems not to have acted as one.[91] This practice the Dundas machine continued under his successor appointed in 1823.[92]

The second appointment made in 1803 was that of William Meikleham to the chair of natural philosophy. He had held the regius chair of astronomy since 1799 and had also been substituting for James Brown, the professor of natural philosophy, who resided in St Andrews.[93] Meikleham had been trying for about three years to arrange a job at St Andrews for Brown so that he might secure the natural philosophy chair but nothing had come of those efforts.[94] He had not, however, been very active in Glasgow. In fact, he treated the astronomy chair as a part-time position. The fine equipment given by Wilson went unused and deteriorated. Meikleham did not observe, taught little and published nothing astronomical. As a lecturer in natural philosophy, he seems to have discontinued the lectures and demonstrations for a non-university audience which had marked the teaching of the natural philosophy professors from the late 1720s until the mid-1790s. While this now mattered less – such lectures were available at Anderson's Institution, where more radical teachers gave them – it was a sign that Glasgow University was no longer reaching out to the city's artisans. David Murray described Meikleham as 'diligent and painstaking, but not brilliant'. He was said to be a better lecturer than his Edinburgh counterpart John Playfair, but he could not point to the long series of texts and scientific works that distinguished Playfair's career.

When Meikleham left the astronomy chair, his replacement was James Couper (August 1752–7 January 1836), minister of Baldernock. He did not immediately resign his kirk upon his appointment. Couper had been seeking a post at Glasgow since 1800, when he was mentioned by the chancellor as one whom the professors would not choose.[95] By 1803, John Millar was gone and Couper was electable. He taught very little and abandoned observations because of the increasing smoke and new building in the areas surrounding the observatory. He seems not to have thought of building an observatory outside of town. When one was put up on Garnett Hill, the men involved in this effort were mostly connected with Anderson's Institution and not the University. Couper held his post until 1836.

At the end of 1803, the masters made Lockhart Muirhead a lecturer in natural history, thus giving Glasgow a chair such as existed at Marischal College and in Edinburgh. Muirhead had been employed by the College as librarian since 1795 and had interests in natural history which qualified him for the post. There seems to have been no political objections to his appointment which in any case lay with the masters. When his chair was converted to a regius chair in 1806, this was done by a Whig administration. It was not the Dundas government who secured his posting.

4. Conclusion

Between the end of 1803 and 1806 there were no other appointments at Glasgow. The University now had only one man of real and lasting distinction, William Richardson, the poet and critic, who had been appointed over thirty years before. The medical men were good but not outstanding; none is remembered today. Here, as elsewhere, the impetus to enlightenment had run out in the political hysteria engendered by the French Revolution and the reactions it had provoked. The normal monopolising tendencies of most machine politicians, most of whom had little concern for excellence, had sapped the vitality of the institutions and made it difficult for men like Jardine to keep up the tone of a College which they could no longer control and which was not protected from mediocrity by outsiders. The promise of the period up to 1765, years which saw introduced into the University men of the calibre of Robert Simpson, Francis Hutcheson, Adam Smith and Thomas Reid, fine and innovative teachers like William Cullen, the Hamiltons, Joseph Black and John Millar, even polite religious innovators such as William Leechman, was not and could not be sustained under a regime such as that of Dundas and the 3rd Duke of Montrose. Their politics was as active in undercutting the Scottish Enlightenment as were the social and economic changes which also worked to erode it.[96] Patronage had made the Scottish Enlightenment possible and brilliant. It was now bringing it to a close.

Notes

1 Thomas Somerville's assessment of his abilities when a student was that he 'excelled chiefly in readiness and fluency of elocution, but he reasoned feebly'. He was fair enough to include Lord Kames's far more generous estimate of Dundas's abilities, which would make him 'an able statesman'. Somerville, *My Own Life*, 1861, p. 40f.

2 There are short accounts of the clubs and of their importance in John Dwyer, *Virtuous Discoures*, 1987, passim; and more sober ones in Fry's *Dundas Despotism*, 1992, p. 57–9.

3 The preface to his book on Voltaire's errors says that he wanted to promote 'liberty, knowledge, and civilisation'. His own point of view was enlightened but not in Voltaire's way. He both admired and feared the works of the Frenchman. Reid, *Divinity Professors*, 1923, p. 278.

4 Millar to Carlyle, 7 September 1782, EUL, Dc.4.41.

5 Ibid.; Joseph McCormick to Alexander Carlyle, 3 February 1783, EUL, Dc.4.41.

6 Joseph McCormick to Alexander Carlyle, 10 February 1784, EUL, Dc.4.41.

7 McCormick to Alexander Carlyle, 3 February 1783, 'Letters to Alexander Carlyle', EUL, Dc.4.41.

8 Joseph McCormick to Hugh Blair, 3 and 10 February 1783, EUL, Dc.4.41.

9 Hugh Blair to Joseph McCormick, 22 January 1783, Watson Autographs, NLS, 588/49.

10 Coutts, *History*, 1909, p. 319.

11 Ibid., p. 338.

12 Scott, *Fasti*, II:38; the Crown was the patron there.

13 Dundas in 1790 noted in a letter to Ilay Campbell that he would help Davidson: 'I have always had him in contemplation as having fair and early pretension to a mark of royal favour.' Davidson had recently been Moderator and would become Dean of the Thistle and a Royal Chaplain whose son would get a regius chair. Succoth Papers, Mitchell Library, Glasgow, TD19/6/208. I thank Dr David Brown for this and subsequent items quoted from this collection.

14 Jardine to Robert Hunter, 1 December 1785, GUL, Gen505.

15 Leven and Melville Papers, NAS, GD26/260/2.

16 Glasgow Minutes, 1 August and 10 October 1787, 10 June 1788, GUA, 26693/254ff; 26693/256ff; 26693/313–40.

17 This account relies on George Thomson, 'Robert Cleghorn, MD', in *An Eighteenth Century Lectureship in Chemistry*, ed. Kent, 1950,

pp. 164–75; Geyer-Kordesch and Macdonald, *Physicians and Surgeons*, 1999, passim, and Macdonald's 'Reading Cleghorn the Clinician', in *Science and Medicine in the Scottish Enlightenment*, ed. Withers and Wood, 2002, pp. 255–79. There are further passing references to him in the same volume of essays in Emerson and Wood, 'The Glasgow Scientific Community 1690–1804', pp. 78–142.

18 Faculty Minutes, 22 December 1761, GUA, 26650. At Edinburgh a similar institution dated from 1762; Forbes Gray, 'An Eighteenth-Century Riding School', *Book of the Old Edinburgh Club*, 1935, pp. 111–59.

19 I thank Dr Esther Mijers for this information.

20 Munn, *The Scottish Provincial Banking Companies*, 1981, p. 43.

21 *Fortuna Domus*, ed. Neilson, 1952, p. 68. In 1796, John Leslie described Millar as a sorry mathematician who was contemplating a career at the English Bar. Leslie to James Brown, 20 January 1796, 'Letters Relating to Edinburgh and the University Life of the Time 1790–1830', EUL, Dc.2.57.

22 Anderson, *The Playfair Collection*, 1978, pp. 35 and 42, n.8.

23 Succoth Papers, Mitchell Library, Glasgow, TD219/6/153–6.

24 Boney, *Lost Gardens*, 1988, p. 205f.

25 Jardine to Robert Hunter, 1 March 1790, GUL, 505.

26 Boney, *Lost Gardens*, 1988, p. 208f.

27 For example, James Jeffrey to William Hamilton, 2 January and 8 May 1783, GUL, Gen 1356/50, 51. See below, p. 309, n. 186.

28 Risse, *New Medical Challenges*, 2005, p. 120.

29 Efforts had been made in 1763 to establish such a chair for Dr John Moore; John Graham to Baron Mure, 10 January 1763, *Mure of Caldwell Papers*, 1883, Part 2: I:165f.

30 Jardine to Robert Hunter, 25 November 1795, GUL, 505/ Box 5.

31 Glasgow Minutes, 26 October 1795, GUA, 26695/53ff.

32 Robert to Henry Dundas, 30 October 1795, Dundas Papers, NLS, 7.

33 Freer is said to have been at Bunker Hill but that is unlikely. His career in the military can be traced in *Roll of Commissioned Officers in the Medical Services 1660–1960*, 1968, compiled by Peterkin and Johnston.

34 Dow and Moss, 'Medical Curriculum at Glasgow', *History of Universities*, 7 (1988), pp. 227–57. This essay also tries to estimate student numbers at the medical school c. 1800 to 1820.

35 I thank M. Michel Faure for a typescript of this letter which does not note its precise source at GUL. The person Anderson then had in mind may have been John Warrock Pursell, his demonstrator and the man whom he named as an executor of his will and clerk to the trustees of the University which he sought to found. It is unlikely that the demonstrator was William McIlquham who was still a student. A more likely man is [?] Meiklejohn, who is said in 1790 to have offered Anderson

£200 per annum for his place; George Jardine to Robert Hunter, 1 March 1790, GUL, Gen 505.

36 There is a description of Anderson's artillery piece in James Muir, *John Anderson*, 1950, pp. 40–68. Anderson designed other military devices depicted in a 1792 print by John Kay entitled 'The instruments of Liberty From the hands of Science'. This is reprinted in Butt, *John Anderson's Legacy*, 2000, p. 8.

37 Minutes of the Faculty, 13 and 21 November 1794, GUA, 26695.

38 Anderson to Principal Davidson, 21 November 1794, GUA, 58355. Headrick's efforts to obtain this chair are recounted by J. H. Burns, 'Twilight of the Enlightenment', *The Scottish Historical Review*, LXXXI (2002), pp. 186–211, 188–92.

39 Glasgow Faculty Minutes, 1 December 1795, GUA, 26695. See pp. 328–34 for the Edinburgh equivalent.

40 Jardine to Robert Hunter, 25 November 1795, GUL, 505/Box 3.

41 Jardine to Hunter, 10 April 1796, GUL, 505/Box 3.

42 John Leslie to James Brown, 20 January 1796, 'Letters Relating to Edinburgh and the University Life of the Time, 1790–1830', EUL, Dc.2.57/207.

43 John Leslie to James Brown, 8 December 1795, Letters, EUL, Dc.2.57.

44 *The Letters of Crito e Letters of Sidney*, ed. Merolle, 1984. The editor believes the letters were by Millar but argues that even if the letters were not, they drew heavily on his work and lecture notes and were thought to be by him.

45 Thomas Reid to James Burnett, Lord Monboddo, 14 April 1796, *Fourth Report of the Royal Commission on Historical Manuscripts*, 1874, p. 519.

46 Allan (or Allen, 1771–1843) was an Edinburgh MD who lectured extra-murally c. 1802 on physiology and sought an academic career but found his way to one barred by his political views. He left Edinburgh to become a physician and secretary in the household of Lord Holland. In that capacity he travelled abroad but continued to write for *The Edinburgh Review*. He became Warden of Dulwich College in 1811 and Master in 1820. I thank Professor James Burns for identifying Allan. See Burns, 'Twilight of the Enlightenment', *The Scottish Historical Review*, LXXXI (2002), p. 190. There is a 'character' of Allan by Henry Cockburn in *Memorials of His Time*, 1909, p. 170f, and a note on him, also by Cockburn, in his 'Account of the Friday Club', in *Lord Cockburn: A Bicentenary Commemoration*, ed. Bell, 1979, p. 188. See also Lawrence, 'The Edinburgh Medical School', *History of Universities*, 7 (1988), p. 268.

47 George Jardine to Robert Hunter, 10 April 1796, GUA, 505/Box 3.

48 Burns, 'Twilight of the Enlightenment', *Scottish Historical Review*, 2002, p. 188.

49 [?] to [?] , Melville Castle Muniments, NAS, GD51/6/1145; this petition also names John Gilchrist Advocate and Provost of Stirling, John Glas[?ford] jr, Alex L[?itt]lejohn, John McKillop, Alexr. McKillop, Wm MacKillop as being his supporters.

50 Robert Dundas to Henry Dundas, 19 March 1796, Dundas Papers, NLS, MS 6.

51 Jardine to Hunter, GUL, 505/Box 3.

52 Archibald Davidson to Lord President Ilay Campbell, 10 April 1796, Succoth Papers, Mitchell Library, Glasgow, TD219/6/274.

53 Headrick to Lord Spencer, 9 June 1796, BL, Althorp MSS, G.23. I thank Professor Burns for providing this information.

54 Leslie to Brown, n.d. [1796], EUL, Dc.2.57.

55 Thomas Reid to Lord Monboddo, 14 April 1796, *The Correspondence of Thomas Reid*, ed. Wood, 2002, p. 235.

56 Meikleham to Lord President Ilay Campbell, 6 May 1801, Succoth Papers, Mitchell Library, Glasgow, TD219/6/310. The Lord President had seconded this scheme.

57 Montrose to Henry Dundas, 29 January 1797, Melville Castle Muniments, NAS, GD51/6/1205.

58 Portland to Montrose, 13 January 1797, Duke of Portland's Papers, Nottingham University Library, PwV 110/263.

59 George Jardine to Robert Hunter, 24 August 1797, GUL, 505/Box 3.

60 Taylor on 17 August 1797 complained to Lord President Ilay Campbell that the College was biased against clergymen, which seems quite unlikely. Succoth Papers, Mitchell Library, Glasgow, TD219/6/282.

61 George Jardine to Robert Hunter, 11 June 1798, GUL, 505/Box 3.

62 George Jardine to Robert Hunter, 31 January 1799, GUL, 505/Box 3.

63 Coutts, *History*, 1909, p. 319.

64 Glasgow Minutes, 7 November 1798, GUA, 26695/268.

65 Cassillis to Dundas, 13 December 1798, NAS, GD51/6/1297.

66 Principal Davidson to Patrick Wilson, 16 January 1799, GUA, 58355.

67 Wilson to Davidson, 27 February 1799, GUA, 58355. Wilson may not have realised that they had not only to sign the Confession but also to be members of the Church of Scotland as Jardine informed him on 9 February 1799; GUL, 505/Box3.

68 Wilson to Davidson, 27 February 1799, GUA, 58355.

69 This appointment was closely watched by John Leslie, who noted that 'Wilson has made a merit of necessity, & has recommended Jackson, because no other person was likely to succeed.' Leslie to James Brown, 19 March 1799, EUL, Dc.2.57/222. In October, when Leslie wrote to Wilson and John Playfair about securing the chair, he knew Jackson was out of the running. Leslie to James Brown, 24 October 1799, EUL, Dc.2.57/22.

70 Wilson to Henry Dundas, 18 March 1799, NAS, GD51/6/1334.

71 James Meek to Archibald Davidson, 18 March 1799, GUA, 58355.
72 Montrose to Wilson, 28 March 1799, GUA, 58355.
73 Principal to Henry Dundas, 1 and 2 April 1799, NAS, GD51/6/1338/1–2.
74 Davidson and Jardine to Oswald, 2 April 1799, GUA, 58355.
75 Davidson to Dundas, 2 April 1799, Melville Castle Muniments, NAS, GD51/6/1287.
76 Henry Dundas to Principal Davidson, 10 April 1799, GUA, 58355.
77 Jardine to Hunter, 5 and 15 May 1799, GUL, 505/Box 3.
78 See below, p. 506.
79 See below, p. 334.
80 James Leslie to Lord Advocate Robert Dundas, 13 August 1799, EUL, La.II. 500/2266.
81 Jardine to Hunter, 16 July 1801, GUL, 505/Box 3.
82 Robert Davidson to Lord President Ilay Campbell, 22 June 1801, Succoth Papers, Mitchell Library, Glasgow, TD219/6/313.
83 The government men in 1802 promised Davidson that he would have his income raised by being made Commissary of Glasgow, but this had not happened by 1809 when he wrote to Ilay Campbell seeking it. He also missed getting the clerkship of the town. He was even willing to give up his professorship to become a Commissioner of Bankruptcy. Davidson to Sir Ilay Campbell, 31 July 1809; William Richardson to Lord President Ilay Campbell, 15 July 1803, Succoth Papers, Mitchell Library, TD219/6/414. Although he continued to badger politicians, Davidson received no further judicial patronage.
84 Jardine to Robert Hunter, 16 July 1801, GUL, 505/Box 3.
85 Mackie, *University of Glasgow*, 1954, **p.** 167. Robert Davidson had dedicated his law thesis to Ilay Campbell, who in 1801 was Lord President of the Court of Session. Mitchell Library, TD219/6/200.
86 Portland to Lord Chief Baron Robert Dundas, 5 June [July], Mitchell Library, TD219/6/314.
87 'A General View of the State of Parties in Gl. College', Succoth Papers, Mitchell Library, TD219/6/294/2. This was sent to Ilay Campbell and lists as friends to the government Principal Davidson, and professors Findlay, MacLeod, Richardson, Jeffrey, Freer and Meikleham; in opposition were John and James Millar, Mylne, Cuming and Brown. Jardine and Young were said to be 'in the middle'.
88 Taylor to Lord President Ilay Campbell, 9 July 1801 and n.d., Mitchell Library, TD219/6/315, 347.
89 William Richardson to Lord President Ilay Campbell, 15 July 1803, Mitchell Library, TD219/6/349.
90 William Taylor to Lord President Ilay Campbell, [?] August and 5 August 1803, Mitchell Library, TD219/6/352, 353.
91 Coutts, *History*, 1909, p. 339.
92 Mackie, *University of Glasgow*, 1954, p. 247.

93 Murray, *The Old College*, 1927, p. 263.
94 Meikleham to Lord President Ilay Campbell, 6 May and 28 November 1801, Mitchell Library, TD219/6/312, 326.
95 Montrose to Ilay Campbell, 20 May 1800, Mitchell Library, TD219/6/301.
96 See R. L. Emerson, 'The Historical Context of the Scottish Enlightenment', in *The Cambridge Companion to the Scottish Enlightenment*, ed. Alexander Broadie, 2002, pp. 9–30.

Part III

Edinburgh University

8

EDINBURGH UNIVERSITY TO 1704

ॐ

1. INTRODUCTION

Edinburgh University was different from the other universities. It was the largest and most prestigious of the universities. It was at the centre of national life and in the most intellectually vibrant place in the country. For at least part of the year, the city attracted members of the political elite who enjoyed the social amenities of the city as they attended court and sought suitors for their daughters and jobs for their sons. The competition for university posts in Edinburgh was greater than elsewhere because salaries and fees were higher (see Appendix 1). Some posts, such as the divinity chairs, virtually assured their incumbents that they would have a church living, sit often in the General Assembly and count for something politically. Medical chairs, once they were established, did not bring much if anything in the way of salary but they did bring increased practices and high fees. This was less true of the law chairs, but these were sometimes steps to judgeships. After c. 1715, many professors also had aristocratic boys living in their homes and paying very well for extra tuition and moral guidance.[1] An Edinburgh professorship translated into prestige and sometimes power.

The number of students in the city was increasingly critical to Edinburgh's prosperity as the century progressed. Student numbers rose from around 400 in 1700 to at least 1,400 by 1800. Since many of them came from outside the city and spent between £15 and £300 per annum, numbers meant money for those catering to them. To attract students, good teachers and a useful curriculum were both necessary. Town councillors and resident gentlemen expected their wishes to be considered; they were both eager to see a useful education provided for their boys. That affected the processes by which chairs were filled in the capital perhaps more than in the other college towns and it accounted for the new chairs added in this period.

The University was distinguished by the degree to which it could be influenced by corporate bodies in the town. It was under the jurisdiction of a Town Council, which gave its professors far less purchase on appointments than was true in Glasgow. Until the 1790s, the Council had the right to appoint to all except the regius chairs and exercised its jurisdiction and oversight through a Council committee and a 'College bailie'. The Council, however, was not quite an independent body. It was elected in autumn elections much influenced by national politicians. The politicians who helped its members expected councillors to follow the advice they were given. This made Edinburgh University more sensitive to national and local politics than other colleges. Few of the Council's choices of professors were really made by the Town Council without the promptings of outsiders.

Lawyers prepared leets from which the Town Council selected law professors; the city's surgeons and physicians gave advice about medical professorships which they expected to be followed and which they had the means to force the Town Council to take seriously. For much of the century, the competition of a second medical school at Surgeons' Hall ensured that good appointments were made at the University. The local clerics expected some consideration in the filling of chairs and they could exact at least a hearing because they gave advice and certified the morals and religion of the men appointed. Edinburgh was the Scottish university most open to outside pressures and influences.

In Edinburgh, too, one can follow the fortunes the Scottish political factions in the awarding of the chairs. The chaos of shifting political coalitions during the years c. 1690–1710 was succeeded by the conflicts between the Argathelians and the Squadrone. Here too the rivalries to administer the kingdom were played out as the factions created by the Union and by the '15 tried to control events for their own benefit. The Union of 1707 made the city fathers more subject to national political struggles than they had formerly been. By 1714, the Argathelians and the Squadrone party struggled for control of the Town Council just as they did for the disposal of most government patronage in Scotland. Here, too, Argathelians came to dominance because they were clever men who possessed a large parliamentary interest which proved useful to Sir Robert Walpole. Of course, it mattered that the 2nd Duke of Argyll was a powerful military leader and that his brother, Lord Ilay, was the organiser and manager of a political machine which efficiently covered more of Scotland than did that of its rivals. The Campbell brothers' superiority as politicians was shown in the general elections of 1715, 1722 and 1727, and repeatedly in the municipal elections thereafter until 1760. By the mid-1720s, Argyll's faction had tightened its hold on Scotland. Here, as in Glasgow, Ilay controlled directly or indirectly most of the patronage dispensed in the University after c. 1725 and until 1761, except for the years 1742–7. Here, too, Ilay's political machine was inherited by his nephew, the 3rd Earl of Bute, who, with his brother, James Stuart Mackenzie, managed Scottish patronage for a few years. The instability of governments in London c. 1763–78 was reflected by the awarding of university jobs to men backed by a variety of patrons who owed allegiance to someone in government but not to an organised, dominant Scottish faction. These conditions allowed the local literati and their friends, the Moderate ministers in the Kirk, to exercise more influence over appointments than had been possible earlier and more than they could exercise in Glasgow, Aberdeen or, perhaps, even in St Andrews. Henry Dundas cooperated with the Moderates but finally put together a machine that made him independent of them. That now-familiar political story was played out in Edinburgh but with differences. Those differences will be traced through the appointments in the various faculties. Divinity, law, medicine and arts were not all treated alike, mainly because of the influences professional men could exercise on recruitment to chairs of interest to them and because of the needs of the government to assure order and obedience in the Kirk and state and in the largest of the Scottish cities.

2. The Revolution Settlement

The purging of Edinburgh University after the Revolution of 1688–90 was accomplished by the end of 1690. About this Visitation we know a good deal because of two accounts left by professors. One account is from the professor of mathematics, David Gregorie of Kinnairdie (24 June 1661–10 October 1708); the other by the outed principal, Alexander Monro, who probably had some help from his colleague, the professor of divinity, John Strachan.

Their troubles, and those of the other Episcopalian and Jacobite masters, began with the Revolution of 1688, which brought the election of a new Town Council by *all* the burgesses of Edinburgh in April 1689. The franchise was normally restricted to those who were in the guilds or the Merchant Company. New Councils normally included men who had served on the previous Council and others coopted by it from leets given in by the guilds. After the royalist councillors had been outed in 1689, a wholly new Council was elected by all the burgesses, including some of the University men. According to Gregorie, only one of the masters, Andrew Massie (c. 1635–c. 1703), voted for the new men or for those elected later as Commissioners to the Estates or Parliament.[2] The College was solidly Jacobite and so bound to conflict with the new Town Council and with the national government. Retribution was not long in coming. The magistrates quickly set out to punish the errant masters through a visitation.[3] Principal Monro saw the Visitation of the Magistrates and the later one by a Parliamentary Commission as the work of Presbyterian enthusiasts who illicitly obtained civil powers and then used them badly.[4]

Pleading poverty, the new Council reduced salaries. On 30 August 1689, David Gregorie's went from 1,000 marks to 600 marks or £400 Scots (from about £55 to £33 sterling). Other salaries were also reduced. James Sutherland (1639–25 June 1719), the botanist, lost his whole salary of £20 but not his place as a professor and keeper of gardens. The masters agreed to a proportional reduction of salaries but they continued to be harassed, although Gregorie and Sutherland seem to have been somewhat protected by HM Commissioner and Secretary of State, George Melville, a former rebel who in 1690 was rewarded with a peerage and became 1st Earl of Melville. By the middle of October 1689, the magistrates had changed some of the College staff. The janitor was replaced, by the brother of the new Dean of Guild, and began to spy on the masters. On 5 November 1689, Gregorie heard that he had been delated by John Young for various offences. It was said that he was to be replaced by Young, who was to have a regius chair of mathematics. Their bad blood went back to Gregorie's election in 1683, an election which became an issue in the Parliamentary Visitation proceedings.[5] On 6 November, Gregorie's friends, Hew Kennedy (?1652–98) and Alexander Cunningham (?–April 1696), were libelled to the Council.[6] On 11 November, Gregorie was told that 'Lady Crawford &c.' was 'resolved to call one Sinclair who is now tutor to my lord Lorn to my place'. In short, he would be replaced by the tutor to the very Whiggish Argyll family.[7] On 13 November, the Town Council ordered that the regents be proceeded against before a Justice of the Peace, a process stopped the next day by the Lords of Session. The new spying janitor was asked if Gregorie and his friends brought women into the College. He seems to have said 'yes'. On 19 November, the rumour that Gregorie brought women into the college was being bandied about. Gregorie and regents Cunningham and [?John] Rowe (c. 1668–?) were said to be unfit for their posts. For believing all this, the magistrates were 'chided' by Secretary Melville. Later that month, Gregorie was told that when there was a Parliament, 'the town would be even with the masters of the coledge'. By then the quarrel had been brought to the attention of the Estates, which had been meeting as a Convention since 15 March 1689 and was turned into a Parliament in June 1689. Neither body sat continuously.[8]

Gregorie and his friends began to defend themselves. Gregorie consulted lawyers, and got letters from a Mr Falconer[9] and from Lord Melville.[10] The last wrote to the Lord Provost, Sir John Hall of Dunglass, about the allegations against Gregorie. Also writing for the professor was George Mackenzie, 1st Viscount Tarbat, an important politician of inconstant loyalties. Meanwhile, the animosity among the masters grew as Massie set upon his suspected Jacobite colleagues. On 1 December 1689, Gregorie was told by the Lord Provost to qualify himself by taking oaths to the new regime or 'give over', i.e. resign. This came after the Lord Provost had talked to William Lindsay, 18th Earl of Crawford, soon to be the praeses of the Parliamentary Visitation Commission for the Universities. Gregorie temporised, saying that since he had been cited by the Visitation Committee of the Town Council, nothing should be done affecting him until after that Visitation had met and sat on his case. The Provost seems to have agreed. The professor reported all this to 'T[arbat] on whose advice he had acted'. The preparation of a proper defence against the Visitation of the Town Council or the Parliament was made more difficult by the College Treasurer, Harie or Henry Fergusson, who temporarily stopped Gregorie's salary. Then on 24 December 1689, Ferguson conveyed to him the Council's order forbidding him to teach publicly, an order Gregorie disobeyed. His income had been reduced and his teaching fees were necessary to him. Things then settled down and there was talk of doing nothing *to* him but little *for* him. It was assumed that he had '150 or 200 guineas from Schollars' and that £40 sterling (720 marks Scots) salary would do for him. The councillors almost certainly exaggerated his income. Even the Whiggish *canaille* felt involved in this matter: 'Will Menzies who raised the Rabble, in a Company had declared himself my enemie & that I ought to comply as my patrons doe.' Gregorie now ran the risk of being rabbled by the Edinburgh mob which had been actively cruel a year or so earlier when it killed men.

Things simmered but started to heat up when the reverend Mr Gilbert Rule (c. 1629–7 June 1701) came to town on 25 January 1690.

The hue and cry after Gregorie went up again. The Town Council found in February that it had no money to pay him. Also in that month, Mr Thomas Burnet (16??–?), one of the regents who may have been wavering, was told by the Episcopalian principal, Alexander Monro (who had never liked him), to do no more teaching.[11] Andrew Massie, the Whiggish senior regent, then told his students not to attend Gregorie's classes.[12] Massie made it difficult for them to do so by lecturing in the very same hours Gregorie taught. The reverend Mr Meldrum (1634–18 February 1709) – he would later be a parliamentary visitor and professor of divinity at Edinburgh – was convinced that regents Burnet and Massie were 'judicious men' and told Gregorie so. By the end of March, Gregorie was no longer speaking to Massie, who was slanging him to all who would listen. Massie also began to harass students like James Kyle[13] who wanted to praise Gregorie in their harangues (orations to the College) or at graduation. Massie called Gregorie's friend Lord Tarbat 'a silly-mad-fool'. Toward the end of that month, the College servitor demanded the garden keys so that masters could not walk there on the Sabbath and thus profane the holy day as Gregorie had been doing. The servitor also complained of the principal for reading the English service on Sundays – something it was imprudent, but not yet illegal, to do. The masters complained to the Town Council of ill usage as the Council continued to consider a visitation of its own. Things were tense and there were problems at the spring laureation of students.

Gregorie was not without important supporters. Among his defenders were some on the Town Council and other more important men: Lords Melville and Tarbat, John Erskine, 11th Earl of Mar; Sir James Ogilvie, later 4th Earl of Findlatter, but then an MP from Banffshire; a recent Lord Provost, Sir Thomas Kennedy; Sir William Hamilton,[14] and Sir James Scougal of Westhall, Commissary of Aberdeen. By March 1690, they had been joined by Alexander Fraser, 9th Lord Salton of Abernethy (aged eighty-six but still hearty), Sir Alexander Seton, SCJ, and by Drs Archibald Pitcairne and [?Archibald] Stevenson.[15] Gregorie had even been defended to the King and Queen by Sir Charles Scarborough, their physician. Sir Charles knew Gregorie because of their shared interest in mathematics.

In late July, Parliament struck its Visitation Commission which by the end of the month had created committees to sit at the several universities. When they embarked on their purge, there was much to sort out, partly because malice had set men to settling scores.[16] Monro said they had solicited 'dirt' which they called *informations* and not *libels*[17] and that they tried the men on biased libels which named no accusers and were too general.[18]

When the Edinburgh committee sat, they had before them a long list of allegations against Gregorie and his friends. Kennedy, it was claimed, was habitually drunk, drunk in sermon time, a swearer, a striker of the janitor's man 'to the effusion of blood' and, like Gregorie, he was politically suspect. Cunningham was said not to have been at communion in the Established Church since the penal laws were first promised to be repealed in 1668 but had frequented the Popish chapel in Holyrood Palace. He too was said to be a drunkard and often absent from classes because of his attendance on Lord Stair. Little is known of their inquisitions but they are likely to have resembled that of Gregorie. They shared Gregorie's circle of friends although neither was as distinguished as he. And they had aristocratic friends who probably tried to protect them. Neither was sacked in 1690 but Cunningham demitted in 1693; Kennedy died five years later.

Gregorie's case begins with the undated 'Articles against Mr Gregorie' drafted and given to him in the summer of 1690.[19] These certainly look like libels. They detailed his religious shortcomings in the form of allegations and sometimes in leading questions. Did he 'declair yt he is not concerned in Religion'? From whom did he last receive communion and where did he attend church? Is he 'ane habituall swearer[,] for instance in trying latly sume experiments wt the air pumpe, he putts in pigeon, & when pumping out the air, the bird begunde to fent, he cryes[,] see ye not? God shoes dieing.' Did he not at Christmas celebrate the day and give his students an eight-day holiday from classes contrary to the usage of the College? The Articles included questions about his moral failings. Was he often drunk? Did he not drink to drunkenness with Kennedy and Cunningham, who could not then walk back to their own chambers? Gregorie had to answer the charge that 'He is known to be ane unclaine persone and hes women often coming att night to his chamber.' Did he not fall out with Kennedy and challenge him with 'many great oaths that if he woud not goe to the yard & fight him he would box him & cugill him lyk a cullione'. Then came his academic sins. Does he properly instruct his forty or fifty students who are learning at differing levels and may not understand his demonstrations? It ended with his political sins: 'Sume two or Three moneths agoe he went to visit ane —— Yeaman present prisoner in the Cannogat Tolboth & ther did Speek very freely agt the present government, and drank to a sheamles oncoss [expense]. Witness the sd Yeoman and his Brother Mr John Yeoman, Witness also Doctor Pitcairne and Mr Kennedy who were both with him and partakers of his guilt &c.' The professor had much to answer and explain. Just how much was made clear on 19 August when a draft of the articles against him was read to him and he made extempore answers which, he wrote, satisfied his friends but put the ministers 'out of countenance'.

The Edinburgh Committee to consider the mathematician's case formally met in the College's Upper Common Hall on 20 August 1690, only three months after the last fighting in Scotland but before it had ended in Ireland.[20] The Committee was composed of noblemen, judges of the Court of Session, a town councillor or two, Dr Rule and another minister, Mr Hew Kennedy, and John Law of Ballarnock, later a regent at Glasgow. It chose as its chairman Sir John Hall of Dunglass, Lord Provost, a man somewhat friendly to Gregory. The clerks were Sir Alexander Gibson and Thomas, the son of Robert Hamilton of Presmannen, who later became a SCJ. Gregorie asked if he should appear in his gown and was told to do so. The *preses*'s first official act was to assert the city's right to visit the University which was controlled by it. That was conceded. The Committee then adjourned the inquiries for a week until 27 August. After it did so, Lord Raith 'seemed very kind' to Gregorie, who believed he also had friends in Sir George Munro, the Earl of Leslie, the Master of Stair and Viscount Tarbat.

In the following week, members of the Committee prepared libels with the help of the professors. Gregorie tells us, 'Mr Massie undertook mine and I really wrote his and Burnets.' That ensured lively cases if nothing else. Gregorie consulted with Tarbat, who warned him against taking any oaths 'untill I be secure intirely both against the venom of the Ministers and town Council, and agt. the proposall of diminisheing my sallarie.' Tarbat lobbied HM Commissioner to the General Assembly, Lord Carmichael, who was disposed to protect Gregory, as were Lord Leslie, Lord Raith, the Master of Stair and 'all the Laymen of the visitation'. Among the ministers, Gregorie counted Mr Kirkton a friend. This was not an enquiry confined to the legal niceties of a court room but a political process in which much of the activity took place outside the chamber. However, it looks as if Gregorie almost from the beginning had a majority of the influential in his favour.

On 23 August, the Visitors asked for the books from which Gregorie taught, 'a report of my method of teaching and 3 years publick lessons'. These he gave them. Cunningham also sent in his.[21] Gregorie's real interrogation began on and after 2 September. On 3 September he gave in written answers to the clerks and responded orally to questions but there was no quorum and no official business seems to have been done. We know what he said.

He began by asking to face his accusers who, he suggested, were malicious calumniators. He vindicated himself from the charge of atheism by saying that he, like all philosophers and reasonable men, had arguments 'from the Nature and Order' of the world to show the existence of God. That was not an answer which would have satisfied all Calvinists. He claimed to be a Christian. He had communicated in the church as it was established [i.e. the Episcopal Church] in Scotland but he called on the ministers of the Commission to tell the others that there is no 'Necessity of frequent communicating', a view common among the zealous men of the Presbyterian Kirk. The charges and the Visitation, he thought, smacked of an inquisition, of the 'Dark and Absourd ages and of those in barbarous inland popish countrys remote from all commerce'.[22]

After dealing with religion he defended his morals. He claimed to be too civil a man to be an 'Habituall swearer' and that the instance given was frivolous. He did not deny swearing but he did deny drinking too much strong ale with Kennedy and Cunningham and said that the charge of drunkenness had 'Miscared from other mans lybells'. He found it ludicrous that he should be charged with bringing women into the College. He denied the charge of being willing to duel with Kennedy or threatening him, saying that the libeller 'fancies me to be the same Hector and Discovers how silly Wild and mean spirited a fellow he is.' He was 'convinced that Your Lordships will allow me to know how to teach Mathematicks better than this informer.' He probably thought their informant was either Massie or John Young. Of the man whom he was alleged to have done out of a job in 1683, he said John Young 'could not add, subtract, multiplie nor divide in numbers, tho he was publiquely invited thereto nor doe I believe that he can yet doe it.'[23] As for keeping Christmas, was he not to have a break after six months of unremitting labour? Moreover, 'Students of quality who have ther friends in or near the city are not easily forced to abridge ther humour so farr at that time of the year as at another.' He denied the visit to Yeoman, 'on the word of a Christian', saying that he had never been 'within the Cannongate tollboth in all my life'. He denied drunkenly speaking against the government but he did not deny the charge altogether. He ended with a stirring call for justice from their Lordships, whom he hoped would bring his accusers to 'condign punishment' because they were 'infamous lyars'.[24]

On 9 September, the Earl of Crawford attended the Edinburgh Committee as a 'voluntier' and sent for missing members to make up the quorum. Were some really ashamed to be there? The Committee then turned its attention upon the principal and professor of divinity, both of whom defended themselves with as much vigour as had Gregorie.

Principal Monro was accused of being a papist, a politically disaffected man, one who neglected family worship, a baptiser without leave, and a defender of the scandalous such as professor Pitcairne who had notoriously ridiculed Presbyterians. The principal rebutted all the charges and used a bit of ridicule himself when he taunted Mr Rule by suggesting that he should write only in Latin because his Latin was so poor it would be noticed while his English was beneath notice.[25] Monro began by saying that he did not need to answer 'Unsubscribed Articles' and that he had a right to know and interrogate his accusers. He pointed to his published works attacking Roman Catholicism. He claimed to have authority for the baptisms he had carried out. He denied being arbitrary and unjust in running the College and said he had resigned the pulpit of the High Church for the reason he gave and that the Committee members should not claim to know his thoughts. He said Dr Pitcairne had ridiculed false doctrine to defend the truth – and he could defend himself. He claimed he would have taken the oaths but would not do so now.[26] He ended his defence by saying that historic usage, freedom of conscience and the priority of the Bible, the word of God, over confessions and other acts of mere men were in his favour.[27]

The professor of divinity, John Strachan, was even feistier in Monro's account. Like Monro, he denied that he had any obligation to answer charges which were not signed. He termed the charges 'libels' and not informations. He questioned the very right of the Commission to sit and did so in a manner which hit at the political and ecclesiological beliefs held and published by Gilbert Rule.[28] Was it a civil body? Why, then, did it include ministers? Their church would not have any bishops in Parliament, so what right had they to mix ecclesiastical and civil power here? If it were an ecclesiastical body, where was the act of the General Assembly authorising it? He accused the Visitors of trying to make him incriminate himself. Strachan admitted that he believed in '*Passive Obedience* and non-Resistance' and he pointed out that he had taken all the oaths tendered to him from 1647 to 1687 but would not take theirs since he would have to swear to uphold the Confession of Faith in ways he could not do. Like the others, he had been accused of theological deviations, in his case preaching reconciliation with Rome, believing in consubstantiation, being an Arminian or Pelagian, setting up the English liturgy, neglecting family worship and marrying people clandestinely. He defended his doctrine by citing his published works and his sermons. He quibbled over Arminianism, saying the Arminians were Presbyterians – as indeed they were. He noted that Massie's view of the presence of Christ in the Eucharist was described by the term 'Bilocation of Bodies', which was close to transubstantiation and as absurd as Massie's alleged disbelief in the Pythagorian theorem and his upholding of judicial astrology! Strachan admitted to using the rites of the Church of England but noted that they were not prohibited any more than the Genevan rites were then prescribed. Both were used by others. He refused to sign the Westminster Confession, holding that it might not contain biblical views on free will and on justification, a sign that he probably was an Arminian. He denied leading an immoral life but said that he had invited Fr Reid, a Dominican priest, to the laureation ceremony in 1687. It was a sharp and honourable defence, one which showed how differently the Edinburgh men were treated by their committee than had been the men at Glasgow.

By 15 September the principal's and divinity professor's libels had been proven and the Committee turned more earnestly to the regents and to Gregorie. Initially they were obstructed by Sir Patrick Hume.[29] Eventually Gregorie was questioned about the behaviour of Kennedy and Cunningham. Like the principal, he denied they had behaved badly; they did the same for him. The Committee asked boys taught by these masters if they heard the professors 'mock the godly' when they were together in 'Baudy houses & taverns with ther masters', a question which may shed surprising light on the diversions of the collegians of the time. They asked fourteen-year-olds if they had seen Cunningham 'committ adultery at Hallyards wods and such like stuff'. Nothing was said to incriminate Gregorie, although David Hume, Lord Crossrig and Mr Rule asked about the women said to have gone to his chamber. This sort of thing went on for several days, with even Massie being subjected to questions about his 'Atheism, Usuary, Drinking, Woaring, backbiting, unnatural [illegible] wt daughter'. 'Cheating his sister' was found not relevant to his case. If Gregorie drew up this libel, he got his own back. On 19 September, both Crossrig and Rule told Gregorie his teaching and dictates were 'very right' and 'that my libell was malitious and false'.[30] His friends Kennedy and Cunningham still faced charges of attending Mass and 'drunkenness and whoring'. Gregorie, now partially cleared, was then offered the oaths on 22 September but refused to take them until he should be cleared of all the charges. When asked if he would take the oaths when he was cleared he refused to answer, saying they could wait and see. His confidence was growing.

After all but two of the St Andrews University professors were deprived on 23 September (see below, p. 375f.), Gregorie made up his mind not to swear the oaths and thought he had persuaded Kennedy and Cunningham to go along with him. They were 'brought over' by Lord Raith. The outing of the principal on the morning of the 24th and the professor of divinity that afternoon may have had some effect. After that they swore, as did Massie. Burnet refused, as did regent John Drummond and the Hebrew professor, Alexander Douglass. Gregorie dined that day with Dr Pitcairne and 'drew up my desirued last speech to the Committee . . . refusing mainly the Confession as contrair to the Reformed Churches & particularly that of England.' In short, he was prepared to leave as an Episcopalian and perhaps as an Arminian. Lord Raith called him to sign in the late afternoon but Gregorie, changing his tack, told His Lordship that he did not wish to be at the mercy of the Town Council with respect to his post and its salary. Raith and Mr Moncrieff, a bailie who came with him, assured Gregorie that the government would protect him and that the magistrates were willing to augment his salary to £100 sterling or 1,800 marks Scots. The professor was adamant, not about the Confession, but now about his rights which he thought the Commission ought to have declared and enforced. He asked for a night to think it all over and said, if denied that time, 'I should infallibly misbehave, and that he [Raith] would have no honour of me.' Gregorie then sought out Lord Tarbat, spoke to the Lord Advocate, and saw Raith again, at which time the professor raised new issues having nothing to do with religion or his salary. He 'told [Raith] that my father was ane old man with a second Wife who would take advantage of me in case of sich whatever[,] that I entreated time untill I might settle affairs with him.' That was granted. Overnight and the next morning there were further negotiations involving Raith, other commissioners, the Lord Advocate, Lords Tarbat, Ruthven, Lothian, the Master of Burleigh, Sir Thomas Kennedy and Dr Pitcairne. About 11.00 a.m. on the 27th, the day the Commission sacked Gregorie's brother James, Lord Cardross called him to the Commission, but he did not go.

The Commission seems to have decided on 27 September that Gregorie's libel had not been proven before the Committee. It recommended that he be given the oaths. He would not take them and in the end he was simply 'passed over'. He was told no further action would then be taken. Instead, the commissioners took action against others. They reluctantly sacked the Glasgow men and appointed George Campbell (c. 1635–3 July 1701) of Dumfries as professor of divinity at Edinburgh University.[31] On the same day, the Commission appointed a Committee for Aberdeen and then adjourned until 15 October, giving Gregorie a longer time to think over swearing the oaths.

While the Commission was not meeting as a body of inquiry, it was not idle. It continued to be lobbied on Gregorie's behalf. Afforced by Mr Massie, and regents John Tran of Glasgow and John Monro of St Andrews, it wrote acts (which were not enacted), made Gilbert Rule principal of Edinburgh and, after comparative trials, gave Edinburgh regencies to William Law (c. 1660–? November 1729) and Lawrence Dundas (c. 1668–c. 1740). Since it took no action with respect to the Edinburgh medical professors, they must have resigned by this time.[32] Alexander Cunningham and Hew Kennedy were the only other teachers besides Gregorie who survived the purge. Both were friends of Dr Pitcairne and other well-placed Jacobites and Episcopalians. Cunningham seems to have been protected by the Master of Stair. Kennedy's friends seem also to have been Gregorie's. Both Cunningham and Kennedy were protected but, in the end, they were willing to swear the new oaths and made less of a fuss over money. Andrew Massie was removed as a trouble maker, not as a political threat. He was then reinstated, so quickly that he did not miss a teaching year.[33]

Gregorie was not happy with the outcome of the Visitation and did not take the oaths, although he resumed teaching in December 1690, having 'resolved to continue untill I be putt out'. His enemies on the Town Council continued to think about ousting him. Even his friend Cunningham began publicly abusing him. Gregorie also fell out with Lord Raith. On 28 December, Lawrence Dundas told him that his own patron, Sir John Foulis of Ravelstone, was 'concerned that [Gregorie] should goe to Rack'. The town would not settle his salary; he would not sign the oaths. By mid-January 1691, the Town Council was again ready to diminish his salary but the principal was telling people that since the Visitation had left Gregorie alone, he would not touch him, suggesting that he thought the Council should follow suit. However, two months later the magistrates were only waiting for the proper moment to set upon him. Then his friend Sir John Hall demitted office under a cloud. During this time Gregorie may well have been seeking other places. On 22 April 1691, he was offered the professorship of astronomy at Oxford and accepted it. He had not been purged and he had not conformed to what was expected of him. Despite his difficulties, he had received a good deal of special consideration and protection, exactly the sort of thing which was lacking for some others who were neither so well born nor well connected. His case is interesting because it shows the shallowness of the religious convictions of some and the tolerance of others, but also suggests that bright men with special skills were not going to be severely hassled by inquisitors unless they acted very provocatively. There was more charity and respect for learning among the men who returned in 1689 than has sometimes been realised.

Gregorie's account of the Visitation at Edinburgh accords with what is known of that affair from other sources. Visitations involved the interested men of power in the area and were political affairs conducted as much behind the curtain as in the hearing rooms. Professors were not backward or unskilful in playing politics. After all, they were from the political classes and came into their offices through politicking of some sort. Gregorie, the son of a northern laird, was exceptional only in being very bright and the friend of more well-born figures than most men. In the presumably partial list of his supporters given above, one finds at least six peers or heirs to peers, six baronets and knights and three town magistrates. If one asks what offices they held, the list is equally impressive: HM Commissioner, former and present judges, Secretaries of State and Lords Provost. These were the sorts of men who placed protégés in the colleges and came to their aid when they were threatened. Some of Gregorie's supporters were, like himself, men from the North; others shared with him the skills and virtuoso interests which made it likely that he would be protected by men such as Tarbat and Stair who were interested in the new sciences, in history and in modern learning generally. Gregorie's friends were willing to use English influence when and if they could find it. While religion and politics were issues, so too were honour and income. He was willing to stay in Edinburgh but his terms had to be met and he stubbornly and cleverly clung to his post long after others might have given way. Part of that was no doubt due to his temperament – most of the academic Gregories were assertive and irascible – but some was due to a sense of honour and to the standing on principle which was so characteristic of the time and place. Gregorie was by birth a gentle-man; he had acted the part.

The Commission appointed as well as extruded. The new men were stalwart Presbyterians much like those at Glasgow.[34] The new principal, Gilbert Rule, had been educated at Glasgow University and once served as a regent at King's College, Aberdeen. Later he had preached in northern England and, when ejected, took a Leiden MD in 1665. He was later imprisoned. George Campbell, the new profes-sor of divinity, was not so different. He too had studied at Glasgow and had been in Holland as a refugee after being imprisoned for a time in the 1660s. Both served on the Visitation Commission to purge the colleges, Rule in Edinburgh, Campbell at Glasgow. Neither man had been unable to compromise in the past. Rule had preached in Dublin (1682–9) while Campbell had been an indulged minister in London in 1672. Both had contacts not only in the Lowlands but elsewhere. Rule's were in the North, but also in the Southeast and in Glasgow. Campbell hailed from Inveraray and knew men in the Southwest, par-ticularly around Dumfries, where he had held a living. Both were related by marriage to others of importance in the management of the Kirk. Both had found patrons in the men who made the revolution. Campbell almost certainly would have been backed by the Earl of Argyll, his 'chief'. Rule had a brother who was a bailie in Edinburgh and other patrons from the livings he had held. Both men were respected scholars. Rule might have wished to 'out' Gregorie but he could also admit he had been a dutiful teacher. Neither Rule nor Campbell were moss-backed men.

The new regent of humanity, Lawrence Dundas, was the younger son of a notable advocate and the former tutor of the sons of an urbane Lord of Session, Sir John Foulis of Colinton, MP and, later, a Privy Councillor. Dundas had probably been abroad as a travelling tutor, most likely in Holland. The other regent, William Law, was the son of a minister of St Giles' and a minor laird. Law was also a Leiden man. He had attended the most liberal and modern university in Holland.[35]

The new men were such as one might expect to come into the most important of the Scottish colleges after a period of turmoil. They rep-resented the magnates and pious lairds who had won. They were tied to the new leaders in the Kirk and to the lawyers then in the ascendant but they were also genteel, travelled and well educated, if not notably modern in philosophic outlook. While they all had Edinburgh con-nections, they knew many outside of the burgh and even had some connections in England, Ireland and Holland. They were to be and were serviceable men.

Officially and legally, their jobs were in the gift of the Town Council but the two professors were appointees of the Visitors. The regents won on trials but the leet for the chair of humanity was set by lawyers and the winner of that trial was closely tied to two legal families. Law won his post over six other men, some of whom were much younger, but he was also the son of the minister of St Giles'. The men who got jobs seem very well sponsored. This was to be the later pattern.

The Town Council was usually filled with reliable men dependent on leading national politicians. From the 1690s until the end of the period covered in this study, the Council seldom acted as 'the absolute patrons and governours' of the University which some have believed it to be.[36] Councillors knew all too well whence came their own security in office and their patronage. The Council seldom crossed those who could help councillors or at least the majority of them. Legal rights to patronage mattered. The city asserted and officially exercised and protected its rights, but the Council was managed by those who held power in Scotland as a whole and it was much influenced by others – ministers, surgeons, lawyers, physicians, the Crown and private patrons – who had or came to have defensible legal interests in chairs after 1690. One should not look at these appointments to the Edinburgh chairs as those of the Town Council but as those which had been negotiated by the kingdom's political managers.

Notes

1 The sorts of extras the boys got are those listed by Colin Maclaurin in a letter to the grandfather of a boy he was boarding: private tuition in classics, history and geometry and its uses, algebra, physics and astronomy and general supervision of his conduct and morals. The family paid far more for the boy's board and special attention than Maclaurin received in salary. Maclaurin to Sir Hans Sloane, 16 July 1741, in *The Collected Letters of Colin Maclaurin*, ed. Mills, 1982, p. 85f.

2 Principal Monro said Massie was much favoured by the parliamentary Visitors who did not enquire into his incoherent theology, poor teaching, lack of discipline, failure to care for the library and, perhaps worst of all, his lecturing from old notes taken from an Aberdeen Jesuit. Those inclined the boys to atheism and scepticism. Those charges were also made against another regent, Thomas Burnet, who, like Massie, had come south from Aberdeen but who was faithful to his royalist views.

See 'The character of Mr Burnet cum notis variorum', AUL, 3017/10/23. I thank Paul Wood for a copy of this document.

3 This and what follows depends on Gregorie Papers, EUL, Dk.1.2[1] /B/23–8; see also Monro, *Presbyterian Inquisition*, 1691, p. 95.

4 Ibid., p. 3.

5 Gregorie was recommended for his post by Sir Isaac Newton, who may also have been supporting him in London at this time. Turnbull, 'Bi-Centenary of the Death of Colin Maclaurin', 1951, p. 4.

6 Kennedy's proper name appears in Gregorie's manuscripts as Hew or Hugh. He had been the rector of the Haddington Grammar School and was a fairly modern man who was interested in Locke and abandoned Cartesianism for Newtonianism in the 1690s. It is not known if he was related to the reverend Hugh Kennedy who served on the Visitation Commission and was the minister of Trinity Church in Edinburgh. Less is known of Cunningham, the son of an Edinburgh merchant. What is known about this pair is to be found in Shepherd, 'Philosophy and Science in the Arts Curriculum', unpublished Edinburgh University PhD dissertation, pp. 68–76, 213, 233, and Forbes, 'Philosophy and Science Teaching in the Seventeenth Century', in *Four Centuries: Edinburgh University*, ed. Donaldson, 1983, pp. 28–37, 34. Shepherd saw Kennedy as the more modern of the two. The friendship of Cunningham and Gregorie with Dr Archibald Pitcairne suggests that here, as in other places, Newton's thought was introduced by medical men and mathematicians. This Alexander Cunningham is not Alexander Cunningham of Blok, as is said by Sir Alexander Grant in *The Story of the University*, 1884, II:280. For proof of this, see John Cairns' forthcoming study of the teaching of law in Edinburgh (hereafter Cairns, *Legal Education in Edinburgh*, forthcoming).

7 This Sinclair is likely to have been Robert Sinclair, who succeeded George Sinclair as the professor of mathematics at Glasgow in 1699. Lord Lorn became the 2nd Duke of Argyll. Lorn was then a boy of twelve or thirteen but already an officer in the army. Mathematicians often taught fortification and gunnery, so Sinclair was not an implausible teacher for the future hero who somewhere learned to point guns and conduct sieges. He had an aptitude for mathematics and Colin Maclaurin and others dedicated mathematical works to him.

8 *An Account of the Proceedings of the Estates in Scotland*, ed. Balfour-Melville, 1955, II:60.

9 This was likely to have been Sir James Falconer of Phesdo, later SCJ.

10 George Melville, 4th Baron and 1st Earl (1690), with the courtesy title of Lord Raith which went to his eldest son, Alexander Melville.

11 The Visitors said Burnet was a papist. Dr Monro denied this but did say that he had tried to keep Burnet out of the College when that regent had been imposed on the College by the Duke of Gordon's interest and the

efforts of John Drummond, the Earl of Melfort. Gordon and Melfort were Roman Catholics. Monro's candidate had been James Martin, who was then teaching at St Andrews. While not openly a Romanist, Burnet was sympathetic to them and had advocated the repeal of penal sanctions against Catholics. In 1686, Burnet had issued theses dedicated to the Duke of Gordon. These condemned the Reformation and maintained the supremacy of a divine right king over Parliament. For these he was given a pension of £25. *Bibliographia Aberdonensis*, ed. Johnstoun and Robertson, 1930, II:500; Monro, *Presbyterian Inquisition*, 1691, pp. 30, 53, 54.

12 DB. Horn thought Massie a poor teacher and a quarrelsome and violent man. Horn says that Gregorie attended church but once a term and that other regents were drunken and the College a place of disorder rather than of learning. Horn may have believed too many of the allegations made to the Visitors. Horn, *A Short History the University of Edinburgh*, 1967, p. 31f.

13 This is the Newtonian iatro-mechanist physician whose name is usually spelt 'Keill'.

14 Possibly Hamilton of Whitelaw who became Secretary of State in 1692.

15 Both were founder members of the Royal College of Physicians and both were active in it during these years. Stevenson was President of the College for some of the years between 1685 and 1694. Pitcairne had been one of the original medical professors appointed in 1685.

16 What follows relies on the Gregorie Papers, EUL, Dk.1.2^1/B/22–8.

17 *Informations* required answers to allegations but were not in themselves charges that would lead to a trial. They might lead to further enquiries and those to libels, or charges on which men were tried. All the professors found this a distinction without a difference and thought the informations were designed to make them incriminate themselves.

18 Monro, *Presbyterian Inquisition*, 1691, p. 8.

19 Gregorie Papers, 'Articles against Mr Gregorie', EUL Dk.1.2.^{1}/B/24. The Articles are annotated: 'This is the original Lybell given to me by Mr Hamilton pressmennens son[,] Clerk to the Visitation. It was written by Mr Massy and Mr Burnet at the instigation of Mr Henry ffergusson.' The latter was the College treasurer. It does not contain another article to which Gregorie had to answer, namely, that he had come by his post at the expense of Mr John Young whom he had outed by 'backbiting him untill I gott his imployment'.

20 Gregorie listed them as including: Robert Kerr, 4th Earl of Lothian; David Ruthven, 2nd Baron Ruthven; Alexander Melville, Lord Raith; John Dalrymple, the Master of Stair; Sir James Hall of Dunglass, Sir William Hamilton, Pitfiver [?Pitfour], Mr Edward Jamison, Gilbert Rule, Mr J[ohn] Law (c. 1662–1718) and Mr Hew Kennedy. Others who later sat with them included Sir Patrick Hume and William Lindsay, 18th Earl of

Crawford, the chairman of the whole Commission. Principal Monro's list of the Visitors included others but he said some were ashamed to participate and did not sit. He adds to Gregorie's list Sir Alexander Swinton, Lord Mersington, SCJ; David Home, Lord Crossrig, SCJ and John [probably Robert] Hamilton [Lord Pressmannan], SCJ. Perhaps the last were the ones too ashamed to sit.

21 For Gregorie's teaching and its Newtonian content, see Eagles, 'David Gregory and Newtonian Science', *British Journal for the history of Science*, 1977, pp. 216–25.

22 The eighteenth century would make more of the argument that politeness depended on trade but here it is clearly alluded to in 1690. Men like Gregorie already shared the perception of John Pocock that civility was a child of commerce: cf. Pocock, *Barbarism and Religion: Narratives of Civil Government*, 1999.

23 What this probably means is that Young could do geometry but was not facile with arithmetic and the generalisation of its principles in algebra.

24 EUL, Dk.1.2^2.25.

25 Monro, *Presbyterian Inquisition*, 1691, pp. 20–8.

26 Ibid., pp. 29–45.

27 Ibid., pp. 45–66.

28 Jackson, *Restoration Scotland*, 2003, p. 176f.

29 Sir Patrick Home of Lumisden, MP, a virtuoso friend of Sir Robert Sibbald.

30 Gregorie Papers, EUL, Dk.1.2^1.26.

31 Campbell's appointment had been facilitated by the General Assembly, which approved his translation from his kirk to the Edinburgh chair; Earl of Crawford to Lord Melville, 1 November 1690, *Leven and Melville Papers*, ed. Melville, 1843, p. 561.

32 They are not generally listed among the professors of that time but there is no clear indication that they were not still on the faculty roster in 1689. Indeed, Monro's account of his hearing suggests that Sibbald was to answer the charges against him which he would only have had to do were he still a professor. However, the fact that Dr Pitcairne appears in Gregorie's account of the Visitation as being in Edinburgh but having already made some arrangements for going to Leiden suggests that he had resigned by the time the Visitors met. That would account for his not being summoned by them. The two other medical professors, Sir Robert Sibbald and James Halket, seem simply to have disappeared. That is not surprising. Sibbald and his two colleagues had been appointees of Charles II and James VII. They would not have been appointed in 1685 unless they had been at least nominally Episcopalians and royalists. Pitcairne was a known Jacobite sympathiser. Cf. Hugh Ouston, 'Cultural Life from the Restoration to the Union', in *The History of Scottish Literature*, ed. Hook, 1989, II:11–32.

33 I thank Dr Esther Mijers for this information. Most of what is known of Massie, an Aberdeenshire man, can be found in Shepherd's unpublished dissertation, 'Philosophy and Science', and in the references to him in *Bibliographia Aberdonensis*, ed. Johnstoun and Robertson, 1930, II:483. A short description of Massie's poor teaching is given in Horn, *Short History*, 1967, p. 32. Horn left a collection of manuscripts concerning the history of the University on which he was working prior to his death in 1969 (EUL, D. B. Horn MSS, Gen 1824). In them can be found materials on the history of each of the chairs, their occupants, and other aspects of the history of the University. This collection contains typescripts of relevant entries from the Town Council minutes which are cited here from the Horn transcripts unless otherwise noted.

34 For biographical details concerning Rule, see Scott, *Fasti*, 1915, I:39–40; for Campbell, see *Bibliographia Aberdonensis*, ed. Johnstoun and Robertson, 1930, II:467. He is also noticed in Wodrow, *Analecta*, ed. Leishman, 1853, III:122.

35 For a recent account of the Dutch universities and their influence on Scotland, see Esther Mijers, 'Scotland and the United Provinces', unpublished St Andrews PhD dissertation. Dr Mijers thinks that the Dutch example was not more important than the memories of Scottish seventeenth-century attempts to create professional chairs and a professorial system of teaching.

36 Arnot, *The History of Edinburgh*, 1779, p. 389.

9

EDINBURGH APPOINTMENTS IN THE FACULTY OF DIVINITY

∽

1. THE PRINCIPALS

The clearest illustrations of political interference in Scottish academic affairs are to be found in the appointments of the principals of the universities. The principals were important national figures who sat often in the General Assembly which met each spring. The Edinburgh principal ordinarily had a hand in the administration of Crown patronage in the Kirk, and might also be important in burgh politics. Principals played a role in administering the patronage of their universities and colleges. They received relatively high salaries. In the aristocratic world of the eighteenth century, the selection of such men could not be left to mere tradesmen and merchants. How the choices were made at Edinburgh can be seen by looking at the men who filled the principality after the death of Principal Rule in 1701.

The first of these men was William Carstares (11 February 1649–28 December 1715). He had been involved in high politics since the 1670s and had become a trusted political advisor to William of Orange in the 1680s. William later made him a Royal Chaplain, a post he retained under Queen Anne. Carstares was helpful to Robert Harley and to various Scottish lords and MPs. His conciliatory temper made his appointment in 1703 one which seemed to all very good. It honourably eased him out of London where he was no longer wanted by a regime which was less Whiggish than William's.[1] The politicians placed in Edinburgh a man with whom they knew they could work and whom they trusted. The Kirk got a man who had been tortured with the thumbscrews and whose orthodoxy was unquestionable.[2] The Scottish universities got much more.

Carstares wanted to remodel the Scottish universities along Dutch lines which were, from another viewpoint, but a return to the reforms proposed and partially effected by sixteenth-century and seventeenth-century Scottish reformers who had looked not only to Holland but to Geneva, Germany and France for their academic models.[3] The most important of those reformers was Andrew Melville, whose university reforms were most notably embodied in the 'novo erectio' which re-chartered Glasgow University in 1577. Melville's personal influence also touched the other universities: King's in 1575, when he helped to reconstitute it; St Andrews in 1580, when he served as principal of St Mary's College and in other offices until he was removed in 1597; and Edinburgh, through his work in the General Assemblies.[4] It was clear to reformers like Melville that the nation needed specialist teachers in Latin, Greek, Hebrew, philosophy and history and others to teach theology, medicine and law. His efforts were directed toward the expansion and specialisation of the university chairs. Regents were to disappear. Scots only needed to provide funds to realise his dreams. During the Scottish Reformation, revenues from confiscated church lands ended up with the Crown, the nobility, a newly created gentry, and a now-married clergy needing more income to support families. The reforms were not carried through but everywhere the reformers' dreams were remembered and remained ideals to be realised. Carstares' espousal them was a reflection of his experience in Holland and of his interests in history and modern learning, but it connected him in the minds of many to the early reformers and to the heroic age of Scottish Calvinism. In 1690 or 1703 this was a distinct advantage for a moderate man whose theological outlook was not as old-fashioned as some of those whom he had to lead.

To Carstares, the Revolution and later the Union offered opportunities to complete the Melvillian reforms. Carstares had worked at this agenda before his appointment and he continued to do so after he became principal at Edinburgh.[5] Regenting ended at Edinburgh in 1708, when specialist professors took over the arts chairs. The curriculum broadened to include better language teaching and history in 1702 and 1719. The modernisation of the materials taught in the arts courses, including the teaching of more science, came at about the same time; so did professional education in law (1707, 1710, 1722) and medicine (1697, 1713, 1720, 1724, 1726). Those changes had his support and progressed during his years as principal. By the end of his life he had accomplished much at Edinburgh and at other colleges where he helped his friends to obtain places.[6] We have seen this in the case of Principal Dunlop at Glasgow and will see some of the same things at St Andrews when we turn to that university. All this made Carstares acceptable to the gentry and to ministers. It also contributed to the modernisation of the kingdom.

Carstares was not only a reformer of universities but a pacifier for a troubled place. His political skills made him a valuable man who could keep order among restless and often lawless folk. He could soothe hotheaded clerics and find compromises which sensible men could embrace. He worked well with politicians of many different sorts, partly because he was not so much a political partisan as interested in defending the interests of the Kirk and inducing all parties to do so. His moderation and wisdom heralded a change in the Kirk which made it possible for many later clerics to accept and further the Scottish Enlightenment. He was one of the greatest Scots of his time.

Carstares was succeeded as principal in 1716 by William Wishart I (1660–11 June 1729), another clerical politician and a popular Edinburgh minister who had studied in Holland and had Carstares' dying blessing. He too was an accommodating man who served as Moderator of the General Assembly in 1706, 1713, 1718, 1724, 1727 and 1728. Like Carstares, Wishart was able to work with any politicians who would allow the Kirk a measure of independence. In 1706 and 1713 he had to get along with the Tory Lord Mar, in 1718 with the Squadrone Whigs and in 1724 and 1727–8 with the Argathelians. Politicians in London and Edinburgh found him agreeable to work with and they had helped him to attain office. In his later years, he became more or less an Argathelian and remained so until near the very end of his career. On 29 September 1715, Lord Ilay, in a letter to [?] Newcastle, noted that in the previous election the Town Council had been 'packed' by the Squadrone. Ilay was the 'packer' of the Council which chose Wishart to be principal.[7]

Wishart was followed by William Hamilton, a more committed partisan and an Argathelian. Hamilton was a moderate who had once been considered for the divinity chair at St Andrews and had held the one in Edinburgh since 1709, when Carstares had had a hand in his appointment. Hamilton supported the Squadrone but he switched when it became apparent that disorder in the Kirk was going to be dealt with better by the Argathelians. They also bought his loyalty. The disorder that worried him was caused by the case of John Simson, which dangerously divided the Kirk and imperilled its relationship with the protecting state. Ilay made Hamilton Chaplain to George II in 1727.[8] In 1727 and 1730 he was for the fourth and fifth times Moderator of the General Assembly where he did Ilay's business.[9] How deeply Hamilton and the Lord Provost of Edinburgh, John Campbell, were concerned in the politics of the Kirk and for whom they acted can be seen clearly in many letters.[10] One where it is strikingly clear is a letter of Archibald

Campbell of Inveraray addressed in 1730 to Lord Milton, Ilay's principal political aide in Edinburgh:

> I have written in the most pressing terms to every one of our Presbitery to Send up their Commissioners; and advised them to direct the Commissioners to waite of My Lord Provost of Edinbr [John Campbell, a man from Inveraray, the chief seat of this Campbell family] & Professor Hamilton, from whom they might receive Directions, with Regarde to any question My Lord Duke [of Argyll] or My Lord Ilay are more or less concerned in.[11]

Archibald and John Campbell, like Hamilton, were only doing what was expected of them to help the Argathelians manage the Kirk in a difficult year. Hamilton's reward for this and other services came in the autumn when he was elevated to the principalship after James Alston, another of Ilay's henchmen, had refused the job. Hamilton was installed as principal in February 1730 but his tenure was short.

When Hamilton died in 1732, Ilay arranged the election of his successor, James Smith (1681–14 August 1736).[12] Smith had served the Dundasses of Arniston, a Squadrone family, but he too had been bought by the Argathelian managers in c. 1727. His new loyalty was rewarded by consideration for the Glasgow principality in 1727 and then by his selection as Edinburgh's professor of divinity in 1732. He was known as one who believed that the authority of the Kirk took precedence over individual consciences. That in a sense was paving the way for Moderates who were less original than many have found them. Smith was elected Moderator in 1733 and then elevated to the Edinburgh principality. He had helped the Crown's managers in the Simson case and had prevented it from causing the damage it might have produced. A recent study of the Simson case sums up Smith's career in these years by saying his 'talents seem to have been those of a negotiator and peacemaker'.[13] He was memorialised after his death as one

> Who now with equal warmth and skill
> Shall heal dissension and fierce discord still.[14]

Men able to deal with the 'hot brethren' were the ones who got these jobs from Ilay and his faction.

When Smith died, Ilay wrote to Lord Milton saying that he hoped 'our friends of the [Town] Council will not enter into any engagements till I come down; I have A great aversion to the frequent changing of the professor of Divinity upon which so much depends when that office is well managed . . . of the people I have yet heard of [I] like [William]Wishart [II] the best & I should be glad you would do him any good you can.'[15] Wishart, the son of the earlier William Wishart, was, at forty-four, much younger than Hamilton and Smith when they had been appointed. Ilay regarded continuity in the posts of principal and professor of divinity as important for the management of the Kirk. Wishart had had earlier dealings with the Argathelians who made him Dean of Faculty at Glasgow in 1730 and dealt with him about an Edinburgh church in 1736.[16] He broke with some Argathelians over the appointment of David Hume in 1744–5 but that was the sensible thing for a believing political cleric to do. The Argathelians were out of power and had themselves split into two groups: one which followed the 2nd Duke of Argyll (d. 1743) and another which, after 1738, remained loyal to Walpole's government and followed the Duke's brother, Lord Ilay. After Ilay returned to power in 1747, the principal supported him. Wishart until 1753 and for nearly a generation solved Ilay's problem concerning the continuity of leadership in the Kirk.[17]

In 1754, Ilay, now the Duke of Argyll, brokered the appointment of John Gowdie (Goudie, Goldie; 1682–19 February 1762), who triumphed over at least three others.[18] George Drummond, the Argathelian Lord Provost, nominated his son-in-law, John Jardine. Lord Milton's candidate was Patrick Cuming (1695–1 April 1776), Ilay's advisor on clerical patronage. The choice of Harry Barclay of Colarnie, one of Ilay's supporters, was William Robertson (8 September 1721–11 June 1793), later famous as an historian. Argyll's choice was Gowdie; he carried the day. Gowdie had been active in opposing the 'Marrow Men', high-flyers in the 1720s. In 1733, he had been on the government's side in the Simson business and it was his casting vote in the Assembly of that year which led to the expulsion of Ebenezer Erskine from his charge and the beginning of the schismatic Associated Presbytery that took out of the Established Church many dissidents.[19] Gowdie did not preach on the sinfulness of men convicted by the law and in need of free grace but on the need to be moral.[20] He had served well and now got a reward which Jardine and Robertson had only begun to earn.

In all these appointments, still formally acts of the Town Council, the Council's opinion does not much figure in the correspondence in which the jobs were settled. The real appointer of the men chosen in 1729, 1733, 1736 and 1754 was Ilay. This was clearly seen at the time, particularly by the man who in 1732 sent a letter to Ilay's supporter, Patrick Lindsay, threatening death to him, Principal Hamilton, William

Wishart II, James Smith and John Gowdie because they were men who had done too well the ungodly bidding of the government managers Ilay and Milton.[21] Cranks are sometimes right.

After Argyll's death in 1761, little changed. His political machine was inherited by his nephew, the 3rd Earl of Bute, who secured the appointment of William Robertson to the principal's chair in 1762. As Baron Mure told Lord Bute, the Town Council's right to appoint 'will make no difference with regard to the disposal of the place . . . It will be equally as your Lordship shall direct' – as indeed it was.[22] This is particularly interesting because Bailie James Stuart, who was to be Lord Provost in the following year, wanted Dr Daniel MacQueen, who was his cousin but also cousin to Lord Bute's wife. Recommending him to Gilbert Elliot of Minto, MP, professor George Stuart cited his lineage, his learning, his popularity and his having the earlier support of Ilay. Bailie Stuart and his friends on the Council were ignored.[23] Robertson, a more polite and accomplished man, was appointed without difficulty, even though other politicians had candidates of their own. The professor of ecclesiastical history, Patrick Cuming, thought he had a claim on the place because it had once been promised to him – or so he said.[24] He was fobbed off with a chair at Glasgow for his bright son, Patrick, and another at Edinburgh for his dull son, Robert. Debts had to be paid; the politicians paid them with jobs allegedly controlled by the others.[25]

When Principal Robertson was replaced in 1793, not by Hugh Blair as many had expected but by George Husband Baird (13 July 1761–14 January 1840), the politics involved were equally clear.[26] Baird was the son-in-law of the Edinburgh Lord Provost of the time and a protégé of the Duke of Atholl who was important to Dundas's electoral success in Perthshire. Henry Dundas assented to this appointment.[27] Baird had not been appointed just because he was an energetic professor of oriental languages who was well liked by his associates in the University or because he was a popular Edinburgh minister.[28] Like other ministers placed around this time, he had preached sermons against the French Revolution. He was a reliable, well-connected man whom national politicians wanted in office in a time of crisis and one whose placement made their electoral politics easier.

2. Divinity Professors

Professors of divinity, like principals, were not picked by the Town Council. Their post was simply too sensitive not to command the attention of the managers for the Crown. The latter's interests lay in having a peaceful Kirk submissive to management, one which would not be torn by factional or doctrinal strife. Managers needed compliant divines who would preach the values they themselves held. Toleration (after 1712) was to be encouraged; patronage of the kirks by heritors and the Crown (it appointed about a third of the ministers) was not to be deplored; commotions over doctrine were to be kept in check so that popular enthusiasm would not make the country ungovernable; addresses to the Crown should not only be loyal but such as to evoke no controversies. The men installed in the divinity chairs upheld such views and inculcated them on those whom they taught.

While George Campbell had been virtually the nominee of the Visitation Committee in 1690, his sponsor for this job seems to have been the Earl of Findlatter, later the Lord Chancellor and Queen's Commissioner to the General Assembly and already an important figure in the government of the kingdom.[29] Campbell's successor in 1701, George Meldrum, was the Trongate Kirk minister. He had once been a regent at Marischal College and had suffered deprivation from his Aberdeen living in the 1680s. He sat on the Visitation Commission for Marischal College in 1695. Three years later, he was made Moderator. Those offices point to good political connections and his skills as a negotiator. Like Campbell and Gilbert Rule, Meldrum was also the choice of the Edinburgh ministers who knew they were supporting a political cleric who was acceptable to ruling politicians. His great accomplishment as Moderator was to assert the independence and privileges of the Kirk in a way the government could accept.[30] He tended to preach that salvation was available to all and not just to the saved who knew (or thought they knew) their condition.[31] This was a modern and tolerant position not much liked by the rigidly orthodox who found fault with John Simson for teaching something like it.[32] Perhaps it was because Campbell believed this that he was more charitable than his brethren to Thomas Aikenhead, the student heretic hanged in 1697.[33] Such attitudes accorded with the views of men like Mar, Findlatter and Ilay. None of them knowingly supported the candidacies of doctrinaire men likely to cause trouble in the Kirk.

In 1709 the Town Council accepted William Hamilton, a man of similar kidney but of more modern divinity.[34] Hamilton was a man whose lectures were characterised by a former student, James Oswald, as teaching 'moderation and a liberal manner of thinking upon all subjects'.[35] What that meant is spelled out by John Ramsay of Ochtertyre who wrote that Hamilton had his students read 'the Great English divines which were universally read, [and who] served as excellent models of composition to young divines'. These would not have been William Ames or Richard Baxter, but John Tillotson and other latitudinarians.[36] He had come from a Covenanting family but his own views were hardly theirs. Carstares liked his moderation, although his first choice may have been another moderate man, William Mitchell. Mitchell was chosen by the Town Council but refused to serve, perhaps because he felt that he lacked the political support to make his tenure a success.[37]

When Hamilton died in 1732, his chair went to James Smith, for some years associated with Ilay and his faction in the running of the Kirk. Smith was very like John Gowdie, who got the post in 1733. In 1754, when Gowdie became principal, Argyll was advised by his friends, Lords Hyndford and Milton, that Robert Hamilton (19 May 1707–3 April 1787), the son of the former principal, should be appointed to the divinity chair. Other gentlemen concurred and this Edinburgh minister was given the post through the Duke's efforts.[38] Hamilton was the brother of Bailie Gavin Hamilton, in whose book-shop the 3rd Duke of Argyll spent many pleasant hours.[39] His appointment, managed by Argyll, was one which helped to show Newcastle and his Squadrone supporters that Argyll was not to be easily ousted from power in Edinburgh or Scotland. Hamilton himself wrote to Milton that he depended on Argyll in getting this post and not on the Marquis of Lothian.[40]

Robert Hamilton held the chair alone until 1779, when he 'retired' by taking an unpaid associate who had the right of reversion. That man was Andrew Hunter of Park and Barjarg (1743–21 April 1809). Hunter was a wealthy evangelical minister related to James Hunter Blair, a principal partner in the Coutts banking house of Edinburgh and London. Hunter Blair had long been a friend and ally of Sir Lawrence Dundas, who in those years controlled the Town Council on which Hunter Blair sat and which named him MP for Edinburgh in 1781. In 1779, Hunter Blair was able to take care of his relative. It helped that Andrew Hunter could afford to teach without pay.[41] Again, the Town Council was compliant but it did not act without outside guidance from and the approval of a dominant politician. In only one of these appointments does the Town Council seem to have exercised its own judgement – and that man would not and did not serve.

3. ECCLESIASTICAL HISTORY

The divinity faculty expanded c. 1702 with the appointment of a regius professor of ecclesiastical history. Regius chair warrants had to be obtained in London and the incumbents were all political appointees. It is not known when, how or through whom the first man, John Cumming (c. 1641–1714), got his posting. Carstares' biographer thought it came through William Carstares.[42] If Carstares was hoping to make Edinburgh University look more modern, polite and Dutch, then ecclesiastical history ought to be offered. It was also a subject close to his own heart.

The next incumbent in 1715 was Carstares' nephew, William Dunlop (1692–29 October 1720), son of Principal William Dunlop of Glasgow.[43] Dunlop's posting came through the good offices of the Duke of Montrose, the chancellor at Glasgow and a leader of the Squadrone faction.[44] Dunlop was later not of his party. His chief qualification for the post was, no doubt, his uncle, but he was also a very bright scholar with some legal training and ability as a preacher.[45] His one notable achievement was a defence of creeds and subscriptions to them, an issue then dividing the dissenting churches in England and the Presbyterians in Ireland. His work justified creeds and supported subscription to them on modern Whiggish grounds.[46] It was designed to prevent in Scotland the sort of turmoil which had come to dissenting churches in England and Ireland and to counter those who believed that one needed to look first to the Bible and not to the Westminster Confession for the statement of what one ought to believe and what one had to teach if one held a post in the Kirk or universities. While Dunlop, like all Calvinists, thought the Bible the ultimate rule of faith, confessions conveniently summed up what most men needed to believe. Ministers who had been admitted to teach and preach according to Westminster standards should not publicly deviate from them and should be suspended if they did. Dunlop's position was stricter than that of his old professor, John Simson of Glasgow. The young professor's position was acceptable neither to the evangelicals (because it put too much faith in the opinions of men) nor to those who would make the standards of belief closer to what they now are among most present-day Presbyterians – Arminian, Socinian, and incoherently lax.

Carstares sought to fill offices with learned and bright men but others were less particular. In 1715, some clearly thought of this office as a reward to political clients. The Marquis of Tweeddale was asked by Alexander Murray of Cringletie to get the post for his brother Archibald. Cringletie wanted this as a reward for his own willingness to stand for the Squadrone in a chancy parliamentary constituency in the election of 1715. Another manager for the Squadrone saw the post as 'a very good way to answer the laird's own expectation till once a good occasion offer.'[47] Six years later, Principal William Hamilton sought the place in lieu of a church; he probably would have treated it as a sinecure and pocketed the £80 a year which it was worth.[48] James Crawford (c. 1682–February 1731), the professor of chemistry and medicine, wanted to combine it with the chairs of Hebrew and chemistry and medicine, which he already possessed, but his colleagues and the Town Council said he could not do this. They would have deprived him of one or both of his other chairs had he got the appointment from the Crown.[49] It probably stayed in his family since it went, instead, to Matthew Crawford (1683–4 June 1736), the son of the former minister of Eastwood who had suffered during the years of Episcopacy in the seventeenth century. Since Matthew Crawford had held office in Glasgow University when it was in the grip of the Squadrone Party, he was almost certainly their man.[50] Thomas Boston reported of Crawford that he held 'patronage was no grievance to the Church' – a point few evangelicals would have accepted but which was of the utmost importance to all the politicians.[51] Whoever supported him had found an apologist for their policies.

In 1737, after Crawford died, Principal John Gowdie told Lord Ilay that the College needed in that chair a dutiful professor who would be politically reliable.[52] Charles Erskine was asked to secure the place for John Jardine, the son-in-law of Lord Provost George Drummond, but that came to nothing.[53] Ilay was solicited by Lady Eglinton for her son's governor or tutor but Ilay gave the place to the man who became, c. 1736, his principal manager of ecclesiastical affairs, Patrick Cuming (1695–1 April 1776).[54] Cuming was reliable but he did not tax himself lecturing on his subject. His seven-year course on ecclesiastical history met once a week to hear a Latin lecture. But Cuming was not the egregious sinecurist he is often made out to be. He devoted much time to 'pastoral theology', to give it its modern name. He taught the elements of preaching and pastoral care.

Cuming's was an interesting appointment for what it tells us about the qualities Ilay prized in professors, especially in divines. Cuming is most often discussed by those interested in the Moderates, on whom he turned toward the end of Argyll's career, and who more or less replaced him as managers of the Argathelian interest in the Kirk. Those scholars tend to see him as a man of no interest, as an old-fashioned man, a dull hack playing politics in the Kirk and as a man of no intellectual force or interest. The character of him given by Ramsay of Ochtertyre is quite at variance with that assessment and is worth quoting since it says a lot about why Ilay and Cuming were successful managers:

> Both he [Cuming] and the Wisharts [William II and his brother, George] were gentlemen by birth – a circumstance which did not make them worse ministers, or spoil their manners and principles. He was a man of great learning and ingenuity and worth, much admired for his pulpit talents. Less philosophical and lively than Dr Wallace, and less English in his strain and language than Dr George Wishart, his own rich store of materials enabled him to shine from the outset as an enlightened useful preacher. His divinity coincided with the Standards of the Church, but his style and arrangements were more polished and pleasant than those of the highly popular clergy. But whilst his orthodoxy was unquestioned, he did not think it incumbent on him to dwell principally on certain errors of the system that led more to strife than to edification. His sermons were pathetic, without affectation of *sentiment*; dignified and nervous in their strain, without being inflated or incumbered with words. Though he had neither time nor inclination to attend to the minutiae of language, he did not neglect the essentials of composition. He was indeed one of those pious and rational preachers whose discourses are directed more to the heart and understanding than to the fancy or humours of men. We may regard him as a happy medium between the old and the new fashioned clergy; for he had the zeal and sincerity of the one, and as much of the elegance and refinement of the other as was necessary.[55]

Ramsay thought him a good teacher but added: 'Perhaps the conversations and counsels of a man who was both an excellent scholar and an excellent critic, were of much greater consequence than his lectures.' In Ramsay's mind, his chief attribute, one which led him to 'power and celebrity', was his 'talent for business'. The man was even-tempered and unruffled, 'temperate and conciliatory' in his language, eloquent when he needed to be and able to carry 'his point without producing an irreconcilable breach' when debating with men whose interest and passions were engaged against him. Ramsay saw him as a man of 'common-sense', 'address', delicacy, 'prudence', courtesy and even humility when that was required. In 1801, Ramsay thought of Cuming as one of the six best preachers of his time.[56] Cuming appears in Ramsay's memoirs as much the same sort of man as Lord

Milton. Both he and Milton were like Ilay, to whom they were answerable. Ramsay, a bit of an evangelical, probably did not share Cuming's theological outlook, but he had an intimate knowledge of Edinburgh and its people which stretched back to 1753 when, as a young lawyer, he attended the Court of Session and the General Assembly. His opinion of the professor is worth considering and makes sense of Cuming's long relationship with the 3rd Duke of Argyll. The Duke, however, was not likely to have applauded Cuming's disapproval of the reverend John Home's *Douglas* and the censure of the clerics who had gone to see that play.

Patrick Cuming resigned his place in 1762 to make way for his son Robert Cuming (c. 1733–88), who got the chair in compensation for his father's failure to obtain the Edinburgh principalship. The younger Cuming's appointment seems to have been opposed by the Lord Provost for the coming year, James Stuart. He wanted the reverend Daniel MacQueen, a more learned historian who had critically reviewed Hume's *History of England*.[57] The Lord Provost was ignored; Robert Cuming was appointed and held the chair for twenty-six years. He is said not to have lectured.[58]

In 1788, Henry Dundas secured the chair for Thomas Hardy of Charlesfield and Navitie (22 April 1748–1 November 1798), who had defended the Moderate Party in a much-admired pamphlet of 1782. Hardy continued his essentially political work after being called to an Edinburgh church two years later. He was a popular preacher but in the end was more known for his practical works, for a notable sermon on the evils of slavery and for political activities, and not for the lectures which he delivered with success and to applause. Like most of the Moderates, Hardy was a friend to order and Tory government. He opposed Painites and the French Revolutionaries. From his own point of view, Henry Dundas had picked well.[59]

When Dundas got to pick another man in 1799, he chose from a field of at least four and seems to have made the choice himself. Dr James MacKnight had the backing of Gilbert Innes, a prominent Edinburgh banker. Lord President Ilay Campbell recommended William Porteous, DD, a Glasgow minister.[60] The evangelical candidate was Robert Walker, the Raeburn skater whose picture graced for some years the walls of many McDonald's hamburger stands in the USA.[61] A fourth man, Alexander Fleming, seems to have been recommended by Adam Ferguson and perhaps Sir James Stuart Denham. Dundas picked Hugh Meiklejohn (1765–11 June 1831). He had the recommendation of the Earl of Hopetoun, who had already presented him to a church living. Hopetoun's letter to Lord Advocate Robert Dundas said of this nominee, his 'principles both religious & political are of the soundest kind – and his Zeal to be useful great.'[62] James Finlayson, the Edinburgh professor of logic and a stalwart Moderate, was named as a voucher for this. Hopetoun wanted Meiklejohn to keep his parish, which he did. Meiklejohn's pursuit of the place was thus helped by his disclaiming any interest in having either an Edinburgh church or a chaplaincy, which the first two men seemed to want. That meant Dundas was able to 'save' patronage for others at the cost of a little pluralism.[63] Such modest men usually had an edge but it also helped to have written a book recommending, as its title proclaimed, *Fidelity to the British Constitution* (1794).

None of the appointees to the ecclesiastical history chair after William Dunlop published anything of significance concerning ecclesiastical history, but all of them were useful to the politicians who appointed them. This chair, like its Glasgow counterpart, did not develop as Carstares had hoped it might. It became instead a near sinecure for clerical politicians and apologists for the status quo, and not a chair training men to justify a Calvinist version of the history of the church. Its career may be reflected in the decline in polemical and apologetic divinity which occurred under such secularists as Ilay and Dundas, a trend the Moderates did not curb but abetted.

4. ORIENTAL LANGUAGES

The last chair considered here is the professorship of oriental languages which, although an arts chair, was principally taken up with the teaching of Hebrew to theologues. The salaries of the Hebrew chairs in eighteenth-century Scotland ranged from £33 to £200, with the largest being paid at St Andrews University.[64] At Edinburgh the salary remained about £80 and was not supplemented by many student fees. Until the mid-century, it attracted few good scholars or willing teachers. Like the principalship and the professorships of divinity, its patronage was legally vested in the Town Council. Like the regents in philosophy, professors were supposed to be competitively tried before they were officially chosen and installed. Initially the post seems to have been controlled by the Edinburgh clerics, but it came to be managed by the politicians from around 1730. This reflects Lord Ilay's efforts to consolidate his power and to establish a stable and monopolising patronage system. This chair was used to reward deserving ministers, but until 1751 it was seldom a place for men of much distinction. This helps to explain the inadequate grounding in the scriptural languages which Scottish divinity students had throughout much of the century.

Its first incumbent, chosen in 1692 after a long vacancy, was Patrick Sinclair (?–?1694). He was the son of a sufferer in the days of Episcopacy who had been a witch-hunter but also a teacher of William Carstares.[65] In 1694, the third son of Principal Gilbert Rule, Alexander Rule (?–c. 1745), was chosen by his father, professor of divinity George Campbell, and the Edinburgh Presbytery. The latter tried his qualifications and saw him installed.[66] Having gone mad by 1701, Rule resigned and was succeeded by John Goodal (?–21 August 1719). Little is known of Goodal but he was said to have been one of three candidates, two of whom were found unqualified on trial.[67] One wonders if they were more unfit than Charles Morthland when he was appointed to the Glasgow chair a few years later.

In 1719, James Crawford, the professor of chemistry and medicine, acquired the chair which he seems to have been qualified to hold. He had been a divinity student at Glasgow and earlier had been recommended for the St Andrews University Hebrew chair. He probably wanted this one because he had few students, a small practice and found the study of Hebrew and other ancient languages diverting. He had the recommendation of the principal and professors. Crawford also campaigned, with a published broadside describing him as 'a Man of so extraordinary a Genius, [as] will not only teach, with Reputation, but prove a distinguishing Ornament to the *Jewish Learning* and Hebrew Language, which are too much neglected among us.'[68] His election was likely a test of the factional support of the Argathelians on the Town Council. He was opposed by George Drummond, then the Edinburgh Treasurer and, since 1715, an adherent to the Argathelian faction.[69] Crawford's family almost certainly had Squadrone connections. That he got the place may have been the most significant thing about his tenure of the chair.[70]

By 1731, this professorship had virtually ceased to be in the gift of the clergy and Town Council and was viewed as a virtual sinecure. Robert Wodrow noted that the place had been 'designed for principal Hamilton when principal' as an enhancement to his income.[71] When Hamilton died, it was sought by Dr Matthew Crawford, the professor of ecclesiastical history and by others. Crawford wanted to add it to his ecclesiastical history chair to increase his income but he had no recommendation from his colleagues. He had already failed as a teacher and had very few students. Robert Wodrow thought he taught only six or seven, partly because he would not give private courses without being paid extra by the divinity students who customarily were not charged for courses preparing them for the ministry. The Town Council was against him.[72] Others sought the place. Colonels John Campbell and John Middleton, both men close to Ilay, wrote to Lord Milton in 1731, with a copy to Ilay, saying:

> Mr [James] Crawford Professor of Hebrew in ye Colledge of Edr[,] Sallary 80 lb[,] is lately dead, the Office in the Gift of the Town Councll. There has been multitude of Applications and different Schemes, some for annexing it to the Office of principall & other's to the Professor of Ecclesiastical History, in order that your Lops may have time to consider what is proper to be done, the Town Councillors have adjourned the consideratn of that Matter till August nixt.[73]

Ilay went to Scotland in the following August and was in Edinburgh by the first week in September.[74] He almost certainly had the disposal of this place. The post was given to William Dawson (?–15 December 1753). Formerly a minister in Newcastle upon Tyne, he was then a minister of the West Kirk where he had been opposed by his colleague, Neil MacVicar, a high-flyer. Dawson was recommended as a moderate man to Ilay, Milton and Lord Provost Patrick Lindsay, one of their henchmen.[75] He held the post until 1751, treating it more or less as a sinecure. If he taught little, Ilay would at least have known how his vote would be cast in the Presbytery and the *Senatus*.[76]

By 1751 things had changed. Dawson, probably by then an elderly man, was forced out in 1751 and died two years later. The teaching of Hebrew was then more prized and there was a demand for better teaching. The divinity students even petitioned the Town Council for the appointment of James 'Rabbi' Robertson (1714–26 November 1795), whom the Edinburgh ministers recommended to the Council. There was also, perhaps, a commercial dimension to this appointment. Robertson seems to have been the first at Edinburgh to teach Arabic and Persian, languages of use to men going into the service of the East India Co.[77] That would have favourably impressed Argyll, who tended to appoint whenever he could men whose merits were displayed in more than one field. Robertson's trial in 1751 is memorable for an alleged quip by the Duke of Argyll, who is said to have attended it: 'I see Gentlemen you have conferred this office according to *Merit*. Pray do not make it a precedent.'[78] 'Rabbi' Robertson held the chair until his old age, when he accepted George Husband Baird as his conjoint and successor in 1792.[79]

Baird was a notable linguist but his father-in-law was, a cog in the Dundas political machine. He was Lord Provost when Baird was chosen for this post. Baird kept his place for only a year, being succeeded by William Moodie (2 July 1759–11 June 1812) in 1793. Moodie too could teach Persian and Arabic but he had been and continued to be useful to politicians. He preached and published sermons against the French Revolutionaries and their Scottish admirers. Dundas and his friends in the Kirk arranged for him to become Moderator in 1799.

The management of the Kirk and of its annual General Assembly were important for the government managers throughout the century. Religious matters, and those who dealt with them, simply could not be left to the Town Council, which might pick the 'unreliable' or 'hot brethren' or 'high-flyers' who would cause trouble because they were immune to management. Believing in their principles and in the will of God as they knew it, the overly orthodox despised both carrots and sticks and paid scant regard to those who offered them. Political managers had to be sure that they appointed docile, Erastian moralists. That policy in the long run caused a decline in the apologetic abilities of the Moderate clergy – and eventually schism in the Kirk – but the Town Council should not be held responsible for those. Few of the appointments were left to the Town Council, which expected to follow, and followed, the orders of its betters.

Notes

1 Dunlop, *William Carstares*, 1964, pp. 101–6. For a sympathetic evangelical account of Carstares, see Fawcett, *The Cambuslang Revival*, 1996. Everyone seems to have thought Carstares 'a great and a good man', as John Cunningham called him in *The Church History of Scotland*, 1859, II:369.

2 Carstares' portraits show his thumbs splayed by thumbscrews in 1684.

3 The Scottish reformers' visions of a complete school system were set out in *The First Book of Discipline* [ed. J. K. Cameron, 1972, pp. 58–60, 129–55], to which *The Second Book of Discipline* [ed. J. Kirk, 1980] added slightly, p. 84f.

4 A convenient précis of his ideas and work can be found in *A Source Book of Scottish History*, ed. Croft Dickinson and Donaldson, 1954, III:408–19.

5 One example of this is the creation of the ecclesiastical history chair in Edinburgh, which dates to c. 1702.

6 These are discussed in Mijers' unpublished dissertation, 'Scotland and the United Provinces, c. 1680–1730', Chapter 3.

7 NAS, SP 54/8/120; see also M. A. Stewart, 'William Wishart', ODNB, 55:863f.

8 The best account of the political involvements of Hamilton and his contemporaries is given by Shaw, *Management of Scottish Society*, 1983, p. 100ff.

9 The moderatorship was the highest and most lucrative position in the Kirk, which men held usually once for a one-year term. On Hamilton's work as Moderator, see Wodrow, *Analecta*, ed. Leishman, 1853, IV:96, 101, 104, 138, 140, 260.

10 Shaw, *Management of Scottish Society*, 1983, pp. 98–107. Shaw gives many more references to the various appointments of James Smith, William Hamilton, John Gowdie, Patrick Cuming and William Wishart II, and shows how these related to the management of the Kirk by Lord Ilay and his friends. They were concerned to secure control of the General Assembly to keep the church and its members quiescent.

11 Archibald Campbell to Andrew Fletcher, Lord Milton, 25 May 1730, Saltoun Correspondence, NLS, 16542/107.

12 Milton to Ilay, n.d., NLS, 16547/176–9; see the life of him by L. A. B. Whiteley, ODNB, 51:185.

13 Skoczylas, *Mr Simson's Knotty Case*, 2001, p. 331.

14 Ibid.

15 Ilay to Milton, n.d. [1736] NLS, 16564/148.

16 George Wishart to Lord Milton, 4 September 1736, NLS, 16568/180; Ilay to Milton, 1 September 1736, NLS, 16564/115; Milton to Ilay, n.d, NLS, 16564/148ff.

17 There are succinct accounts of his career by M. A. Stewart, 'Principal Wishart', *Records of the Scottish Church history Society*, 2000, pp. 60–102, and in the ODNB, 55:864–6.

18 Gowdie seems to have been Ilay's second choice in 1733, but he was ranked ahead of James Alston in 1736. Ilay to Milton, 1 April 1736, NLS, 16564/115; Milton to Ilay, n.d. [1733], NLS, 16547/176–9.

19 Lachman, *The Marrow Controversy*, 1988, pp. 159ff, 343; Drummond and Bulloch, *The Scottish Church*, 1973, p. 41.

20 He taught the Ten Commandments not as convicting men of sin, but as a guide to living. *Memoirs of the Life of Thomas Boston*, ed. Morrison, 1899, p. 274.

21 Shaw, *Management of Scottish Society*, 1983, p. 103.

22 Quoted in Emerson, 'Lord Bute and the Scottish Universities', in *Lord Bute*, ed. Schweizer, 1988, p. 157ff.

23 George Stuart to Gilbert Elliot, 20 February 1762, Minto Papers, NLS, 11016/13. Stuart succeeded George Drummond as Lord Provost in 1764.

24 Robertson's polite accomplishments were not irrelevant because the University, or rather those concerned with it, were then trying in other ways to become more fashionable. One move in that direction was the establishment of 'an Academy of Riding' in which 'young Gentlemen will be initiated in the principles of useful Knowledge and at the same time exercised in all those liberal accomplishments which qualify a man to appear in the distinguished spheres of life.' Allan Ramsay II to Sir Alexander Cunningham Dick, 31 January 1762, Papers of Sir Alexander Dick, NAS, GD331/5/19.

25 Until Jeffery Smitten's collected correspondence and life of Robertson appear, the best sources on his appointment are: Sher, *Church and University*, 1985, pp. 93–119; Jeremy Cater, 'The Making of Principal Robertson', *Scottish Historical Review*, 1970, pp. 60–84; Brown, 'William Robertson (1721–1793) and the Scottish Enlightenment', in *William Robertson*, ed. Brown, 1997, pp. 7–35. These list more studies of particular professors and principals.

26 Blair denied that he had sought the place but then said he believed he had 'the voice of the Public' and his colleagues. Blair to [?], 18 March 1795; 18 July 1795, Lee MSS, NLS, 3431/232f, 234.

27 Fry, *Dundas Despotism*, 1992, p. 184.

28 See the entries on Baird in Kay, *A Series of Original Portraits*, ed. Paton, 1877, II:412–15.

29 *Moderators of the Church of Scotland*, compiled by Warrick, 1913, pp. 92–112.

30 *Memoirs of Boston*, ed. Morrison, 1899, p. 164. In 1706 he helped the government by arguing that the Kirk should not oppose the Union. Dunlop, *Carstares*, 1964, p. 116.

31 Skoczylas, *Mr Simson's Knotty Case*, 2001, p. 96.

32 *Moderators of the Church of Scotland*, compiled by Warrick, 1913, pp. 240–57; his theological position seems not unlike that of John Simson as presented by Skoczylas in *Mr Simson's Knotty Case*, 2001.

33 Meldrum had pleaded for clemency to Thomas Aikenhead. Michael Hunter, ' "Aikenhead the Atheist" ', in *Atheism from the Reformation to the Enlightenment*, ed. Hunter and Wootton, 1992, pp. 221–54, 234. After Aikenhead's hanging, Principal Rule had the 'atheistic' books of the College locked up in a college attic. In 1703, the Town Council decreed they were only to be taken out to be read only with their warrant; *Extracts from the Records of the Burgh of Edinburgh 1701–1718*, ed. Armet, 1967, p. 49.

34 Skoczylas, *Mr Simson's Knotty Case*, 2001, p. 97.

35 Henry Sefton, 'William Hamilton', in DSCHT, p. 391.

36 John Ramsay of Ochtertyre, Ochtertyre MSS, NLS, 1635/1324f.

37 'Memoirs of the Reverend John Brand', NLS, 1668.

38 Argyll to Lord Milton, 15 January 1754, NLS, 16685/131; Hew Dalrymple to Milton, 1 December 1715, NLS, 16682/151; D. B. Horn, 'Manuscript History of Edinburgh University', EUL, Gen 1824, 'Divinity', p. 23. Hamilton's lectures were based on the works of Benedict Pictet, but he also gave the students some biblical criticism, criticism of their writing and speaking styles and 'exhibited favourable evidence of his temper, liberality and good taste'. Somerville, *My Own Life*, p. 18.

39 Balfour-Melville, *The Balfours of Pilrig*, 1907, p. 131f.

40 Robert Hamilton to Milton, 8 October 1754, NLS, 16688/13.

41 Kay, *Portraits*, 1877, I:298–302. Later, Hunter Blair kept his seat with the assistance of Henry Dundas, to whom his allegiance shifted after Sir Lawrence died in 1781. Henry Dundas made the banker Lord Provost in 1784.

42 Dunlop, *Carstares*, 1964, p. 105, n.3.

43 Carstares had hoped as early as 6 July 1710 to get such a chair for a nephew, either Andrew or William Dunlop. He reminded his friend, Principal Stirling of Glasgow, that his nephew still wanted 'that post secured to him with you which [the professor of ecclesiastical history] Mr Cummin hath with us and I doubt not but he will fitt himself for it.' Carstares to Stirling, Stirling Letters, GUL, Gen 204/3/113.

44 William Carstares to William Dunlop, 13 January 1715, quoted in Story, *William Carstares*, 1874, p. 361; EUL, Gen 1824, miscellaneous notes and 'Ecclesiastical history', p. 4; William Scott to James Anderson, 2 December 1714 and 5 March 1715, Anderson Papers, NLS, Adv.MS 29.1.2/180–3.

45 Historians often had legal training. This familiarised them with feudal documents and the means of interpreting them. Humanistically trained civilians had imbibed a view of the Roman law evolving over time in response to changing manners and other conditions. This disposed them to historical work. As clerics looking neither to Rome nor Canterbury, they were also sensitive to issues of national honor.

46 What there is on and by Dunlop is noticed by D. F. Wright in DSCHT, p. 264f.

47 Quoted in Sunter, *Patronage and Politics in Scotland*, 1986, p. 73; *The House of Commons 1715–1754*, ed. Sedgwick, 1970, I:401f.

48 Milton to Ilay, March 1731, NLS, 16547/169.

49 Wodrow, *Analecta*, ed. Leishman, 1853, IV:212.

50 He is probably the 'Mr Crauford' who sought the Glasgow chair of history in 1718 and who is described by William Dunlop as a 'servt. of the Chancellor' of Glasgow University, James Graham, 1st Duke of Montrose, one of the Squadrone leaders; Letters of Andrew and William Dunlop, GUL, Gen 83.29.

51 *Memoirs of Boston*, ed. Morrison, 1899, p. 288.

52 EUL, Gen 1824, 'Ecclesiastical History', p. 6; Milton to Ilay, 11 November 1736, NLS, 16564/98.
53 Robert Laurie to Erskine, 29 May 1739, Erskine-Murray Papers, NLS, 5074/144.
54 Henry Sefton, 'Patrick Cuming', in DSCHT, p. 227.
55 John Ramsay of Ochtertyre, *Scotland and Scotsmen in the Eighteenth Century*, ed. Allardyce, 1888, I:250–4. See also Ochtertyre MSS, NLS, 1635/1/344 and 1635/2/58. Ramsay's view of him is shared by Whiteley, his biographer in ODNB, 14:626f. Whiteley stressed his conciliatory nature, his success as a politician and his willingness to see clerical stipends raised in 1749 and after. At the same time, he noted that he was totally dependent upon Ilay's support of him for his power.
56 *Letters of John Ramsay of Ochtertyre 1799–1812*, ed. Horn, 1966, p. 34.
57 Professor George Stuart to Gilbert Elliot, MP, 20 February 1762, Minto Papers, NLS, 11016/13.
58 Bower, *History of the University of Edinburgh*, 1830, III:273.
59 Fry, *Dundas Despotism*, 1992, p. 184; Thomas Hardy to Henry Dundas, 11 April 1793, EUL, La. II.500.
60 Robert Dundas to Henry Dundas, 24 November 1798, Dundas Papers, NLS, 6/222; Scott, *Fasti*, III:443; Strang, *Glasgow and Its Clubs*, 1864, p. 302f.
61 Robert Walker to Henry Dundas, 24 December 1798, Melville Castle Muniments, NAS, GD51/6/1303.
62 Lord Hopetoun to Robert Dundas, Lord Advocate, 10 January 1799, EUL, La. II.500/1773.
63 Hopetoun to Dundas, 23 November 1798, Melville Castle Muniments, NAS, GD51/6/1287.
64 The total income of the professors was greater since they collected 'diet money', perquisites and some fees.
65 Dalzel, *History of Edinburgh University*, ed. Laing, 1862, I:237.
66 Ibid., II:249; Town Council Minutes, 2 February 1695.
67 Bower, *History of the University of Edinburgh*, 1817, I:12.
68 *A Memorial Concerning Doctor Crawford*, Edinburgh, 1719; NLS, Pamphlet Series 1.10.158.
69 Bower, *History*, 1817, I:12.
70 Wodrow, *Analecta*, ed. Leishman, 1853, IV:212.
71 He might also have seen this as a way of restoring some teaching to the principal.
72 Wodrow, *Analecta*, ed. Leishman, 1853, IV:212.
73 Cols John Campbell and John Middleton to Milton, NLS, 16547/169.
74 This comes from a life of the 3rd Duke which I have been preparing.
75 John Nisbet to Lord Milton, 12 July 1732, NLS, 16551/15.

76 Dawson's father-in-law, John Keir, was a sometime Convener of the Trades and a member of the Town Council; Lorimer, *The Days of Neil M'Vicar*, 1926, p. 94.

77 This may be because he had so little custom from the divinity students, who, according to Thomas Somerville, 'little cultivated, or altogether omitted' Hebrew classes. Somerville had better things to say about the other teachers at Edinburgh from 1756 until the early 1760s. Somerville, *My Own Life*, 1861, p. 18.

78 The story is related by Ramsay of Ochtertyre [NLS, MS 16351/2/10] and is not wholly unlikely. Argyll was something of a linguist able to read perhaps eight languages [in order of fluency, English, Latin, Greek, French, Spanish, Italian, Dutch and German]. Hebrew was an arts course in his time and it is conceivable that he might have picked up some Hebrew. His sense of humour was such that the remark is plausible. Robertson had studied at Oxford and Leyden, which would have recommended him to his lordship, who tended to favour Leyden men. See also Cater, 'James Robertson, 1720–1795', unpublished PhD dissertation, 1976.

79 There had been a request on 28 June 1791 from Robert Jackson to Henry Dundas to split the chair into one of Arabic and Persian, for those who wished to learn languages useful in trade or imperial service, and another teaching biblical languages useful to ministers: Melville Castle Muniments, NAS, GD51/6/898.

10

CHAIRS OF INTEREST TO LAWYERS

1. HUMANITY

The arts faculty was for a long time principally constituted by five regents. The junior member of this group, the humanist, taught humanity or Latin; the rest taught all the other subjects studied by arts students – Greek, philosophy and, before there was a mathematics professor, mathematics. Scottish lawyers had long taken a special interest in the teaching of Latin because their classes were given in Latin. The professors on the continent, where Scots lawyers generally trained before the 1730s, also taught background courses on Roman history, which was useful to those studying civil law. These courses were given in Latin.[1] The lawyers asserted their interest in the humanist's post by providing an endowment for it in 1597. This led to the creation of a body nominating candidates for this chair. It was composed of a Writer to the Signet, an advocate, two Lords of Session, and two town councillors. The Town Council picked men from the leet this committee presented to it. After 1690, humanists were to be appointed by the Town Council only after trial by their future colleagues. For some years the trials were real. Several men sometimes competed and the man with the highest grade in the 'comparative trial' won the job. This gave the professors who served as judges some purchase. They were not the only ones to be involved, since the town ministers also sometimes served as judges and had the right to ascertain the orthodoxy and morals of the candidates for all the chairs and to advise on all appointments. Appeal from their decisions lay to the courts of the Kirk and to the civil courts. In 1690, the Edinburgh regent of humanity was elevated in status to become equal to the other regents, although in precedence he was still ranked lower than the regents of philosophy and did not receive as high a salary. His fees were probably as great since he taught about 50–70 students.

Lawrence Dundas (c. 1668–c. 1740) was tried by the professors and regents along with four others in 1690 and came first. He was appointed for five years but in fact remained until 1728, when he resigned. Dundas had tried to resign in 1725, stipulating that his successor should be an unnamed member of the Faculty of Advocates. The Faculty refused to accept this arrangement.[2] Two years later, Adam Watt (c. 1706–30 March 1734), the son of the Edinburgh Town Clerk, was tried after the Town Council and the lawyers agreed to appoint him conjoint professor of humanity with Dundas if he were found qualified – which he was.[3] Watt had probably trained as a writer or solicitor. He taught for fees, while the salary went to Dundas as retirement income. When Watt died before Dundas in 1734, another conjoint appointment had to be made. The Faculty of Advocates again insisted that whoever received the place should continue to assign the salary to Dundas. Four people seem to have been in contention for the post.

Watt's deputy tried to secure the place but found no important backers. Three classicists teaching elsewhere were then sounded.

Sir John Clerk of Penicuik, a political dependant of the Marquis of Queensberry, tried, but failed, to interest Thomas Blackwell II in this post.[4] Blackwell was the professor of Greek at Marischal College and a man familiar with literary circles in London. He had been eager to make a literary reputation as, indeed, he did, but he was unwilling to take this chair.

Other lawyers offered it to Francis Pringle, professor of Greek at St Leonard's College, St Andrews University. He was a good teacher but not an unimpeachable Calvinist. For him were David Scot of Scotstarvit, Sir Walter Pringle, Lord Newhall, SCJ; Lord Provost Patrick Lindsay and 'other men of power'.[5] Scotstarvit was then in opposition to the government;[6] Newhall had been a Squadrone supporter; Lindsay was an Argathelian. Politicians could cooperate to secure the best man available to train future lawyers, a consideration for them all. That was the principle allegedly followed in appointments to the law chairs. Pringle, like Blackwell, declined the unsolicited offer made to him, so the University failed to get an accomplished, urbane man who was also a musician.

The chair finally went to John Ker (?–20 October 1741), the professor of Greek at King's College, Aberdeen, who was translated without a trial. This was customary when a man was already teaching in a university. To have tried him would have been to insult King's College, since it would have implied that his ability to teach was questionable. Ker had many Edinburgh friends because he had been a master in the High School c. 1710, a place also in the gift of the

Council. With him the city secured a first-rate classicist, one of the last of the eminent Scots Latin poets, and a teacher respected by Jacobites, Whigs, Episcopalians and Presbyterians, in fact by men of all factions who wanted their boys to be well taught. The lawyers had looked for and found excellence but it is curious that they had to raid other colleges to get it. Again, the Town Council did not make the choice but ratified a choice made for it by others.

In 1741, Ker died and an appointment committee was struck. It named George Stuart of Midlum Mill (August 1711–18 June 1793) and Sir James Foulis. The former was backed by the judges and advocates, including Lords Milton and Minto. Thomas Ruddiman, the learned librarian of the Faculty of Advocates and the author of a notable Latin grammar, was also vocal in support for Stuart.[7] The Town Council votes were split, while the Writers to the Signet wanted Foulis, who was described as 'the popular candidate'.[8] The University professors preferred Robert Hunter (c. 1703–27 May 1779), who had been deputising for the recently dead incumbent, but he was not really in contention. Lord Milton, speaking for the judges, insisted on a trial which was not carried out because the two contenders, in an unprecedented move, each held the other sufficiently or equally well qualified. When the vote was held, Stuart won. Principal Wishart protested that no trial had taken place and this was not to become a precedent. By then, William Scott, the Greek professor, had died and the professors could be placated by giving his chair to Hunter.[9] The Council once more endorsed settlements made for it by others.

In 1775, the humanist's chair went to John Hill of Kinglassie (27 April 1747–7 December 1805), the St Andrews humanist, who made a retirement deal with George Stuart after Robert (later Sir Robert) Liston had decided not to buy out Stuart for £500, which seems to have been his asking price.[10] This presumed that Stuart or his purchaser had the influence to move the Council to give its permission for a transaction which was not at all uncommon in other Scottish universities but was somewhat uncommon in Edinburgh, where the University men could generally not effect such arrangements until later in the century. In this case, both Stuart and Liston were protégés of the Elliots of Minto. Hill was related by marriage to a number of prominent Moderate clerics at St Andrews.[11] He was not tried because he was a sitting professor. That the chair was sold shows how little the Town Council counted in this transaction.

The provision for trials in the five appointments to this chair resulted in only one real trial – that of 1690. In every other case this chair was filled by what were in effect patronage negotiations among men looking after their own. Among these men, the advocates were the most important on the committees that drew up the leets. Having found a competent classicist, the lawyers then got the city fathers to appoint him.

2. Universal and Civil History and Roman Antiquities

The story was somewhat different in another chair, which the lawyers did not deem crucial to their success in the practice of the law. That was the chair of universal and civil history and Roman antiquities created in 1719 by the Town Council, which came in time to fill it by choosing from a leet provided by the Faculty of Advocates.

The idea for such a chair went back at least to 1688, when the draft for a new University charter called for the creation of a history chair. Nothing came of that, although one might have expected the town's antiquaries to have been much in favour of it.[12] In 1691, Principal Rule 'proposed to the masters to recommend Dolhulsius a German to be ordinary professor of historie & politicks & extraordinary professor of theologie in this Coledge'.[13] Principal Rule and regents Law, Massie and Cunningham were for it but it was opposed by the professor of mathematics, David Gregorie, by the humanist, Lawrence Dundas, and by Hew Kennedy. Those opposed had personal interests in history. Gregorie seems even to have collected old Scottish manuscripts. Rule's proposal went nowhere.

The idea was kept alive in Edinburgh not only by divines but by lawyers who had an interest in the teaching of civil history as a background to Roman law or the laws of their own nation. In Edinburgh, the first surviving indication that the subject was formally taught is found in the 1704 teaching regime of John Spottiswoode, who gave extramural law courses in the city. He expected his students to have a knowledge of history and appointed a teacher to instruct them in Roman history as a background to his civil law courses.[14] In 1707, another sign of interest came when Sir David Nairne, Mar's secretary, wrote to William Carstares that a professorship of history was 'Not Convenient at this time'.[15] Carstares, who had likely arranged one for the clerics, now sought one for the lawyers and others. The timing suggests he was also trying to get a bit more from the government for the University before the Union with England. There were doubtless too many good projects to be funded before the official end of the independent and separate Scottish state to allow a history chair to be founded. Edinburgh waited from 1688 until 1718 for such a chair to be created. At Glasgow William Jameson had one in 1692. In the meantime, several men taught history extramurally from 1711 to 1717, thus satisfying the demands of the lawyers and keeping alive the idea that the University needed a history chair.[16]

In 1716, Edinburgh Town Council was given an ale duty, part of which was to be used to pay the professor of civil law, to whom a grant was made in 1717.[17] In August 1718, the Council chose to make money from this source available to Charles Mackie (31 March 1688–1770), then a travelling tutor who had spent time at Groningen (1707–8), Utrecht (?) and Leiden (1715–19).[18] Mackie had been brought up for some time in the household of Principal Carstares, his uncle by marriage. This is not irrelevant to his appointment. Carstares was interested in history,[19] owned many history books,[20] made his brother-in-law, William Dunlop, Historiographer Royal in Scotland (1693), and may have helped secure the ecclesiastical history chair for Glasgow University. He certainly intended to have history taught in Edinburgh University as it was in Holland. There it was taught in the faculties of arts, law and divinity.[21] The Town Council's creation of this chair reflected past interests in the subject by divines, lawyers and others.

Mackie was a polite man who had been seeking a professorship since at least 1716, when Colin Drummond wrote to him to return home from Holland because jobs were to be had owing to the purge of Jacobites who had taught in colleges before the rebellion of 1715.[22] Mackie had attended Dutch law and history lectures with the boys he had in charge. He and they heard some of the notable Dutch professors of history such as Michael Rossal and Pieter Burman. The fathers of the boys with whom he travelled belonged to the Squadrone interest which was then in power in the country as a whole and by 1718–19 had a good chance of controlling the Edinburgh Town Council, although in the end it failed to do so.[23] The most prominent of the men whose sons Mackie tutored were Lord Leven and the Marquis of Tweeddale.[24] They, along with Carstares' old friend, John Leslie, 8th Earl of Rothes, were his most likely sponsors for the new chair. Mackie's family had long been tied to these men and his Fifeshire forebears had been patronised by the families of Leslie and Melville. Indeed, it was Rothes in 1716 whom Colin Drummond told Mackie would secure a living for him were he to come home. Although the Edinburgh Lord Provost was a Campbell, power had been shifting away from the Argathelians and they could probably not have affected this choice which again seems to have not been made by the Town Council.

Mackie's original appointment in 1720 was as professor of universal history, but in 1722 he was given a new commission as 'professor of Universall Civill History and the History of Scotland in particular and of Greek[,] Roman and British Antiquities'– a grant wide enough to satisfy the most ambitious. For teaching all that, he was given £100 plus his fees.[25] His chair was an arts chair but most of his students were boys intending to become lawyers mixed with a few others who were generally to become ministers. His income from his post in good years would have been about £150, to which he usually added more derived from the keeping of students.[26] Mackie's income for a year from all sources was perhaps £200, a very good academic income. No professor holding the chair until the 1780s is likely to have equalled this academic income. By 1799 the chair carried a salary of £166.

After Mackie's appointment, the Faculty of Advocates gained control of the nominations for this place and tended to use it to take care of well-connected junior members of the Faculty, men who had an interest in history and who seemed in need of steady employment. The advocates' control rested on the 1722 Act of Parliament which gave them rights of nomination to the chair of history and to the two law chairs whose incumbents were picked by the Town. The Faculty of Advocates was in each case to present a leet of two, from which the Town Council was to appoint one.

Things did not go quite as they should have gone. When Mackie wanted to retire in 1753 he tried to name his successor, but was told that a leet was necessary for his reappointment with a conjoint professor. This presented no problems to inventive men. Mackie picked an advocate, John Gordon of Buthlaw (? May 1715–? July 1775), and the Faculty approved the name of a second man, James Hamilton, who would not serve. The Town had the required two names but was deprived of its right to make a real decision.[27] This was followed by a slightly more sordid transaction in 1755 when the chair was given to another young and impecunious advocate, William Wallace of Cairnhill (c. 1732–28 December 1786).

Before 10 June 1754, Mackie's old student Alexander Boswell, who in the following year would be made Lord Auchinleck, SCJ, was managing a deal with Mackie and the Faculty to get the job for Wallace. This involved seeking the support of Auchinleck's Ayrshire neighbour, the Earl of Loudoun, a Campbell in Argyll's camp.

Loudoun was to write to Lord Milton asking for the support of both Milton and Argyll. Milton wanted his son promoted to the rank of major; a majority was on offer in Loudoun's regiment. Everything seems to have been worked out to the satisfaction of the principals by the time Mackie wrote to the Town Council on 2 December 1754 asking them to allow Wallace to succeed to the conjoint appointment. To ensure that nothing went wrong, Ilay Campbell, another young advocate, was also nominated. He probably promised not to accept the post should it be offered.[28] All that may not really have been necessary since Wallace was in 1754 an Assessor to the Edinburgh Magistrates. He would later become Sheriff of Ayr and an undistinguished Keeper of the Advocates' Library.[29]

In 1764, the now-familiar drill was repeated. The new conjoint professor was John Pringle (25 November 1741–14 February 1811). Pringle induced Mackie to write to the Town Council asking for a colleague. The Faculty sent up two names, of whom one, William Baillie, would not serve. Pringle was accepted.[30] Mackie finally retired altogether in 1767, leaving Pringle as the sole holder of the chair.

In 1780, Pringle sought a colleague and found one in Alexander Fraser Tytler (15 October 1747–5 January 1813), who is said to have obtained the post through the favour of Henry Home, Lord Kames.[31] Tytler held the place until 1800, at which time Dundas allowed his old friend's son, William Fraser Tytler (10 September 1777–4 September 1853), to succeed.[32] William Fraser Tytler remained the nominal professor until 1821, when he resigned.[33] He was not a diligent teacher but, toward the end of his tenure, he did allow his younger brother, Patrick (30 August 1791–24 December 1849), to lecture in his place. Patrick was a good historian who produced a history of Scotland from c. 1240–1603 resting on what then passed for critically evaluated sources. Few did more for Scottish history in the early nineteenth century than this now-neglected man.

Others had tried for the place Tytler got. The reverend John Logan was apparently encouraged to seek the post by some of the University men, including Principal Robertson and professors Hugh Blair and Thomas Hardy. Logan had other friends among the prominent literati such as Adam Smith and Alexander Carlyle.[34] Logan gave extramural lectures in 1779 at St Mary's Chapel but he did not get the Faculty's nod. His biographer said it was because, 'It had been the invariable practice of the patrons to present a member of the Faculty of Advocates.'[35] That also excluded Gilbert Stuart, the turbulent son of the humanist George Stuart, who would have had the backing of the political faction headed in Edinburgh by Sir Lawrence Dundas and perhaps that of the Elliots of Minto.[36]

The appointments to the chairs of humanity and history are interesting in several ways. First, the politicians who counted nationally tended to leave the Faculty of Advocates to act as it saw fit with regard to the chair it had endowed but also to the history chair. They also tended to do that in the patronage of the law chairs where the leets could be, and sometimes were, arranged in the same manner but with consequences of more interest to the lawyers. Second, the history chair, after Mackie left off teaching, was seen as a stepping stone to something else, not as a place of importance in itself. Gordon secured a law chair and vacated his history profession. Wallace kept his post for a decade, surrendering it to become a law professor. Pringle, in effect, resigned in 1780 to become Sheriff of Stirling. Alexander Fraser Tytler quit because he was to be made a Lord of Session in 1802. His successor, William Fraser Tytler of Balnain, gave over lecturing to sit as a judge in Inverness and to practise law in Edinburgh. These professors were thinking more about advancement in the law than academic distinction. None of them save the Tytlers were men with literary reputations or notable as teachers. The lawyers used the chairs to take care of lawyers, with the consequence that the history chair became almost a sinecure.

There was perhaps another reason for the decline of the chair. There was a clear shift in historical interests among lawyers from Roman and ancient history to Scottish history.[37] As Scots law developed during the eighteenth century, it oriented itself more toward England and less toward Rome and the continental countries. English and British history became of greater interest. This change can be most clearly seen in the teaching of John Millar at Glasgow. His original work in historical jurisprudence centred on post-Roman European developments, but his later work was on English constitutional history. This downplayed universal and Roman history, which were now served by more and better textbooks than had existed when Mackie began teaching. The history which mattered most was British history and, for men who were North British in outlook, that meant not paying as much attention to ancient and universal history which included large dollops of ecclesiastical history. Edinburgh University was to become important for science and medicine but not for historical studies. Finally, although the town's taxes paid for the post, the town had after the first appointment no say about the men who held this office in the town's University. It also does not seem to have cared.

3. THE LAW CHAIRS

Good Latin and some history were among the desiderata set out by lawyers when they thought about the education of lawyers. Those subjects had been on the mind of Sir George Mackenzie, the founder of the Advocates' Library, and of John Spottiswoode who had taught extramurally in the city.[38] After 1708, the lawyers were interested in the chairs actually teaching law – public law or the law of nature and of nations, civil law and canon law. Those chairs had rather different careers.

4. PUBLIC LAW

The public law chair was created by the Crown on 11 February 1707. It was designed to supply a felt need among those who wanted to see a polite and complete law programme taught in the city.[39] Teaching natural law and the law of nations was teaching material used in legal arguments presented in Scottish courts. In more cynical terms, it was a scheme concocted in 1706 by regent William Scott to get some of the money provided by Queen Anne's Bounty for himself and for his friend, Charles Erskine (1680–5 April 1763), then another regent[40] (see below, p. 335). Scott wanted £50 as a salary for his Greek professorship, which was not well paid (see Appendix 1). He believed Erskine might get £100 for himself as a professor of public law. Such things seemed possible, as many raided the treasury prior to the ending of Scotland's independence. Erskine was to approach 'his friends at Court', mainly his relative, John Erskine, the Earl of Mar, who would do their business. As an earlier historian of the affair noted, it recognised 'the active part which his connections had taken in regard to the union of the two Kingdoms'.[41] Mar was willing to help and enlisted the aid of the other Secretary of State, Hugh Campbell, 3rd Earl of Loudoun, and of the Queen's Commissioner to Parliament, James Douglas, 2nd Duke of Queensberry, Erskine's original patron.[42] That put three powerful family connections behind the scheme. Despite opposition from the Town Council, the chair was created by a royal warrant and Erskine received a commission as its first incumbent. He was admitted on 13 November 1707.[43] Erskine managed to do well for himself but Scott was left with nothing but 'a bare letter without a sallary' – that is, a letter appointing him as an unfunded regius professor. He got only his hoped-for title, since Erskine never gave him any of his salary as Scott believed he would do.[44]

Erskine had not qualified as a lawyer when he was appointed but he had been teaching moral philosophy and so was not quite as unprepared as his lack of a qualification in law might suggest. Because his pay did not start for some time, he, like Charles Morthland at Glasgow at about the same time, went off to Leiden to study what he was to teach.[45] He passed advocate in 1711 after two or three years in Holland. Erskine may have taught for only one year but he kept the post until 1734.

By 1734, Erskine, although only a sinecure professor, had become a good lawyer, an MP, Solicitor-General and, after c. 1724, one of the chief aides of Lord Ilay in the management of the kingdom. He had no trouble getting permission from the Crown managers, Ilay and Milton, to sell his place to a long-time protégé and future son-in-law, William Kirkpatrick of Shaws and Allisland (1705–22 May 1778).[46] Erskine may have been encouraged to do so since selling created one more place for his friends to bestow in an election year. The placing of Kirkpatrick also aided Ilay in his quest for the Dumfries parliamentary seats. Kirkpatrick bought the chair at about five years' purchase for £1,000 with the blessings of the Lord Advocate, Duncan Forbes. Kirkpatrick may have wanted a judicial post. When he got one in 1738, he sold the chair for £1,000 to George Abercromby of Tullibody (1705–8 June 1800). This may have been partly motivated by Ilay's electioneering in Dumfriesshire and Perthshire.[47] The sale had been managed by Charles Erskine and Lord Milton, who would not have acted without the approval of Ilay who customarily made the arrangements for the transfer of regius chairs in London.

Abercromby held the chair for twenty-four years, giving private lectures on Grotius's *de Jure Belli ac Pacis* from the late 1730s to the early 1750s.[48] By then the chair had become principally a means of rewarding a useful lawyer whose needs could not be met with legal patronage of another sort. Those who hoped that the University would teach jurisprudence did try to ensure this with schemes to appoint a philosopher when the chair was next for 'sale'.

In 1758, David Hume, John Jardine and some of their friends devised a complex scheme to provide a professorship for Adam Ferguson. Adam Smith was to buy this chair from Abercromby and vacate his moral philosophy professorship at Glasgow. Ferguson was to take that, whose worth was estimated at £130 a year. Abercromby was asked by Lord Milton if he would sell and for how much. His price proved too high.[49] There was politics involved in this transaction, since in 1759 Abercromby disposed of the chair to his son-in-law,

Robert Bruce (24 December 1718–8 April 1785). Bruce was a brother-in-law of Sir Lawrence Dundas, MP, an enemy of the Argathelians. Dundas is likely to have arranged for this appointment in London. Bruce lectured regularly to large classes[50] but he surrendered his place upon being made a Lord of Session in 1764.[51]

It was then secured by James Balfour of Pilrig (1705–6 March 1795) who gave up his posts as professor of moral philosophy and Sheriff-Substitute of Edinburgh.[52] This transaction was also part of an elaborate plan to provide for Adam Ferguson. He took the moral philosophy chair which Balfour had filled. James Russel took the natural philosophy post then held by Ferguson.[53] Russel was thought to have supplied part of the money with which Balfour was bought out. The public law chair was thus treated as patronage bestowed in lieu of a judgeship or other place worth about £200 a year. Balfour probably did not lecture. When Balfour sold out in 1779, his price was the less dignified, but more lucrative, post of Procurator-Fiscal to the Commissary Court of Edinburgh.[54]

The purchaser of the chair was Allan Maconochie of Meadowbank (26 January 1748–14 June 1816), a relative of Principal Robertson and friend of Henry Dundas, who rewarded him for legal and political support given during Dundas's attempts to repeal disabilities on Roman Catholics in Scotland.[55] Maconochie paid £1,500 for the post and lectured even after he came to hold judgeships. His lectures changed the nature of the material taught from a Grotian and rational approach to natural law to a Smithian emphasis on the historical evolution of law now seen as based in the feelings and the development of social institutions. This mirrored what John Millar was doing in Glasgow.[56]

In 1796 Maconochie sold the chair to Robert Hamilton (19 April 1763–13 December 1831). That sale was arranged by Henry and Robert Dundas, Lord Advocate.[57] Hamilton may never have taught, although classes by him were advertised in some years.

Sir Alexander Grant thought this professorship originated in the idealism of Carstares who would have had the subject taught as it was in Holland, but it was something of a boondoggle from the start.[58] Only three of its incumbents – Abercromby, Bruce and Maconochie – lectured for any period of time. The post was used in lieu of judicial offices to reward young lawyers belonging to the faction which dispensed patronage for the Crown in Scotland. At best it gave a place to 'deserving' young men and thus helped in the political management of the kingdom; at worst it wasted money which would have better spent on other things. Too convenient for the politicians to abolish, it lasted for about a century as a chair almost useless to students interested in the subject. This was not the fault of the Town Council, which had nothing to do with appointments to this chair, whose establishment it had opposed. The councillors only admitted men to office once they had secured the Crown's warrant.

5. CIVIL LAW

The civil law chair was very different because it actually trained lawyers and required a bright, conscientious, able man who wanted to teach. This did not eliminate all political considerations but politics seems not to have been the decisive determinant of who got this place. When the Town Council established the unfunded chair, it went to a successful extramural law teacher in Edinburgh, James Craig (1672–14 August 1732).[59] He was descended from a long line of Scots lawyers going back to Sir Thomas Craig, the great legal writer who served James VI. When James Craig was nominated by Principal Carstares in 1710, he was one of several men who were teaching law in Edinburgh during those years.[60] They are described by John Cairns but with no indication that there was a contest for the chair. It is likely there was since several of the other men had powerful patrons. For various reasons, the others were all more or less ineligible. In 1715, Craig was raised in status, if that is the right phrase, by being named by the Crown to be professor of civil and canon law. His elevation was secured by Carstares and the Duke of Montrose.[61] This made Craig a regius professor and gave him security of tenure for life (which he had previously lacked), thus making him the equal of the Glasgow professor of law who held a regius chair. Craig taught until he died in 1732.[62]

Craig was followed by Thomas Dundas (26 April 1706–25 December 1784), who won the post in a field of at least six.[63] Lord Ilay chose not to interfere in the appointment, perhaps thinking he would gain more respect and gratitude from the advocates by allowing them to act freely.[64] Advocates belonging to his faction backed Dundas but he was also supported by the Squadrone leader, the Marquis of Tweeddale.[65] Both sides believed he was the best man but he himself became a partisan who later served Tweeddale as an informant on affairs in the University which the Marquis tried to manage.

In 1745, when Kenneth Mackenzie (4 September 1699–13 August 1756) bought the place from Dundas for £1,000, the chair went to a known Squadrone man from a Jacobite family who was opposed by Argathelians. In 1745, the Squadrone was struggling to secure a firm hold on Scottish politics and patronage but Ilay, now 3rd Duke of Argyll, was out of power and had been for three years.[66] The leet sent to the Town Council contained the names of Mackenzie and Alexander Boswell. They had been unanimously chosen but the leet was carried up to the Town Council by two Squadrone lawyers. Boswell seems in this case not to have been a dummy candidate but one who truly wanted to teach or at least to cause trouble to the Squadrone men.[67] Mackenzie kept the chair until 1755, when it went to Robert Dick of Kirkfield (?–17 February 1796). He may have purchased the post and certainly owed it in part to Lord Milton.[68] The chair had been sought by at least two other men, one of whom resigned the history chair to compete for it.[69] Dick held the chair until 1792, when he became a conjoint professor with a bright young lawyer, John Wyld (Wild or Wilde; c. 1764–6 February 1740), who came in with the blessings of Henry Dundas who had been impressed by his writings against would-be Scottish revolutionaries.[70] Wyld became deranged in the late 1790s and was replaced in 1800 by another Dundas appointee, Alexander Irving of Newton (12 October 1766–23 March 1832), later Lord Newton, SCJ.[71]

All of these men had good political connections but they were chosen for their merits as well as for their political allegiances. All were decent teachers who enjoyed the respect of their colleagues at the Bar, and at least two had reputations outside Scotland.

6. Scots Law

The story was much the same in the chair of Scots law. The first appointment, made in 1722, went to Alexander Bayne of Rires, a former Leiden student. He was a polite and accomplished man probably connected with the Squadrone, as were some of his friends such as professor Francis Pringle.[72] Bayne had been for some time in London where he may have contributed essays to the *Guardian*.[73] In 1715, he was Secretary to the Admiralty Court in Edinburgh.[74] By 1722, Bayne had taught privately with success, although Allan Ramsay sr thought him 'very ignorant of law'. James Boswell reported that Lord Kames also had a low opinion of Bayne's talents but neither Ramsay, Boswell nor Kames were his students nor men who knew him well.[75] They were also not allied with Bayne's likely patrons.[76] The Faculty of Advocates is said to have requested his appointment.[77] John Erskine of Carnock and Cardross (1695–1 March 1768) seems to have been the other person short-listed for the post when Bayne was appointed. In the light of his later career as teacher and legalist, Erskine, young as he was, may well have had hopes in 1722.

When the chair was filled again in 1737, there was competition among the lawyers. James Balfour sought the aid of Sir John Clerk, possibly hoping for the support of various Douglases since Clerk was the political handyman of the Queensberry family.[78] Archibald Murray's brother, Alexander, the laird of Murrayfield, solicited Lord Milton, so there was also lobbying for the post by men who assumed that Ilay would play a role in its disposal.[79] The appointee, John Erskine, was certainly the best of the candidates. Erskine's family was influential but the man's own intelligence may have been his best recommendation to men like Lord Milton who had been at Leiden c. 1715 while Erskine was also a student. The professor became a notable systematiser of Scots law and the writer of a great text on the subject.

Erskine resigned in 1765 but the wheeling and dealing for his place began earlier. On 10 December 1764, George Wallace wrote to Sir James Grant soliciting support in the Faculty of Advocates; a day later he wrote directly to Lord Milton.[80] His father, the reverend Mr Robert Wallace, at about the same time wrote to James Stuart Mackenzie, the manager of patronage in Scotland for the London ministry. For more than seven months, George Wallace struggled to find votes to make his fortune, but on 18 July 1765 he wrote to Sir James that he would have to quit having found too little support.[81] He said that another candidate had withdrawn so as to make his task more difficult. Wallace was passed over, perhaps because Stuart Mackenzie did not 'care to be meddling one way or another in the Professorships appointed by the Magistrates.'[82] If he believed that, it is another sign of his limitations as a patronage manager; or, equally plausible, it shows him trying to imitate his uncle, Ilay. In the end, five other men probably sought the place: (?David) Kennedy, Alexander Wight, John Gordon, Ilay Campbell, and William Wallace of Cairnhill (c. 1730–28 December 1786). Campbell was second on the leet and may not have been a real choice.[83] The man who secured the place, William Wallace, was Keeper of the Advocates' Library and vacated the chair of history to teach Scots law. He was a popular and clever man but he left no works other than a few humorous verses of no distinction.

Wallace's successor in 1786 was David Hume of Ninewells (27 February 1757–30 August 1838), the nephew and namesake of Scotland's greatest philosopher. The second name on the leet was that of Henry Dundas's nephew, Robert Dundas, then the Solicitor General and serving as Henry's manager in Scotland. He was surely not interested in the chair[84] but he seems to have solicited support. Alexander Gordon of Culrennan on 28 November asked him to vote for Hume but, two days later, Robert Dundas wrote to Sir William Fraser, to whom he had applied for support, saying that 'Mr Robertson having yesterday withdrawn from the contest, Mr Hume will in all probability be unanimously named to the vacancy: So that I must relieve you from all further trouble, & request your forgiving me that I have already occasioned you.'[85] Having votes in his pocket would allow him to give them to a favoured candidate. He might have had to struggle to be named second on the leet. Hume, with the help of the Dundas machine, beat William Robertson jr, the son of the principal, and became the chair's second great incumbent.[86]

The professor of Scots law was an important figure in Edinburgh, but the Council never got to choose him except in so far as it fulfilled the formalities of granting the commission. There was some politicking for the post and some of it was done by the men who steered the 'gravy train' but, in general, the advocates were left to do as they would and the politicking seems as much concerned with candidates' personal abilities as with their party affiliations.

Notes

1 Cairns, 'Rhetoric, Language and Roman Law', *Law and History Review*, 9 (1991), pp. 31–58, 32.
2 *The Minute Book of the Faculty of Advocates*, ed. Pinkerton, 1980, II:90, 93.
3 Ibid., II:107f, 148. Town Council Minutes, 30 June 1725.
4 Thomas Blackwell II to Sir John Clerk of Penicuik, 29 April 1734, NAS, GD18/5036/32.
5 'Mr Pringles Book', SAUL, LF1111.P81C99, pp. 135–7. For Lindsay, see Shaw, *Management of Scottish Society*, pp. 76, 94, 98.
6 *History of Parliament*, ed. Sedgwick, 1970, II:412f.
7 George Stuart had a small estate which adjoined the Minto property and was bought by that family in 1772. Lord Minto was Stuart's patron, as is shown by many letters between the professor and the family in the Minto Papers and by the testimony of Ramsay of Ochtertyre: Ochtertyre MSS, NLS, 1635/1/327.

8 Ibid., 1635/1/327. Ramsay's verdict on Foulis was that he 'was not the best qualified for the office'. NLS, 1635/1/324f.

9 Charles Mackie to Lord Balgonie, 9 January 1742, Leven and Melville MSS, NAS, GD26/13/615. Mackie's letter contains a satiric poem on the affair by William Wallace of Cairnhill which much offended Lord Minto. See also: Chalmers MSS, NLS, ADV. MS 21-1-11; Horn MSS, EUL, Gen 1824, 'Humanity', p. 10; Dalzel, *History*, ed. Laing, 1862, II:370, 409; Grant, *Story of the University*; 1884, II:31ff; *The Minute Book of the Faculty of Advocates*, ed. Pinkerton, 1980, II:183.

10 Dalzel, *History*, ed. Laing, 1862, I:9. Liston had sought the humanity chairs at St Andrews and Glasgow in 1773 (see pp. 161–4) and had already held a diplomatic post. Stuart's price was presumably the value of the salary and fees for five years. If this is the case, then his fees would have come to less than £50 a year, with the difference being made up out of incidentals and salary. William Zacks has estimated Stuart's income from fees at about £40 a year; his salary in 1760 was £52. A portion of his income probably came from being a minor laird and perhaps more from pensions from earlier tutoring and from the boarding of students. He left an estate of over £5,000 which included the sale price of his land. Zacks, *Without Regard to Good Manners*, 1992, p. 4.

11 Minute of 29 April 1782, Marischal College Minute Book 1729–90, AUL, M.41; Horn MSS, EUL, Gen 1824, 'Humanity'; Grant, *Story of the University*, 1884, II:319; Dalzel, *History*, ed. Laing, 1862, I:9.

12 The city had had an active antiquarian club in the 1680s led by the Lord Advocate Sir George Mackenzie and later on by Sir Robert Sibbald. Emerson, 'Sir Robert Sibbald ... and the Origins of the Scottish Enlightenment', *Annals of Science*, 1988, pp. 41–72, 55.

13 David Gregorie Papers, EUL, Dk.1.2.2b [1691].

14 Cairns, 'John Spotswood', in *Miscellany Three*, Stair Society, Edinburgh, 1992, pp. 131–59, 145f.

15 Nairne to Carstares, 4 December 1707, Carstares MS, EUL, DK1.1.2; some months earlier, Carstares had been consulted by the Earl of Glasgow about the Historiographer Royal's place. Queensberry and the Secretaries of State sponsored David Simson for the post, which he received in 1708. Nairne and Lord Glasgow seem to have supported a Mr Walker. The Earl of Glasgow to Carstares, 2 August 1707, EUL, DK1.1.2; see also Hay, 'The Historiographers Royal in England and Scotland', *Scottish Historical Review*, 30 (1951), pp. 15–29.

16 For an account of those teachers and references to their advertisements in the Edinburgh papers, see Cairns, *Legal Education in Edinburgh*, forthcoming.

17 Grant, *Story of the University*, 1884, I:285.

18 Mijers, unpublished dissertation, 'Scotland and the United Provinces', Chapter 6. Dr Mijers thinks Mackie was unlikely to have done more than visit Utrecht, since his letters show he did not know the city well. Her account of Mackie is presently the best available; it is also forthcoming in *'News from the Republic of letters': Charles Mackie, Scotland's First Professor of history and the Netherlands* (Brill, 2008).

19 Dunlop, *Carstares*, 1964, p. 83.

20 I have not seen a full catalogue of his library but many of his books are noticed in the correspondence between William and Andrew Dunlop. After Carstares' death in 1715, they discussed the sale of his books and those they each might want. Both were interested in history. Andrew was then thought of as a possible appointee for the ecclesiastical history chair at Glasgow University. See 'Transcripts of Thirty-six, 1715–1720', prepared in 1932 by J. G. Dunlop; GUL, Gen 83.

21 See Cairns *Legal Education in Edinburgh*, forthcoming, and Mijers, 'Scotland and the United Provinces', Chapter 5.

22 For Mackie, see Cairns, 'Rhetoric, Language and Roman Law', *Law and History Review*, 1991, pp.31–58; Sharp, 'Charles Mackie', *Scottish Historical Review*, 1962, pp. 23–44; Drummond to Mackie, 12 September 1716, Mackie Papers, EUL, La.II. 91. The jobs in question were at Aberdeen and possibly St Andrews, where a purging of Jacobite masters was expected.

23 Drummond to Mackie, ibid.; Cairns, *Legal Education in Edinburgh*, forthcoming; *The Lord Provosts of Edinburgh 1296 to 1932*, ed. Whitson, 1932, p. 62.

24 Rothes is identified as a Squadrone man by Shaw, *Management of Scottish Society*, 1983, p. 50.

25 That was £50 more than it was worth when first set up in 1720.

26 Mackie may also have had other resources since he died quite well off.

27 Mackie to the Town Council, 2 and 7 December 1753, EUL, La.II. 90.2; Dalzel, *History*, ed. Laing, 1862, II:433; Grant, *Story*, 1884, II:367.

28 William Wallace to Lord Loudoun, 7 February 1754, 10 June 1754, Mount Stuart House, Isle of Bute, Loudoun MS, 1754/VIII; Charles Mackie to Loudoun, ibid.; Alexander Boswell to Charles Mackie, 20 November 1754, NLS, 6686/77; EUL, 588/131; Charles Mackie to Edinburgh Town Council, 2 December 1754, EUL, La.II. 90.2.

29 *The Faculty of Advocates in Scotland 1532–1943*, ed. Grant, 1944, p. 214.

30 Dalzel, *History*, ed. Laing, 1862, II:435; Town Council Minutes, 27 July 1764; Pringle to Mackie, 22 November 1765, EUL, La.II. 91.

31 EUL, Gen.1824, 'History', p. 18.

32 Fry, *Dundas Despotism*, 1992, p. 184.

33 Grant, *Story*, 1884, II:368f.

34 Writing to Alexander Carlyle on 25 January 1780, Logan begged 'that you will mention my affair with warmth to Mrs Home, Dr Ferguson & Dr Smith. If I have not the aid of my friends I must begin the world de novo' – as indeed, he had to do. Logan came to believe that Robertson had undercut his chances and favoured Tytler, a friend of his son, William. EUL, La.II. 419/2 and La.II. 419/1.

35 'Life of Logan', in *Logan's Sermons*, [1783], pp. xxiii–xxv. This brief 'Life' is anonymous and no editor is given for the volume.

36 Zachs, *Stuart*, 1992, p. 109f.

37 Mijers, 'Scotland and the United Provinces' analyses the parallel change among the Dutch in Chapter 6.

38 Spottiswoode's papers at the NLS have a good deal on these topics: see Cairns, *Legal Education in Edinburgh*, forthcoming, and 'John Spotswood', in *Miscellany Three*, Stair Society, 1992, pp. 131–59; and Cairns, 'Sir George Mackenzie, The Faculty of Advocates & the Advocates' Library', in *Oratio Inauguralis in Aperienda Jurisconsultorum Bibliotheca Sir George Mackenzie*, ed. Cairns and Cain, 1989, pp. 19–35.

39 Cairns, 'The First Edinburgh Chair in Law – Grotius and the Scottish Enlightenment', *Fundamina*, 2005, pp. 32–58; this is also available at http://www.law.ed.ac.uk/Tercentenary/documents. My page citations are to that version. See also Cairns, *Legal Education in Edinburgh*, forthcoming.

40 There is no biography of Erskine, but see 'Charles Areskine' in *The House of Commons 1715–1754*, ed. Sedgwick, I:420, and Cairns, *Legal Education in Edinburgh*, forthcoming. I have retained the Erskine spelling here because it was most commonly used in the period but not by him.

41 Bower, *The History of the University of Edinburgh*, 1817, II: 65.

42 Cairns, 'The First Edinburgh Chair in Law', Tercentenary documents, pp. 9–15. Cairns says that Principal Carstares should also be thought of as involved in the creation of this chair; Cairns, *Legal Education in Edinburgh*, forthcoming.

43 The professorial rights of Alexander Cunningham of Blok to be, by Act of Parliament, professor of civil law in Scotland were carefully protected by the grant to Erskine: copy of Erskine's grant, AUL, Crown Tower MSS, Box 43.

44 Scott to James Anderson, 2 December 1723, James Anderson MSS, NLS, Adv. MS 29.1.2/180. Dalzel believed that Lord Ilay also had a hand in this; Grant, *Story*, 1884, II:314.

45 The funds to pay his salary were not yet available. He went abroad with the permission of the Provost, Magistrates and Town Council, permissions secured by Mar. Cairns, *Legal Education in Edinburgh*, forthcoming.

46 With Ilay's backing he became an became an MP in 1736 and served for two years, after which he became a Principal Clerk of Session. Kirkpatrick's tenure is discussed by Cairns, 'The First Edinburgh Chair in Law', Tercentenary documents, pp. 15–18.

47 Cairns, 'The First Edinburgh Chair in Law', Tercentenary documents, p. 18.

48 Grant, *Story*, 1884, II:314; Cairns, 'The First Edinburgh Chair in Law', Tercentenary documents, pp. 18–22.

49 Ferguson to Milton, 29 June and 11 July 1758, NLS, 16702/26, 234; John Home to Milton, 11 August 1758, NLS, 16703/28; Home to Milton, 16 August 1758, NLS, 16705/234; Sher, *Church and University*, 1985, p. 106; Cairns, 'The First Edinburgh Chair in Law', Tercentenary documents, p. 21f.

50 Ibid., p. 23.

51 He seems to have wanted to sell to Gilbert Stuart but Principal Robertson prevented this and brought upon himself the enduring and vocal hatred of the slighted man. Stuart thereafter deplored Robertson's work and derided his scholarship. Zachs, *Without Regard*, 1992, p. 105; Kerr, *Life and Memoires of Smellie*, 1811, II:501. See also Cairns, 'The First Edinburgh Chair in Law', Tercentenary documents, p. 24f.

52 Cairns thinks this appointment, and Bruce's elevation to the Court of Session, may have been affected by the political interests of the ministry for whom Bute's brother was the Scottish manager. Cairns notes that Balfour either lectured in some years or that others advertised lectures to be given by him as a way of inducing his resignation. 'The First Edinburgh Chair in Law', Tercentenary documents, pp. 27–30.

53 Sher, *Church and University*, 1985, pp. 117–19.

54 Gilbert Stuart tried to secure the post in 1766–7 and again ten years later, when the post may have been promised to him by Henry Dundas who was then not able to secure it for him because of the machinations of Principal William Robertson. Zachs, *Without Regard*, 1992, pp. 33f., 105–8; Cairns, 'The First Edinburgh Chair in Law', Tercentenary documents, p. 28f.

55 Ibid., pp. 30–8.

56 Cairns, 'The First Edinburgh Chair in Law', Tercentenary documents, pp. 31–9; Sher, *Church and University*, 1985, p. 140.

57 Hamilton to Henry Dundas, 24 December 1798, Melville Castle Muniments, NAS, GD51/6/1145; Cairns, 'The First Edinburgh Chair in Law', Tercentenary documents, pp. 38–41.

58 Grant, *Story*, 1884, I:232f.

59 Cairns, *Legal Education*, forthcoming. Cairns has some material on his early career.

60 Cairns, *Legal Education in Edinburgh*, forthcoming.

61 Ibid.

62 Ibid.; Horn MSS, EUL, Gen 1824, 'Civil Law'.

63 Dalzel, *History*, ed. Laing, 1862, II:402; EUL, Gen 1824, 'Civil Law', p. 6; Lord Milton to Ilay, 28 November 1732, NLS, 16548/99.

64 Ilay to Milton, 28 November 1732, NLS 16548/99.

65 Robert Dundas to Tweeddale, 14 August 1742, Yester MSS, NLS, 7049/45.

66 The atmosphere at Edinburgh in those years is described in Emerson, 'The "affair" at Edinburgh and the "project" at Glasgow', in *Hume and Hume's Connexions*, ed. Stewart and Wright, 1994, pp. 1–22; Stewart, 'The Kirk and the Infidel: An Inaugural Lecture', 1994. See also 'A Diplomatic Transcription of Hume's "volunteer pamphlet" ', eds Box, Harvey and Silverthorne, *Hume Studies*, 2003, pp. 223–66.

67 Argyll arranged Boswell's 1754 appointment to the Court of Session; Murdoch, *The People Above*, 1980, p. 56.

68 EUL, Gen 1824, 'Civil Law'; Dalzel, *History*, ed. Laing, 1862, II:426; Patrick Cuming to Lord Milton, 3 January 1754, Saltoun MSS, NLS, SB 80.

69 Grant, *Story*, 1884, II:367.

70 Fry, *Dundas Despotism*, 1992, p. 184.

71 Ibid.

72 Pringle wrote a touching obituary for his friend, 'The Commonplace Book of Francis Pringle', SAUL, LF111.P81C99/39. Pringle's family had been the recipients of much patronage doled out by the Squadrone.

73 *The Guardian*, ed. Stephens, 1982, pp. 32, 655, 661.

74 Cairns, *Legal Education in Edinburgh*, forthcoming; Miège, *The Present State of Great Britain . . .* (3rd ed., London, 1715), Part II:165.

75 Walker, *The Scottish Jurists*, 1985, p. 204.

76 The Petition is in Edinburgh Council Archives, MacLeod, Bundle 9, Shelf 36, Bay C.

77 There is no record of this in the published minutes.

78 Bower, *History*, 1817, II:374f; Chambers, *A Biographical Dictionary*, 1856, II:265; James Balfour to Sir John Clerk, 27 June 1737, Clerk of Penicuik Papers, NAS, GD18/5413.

79 Alexander Murray to Milton, 28 April 1737, NLS, 16571/105a.

80 George Wallace to Sir James Grant, 5 February 1761, Seafield MSS, NAS, GD248/49/2; George Wallace to Lord Milton, 11 December 1764, NLS, 16732/127.

81 Among his supporters was William Johnstoun Poultney. George Wallace to Sir James Grant, 18 July 1765, NAS, GD248/672/54.

82 Stuart Mackenzie to Baron William Mure, 31 December 1764, *Mure of Caldwell Papers*, 1883, Part 2, I:282.

83 Dalzel, *History*, ed. Laing, 1862, II:235, 426; Walker, *Scottish Jurists*, 1985, p. 278.

84 Zachs, *Without Regard*, p. 207; Fry, *Dundas Despotism*, 1992, p. 184; Walker, *Jurists*, 1985, p. 317.
85 Robert Dundas to Alexander Gordon, 30 November 1786, papers of Sir William Fraser, NAS, GD397/2/8. Robert Dundas to Alexander Gordon, 28 November 1786, NLS, 3834/16f. I thank Dr David Brown for these references.
86 Horn MSS, EUL, Gen 1824, 'Civil Law'.

11

SURGICAL AND MEDICAL CHAIRS

৶

1. INTRODUCTION

The medical chairs were similar to those in law and unlike the ones in divinity.[1] Deference was shown to the assessments of competence made by practitioners but a candidate's politics and his connections were always of interest. But patronage to the medical chairs was a more complicated matter because there were more interests to consider. Surgeons and physicians, like writers and advocates, had corporate interests to protect. So too did the University and the town as the numbers of medical students increased to become of great economic importance. By the end of the eighteenth century, the medical school in Edinburgh had brought well over a million pounds to the city's economy.[2] Students from time to time also influenced appointments, as did men who taught extramurally. The Council preserved its rights to create chairs teaching the same subjects as the regius professorships created by the Crown, which meant the livings could be made worthless if the Crown's appointees were not liked. However, as with the law chairs, the Town Council exercised little independent judgement and did not really pick the appointees. How complex all this could be is perhaps best seen in the oldest of the medical chairs, those of botany and anatomy.

2. BOTANY AND *MATERIA MEDICA*

The chair of botany had a double origin. By the end of the seventeenth century Edinburgh had many apprentices to surgeons and physicians who needed someone to teach them botany and pharmacy.[3] And the Crown, town and University needed to have a competent keeper or keepers of their various gardens.[4] In 1670, Sir Robert Sibbald, MD and two of his friends appointed James Sutherland (1639–25 June 1719) their gardener for a new but small private garden (it was only 40 feet by 40 feet). By 1675, this had expanded to a plot 300 feet by

190 feet. In the following year, Sutherland was made Intendant of the Physic Garden by the Town Council, with an annual salary of £20, and a new status was given him. He was 'joined with to [sic.]' the professors teaching in the College, where he would thereafter give botany courses to students and to the apprentices of the surgeons and physicians. That right was worth about £20 yearly. Twenty years later he founded another garden near the College buildings where he taught and in the same year he assumed the direction of the Royal Garden at Holyrood Palace. Those places, all patronage positions, allowed him to deal in plants on the side. In 1699, he became King's Botanist and in 1710 regius professor in the city but not in the College. Collectively, his posts were worth about £90–100 annually in 1706, to which should be added the unknown profits from the sale of plants. His income equalled or exceeded that of the regents and was partly spent on his numismatic collection and on books related to his virtuoso interests. When he resigned his College chair in 1706, along with his control of the Physic Garden and the College Garden, he kept his other titles until 1714, when his royal warrants were not renewed by George I.

Sutherland's accomplishments created a situation in which no one group could control the nomination to the University's chair of botany. Any group had to negotiate with others who expected to be considered and consulted. If they were not consulted, the appointment might not be worth having. The Incorporation of Chirurgeons [sometimes called the Company of Surgeons and, after 1778, the Royal College of Surgeons of Edinburgh] had a near veto over the appointment to the University's chair because it specified the person with whom surgical apprentices were to study botany. Those apprentices constituted the principal market for the professor's skills. The surgeons could render the chair nearly worthless to an incumbent they neither liked nor approved. The Town Council could deny the use of the best, but not the only, garden in the city and could appoint someone who did not hold the regius chair. The Crown could always give the posts of Royal Botanist, Keeper of the Holyrood Garden and regius professor in the city or in Scotland to someone other than the choice of the surgeons or the Town Council, thus establishing another school of botany in the burgh. This probably would have happened c. 1715 had William Arthur not been involved in the uprising of 1715. Finally, the University men could make life difficult for anyone not suiting the professors. A man might find his classes scheduled at inconvenient times or even have the students barred from attending them. Politicians who brokered the arrangements leading to appointments reconciled the divergent interests.

When Sutherland resigned his University post in 1706, he was followed by Charles Preston (12 July 1660–December 1711), who in the previous year had applied to the Company of Surgeons for the privilege of teaching the apprentices and had received it.[5] His success as a teacher may have been a partial cause of Sutherland's resignation, since the Surgeons' Company had stipulated its apprentices were to attend Preston and only Preston.[6] That would have reduced Sutherland's income from teaching fees if the now elderly man were still teaching. A few months later, Preston was made professor of botany in the University, with the Town Council noting in its appointment that his 'abilitie and qualifications . . . for teaching thereof being sufficiently knowen', he had not been tried for ability.[7] In this instance, the comment was more than the usual puff for a favoured man.

Preston had studied at Leiden but took his MD degrees first at Reims (1696) and then at King's College, Aberdeen (1699), so that he might more easily become a FRCPE. He was a virtuoso known in Leiden to Paulus Herman and in Paris to Joseph Pitton de Tournefort and to men in the Académie royale des sciences. He attended at least one meeting of the Académie in 1699.[8] He was in contact with James Petiver, Leonard Plunket, John Ray and others in the circle of Sir Hans Sloane in London. Preston, despite his present obscurity, was one of the best-educated and well-connected Scottish scientific virtuosi of his time. He was friendly with Sir John Clerk of Penicuik, a neighbour of Preston's family who was then a manager for the Duke of Queensberry's interest and soon to be a leading intellectual in Edinburgh. The doctor knew all the Edinburgh men of learning, many of whom were gathered in the medical corporations and in the virtuoso clubs sustained by his friend Sir Robert Sibbald.[9] His father, Sir Robert Preston, was a well-placed Edinburgh lawyer and SCJ.

When Charles Preston died in 1711, he was succeeded by his younger brother, George (1665–16 February 1749), who had trained as a surgeon-apothecary. George Preston had served as a military surgeon (1691–?)[10] and when appointed was Surgeon Major to the Forces in Scotland (1703–?). He had sought and received the support of the Incorporation of Chirurgeons. Preston probably also inherited things which his brother had added to the garden, things which would stay there only if he were to be appointed. It may also have mattered that he had not been fully paid for acting as Surgeon Major. By 1707, he was owed four year's back pay; his debt was still unpaid in 1712.

Preston began enthusiastically by building a new greenhouse. Two years later he asked James Erskine, Lord Grange, SCJ, to be put on 'the Establishment of Guards & garisons' which would allow him to 'improve the science of Botany'.[11] The city tried to help him get a grant in 1715 but his work was not supported.[12] What he wanted was the £50 given to the King's Botanist, which went in 1715 to William Arthur, MD.

Neither of the Preston brothers got the regius professorship in the city or the Keepership of the Royal Garden. These offices went to William Arthur (1680–c. November 1716)[13] as political gifts from his relatives, Sir John Clerk, Sir John Inglis and Adam Cockburn, Lord Ormiston, SCJ, three men in office and with ties to Scottish political factions.[14] Arthur had not yet begun to teach when he became involved in the 1715 effort to take Edinburgh Castle for the Jacobites. Had Arthur taught, George Preston would have found a rival earlier than he did. As it was, Arthur fled the country in 1715 and died in Rome in the autumn of 1716. His death did not help George Preston since Arthur's replacement was not himself but Charles Alston (21 October 1683–22 November 1760), who secured Arthur's posts through the intervention of the Duchess of Hamilton.[15]

When George Preston got neither grant nor office, he began to lose interest in his profession. By the early 1720s he was neglecting his students. After 1724, he ceased to have any connection with the College garden.[16] By 1738, when he resigned his professorship, he had long been all but inactive as a teacher but not as a botanist. In the 1730s he was still reading papers to The Honourable Society for Improving in the Knowledge of Agriculture in Scotland and dispensed seeds to its members. He was noted in their minutes as one who was 'to carry on the silkworm manufactory', a Lockean project or dream shared by men in Britain and America.[17] Alston had started life as a writer or solicitor and servant to the formidable Anne, Duchess of Hamilton. She secured his first positions for him, after which he went to Leiden to qualify for his place. Alston was yet another professor who went to Holland to perfect the skills he needed to teach. He studied medicine, took his MD at Edinburgh in 1719 and began to teach. From June 1720 until he secured the University chair in 1738, he taught in the King's Garden and in the winter gave a course in *materia medica*.[18] By the mid-1720s, Alston seems to have been the only important teacher of botany and *materia medica* in the burgh. His primacy was confirmed by his reappointment in 1727 as King's Botanist, a post for which the Earl of Ilay had the nomination but which the Hamiltons would have been soliciting for Alston. He was a good teacher who quickly acquired an international reputation as a botanist. When Preston resigned his professorship in 1738, Alston seems to have been everyone's choice to become professor. No one else could make the post pay as well as he. Lack of competition for the place suggests that he had the backing of influential men. While it must remain a speculation, Ilay, a keen botanist, is likely to have helped him to his chair. He probably had support for the post by some at the University and by those with whom he sat in the Philosophical Society of Edinburgh. Alston had been associated with the medical professors for many years before he became officially their colleague and he was an ornament to the recently established Edinburgh Philosophical Society. Its officers included: the Earl of Morton, President; Sir John Clerk and Dr John Clerk of Listonshiels, Vice-Presidents; Colin Maclaurin and Alexander Monro, Secretaries – all notable men with influence.[19] The Hamiltons too are likely to have aided him, since his appointments and his success as a teacher saved them a retirement salary for his former service to the Duchess. By 1738, all the offices that counted were again in one man's grip.

When Alston died in 1760, the Incorporation of Surgeons recommended Dr John Hope (10 May 1725–10 November 1786), who became in April 1761 King's Botanist, Keeper of all the gardens and professor of both botany and *materia medica*. He claimed that his success in winning office was owing to the aid he received from the 3rd Earl of Bute.[20] Bute was a talented botanist and a knowing man in several sciences. He could recognise scientific merit when he met it. Hope later received the Council's appointment as their professor as well, but their hand had been forced.

Hope deserved his post.[21] He was a talented teacher and, like his predecessors, served the needs of collectors and amateur botanists. He too was a member of the Edinburgh Philosophical Society and promoted and ran the Edinburgh Seed Society, which was a sort of subsidiary of it.[22] He was able to keep Edinburgh very much in the international network of eighteenth-century botanists and medical men. His students went away having been trained as collectors, taxonomists and some of them as plant physiologists. Many became important collectors in the Empire; some established gardens in America, the Caribbean and India.

During Hope's tenure, he changed the character of the chair. In 1768 it was split, with Hope retaining what was now a regius chair of botany in the University, one which was joined to the Keepership of the Royal Garden and the office of King's Botanist in Scotland. Dr Francis Home (17 November 1719–15 February 1813) secured the place of professor of *materia medica*, whose patronage legally vested in the Town Council. The chair of botany and *materia medica* seems to have been split partly because Hope believed that systematic botany and plant physiology had less relation to *materia medica* than formerly. The latter was now as much mineral- as plant-based and required a chemist as much as a botanist to teach it. There were other reasons too.

Home was, like Hope, a one-time army surgeon who had taken an MD at Edinburgh (in 1750) and wanted to teach.[23] He had long sought a university chair and had somewhat shaped his career to promote his prospects. He had done chemical analyses for the Board of Trustees for Fisheries and Manufactures during the 1750s. These had resulted in the better bleaching of linens with dilute sulphuric acid, which led to an expansion in the linen trade. Home was also interested in improving agriculture, a topic on which he wrote. He produced a number of useful chemical and medical texts. In addition, he was some sort of a cousin to Lord Milton and deeply believed he should be rewarded for his good works. He had sought the chair of chemistry in 1755 with the aid of Milton and Lord Marchmont (his family name was Home), but it went to William Cullen when the Duke of Argyll 'employed the weight of his whole interest in favour of Dr Cullen'.[24] In 1761, Home drafted a memorandum which appointed himself 'Professor of Philosophick Agriculture in the University of Edinburgh' and gave him a small experimental farm on which to show the best techniques not only to University students but to the 'Children of the Tenants of the Annex'd Estates'.[25] He seems to have modelled his plan on a royal farm in Denmark. Nothing came of that scheme. Between 1764 and 1766 he sought John Rutherford's (1 August 1695–6 March 1779) professorship of the practice of medicine or Cullen's chair of chemistry. He had the support of John Home, the friend of Lord Bute,[26] of James Coutts, the MP for Edinburgh,[27] and of the now nearly senile Lord Milton and his replacements as manager, James Stuart Mackenzie and William Mure, Baron of Exchequer.[28] But Home was opposed by the College professors, including Hugh Blair and Principal Robertson. They wanted and got Joseph Black, whom they regarded as a more respectable literary man.[29] In the end, supported by Kames and other medical men who warned off competitors, Home received the *materia medica* chair.[30] Since Hope had kept the salary attached to the old chair, Home was dependent on fees for his professorial income.[31] By the time he retired he had a small estate, Cowdenknowes in Berwickshire. Home's son, James (1760–5 December 1844), followed him in 1798 in what by then had become, thanks to the numbers of fee-paying students, a very lucrative position.[32] His succession was acceptable to the medical faculty and to the political manager, Henry Dundas, who took credit for the appointment.[33]

John Hope was succeeded in the botany chair in 1786 by Daniel Rutherford (3 November 1749–15 November 1819), who defeated two others.[34] The town made clear its claim upon the chair by also presenting Rutherford to the town's chair of botany and then admitting him as the regius professor of botany in the University. The Crown might appoint but the town maintained its right to present a man who had its blessing and the custom of the Edinburgh surgeons.[35] Rutherford's patent had been obtained through the good offices of Henry Dundas.

In all these appointments, respect was paid to professional accomplishments and public usefulness. All the professors of botany had or established reputations and connections outside the kingdom and all of them did useful things. They worked on improvement projects, gave plants to the aristocrats with large gardens and reforestation projects and were helpful to businessmen. The appointments to these chairs were ones which enhanced the city's reputation as a teaching centre and made it a prominent node in the botanical and chemical networks of the century. They also promoted the collection of commercially useful plants abroad and the search for those which could and did expand the pharmacopeia. The appointees were picked for the Town Council by medical men and political figures.

3. ANATOMY

The surgeons had a greater interest in the chair of anatomy. Before the end of the seventeenth century they had established procedures for the teaching of anatomy[36] and later claimed to have recommended all the anatomists who taught in the burgh beginning in 1695.[37] They had acted in 1705 to protect their teaching monopoly by setting up a 'professorship' and preventing a stranger from teaching anatomy in the town. They made the surgeon Robert Elliot (?1669–1717) their recognised teacher. The Town Council added to his status in the burgh by making him Keeper of the University Museum, with a salary of £15,[38] but he was not made a professor in the University.[39] He kept his post until his death in 1715.[40] Elliot had been a student of Archibald Pitcairne at Leiden. His appointment probably showed the determination of the surgeons to have available in the city teachers of modern anatomy and iatro-mechanical physiology as Pitcairne taught it.[41]

On 5 August 1708, Elliot was joined in his profession by Adam Drummond (?1679–1758), another young surgeon whose own most distinguished pupil was professor John Rutherford. After Elliot's death, Drummond was given as an associate the surgeon John MacGill (or McGill; ?1660–1734). Like the other surgeons, both taught sporadically from 1717 until they resigned to make way for Alexander Monro (8 September 1697–10 July 1767) in 1720.[42] All this looks as if the surgeons had looked after their interests by themselves[43] but, as was the case with the botanists, politicians were also involved, even though some of the posts were not University jobs and the salaries they carried were very small. One must remember that every honourable post increased the practices and incomes of their holders. In the crowded, competitive world of Scottish medicine, no advantage was too small to pursue.

In 1708, before Adam Drummond was added as a conjoint professor, Dr Archibald Pitcairne, who had long been associated with the Surgeons' Company, asked the Secretary of State, John Erskine, 11th Earl of Mar, to help Drummond.[44] Pitcairne was not the only one looking for this appointment. Someone named Erskine also solicited from Mar and his brother, James Erskine, Lord Grange, SCJ, an appointment as a professor of anatomy and physic. This was to go to the brother of George Erskine of Balgowny. Neither Mar nor Grange thought this practicable at that time.[45] By 1709, Dr Pitcairne wanted a regius chair of some sort – either in the town or University – created for Drummond. He was willing to have a patent for the chair even if it omitted any salary. This was partly because he feared the aspirations of another man, —— Abercromby, who in 1709 was trying to obtain something of this sort with the support of the former Chancellor of Scotland, the Earl of Seafield.[46] Two years earlier it might have been possible but now such a chair could not be created in Scotland but would need the approval of English politicians who were not likely to give it. What this shows is that the creation of a chair of anatomy was something wanted by several which in 1708–9 involved national political factions and was not something that was going to be left only to the Edinburgh Surgeons' Company and the Town Council.[47] It was as much a matter of political patronage as of professionalisation among aspiring surgeons. The new post, could it be secured, would show which politicians could give status and money. It would be a political matter, and not just because some public funds would be used to pay for it.

That this situation persisted is suggested by the appointment of MacGill in 1716. His appointment looks like a reward for his service in the '15. He had met Lord Ilay by that time and may have treated his wounds at the Battle of Sheriffmuir. Later he became his personal physician in Scotland.[48] MacGill's brother, Alexander, an Edinburgh architect who died in 1734, was also connected with the Campbells. Between 1716 and 1734, Alexander MacGill worked for the Duke of Argyll, for Lord Ilay and Lord Milton. He built a number of civic buildings in Scotland about which they also would have had some say. He was admitted a burgess in their town of Inveraray in 1720. When John MacGill got his post as anatomist from the Incorporation of Surgeons, he would surely have had the backing of Argyll, Ilay and men in their faction. The place would have rewarded a friend by enhancing his status and increasing his income. While we have no clear evidence that this is why he was chosen, it is pertinent to note that in 1717 the Lord Provost of Edinburgh was John Campbell, an Inveraray man whose position was owed to the rising power in the city of the Campbell brothers. By 1715, they could control enough of the elections to the Edinburgh Town Council to secure a majority. Lord Provost Campbell and the Council should be thought of as agents and not as men acting independently or primarily in the interest of the Incorporation of Surgeons. Men like Ilay concerned themselves with the appointments of tide-waiters (ordinary customs men whose posts were worth only £5–10 to which were added perquisites and opportunities for illegal enrichment) so were not likely to let this place go without trying to determine who received it.

This pattern seems to have been repeated in January 1720, when Alexander Monro (8 September 1697–10 July 1767) got his place, first during the pleasure of the Council and then, in 1722, for life and good behaviour.[49] The University with an anatomy professor was now able to compete with Glasgow, where the latter subject had been more regularly taught in some fashion for six years and where in March 1720 another Leiden graduate, Thomas Brisbane, was appointed to the chair of botany and anatomy.[50] Monro, a young man trained at Leiden, London and Paris, was supported by the Incorporation of Chirurgeons and by the Royal College of Physicians. Both bodies urged the Town Council to appoint him. Significantly, both incumbents appointed by the Surgeons' Company and the town resigned to make possible Monro's appointment. Monro's father, John, lost a minor city job, which made it easier to patronise his son.[51] This was a political deal involving several interested parties.

The best account of the Monro appointment is that of E. A. Underwood, who, like others, gives too much credit for the founding of the Edinburgh medical school to John Monro and Lord Provost George Drummond. Alexander Monro I's appointment is seen as a crucial step in a plan devised by John Monro to create a medical school in Edinburgh University. Retailers of this yarn have retold it principally because of their belief in the accuracy of the self-aggrandising *Memoirs* left by Alexander Monro I.[52] This old story was given an enormous push by the publication of Alexander Monro I's autobiographical essay in 1954 by H. D. Erlam.[53] The legend rests on Monro's word, but that has no independent corroboration and there is much to suggest that it is biased if not altogether false. Underwood and others have retold it but have offered no new evidence to buttress Monro's claims, which are implausible given the way Scottish politics was then pursued. There was also a behind-the-scenes story which has not been noticed by those who have considered this matter.[54] It is time to look at the creation of this chair from other angles. There is more to the story than the hopes of John Monro to establish a medical school in the city with the aid of his friend George Drummond.

The requirements of a better education for the city's many apprentices were apparent to both surgeons and physicians and had been since the seventeenth century.[55] The needs were partially met by the teachers of botany after c. 1675, by the erection of a professorship of botany in the University in 1676, and by the appointment of a Royal Botanist in 1699. The attempt to create medical chairs in 1685, when Drs Sibbald, Pitcairne and Halket were appointed professors of medicine, also recognised the need for medical education to be carried on in the University. By the 1690s there were more moves in this direction. The new facilities available at the Surgeons' Company in the 1690s provided places where lectures on anatomy, chemistry and medicine could be and were given.[56] There was a proposal by someone in 1704 to establish an infirmary in Edinburgh. The houses of Old Greyfriars were to be converted into a hospital which would possess an apothecary's shop. The physician to be employed there was also 'to be A professor of medicine to be instituted, and in the mean tyme, the College of physitians is to appoint one who is to attend as long as the[re is no] apothecary & is to have a proper chamber in ye house – minister, governor, surgical operations take place, serves a 12 mile radius if they will tax themselves for it.'[57] All that would have required action by at least the Town Council. Since the proposal was one of many for the revival of Scotland's prosperity and civic health, interventions by the Scottish Parliament were also likely to have been in the mind of the writer of the proposal.

The creation of a 'profession' of anatomy in 1705 was but another step toward medical education in the city. So too was the granting of the University's first medical degree in 1705.[58] Extramural classes were announced by Dr Sibbald in 1706 and recognised the demands for better and more teaching.[59] As we have seen, others were thinking about medical and anatomical chairs by 1708–9. In 1713, the University finally got a medical chair when Principal Carstares obtained the chair of chemistry and medicine. Those steps surely had been taken with an eye on developments at Glasgow. There the University was beginning medical education and both universities were competing for dissenting students. Glasgow's appointments had involved politicians. In a place where all public and semi-public jobs were given out with calculation and where the 'men of power' sought to monopolise their distribution, it simply does not make sense to regard the appointment of Alexander Monro I as the work only of his father and his friend George Drummond who hoodwinked the Town Council into making a new chair in the University. That was not the way things were done. If there was hoodwinking to be done, it would have had higher sanction. Moreover, Monro's recommendation by the Surgeons' Company in January 1720 would by itself not have allowed him to displace the friend and physician of a powerful political figure unless the office holder and his patron saw it in their interests to allow a new man to take the job. Alexander Monro I tells us that Adam Drummond had promised to demit his half of the place after having seen fine anatomical specimens sent home by Alexander to his father from London in 1718.[60] But Ilay and his brother were struggling with politicians in the Squadrone faction for the control of all the patronage of Scotland between 1718 and 1722. Their protégés were walking symbols of their influence and power; they were unlikely to surrender any gains. Men so conscious of such things, and of the means of displaying and maximising their power, were unlikely to let any of it slip. MacGill could not have been forced out. If he wished to go, then he and Drummond would surely have consulted those who really appointed them. Monro's appointment should be seen as one negotiated with John MacGill and Adam Drummond, but also with Ilay or his managers and whoever had backed Adam

Drummond for his post in 1717. It should be seen as one in which the majority of the town fathers were led by Lord Provost John Campbell, and not only by George Drummond, Treasurer (1718–20) and Old Dean of Guild (1720–1), who would not become Lord Provost until 1725. Drummond was never his own man until the very end of his life after Lord Ilay had died and his political machine had been taken over by others less efficient. When Monro became a professor of anatomy, the Town Council appointed a man from an impeccable Whig background to an insecure post.[61] They also put him in the University but one should not see this as an inadvertent or a shifty manoeuvre by George Drummond. The commissions of professors were carefully written by a corporation clerk or lawyer, so this is simply unlikely. George Drummond may have played a visible part but he was only one of the Argathelian agents in Edinburgh and less important than Lord Provost Campbell or Duncan Forbes. We have no reason to think this appointment was treated differently from others in the same period. These show interfering politicians carefully supporting their own.[62]

There is a more likely scenario. John Monro, a landless surgeon of little influence and status, was cousin to Duncan Forbes of Culloden, the Sheriff of Midlothian and Advocate Depute. Forbes was the friend and political ally of the Campbell brothers. Monro is likely to have gone to him to say that it would be a good thing if his bright and well-educated son, Alexander, were to get a chance to teach. Forbes and his friends in the Argathelian Party could then have worked to arrange this once they saw some political benefit in the scheme. There was some. The two men who held the anatomist's post were willing to give it up; they had had their benefits from it. John Monro, a military surgeon and a volunteer in the '15, would be rewarded for his service to the government with a job which would survive him. And he would vacate a post to which another might be appointed. The younger man would have a chance to show his talents, which many thought substantial. Making him a professor would please those who believed the University ought to expand its teaching of the professional subjects. Unlike his predecessors, he would teach more and regularly. Drummond and MacGill had not been lecturing steadily for fees but demonstrating anatomy on several corpses a year with apparently no lectures between anatomies. Alexander Monro's post in the University promised better lectures for which there was a market which would augment his slim income from a new practice. This novelty would not hurt those who promoted it and might be a considerable benefit to the

University and burgh. It would cost the lieges very little. However it was managed, it would not have been managed only by George Drummond and John Monro for their private ends.

Political considerations are also likely to have affected the Council decision on 14 March 1722 to change Monro's office from being one held during pleasure to one held for life during good behaviour.[63] This decision came a week before the parliamentary election and during the term of Lord Provost John Wightman, an Argathelian who would have been looking after the interests of his faction. In 1722, the Argathelians were straining to extend their control of every burgh by any means they could find. If the Earl of Ilay thought his agents should consult him about minor posts, it is unthinkable that he or others close to him should not have been consulted when his friends on the Town Council handed out a potentially more valuable place. That would not have happened without the concurrence of politicians more important than George Drummond.

Later appointments to this chair were little different, and not just because they went to the son and grandson of the first professor. Alexander I was a skilled anatomist who had learned to make fine wax preparations and eventually accumulated a large and valuable collection of teaching materials without which no one could teach anatomy. Alexander II (20 March 1733–2 October 1817), like his father, was extremely well trained, bright and ambitious. He inherited the collection of teaching preparations his father had amassed. This needed to be kept in the city, but the younger Monro might, if not appointed to the chair, move to the Surgeons' Hall and use his collection for extramural lectures.[64] Or, were he not to be appointed professor of anatomy, he might simply leave the city as his brother Donald had done and take away the collection. That would be bad for the University's medical school, particularly since Monro, *secundus*, by 1754, had begun to acquire a reputation as an anatomist even though he was then only twenty-one. Alexander Monro I promised to train his son and to share the burdens of office with him for some time. He did so until his final resignation in 1764. Alexander Monro II owed his appointment to those factors and to the recognition that he was a man who could bring custom to the school. In 1754, the Town Council was again headed by George Drummond and most of the councillors were loyal to Ilay, now the Duke of Argyll.

Alexander Monro II was a better teacher and researcher than his father. He held the post until 1798, when Alexander III (5 November 1773–10 March 1859) became assistant to his father and then, in 1800, conjoint professor with him. *Tertius* held the post until 1846. The reasons for the appointment of Alexander III as a conjoint professor with his father were essentially the same as those which led to Alexander II's appointment. He had been well trained and possessed the collection of teaching materials which could not be matched in Scotland and was probably equalled for much of this period in Britain only by the ones collected by William and John Hunter for the use of their medical school in London.[65] It did not hurt that Alexander II occasionally dined with Robert Dundas and had voted for Dundas's candidates in 1796.[66] Still, there must, however, have been some uncertainty about the filling of the chair in 1798. Benjamin Bell, a distinguished Edinburgh surgeon, wrote to Lord Advocate Robert Dundas soliciting the post for Dr John Barclay, then the teacher of anatomy at the Surgeons' Hall. He would have been a better choice since Alexander III was neither a brilliant teacher nor a great researcher. He added little of value to the collection, which by the mid-nineteenth century was not what it once had been nor as necessary for teaching. There were to be other Alexander Monros who taught anatomy but in Edinburgh the line ended with him, though not until 1846.

4. SURGERY, CLINICAL SURGERY AND MILITARY SURGERY

In 1777, a chair of surgery was annexed to the chair of anatomy by the Town Council. The establishment of this chair had been requested by students in 1773 and the Surgeons' Company had considered the problem for some time. In 1777, the Surgeons' Company asked Sir Lawrence Dundas, the MP for Edinburgh, to obtain a royal warrant for a chair of surgery. He gave in their petition but it was not supported by the University or the man whom the government trusted more – Henry Dundas, the Lord Advocate, who was then on the verge of consolidating his hold on Scottish politics. Henry Dundas would not support the Incorporation or its chosen man, James Rae, a surgeon who had the distinction of being the first to teach dentistry in the burgh.[67] Alexander Monro II, who from self-interest had opposed this new creation, triumphed and added to his old title that of professor of surgery. The trouble was that he was an anatomist and physiologist and neither an operating surgeon nor a member of the Royal College of Surgeons of Edinburgh.[68] All the title meant was that his monopoly had been extended and upheld by politicians eager to tell the surgeons where real power in the city lay but who cared little about the teaching of surgery in the University. Alexander Monro II would not, could not, teach surgery, but his monopoly continued until a period of warfare placed a premium on the training of surgeons for the army and navy which ended it in 1803.

War led to the increased teaching of surgery by men at the medical school at Surgeons' Hall. James Rae was followed by others: the distinguished surgeon and author, John Aitkin (1779–?), James Russell (1786–93), and in the late 1790s by the eminent anatomists and writers, John (1763–1820) and Charles Bell (1774–1842).[69] In a letter to Robert Dundas soliciting the creation of a University chair of surgery in 1793, Russell not only noted that he had given ten well-attended lecture courses in clinical surgery from 1786 to 1793 but that the lack of a chair of surgery was 'a chasm' in the education offered at the University. Providing for such instruction would increase enrolments and would even add to the income of Alexander Monro II, since it would raise the demand for anatomy lectures.[70] Russell wanted the regius chair he sought to carry a salary of £100.[71] His proposal was given serious consideration, since it was approved by the Lord Advocate, Robert Dundas; the Solicitor General, Robert Blair of Avonton; Lord Chief Baron, James Montgomery; John Davidson, W. S. and Agent for the Crown; and John Hunter, Surgeon General of the Army. Despite that impressive support, nothing came of it. It was only in 1803 that Edinburgh got a regius chair of clinical surgery. Three years later, James Russell (1754–14 August 1836) was appointed to the chair. He also became Consulting Surgeon to the Royal Infirmary, where, having no patients of his own, he commented on the cases of others.[72] The chair of military surgery was a place which, like many others, was created by a new ministry to gratify one of its followers. The first regius professor of military surgery was John Thomson (15 March 1765–1 October 1846), who from 1804 had been the professor of surgery to the Royal College of Surgeons. He owed his University professorship to the Whiggish Earl of Lauderdale, whom he had once tutored in chemistry, and to Earl Spencer.[73] Only with a change of ministers in London, and the temporary ouster of the local Edinburgh Tories, had it been possible to break the monopoly of the Monros. These new establishments were the culmination of a long agitation by the Royal College of Surgeons for the provision of better education for surgeons in the University. They marked steps in making the profession a learned as well as a manual one and they were taken with recent Parisian precedents in mind. The College was well aware that Paris and London were better places for the education of an operating surgeon than was Edinburgh.

The surgeons also had a clear interest in the chair of midwifery, to which they recommended but whose incumbents tended to have recommendations from, and to be members of, the Royal College of Physicians. That chair will be discussed below under the medical chairs.

5. CHEMISTRY TO 1726

The first of the medical chairs established after the failure of the original medical professorships in 1685 was the chair of chemistry and medicine, which was created by the Town Council in 1713. The background to this creation is often said to be the general interest in establishing professional education in Edinburgh on the Dutch model, a cause which Principal Carstares had taken up. Of equal or greater importance was the rivalry with Glasgow University and the competition for students. Glasgow University, late in 1712, decided to seek the establishment of regius chairs of medicine and law.[74] By August 1713, that University had secured its medical chair and was actively looking for a man to fill it, although it would not make an appointment until June 1714. What Glasgow had secured, Edinburgh wanted. By 22 December 1713, Edinburgh's Town Council had, at Carstares' urging, appointed Dr James Crawford (c. 1682–February 1731) as its first professor of chemistry and medicine.

Crawford was a local man from Leith, a Leiden MD who also held the same degree from King's College, Aberdeen, where his sponsor had been Archibald Pitcairne. Like Pitcairne, he was something of a virtuoso, with serious interests in both languages and history.[75] Between July and November 1713 he had been travelling outside Scotland, but upon his return he lost no time in making his request for the post.[76] He petitioned Carstares for its creation and got the endorsement of the College professors and of the Fellows of the Royal College of Physicians of Edinburgh. Crawford was later opposed by Argathelians, which suggests that he did not have their support for this position but relied instead upon the 1st Duke of Montrose and his friends from whom he later expected favours. As we have seen (p. 58), Crawford applied for the Glasgow chair of medicine, possibly because it carried a salary of £50 whereas no salary was attached to his Edinburgh position.[77] The Edinburgh Town Council on 16 January 1714 gave Crawford permission to take the Glasgow medical chair if he wished and if he could get it.[78] In the end, he did not seek the place or else rejected Glasgow's offer. This suggests that his expectations of class fees in Edinburgh were not high and that, in 1714, Glasgow looked as likely to develop as an academic teaching centre as did Edinburgh. In the long run, Glasgow's ambitions were not pushed by the Faculty of Physicians and Surgeons, while those of the University of Edinburgh had the backing of the city's medical corporations and the politicians.

In both cities men continued to think about the creation of medical schools. Edinburgh men were prompted to do so partly because applications for the MD degree continued to come to the University even though it lacked a proper medical faculty. Each time the University granted a degree, it had to ask examiners to come in from outside its walls to aid Dr Crawford when he examined candidates for the MD degree.[79] There were also other reasons which related to the practical accomplishments of the teachers of medicine in the burgh. By 1720, Charles Alston was teaching botany in the town; Monro had a University anatomy class, although he actually taught in the Surgeons' Hall until 1725.[80] Crawford was at least sometimes teaching chemistry and pharmacy in the College.[81] What was lacking was teaching of both the theory and practice of medicine, for which there was a clear demand. Dr William Porterfield (1696–21 July 1771) resolved to meet that perceived need. He announced his intention of doing so in 1723 and was encouraged by the Royal College of Physicians. The Town Council appointed him professor of the theory and practice of medicine in August 1724. Porterfield, about twenty-eight in 1724, could have taught both the theory and practice of medicine as professor Johnstoun was expected to do in Glasgow. The Council's appointment, made while Lord Provost Campbell was in office, bound Porterfield to 'give Colleges regularly, in order to the instructing of Students in the said Science of Medicine.'[82] But Porterfield did not lecture in 1723–4 and he seems not to have done so in 1724–5. He also did not examine candidates for the doctorate with professor James Crawford.[83] It may be that Porterfield overestimated his market or, more likely, that others were more successful in serving it. By 1725–6, when Lord Provost Campbell was replaced by that equally good Argathelian, George Drummond, Porterfield had ceased to be a professor. What happened to Porterfield is an intriguing question which has no sure answer. A very plausible guess can be made about why he left his chair.

In 1726, the Visitation Commission which sat at Glasgow insisted that the medical professors there should teach whenever five students requested their services.[84] As we have seen, the Commission was run by Ilay who sat with it and who had packed the Commission with men who enjoyed his favour, men such as Lord Milton, Charles Erskine, Lord Provost Campbell, the reverend James Alston and Principal William Wishart, all of Edinburgh. As we have seen, this Commission was designed to bring a recalcitrant institution under Ilay's control.[85] One way of bringing pressure to bear on professors was to make them perform the duties required by their commissions. Such pressure was applied to professors Brisbane, Johnstoun and Forbes. All were threatened with sanctions if they failed to teach. If this attitude prevailed in Edinburgh, where Ilay's men were fully in charge of the Town Council, then Porterfield may well have been told to teach or go. Ilay would have had no compunction about the dismissal of Porterfield. What happened to the professor remains unclear, but he probably resigned or got sacked along with less-than-diligent James Crawford, who disappears as a medical professor by 1726 when new teachers of chemistry were appointed.[86] What is notable is that Porterfield and Crawford had both, by 1725, found competition from two sets of extramural teachers who appear to have taken over the market for their skills.[87]

6. THE FOUNDING OF A MEDICAL SCHOOL

Alexander Monro ascribed to his father a leading role in the planning and creation of the medical school, but the time was ripe and the political conditions were favourable for its creation. Monro's efforts were not needed and do not explain the founding of the medical school.

In 1721, Dr John Rutherford may have taught chemistry in Edinburgh.[88] That same year saw the publication of a pamphlet again advocating the building of a public subscription hospital in Edinburgh.[89] One function of the hospital was to be the training of medics. John Monro was urging his son to teach medicine about the time Porterfield was appointed in 1724.[90] Clearly there was thought to be an effective demand for medical teaching. That same year a set of four young doctors – John Rutherford (1 August 1695–6 March 1779), Andrew Sinclair (or St Clair) (c. 1698–25 October 1760), Andrew Plummer (1698–16 April 1756) and John Innes (1696–12 December 1733) – had the same idea. In the autumn of 1724, they advertised in the *Caledonian Mercury* lectures on the theory and practice of medicine which were to begin on 10 November.[91] They promised to teach chemistry in the following year, by which time they had acquired a house for use as a laboratory and rights to the use of the College 'physic garden' to sustain a pharmaceutical business they planned to conduct and which they soon started. Their chemistry lectures began in February 1725.[92] For the teaching of anatomy they would have relied on Alexander Monro and on Charles Alston for the teaching of botany and *materia medica* since there is no indication that George Preston or anyone else was actively teaching these subjects.

The following year saw the appearance of competitors, a duo composed of Dr William Graeme (1701–45) and Dr George Martine (1702–41). They had almost certainly met as medical students at Leyden in c. 1720, where they would have met one or all of their rivals in the competing foursome.[93] Graeme was lecturing on the practice of medicine by, if not before, the autumn of 1725, when he was given the rooms at the Surgeons' Hall vacated by Alexander Monro in October of that year. Martine joined him there some time in 1725 – probably in the autumn since medical lectures generally began in October or early November.[94] Martine taught some anatomy, some chemistry and the theory of medicine or physiology.[95] They lectured for about two years. The fact they taught more than one year points to a market that demanded lectures on anatomy, medicine and chemistry and was large enough to employ six men. Graeme later bragged that he and Martine had as many students as the foursome with whom they competed.[96] This could last only so long as neither set was university professors. By 1728, Graeme had moved from Edinburgh to London, where he published 'A Proposal to teach the Theory and Practice of Physick, in a Course of lectures' (1728). The next year, he produced a short work on the study of medicine and seems to have continued teaching and practising in London. He became an FRS in 1730. Martine gave up lecturing in Edinburgh either in 1727 or 1728. He returned to St Andrews, where he practised and experimented until 1739/40. He became a member of the Philosophical Society of Edinburgh and an FRS in 1740. In the same year, he secured a post as a military doctor, a place which soon cost him his life at Cartagena.

A market great enough to give employment first to at least four men and then in 1725 to eight men was great enough to recognise with university chairs. Independent of Monro's efforts, the young physicians eager to teach were hoping for places in the University.[97] As we shall see, the political conditions were also favourable for their creation.

Both sets of men tried for university posts but the political ties of the duo all ran the wrong way for men looking for places in the gift of a Town Council which owed fealty to the Argathelians. Martine came from a minor Jacobite family settled in St Andrews where, as a student, he had rung the University's bells for the Pretender during the '15 and where he and others, flourishing pistols, had threatened a college porter and his wife (see below, p. 415). Things like that were remembered, particularly by Ilay's enemies who for years accused him of being a secret Jacobite or at least soft on the Jacobites. Graeme was also some sort of kinsman of the Squadrone-supporting James Graham, 1st Duke of Montrose; 'Graham' was a spelling of the surname under which the doctor also appears. After he moved to London, Dr Graeme served Montrose as a physician and was in attendance at his death in 1742.[98] Such men could not expect help from Ilay or his friends on the Town Council. The duo were also not likely to be able to call on any important political supporters who could help them. Lord Provost Drummond might tell Professor William Cullen in 1756 that the choice of one set of young men over the other had been difficult to make, but Drummond's difficult choices were usually made in his patron's interest. It was not in Ilay's interest to see appointed a Graeme or a man who had been a Jacobite.

The other four seem politically quite differently situated. Andrew Sinclair was some sort of cousin to Andrew Fletcher, Lord Milton, by then Ilay's Edinburgh manager.[99] Plummer in 1742 was listed as a strong supporter of the Argathelians and he is likely to have been so earlier since his estate lay in Selkirkshire, which was pretty much in the Argathelian's political grasp after 1722.[100] John Rutherford came from the same area. He had been looking to a teaching career since 1721, when he applied for the new medical professorship established at St Andrews by the 1st Duke of Chandos, a man friendly with Ilay and rather like him. Rutherford's application in 1721 had been supported by James Erskine, Lord Grange, then one of Ilay's political allies.[101] About John Innes less is known, but he did get a minor city job, Physician to Heriot's Hospital, in 1730 when the patronage was controlled by Ilay's friends.[102] The little that is known of their politics suggests that these men were of, or in, Ilay's party and could expect his backing, while the other two could not.

In another way which counts, the duo of Martine and Graeme were also less well-positioned to apply for the University positions. Graeme was a member of the Surgeons' Company but Martine was affiliated with no Edinburgh medical corporation. The University was unlikely to support giving a medical chair to a man in the surgeons' guild because that would not have given the University the prestige it needed to attract men to study in Edinburgh. The surgeons were tradesmen represented on the Town Council and they would not have provided as much socially impressive support as the more dignified Royal College of Physicians to which the foursome belonged and whose endorsement they secured.

One must also not underestimate the very tense political atmosphere in which these appointments were considered and made. After the elections of 1722, Ilay tried hard to oust his Squadrone opponents from the administration and control of *any* Scottish patronage, but he had not yet done so. Edinburgh in 1725/6 was gripped by the furore created by the Malt Tax imposed in 1725. The imposition of the tax set off riots in Glasgow and Edinburgh when collections were attempted. Ilay came up from London to see that this new law was enforced despite the opposition of the judges on the Courts of Session and Justiciary, notably the opposition of Adam Cockburn of Ormiston, the Lord Justice Clerk, who normally headed the latter court which handled criminal cases.[103] Ormiston was a Squadrone man. Ilay arrived in the city on 16 August 1725. Within a month he had forced the striking brewers to brew again and to pay their taxes. Halfway through this period, the Duke of Roxburghe, a Squadrone man and the King's personal friend, had been sacked as Secretary of State for Scotland. The news reached Edinburgh by the end of August. It soon became apparent that Walpole had given the Earl a nearly free hand to manage most things in Scotland as he saw fit. For Ilay that meant punishing some, rewarding others, and showing that he had a near monopoly of government patronage other than that belonging to the Treasury. He was the man to whom most Scots should look for favours. His actions showed he would prevail and that he could secure places in the universities. He did so at Glasgow through the Visitation of Glasgow University and his defence of professor John Simson.[104] In the Universities of Aberdeen[105] and St Andrews,[106] he did so by appointments and the defence of other alleged heretics.

The Edinburgh civic elections of 1725 were prepared for in this atmosphere. Although rancorous, they were carefully planned to return men through whom Ilay could control the burgh. Control of the Town Council meant control over University appointments. Ilay was very much a participant in those elections since he did not return to London until 17 November 1725, by which time they had occurred. How closely he watched these and how prepared he was to reward and punish medical men can be seen in a letter written to the Duke of Newcastle dated 16 September 1725. This letter is worth quoting at length because it suggests that a man so interested in what the town councillors were doing in the aftermath of the Malt Tax Riots would have known and approved of actions which have been attributed to George Drummond rather than to the man he served. If there were jobs to be handed out, and men to be sacked or punished in this period, they would have had Ilay's approval:

Some days agoe a secret design began to discover it self in this City of over-turning the Present Magistrates & all their interest at the new Elections, & in particular of putting at the head of the Mechanick corporations [the crafts guilds] a very active person who I think is a Jacobite, & whose brother was in the late Rebellion: the office intended for him is called Deacon conveener, & the Man is one Eaton a Goldsmith: this officer amoung other privileges has the keeping of the Standard of the Tradesmen [the 'Blue Blanket'], which in cases of insurrections is held in veneration amoung them to a degree that is incredible; this fellow had a majority amoung those of his own trade, got himself chosen their deacon (or Chief) & had made such interest amoung the deacons of the other trades, that he thought himself sure, but the present Magistrates & Town Council having a right to appoint one of the deacons to be extraordinary (as they call it) whereby such person has no vote in the Town Council but in disposing of publick money, they named, by a majority this Eaton to be extraordinary deacon: when the Assembly of deacons met to chuse their deacon con-veener, there was the utmost effort made by the enemy to chuse this person, but, as it had been forseen, some of his friends thought it would be an affront to their body to put at their head [one] who had hardly any vote in the Town Council, this brought the Votes to an equality, & consequently to the casting vote of the present deacon Conveeneer, who is one Keir a Baker by trade, & who has been very usefull during the late distractions; upon this they quarrelled to that degree among themselves that nothing but this Keir's putting an end to the meeting by declaring the Vote against Eaton could have prevented some disturbance. I am ashamed of troubling your Grace with such minute circumstances, but as the Elections in this City are of the last consequence to his Majesties service in Scotland, I think it my duty to watch every step in them as narrowly as possible, & I believe all will go very well: the Enemies of the Government seem to think it absolutely necessary to leave nothing undone that can prevent the abating of the present seditious humour of the People, & therefore daily spread some false report to keep up the disaffection: they endeavour to preswade the people that the present ministry will very soon be overturned, & name some persons in England (whom your Grace may easily guess) who will be put into power & will ease this Country of the Malt Tax . . .

. . . In the present contest in this City relating to their Elections, Mr John Macgill Surgeon & Apothecary has been very active & usefull, he has always been zealous for the Government, & at the late Rebellion he served as a voluntier; I would beg leave to recommend him to the office of his Majesties Apothecary (40 lb per Ann.) Which is possess'd at present by one Henry Hepburn a near relation of the Justice Clerks, he has instead of assisting the Magistrates amoung those of his trade, absented himself out of Town during the whole time of the late disorders & and present contests.

I am My Lord very confident that a proper distribution of the favours of the Government to those who deserve well, with an absolute exclusion to all who oppose or show an avowed indifference in his Majesties service will soon bring this Country to a sense of their duty . . .[107]

A man who so closely watched Edinburgh politics in 1725 would not have ignored the creation of new chairs in the University or have been indifferent to who got them. There is every reason to think that the men chosen for the professorships were chosen with an eye to their and their families' politics. Professors Porterfield and Crawford may have suffered deposition for their politics as well as their nonfeasance. It would have been almost unprecedented and unnatural for the four appointments to be made by the town councillors without consulting their betters, particularly since these posts were contested and worth contesting. If Ilay was giving favours on behalf of the government and excluding the unworthy from office, he would have been consulted about the plans of the foursome whose jobs collectively were worth far more than the post of King's Apothecary.[108] Since the Earl was in the city when such things were likely to have been considered, he would have written no letters about them. It is unsurprising that there are none in the papers of Lord Milton.

Finally, there was another reason for Ilay to be interested in and consulted about the foursome who applied for Town Council favour on 1 February 1726. Ilay himself had serious interests in chemistry and medicine, to which his honorary MD from King's College, Aberdeen (1708) attested. To give a peer and a trained civil lawyer a medical degree, rather than a DCL or LLD, shows a solicitude for a particular interest which should not be missed. The Earl's library also shows how interested in medicine and chemistry he really was. By 1726, he had a sizable collection of medical and chemical books and had proven himself to be a competent amateur chemist and a man with many other scientific and mathematical interests.[109] The men seeking to be professors were men of the same kidney but the foursome had an edge.

Martine was no narrow specialist. He was interested in anatomy, chemistry, mathematics and physics and eventually published in all those fields. He was later known for his edition of Eustachio's anatomical works and commentaries.[110] He lectured on anatomical topics in one of the years he taught in Edinburgh. But the University had an anatomist who was already teaching and was probably cooperating with the competing foursome.[111] Martine also had been a successful teacher of chemistry since his brother, Arthur, told William Wilson in 1755 that William Cullen should be advised to teach in Edinburgh whether or not he had an appointment because George Martine had 'success in that way against a greater opposition'.[112] Martine's interests in chemistry were theoretical and ran to heat and to the practical problems of measuring its intensity and quantity.[113] In all this he was a forerunner of Joseph Black, who used his published work on heat as a text in his own course at Edinburgh after 1766. This would not have looked particularly useful to men like Lord Provost Drummond and his patrons. Unlike Cullen and Black, Martine is not known to have supplemented his theoretical interests with chemical consulting for businessmen. The councillors and Ilay in 1726 would have been more impressed by the pharmaceutical company run by the four other young chemists, or the ability, which Plummer displayed later in life, to do chemical assays of mineral ores.[114] Martine's interests in physics and mathematics may also have seemed irrelevant in a College which had just acquired an even better physicist and mathematician in the person of its new professor of mathematics, Colin Maclaurin. Graeme had more limited interests, being primarily a medical man concerned with the practice and the teaching of medicine. In his university appointments, Ilay usually favoured the many-sided person who could be publicly useful over those with more narrow interests who were less likely to do publicly useful things.

The four MDs by 1726 had all taught some aspect of medicine and they were all chemists whose chemical knowledge was being put to commercial or public purposes. Ilay would have found this a point in their favour.[115] He later backed a number of chemists in their efforts to improve bleaching and other industrial processes in Scotland. Chemistry and the ability to teach and use it may have been of greater importance in other ways which have not been noticed. The foursome all taught the subject jointly in the University, where for some time after 1726 they *jointly* replaced the professor of chemistry, James Crawford.[116] They had a laboratory of their own in which they could teach chemistry and pharmacy, while the University did not have one which was adequate. Crawford had had rooms in the College but he seems to have had no laboratory supported by annual grants from the town or College. That this mattered is suggested by a letter of George Drummond to William Cullen in February 1756. Drummond wrote: 'At that time I should have cheerfully come in to the Town's accomodating them with a laboratory, if our finances would have admitted of it.'[117] The cost of employing men possessed of a laboratory would in the long run have been less than employing men lacking one which the town would be expected to provide and maintain.

The town had already encouraged this foursome of young doctors. When the four petitioned the Council for their posts, they referred to the fact that they had 'undertaken the professing and teaching of Medicine in this City, and, by the encouragement which the Council had been pleased to grant them, had carried it on with some success.'[118] As successful men, they were asking for further favours, not initial ones. The four had taught longer, had apparently found an audience, and had survived the competition of their rivals. George Drummond when he wrote to Cullen in 1756 saying that both sets of doctors petitioned the Town Council for appointment to the University and that the Council 'were only making a trial, and were somewhat uncertain about its success',[119] was perhaps alluding to the fact that the four had had some encouragement and were now being given more. But Drummond was quite wrong about the tentative nature of the appointments given to the men who got 'a preference in our choice'. They were appointed for life on good behaviour. Moreover, the men who received the appointments in 1726 were regarded by the College as constituting a 'Faculty'. On 1 November 1726, the minutes of the RCPE record the thanks of the University, conveyed by professors Robert Stewart and Colin Drummond, for having in the past supplied examiners for degree candidates. The went on to say, 'now that there was a sufficient number of Professors of Medicine to make a Facultie of Medicine . . . they would no longer trouble the Colledge [of Physicians] any more upon that head.' The Town Council also seems to have regarded the new appointments as creating a Faculty, since it said that medicine in all its branches could now be taught there and the 'Professors of that Science may by themselves promote students to their degrees, with as great solemnity as is done in any other College or University at home or abroad.'[120] Drummond's recollection of the appointments as tentative and a trial may reduce his understanding of a permanent place as one which was funded – not an unlikely way for a placeman like Drummond to regard a post. This finds some support in Dr Graeme's 1729 claim to have 'been for three Years publickly Teaching, in a Place [Edinburgh] where, though Physick <u>has</u> no settled Establishment for a Professor, yet it is much studied and well understood.'[121] That may have reflected Graeme's knowledge that none of the professors had a salary and only two of them could sit and vote in the Senatus. This they were to do by turns.

Given the way things had been done in the past when chairs were created or were up for filling, one can be reasonably sure that Lord Provost Drummond and John Monro did not engineer either Alexander Monro's or these appointments by themselves.[122] The divinity chairs all had been politicked for. That was less true of the law chairs but they too went to well-connected men, men about whom the Council had no choice. The chair of botany was little different. When the chair of chemistry and medicine was created in 1713, it seems to have been created partly in imitation of the Glasgow foundation. This regius chair came through the Secretary of State for Scotland. Later, in 1715, Montrose was asked to find a salary for Professor Crawford.[123] When the Edinburgh chair of anatomy was created in 1720, Ilay's friends were involved. Lords Provost John Campbell and George Drummond were involved in the creation of the chairs of anatomy and medicine; both were Argathelians. The likeliest conclusion is that the creation of the Edinburgh medical faculty was a political job carried out by Argathelians with the support of their leaders. There is some slight confirmation of this in an obituary of Lord Ilay. There he is credited with the creation of *several chairs* in the Scottish universities. The only *one* which he is known to have created is the Glasgow chair of practical astronomy. The obituary is accurate in other respects, which leads one to think that the Edinburgh chairs should be added to his list and that we should all think less of John Monro and George Drummond, who were only among the supporters of a general movement to establish medical education in the city.[124]

7. MIDWIFERY

Finally, we must look at the professorship of midwifery created in the town for Joseph Gibson (c. 1698–c. January 1739) in 1726. Gibson held an MD but practised as a surgeon in Leith.[125] He was Library Keeper to the Surgeons' Company, in succession to Alexander Monro.[126] Gibson was also an Episcopalian, which would not have made him eager to subscribe to the Westminster Confession as a professor in any Scottish university would be expected to do.[127] This may be why he was not made a member of the University while his successor was. Both of them taught some medical students and not just the local female midwives. Gibson's skills, and his political connections, must have been good since religious deviants were seldom preferred. His skills were attested to by both the Incorporation of Surgeons and the Royal College of Physicians, which supported his petition to the Town Council for the post he received.[128] Unfortunately, nothing more is known of him.

About his successor, Robert Smith (1705–74), we know marginally more. He was recommended by the Surgeons and was appointed as a professor with the right to sit in the Senatus. He successively married two women bearing the names of Jacobite families but he himself was a member of the Revolution Society which annually celebrated the Whiggism of its members. Smith was polite enough to have belonged to the Musical Society and sensible enough to have made a politic resignation in 1756 for Thomas Young (c. 1728–3 February 1783), who got what was widely thought to be a political job.[129] Glasgow's professor John Anderson and its sometime rector, John Graham of Dougalston, both saw Young's appointment as a political reward to one of Argyll's men who had done useful work while sitting on the Town Council as the representative of the Surgeons' guild. Young was also the son of a distinguished extramural teacher of medicine, George Young. Thomas could have found politically important backers in the clubs to which he belonged: the Revolution Society, the Music Society and the Edinburgh Philosophical Society. He married a daughter of a Dr Thomas Gibson. When he took a conjoint successor in 1780, it was Alexander Hamilton (1739–1802), a learned, wealthy, land-owning surgeon who had recently headed his guild and served on the Town Council. Hamilton had published a number of things including a textbook on his subject. He in turn took his son, James (1767–14 November 1839), as assistant and conjoint professor in 1798[130] and resigned in 1800 two years before his death.[131] His son was allowed to succeed partly because the Hamiltons had sustained the Edinburgh Lying-in Hospital largely out of their own pockets. It was a needed teaching facility and the easiest way to keep it readily available to students was to appoint James Hamilton who, in any case, would have been a strong candidate. As with the anatomy chair, tangible assets, including the wickerwork teaching dummies of pregnant women, figured in this appointment, which, like that of his father, Henry Dundas reckoned he had determined.[132] All the midwifery professors were well thought of by their fellows; they all published but in at least three cases the politicians who chose them are also clearly visible.

8. CHEMISTRY AFTER 1726

When the four young men were appointed in 1726, the chairs of medicine and chemistry were not tied to any one man; all four taught chemistry at some time, although Innes and Plummer seem to have been the chief teachers of the subject. After Innes died in 1733, Plummer usually taught alone until 1754, when his health failed. Then Joseph Black taught for him for a short time. Plummer's tenure was notable for the teaching of pharmacy. As a pharmacist, he was the inventor of the widely used 'Plummer's Pill' which remained in the bags of physicians until the end of the nineteenth century and which helped to make him affluent and allowed him to leave off medical practice before 1751. He acted as a chemical analyst for the Philosophical Society of Edinburgh, which he served as Secretary c. 1737–c. 1749. In 1742, he offered to analyse samples of ores sent in by would-be improvers. His career established a precedent which required the chair to be publicly useful not only to physicians but also to industry. That was why, in 1751, when there were rumours that Plummer would give up his teaching as well as his practice, Cullen thought he would himself be an ideal man for the place.[133] When the chair of chemistry had to be filled, after Plummer became incapacitated, that would be kept in mind.

There were several real candidates for the post in 1754–5.[134] Joseph Black (16 April 1728–6 December 1799) was the weakest. Having just finished his medical degree, he had no prominent medical backers save the professors who had taught him, including Plummer who had employed him as a deputy.[135] The College men did not like the way William Cullen (15 April 1710–5 February 1790) was being parachuted into their institution without a deal worked out to protect Plummer's interests. They wanted Black but they had no votes.[136] Outside the College, Black seems to have had two political supporters. One was William Alexander, Lord Provost in 1752, and MP on the Argathelian interest in 1754. The second was Black's cousin, James Russel, a prominent Edinburgh surgeon, who in 1755 sat as a Trades Councillor representing the Incorporation of Surgeons. The struggle for the chair was a struggle between men committed to the same faction, which made it easier for the better, or senior, man to win.

A more formidable candidate than Black was Francis Home, whose chief supporter was his relative, Lord Milton.[137] In the end, Milton did not persuade Argyll to appoint Home, who deferred to Milton's judgement that he should not contest the place but wait until one could be found for him.[138] That left William Cullen, whose candidacy was pushed by many. Henry Home, Lord Kames, lobbied councillors, physicians, professors and Lord Milton.[139] William Hunter in London wrote to Argyll.[140] Others spoke to town councillors, to John Maule, who had been Argyll's secretary before the Duke made him a Baron of the Scottish Exchequer, and still others to the professors. All those recommendations were in the end directed to Argyll.[141] According to Robert Chambers, 'At this critical juncture of affairs, the duke of Argyle arrived in Edinburgh, and employed the whole weight of his interest in favour of Dr Cullen.'[142] Cullen became conjoint professor with Plummer in 1755 and succeeded to the chair on Plummer's death in the following year. Once more, the Council ratified Argyll's personal choice.[143]

When Cullen moved to a medical chair in 1766, the chemistry post went to Joseph Black, who had spent a decade teaching medicine and chemistry at Glasgow University. He was everybody's candidate and unanimously chosen, which we know from the correspondence of Baron Mure. He had watched Black's selection as more than a disinterested observer since he was now more or less the patronage manager for the ministry in London.[144] Black said he owed his post to Dr Cullen, Principal Robertson and other friends.[145] By then, the Town Council needed to appoint the best man who could be found and the politicians understood that. All agreed Black was best.

In 1795, when Black sought to retire by taking a conjoint professorship, merit was less regarded than loyalty. Black initially backed his assistant, John Rotherham, to succeed him. Rotherham had been making interest among the Town Councillors by the beginning of 1794. However, Henry Dundas and his friends wanted to give the chair to Dr Daniel Rutherford, with Thomas Charles Hope coming from Glasgow to Edinburgh to assume Rutherford's chair of botany. Neither was well qualified for the posts the politicians wanted them to have. Lord Advocate Robert Dundas, Henry Dundas's patronage manager, suggested that Rotherham could be provided for at Glasgow in the chair of botany which was not in fact vacant. That suggestion at least recognised Rotherham's period of study of botany with Linnaeus at Uppsala. Robert assured Henry that the MP for Edinburgh would find the Edinburgh Town Council reasonable enough when it was pointed out that other patronage could be found for Rotherham whom the Councillors liked and wished to help.[146] Neither Black, Rotheram nor Henry Dundas had their way, but neither did the town councillors.

In October 1795, Lord Provost James Stirling told Robert Dundas 'that the succession to Black's Class was a matter so fixed, that it was impossible to interfere.' What this meant was that the medical and scientific community had found the man they and, by then, possibly Black regarded as best. The Town Council was told he was Thomas Charles Hope (21 July 1766–3 June 1844).[147] To have opposed this nomination would have appeared to be working against the best interests of the Medical School and, thus, against one source of the city's prosperity. That could not be done. The Dundas connection put the best face on the matter they could and agreed to his appointment.[148] Hope was not only better connected in Edinburgh than Rotherham but he also had a better record as a research chemist, even though he never realised his early promise as a practical researcher.[149] Rotherham was taken care of by Henry Dundas at St Andrews[150] (see below, pp. 500–2).

9. The Institutes or Theory of Medicine

In 1726, the chairs of the institutes or theory of medicine and of the practice of medicine had gone initially to John Rutherford and Andrew Sinclair, with the latter eventually becoming the man who generally taught theory. Sinclair had a mad wife and was in fragile health himself. Around c. 1744–7 he was forced to leave his chair because of his own health and that of his wife. Robert Whytt (6 September 1714–15 April 1766) then served as his deputy. Like Sinclair, Whytt taught both the institutes and the theory and practice of medicine and perhaps chemistry. He published notable papers on lime water.[151] The young doctor was a bright man but his connections in Edinburgh were also excellent. His first wife was the daughter of James Drummond of Blair Drummond and thus distantly related to Lord Provost Drummond and more closely related to Henry Home's [later Lord Kames'] wife who came from the same family. Whytt's second wife, whom he married in 1743, was the sister of James Balfour of Pilrig. Through that family he was related to Gavin Hamilton, an important publisher and town councillor, to professor William Cleghorn and to Glasgow's William Leechman. Whytt owned a small estate in Fifeshire where he had a vote. Not surprisingly, he had support from Argathelians. His biographer says, 'Provost Drummond was instrumental in placing Whytt in the chair, and in seeking the consent of the Duke of Argyll, through his delegate Lord Milton.'[152] This was the normal way in which Drummond interfered in University affairs as long as the great Duke lived.

When Whytt died in 1766, William Hunter approached Lord Bute on Cullen's behalf and Lord Kames made representations to others. These men very likely had as much effect on the outcome of the election as did the request of the medical students that Cullen be translated to this chair.[153] When he left it, to become the sole professor of the practice of medicine in 1773, there was a contest for the vacated chair which involved Drs Alexander Monro Drummond (by 1745–13 September 1782), Gregory Grant, William Buchan, Dr ___ Rutherford, Andrew Duncan and James Lind (17 May 1736–1812).[154] Drummond was picked after the Town Council sought the advice of the medical faculty members who gave him the nod. With a name such as his, it should surprise no one that he was chosen. Drummond did not come to an immediate decision about the medical chair. He was unwilling to give up his position as Physician to the King of Naples and remained in Naples until 1782, when he died as the result of a fall from his spirited horse. He dithered for three years, during which the chair was filled by deputies. James Gregory (January 1753–2 April 1821), then still a student, lectured for the remainder of the year in which his father had died. He presumably read his father's notes from December until the end of the course in May. Andrew Duncan (17 October 1744–5 July 1828) deputised in 1773–4,[155] 1774–5 and 1775–6. By then Drummond had made up his mind and there was a contest for the chair.[156]

James Gregory and Duncan contested the chair, which was also sought by a number of others who dropped out of contention early. Gregory won. Duncan attributed his choice to a 'powerful connexion' and to 'political interest'.[157] He was so angry and aggrieved that he published in the *Medical Commentaries*, which he edited, the following statement about appointments:

All that Dr Duncan wished for was that the magistrates should as formerly, send to the professors a list of the candidates that might offer, requesting their opinion which of them they believed was the best qualified for discharging the duties of that important office in all its branches; or, if they had any particular reason for not thus consulting the professors, that they should take the opinion of the colleges of physicians and surgeons at large on the same question. But in place of this, the Lord Provost put a question

304   ACADEMIC PATRONAGE IN THE SCOTTISH ENLIGHTENMENT

to the Medical Professors, asking whether they had any objection to
Dr James Gregory. To which the Professors returned an answer in writing,
informing him that they had no objection to Dr Gregory.[158]

The Lord Provost had, in effect, ruled out a competition because he
knew in advance the answer he wanted and the one they had to give.
Gregory had taught successfully when he had lectured; his former colleagues could hardly insult him by saying 'No'. The Lord Provost,
James Stoddart, was later one of Henry Dundas's men and in 1776 was
opposed to Sir Lawrence Dundas, whom his distant cousin, Henry, was
trying to oust from importance in Edinburgh politics. His manoeuvre
prevented the normal negotiation of the place. Duncan later became a
Foxite Whig and seems to have remained opposed to Henry Dundas
for many years. In 1789, Duncan had the dying blessing of William
Cullen when he took the chair which Gregory left to assume the chair
of the practice of medicine – also with Cullen's blessing.[159]

These appointments show a deference to medical men but only one
appointment seems not to have involved at least one prominent political figure. Again, the Town Council's only role was to take the good
advice which came from the town's most prominent and respected
physicians and surgeons and from its politicians. Everyone recognised
that the prosperity of the city depended heavily on the reputation of
the medical school, which could be kept up only through the appointment of good men.

10. THE PRACTICE OF MEDICINE

As we have seen, the duties of the chairs of the theory and practice of
medicine were initially shared. Sinclair and his successor, Robert
Whytt, both lectured with John Rutherford until some date unknown,
after which Rutherford became the sole professor. By 1764,
Rutherford, who had been teaching since c. 1721 and regularly for
forty years, was ready to retire. He tried to arrange for Francis Home
to succeed him.[160] Home's 'Memorial to Lord Milton' asking for the
job is interesting because it sets out the grounds on which he and
others now thought the medical posts should be awarded – public
service, successful practice and authorship:

That I have these 16 years [he resigned as an Army surgeon in General
Cope's Regiment in 1748] been preparing Myself for this Class; have all
the Lectures ready writt. & have Reduced them into aphorisms & published them 6 years agoe. There never was a Professor in the Colledge that

had done so much before he got it, nor even afterwards. That makes the Opposition to me at present most Singular.

I think if things were more equal that the Country owes me a favour for establishing on a firm footing so essential a part of the Linen Manufacture of this Country as Bleaching. That the Present opposition arises from the Ambition of the Principal [William Robertson] & the Disappointment of the late Provost [probably George Drummond].[161]

Home had support from Lords Milton and Kames, Baron Mure, John Home (he had influence with the 3rd Earl of Bute) and, for a time, from James Coutts, MP for the city, a man whom Bute favoured.[162] He was opposed by the 'College People', which meant the medical faculty, the principal and many students. They wanted Cullen in this chair or, if that were not possible, for Black to be appointed. Lord Bute's brother, James Stuart Mackenzie, then the government's chief patronage manager for Scotland, switched his support to Cullen in September but Rutherford would have none of it and soldiered on.[163] Cullen, disappointed, went into Whytt's old chair.

In 1766 Rutherford picked another man, John Gregory (3 June 1724–10 February 1773), to succeed him and resigned once the Lord Provost, James Stewart, had indicated his willingness to back Gregory.[164] Gregory was a popular and well-connected man who had held professorships in King's College, Aberdeen before coming to Edinburgh, where he had practised for two years. His friends in Aberdeen and London, where he had also practised, included many intellectuals but it is unclear why he so impressed Rutherford. They may have shared a common religious perspective. Or perhaps everyone was willing to humour the aging Rutherford (he was 71) to get rid of him. Gregory kept the chair until his death in 1773, but from 1769 on he alternated with William Cullen so that students who stayed two years could hear their lectures on both the theory and the practice of medicine.[165]

When Gregory died in 1773, Cullen kept the practice chair which was the more lucrative and prestigious; he held it until just before his own death on 5 February 1790. Before he died, he knew of, and approved, the Town Council's decision to appoint James Gregory (January 1753–2 April 1821) as his successor.[166] Gregory had petitioned the Council for this post. Here again a famous medical professor named the man to succeed – a clear testimonial of the Town Council's willingness to be guided by its most renowned professor. With Cullen's immense prestige, the town could hardly make an issue of an appointment which might bring much money to the burgh.[167]

Henry Dundas agreed to this too.[168] The medical men, the other professors, knowledgeable outsiders, even the students now had more to do with the picking of these men than did the town councillors or even a politician as strong as Henry Dundas.

11. Natural History

In Edinburgh as in Europe generally during this period, natural history was closely associated with medicine since many of its concerns dealt with life.[169] Natural history constituted a part of a general science education but one still tied to medical faculties. In Edinburgh, the natural history chair was associated with the medical school. The chair was created by royal patent on 13 March 1767 and was given to Dr Robert Ramsay of Blackcraig (1735–15 December 1778). It had been in the works from at least 1763–4, when various men around Edinburgh began to worry about the University Museum which was fast disappearing through neglect.[170] By 1764, Andrew Ramsay wrote to Lord Loudoun thanking him for recommending his brother, Dr Robert Ramsay, to someone, probably another Campbell since Robert Ramsay went abroad with the son of the Earl of Breadalbane shortly after this. According to the 11th Earl of Buchan, the regius chair was obtained for Ramsay by Breadalbane.[171] Professor John Hope thought that his friend the Earl of Loudoun also had had a hand in Ramsay's appointment.[172] These related noblemen very likely secured the creation of the chair. What politicking took place to found this chair was done quietly in London, since Ramsay's appointment seems to have come as a surprise to those to whom he presented his patent in 1770. Some politicking would have been required since its foundation meant finding money to fund the stipend of £70 a year. When appointed, Ramsay asked the Town Council that he be made Keeper of the University Museum.[173] The Council complied but reserved to themselves the right to make rules for him and to create a parallel chair of their own should they choose to do so.

Ramsay was a failure as a teacher but he was not without connections in the scientific world. He had himself made the grand tour.[174] He knew intellectuals in Holland, France and Switzerland. A letter from him to Sir Alexander Dick in 1766 mentions his meeting Count Carburi, the professor of chemistry and medicine in Turin, who had toured Scotland in the previous year. Ramsay could have done more, but he died in 1778 having given no lectures and done little about the museum.

As early as 1775, moves were made by others to come by this post. William Smellie, the century's most learned Edinburgh printer and the editor of the first *Encyclopedia Britannica* (1771), was one of those who sought it. He had studied medicine, was a respectable botanist and eventually translated some of Buffon's work into English. For a while he had the backing of Lord Kames.[175] Unfortunately for Smellie, Kames had used his influence for candidates for parliamentary seats backed by men other than Sir Lawrence Dundas in Stirlingshire and Argyllshire.[176] Sir Lawrence, then MP for Edinburgh, 'had the power to nominate' but would have nothing to do with Kames's friend. By early 1776, a majority of the Town Council was for Smellie, who was warned not to approach Henry Dundas, MP for Midlothian and the enemy of Sir Lawrence. Henry too was opposed to some of Smellie's friends.[177] Kames still seems to have been for Smellie in 1777 but by early 1778 he had switched his support to John Walker (1731–31 December 1803), the minister of Moffat, a first-rate botanist and a naturalist who had surveyed the Highlands for the Kirk in 1764 and 1771.[178] Walker belonged to the Moderate Party in the Kirk and was a prominent, though usually absent, member of the Philosophical Society of Edinburgh. By 1778, Walker could count Principal Robertson, Lord Provost Walter Hamilton and the party of Sir Lawrence Dundas in his interest.[179] Smellie recalled that his friends, probably the Earl of Buchan, 'applied to Lord SUFFOLK in my favour'. Suffolk was the Secretary of State and would normally have been approached by the MP for Edinburgh or some other person having the confidence of the government. This was a last-gasp try for the job. 'Dr Walker's political interest was strongest and I lost the chair.'[180] This was a marginal science chair and as such not handled like the chairs from which medicine was taught.

Late in February 1778, John Walker told Sir David Dalrymple, Lord Hailes, that he hoped to get the chair through a complex deal which involved securing the chair and the parish of Colinton at the same time. He had the active support of the Earl of Hopetoun, Sir John Pringle, PRS, Lord Provost Walter Hamilton and presumably Dalrymple.[181] Walker wrote to Kames on 7 March 1778 that the chair was to be 'sold' and asked him to resist the sale. Presumably Ramsay would resign for a payment if the men who could dispose of it were willing to appoint a man willing to buy Ramsay's interest. The price was said to be £700, ten years' purchase – a rather steep price for a dying man's post.[182] The would-be purchaser was Daniel Rutherford (3 November 1749–15 November 1819). He was twenty-nine and might live to recoup the cost. Another of the 'numberless others' who sought the place was William Cullen's son Henry. He started too late to really make much of a run for the chair, even though his father's influence would have counted for much.[183] In the end the chair was not sold but won by Walker's politicking.

The awarding of this bit of patronage led to considerable bitterness between Foxite Whigs, who looked to Lord Buchan and his politician brothers, Thomas and Henry Erskine, and the increasingly Tory party forming around Henry Dundas and the Moderates in the Kirk led by William Robertson. By 1783 it had led to the formation of two royally chartered societies in the burgh, The Royal Society of Edinburgh, sponsored by the Edinburgh establishment, and the Society of Antiquaries of Scotland, which had grown out of a 1780 Society of Antiquaries of Scotland formed by Buchan.[184] Walker, Principal Robertson and most of the University professors opposed the formation of the SAS in which Smellie became an officer and was appointed to give lectures on the philosophy of natural history. Walker objected to these. Their substance later appeared as Smellie's two-volume work, *Philosophy of Natural History* (1790, 1799). Walker became an active professor of natural history, working until 1800 when he took as his deputy Robert Jameson (11 July 1774–19 April 1854) who succeeded him in 1804.

Jameson, one of Walker's best pupils, shared with him an interest in the Highlands and Islands where both of them had done significant work. Jameson did not lack competition for the chair, which he occupied from 1804 until his death in 1854. None of it was very serious because by 1804 Jameson had an impressive series of accomplishments and impeccable sponsors. He had published several books on Scottish mineralogy and was the leading Scottish 'Neptunist' or Wernerian geological theorist. He had also written many articles for *Nicholson's Journal of Natural Philosophy*. He was helped into his chair by the distinguished chemist Charles Hatchett and by Sir Joseph Banks, PRS. Both advised Dundas that Jameson was the best man for this position.[185] Edinburgh chairs were now of interest to men in London as well as in Scotland, another sign of the growing integration of two societies. Jameson went on to teach generations of medical and arts students and numerous auditors. Walker had not had large classes but Jameson during a long career lectured to 100 or so each year and counted among them most of the great names in all areas of British natural history for a very long time. He also fulfilled Walker's hope of creating a first-class museum. When Jameson died, only the

British Museum had a larger collection of natural history specimens than was possessed by the Edinburgh University Museum. He also excluded from the use of this Museum those with whom he disagreed and was unpleasant to others in diverse ways.

12. THE CHAIR OF AGRICULTURE

This chair was not of particular interest to physicians but it is conveniently covered here for two reasons: it offered a course taken by veterinarians, most of whom trained as MDs; and it was initially somewhat tied to the chair of natural history in the minds of many because of professor Walker's interest in agriculture. He was a leading member of the local agricultural society and tried initially to secure this place for himself, protesting that the chair infringed on his department. Its founder, Sir William Johnstone Pulteney, ignored his protests.[186] Instead, he presented the chair to Andrew Coventry, MD (February 1764–1830), a doctor of horses as well as people and a man more attuned to the developments in the teaching of agriculture in Europe than was Walker.[187] Sir William had been solicited by others for the nomination but it went to a man from the Borders who had the support of other Borderers, among whom were Sir William's old friends Sir John Pringle, PRS, and Andrew Pringle, Lord Alemore, SCJ. Coventry's father was minister in Pringle's family's parish.

The medical school professors were no more appointed by the Town Council than were the others examined earlier. Surgeons, physicians and professors had a good deal to say about the selections but politicians were usually also in evidence.[188] The school had an orientation to hands-on medicine which did not preclude the theorising of men like Cullen. Perhaps that accounts for the fact that about half of the chairs of medicine were filled by men who had first qualified as surgeons.

Notes

1 This chapter partially reproduces Emerson, 'The Founding of the Edinburgh Medical School', *Journal of the History of Medicine and Allied Sciences*, 2004, pp. 183–218. I thank Oxford University Press for allowing me to reuse material printed there.
2 Emerson, 'Numbering the Medics', unpublished paper.
3 Dingwall, *Physicians, Surgeons and Apothecaries*, 1995, p. 70. See also Cunningham, 'Sir Robert Sibbald and Medical Education, Edinburgh, 1706', *Clio Medica*, 1979, pp. 135–61; his 'The Medical Professions

and the Pattern of Medical Care', in *Heilberufe und Kranke*, ed. Eckhart and Geyer-Kordesch, 1982, pp. 9–28; and Cunningham's less perceptive 'Medicine to calm the mind', in *The Medical Enlightenment*, ed. Cunningham and French, 1990, pp. 40–66.

4   What follows relies upon Fletcher and Brown, *Botanic Garden*, 1970, pp. 7–19.

5   Fletcher and Brown, *Botanic Garden*, 1970, p. 28f.

6   Ibid., p. 28.

7   *Extracts from the Records of the Burgh of Edinburgh*, ed. Armet, 1967, p. 121.

8   See his correspondence edited by Cowan in 'The History of the Royal Botanic Garden, Edinburgh – The Prestons', *Notes of the Royal Botanic Garden, Edinburgh*, 1935, pp. 63–131; MacGregor, *Sir Hans Sloane*, 1994, p. 127 and Sturdy, *Science and Social Status*, 1995, p. 294f; Guerrini, 'George Preston', ODNB, 45:254f.

9   Emerson, 'Sir Robert Sibbald', *Annals of Science*, 1988, pp. 41–72.

10 Fletcher and Brown, *Botanic Garden*, 1970, pp. 31–3.

11 George Preston to Lord Grange, 10 April 1714, Mar and Kellie Papers, NAS, GD124/15/1122.

12 George Preston, n.d., 'To the City and College of Edinburgh', Montrose Papers, NAS, GD220/5/1910/7 and Lord Provost George Warrander to the Duke of Montrose, 18 January 1715, NAS, GD220/5/1910/6. See also, Fletcher and Brown, *Botanic Garden*, 1970, pp. 32–5.

13 Arthur had an MD from Utrecht (1707) and a second MD from St Andrews given in 1713. St Andrews University Minutes, 1 June 1713, SAUL, UYUY 452/2.

14 Fletcher and Brown, *Botanic Garden*, 1970, p. 24. Clerk would have had support from the Duke of Queensberry, while the others were members of the Squadrone faction which had helped them into offices.

15 Charles Alston, 'The Family of Alston,' EUL, La.III.375/55; Fletcher and Brown, *Botanic Garden*, p. 38f.

16 Fletcher and Brown, *Botanic Garden*, 1970, p. 35f; Guerrini, 'George Preston', ODNB, 45:256f.

17 The known paper titles deal with madder (1732), hedging with 'apple-rose' (1733), barometers (1734), a report 'on the silk worm manufactory' (1735), distilling and the preparation of saffron (1736). 'Transcript Minutes of the Society for Improving in the Knowledge of Agriculture of Scotland, 1731–36', Library of the Royal Highland Society. These incomplete minutes are what survived a nineteenth-century fire. I thank the Library's former Keeper, Mr William Johnston, for bringing these to my attention and the Society for permission to quote from them.

18 Fletcher and Brown, *Botanic Garden*, 1970, p. 39. There is no independent evidence for the claim by Alexander Monro I that John Monro

induced him to lecture. This claim was made not only in the autobiography left by Alexander Monro I but also in the life of him written by his son Donald which prefixes *The Works of Alexander Monro, MD*, 1781, p. ix. Lecturing was an obvious thing to do when an unserved market existed and when Alston already controlled a garden which a lecturer required.

19 A list of the known Society's members is given in Emerson, 'The Philosophical Society of Edinburgh 1737–1748', *British Journal for the History of Science*, 1979, pp. 154–91.

20 Emerson, 'Lord Bute and the Scottish Universities', in *Lord Bute*, ed. Schweizer, 1988, p. 150ff.

21 The best account of Hope is that of A. G. Morton, 'John Hope', a 1986 pamphlet published by the Royal Botanic Garden, Edinburgh.

22 Emerson, 'The Edinburgh Society for the Importation of Foreign Seeds and Plants, 1764–1773', *Eighteenth-Century Life*, 1982, pp. 73–95.

23 His thesis on remitting fevers was fulsomely dedicated to the Earl of Ilay. I thank Dr Michael Barfoot for this information.

24 Grant, *Story*, 1884, II:394. See also Home to Lord Milton, 1 October 1755, NLS, 16692/55 (this letter says that Ilay's interest will fill the chair) and Home to Milton, 1 October 1755, 16692/99. There are many other letters dealing with this appointment in the Saltoun Correspondence for 1755 and in the Thomson/Cullen Papers, GUL, 2255.

25 NLS, 17603/52.

26 Sher, *Church and University*, 1985, p. 218.

27 NLS, 17603/64; Blair to Hume, 15 November 1764. Hume papers formerly at the Library of the FRSE but now deposited at the NLS.

28 James Stuart Mackenzie to Baron Mure, 4 August and 24 September 1764, *Mure of Caldwell Papers*, 1883, I:262 and 267.

29 Joseph Black to John Black, 30 June 1766, Correspondence of Joseph Black, EUL, Gen 874/5/17; Hugh Blair to David Hume, 15 November 1764, Hume Papers now at the NLS.

30 Dr David Skene of Aberdeen, a good botanist and naturalist, had been offered the post by his friend John Hope but was then told it would go only to Home. John Hope to David Skene, 5 and 28 December 1767, and 11 April 1768, Skene Correspondence AUL, M 38; Alexander Thomson, 'Biographical Sketch of David Skene, MD of Aberdeen', 1859, pp. 3–16; Lenman and Kenworthy, 'Dr David Skene, Linnaeus, and the Applied Geology of the Scottish Enlightenment', *Aberdeen University Review*, 1991, pp. 32–44 and 231–7; *The Minutes of the Aberdeen Philosophical Society 1758–1773*, ed. Ulman, 1990; *Thomas Reid on the Animate Creation*, ed. Wood, 1995, pp. 4, 11, 12, 19, 20, 57.

31 The details of what Hope was asking for are set out in his letter to Skene, 28 December 1767, Skene Correspondence AUL, M 38.

32 Francis Home was described in 1788 as 'an old rich batchelor [i.e. widower]', *View of the Political State of Scotland*, ed. Adam, 1887, p. 72. His class fees in 1796–7 came to £198, to which one would have to add some incidental monies from the College and his income from a practice – perhaps as much as £200 more. Later in his career his enrolments were as high as 310. Morrell, 'The University of Edinburgh in the Late Eighteenth Century', *Isis*, 1971, p. 165; James Home,' G. T. Bettany and Claire L. Nutt , ODNB, 27:883, 2004.

33 Fry, *Dundas Despotism*, 1992, p. 184.

34 They were Robert Langlands and Thomas Charles Hope who was too young to hold a chair legally. The following year Hope was appointed lecturer in chemistry at Glasgow. George Home to Patrick Home, MP, 12 November 1787, Hume of Wedderburn MSS, NAS, GD267/1/12/16; *An Eighteenth Century [Glasgow] Lectureship in Chemistry*, ed. Kent, 1950, p. 156.

35 Fry, *Dundas Despotism*, 1992, p. 184.

36 The history of this early teaching is recounted by Kaufman, *Medical Teaching in Edinburgh*, pp. 7f, 17f.

37 RCSE, Minutes, 4 August 1777.

38 One wonders if the museum already contained teaching specimens and preparations which were recognised as important to the teaching of anatomy.

39 Underwood, *Boerhaave's Men*, 1977, p. 95; 'Act in favour of Robert Elliot, surgeon', *Extracts from the Records of the Burgh of Edinburgh*, ed. Armet, 1967, p. 109.

40 The fullest account of Elliot is in Underwood, *Boerhaave's Men*, 1977, pp. 90, 91, 94, 95, 97, 104. Others say he died in 1714; *Eighteenth Century Medics*, compiled by Wallis and Wallis, 1988, p. 186.

41 After 1698 there were occasional anatomies in the Surgeons' Hall and in 1702 Alexander Monteith gave some sort of instruction in chemistry. Dr Pitcairne also lectured briefly on anatomy and physiology. Anderson, *The Playfair Collection and the Teaching of Chemistry*, 1978, p. 3.

42 Underwood, *Boerhaave's Men*, 1977, pp. 94–7, 104f.

43 Dingwall is one of many who present this as a story of medics pursuing professional ends; Dingwall, *Physicians, Surgeons and Apothecaries*, 1995, p. 77f.

44 Pitcairne to Mar, 4 November 1708, Mar and Kellie MSS, NAS, GD124/15/755/3.

45 —— Erskine to Mar and Grange, 5 February 1708, NAS, GD124/15/754/6.

46 Pitcairne to Mar, 24 January 1709, NAS, GD124/15/755/4.

47 Just before the Union of 1707, Mar had secured for Edinburgh the chairs of the law of nature and of nations and the unfunded regius chair

of Greek. At St Andrews, money was made available for the chairs of mathematics and ecclesiastical history which had been established earlier but were not regularly funded.

48 Lindsay and Cosh, *Inveraray and the Dukes of Argyll*, 1973, 'McGill', pp. 351, n.62; 422.

49 Comrie, *History of Scottish Medicine*, 1932, I:295.

50 Geyer-Kordesch and Macdonald, *Physicians and Surgeons in Glasgow*, 1999, p. 194.

51 Underwood, *Boerhaave's Men*, 1977, pp. 88–97; for Monro's appointment, see also Wright-St Clair, *Doctors Monro*, 1964, pp. 27–36. For an example of Monro's unreliability, see Emerson, 'The Philosophical Society of Edinburgh 1737–1747', *British Journal for the history of Science*, 1979, pp. 167–71.

52 'Alexander Monro, *primus*,' ed. Erlam, *University of Edinburgh Journal*, 1953–4, pp. 77–105, 80–6; see also Donald Monro's life of his father prefixed to *The Works of Alexander Monro*, 1781.

53 'Alexander Monro, *primus*,' ed. Erlam, *University of Edinburgh Journal*, 1953–4, pp. 77–105.

54 The first to use Monro's account was Alexander Bower, *The History of the University of Edinburgh*, Vol. II (1817). Among the influential works in which it is accepted are: J. Struthers, *Historical Sketch of the Edinburgh Anatomical School*, 1867, pp. 4–22; Grant, *Story of the University*, 1884, II:385f; Comrie, *History of Scottish Medicine*, 1932, I:294; Gray, *History of the Royal Medical Society*, 1952, pp. 7–9; Wright-St Clair, *Doctors Monro*, 1964, pp. 28–37; Guthrie, *Extramural Medical Education in Edinburgh*, 1965, p. 10; Christie,'The Origins and Development of the Scottish Scientific Community, 1680–1760', *History of Science*, 1974, pp. 122–41; Morrell, 'The Edinburgh Town Council and its University 1717–1766', in *The Early Years of the Edinburgh Medical School*, ed. Anderson and Simpson, 1976, pp. 46–60; Lawrence, 'Early Edinburgh Medicine: Theory and Practice', ibid., pp. 81–94; Underwood, *Boerhaave's Men*, 1977, pp. 88–97; Chitnis, 'Provost Drummond', in *The Origins and Nature of the Scottish Enlightenment*, ed. Campbell and Skinner, 1982, pp. 86–98; Cunningham, 'Medicine to calm the mind', in *The Medical enlightenment of the eighteenth century*, ed. Cunningham and French, 1990, pp. 40–66, 64f; Dingwall, *Physicians, Surgeons and Apothecaries*, 1995, p. 231; M. Kaufman, *Medical Teaching in Edinburgh*, 2003, p. 7f.

55 Stott, 'The Incorporation of Surgeons and Medical Education', unpublished PhD dissertation, 1984; Dingwall, *Physicians, Surgeons and Apothecaries*, 1995, passim.

56 Goslings, 'Leiden and Edinburgh', *The Early Years of the Edinburgh Medical School*, ed. Anderson and Simpson, 1976, pp. 1–18; Anderson, *The Playfair Collection*, 1978, p. 3f. Kaufman, *Medical Teaching*,

2003, discusses and sometimes maps the various places where instruction was given during this period.

57 Papers of John Spottiswoode, NLS, 2933/131. The entry is dated 1 May 1704.

58 See Underwood, *Boerhaave's Men*, 1977, p. 98.

59 Cunningham, 'Sir Robert Sibbald and Medical Education', *Clio Medica*, 13 (1978), pp. 135–61.

60 Underwood, *Boerhaave's Men*, 1977, p. 103.

61 The Monros were a Whig clan. John Monro and his son were said to have attended the government wounded in 1715, although this is not noticed in Alexander Monro's short autobiographical sketch.

62 See the accounts of the placements of William Dunlop (1715), Principal William Wishart (1716), James Crawford (1719), Charles Mackie (1719–20), Matthew Crawford (1722) given above and that of Colin Maclaurin (1725) given below. The same patterns are evident in the other Scottish colleges, as can be seen in the other parts of this study and in Emerson, *Professors, Patronage and Politics*, 1991.

63 Wright-St Clair, *Doctors Monro*, 1964, p. 35; *The House of Commons, 1715–1754*, ed. Sedgwick, 1970, I:398.

64 In 1777, Alexander Monro II valued his anatomical collection at £1,000, 'All of which he proposes to leave at his death to the University', a proposal he seems to have forgotten by the time he died in 1817. 'Petition for Doctor Alexander Monro 1777', Lothian Medical Archive, EUL, GD1/1/75/2. I thank Michael Barfoot for bringing this document to my attention.

65 Benjamin Bell to Robert Dundas, 19 November 1798, EUL, La.II. 500/2185f.

66 Alexander Monro II to Robert Dundas, 18 and 30 May 1796, EUL, La.II. 500/878; II. 500/2430.

67 RCSE, Minutes, 23 October 1773, 6–30 October 1776, 27 November 1776, 16 December 1776, 1 May 1777, 4 August 1777, 10 August 1778. Sir Lawrence Dundas to the Surgeons' Company, 21 May 1777; Henry Dundas to the Surgeons' Company, 21 May 1777: these letters are included in the Minute Book.

68 Its Charter as a Royal College dates from 1778.

69 Morrell, 'Medicine and Science in the Eighteenth Century', in *Four Centuries of Edinburgh University Life*, ed. Donaldson, 1983, pp. 38–52. Most of the teachers can be followed in the various chapters of Kaufman, *Medical Teaching*, 2003.

70 Aitkin is listed in Comrie, *History of Scottish Medicine*, 1932, II:629, but Russell is not on his list. James Russell to Robert Dundas, 20 April 1793, EUL, La.II. 500/305–12, and James Russell to James Montgomery, 16 January 1794, EUL, La.II. 500/313f.

71 Ibid.

72 Grant. *Story*, 1884, II:437ff.

73 Lawrence, 'The Edinburgh Medical School', *History of Universities*, 7 (1988), p. 283 n.46.

74 The University of Glasgow had corresponded with the Earl of Glasgow and perhaps with the Earl of Loudoun about the founding of a medical chair as early as 6 July 1706; John Stirling to Glasgow, GUL, MS Murray 650/3. That was not long after the founding of the Edinburgh city chair of anatomy and about the time at which Sir Robert Sibbald announced a course of medical lectures in Edinburgh. Stirling was still pursuing this project in 1709, when he thought that a 'Mathematical and Physical design' might be funded; George Ridpath to Stirling, 20 December 1709, GUL, MS Murray 650/3. Three years later, the College petitioned the Crown for the creation of a chair; Coutts, *History*, 1909, pp. 186, 192. See also Geyer-Kordesch and Macdonald, *Physicians and Surgeons*, 1999, p. 194ff.

75 Horn MSS, EUL, Gen 1824, 'Chemistry', p. 2; RCPE, *Minutes*, 14 April 1713; Wright-St Clair, *Doctors Monro*, 1964, p. 25.

76 Peel Ritchie, *The Early Days of the Royall Colledge of Phisitians*, 1899, p. 284.

77 In 1715, the College wrote to Montrose seeking a salary for the professor. It asked that the office of HM Physician in Scotland 'be annexed to the said professorship', now simply called a professorship of medicine. 'Memorandum to Montrose', Charles Mackie MSS, EUL, La.II.676.

78 Carstares to John Stirling, 16 and 21 January 1714, GUL, Murray 650/1.

79 Those examined are listed in Peel Ritchie, *The Early Days*, 1899, pp. 282–300, passim; see also Craig, *History of the Royal College of Physicians of Edinburgh*, 1976, pp. 363–6.

80 Fletcher and Brown, *The Royal Botanic Garden*, 1970, p. 39; Wright-St Clair, *Doctors Monro*, 1964, p. 36; Anderson, *The Playfair Collection*, 1978, p. 41.

81 What is known of Crawford's teaching is summarised by Anderson, ibid., pp. 4f, 142.

82 Quoted in Peel Ritchie, *The Early Days*, 1899, p. 298. The Lord Provost of that year was John Campbell, so the chair was established during the ascendency of Lord Ilay.

83 Peel Ritchie, *The Early Days*, 1899, pp. 295–8.

84 Mungo Graham to Principal Stirling, 3 February 1719, GUL, Murray 650/1; Coutts, *History*, 1909, p. 208. This shows that the 'supposed lack of teaching' by the medical professors was not merely a nineteenth-century calumny originating in Thomas Thomson's *Life of Cullen*, 1832 and 1859, as Geyer-Kordesch and Macdonald have claimed: *Physicians and Surgeons*, 1999, p. 196.

85 Coutts, *History*, 1909, p. 204.

86 Underwood thought Porterfield might have been prevented from getting students by John Monro but, if that were the case, then we would surely have heard that he at least tried to give courses in the years they are presumed by Underwood to have failed. No indication that he did so has been found. Underwood, *Boerhaave's Men*, 1977, p. 112.

87 James Crawford taught off and on but perhaps was not doing so regularly by c. 1725/6. Crawford last examined a candidate for the MD degree on 4 May 1725, so he was a professor until then. His chair was treated as vacant and filled in 1726. Crawford did continue in his Hebrew chair where he served a real market. He lived until 25 November 1731, when Charles Mackie recorded his death: Charles Mackie, 'Index funereus 1727–1736', SAUL, 36987.

88 If he did, it was perhaps as James Crawford's deputy. Doyle, 'James Crawford, MD', 1981, p. 6.

89 Anon., 'An Account of the Rise and Establishment of the Infirmary', p. 2. This 1730 pamphlet contains a list of the original subscribers – 464 of them. This was a popular project largely managed by Argathelians.

90 'Alexander Monro, *primus*', ed. H. D. Erlam, *University of Edinburgh Journal*, 17 (1953–4), pp. 77–105, 84.

91 *The Caledonian Mercury*, 29 October, 1 and 5 November 1724, cited by Anderson in *Playfair Collection*, 1978, p. 5; Wright-St Clair, *Doctors Monro*, 1964, p. 39 n.5, cites advertisements in *The Caledonian Mercury* for their lectures giving other dates – 29 September 1724 and 4 October 1725. Monro *primus* said that Graham and Martine began to teach in the same year, 'Alexander Monro, *primus*', ibid., p. 84. This seems unlikely; see Mackenzie, 'George Martine', *Journal of Thermal Analysis*, 35 (1989), p. 1825.

92 Underwood, *Boerhaave's Men*, 1977, p. 111.

93 Ibid., pp. 110–19, passim. Martine was the only one of the six not to have a continental degree. He took his MD at St Andrews, with which his family had long been closely associated.

94 Mackenzie, 'George Martine', *Journal of Thermal Analysis*, 1989, pp. 1823–36.

95 George Martine to James Douglas, 4 August 1735, EUL, Gen 505 (12) D626/3. This letter mentions his 1725 'publick lectures' at Edinburgh; Erlam, 'Alexander Monro', *University of Edinburgh Journal*, 1953–4, p. 84.

96 Graeme said he had taught in Edinburgh for three years. Graeme, *An Essay on the Method of Acquiring Knowledge in Physick*, 1729, p. 29.

97 For an account which concentrates on the Royal Infirmary and gives more credit to Lord Provost Drummond, see Chitnis, 'Provost Drummond and the Origins of Edinburgh Medicine', in *Origins and Nature*, ed. Campbell and Skinner, 1982, pp. 86–97. This is somewhat

derivative from Baird's 'George Drummond, an Edinburgh Lord Provost of the Eighteenth Century', *Book of the Old Edinburgh Club*, IV, 1911, pp. 1–54, and can be usefully supplemented by two pamphlets: Michael Hook et al., *Lord Provost George Drummond*, 1987, and *Edinburgh's Infirmary: A Symposium*, no ed., 1979.

98 Lord Graham to Mungo Graham of Gorthy, 15 January 1742, NAS, GD220/5/917/5.

99 Horn MSS, EUL, Gen 1824, 'Medicine', p. 12.

100 Thomas Hay to the Marquis of Tweeddale, 27 April 1742, Yester Papers, NLS, 46/91. Plummer, adhering to Ilay and his friends, had refused to vote his shares in the Bank of Scotland for the Marquis to become Governor of the Bank. The Bank of Scotland was used to bolster the Squadrone faction; the Royal Bank supported Argathelians.

101 Allan Logan to James Erskine, Lord Grange, 11 October 1721, Mar and Kellie MSS, NAS, GD124/15/1214; St Andrews University Minutes, 4 December 1721, SAUL, UYUY 452/3.

102 This position paid little but in 1755 it was a matter of concern to the Argathelians who filled it in that year. It would have been so thirty years earlier. George Drummond to Lord Milton, 18 October 1755, NLS, 16692/219.

103 What follows relies heavily upon Wehrli, 'Scottish Politics in the Age of Walpole', unpublished PhD dissertation. Ilay enforced the law through his own actions as a Justice of the Peace and as Lord Justice General. He bypassed the Justiciary Court because in it he lacked a majority among the judges. Without that he could not get convictions.

104 At Glasgow, the assertions of his power also came in the selection in 1727 of Neil Campbell as principal. See also Skoczylas, *Mr Simson's Knotty Case*, 2001, passim.

105 Emerson, *Professors, Patronage and Politics*, 1991, pp. 45–58.

106 At St Andrews, Ilay's men defended Alexander Scrymgeour, for whom they tried to find an honourable way out of his troubles with the local clerics. See Skoczylas, 'The Regulation of Academic Society', p. 185f.

107 Public Record Office, London, Ilay to Newcastle, 16 September 1725, SP 54/16. I thank Dr Andrew Cunningham for transcribing this letter for me.

108 The professors had no salaries but they could expect fees from students and increased practices. The King's Apothecary made most of his money selling medicine to the forces in Scotland.

109 Emerson, '*Catalogus Librorum ACDA*', in *The Culture of the Book in the Scottish Enlightenment*, ed. Oldfield, 2000, pp. 3–39, 29–31; ——, 'The Scientific Interests of Archibald Campbell', *Annals of Science*, 2002, pp. 21–56.

110 George Martine to Dr James Douglas, 4 August 1735, GUL, Gen 505 D 626/3. Martine's work on Eustachio was printed in 1755 by Alexander

Monro I; a list of his other publications is given by Mackenzie (*Journal of Thermal Analysis*, 1989, p. 1835) but it omits a pamphlet sometimes attributed to him: *An Examination of the Newtonian Argument for the Emptiness of Space and the Resistance of subtile Fluids*, London, 1740. In metaphysics he was not an orthodox Newtonian.

111 Wright-St Clair, *Doctors Monro*, 1964, p. 39.

112 William Wilson to William Cullen, n.d. [1755], Thomson/Cullen MSS, GUL, 2255/73.

113 His work on animal heat was published in both English and Latin and stirred other Scots to investigate this topic.

114 *Scots Magazine*, vol. 5, August 1743, p. 385.

115 This story is told by Emerson, 'The Scientific Interests of Archibald Campbell', *Annals of Science*, 2002, p. 45f.

116 'That the Chemical colleges be begun the first Saturday of febry by Dr Plummer to be continued every Saturday in the following order viz. Dr Plummers for february[;] Dr St Clair for March Dr Inness for aprile and Dr Rutherford for May[;] That on the second thursday of march there be two chemical Theses given out by Dr St Clair, two chemico:physiological by Inness, Two Physiological by Dr Rutherfoord, and two Practical by Dr Plummer each of these at eight days intervals.' 'Minutes of the Professors of Medicine and Partners of the Chemical Elaboratory in Edinburgh', 26 January 1731, EUL, Gen 1959. This regime was still in place in 1730 when John Boswell took chemistry from St Clair, Innes, Rutherford and Plummer and the practice of medicine from Plummer and Innes. See Joy Pitman, 'The Journal of John Boswell: Part I', *Proceedings of the RCPE*, 1990, pp. 67–77, 73. This distribution of functions is at odds with the Town Council's initial assignment of the chair of chemistry to Plummer and Innes, of the chair of theory of medicine to St Clair and of the chair of the practice of medicine to Rutherford. Craig, *History of the RCPE*, p. 93. This distribution of functions was corrected on 9 February 1726 when the men were given 'full power to all of them to profess and teach medicine in all its branches', NLS, 17603/36. Peel Ritchie believed that Rutherford and Innes shared the theory and practice chairs. Peel Ritchie, *Early Days*, p. 302. His belief is borne out by a letter concerning the appointment of Robert Whytt which says that Andrew St Clair had replaced Innes in teaching chemistry and asks that Whytt be made professor of the theory and practice of medicine and of medicine and chemistry: 'Notes on Universities', NLS, 17603/37. This accords well with Whytt's publications, which dealt with chemistry, anatomy and physiology. Plummer seems to have taught chemistry by himself only after 1733–4. In 1734, the partners bought for £230 10s 8d 11/12 the share of the pharmaceutical company held by the recently deceased Innes. This is presumably £ Scots, which would equal about £18 sterling. The partnership would

have been worth roughly £80 if the company was held in equal shares. Most of the assets would have been in stock, chemicals and simple apparatus.

117 Quoted by Cunningham in 'Medicine to calm the mind', in *The Medical enlightenment of the eighteenth century*, ed. Cunningham and French, 1990 p. 57.

118 Cited in Grant, *Story*, 1884, p. 310.

119 George Drummond to William Cullen, 3 February 1756, GUL, MS 2255/1–47.

120 Peel Ritchie, *The Early Years*, 1899, pp. 300–2; French, *Robert Whytt*, 1969, p. 8. The Faculty of Medicine formally appeared in 1730 when the professors of medicine and anatomy were granted this status by the Senatus Academicus, but it was much later, in the 1770s, when a dean was appointed.

121 Graeme went on to say that he had been 'more followed than I could pretend to deserve, seeing that there were others very well qualified, and of equal Standing, teaching in the same Manner with myself', *An Essay on the Method of Acquiring Knowledge in Physick*, London, 1729, p. 29. The pamphlet then outlined his and Martine's course and presumably the one he and the foursome gave in Edinburgh – 'history of Physick', anatomy, physiology, theory of medicine, health, diseases and their signs and cures, and the practice of medicine. All this was expounded in London, in English, to an audience made up of men who would become physicians, surgeons and apothecaries. I am grateful to Michael Barfoot for bringing his pamphlet to my attention.

122 The role which has been claimed for Drummond exaggerates his importance and nowhere more so than in the character of him given by Grant, *Story*, I:363–74. The most valuable thing we can take from this is Grant's assurance that the election of sixteen professors was managed by Drummond while he was Lord Provost and the fact that the surnames of his first two wives was Campbell. He was first associated with the Dukes of Argyll in c. 1705 when he worked on calculations of the relative wealth of England and Scotland, calculations related to the union of England and Scotland. Somerville, *My Own Life*, 1861, p. 46; Michael Hook, 'The Formative Years', in *Lord Provost George Drummond 1687–1766*, Edinburgh, 1987, p. 1; T. C. Smout in a 1978 lecture to the Edinburgh District Council gives his birth date as 1681 and says that he had been calculating relative wealth since 1699 when he was employed by Sir John Clerk, Smout, 'Provost Drummond', typescript held at NLS. In the same lecture Smout says that some contemporaries believed 'he could never get any appointment in the college or town without Lord Milton's approval' (p. 16).

123 'Memorandum to Montrose', EUL, La.II 676/182. This asked that Crawford be made the Physician to the King in Scotland, which would

have given him a salary of £100 a year. The idea did not die. On 8 July 1733, Ilay secured this fund which was then divided between the three professors of medicine at Edinburgh.

124 'As [Ilay] was well acquainted with all the branches of Learning, He got several New Professions established in Several Universitys of Scotland, and particularly encouraged the Professors of Physick in the University of Edinburgh, which is now a School for that Science, famous all over Europe and America.' 'A Character of His Grace Archibald Duke of Argyll 1761', NLS, 17612/218. Other chairs in which he may have had a hand were the Marischal College chair of oriental languages and the chairs 'fixed' to specialised professors at Glasgow in 1727 and at Marischal in 1754.

125 Where he got his MD degree has not been found, but D. B. Horn thought he had one; Horn MSS, EUL, Gen 1824, 'Midwifery', p. 2.

126 Wright-St Clair, *Doctors Monro*, 1964, p. 34.

127 *Register of the Episcopal Congregation in Leith 1733–1777*, ed. MacIntyre, 1949, p. 81.

128 Grant, *Story*, 1884, I:315.

129 *Mure of Caldwell Papers*; 1883, Part 2, I:163–6.

130 The Town Council's decision to allow this can be found in the Papers of Reverend Dr Archibald McLea, NAS, GD1/456/163.

131 Under this somewhat ungenerous arrangement Alexander Hamilton kept half of the teaching fees but his son James got the right to all the apparatus. 'Miscellaneous papers relating to the Edinburgh professors of anatomy and midwifery: Alexander Monro II, Thomas Young, and Alexander and James Hamilton and to their appointments', EUL, Lothian Medical Archive, GD1/1/75/5–6.

132 Fry, *Dundas Despotism*, 1992, p. 184.

133 William Cullen to William Hunter, 9 August 1751, GUL, 2255/185. Cullen noted that Plummer had planned to make way for one of his own students, Dr Thomas Elliot, who died around this time. Plummer's books and manuscripts were purchased by another old student, Dr Adam Austin, who was also a chemist and may have hoped for the chair. He had trained in Edinburgh as a surgeon with Adam Drummond and became a member of the Surgeons' Company in 1749, the year in which he also took a Glasgow MD. He practised as a surgeon and noted that, at 'almost at the Summit' of his profession in Edinburgh, he made only about £300 a year. By 1756 he had become a military surgeon serving in America as a hospital mate. A year later Austin tried to secure a post at the Greenwich Hospital. Like many former surgeons who left the services, he began to practise as a physician. He entered the RCPE in 1762. In the following year he became Military Inspector at the Royal Infirmary, a post reserved for an MD. This place he held until his death in 1773. Austin belonged to the Philosophical Society of

Edinburgh and was a polite man married to the daughter of Lord
Somerville. Peterkin and Johnston, *Roll of Commissioned Officers*,
1968, I:24; Austin to Gilbert Elliot, MP, 6 January 1757, Minto Papers,
NLS, 11008/32f.

134 Francis Home to My Lord [?Milton], [?1] October 1755, NLS,
166692/99.

135 Chambers, *Lives of Eminent Scotsmen*, 1856, II:28; Arthur Martine to
William Cullen, n.d. [1754/5], GUL, 2255/72; Grant, *Story*, 1884,
II:394; Francis Home to Milton, [?] October 1755, NLS, 16692/99.

136 Hugh Blair to David Hume, 15 November 1764, NLS, 23153/54.

137 NLS, 16692/99; Grant, *Story*, 1884, II:394.

138 That Milton promised to provide for him seems to be the meaning of
an obscure sentence in a letter of William Wilson to William Cullen,
n.d. [1755]: 'He [Arthur Martine] said nothing to Milton wt respect to
Dr Hume or the Manner of providing him.' Thomson/Cullen MSS,
GUL, 2255/73.

139 Kames to Milton, 6 September 1755, NLS, 16692/75. The best account
of this is Donovan's in *Philosophical Chemistry*, 1975, pp. 70–6. See
also George Drummond to Cullen, 3 February 1756, GUL, 2255/20,
which has details about the opposition to Cullen and about what he was
expected to pay for Plummer's equipment – £120. This is less than the
£136 he was given in his first year at Glasgow to equip a laboratory.
Donovan, *Philosophical Chemistry*, p. 63f. Even making allowance for
the second-hand nature of what was bought, the Glasgow establishment
seems to have been the superior one at this point.

140 Brock, 'The happiness of riches', in *William Hunter*, ed. Bynum and
Porter, 1985, p. 47.

141 Arthur Martine to William Cullen, n.d. [1755], William Wilson to
Cullen, 20 September 1755, GUL, 2255/72f.

142 Chambers, *Lives of Eminent Scotsmen*, 1856, II:27.

143 The choice of Cullen in the end embarrassed the Duke and made him
very angry. The doctor had accepted his Edinburgh office and a patent
had been drawn for Robert Hamilton to succeed him at Glasgow, but
Cullen had not resigned his Glasgow chair – as Argyll had told
Newcastle he had done. This made Argyll a liar, not something he
would be in dealing with Newcastle who had tried and was still eager
to oust him from the handling of Scottish patronage. The story of this
incident is told by William Rouet who had never seen 'his Grace so
much out of humour', so much in fact that he said 'That if he found
himself fool'd in this affair, it was the last time he should ever give ye
least ear to any recommendation from our University' – another indication, if one were needed, that he tried to accommodate the professors' choices of men they considered fit for the positions. Rouet to
[?Robert Simson], 11 March 1756, GUA, 30492.

144 Principal and professors of Glasgow College to Baron Mure, 5 May 1766, *Mure of Caldwell Papers*, 1885, Part 2, II:84.

145 Joseph Black to John Black, 30 June 1766, EUL, Gen 874.5.

146 Robert Dundas to Lady [?J] Dundas, 17 January 1794, Dundas Papers, NLS, 6.

147 Mackie, *The University of Glasgow*, 1954, p. 232.

148 Robert Dundas to Henry Dundas, 30 October 1795, Dundas Papers, NLS, 7; Fry, *Dundas Despotism*, p. 184; Kerr, *Memoirs of the Life of William Smellie*, 1811, II:333–5.

149 Anderson, *The Playfair Collection*, 1978, pp. 36–45.

150 James Stirling to Robert Dundas, 4 November 1795; Robert to Henry Dundas, 5 November 1795; John Hill to James Stirling, n.d. [November 1795]; William Barron to Robert Dundas, 7 November 1795, all in the Dundas Papers, NLS, 7.

151 French, *Robert Whytt*, 1969, pp. 8, 17–26; French is incorrect in saying that Innes became ill in 1743; he had died in 1733.

152 Ibid., p. 8.

153 Chambers, *Biographical Dictionary*; 1856, II:30; Dalzel, *History*, ed. Laing, 1862, II:439.

154 Dalzel, *History*, ed. Laing, 1862, II:443; Kerr, *Life of Smellie*, 1811, I:262; Comrie, 'John and James Gregory', *University of Edinburgh Journal*, 1936–7, pp. 126–30.

155 Comrie says that Francis Home taught in 1773–4 but his account seems garbled: *History of Scottish Medicine*, 1932, II:311; see Rosner, 'Andrew Duncan, MD', 1981, p. 5; Rosner, 'Andrew Duncan, the elder', ODNB, 23:673–5.

156 Duncan took a St Andrews MD in 1769 and in the following year sought the St Andrews medical chair with the help of William Cullen, the Edinburgh medical faculty and others in the profession (see below, p. 475f.). *Mure of Caldwell Papers*, 1885, Part 2, II:176; Minutes of the University of St Andrews, 6 December 1770, SAUL, UYUY 452/8; Chambers, *Biographical Dictionary*; 1856, II:170; James Flint to Henry Dundas, 25 October 1790, Melville MSS, SAUL, 4438; Wilson, 'The Gregorys and Andrew Duncan', p. 160; Bower, *History*, 1830, III:200.

157 Chambers, *Biographical Dictionary*, 1856, II:170.

158 *Medical Commentaries*, 4:1:99–107 (1777). Duncan's statement that the medical professors had played a large role in earlier appointments is interesting since it is explicit evidence of their concern to appoint men who would keep up the enrolments. If he was correct, then at least the appointments of Cullen (1755), Thomas Young (1756), John Hope (1761), Black (1766), John Gregory (1766), Francis Home (1768) and Drummond (1773) probably had professorial input.

159 Duncan noted this again in the *Medical Commentaries*, 15 (1789), p. 499. Henry Dundas had to allow this appointment because Duncan

had become such a notable extramural lecturer that his politics could be ignored.

160 Richard Sher, 'Church, University, Enlightenment: the Moderate Literati of Edinburgh, 1720–93', PhD dissertation, p. 217f; Hugh Blair to David Hume, 15 November 1764, RSE Hume MSS now in the NLS, III:54.

161 Home to Lord Milton, November 1764, NLS, 17603/64.

162 Blair to Hume, 15 November 1764, RSE Hume MSS now in the NLS; James Stuart Mackenzie to William Mure, 4 August 1764, and James Coutts, MP, to Mure, 17 December 1764, *Mure of Caldwell Papers*, 1883, I:262 and 278. Coutts says that, given the character of the College, he would favour 'the prosperity of such a Colledge' over the promotion of his own brother.

163 James Stuart Mackenzie to Baron Mure, 24 September 1764, *Mure of Caldwell Papers*, 1883, I:267.

164 Bower, *History*, 1885, Part 2, II:200.

165 All this reflected the students' desire to have Cullen teach the practice of physick and Gregory take over the theory chair. They also wanted Black to teach chemistry. J. Gordon Wilson, 'The Gregorys and Andrew Duncan', *University of Edinburgh Journal*, 9 (1938), pp. 160–3.

166 Town Council Minutes, 3 December 1789; *Medical Commentaries*, 15 (1790), p. 499.

167 Joseph Black in 1788 estimated that a Russian medical student 'who is to appear like a Gentleman's Son' would need to spend for two quarters £51 2s 0d, while the most penny-pinching would spend only ten pounds less. These sums included £5–10 for travel costs from St Petersburg but they included few incidentals. Black to Princess Daskova, 21 March 1788, Black Correspondence, EUL, Gen 873/111.

168 Fry, *Dundas Despotism*, 1992, p. 184.

169 Brockliss, 'Science, the Universities, and Other Public Spaces', in *The Cambridge History of Science*, vol. 4, ed. Porter, 2003, IV:44–86, 69–71.

170 Principal Robertson to Gilbert Elliot, 8 January 1763; Minto Papers, NLS, 11009/163; Kerr, *Life of Smellie*, 1811, II:106f.

171 Andrew Ramsay to Loudoun, 14 October 1764, Uncatalogued Loudoun MSS, Mount Stuart House, Isle of Bute; Buchan MSS, GUL, 502/66.

172 Hope to Loudoun, n.d. [1766], Uncatalogued Loudoun MSS, Mount Stuart House. Hope, the founder and conductor of the Edinburgh Seed Society, provided a focus for the botanical and natural history interests of others in Edinburgh and for the Scottish activities of Bute, Stuart Mackenzie, Loudoun and their circle of foresters, plant collectors and gardeners. Emerson, 'The Edinburgh Society for the Importation of Foreign Seeds', *Eighteenth Century Life* (Special Issue), 1982, pp. 73–95.

173 Grant, *Story*, 1884, I:319, 374–8.
174 Robert Ramsay to Sir Alexander Dick, 2 September 1766, Cunningham-Dick papers, NAS, GD331/11.
175 The tale of Smellie's candidacy has been told by Paul Wood in his Introduction to Smellie's *The Philosophy of Natural History*, 2 vols, 2001, p. xiiff.
176 Kerr, *Life of Smellie*, 1811, II:90.
177 Ibid., I:93, II:95.
178 John Walker to Kames, 2 February 1778, EUL, La.III. 352/4; Walker to David Dalrymple, Lord Hailes, 28 February 1778, New Hailes Papers, NLS, 7228/24.
179 Walker to David Dalrymple, Lord Hailes, 28 February 1778, NLS, 7228/24.
180 Kerr, *Life of Smellie*, II:106f.
181 John Walker to Lord Hailes, 28 February 1778, NAS, 7228/24.
182 Walker to Kames, Abercairny MSS, NAS, GD24.1.581/f3–4.
183 Kerr, *Life of Smellie*, 1811, II:98; Walker to Kames, 2 February 1778, EUL, La.III. 352/4.
184 Emerson, 'The Scottish Enlightenment and the End of the Philosophical Society of Edinburgh', *British Journal of the History of Science*, 1988, pp. 33–66.
185 Eyles, 'Robert Jameson', DSB, 7:69–71.
186 James Anderson to George Culley, 20 April 1791, EUL, Dc.2.76/6.
187 See Eric Richards, 'Agriculture', in *Oxford Encyclopedia of the Enlightenment*, 2002, I:32–8, 37.
188 By far the best account of the medical school at the end of the century is by Christopher Lawrence, who argues that the really creative medical men in the city by 1790 were teaching extramurally, usually at Surgeons' Hall. These men were more influenced by French medicine and practice. Lawrence, 'The Edinburgh Medical School and the End of the "Old Thing" 1790–1830', *History of Universities*, 7 (1988), pp. 259–86. He also has a realistic assessment of the importance of patronage and of the role played by the Town Council (p. 260ff.).

12

THE ARTS CHAIRS

ↄ

1. MATHEMATICS

Having looked earlier at the appointments of 1690, we need now to consider the later appointments to chairs from which were taught the subjects of the core curriculum other than Latin: Greek, mathematics and philosophy. Most is known about the mathematics appointments, which were always made with an eye to the competence of the appointees. This may even have counted more than politics, which was never altogether lacking.

The first of the men appointed to the new chair in 1674 was said to have been at least partially picked by Sir Andrew Balfour, a virtuoso who, with Sir Robert Sibbald, is regarded as one of the founders of the Botanical Garden in Edinburgh:

> [Balfour] had a principal hand in procuring the Mathematical Chair, in the College of Edinburgh for Mr James Gregory, the celebrated inventor of the reflecting telescope. After his death, he procured the same office to Mr David Gregory, his nephew, who was afterwards called to be Professor of Astronomy at Oxford. And upon his removal, he had the place filled by Mr James Gregory, his brother, then Professor at St Andrews; and who in an inaugural oration, had there first announced the Newtonian philosophy in Scotland.[1]

Professor John Walker may not have got his story quite straight but it is interesting to think that this chair had from the first been filled by the local intellectuals and not by the choice of the town councillors.[2]

When David Gregorie resigned his mathematics chair in 1691 and went to Oxford, he was replaced by his younger brother, James Gregory (1666–1742), who had taught briefly at St Andrews but was outed by the St Andrews Visitors for 'contumacy' on 27 September 1690.[3] James Gregory was not only a competent mathematician but had, like his brother David, already introduced Newtonian philosophy to students.[4] Like his brother, he had interests in science and history. Abroad Gregory knew members of the Jardin des Plantes and the Académie des Sciences of Paris.[5] In England he was acquainted with, and visited in 1697, men in London, Oxford and Cambridge.[6] His friends in Edinburgh included Drs Andrew Balfour, Archibald Pitcairne and Sir Robert Sibbald. Among his politician friends were virtuosi such as Viscount Tarbat, to whom Gregory's 1690 theses were dedicated. Correspondence mentioning James Gregory exists in the *Mar and Kellie Manuscripts* showing that he had amicable relations at a later date with Lord Mar and his brother, James Erskine, Lord Grange. By 1707, Gregory had come by a place in the Mint and had at his death a small pension from, or place in, the Excise.[7] All this points to a well-connected man who in 1691 could seek the Edinburgh post even though his Jacobite associations were known and he had been punished along with the other men at St Andrews in the previous year. Who exactly sponsored him is unknown, but it may be significant that Sir John Hall of Dunglass, David Gregorie's friend, had again become Lord Provost in the autumn of 1692.

James Gregory died in 1742 but long before that time he had employed deputies to teach for him. The reverend Robert Wallace (7 January 1697–29 July 1771) taught his courses in 1720 and George Campbell (before 1700–after 1744?) is likely to have done so in 1723–5, when David Hume was probably one of his students.[8] Gregory was willing to retire and did so in 1725 in favour of Colin Maclaurin (February 1698–14 June 1746). Maclaurin and Gregory were appointed conjoint professors in November of that year. Maclaurin had, in effect, bought the post for a flat sum totalling 'betwixt 260 and 270 lib. St'.[9] What made this possible was the fact that Maclaurin was a man very well connected with Scottish politicians.[10] Maclaurin later acknowledged that he had had patronage from both the Squadrone and the Argathelians, although he was not a party man.[11] His chair at Marischal College had been secured in 1717 on a recommendation from his Glasgow teachers even though, at nineteen, he was below the legal age of appointment which was twenty-one.[12] By about 1720, he had met in London the Duke of Argyll and his brother, Lord Ilay. He kept in touch with both brothers as befitted a man from Argyllshire whose family had long been patronised by the Campbells of Inveraray. In 1722–4, Maclaurin, now with an international reputation as a mathematician/physicist, went off as a travelling tutor with Lord Polwarth and became a largely absentee professor at Aberdeen. This job tied him to politicians sometimes opposed to the 2nd Duke of Argyll. His later claims to be apolitical may have been overstated but a mathematician who was simply a Squadrone man would not have got a post in Edinburgh in 1725. The Argathelians were then too interested in consolidating their control of the town its institutions. Appointing a well-known mathematician from Argyllshire would have appealed to the Earl of Ilay and the Duke of Argyll, who were both amateur mathematicians and willing to be his protectors. Ilay shared Maclaurin's interests in astronomy, optics and telescopes and in improvements.[13] In 1732, Maclaurin hoped that their connection would be worth a job in the Exchequer. It was not.[14] Perhaps this is why, in 1742, he dedicated his *Treatise of Fluxions* to Duke John, then in opposition, rather than to the Earl of Ilay, who seems to have been the better mathematician.[15] Maclaurin's abilities, their mutual interests and the political situation would have facilitated his appointment as much as Newton's letter to the Town Council recommending Maclaurin and offering £20 a year toward his salary.[16]

When Maclaurin died in 1746, he was followed in office by Matthew Stewart (1717–23 January 1785) who was a minister living in Roseneath, a parish given to him by the 2nd Duke of Argyll. There is little question who his patron was since there was correspondence about the job between Patrick Cuming, Ilay's manager of church patronage, and, probably, Charles Erskine. The letter offers a revealing glimpse into the appointment process in 1746, when the Argathelians and the Squadrone were vying to be the King's chief servants in Scotland. Cuming wrote recommending Stewart, saying that he had had Maclaurin's blessing as the latter lay dying, and

> since that time [had been recommended] by Mr [professor Robert] Simpson at Glasgow two excellent Judges[.] One [James] Williamson in England has been talked of as a very Sufficient Man[.] Mr Craigie Professor of Hebrew at St Andrews has been soliciting and Spoke to me but I kept my Selfe Free[.] He is a relation of the late [Lord] Advocate [Robert Craigie] And therefore will have a partie [the Squadrone] to Support his Merit.

Cuming vowed to support whomever the 3rd Duke of Argyll might choose and noted that before the appointment could be made, a municipal election would intervene. He clearly expected the councillors backed by the Duke to follow his wishes in the choice they made.[17] He, of course, knew that Professor Simson was an old friend of Argyll.

Others were also soliciting. Lord Morton's candidate was one of his protégés, Alexander Bryce, a country minister who was a keen amateur scientist.[18] Bryce was a competent astronomer who in 1741–2 produced a map of northeast Scotland which was a by-product of his earlier trip to survey Orkney which then belonged to the Earl of Morton to whom the map was dedicated.[19] Dr John Stedman sought the support of Charles Mackie through a friend who undoubtedly wrote to many others.[20] This suggests that the University professors played some minor role in this and perhaps other appointments. David Hume thought that if either Williamson or Robert Hamilton, later professor of divinity, were chosen, then 'we shou'd be sure of a good Professor'.[21] His comment likely reflects discussions among the literati. There was even a Jacobite candidate, James Stirling, the manager of the Leadhills Mine, which was owned by the Earl of Hopetoun. The Earl was no Jacobite but he was a keen amateur astronomer and knew Stirling to be a man with a European reputation as a mathematician who ought to be considered.[22] Argyll's pick, Matthew Stewart, got the post and the Duke soon after resumed his role as the manager of most government patronage in Scotland.

By 1772, Stewart had gone bankrupt and had lost funds entrusted to him for the building of an Edinburgh Observatory. He was also said to be in ill health.[23] It behoved him to resign and leave town but he needed an income and he needed to take care of his brilliant son, Dugald (22 November 1753–11 June 1828). The solution to his problems came with the appointment of his nineteen-year-old son as his deputy and then with their appointments as conjoint professors in 1775 after Dugald had come of age. This deal was facilitated by someone but by whom is unknown. The Stewarts were likely to have been loyal to the MP for Edinburgh, Sir Lawrence Dundas, whose men ruled the Town Council in those years, but they had other powerful friends.

In 1785, the mathematics chair went to Adam Ferguson (20 June 1723–22 February 1816) in a swap with Dugald Stewart which the Town Council approved. This was really a retirement deal for Ferguson who did not teach mathematics but became a conjoint professor with John Playfair who did. Playfair (26 February 1748–20 July 1819) had for some time been an assistant and deputy to Nicholas Vilant, the disabled professor of mathematics at St Andrews where, by 1785, Henry Dundas had a considerable political interest and where, three years later, he would become chancellor. Dundas patronised other Playfairs and claimed to have arranged this appointment in Edinburgh.[24]

The placing of the next professor, who also became a conjoint professor with Ferguson, was a *cause célèbre* because the man who eventually won in 1805, John [later Sir John] Leslie (10 April 1766–3 November 1832), was opposed by two ministers, a Moderate and an evangelical, each of whom had the backing of their respective parties.[25] The other two candidates were Thomas Jackson and a Dr Thomson who has not been identified.[26] To settle this matter took over a year.

The Moderate man, Thomas MacKnight, had the backing of his party which had worked easily with Henry Dundas. MacKnight had published nothing of scientific substance but he had some knowledge of mathematics and had been an active Moderate minister in Edinburgh involved with the running of the Kirk. He was at best a shallow philosopher and not much of a mathematician. The evangelical was Thomas Chalmers, later known for his economic and religious writings and for leading the 1843 Disruption. He was then a young man who looked very much like a promising scientist. His qualification for the post was a good general knowledge of science and having, like Playfair, taught mathematics for Nicholas Vilant in the late 1790s or early 1800s. He had filled in for other teachers there as well.[27] Thomas Jackson had deputised for professor James Brown at Glasgow, and had been recommended a bit earlier for the astronomy chair there by its incumbent, Patrick Wilson. Jackson dropped out of the running very early.

Leslie was clearly the best qualified of the five. He had published papers in mathematics and had written extensively on electricity and heat from the standpoint of the common-sense philosophers. He was appreciated by the scientists of his time in Scotland and elsewhere.[28] He had tutored, lectured, written and travelled widely in Europe and America and had been for a time connected with the Wedgwoods and their circle of industrialists and scientists. He shared their interests in practical science. Leslie won the Rumford Prize from the Royal Society of London in 1805 and two years later was made an FRSL. He was best qualified for the chair of natural philosophy at Edinburgh and that is the one he probably had his eye on in 1804 as its incumbent, John Robison, was failing and trying to resign. Both Leslie and Chalmers had also applied to succeed John Rotherham as professor of natural philosophy at St Andrews in 1804 and both were friends of James Brown, whose correspondence supplies much of the information about this contest for the professorship.[29]

The contest was made exciting because the Town Council had the freedom to choose and to exercise its powers of appointment in this election. Henry Dundas was about to be impeached and government influence in the town was at a low point. The councillors were able to ignore the politicians and make up their own minds – or as Leslie put it, 'act on views of public utility'.[30] What they did and how they did it became something of a harbinger of nineteenth-century appointments in which many of the same procedures were followed, as has been shown by scholars who have looked at appointments in that period.[31]

Leslie probably did not care whether he received the chair of natural philosophy or mathematics. Playfair and Leslie had talked to Robison about the St Andrews post in 1804 and may well have sounded him in November of that year about the natural philosophy chair which Robison still held.[32] He died on 30 January 1805. On 2 February, Leslie wrote to Brown that he had begun his Edinburgh canvas but for which chair is not clear. He wrote to Brown early in February 1805, well into his campaign, that John Playfair might take the natural philosophy chair, leaving the way clear for him to pursue the one in mathematics. This happened. Playfair was admitted to his new post on 30 March 1805, having gained it some time earlier. Leslie planned to have references sent from professors John Hunter and Nicholas Vilant at St Andrews and more from men in Edinburgh. He added: 'Nor have I neglected some political channels that have lately opened to me.'[33] Four days later he asked Brown to 'try to stir a little – to counter act at least any rumours that may be circulated to my prejudice about religion or politics.'[34] Since Brown's religion and politics were nearly as Whiggish and radical as his own (but less vocal), this was not likely to be very helpful. What it shows is that Whigs who had had any sympathy for the French Revolution and who were not wholeheartedly in the Moderate interest were anathema to the Tory Moderates supporting MacKnight. By the end of the month, Leslie had named a principal villain, the professor of logic, James Finlayson (15 February 1758–28 January 1808), who had preached a Fast Day sermon on 20 February in which he had 'insisted upon the danger and Sinfulness of appointing people of suspicious Principles to preside over the Education of the Young.' Finlayson implied that Leslie was an infidel for accepting Hume's view of causation.[35]

Finlayson was an old friend and protégé of Henry Dundas, one who helped him in the management of the Kirk. The managers of the Kirk had by then bruited it about this they would not allow Leslie to sign the Confession of Faith before the Edinburgh Presbytery. They assumed this would disqualify him for appointment since it was believed they had a legal right to veto the appointments of the heterodox. This would clear the way for MacKnight, whom they wished to retain his church living in addition to getting the chair. Despite all this, Leslie thought he was ahead in the competition for town councillors' votes which he now openly sought. To help secure these votes, he formally denied and rebutted Finlayson's charges on 22 February and sought support from ministers including the University's professor of divinity.[36] It helped him that some town councillors were unwilling to have MacKnight, as is made clear in a letter from Thomas Chalmers to Brown written on 24 January 1805 after a visit to Lord Provost Fettes. Chalmers found him 'determined to resist MacKnight unless he gives up his Church', something he was willing to do but his supporters were not willing to allow him to do.[37] MacKnight's or his friends' great sin was wishing to have two patronage positions giving him votes in both the Edinburgh Presbytery and in the Senatus Academicus. This would benefit his political friends and was quite in keeping with Moderate views on pluralism, but it was greedy and showed a willingness to monopolise power which was disliked even by men almost equally venal. Chalmers saw Leslie as his most formidable opponent, even though the Lord Provost knew of Leslie's suspect political and religious views.[38] The Council was looking for the man who could best attract students. Some University men also wanted such a man. The election was delayed. Leslie had his medals sent to Edinburgh 'to shine before the magistracy'. He counted his votes and believed he saw a victory in sight.[39] The Deacon of the Surgeons had defended him; professors who had opposed him now even bowed; old George Dempster, once an MP but now living retired in St Andrews, thought well of his book. By March he could write:

> My success is almost certain. A very few days will decide it. I have fought a very hard battle with McK[night] & and the whole set of soi-disant moderates; & I begin to think much better of the wild party [the Evangelicals] than ever. When we meet, I shall amuse you with the infamous manoeuvres of the high church [Moderate] party. Their engines have recoiled upon them, & they have sunk in the public opinion . . . Richie [David Ritchie, later professor of logic] has behaved very ill. My medals came yesterday – & on Friday perhaps something will be done.[40]

The committee of the Town Council responsible for the University met on 9 March and recommended Leslie over MacKnight by a vote of 15 to 2. By then he seems to have had support from Francis Rawdon-Hastings, Lord Moira, the Commander-in-Chief in Scotland, from Charles Hope, the Lord Justice Clerk (an old Dundas friend) and from others who were put off, as Hope had been, by 'the Moderate Jesuits'.[41] When the time came to elect the new professor on 13 March, every Foxite Whig, many Evangelicals and many who just disliked clerical monopoly and the arrogance of the Moderates urged town councillors to vote for Leslie. They did. But the 'Jesuits' were not through with Leslie. When he went to sign the Confession of Faith a few days after his election, he was refused. Leslie then appealed their action in the courts of the Kirk. By mid-March some began to argue that the minister's right of *avisamentum* had been allowed to lapse under Principal Robertson and that an inquisition into Leslie's beliefs would not be tolerated.[42]

There had been no great split among the Edinburgh ministers until after Leslie had been refused the chance to sign the Confession. When the ministers met on 22 March, the Evangelicals were willing to accept Leslie's explanations and the letters supporting his orthodoxy, while the Moderates were not. On 27 March, the matter went to the Edinburgh Presbytery, which voted to proceed with the case and sought a stay of proceedings from the Court of Session concerning Leslie's installation. This action had been taken without the knowledge of the Evangelicals and was a huge tactical mistake. The Moderates had been shocked by the defection of old friends and by the split among the ministers about the *avisamentum*. Another shock now came in the form of the dismissal of their petition by the Lord Ordinary who said they had only the right to advise, not the power to veto an appointment. Their advice might be ignored. There was no case to go to any civil court.[43] Leslie then refused to deal with the Moderates or to appear before the Edinburgh Presbytery since there were now no charges for him to answer. The non-case then made its way to the Synod of Lothian where Henry Grieve's motion stating the Moderates' demand for a stay and recognition of their right to block an appointment was carried against the votes of the Evangelicals. Whigs and Evangelicals were now united in backing Leslie and appealed to the decision of the General Assembly.[44]

While all this was going on in April and May, pamphleteers were active in attacking Leslie. Dugald Stewart and others appeared in print on his side – partly to settle scores of their own. The debate saw the high flyers, who had once attacked Hume, now defend him and Leslie as men whose arguments about causation and the rational basis for religion either supported evangelical religious views or were neutral with regard to religion. Both they and Hume, they said, held religion to rest on non-rational foundations – in their case, grace; in Hume's, probably feelings and delusions which he had been at pains not to spell out too clearly and masked with the rhetoric of Calvinist fideism.

When the General Assembly got the case in late May 1805, the decisive factor was the evangelical vote, which carried the day by 96 to 84. Evangelicals, who could not elect their own man, Thomas Chalmers, were angered by the Moderates' treatment of them and supported Leslie. Like him, many of them were Foxites and not Tories interested in propping up the Dundas political machine. They were looking to the next ministry and to a regime in Scotland run by Henry Erskine and his friends who were of their persuasion. The General Assembly voted for the Whigs and MacKnight looked the fool.[45] Leslie was then admitted to his chair.

The behaviour of the Dundas politicians and the Moderates is usually seen as mean-spirited and foolish but there was more to this fight. We should see it as what it seemed to be – the last gasp of Henry Dundas's machine. It was worth fighting hard, even unfairly, since the fate of the party seemed at stake. Dundas was about to be impeached and his machine was fighting not to go down with him. Ian Clark has well described the religious issues which the case raised. He claims it foreshadowed many of the problems which were to bedevil the Kirk in the nineteenth century – Erastianism, patronage, pluralism, the independence and increasing secularism of the schools and universities, the rational or irrational bases of personal religion and the kind of Christianity one should teach and sanction in the country. He sums this up nicely at the beginning of his article and then goes on to write:

> Ecclesiastical and secular politics played an important part in the struggle, but what was really at stake was 'moderatism' as a theological and ecclesiological system. In the arguments put forward by the opposing parties two radically different religious positions came into conflict. The whole framework of 18th century 'rational' religion was shaken by Leslie's supporters, and many of the presuppositions upon which Moderatism had hitherto rested were destroyed. At the same time the opponents of the Moderate Party profited from the disastrous way in which the Moderate leaders handled the case. Thus from the point of view of church politics and of theology, Leslie's appointment was to have a considerable and direct effect.[46]

It is also a case which offers us an example of the kinds of conflicts that prudent managers of patronage kept from occurring. When the ties of management were weak, as they were in 1804–6, foolish and overweening men did politically stupid things which brought chaos. Whatever we may think of the ideological politics Dundas espoused, he knew how to keep order and how to keep his wayward supporters from subverting his intentions and ends. In 1805 he lacked the power to do so and turmoil followed.

2. ASTRONOMY

The Dundas machine and the Moderates would have filled the mathematics chair with an incompetent; twenty years earlier they had put into the astronomy chair a man who would not teach because he had no observatory and had none because they would not finance it. The regius chair of astronomy had been created by the Crown in 1785 on 'the advice and consent of the Lord Chief Baron, and the other Barons of Excheque'.[47] The Lord Chief Baron, James Montgomery, enjoyed the favour of the Dundases of Arniston throughout his career. Most of his judicial colleagues on the Exchequer Court were also the appointees of Henry Dundas, without whose support the chair would not have been created. Dundas claimed credit for this appointment.[48] The Town Council resented this creation and refused to fund an observatory for Dr Robert Blair (1748–22 December 1828), even though he was a relative of Lord Provost James Hunter Blair. The burgh would not finance one because a private group was trying to build a private venture observatory on Calton Hill. The government in London did nothing so Blair treated his post as a sinecure office for the next forty-three years.[49] In Glasgow, the professors in 1784 had secured their chair for a very active man who tried at the end of his career to ensure that the chair remained a useful one. The Glasgwegians were defeated by the obstinacy of the 3rd Duke of Montrose; Edinburgh's astronomer did little to make his chair effective and the politicians there seem to have regarded this as acceptably normal. It is not surprising since it was this same political party that appointed a sinecurist to the professorship in Glasgow.

3. GREEK

The other arts chairs were those of the professors of Greek and philosophy. The story of the origins of the Scottish Greek chairs has been told elsewhere.[50] Here it will suffice to note that although this chair had been mandated by the University Commissioners in 1700, the first incumbent was forced on a Town Council reluctant to create the chair. A royal warrant appointing William Scott (1672–August 1735) to the new chair was sent up in 1708. The Crown gave Scott a regius professorship for himself but it provided no permanent fund for his chair which remained like all the other former regencies, funded by and legally controlled by the Town Council.[51] Since Scott was a well-connected man who had been helpful to politicians before the Union, this must have been very disappointing.[52]

Even before he was installed, Scott sought funds for his new post. In 1707, a petition for a fund for the Greek chair went from the University's professors to the 1st Duke of Buccleuch, the Queen's Commissioner. It asked for 400 marks in salary (about £33 sterling) for a Greek professor.[53] As we have seen (see p. 260), this was related to the establishment of the chair of public law. Scott and his friend Charles Erskine hoped that two chairs would be funded before Scotland disappeared as an independent country. There was some urgency in all this, not only because Scott and Erskine were among many trying to get a bit of the gravy ladled out as the country dissolved, but also because Scott's own finances were in disarray and he needed more income. He eventually sold the family estate, but not before he had borrowed 18,000 marks (£990) from Sir James Steuart. Steuart, the Lord Advocate, was a close relative by marriage, who had lent with no security. Getting a better living for William Scott was one way to secure it.[54] When Scott was appointed in 1708, his family probably thought it was being rewarded for its support of the Union. A younger brother was being taken care of by those who could do so and a relative was being given greater assurance that he would indeed get his money back. The additional money never came. Scott remained unsatisfied but continued to push his claim. In 1714, 1715 and 1723 he was dealing with politicians for an augmentation of his salary.[55] He seems to have got nothing. What he did get in the end was to pass the post on to his son, William II (?–December 1729). William II became professor of Greek in 1729. This deal had the approval of Lord Ilay and the man whom Ilay had made or would soon make principal, William Hamilton.[56] The younger Scott was tried by Hamilton, Charles Erskine and Colin Drummond, three of his father's friends and colleagues. There were no other known candidates.[57] Unfortunately, the second William Scott lived only a few months longer. At his death, the post reverted to Colin Drummond (?–d. 1752) who claimed it as senior regent. The other known candidate at that time was George Turnbull who had taught at Aberdeen. He was not given a look-in.[58]

In 1738, the Greek chair was again vacant because Drummond, who had taught for thirty years, was now ailing and ready to enjoy at least semi-retirement. His deputy, Robert Law of Elvinston (?–1 November 1741), the son of the former regent and professor of moral philosophy, William Law, secured the post after trial by the professors of philosophy, the ministers and the principal.[59]

When Law died in 1741, Drummond found another conjoint colleague in Robert Hunter (c. 1703–27 May 1779). He was chosen to placate the professors as has been noted above (p. 254). Hunter came in without a trial. He kept the place until 1772, when it went to his deputy, Andrew Dalzel (6 October 1742–8 December 1806).[60] Dalzel had been tutor to the son of the Earl of Lauderdale, who may have given him the £300 which it took to persuade Hunter to accept only half his salary and leave the fees and a reversionary interest to Dalzel.[61] Dalzel was also, as he tells us, recommended by his cousin by marriage, Principal Robertson.[62] Dalzel passed on the chair to his assistant, George Dunbar (1774–6 December 1851). Dunbar had the support of two of Henry Dundas's friends, Lord Provost Fettes and Allan Maconochie, Lord Meadowbank, SCJ, the professor of public law. Dundas claimed the credit for the placing of this man.[63]

Political influence marked most of the appointments to the chair of Greek but in some the professors themselves played important roles and were the judges of competence as well as nepotists. As usual, the Town Council approved what others had decided for it.

4. The Regents, 1695–1707

The remaining chairs were the regencies and the professorships of philosophy. The appointments made in 1690 were ones for which men competed. William Law of Elvinston was appointed after a comparative trial in which six other men were found wanting. Two of those men, William Forbes and Robert Stewart, eventually became professors: Forbes in the law chair at Glasgow, Stewart as a regent at Edinburgh.

In 1695, when the next regency opened, it was William Scott who was chosen over three unknowns in a comparative trial. One cannot say that the trial was rigged but his contacts could not have been a hindrance to his success.

In the same year John Rowe (c. 1667–after 1700), a St Andrews regent, was translated to Edinburgh without trial. Nothing definite has been found about his selection but he had relatives in Edinburgh and a brother who was a chaplain to the Earl of Haddington. Rowe was tied by heritage and marriage to many people who had suffered in the period prior to the Revolution.[64]

When the Town Council appointed the next regent in 1701, after an eight-day trial, it picked Charles Erskine from a field of four. The rejected candidates included William Hay, the son of a merchant, Kenneth Campbell, a servant of the Argyll family, and John Beaton, a servant of John Forbes, the Laird of Culloden.[65] All would have had some political support for the job they sought through competition. Erskine probably deserved to win. He was a bright and widely cultured man who later had improving interests, but he could have expected help from the Earl of Mar, then the most powerful patron of the time and a man to whom the college looked for favours.[66]

Two more regents were chosen before the Town Council ended regenting on 16 June 1708.[67] The first one was Robert Stewart (c. 1672–10 July 1747) who, as we have seen, had tried for a regency in 1690. He was then underage (only about eighteen) and failed in the competition. In 1703, when he tried again, he was an experienced travelling tutor who had spent time abroad. He may also have studied medicine in the interval. His uncle, now the Lord Advocate, and his uncle's friend, William Carstares, recommended him to those who needed advice.[68] Stewart was elected without a real comparative trial but 'with the advice of the ministers'. One of the historians of the University, Alexander Bower, should have the last word on this case: 'His qualifications were well known; and, besides, his uncle, Sir James Stewart was at the time Lord Advocate of Scotland.'[69] Robert Stewart was an innovative lecturer impressed by Boyle and Newton. He founded a special library for the natural philosophy students.[70] He also had antiquarian interests shared with his close friend Robert Wodrow, the historian, whose piety and ecclesiastical politics he shared.

No comparative trials involving real contests between disputants were held after that date in Edinburgh. The reasons why were stated in the following year by Sir James Steuart in a letter about a Glasgow regency:

> But the truth is this comparative triall as they call it is not so much now esteemed and its likeways observed that it hath rather greater inconveniences than a well advised judicious election ffor it is oft time found that he that prevaills in the dispute is not so deserving of the place and this occasions much murmuring. And therefore I can only say that as your case is circumstantial were I of your faculty I would concurr to settle this office and place without dispute.[71]

This was a quasi-legal opinion, which helps to explain why later trials were merely trials of competence, usually just formalities.

In 1707, Colin Drummond (?–c. 1752), another well-educated travelling tutor, was chosen. There is no hint of a comparative trial, although he was tried for competence by the professors and ministers. Drummond's family, the Drummonds of Megginch, was one from which Adam Drummond, the Surgeons' professor of anatomy, also came and came to office at about the same time.[72] The Drummonds lacked the clout of Robert Stewart's family but Colin Drummond was the son of a well-heeled laird and related to a one-time Lord Provost who had held power in the 1680s. He himself was a fairly well-off man who raised a company at his own expense to fight in the '15. He led it against the rebels. A man of that sort would not have been friendless when much younger.

In 1708, when the chairs were 'fixed' or converted into chairs filled by specialist professors, the regents chose their chairs in order of seniority and with an eye to their own interests and to the likely value of the positions. William Law took the chair of moral philosophy. His teaching showed that morals depended upon a knowledge of God and his laws. Stewart chose the natural philosophy chair. In addition to science of a modern sort, he included pneumatics (the study of spirits conceived as natural bodies) and ethics. His course thus had a strong religious emphasis and used its science to support design arguments. The chair of logic went to Drummond who taught logic and metaphysics in a very traditional way until 1730, at which time a new man was chosen.[73]

5. LOGIC AND METAPHYSICS

Drummond's replacement in the logic chair was John Stevenson (c. 1695–12 September 1775), the former tutor of Lord Balgony, heir to the Earl of Leven. He had four known competitors for the chair: Robert, the son of Principal Hamilton; James Balfour of Pilrig, who later served as professor of moral philosophy; John Lees, who was picked as a deputy by William Scott to teach his son's classes; and Thomas Johnstoun, about whom nothing has been found. This information comes partly from the papers of Lord Milton, showing that the Argathelians were interested in the outcome which they probably did not determine.[74] Andrew Dalzel's *History of the University* described the decision as involving a trial of some sort but surely only one of Stevenson's competence.[75] Stevenson turned out to be a fine choice and one popular with students. He modernised the logic course by using Wynne's *Abridgement* of Locke's *Essay*, and began to teach rhetoric and criticism in an exciting fashion.[76] Late in his career (c. 1773) he introduced the philosophy of Thomas Reid to his students. This began the teaching of Common Sense philosophy at Edinburgh. It became, in time, *the* Scottish philosophy here and elsewhere.[77] The Scottish academic philosophy most taught in the late eighteenth century was not that of Hutcheson and Smith but the philosophy of Thomas Reid and Dugald Stewart.

In 1774, when Stevenson wished to retire, he requested as a conjoint professor John Bruce (1775–16 April 1826). The Town Council merely asked the Senatus about the young man's qualifications. These were held to be good. The professor's wish was granted and Bruce succeeded him. He was appointed after a perfunctory trial of competence which seems to have been but a formality to comply with the rules.[78] Bruce had been a founder of the Speculative Society [79] which Henry Dundas joined not long after its inception.[80] In later life, Bruce was much indebted to Dundas for a string of positions and served him as a secretary and literary man of all work, perhaps even publishing under his own name materials dictated by Dundas.[81] It is unlikely that Bruce was without political support in 1774 and more likely that it came not from Sir Lawrence Dundas but from the Lord Provost, James Stoddart, who later supported Henry Dundas. Bruce arranged to leave office in 1786, to serve as tutor to Dundas's son. He retired as conjoint professor with James Finlayson (15 February 1758–28 January 1808), who also had been tutor to a number of well-born boys and had the support of the Duke of Atholl, to whom one of his charges had been related.[82] Henry Dundas took credit for brokering his appointment.[83]

6. MORAL PHILOSOPHY

The story of the moral philosophy chair was little different.[84] After William Law's tenure from 1708 to 1729, the chair went to William Scott who claimed it as senior regent. He was examined by the principal and several professors in a 'private trial', since he had been teaching in the chair of Greek which was not a philosophy chair although still technically a regency, as were the other philosophy chairs.[85] His trial preserved without question the right of the masters to try candidates for this office. Scott was enough of a politician to resign at a time opportune for others as well as himself and in 1734 the post went to Dr John Pringle (10 April 1707–18 January 1782), who became conjoint with Scott who had nominated him.[86]

Scott's resignation and the nomination of John Pringle were very likely moments in a political job. The Pringles were a Selkirkshire family with members in Parliament where, until 1734, they supported the government. This meant that they had recently been in Ilay's camp or willing to vote with him, just as they had earlier voted with the Squadrone, to which members of the family owed legal appointments. The family was also well represented in the Faculty of Advocates and on the courts. When professor Francis Pringle of St Andrews was offered the Edinburgh humanity chair in 1733–4, it was in part because of the Pringles' influence in the legal community. Francis rejected the offer. There was a parliamentary election on 20 May 1734 which changed the family's allegiance in Parliament until c. 1753[87]. They went into opposition after the election and may have been wavering in 1733–4. If the offer of the professorship to Francis Pringle was connected with an election deal to keep the family loyal to the government, then, when Francis rejected it, some other sweetener would have had to be found. The offer to John Pringle, MD, made by February 1734, should be seen in this context. The Town Council's reluctance to appoint Pringle seems clear. The Council was dominated by Ilay's friends and presided over by his man, Lord Provost Patrick Lindsay. Ilay might allow or even need the appointment but the Council forced Pringle to 'give some Specimen of his fitness for it by having a publick discourse upon some subject relating to the Said Profession.' This he gave in 'The Common Hall'.[88] In the recent past, such demonstrations had not been usual. This may have been designed to show that a physician was qualified to hold the post which formerly had gone to men more interested in religion and natural law than a physician might be. Dr Pringle was later given by the Town Council rather demeaning rules governing what he was to teach and his rights to practice medicine while holding the chair were limited.[89] The Council wanted no negligent teacher and sought to ensure that he performed his duty. They had judged their man better than his sponsors. Between 1742 and 1745, Pringle was away from Edinburgh serving as a military doctor in the Netherlands. His post was filled by deputies, George Muirhead, later the Glasgow professor of humanity, and William Cleghorn (c. 1718–23 August 1754), who succeeded Pringle. For some of that time the post was sought by David Hume, who was supported by Lord Provost John Coutts and others on a Town Council once more loyal to the 2nd Duke of Argyll than to his brother Lord

Ilay. Argyll had gone into Opposition in 1737/8. Because of that, Ilay was not able to obtain in the elections of 1741 enough seats to keep Walpole's government in office. It fell in 1742. After that, the Squadrone faction came to control patronage in Scotland.

Like the Argathelians before them, the Squadrone in 1742 sought to create a system of management which would give them control of all the Scottish institutions. In this they were not notably successful. They were not talented politicians and they faced the entrenched opposition of their enemies. The Edinburgh Town Council proved one institution they could not dominate. It divided with some councillors loyal to the Squadrone men, some loyal to the 2nd Duke of Argyll, some loyal to Ilay and others who watched to see how the wind would blow. Split into several groups, the Council was unmanageable and the selection of a professor to replace Pringle was from the beginning a politicised business which did not go well for the Squadrone. Hume was also a problem to his friends because he was not, in the minds of many, an obvious choice to teach moral philosophy. He was religiously suspect; his moral theory was wholly secular and seemingly non-normative; even his life and conduct seemed reproachable. Had he not fathered a brat in the 1730s?[90] In the end, Hume was defeated. His friends had acted neither decisively nor quickly enough when they might have got him appointed. Hostile ministers objected to his philosophy and religious stance, which they took to be at best deistic. Politics and religion put paid to Hume's chances. His failure did not help in 1751–2 when he was considered for a post at Glasgow University.

The man who triumphed over Hume was William Cleghorn (c. 1718–23 August 1754). The Squadrone men opposed Hume but they were not particularly effective in their support of Cleghorn. He was helped by his brother-in-law on the Town Council, Bailie Gavin Hamilton, and by his kinship to many in the intellectual community. In the end he was the candidate of his friends, the Squadrone men and the local ministers, with the exception of the three chief clerical politicians. When the *avisamentum* was given by the Edinburgh ministers, Robert Wallace, who acted for the Squadrone, Patrick Cuming, Ilay's man, and Alexander Webster, the high-flying leader of the Evangelicals, all supported Hume.[91] They respectively took him to be a sensible empiricist and sceptic, a member of Cuming's political party, and a fideistic thinker whose work posed few threats to those who believed religion rested on faith given by God's grace – which was just what Hume ironically claimed.

When Cleghorn died, the post went to one of his brothers-in-law, James Balfour (1705–6 March 1795), who earlier had sought the chair of logic and who, as a relative, not unnaturally had Cleghorn's 'dying voice'.[92] Balfour was from a pious family which was very well connected. He was active as an advocate and minor judge. Like Cleghorn, he would have been helped by relatives. Robert Whytt was a brother-in law; so too was Bailie Gavin Hamilton who, by that time, was also very friendly with the 3rd Duke of Argyll.[93] Another brother-in-law was professor William Leechman of Glasgow. Balfour was related by marriage to the Elliots of Minto but also to the family of Neil MacVicar, a notable high-flying Edinburgh minister who had come originally from Argyllshire.[94] Another more distant connection was with the Melville clan in Fifeshire. Balfour's connections thus ran into the evangelical clergy, the supreme courts and to men with political influence such as Gilbert Elliot, MP for Selkirkshire.[95] Of perhaps more interest was the fact that another brother-in-law, the surgeon James Russel, was not only a member of the Town Council in 1754 but Convener of the Trades when the appointment was made. All this should not obscure Balfour's talents and qualifications, but his relatives and friends help to explain his career.

The new professor was a polite man who, as a student in Leyden, had taken not only law courses but others in history and philosophy, botany and chemistry. Such a virtuoso would have appealed to the 3rd Duke of Argyll who is, however, not known to have been involved in his appointment. The chair may have come to Balfour in lieu of preferment in the courts, which he seems always to have been seeking. He treated the chair almost as a sinecure, giving only a few lectures a year, some of which he turned into a book against Hume.[96] He was not admonished by the Town Council to be attentive to his duties as a teacher as Pringle had been. When Balfour left this post in 1764, it was for the even less demanding chair of public law, which he kept until he was given, in 1779, the lucrative but not onerous office of Procurator Fiscal of the Edinburgh Commissary Court.

Adam Ferguson's friends secured the morals chair for him in 1764 in an intricate set of changes which ended a long campaign on his behalf. As early as 1756, John Home had approached Lord Milton about getting a professorship of eloquence created at Edinburgh for Ferguson.[97] In 1758, David Hume and William Johnstone Pulteney (later Sir William) had schemed to get Adam Smith to buy out the Edinburgh professor of public law, thus vacating his Glasgow post which they believed Ferguson could obtain. Ferguson's friends knew they would need the support of politicians for this transaction and they knew where to find it:

> We are certain, that the Settlement of you here & of Ferguson at Glasgow woud be perfectly easy by Lord Milton's interest. The Prospect of prevailing with Abercrombie [the professor of public law] is also very good: For the same Statesman [Lord Milton], by his Influence over the Town Council, coud oblige him [Abercrombie] either to attend [that is, to teach], which he would never do, or dispose of the Office for the Money which he gave for it.[98]

This scheme did not work out. Neither did another.

In 1759, Hume, William Robertson, John Jardine, Gilbert Elliot, MP and Lord Milton planned to secure William Rouet's Glasgow chair of ecclesiastical history for Ferguson.[99] This came to nothing, partly because it was entangled with Rouet's dealing with the Earl of Hopetoun whose boys he was going to serve as a travelling tutor. Argyll, as we have seen (p. 135), was involved in this Glasgow appointment. He wanted the chair's salary retained by Glasgow University for his own protégé, Alexander Wilson. He did not want it used to subsidise the Earl of Hopetoun's tutor. Hopetoun was not among his political friends. Argyll was also feuding with his nephew, Lord Bute, who backed Freguson's candidacy. He would give Bute nothing.[100] It all terminated with Ferguson's appointment to the Edinburgh chair of natural philosophy, a chair which had been sought by James Russel.[101] That appointment involved both Lord Milton and George Drummond, again Lord Provost. How they proceeded with the job is made clear in a letter of Drummond to Milton which gives a rare glimpse of just how such appointments were 'made' by the Edinburgh Town Council:

> I had 9 of the Councill, some of whom I had talkt to separately. I found an opportunity to read your letter to them in a body – and Explained several paragraphs thereof, Russell has the caracter of being the best natural philosopher in the country, and to do him justice, his succeeding [John] Stewart in that profession would raise the reputation of our university. This made several of our friends point at delaying the naming fergusone, for some time; in order to bring about the double scheme, being informed that Mr Balfour was to come to me, with proposals, but a very little reasoning Convinced them that the way to do good to the Colledge and to get Russell, was, in the first place, to posess our selves of Ferguson with unanimity and dispatch. Yesterday, we were 17 here, who all of them, heartily agreed in the measure, so to morrow I am to move the Councill to call our clergy together for their avisamentum, on Friday next, and, The

Wednesday following we will Elect Fergusone, unanimously, By the Merchts, and I imagine even by the trades too[.] I think it right your Lordship, should know that Russells reputation has given occasion to the Duke's being address'd – I have reason to say, without his [Russel's] knowledge, by more than one Connoisseur, for his Graces countenance to him, and that the Duke spoke favourably of him.[102]

Drummond voiced the Council's concern for the reputation of the University, but he was doing Milton's bidding. It is also clear that he believed Russel's ability as a scientist would weigh considerably with the Duke of Argyll. Argyll's apparent approval of the candidates was the sort he gave in other cases where he did not care who was picked so long as the choice lay among his own meritorious followers. Milton backed Ferguson, to whom he had obligations incurred by Ferguson's having been abroad with his own somewhat deranged son. Drummond recognised that to get something done now was less risky than waiting until one might get all one wanted. In the meantime, men might die, go out of power or change party. Things went as planned. Ferguson was secured but not for the right chair. Russel was unprovided for but would wait. Balfour remained the impediment to improving the University and pressure was put on him to leave.

In March 1761 (shortly before Argyll died in April), Balfour was pressed by the Lord Advocate, Thomas Millar, another Argathelian, to resign or swap the moral philosophy chair for the chair of public law.[103] He refused, 'for which the whole town are exclaiming against him'.[104] More correspondence followed but he would not budge, even though another protégé of Argyll, George Lind, thought Balfour might be made Commissary Clerk.[105] In 1762, Ferguson sought the principalship at Edinburgh along with five others: the high-flyer Daniel MacQueen, George Wishart, Hugh Blair, Patrick Cuming, and William Robertson who got the place. Robertson was backed by Lord Bute, the favourite of the new King and the new government leader. Ferguson had had initial support from Lord Milton and Campbell of Ardkinglass, one of the most important of the Argyllshire Campbells.[106]

The following year, 1763, Robertson wrote to Gilbert Elliot that he had tried to get for Balfour the post of Sheriff-depute in Edinburgh, but this had come to nothing because that judge had not resigned. He hoped Bute might be able to help.[107] Nothing happened, but the old notion of a switch and swap was reconsidered early in 1764. In the opinion of James Stuart Mackenzie, Bute's brother, who now had the management of patronage, 'the whole Movement depends on the pleasure of the Crown' which could give the clerkship of the Commissary Court to Balfour. Instead, he got the chair of public law, once again showing that this was, in the minds of the politicians, equivalent to a bit of judicial patronage worth now about £300 a year. Ferguson succeeded Balfour; Russel stepped into Ferguson's place.[108] We know a great deal about this appointment but others may have been made after rather similar bargaining during the years in which the 3rd Duke of Argyll held sway.

In 1772, it looked as if the always restless Ferguson might abandon his chair or be forced out should he get a post with the East India Company.[109] Failing to get the East India Company job, Ferguson took up a position in the summer of 1773 as travelling tutor to the son of Lord Chesterfield.[110] The rumours of Ferguson's going to India, his departure for the continent and then his sacking by the Town Council (it was later rescinded) led to many seeking his place. Among those who tried for it were James Beattie, professor of logic and moral philosophy at Marischal College, Henry Grieve, the Moderate minister of Dalkeith who would later seek posts at Glasgow and St Andrews, and William Wight, the Glasgow professor of ecclesiastical history. Beattie later denied that he had sought the post, but he had and had done so with support in England from the King, Lord Dartmouth, the Archbishop of York (a brother to Beattie's friend, Thomas Hay, Earl of Kinnoul), William Murray, Lord Mansfield, the Lord Chief Justice and some London 'bluestockings'.[111] He also had the support of Lord Lyttleton, who wrote to Sir David Dalrymple that he would help Beattie if he could but that writing to Principal Robertson was out of the question in this case.[112] In Edinburgh, Beattie's friends included General Sir James Augustus Oughton (the Commander-in-Chief in Scotland), David Dalrymple, Lord Hailes, SCJ, and almost certainly his brother, John Dalrymple. The last was Lord Provost when this business started. In the University, Beattie had had two friends. Dr John Gregory, his old colleague from Aberdeen, was one but Gregory died in 1773. The other was the professor of humanity, George Stuart. In the town, 'several of the Council of Edinburgh', including the bankers James Hunter Blair and Sir William Forbes, another man from the Aberdeen area, were friendly to Beattie.[113] These people included some of notable piety of a Scottish Episcopalian/Anglican sort and, perhaps, in Scotland, of a slightly evangelical flavour. They were also mostly outsiders whose views on education were less oriented to utilitarian and practical subjects than were those of most in the College or burgh. All that may have made the candidacies of Henry Grieve and professor Wight, who had been a preacher before he got his Glasgow history chair, of greater interest to the literati who were not Episcopal in their leanings. Adam Ferguson wanted Grieve to teach for him. He noted his competence but not that they shared a common interest in the fortunes of the Moderate Party. Baron Mure worried that Wight and Grieve would divide the Moderates and that Beattie would squeak through.[114] James Mackintosh (later Sir James) sought Ferguson's post in 1774 but he did not get a look-in.[115] In the end Ferguson did not leave but returned and taught almost steadily until 1785, when he retired to the chair of mathematics. Dugald Stewart then got Ferguson's blessing and that of Henry Dundas. Stewart retained the moral philosophy chair until 1809, when he gave up teaching and became conjoint professor with Thomas Brown. Stewart resigned finally in the 1820s.

The contests for the moral philosophy chair were, in general, not about the views of the men chosen but about their character and how well they fitted into a Scotland dominated by cliques in the Kirk and among the politicians only some of whom were on the Town Council. In natural philosophy things were a bit different, since competence of no ordinary kind was increasingly an issue.

7. NATURAL PHILOSOPHY

The history of the natural philosophy chair was entwined with that of the chair of moral philosophy. Robert Stewart, its first incumbent, came to it from a regency when the chairs were fixed in 1708. Stewart continued to teach some moral philosophy from his new chair since his course purported to prove the existence of God from the design and order of nature and, in pneumatics, to sketch the bases for a moral philosophy with a discussion of spirits, including the human soul. By the time he retired, he probably had come to focus more on physical matters and left the teaching of the metaphysical bases of morals mostly to the other philosophy professors.

When Stewart resigned in 1742, he became a conjoint professor with his son, John (1712–2 May 1759), a Reims MD, who had been helping him to teach the course.[116] Ilay expressed qualms about allowing sons to succeed their fathers, which is perhaps why the Town Council also balked. It expressed a fear that the chair would become hereditary.[117] In the end, John Stewart was supported by a number of the professors but subjected to a trial of his abilities before the Town

Council by Principal Wishart, Colin Maclaurin, Colin Drummond and the city's ministers.[118] This might have allayed suspicions that the appointment was just another bit of nepotism, but not to have found him qualified would have harmed the College in which he had been teaching for some time. He was promptly installed and taught until 1759, when Adam Ferguson succeeded him. Ferguson had as his only known competitor James Russel. Russel took over the chair in 1764 in the deal discussed above (see p. 343f.). He held it for nearly ten years, dying just as classes were about to start in October 1773, at which time there was a lively contest for the post which swollen enrolments had made much more valuable. Indeed, the contest was so hot that it was reported in the newspapers.[119]

Adam Ferguson taught the class for a short while before he left to accompany Lord Chesterfield's son on the grand tour. He recommended as his replacement James Lind, the son of Argyll's old friend and sometime chemist, Alexander Lind of Gorgie. James Lind was a young physician of promise who had spent a short time in India in the early 1760s. He purchased scientific instruments for the Earl of Loudoun,[120] aided Andrew Pringle, SCJ, in his observatory at Hawk Hill[121] and was, for a few years, active in the Edinburgh Philosophical Society.[122] He had organised the Society's observations of the Transit of Venus in 1769. In 1772, he accompanied Sir Joseph Banks to Iceland when Banks abandoned a second trip to the South Seas on which Lind was to have gone. The doctor had published papers in the *Philosophical Transactions of the Royal Society of London* and would later work on and publish papers on the rifling of ordnance. Later still, he became Physician to George III at Windsor Castle. Lind's friends sought the backing of Sir Lawrence Dundas, MP for the city.[123] There would have been a number of other well-known and influential local figures from the Philosophical Society who would have thought him a fit and desirable man to appoint. Even Sir William Forbes thought, in October 1773, that he stood the best chance of getting the appointment. The *Glasgow Journal* rated Lind's chances best in late October and said that the man with the next best chance was the reverend Neil Roy, minister of Aberlady.

Roy was the brother of General (then Colonel of Engineers) William Roy, who was in charge of the military survey of Scotland and left interesting antiquarian manuscripts. Neil Roy had graduated MA from Glasgow in 1750 and was honoured forty years later by his alma mater with a DD. It is not known why he would have been a favoured candidate. The *Journal* also thought that very much in the running for the place were James Williamson, then professor of mathematics at Glasgow University, and a Mr Wright. This was perhaps William Wright, sometime Honorary Surgeon General of Jamaica and a notable naturalist who belonged to the Edinburgh Philosophical Society, the American Philosophical Society and late in his life to the Wernerian Society of Edinburgh. Another name given in the Glasgow paper was that of Ebenezer McFait. An Edinburgh MD, he had been a travelling tutor and for about twenty years had given extramural courses in the burgh on many topics – Greek, Latin, mathematics, geography and natural philosophy. He too was a distinguished member of the Philosophical Society, which he had joined about 1752. By 1773 he had published a number of papers on natural philosophy and a work on Plato.

Other applicants included William Buchan, the celebrated author of *Domestic Medicine* (1769),[124] and Alexander Keith of Ravelstone, WS, whose chances also looked good to Sir William Forbes in October 1773. Keith was a sometime Treasurer of the Philosophical Society and was interested in instruments and the measurement of heat. He later founded the Keith Prize, awarded by the Royal Society of Edinburgh. Another seeking this place was Robert Hamilton, Rector of the Perth Academy and later the professor of natural philosophy and mathematics at Marischal College, Aberdeen. Hamilton, the son of Bailie Gavin Hamilton, was well qualified, had practical interests and abilities and had no lack of relatives in the city to argue for his appointment. He, like Lind, was something of a protégé of Lord Kames.[125] Hamilton may have been the choice of the magistrates.[126] If Beattie was a candidate for this chair, as his friend and biographer Sir William Forbes thought, he was outclassed as a natural philosopher by all of those men and certainly by the man who got the post – John Robison.

In the end the Edinburgh professors seem to have been taken with the suggestion made before October 1773 by professor William Wight of Glasgow that John Robison be hired.[127] Besides Principal Robertson, Robison [his name had been changed from *Robertson* to *Robison* so as to spell it as it was pronounced] had the support of William Cullen and Joseph Black, who would have known him through their connections to Glasgow University. He is said to have been picked by a committee of professors as the most fit and seems to have had the job by 24 February 1774.[128] Robison by then had had experience as a teacher of chemistry at Glasgow University. As a midshipman, he had been a tester of Harrison's chronometer and a surveyor of the St Lawrence River. He had been an instructor in natural philosophy and mathematics at the naval academy in St Petersburg, where he had met Leonhart Euler and other academicians in the Academy. He was certainly qualified. Forbes's letter, cited above, makes it clear that the Town Council was seeking the person who could do the most for the University's reputation and bring the largest number of students to the city. Robison was the one to do that because of his ties to men beyond the kingdom. After his appointment, he accounted for the handful of Russian students who annually attended the College. Some of them lived with his family. He held the place until his death in 1805, by which time he had become a very well-known figure in the world of science and what might be called engineering. He employed a teaching deputy in his later years.[129] William Greenfield taught for him in the years 1793–9.

Robison was succeeded by John Playfair, who was promoted from his mathematics chair.[130] This was a move which it would have been difficult to prevent because he was at this time the most visible and capable of the Edinburgh men of science. His supporters for this post included those who secured the professorship of mathematics for his friend John Leslie, whom he supported in print with a pamphlet which belittled the scientific accomplishments of Leslie's opponent.

8. RHETORIC AND *BELLES LETTRES*

John Home had sought the creation of such a chair for Adam Ferguson in 1756. Lord Milton was consulted but nothing happened until after Argyll died and Lord Bute took up this issue. Argyll had little interest in rhetoric except as it was employed by classical orators. Bute in this respect was a more modern man. The chair of rhetoric and *belles lettres* was established by the Crown in 1762. This regius chair foundation recognised the fact that for about ten years extramural lecturers had found an audience in Edinburgh for the topics discussed from this chair. Adam Smith (1748–51),[131] Robert Watson (?1752–6)[132] and Hugh Blair (1759–60) had all lectured to respectable audiences. They gave courses modelled on those taught in Holland and France but theirs were more innovative and modern in their approaches to rhetoric and in their analyses of literature. Smith continued such lectures after he was appointed at Glasgow in 1751 and Watson did the same thing at St Andrews, where he was made professor of moral philosophy in 1756. Blair's success had been rewarded with an unpaid professorship of rhetoric and *belles lettres* established by the Town Council in 1760.[133] In 1762, Bute was prepared to reward Blair's service as a lecturer (and probably his political work for the Moderate Party) by creating and endowing a chair to which the rights of appointment would vest in the Crown.[134]

After a long and active career, Blair took a colleague in 1784. He was William Greenfield (?–28 April 1827), a young and accomplished cleric who had been looking for academic posts since 1778.[135] In 1798, Greenfield was detected in some sort of misconduct, almost certainly sexual in nature. He left Edinburgh stripped of his reputation and all that it had brought him – his University and church livings, the office of King's Almoner and his doctorate in divinity. He had even been Moderator of the General Assembly in 1796. Once he had fled the city, he lived under an assumed name in England. There was an intense competition to succeed him as conjoint professor with Blair. In the short run no one did. After Blair's death in 1800, those who sought the Crown's warrant included Robert Walker, a local minister who believed he had the 'good wishes of the University and of the present Magistrates of Edinburgh', Thomas MacKnight, who was a friend of Blair, Dr—— Robertson and someone un-named.[136] Henry Dundas, after offering the place to Sir Walter Scott,[137] gave the professorship to the reverend Andrew Brown, minister of St Giles', who made so little of it that by 1826 the Commissioners of the University Commission could reasonably suggest the abolition of the chair.[138] Blair's belief that a man teaching mainly for fees would exert himself and shine had proven to be a delusion.

9. CONCLUSION

The Edinburgh University chairs were usually sought and filled by men well qualified for their places, men who often had a diversity of interests. They generally taught regularly and well, were useful to the city or country in various ways, and sometimes even made contributions to knowledge or literature which increased the reputation of the institution and drew more students to the city. The system worked. However, it is equally clear that the system was not one run by the town councillors but by the politicians to whom the councillors owed their places and whom they served. While the Council formally made most appointments, the foregoing account has shown that generally the Council ratified a nomination which had been offered, if not dictated to it, by other more important politicians.

The fact that the Town Council of Edinburgh did not, except as a formality, choose many of the men who taught in its university may well have been a blessing. The political patrons and the Edinburgh professional men were generally among the most enlightened and secular-minded of the Scots. They were the ones who insisted, for their English friends, that Scots be tolerant. In their own names, they made the college modern, forward-looking, an improving institution able to educate boys to make careers furth of the kingdom but capable of changing it if they chose to stay in Scotland. Edinburgh University offers evidence of their influence and of their success in changing Scotland. The man most responsible for this, here, as at Glasgow, was the 3rd Duke of Argyll, whose patronage did so much to make the Scottish enlightenment brilliant.

No university in Scotland was more politicised than Edinburgh. However, the nature of the politicking usually allowed political brokers to secure the man whom they thought to be best qualified. It helped that the patrons such as Ilay and Bute could pick from many candidates. There were 124 men appointed or confirmed from the time of the Visitation Commission in 1690 until the end of 1806.[139] We know that at least 148 other men competed for these posts, even though we do not know all who sought places here. The total number of competitors, excluding the ringers whose names went forward on leets for law chairs which they had no intention of filling, may well have been two or even three times as many as the known appointees. Choosing from among the able who were recommended by patrons of about equal importance, the managers could often please themselves so long as they served men in their own connection. Of those appointed, only about a dozen at Edinburgh seem to have been appointed without the intervention of an important politician. This University was shaped more by the Squadrone lords, Lord Ilay and Henry Dundas than by any others including William Carstares. At least twenty-five appointments fell to Ilay and his friends, a number closely rivalled by the less distinguished twenty or so who owed their Edinburgh jobs to Henry Dundas. The Squadrone lords collectively accounted for about ten and Principal Carstares for perhaps seven more. Bute weighed in with six. For a few years in the 1760s and 1770s, the Edinburgh literati and the Moderates in the Kirk, working with or through their political friends, were important. After 1785, the Edinburgh record was less brilliant as nepotism and political concerns over political loyalty became more common. The candidates themselves were men who were often of about equal accomplishment at the time one of them secured a post. There are not a large number of obviously better-qualified men among the rejects – something which is also true of the rejects of the other universities.

The Town Council was most important as the protector of the town's economic interests. As such it may have forced up the quality of the men chosen for the chairs. It was usually docile but understood its power – as did those who dealt with it. The town councillors who hired T. C. Hope or John Leslie demanded that professors be efficient and good. The Council, however, was usually reluctant to act in the way it did in 1805 because it generally lacked the independence which it had in that year of uncertainty about the political leadership of the country. In 1805, when controls over it were relaxed and it was for a time independent, it did what it ought always to have done and did in the myth of its dominance spread by men like Sir William Forbes. It considered the town's prosperity and the meritorious men who could promote it. In doing so it set a pattern which was to be followed more often after 1833, when the Dundas machine finally imploded. Still, despite nepotism and appointees dictated by ideology, the teaching staff was often brilliant and did not seriously deteriorate until after 1780.[140]

The burgh derived a lot of money from the University students, so it was concerned to have good appointees. In the 1690s, enrolments of arts students stood at about 300, but by c. 1800 they had about tripled to between 1,000 and 1,300. Divinity students increased marginally to perhaps 100 in residence at any one time.[141] Medical students in the town grew at an astonishing rate. Even before the founding of the medical chairs in 1726, the city had about twenty-five boys studying with or serving surgeons in any given year, with probably a few more doing the same thing with physicians. By the early 1800s there were over 1,000 men taking medical courses in the city.[142] Probably over 12,000 men got some medical instruction at a Scottish university during the century; most obtained it in Edinburgh.[143] In 1700, the value of the non-medical students to the city might have been somewhere around a minimum value of £5,200, while the medical apprentices would have added perhaps £500 more, coming to a minimum total of £5,700.[144] By c. 1810, the arts, divinity and law students brought into the city over £51,700, while the 1,000 medical students would have accounted for perhaps £62,000. The annual value of university and extramural teaching to the town by then can be estimated as at least £113,000. During the period 1700–1800, it must have amounted to more than £1,250,000. As student numbers grew, it became increasingly obvious to all who were involved in appointments that good men had to be selected.

There were some differences in the ways in which the chairs were handled. Those most sensitive to professional pressures were the best served. The most meritorious were appointed in the sciences, medicine and law, but less often in divinity and the arts faculty. The recommendations of medical men, lawyers and scientists counted but, it seems, anyone could teach Latin. The notion that special knowledge was required to teach logic and morals probably did not come until about 1760 and even then there was a surprising lack of specialisation in the holders of arts chairs. Men like Adam Ferguson were willing to teach rhetoric, history and natural or moral philosophy. What seems to have mattered most was character and social abilities.

The patronage of Edinburgh University defined, more than that exercised elsewhere, what Scots would become. They chose to see their universities become not the rather somnolent colleges and halls which graced the banks of the Isis and Cherwell or the Cam, but bustling schools which by the 1720s had many notable and often polite and well-travelled men teaching at them. This was a necessity for a people poorer than the English. Scots often had to struggle outside the kingdom for their incomes. They needed educations that would allow them to succeed. The educational demands of the professional classes and the landed gentry, much more than the opinions of any town councillors, made Edinburgh University what it became. Those demands were negotiated and met by successful politicians who constantly interfered in the colleges. But this is what allowed the country to become reflective of the outlook of men like Ilay. Their interest in science and medicine, their secularism and delight in what was utilitarian and modern, helped to make the country of 1800 very different from the one which Lord Archibald Campbell had known as a young student at Glasgow in the 1690s or as a fledgling politician in Edinburgh in 1705. The Earl of Ilay, and others not so different, presided over the selections of professors in Edinburgh and elsewhere which transformed the country in the process. The Town Council of Edinburgh was generally a passive presence in these negotiations. At most, it can be praised for not causing problems for its betters.

Notes

1 'Essays on Natural History', p. 360, 'John Walker, Papers and Transcripts', Royal Botanic Garden, Edinburgh.

2 Grant, *Story of the University*, 1884, I:374. Balfour may have been humoured, since he was leaving to the University his extensive cabinet which formed the Musaeo Balfouriana. Its four presses, two cabinets, two chests of drawers, instruments, artifacts and books are described generally by Bower, *History of the University*, 1817, II:22f.

3 A. G. Stewart thought James Gregory had resigned but his brother David said he was sacked for 'contumacy.' Stewart, *Academic Gregories*, 1901, 84f; see also David Gregorie Papers, EUL, Dk.1.2²/26.

4 Awareness and approval of Newtonian ideas in Edinburgh dated from at least 1689 and David Gregory may have defended them earlier than that. Russell, 'Cosmological Teaching', *Journal of the History of Astronomy*, 1974, p. 129.

5 Sibbald, *Memoria Balfouriana*, 1699, p. 82f; EUL, DK1.2¹/90. His Parisian acquaintances seem to have included the botanist Joseph Piton de Tournefort and Guy Crescent Fagon, a notable chemist. The Gregorie brothers knew many English scientists even before David became a professor at Oxford: *David Gregory, Isaac Newton and Their Circle*, ed. Hiscock, 1937.

6 *The Correspondence of Isaac Newton*, ed. Turnbull et al., 1959–77, II:204, n.19.

7 Colin Maclaurin to Martin ffolkes, 25 March 1731, *The Collected Letters of Colin MacLaurin*, ed. Mills, 1982, p. 33.

8 Dalzel, *History*, ed. Laing, 1862, II:395; Wodrow, *Analecta*, ed. Leishman, 1853, IV:215.

9 Maclaurin to Martin Folkes, 25 March 1731, *The Collected Letters of Colin Maclaurin*, ed. Mills, 1982, p. 33.

10 Newton's offer to the Town Council is printed in the short biography of Maclaurin by Patrick Murdoch contained in his edition of Maclaurin's *An Account of Sir Isaac Newton's Philosophical Discoveries*, 1968, pp. iv–v, and in *The Correspondence of Isaac Newton*, ed. Turnbull et al., VII:336. Maclaurin's salary when he was appointed was £50, of which Newton offered to pay £20. Newton to Lord Provost John Campbell, [November 1725]. See also *The Collected Letters of Colin Maclaurin*, ed. Mills, 1982, p. 33. Again, a Campbell had a finger in this and was looking after an Argyllshire man.

11 Colin Maclaurin to Mungo Graham of Gorthy, 15 March 1740, Montrose Papers, NAS, GD220/5/1500.

12 Emerson, *Professors, Patronage and Politics*, 1991, p. 36.

13 *The Collected Letters of Colin Maclaurin*, ed. Mills, 1982, pp. 171ff, 252f; Records of the Town Council of Edinburgh, 6/V/52.

14 Ibid., p. 32.

15 Both brothers had mathematical works dedicated to them but Ilay was the one who seems most to have sought the company of mathematicians. Taylor, *Mathematical Practitioners*, 1966, pp. 58, 72, 118, 119, 182.

16 This letter would have been received by either Lord Provost John Campbell or George Drummond.

17 Patrick Cuming to [?], 13 August 1746, Mar and Kellie MSS, NAS, GD124/15/1565. See also Matthew Stewart to John McLea, 1746, Papers of John McLea, NAS, GD1/456/163; 'Essays on Natural History', p. 360; John Walker, 'Papers and Transcripts', Royal Botanic Garden, Edinburgh. The Craigies were a Squadrone family. Their political interest had recently been led partly by Robert Craigie of Glendoick. That Maclaurin had named possible successors is also made clear in a letter by his colleague, John Stevenson, who noted that 'the world at least will pay a considerable regard to his judgment, whatever our Patrons may do'; Stevenson to William Wishart, 23 June 1746, EUL, La.II. 115.13.2.

18 John Ramsay of Ochtertyre, Ochtertyre MSS, NLS,1635/II/1379.

19 The map is noticed by C. W. J. Withers in *Geography, Science and National Identity*, 2001, p. 149 and by Emerson, 'The Philosophical Society of Edinburgh, 1737–1747', *British Journal for the History of Science*, 1979, p. 78. One of the other projects of the Orkney expedition was to measure a degree of the earth's surface to confirm – or refute – Newton's claims about the shape of the earth, claims which recently had been supported by a French expedition to Lapland led by Maupertuis.

20 Sarah Bruce to Charles Mackie, 19 September 1746, EUL, La.II. 91.

21 David Hume to Henry Home, Lord Kames, 24 July 1746, *New Hume Letters*, ed. Mossner and Klibansky, 1954, p. 21.

22 Bower, *History*, 1817, I:357.

23 David J. Bryden, 'The Edinburgh Observatory 1736–1811', *Annals of Science*, 1990, pp. 445–74, 457.

24 Fry, *Dundas Despotism*, 1992, p. 184. See also Jane Fagg's 'Biographical Introduction' in *The Correspondence of Adam Ferguson*, ed. Merrolle et al., 1995, I:lxxiiif. It is unlikely that after 1790 Playfair could have been appointed because of his political views.

25 Ibid., I:lxxiv.

26 John Leslie to James Brown, 2 February 1805, EUL, Dc. 2.57/245. Thomson may have been John Thomson, later professor of military surgery.

27 Cant, *The University of St Andrews*, 4th edn, 2002, p. 124.

28 Richard Olsen, *Scottish Philosophy and British Physics*, 1975, pp. 194–219; Olsen, 'John Leslie', DSB 8:261f; Jack Morrell, 'John Leslie', ODNB, 33:462–4.

29 Leslie to James Brown, n.d. [1804], EUL, Dc.2.57/97 and 142; Leslie also had sought the Glasgow chairs of natural philosophy (1796) and astronomy (1803) and possibly, before that (1795), the chair of mathematics. At St Andrews he had tried for the natural history and natural philosophy chairs. Leslie to Brown, 20 January 1795; n.d.; 24 October

1799; 16 November 1804; 19 November 1804; 23 November 1804, EUL, Dc.2.57/207, 209, 226, 237, 241, 243.

30 Leslie to James Brown, 2 February 1805, EUL, Dc.2.57/245.

31 Sheets-Pyenson, 'Horse Race: . . . the Edinburgh Natural History Chair in 1854–1855', *Annals of Science*, 1992, pp. 461–77; Michael Barfoot, 'To ask the Suffrages of the Patrons', *Medical History*, 'Supplement', 1995.

32 Leslie to James Brown, 23 November 1804, EUL, Dc.2.57/243.

33 Leslie to James Brown, 2 February 1805, EUL, Dc.2.57/245.

34 Leslie to James Brown, 6 February 1805, EUL, Dc.2.57/247.

35 Leslie to James Brown, 28 February 1805, EUL, Dc.2.57/52f.

36 Clark, 'The Leslie Controversy, 1805', *Records of the Scottish Church History Society*, 1963, pp. 179–97, 181.

37 Ibid., p. 180.

38 Thomas Chalmers to James Brown, 24 January 1805, EUL, Dc.2.57/54.

39 Leslie to James Brown, 15 February 1805; n.d.; EUL, Dc.2.57/115, 127.

40 John Leslie to James Brown, n.d. [March 1805], EUL, Dc.2.57/157.

41 Leslie to James Brown, 25 March 1805, EUL, Dc.2.57/250.

42 Clark, 'The Leslie Controversy, 1805', *Records of the Scottish Church History Society*, 1963, p. 181.

43 Clark, 'The Leslie Controversy, 1805', *Records of the Scottish Church History Society*, 1963, p. 182.

44 Ibid., p. 183f.

45 Michael Fry sees this, wrongly I believe, only as a defeat for those who sought clerical domination in the University and not a defeat for Henry Dundas. Fry, *Dundas Despotism*, 1992, p. 297.

46 Clark, 'The Leslie Controversy, 1805', *Records of the Scottish Church History Society*, 1963, p. 179.

47 Grant, *Story*, 1884, I:339.

48 Fry, *Dundas Despotism*, 1992, p. 184.

49 Bryden, 'The Edinburgh Observatory', *Annals of Science*, 1990, pp. 445–74.

50 Stewart, 'The Origins of the Scottish Greek Chairs', in 'Owls to Athens', ed. Craik, 1990, pp. 391–400, 395.

51 Ibid., p. 395.

52 William Scott was the son of James Scott of Bristo, steward and servitor to James Scott, the 1st Duke of Buccleuch. Scott of Bristo fathered nineteen children and, not surprisingly, died in debt in 1692. William was his youngest surviving son. In addition to being related to the Lord Advocate, Sir James Steuart, Scott had well-placed brothers. James became a diplomat at Hanover; George was the secretary to a politician in London; David was an Edinburgh bookseller. In 1706, George

Scott introduced Daniel Defoe to 'the great folks Viz: Ld Stairs, Lord president [Sir Robert Berwick], Sir David Darm [Dalrymple], Ld Rosebery & others'. He claimed some of the credit for Defoe's writing 'an essay at removing national praejudices agt a uniuon with Scotland'. William Scott played a role in this good work. The Greek chair was almost certainly meant to pay for the Scotts' efforts. George to William Scott, 14 May 1706, EUL, La.II. 63. This contains a Scott genealogy.

53 Stewart, '*Owls to Athens*', ed. Craik, 1990, p. 395.
54 James Steuart to William Scott, 29 June 1709, EUL, La.II. 63.
55 Thomas Scott to William Scott, 30 March 1723; Thomas Scott to William Scott, 9 November 1723, EUL, 5072/153ff; James Scott to Lord Townshend (copy), 13 July 1723; George Scott to William Scott, n.d. [1723?], NLS, La.II: 63 In 1723 the Town Council, under Lord Provost Campbell, agreed to give him £300 'to be applyed for the benefite of his children in any manner he can devise' and it asked that the £100 salary which had been authorised earlier should be paid to him. John Campbell to [? Duke of Newcastle], 31 December 1723, PRO, SP54/14. I thank Dr Andrew Cunningham for a transcription of this letter.
56 Lord Milton to Ilay, n.d. [c. 1730], NLS, 16547/176–9; Wodrow, *Analecta*, ed. Leishman, 1853, IV:260.
57 Dalzel, *History*, ed. Laing, 1862, II:392.
58 Grant, *Story*, 1884, II:323; George Turnbull to Charles Mackie, 10 January 1730, EUL, La.II. 91.
59 Dalzel, ed. Laing, 1862, *History*, II:408.
60 A description of the trial is given in Minutes of the Town Council, 14 December 1772.
61 Dalzel says that he secured his post through the Earl's influence with the Town Council; *History*, ed. Laing, 1862, I:13. See also Grant, *Story*, II:324; Chambers, *Biographical Dictionary*, II:60; Horn MSS, EUL, Gen1824, 'Greek'.
62 Dalzel, *History*, ed. Laing, 1862, II:12.
63 Fry, *Dundas Despotism*, 1992, p. 184.
64 Scott, *Fasti*, V:131 and the entries to which it leads.
65 Dalzel, *History*, ed. Laing, 1862, II:273.
66 John Cairns, 'Charles Erskine', in *Legal Education in Edinburgh*, forthcoming.
67 *Charters, Statutes, and Acts of the Town Council and the Senatus 1583–1858*, ed. Morgan and Hannay, 1937, p. 166.
68 Dalzel, *History*, ed. Laing, 1862, II:285.
69 Bower, *History*, 1817, II:32.
70 The library is discussed by Michael Barfoot, 'Hume and the Culture of Science in the Early Eighteenth Century', in *Studies in the Philosophy of the Scottish Enlightenment*, ed. M. A. Stewart, 1990, pp. 151–90.

There were by c. 1750, in addition to the University Library, theological, classical and medical libraries maintained by students and professors at the College. The medical collections are noticed in Bunch, *Hospital and Medical Libraries in Scotland*, 1975. Bower said the Theological Library was begun by George Campbell in 1698 and had around 1,100 volumes in 1719. Bower, *History*, 1817, II:92.

71 Sir James Steuart to Principal John Stirling, 14 September 1704, Murray MS, GUL, 650/I.

72 There are details concerning his portrait by an unknown artist and a short sketch of his life, by Peter McIntyre, in *University Portraits*, compiled by Talbot Rice, 1957, I:50–2. McIntyre makes him a member of the Rankenian Club, which is plausible but doubtful. There is no definitive surviving list of the members of this club. For accounts of some its members, see M. A. Stewart, 'Berkeley and the Rankenian Club', *Hermanthena: A Trinity College Dublin Review*, 1985, pp. 25–45.

73 Stewart, 'Hume's Intellectual Development, 1711–1752', in *Impressions of Hume*, ed. Frasca-Spada and Kail, 2005, pp. 11–57.

74 Lord Milton to Ilay, [n.d.], NLS, 16547/176–9; Milton to Ilay, [n.d.], NLS, 16548/105; EUL MS Dc.1.4.1$^{1-2}$.

75 Dalzel, *History*, ed. Laing, 1862, p. 400.

76 Wynne, *An Abridgement of Mr Locke's Essay concerning Human Understanding*, 1st edn, 1696; subsequent editions in 1700, 1731, 1752, 1770. This was a widely used introduction to Locke's philosophy.

77 Wood, ' "The Fittest Man in the Kingdom" ', *Hume Studies*, 1997, pp. 277–313.

78 Edinburgh University, Senate Minutes, 25 January 1774, in Dalzel, *History*, ed. Laing, 1862, II:444.

79 Henry Paton, 'Letters from John Bonar to William Creech concerning the Formation of the Speculative Society', *The Book of the Old Edinburgh Club*, 1912, pp. 163–90.

80 Fry, *Dundas Despotism*, 1992, p. 22.

81 Ibid., p. 196.

82 Chambers, *Biographical Dictionary*, 1856, II:319; Horn MSS, EUL, Gen 1824, 'Logic'.

83 Fry, *Dundas Despotism*, 1992, p. 184.

84 See also Richard Sher, 'Professors of virtue: the Edinburgh chair', in *Studies in the Philosophy of the Scottish Enlightenment*, ed. Stewart, 1990, pp. 87–126. This has numerous additional references to manuscripts concerning the patronage of the chair. Like Paul Wood, I am sceptical of Sher's claim that the Edinburgh chair was so marked by practical moralising that little moral anatomy was done by its incumbents.

85 Grant, *Story*, 1884, II:323. The fact that he was tried may show an intent on the part of his examiners to affirm his right to the chair in the

face of opposition from men led by James Alston. Cf. Lord Milton to Ilay, [n.d.], NLS, 16547/176–9.

86 Dalzel, *History*, ed. Laing, 1862, II:403.
87 *House of Commons, 1715–1754*, ed. Sedgwick, 1970, I:393.
88 Senate Minutes, 10 January 1734.
89 Town Council Minutes, 25 February 1734.
90 Mossner, *The Life of David Hume*, 1980, p. 81.
91 See Emerson, 'The "affair" at Edinburgh and the "project at Glasgow"', in *Hume and Hume's Connexions*, ed. Stewart and Wright, 1994, pp. 1–22. Since writing this I have concluded that there were probably four factions on the Council: Ilay's men, who were neither led by Lord Provost Coutts, a member of 'the Duke of Argyll's Gang', nor very numerous; Argyll's friends; the Squadrone men; and the indifferent who waited to see how the balance of power would tip. See also M. A. Stewart, *The Kirk and the Infidel*, 1994.
92 Grant, *History*, 1884, II:338f.
93 See: Balfour-Melville, *The Balfours of Pilrig*, 1907, pp. 75, 108f, 131f. Ilay's trips to Scotland, always frequent, became almost annual after he inherited his dukedom in 1743. He began spending more time in Edinburgh than he had previously done. Gavin Hamilton's bookstore became one of his haunts.
94 Sher, 'Professors of virtue', in *Studies in the Philosophy of the Scottish Enlightenment*, ed. M. A. Stewart, 1990, p. 138f.
95 Elliot was consulted about the deal which ended Balfour's tenure of the chair. Patrons were often consulted, which suggests that he had had a hand in the securing of the post in 1754, just as he had interfered in 1745. Ibid., p. 118.
96 Somerville, *My Own Life*, 1861, p. 168. Balfour's book is entitled *A Delineation of the Nature and Obligation of Morality with Reflexions upon Mr Hume's Book . . . Principles of Morals*, Edinburgh, 1753.
97 Home to Milton, August 1756, cited by Jane Fagg in her 'Biographical Introduction' to the *Correspondence of Adam Ferguson*, ed. Vincenzo Merolle et al., 1995, I:xxvi and I:cii, n.29.
98 Hume to Smith, 8 June 1758, *The Letters of David Hume*, ed. Greig, 1969, I:279f. This letter is interesting for its assertion that the man who could effect the switch was Milton and not Argyll. There are other indications that in the last years of his life, Argyll was less active in university affairs outside Glasgow and Aberdeen, but they are only suggestive of a diminished role for a man who still engaged in politics and all the other business which he had pursued during a long life. He remained active and mentally alert until the end of his life. Milton remained his servant.
99 Hume to Smith, 12 April 1759, *The Letters of David Hume*, ed. Greig, 1969, I:304; Hume to William Robertson, 29 May 1759, *New Hume Letters*, ed. Mossner and Klibansky, 1954, p. 55f.

100 Adam Ferguson to William Cullen, 17 April 1759, GUL, 2255/24; Fagg, 'Biographical Introduction', p. xxxf; Sher, *Church and University*, 1985, pp. 117–19.
101 Ibid., p. 106f.
102 Drummond to Milton, 26 June 1759, NLS, 16708/259.
103 Shaw, *The Management of Scottish Society*, 1983, p. 184.
104 Millar to Lord Milton, 19 March 1761, NLS, 16721/24.
105 Sher, *Church and University*, 1985, p. 118.
106 There is much correspondence about this in the Saltoun Correspondence, most of it noted by Fagg, Sher or by Cater in 'The Making of Principal Robertson in 1762', *Scottish Historical Review*, 1970, pp. 60–84.
107 Robertson to Gilbert Elliot, 8 January 1763, NLS 11009/63; other letters to and from Baron William Mure about this appointment appear in the *Mure of Caldwell Papers*, Part 2, vol. I.
108 Fagg and Sher, cited above; Blair to Hume, 6 April 1764, NLS, Letters to David Hume formerly held at RSE but now in the NLS.
109 George Jardine at Glasgow immediately moved to secure this chair should Ferguson have to give it up. Jardine to Baron Mure, Mure MSS, NLS, 4945/165.
110 This incident and its aftermath are succinctly described by D. D. Raphael in *The Times Literary Supplement*, 2 March 1985, p. 15; the longer version of the story with the supporting documents is found in Raphael, Raynor and Ross, ' "This very awkward affair" ', *Studies on Voltaire and the Eighteenth Century*, (278), 1990, pp. 419–63. Had Adam Ferguson not gone abroad with Lord Chesterfield's son, John Jardine, another who aspired to professorships, probably would have done so. George Jardine to Robert Hunter, 24 February 1774, GUL, Gen 507.
111 The efforts made on Beattie's behalf are described by Cater, 'General Oughton *versus* Edinburgh's Enlightenment', in *History and Imagination*, ed. Lloyd-Jones, Pearl and Worden, 1982, pp. 254–71.
112 Lyttleton to Dalrymple, 5 March 1772, New Hailes MSS, NLS, 7228/23.
113 Cater, 'General Oughton', in *History and Imagination*, ed. Hugh Lloyd-Jones et al., 1982, pp. 254–71; *James Beattie's London Diary*, p. 9; Baron Mure to John Jardine, n.d. [1772], *Mure of Caldwell Papers*, 1885, Part 2, II:301. Mure described 'Beatty of Aberdeen (whom every man of a liberal way of thinking would wish to oppose)' as someone who should not be appointed. It was a comment motivated by friendship for Hume, whom Beattie had traduced in print. There is an account of this affair in Sir William Forbes's *Life of Dr Beattie*, 1824, pp. 173–78. Forbes believed that Beattie first had been offered the chair of natural philosophy, then vacant by the death of James

Russell, but it seems reasonably clear from other sources that the chair in question was always Ferguson's chair of moral philosophy. Sher has an account of this in 'Professors of virtue', p. 138; so does Fagg, 'Biographical Introduction', p. xlivff. Beattie's own accounts of this affair should not be read in the severely edited letters printed by Forbes in *The Life of Dr Beattie*, 1st edn, 1806, but in the originals found in NLS, Fettercairn Papers, ACC 4796 Box 94 and at AUL in the Beattie Manuscripts, especially AUL, 30/1/201–50.

114 *Mure of Caldwell Papers*, 1885, Part 2, II:294, 301; Dalzel, *History*, ed. Laing, 1862, II:44.

115 O'Leary, *Sir James Mackintosh: the Whig Cicero*, 1989, p. 10.

116 Dalzel, *History*, ed. Laing, 1862, II:410.

117 Bower, *History*; 1817, I:336.

118 Dalzel mentions Colin Drummond, Colin Maclaurin, Charles Alston, Alexander Monro, Andrew Plummer and William Porterfield; all but Drummond were prominent members of the Philosophical Society of Edinburgh, as was Stewart.

119 See the *Glasgow Journal* (No. 1676, 21–28 October 1773). I thank Paul Wood for this information.

120 James Lind in a letter to Lord Loudoun of 24 November 1773 asked the Earl to support his application for the job: Uncatalogued Loudoun Papers, Mount Stuart House, Isle of Bute; Grant, *Story*, II:352.

121 James Lind to Lord Loudoun, 27 August 1769, Uncatalogued Loudoun Papers, Mount Stuart House, Isle of Bute.

122 Emerson, 'The Philosophical Society of Edinburgh 1768–1783', *British Journal of the History of Science*, 1985, pp. 255–303.

123 Sir William Forbes to James Beattie, 19 October 1773, AUL, 30/2/154.

124 Horn MSS, EUL, Gen 1824, 'Natural Philosophy', Buchan was also seeking a medical chair at about the same time: see above, 'Institutes of Medicine', (p. 303).

125 Chambers, *Biographical Dictionary*, 1856, II:577.

126 Robison believed that the Town Council harboured resentment against him 'for having come into the university in opposition to their own' – another indication of how infrequently they made choices and how much their hands were tied. John Robison to William Windham, 17 July 1799, Wyndham papers, BL Add. MS 37915/74/98. This letter describes the ways in which the Town Council dictated to Robison the terms on which he might take an assistant, William Greenfield, who had been since 1784 conjoint professor with Hugh Blair in the rhetoric chair. Later letters in this collection describe Robison's dealings with subsequent assistants. I thank Paul Wood for a copy of this and other letters from this collection.

127 George Jardine to Robert Hunter, 24 December 1774, GUL, Gen 507, Box 1.

128 George Jardine to Robert Hunter, 24 February 1774, GUL, Gen 507, Box 1.

129 Robison to[?], 14 June 1799, Wyndham papers, BL, Add. MS 37915, 74/85.

130 It is likely that John Leslie and perhaps Thomas Chalmers sought this chair. See the section on the mathematics chair (above, pp. 328–34).

131 Ian S. Ross, *The Life of Adam Smith*, 1995, p. 83.

132 Wilbur S. Howell, *Eighteenth-Century British Logic and Rhetoric*, 1971, p. 544.

133 Grant, *Story*, 1884, p. 358; Sher, *Church and University*, 1985, p. 109.

134 The story of the creation of this chair has been well told by Sher, *Church and University*, 1985, p. 115ff.

135 Beattie MSS, AUL, 30/2/542.

136 Robert Walker to Henry Dundas, 24 December 1798; MacKnight to Henry Dundas, 15 January 1799, NAS, GD51/6/1303. Walker's beliefs are discussed by McIntosh in *Church and Theology*, 1998, pp. 176–95, 199–05.

137 Talbot Rice and MacIntyre, *The University Portraits*, 1957, I:24.

138 Grant, *Story*, 1884, p. 359.

139 This excludes Joseph Gibson but counts, I hope, all the conjoint professors who were appointed with those already holding a chair. Many of the men ultimately appointed had competed for more than one post.

140 Morrell, 'Medicine and Science', *Four Centuries of Edinburgh University Life*, ed. Gordon Donaldson, 1983, pp. 38–52.

141 The number of Edinburgh divinity students was always greater than the number actually in the city because many attended irregularly while tutoring or doing something else.

142 Dingwall, *Physicians, Surgeons*, 1995, p. 24. See also Morrell, 'The University of Edinburgh in the Late Eighteenth Century', *Isis*, 1971, pp. 159–71, 165; Hamilton, *The Healers*, 1981, pp. 118–22; Emerson, 'Scottish Universities', *Studies on Voltaire and the Eighteenth Century*, 1977, pp. 453–74. Page 473 gives likely Scottish university enrolments for selected years, 1700–1800 inclusive.

143 Emerson, 'Numbering the Medics', unpublished paper.

144 This figure assumes that there were, in 1700, 400 students paying on average 3 guineas for class fees and £10 for living costs each year for a total of £5,200. The thirty or so medical students would have paid in apprenticeship and other fees and expenditures about £10 yearly, coming to perhaps £300. By the late eighteenth century the 1,200 or so arts and divinity students would have spent over £20 each on living and other expenses and about £10 each on tuition, coming in all to £36,000. The eighty or so law students might add a minimum of £500 in tuition and £3,200 for living, or £3,700. The 1,000 medical students we might assume to be each paying at least £6 in fees (£6,000) and £50

in other costs (£50,000), for a total of £56,000. Morrell's calculation of the medical fees paid at the university in 1798–9 came to £3,516, to which we would have to add the fees paid at the Surgeons' Hall School and for other courses at the University taken by men interested in other subjects. Morrell, 'The University of Edinburgh in the late Eighteenth Century', p. 165. In the 1750s, the approximately 400 medical students alone contributed a minimum of £16,400 for one year. By 1800, students generally were probably leaving in the city annually between £80,000 and £100,000.

Part IV

St Andrews University

13

THE ARTS CHAIRS, 1690–c. 1715

෨

1. THE UNIQUENESS OF THE PLACE AND ITS INSTITUTIONS

St Andrews and its University was unlike the other Scottish university towns and their universities. The history of the University and its colleges in this period has been poorly preserved and is not well known. There are for this period no great printed collections of documents comparable to the *Munimenta Universitatis Glasguensis* (1854) or the similar volumes for the Aberdeen universities published by the Spalding Club (1854–98). One cannot find in print a record of much of the official life of the University during the eighteenth century or dense descriptions of the local society in which it operated. There are only the rather slim, although useful, histories of the University by James Maitland Anderson and Ronald Cant. Robert Smart's *Biographical Register of St Andrews University 1747–1897* (2004) has only recently appeared to supplement the printed matriculation rolls. The latter are less complete and useful than those existing for the other Scottish colleges save Edinburgh.[1] There are few collections of printed records comparable to those for Edinburgh University. Until after 1747 and the union of the arts colleges, St Andrews livings did not pay enough to be of great concern to the politicians. With the absence of many notable professors and with relatively few graduates, less attention has been paid to the colleges. This reflects the recruitment of professors and students from less socially and intellectually prominent families and their patronage by families whose archives have not been published or preserved in readily accessible places. The professors left little which has come into Scottish archives or been printed. Worse yet, there are very few published or manuscript sources holding the wealth of information on local families such as one finds elsewhere. This is partly owing to the structure of the genteel society in the University's hinterland. It had fewer large and important families and more small landowners than did the areas around Aberdeen or Glasgow. The Grahams and Hamiltons of Glasgow had no local Fifeshire counterparts. One simply has less to work with in St Andrews despite its possession of three colleges.

There is no good burgh history of St Andrews, which was in 1700 a small royal burgh of about 4,000 people with perhaps 945 dwellings, of which 159 were reported to be ruined in 1728.[2] St Andrews was in a declining region which did not benefit from the economic changes which transformed other parts of the country during the century.[3] It did not and could not become a rich industrial or trading town or even a prosperous fishing port. This town stagnated and regressed.[4] There was a rural air about St Andrews lacking even at King's College, Aberdeen. Indeed, some of the indwellers farmed fields adjacent to the town and stabled livestock and stored their carts within the walls. As an economic centre, St Andrews lacked wealthy and influential men with the motives and means to interfere in the appointment of men in the University and its three colleges or even to leave them considerable legacies.

The burgh was not much of a social centre for the aristocrats of the surrounding countryside. Late in the period, a few men, like George Dempster, formerly an MP, and professor Adam Ferguson, retired there but cold, windswept St Andrews was not a general resort of the local gentry. The University did not attract many aristocratic boys from any distance to study at its colleges. They went to nearby Edinburgh or to Glasgow or, late in the century, south to England. While the city had a Commissary Court, it had no corporations for legal practitioners or medical men. There was no pressure to teach law in the University and the medical chair should be seen primarily as a fund-raising foundation, not a teaching one. The town's decline was hastened by the end of episcopacy, which had deprived the University of its resident archepiscopal chancellor. The Synod of Fife and the Presbytery of St Andrews met in the town and sometimes tried to interfere in divinity appointments, but they were relatively uninfluential in the University as a whole. In the early part of the century, the colleges were not very sympathetic to the strict Calvinism preached by the local ministers. In neither half of the period were the professors close to or dependent upon the local ministers. The principal of St Leonard's College and later the principal of the United College usually sat with them in the Presbytery as the minister of St Leonard's parish. Sometimes a local minister was honoured by the University but this tended to be when the University men found him personally congenial and not because he represented views held by men in the burgh or its Kirks which the professors felt inclined to respect.

St Andrews was almost insignificant politically and lacked the dominant position among its set of parliamentary elective burghs (the Perth Burghs) which Aberdeen and Glasgow enjoyed in theirs. This was partly because the burgh was too poor to be independent. This made it easier for outsiders to control it. The Provost's place was often held not by a local merchant but by a local nobleman or a cadet member of a noble family.[5] No figures such as Lord Provost Drummond in Edinburgh or Provost Cunningham in Glasgow could arise. The local important Fifeshire political families – the Leslies, Melvilles, Anstruthers, Wemysses, St Clairs, and the Scots of Scotstarvit – were active in the town's politics and could not be ignored. Until 1761, Murrays, Lindsays, Haldanes and Leslies dominated its parliamentary interest and after that George Dempster, MP. These men, all non-residents, tended to have their way until Dempster's retirement from Parliament in 1790. Then Henry Dundas and his friends became the dominant men. Until 1745, these men were often Jacobite in outlook, and reluctantly voted for Whigs, or they belonged to the Squadrone during years when Ilay was the country's chief patron. They and the colleges were to some extent excluded from the gravy trains conducted by the Squadrone lords or by the Argathelians. Even after 1745 the burgh counted for too little to get much for itself or the colleges located within it.

The burgh was more dependent upon its colleges than they were upon the town, a fact that even made it thinkable in the 1690s for the masters to consider moving the University to Perth.[6] The colleges were politically involved but they remained somewhat isolated from the politics of the town. This was owing partly to a University rule which prevented its members and officers from holding town offices, but there was also little inducement to seek them. The burgh also had a cumbersome sett or constitution which did not make it easy to produce a stable, active and local municipal oligarchy including men from the colleges. All these factors worked to limit town and gown involvements which elsewhere benefited colleges.

The University was also peculiar in not having many important noblemen concerned with its affairs during this period. It was unlike Marischal College, where the last Lord Marischal was followed in c. 1725 by Lord Ilay, exercising the rights of the office without the title, and then by Lords Bute, Mansfield and Auckland. Neighbouring King's had locally important men as chancellors and rectors when it bothered to appoint them. The lack of interested and distinguished outsiders playing important roles in the corporations between c. 1710 and 1765 meant that St Andrews University and its colleges lacked the sort of lobbyists and solicitors which Glasgow, Edinburgh and Marischal College could always find. This was a place which, like King's College, would remain underfunded and undistinguished throughout most of the eighteenth century, even though it educated many bright men and appointed some distinguished professors who were then sometimes lost when opportunities opened elsewhere. This was also the case in Old Aberdeen.

Until the 1750s, the University had, in comparison with the other colleges, a smaller and, for much of the period, a shrinking recruitment area for students. It was hemmed in by the areas dominated by the flourishing colleges in Aberdeen and Edinburgh, towns which were expanding and providing more students to the local colleges.[7] St Andrews suffered generally declining enrolments until after the union of the arts colleges in 1747. Chairs at St Andrews were eagerly sought, but generally by local men and not outsiders attracted by the incomes as they were at Glasgow and Edinburgh. The small salaries and scant fees of the professors inhibited the recruitment of notable men.[8] The St Andrews colleges were not staffed by the brightest and the best. When such masters chose colleagues, they, like members of mediocre departments in universities today, did not risk making brilliant appointments. External patrons who cared about the quality of appointees were not as active or effective at St Andrews as elsewhere.

The colleges's ability to attract first-rate men was further undermined by the fact that they had two chairs filled by private patrons. The Kennedys of Cassillis and the Scots of Scotstarvit usually appointed protégés as humanists.[9] These were seldom men of much distinction, however good they had been as family tutors or as ministers in parishes where their patrons or their friends earlier had placed them. Once installed as teachers, they were often promoted into better-paying chairs and their patrons again made appointments. These masters seemed to elect men indebted to, or supported by, their own patrons. This was one means by which Jacobites were introduced into the foundations. Certainly some of the men complained of as Jacobites – Colin Vilant, Ninian Young and Alexander Scrymgeour – came into the arts colleges on appointments from private patrons.

At St Mary's College, the divinity school, things were little better. Those chairs were all in the gift of the Crown and were more purely political appointments. As in the other colleges, only the principal and professor of divinity had to be really competent men who could also politick for those who placed them. The professors of Hebrew and ecclesiastical history could be and were less competent and sometimes the holders of more or less acknowledged sinecures. This too worked to introduce mediocrities.

The chair of medicine after c. 1760 was little better. The incumbents, after the first, did not publicly lecture, although some of them may have had apprentices or others whom they taught privately.[10] The professor's principal job was to examine men for degrees, which by the end of the period took up a great deal of time but was hardly demanding work. The fee for the MD degree was at first about £5 for a degree awarded after an often cursory examination. This money was shared. About a third went to the professor and the rest to a scrivener, to the library and to the professor's colleagues. In 1747, the fee rose to £10.[11] Between 1696 and 1810, 1,103 MDs were awarded, benefiting the University by many thousands of pounds.[12] Other signs of the poverty of the University and its colleges can be found in the colleges' sales of their feudal superiorities[13] and the sale of some of St Salvators' silver in 1757 to contribute to a building fund.[14] In these actions, the masters were like those at King's College. They too sold superiorities and patronages in 1752 and 1765 for the political benefit of their friends and then the College bells when they wished to give themselves a 'bonus'.

St Andrews was also different from the other universities because of the complexity of its structure. Until 1747 it had three colleges, but after that date two. The colleges were independent corporations within the University which, like the universities in Glasgow and Aberdeen, had a chancellor, vice chancellor, rector, deans and a Senatus Academicus which acted on University matters. The chancellor, until the Revolution of 1688, had usually been the Archbishop of St Andrews, the Primate of Scotland. He gave the University prestige which it lost when episcopacy was abolished in the Established Church in 1690. The chancellor was also 'Conservator of Privileges'. This office dated from the mid-seventeenth century and gave powers of reform rather like those which at Glasgow were assigned by its charter to the visitors. The chancellor granted the higher degrees (a function delegated by him to the vice chancellor) and acted as the head of the corporation, often serving as the mediating figure with government officials when business was to be done. Chancellors had few other clearly defined powers and, as Lord Ilay had pointed out to men in Glasgow, the office might belong by right to the Crown. Despite that, after 1690, the Senatus elected the chancellor for life, but none was elected until 1697 when John Murray, Earl of Tullibardine and later 1st Duke of Atholl, was chosen to fill the post and to protect the University from what it saw as the harassment of the town. Tullibardine solicited appointments and seems to have approved of the negotiations with the town fathers of Perth, to which the University considered moving in 1697–8.[15] When the Archbishop was deposed, the University and its colleges also lost more financial resources than seems to have been the case at Glasgow and King's College.

After 1690 there were no outstanding and powerful chancellors like those at Glasgow to lobby the government for grants to make up the revenues lost earlier. Most of the chancellors seem to have been less interested or involved with the affairs of the University than those elsewhere, partly because they were often absentees. Atholl, chancellor 1697–1724, appointed a vice chancellor who acted for him on most matters until the Duke's death in 1724.[16] So did his successor, James Brydges, 1st Duke of Chandos (1673–1744), an English peer who was honoured with this office (1724–44) for establishing the Chandos Professorship of Medicine. He was sometimes useful in London but he did little in St Andrews. Even in London the real business concerning appointments between 1725 and 1761 generally was done by the Earl of Ilay and the Duke of Newcastle and, after 1761, by the political managers who replaced them. Chandos's deputies, like Atholl's, were college heads. The Duke of Cumberland (1721–65), a younger son of George II, was chosen as chancellor in 1746 and served until 1765. During this time he was often abroad and did little except to intervene in a regius appointment. The institution had no effective chancellors until its livings had so increased in value as to make Scottish politicians interested in them.

Thomas Hay, 8th Earl of Kinnoull (1710–87), who held the place from 1765 to 1787, was different. He also lived not far away in Perthshire and was a good influence on the institution. A friend of Edinburgh's Principal Robertson and the Moderate literati, Kinnoull was a pious man, active in civic affairs and the management of the United Kingdom. He expended considerable energy on University appointments at St Andrews and elsewhere. The Earl established prizes for each class in the United College funded by a donation of £100. These prizes he gave out on visits during which he sometimes enriched the Library. He was followed (1788–1811) by Henry Dundas, later 1st Viscount Melville (28 April 1741–27 May 1811), whose influence on the place was baneful.

The rector throughout the period had to be the head of one of the colleges or either the professor of divinity or ecclesiastical history.

There were no more than five men at any time who were eligible for the post and after 1747 only four.[17] In the first half of the period, the office tended to be rotated among the principals, with Provost Robert Ramsay holding it most often; after 1747 it was usually held by the principal of St Mary's College but sometimes by the professor of divinity. Rectors were usually elected without difficulty by a 'general congregation of masters and students', in reality by the masters and the students who had been matriculated for two years of whom there were few. In this meeting, the old rector had a casting vote. Rectors presided over the rectorial court where their assessors were other professors whom they named. The rector chaired the Comitia or Senatus Academicus if he was vice chancellor, as he often was. This body controlled University finances and did most University business, including making the appointments of the Chandos professor of medicine who was a University professor attached to no college until 1747. The act of union incorporated him into the United College. The senate made regulations, managed the library, appointed University officers such as the librarian, clerk and quaestor, and did a miscellany of things like setting fees for matriculation and granting degrees. Arts degrees were conferred by the faculty of arts but the Senatus granted all the rest. It bought instruments and other pieces of equipment, entertained visitors like Ben Franklin, Dr Johnson and James Boswell, and addressed the King from time to time.[18] In short, it was the means by which the professors and masters ran things which did not belong to the colleges. The chancellors were not powerful outsiders who played independent and important roles in the management of the University until 1765. The vice chancellors and rectors were usually professors who looked after their colleagues' interests and were expected to do just that. They lacked the independence which rectors at Glasgow and King's College sometimes showed.

The faculties were treated effectively as committees of the Senatus chaired by their deans.[19] The deans of faculty were alternately the heads of the arts colleges and then, after 1747, the principal of the United College. The dean of the faculty of divinity was the principal of St Mary's. Medicine does not seem to have had a formal faculty but the professor of medicine functioned as a dean when he promoted men to doctor of medicine degree. Deans did little but promote men to degrees but their formal powers included supervising and directing the course of studies and examining for degrees. With the chancellor often an absent figure acting by a professorial deputy, and the rest of the University's officers themselves professors, it is not surprising that the place was an inbred institution in which men looked after family interests more than was possible at any of the other schools save King's College, Aberdeen.

The Colleges of St Salvator's and St Leonard's were, like St Mary's College, self-governing bodies which managed their own funds, looked after their bursars and students and taught the courses appropriate to them. The arts colleges elected their members save for the principals, whom the Crown appointed, and the humanists who were appointed by private patrons. After the union of 1747, the masters of the United College also elected the professor of medicine who had been incorporated in the United College. In none of the St Andrews corporations was there a sustained and effective outside influence other than that exercised by the patrons of the humanity chairs and the occasional interventions of Visitors appointed by the Crown. The first of these bodies which concerns us is the Parliamentary Visitation Commission of 1690.

2. The Purge of 1690 and the Revolution Settlement

The Committee of the Visitation Commission which sat in St Andrews to consider the affairs of the University was more severe than those which sat elsewhere.[20] It had to be since the professors, except for one, had all publicly supported King James and had signed an address urging others to do so.[21] The Archbishop, the professors and regents had been more loyal to the Stuarts, or at least more vocal about their allegiances, than those elsewhere. They continued to be egregious. When the masters were required to appear before the Visitors in their gowns, they attended in state:

> . . . the Masters, Professors and Regents made their appearance before them more like persons that would seem to have Power and Authority over the Commissioners of Parliament, than like persons who were accus'd as Delinquents, or punishable, having come in all their Formalities, the Mace and Sword carried before them: This they did for two days, until they were forbid to do so any more. The first thing they did after their appearance, was to decline the Authority of the Commission of Parliament, and then to enter their Protestation against the Commissioners Authority and Proceedings; which is such a degree of arrogance, that by our Law is accounted little less than Treason to decline the Authority and Jurisdiction of Parliament, and in due time they will be proceeded against as their Insolence deserves. They refused to give an Inventory of, or to exhibit the Registers and Records of the University, so that the Commissioners were

obliged at length to break open the Doors and the Gate of one of the Colleges, before they could be admitted into it. Of all this, report is made to the Parliament, and to the Privy Council . . .[22]

Those interrogated delayed and obstructed the Visitors as best they could. They deeply resented being questioned about their religious beliefs and morals, about their teaching, the oaths they had required of students and graduands, and about their stewardship of the funds and lands which sustained the endowments. While some professors queried the right of some of their accusers to act, others found it opportune to be out of town, and all of them seem to have tried to evade difficult questions. They said they had clear consciences about their past conduct. They were also well aware that grudges from the past were being settled by local men who were good Presbyterians and now better Whigs.

The professors and regents could not have been much surprised when the Visitors concluded

that the Rector, principalls and regents of the universitie have been negligent in keeping good order in the said universitie and that some of them are guiltie of gross immoralities as appears by the depositiones of witnesses heirwith produced . . . that the Rector, principals, professor of Hebrew, and all the regents (except the said Mr John Monroe) are guiltie of contempt of authority of this meiting, dissaffectione to the government of church and staite now established by law, as lykewayes the said Rector, principalls, the professor of Hebrew, the professor of Mathematticks, who is alsoe dean of facultie of Airts, haveing refuised to sign the confessione of faith ratified in the second sessione of this current parliament, to suear and signe the oath of alleadgeance, signe the bond of assurance and to submit to the church government now established by law, have rendered themselfes incapable to officiat in the said universitie.[23]

The Visitors of 1690 meant to clean house and did so. They sacked every teaching member of the University save John Monro. The principals and professors, like some in Edinburgh, had resisted with style. They continued to do so before the full Commission in Edinburgh.

The full Commission was willing to be more lenient. As late as 26 September 1690, the university men were given a final chance to recant, sign the oaths and continue in office.[24] In the end, they would renounce neither their political nor religious beliefs by signing the new oaths and assurances. They were 'all deprived by one sentence for being highly disaffected to the Government & refusing the oaths.'[25] When it was all over, there followed a strange scene in Edinburgh which shows how unsettled the times really were: 'Att Night when they went home they were almost worshiped in the streets by persons of all ranks.'[26] It is an image which recalls those who left the General Assembly in 1843 led into schism by Thomas Chalmers, a St Andrews alumnus.

The vacated professorships were filled by competitive examinations held after 29 October 1690. These competitions were advertised by printed notices posted on church doors throughout the country. The new men would be chosen or imposed by 'his Majesty's delegates' from those who competed and the University would be restocked with reliable professors and masters.[27] The trials in 1690 involved, here as elsewhere, disputations and 'examination as otherwayes as the judges of the said University or Colledge think fitt.' But the examiners were to have an eye to 'the dignity and Merit of the parties Competing' and to their 'good Life and Conversation[,] their prudence f[riend]ships for ye place[,] affection for the Government of Church and State now Established'.[28] One suspects that the Commissioners also noted the 'dignity and Merit' of those who recommended the candidates but this cannot be shown. Who actually tried the men is also uncertain; perhaps it really was the Commissioners, as William Carstares suggested in 1708.[29] They included learned ministers who could have done so.[30] The trials were to form the pattern for future appointments save those to professorial and divinity chairs, but no other comparative trials seem to be recorded for St Salvator's until 1713. At St Leonard's, they seem to have been held but few names of unsuccessful competitors have survived. At St Salvator's, the College was fully staffed and running normally in 1691 and at St Leonard's by the following year. The full complement of professors was not reached at St Mary's until 1708. Here, as elsewhere, the Visitation Commission continued its oversight and meddling at least until 1702.

3. The First Principals

At St Mary's, as at the other colleges, the first person appointed after the Visitation was a new principal, the reverend Mr William Vilant [or Violant] (c. 1630–93). Vilant was the youngest son of a French émigré who became chamberlain or steward to the Earl of Strathmore. Principal Vilant seems to have graduated MA at St Andrews in 1649 and so was probably in his early sixties at the time of his appointment. He had been ordained in 1656 to the royal living of Ferry-Port-on-Craig, a local parish near Leuchars. Because of his theological views, Vilant was deprived in 1662 and finally deposed in 1665.[31] For some years, he was chaplain to the very orthodox Earl of Cassillis. Robert Wodrow thought him at some time chaplain to the Duke of Lauderdale and noted his controversies with Episcopalians.[32] Indulged at Cambusnethan in 1669 (where he was almost certainly put in by the interest of the Duke of Hamiliton), Vilant supported conventicles and was again deposed in 1684. After his second deposition, he may have served for a while as chaplain to other noblemen. Despite his theological views, he was no enthusiast but a polite and moderate[33] man who was not out of place in the dining room of the Duke of Hamilton.[34] At the Revolution, he was chosen to sit in the General Assembly of 1690 and in mid-July 1690 he was appointed to his principalship. He was not installed until the following year. Vilant was a reliable man capable of heading a divinity school. The Visitors opted here, as at the other colleges, for a temperate man who had suffered and who would teach the Calvinist views they now sought to impose. He may have taught alone until his death in 1693. Principal Vilant was the first of a line of Vilants who would teach at St Andrews into the nineteenth century.

Principal Vilant was followed to St Andrews by another short-tenured man much like himself, Alexander Pitcairne (1622–c. September 1695), who in 1690 became provost of St Salvator's.[35] He had graduated MA at St Andrews in 1643, after which he taught as a regent at St Salvator's from 1648 to 1656. Ordained in 1656 to the parish of Dron in Perthshire, a royal living, he had been deprived in 1662, being, as someone said, 'an eyesore to the Episcopal clergy'.[36] Although deprived he was protected by Bishop Robert Leighton who respected his learning and irenic disposition. Pitcairne remained in Dron until c. 1680, at which time he fled to Holland where he remained until 1687.[37] He returned to Dron in 1690–1 but was quickly moved to the headship of his old college in a town where he had connections. Pitcairne had philosophical interests. He wrote a compendium of Aristotelian and Cartesian philosophy, which he dedicated to Robert Boyle, and bought for the University library works by Tycho Brahe, Fénelon, Bishop Stillingfleet and issues of the *Philosophical Transactions of the Royal Society of London*.[38]

The third principal, appointed to St Leonard's College in 1691, was William Tullideph (c. 1626–September 1695), a Covenanter from Cupar, Fife who had served on the Commission of Visitation. His relatives and descendants also served the University for over eighty years. He too held a St Andrews MA given to him in 1641 and had taught at his college, St Salvator's, as a regent while Pitcairne had been teaching there. The three principals were old acquaintances. Like the others, Tullideph had been ordained to a royal living, at Dunbog, in 1657, had been deposed in 1662, indulged later at Kilbirnie (1670–84) and deprived and then imprisoned. After the Revolution, he preached at Wemyss until 1691. He then became principal and the minister of St Leonard's parish in St Andrews. At Kilbirnie, the principal heritor was the 18th Earl of Crawford, in 1690 a Lord of Treasury, one of the Commissioners for settling the Kirk and praeses of the Visitation Commission of 1690 and so a Visitor at St Andrews. In Wemyss the chief heritor was the Earl of Wemyss.[39] All three principals needed political support for their office. We know that Tullideph was backed by well-born men, including Sir George Mackenzie, 1st Viscount Tarbat,[40] and probably by the Earl of Melville, and David, Lord Leslie, Lord Raith. Tarbat and Raith had both sought to protect David Gregorie when others wished to out him at Edinburgh in 1690.[41] Tullideph seems to have been a man able to work with those who did not wholly agree with his principles. At St Mary's the next appointment saw provost Pitcairne succeed the deceased Vilant. There were no other appointments until 1696. These men were not as interesting as the men appointed at Glasgow but they were not without virtues and accomplishments. They had had influential patrons early in their careers. Two had been abroad. None seem to have been vindictive or mean-spirited Calvinists such as are sometimes said to have been put into the universities by the Visitors.

4. OTHER APPOINTMENTS AT ST SALVATOR'S AND ST LEONARD'S COLLEGES, 1691–c. 1693

At St Salvator's, John Kennedy, 7th Earl of Cassillis, a member of the Commission of Visitation and one on the St Andrews Committee, appointed Alexander Scrymgeour to be humanist.[42] The place was his to give since its patronage belonged to the Kennedys of Cassillis. Scrymgeour, an alumnus of St Salvator's, was later said to be both a Jacobite and Episcopalian but his initial sponsorship makes that unlikely in the 1690s.[43] Scrymgeour was a local man and later became de jure 4th Earl of Dundee. He was a learned man with particular interests in languages (he seems to have known Hebrew well enough to have thought of teaching it) and history. He served in this post for about two years, after which he was promoted to be a regent of philosophy.

Other regents had been appointed with Scrymgeour in 1691 but little is known about them save that they seem to have been interested in logic and metaphysics. They prepared the courses on logic and metaphysics which they and others hoped would become the standard Scottish texts in these subjects and received funds from vacant stipends to print the volumes. Their books appeared in London in 1701.[44] One of them, John Arrot (c. 1668–after 1722), held his regency until 1705 when he resigned. Arrot married and may have been the man of the same name who became factor to the Archbishopric.[45] If he was, then he was probably well connected with local political figures. He seems to have remained in touch with the College men into the 1720s.[46]

A second regent, Alexander Monro (c. 1652–December 1697), had trained as a writer in Edinburgh but gave up that life to accept a teaching post. The most likely reason for his switch of careers was that he could now take the oaths required of teachers.[47] He was well enough connected to be made provost of St Salvator's in 1694 and three years later became vice chancellor, an appointment he owed to the Marquis of Tullibardine.[48] Monro was probably a relative of John Monro, the only man not deposed by the Visitors and who, in 1690, sought the principality at St Leonard's.

A third regent, Robert Ramsay (c. 1666–25 January 1733), is not a well-known man. He was almost certainly a relative of Henry Ramsay, a St Leonard's master. Like the Vilants and Tullidephs, Ramsay seems to have had relatives in the other arts college. Robert Ramsay became provost of St Salvator's and served the University as rector for nineteen years. Monro and Ramsay both had connections with men who could be useful to them and to their colleges.

The last man to be named a regent in 1691 was William Young the younger of Kirkton (c. 1665–24 November 1746). He succeeded Ramsay as provost in 1733 and like others founded an academic dynasty.[49]

At St Leonard's, John Monro (?–1697) was the sole regent to survive the purge of 1690. He was not made principal, as he wished, but in the following year his loyalty was recognised when he was named dean of faculty. Monro was joined in that year by Thomas Tailzour [Tailyeour or Taylor] (?–c. 1708/9), John Rowe (c. 1668–after 1700) and John Craigie (c. 1672–March 1732). Unlike the Glaswegians, these men are not known to have had virtuoso interests but they had records which attested to their orthodoxy.

Tailzour was the son of a dissenting minister in Ireland, James Taylor, and was probably related to the wife of Principal William

Tullideph, Helen Tailyeour. He was noticed by the reverend George Turnbull as 'the learned and faithful Mr Thomas Taylor who had a deep, distinct and long exercise under Mr [Thomas] Hog's ministry and in the end got a clear and safe out-gate and was there after an eminent and shining light both in Scotland and Ireland.'[50] Thomas Halyburton (25 December 1674–23 September 1712), who came under Tailzour's care, remembered him as 'a man very capable, and very careful of and kind to me'.[51] Like his father, he may have ministered in both Scotland and Ireland prior to the Revolution and may have studied with Hog in Holland. In 1707, Tailzour seems to have taken a St Andrews MD after the defence of a thesis. It is significant that he was actually examined by five physicians because in 1705 the University had told the Royal College of Physicians in Edinburgh that it might name five doctors to examine candidates for the MD degree at St Andrews.[52] When Tailzour took his degree, on 28 November 1707, he appears to have been the first man to do so under this arrangement. The only other indication that he had interests in science is his appointment to a committee to deal with the terms of employing the mathematician, William Bethune [Beton or Beaton], in 1707.[53] Taylor was dead by 12 January 1709.

Rowe was the son of the minister of Ceres, a nearby parish later in the gift of the Earls of Crawford. His mother was Jean, daughter of Robert Blair, the minister of St Andrews, a relation which tied him to the reformer Robert Blair and in the future to Hugh Blair, the Moderate minister of Edinburgh, whom he did not live to meet and would not have approved had he done so.[54] He resigned his St Andrews living and was translated to Edinburgh University, where he was admitted as a regent on 9 August 1695. Rowe had a brother who was chaplain to Thomas Hamilton, 6th Earl of Haddington, a relative by marriage to the Leslies, the family of the Earls of Rothes.[55] That Rowe had support from Leslies and Hamiltons when he went to Edinburgh is suggested by his replacement, John Loudoun, another protégé of those families. Rowe served in Edinburgh as a regent until 1700, when he resigned. He died a short time later.[56]

The last of the early regents was John Craigie, who c. 1700 either inherited or was able to buy the small estate of Lahill (or Lawhill), part of which he called Dunbarnie after his family's estate in Perthshire. He was a cousin of both Lawrence and Thomas Craigie, respectively a Squadrone lawyer of importance and a professor who taught at both St Andrews and Glasgow. John married into the Lindsay family and had a son who, like other Craigies, became an advocate and twice married well, the first time into an important Squadrone family, that of Sir John Inglis of Cramond.[57] John Craigie, like Rowe, would not have lacked local sponsors.

The last man appointed, humanist Gilbert Cunningham, owed his place to the private patron of his chair, Scot of Scotstarvit. Cunningham had been a minister in Kinghorn, whose patron was the Jacobite and Episcopal Earl of Strathmore, who had employed Principal William Vilant's father. Cunningham is remembered as a teacher of Thomas Halyburton and as one of the few professors in the century to go mad, which he did shortly before his death in 1694.

With these appointments the faculties were reconstituted and functioning, and the normal processes of appointment by the Crown, by patrons and by co-option could resume. As they did, the kind of men appointed did not change. The masters tended to name local men who were often their kin.

5. College Appointments to 1716

In 1693, two appointments were made at St Salvator's College. In September, Alexander Scrymgeour was promoted from humanist to regent. This allowed the Kennedys of Cassillis to appoint another humanist. Those who made Scrymgeour a regent in September 1693 do not appear to have been related to him or beholden to his family, but they may have been happy to gratify the Kennedys who on 24 March 1693 appointed his replacement, Gershom Carmichael. He retained the post very briefly and was gone by September 1693. Carmichael is unlikely to have taught at all, but he benefited from his appointment since he could accept another academic post without trial. He left to continue his studies at Glasgow University.

Cassillis in appointing Carmichael would have been mindful of his background. He came from a family which had suffered and been exiled from Scotland. In 1692–4, his stepfather, James Fraser of Brea, held the living in Culross and was an important figure in the General Assemblies of those years. This would have weighed with the pious head of the Kennedy family. Carmichael later secured his Glasgow University post through the good offices of the Duke of Hamilton and his own relative, John, Lord Carmichael, who had been Lord Privy Seal (1689), HM Commissioner to the General Assembly (1690), Chancellor of Glasgow University (1692) and in 1693 had just been given command of a regiment. He could have helped his young relative, but who besides Cassillis actually did help him to a St Andrews post is unknown.

No other humanist was appointed until 1695, when the position went to William Vilant II (c. 1660–21 January 1759), son of the recently dead William Vilant, principal of St Mary's College.[58] The Kennedy family had again looked after one of their own.

Scrymgeour's advancement had been made possible by the elevation of the provost of St Salvator's, Alexander Pitcairne, to the principality of St Mary's in 1693. Pitcairne was followed in his provostship in 1694 by Alexander Monro, the former Edinburgh writer. That Tullibardine made him vice chancellor in 1697 may offer a clue as to the reason for his election to the provost's chair. His tenure was short. He died in 1697 and was succeeded by regent Robert Ramsay. Ramsay served as provost from March 1698 until his death in 1733. In him, the masters had selected one of their own. They replaced him as regent in November 1697 with Thomas Forrester (c. 1677–21 June 1707), about whom little is known save that his local connctions were excellent. His father, Thomas Forrester (1635–4 July 1706), was made principal of St Mary's in January 1698.[59] If the younger man was like him, he was a radical Whig, a serious Calvinist, and one who would have no truck with episcopacy.

In c. 1705 John Arrot resigned and was replaced by Patrick (or Peter) Haldane (1683–10 January 1769), the second son of John Haldane of Gleneagles, MP, and his wife the Hon. Margaret Forrester, daughter of Lord Forrester. Haldane was made the first professor of Greek. The chair had been mandated by the Commission on the Universities in 1700[60] but St Salvator's had not implemented the decree to teach Greek from a fixed chair. It had not done so because of fears that there would be few students and, indeed, the Greek professor had few students and thus low fees and a low salary. No plum position, this chair provided a living for a younger son who in 1704 had sought a Glasgow regency with the backing of the former Lord Carmichael, now 1st Earl of Hyndford.[61] This posting was patronage for a family with an important electoral interest in Perthshire which needed to take care of a younger son. Patrick Haldane held this post until April 1707, when he resigned and was followed in the chair by his cousin James Haldane (c. 1686–17 January 1727). By the time he left the chair of Greek, Patrick was no longer interested in being a professor but had become an opportunist who used his posts, not for academic achievement, but to advance the career he would make in politics and law. He used his salary to subsidise his study of law and became an absentee. James Haldane, the son of a lesser laird of the Haldane family, seems a more serious man. He kept the Greek chair until 1721, when he was translated to the chair of ecclesiastical history at St Mary's.[62]

In 1707, after the death of regent Thomas Forrester, the College appointed Henry Ramsay. He was the son of another local laird, George Ramsay of Gallary in Coupar, Angus and a probable relative of Provost Ramsay.[63] Unlike most Old College regents, Henry Ramsay had studied at St Leonard's and then was listed as a divinity student at St Andrews from 1701 to 1706. He had not found a kirk but had come by something better. Ramsay held his place until 1744.[64] After him there was only one more appointment before 1716, that of James Duncan who became regent in 1713.

Duncan replaced Alexander Scrymgeour, who had moved on to become the first layman made a professor of divinity at St Mary's. Duncan had six competitors for the post of regent, all of whom seem to have been interviewed before 'Auditors' – perhaps rather different figures than the examiners in a comparative trial involving written theses as well as disputations. The runner-up was Patrick Clow, the tutor to the son of Lord Rothes, who, as a consolation prize, soon got a church in Rothes's gift.[65] Duncan may have been chosen by the masters but he probably also had had the countenance of John Leslie, 9th Earl Rothes.[66]

St Leonard's was a less happy place than St Salvator's, one in which tensions caused by appointments spilled over into lawsuits which left bad feelings. The principals there were not always local men and some regents were clearly not as politically reliable and religiously orthodox as others would have had them be. Initially the appointments made at St Leonard's were given to men who were unimpeachably Whiggish and orthodox. That changed over the next few years but not because of the principals.

The principals, like those at other colleges, were Crown appointees and they resembled the appointees of the Visitation Commission. George Hamilton of Cairns (1635–1712), appointed to the principalship in 1695, served for about a year before going to preach in the High Kirk of Edinburgh. Earlier he had been minister of Newburn, a parish in which relatives of the regent John Craigie were the principal heritors and in which Hamilton's father had preceded him as minister. The parish had a reputation for enthusiasm in the eighteenth century. In 1699, Hamilton was Moderator of the General Assembly. St Andrews was not able to keep this active cleric.[67]

Hamilton was followed by John Anderson (1630–February 1708), who served the College from 1697 until his death. Anderson was an older man who in 1662 had been deprived of the living in Auchtergaven, which he had held since the 1650s. He spent the years 1671 to 1688 in Ireland, where he would have known or known of Thomas Tailzour. He returned to his original parish by 1690, but he came to the College from the parish of Leslie where the principal heritor was the 8th Earl of Rothes. It would be surprising had that family not sponsored their own minister. That Tullibardine made Anderson his vice chancellor in 1707 suggests that Anderson had the interest of at least another local nobleman. When he died in 1708, a man who was a relative outsider was imposed on the College in the person of Joseph Drew (1663–13 September 1738).

Drew was the son of a Glasgow merchant and had held the living of New Monkland in Lanarkshire. In 1701, Drew moved to Markinch in Fife where the heritors included the Earls of Rothes, Leven and Melville (members of the Leslie clan) and members of the Wemyss family. None of them is known to have helped him to his new post. He found local support in the Presbytery of St Andrews.[68] His principal recommendations for his new place were undoubtedly that he was the brother-in-law of William Carstares (he came from a Fifeshire family) and was religiously and politically loyal.[69] Carstares secured Drew's place through the Earls of Mar and Loudoun.[70] That was done 'wtout advice Consent or Concurrence of the Regents of that Society', who resented it just as they resented Drew's later high-handed actions regarding later appointments.[71] His posting gave Carstares influence in St Andrews rather like that he had long enjoyed at Glasgow. Unfortunately, this man was no Principal Stirling. The man whom Drew defeated for the position was probably Colin Vilant. He had been recommended for the post by David Erskine, later Lord Dun, SCJ.[72] Drew became a rather embattled figure at St Andrews.

The Scots of Scotstarvit between 1694 and 1706 appointed three humanists and by c. 1707 had three appointees in the College. The first, Colin Vilant (c. 1668–c. 1716), was a 1682 graduate of St Andrews whose career prior to his appointment as the St Leonard's humanist in 1694 is unknown. He was the brother of William Vilant, the humanist at St Salvator's, and both were surely relatives of Principal William Vilant of St Mary's, who had died in 1693. In the following year, Colin Vilant sought the regency vacated by John Rowe who had resigned upon gaining an Edinburgh regency. Why Vilant was denied his place is interesting and affords a glimpse of how things might go even when comparative trials were held. He competed for the post with John Loudoun (c. 1666–1 November 1750). Vilant was clearly the candidate whom the masters thought did best on the examinations:

> But of a humble Respect to, & Veneration for the noble & Honble Families of Rothes & Haddington, [the masters] are satisfied that the sd Mr Colin shall Cede in his Right to make Way for Mr John Loudoun Governour to My Lord's Lesly and Haddington. And do moreover promise that ye sd Mr Colin thus Ceding for this Time shal wtout any Tryal, Impediment, Debate, Delay, Hinderance or Molestation whatsoever, & that not with standing what somever pretensions or Recommendations in the Contrair, or in Favour of any other, providing he will accept; be admitted to & settled in the next Vacancy that shall happen in the fors'd Col. Of St Leonards of a Profession of Pphy.[73]

Principal Tullideph and one master disagreed. Again Principal William Carstares' comments are revealing:

> . . . since the Revolution there have been only three vacancies, two of which were supplied unanimouslie without any comparative trial [those resulting in the appointments of Vilant and Francis Pringle], in the admitting the third [John Loudoun] there was a tryall and the Regents were allowed by the principal to vote and upon the vote he and they disagred and he would not for some time consent to what was carried by the plurality but at last yeilded.[74]

Uncertainty still existed about how regents were to be chosen. The principal seems to have favoured Vilant who had done best on the examinations and thought his opinion was equal in weight to the votes of the majority of the masters. The masters wanted the candidate backed by men who had done things for the University in the past and who might do more for the College. It also looks as if an old Calvinist was not about to have a polite tutor enter the College when he could favour the relative of a colleague who, like himself, had suffered for his dislike of episcopacy and the arbitrary government of a Catholic King. Principal Tullideph clearly did not suspect Vilant of views about church government later attributed to him – views said to favour episcopacy. Comparative examinations would later fail at Glasgow and Edinburgh but they seem to have had their first subversion at St Andrews in this case where interest triumphed over learning.[75] When John Monro died in 1697, Vilant succeeded him as a regent just as he had been promised he would.

Vilant was replaced as humanist in 1697 by James Preston (?–1707).[76] Preston published *The History of the World from the*

Creation to the Birth of Abraham (1701), which was noticed in the *Philosophical Transactions of the Royal Society of London.*[77] He was teaching by deputy in 1699 when Daniel Stark took his class. It is not known why the Scott family appointed him.

When John Loudoun left St Andrews for Glasgow in 1699, there were nine candidates for his vacant regency but only one other is known, Charles Erskine (Arskine or Ærskine).[78]

Erskine was the third son of Sir Charles Erskine of Alva, a Stirlingshire laird with Jacobite leanings, another of whose sons, Robert, became Physician to Czar Peter and was embroiled in Jacobite plots. Charles Erskine attended St Salvator's College and took a BA there in 1696.[79] He may then have studied briefly at Edinburgh.[80] In 1699, he returned to St Andrews and after a term's residence took his MA. The University Minutes for 10 June 1699 say that he had 'lately given sufficient proof of his fitness to commence Master of Arts in A Comparative tryal for a profession in St Leonards College where he acquit himself to satisfaction.'[81] Having an MA was a requirement for the post. It was useful when Erskine later sought to be and became a regent at Edinburgh. However, on 18 February 1700, the regency for which he competed went to Francis Pringle (c. 1680–3 April 1752), like Erskine, a polite and accomplished man. Pringle's comment on the comparative trial is revealing. He said he won his place on 'fair trial, without any demand of Money upon Success'.[82] This probably means that he was not expected to buy out the regent he replaced, John Loudoun, or to repay the College for any portion of the salary it had paid to Loudoun after he left for Glasgow. What it surely says is that some trials were seen as unfair and that some chairs were costly to come by. Despite his comments, it is hard to believe that the numerous members of his family had no influence on his success. Among them were rising men in the legal professions in Edinburgh and others well connected by marriage and blood to various families much like their own in the Borders.

Pringle was descended from the Covenanting laird of Stichell in Roxburghshire. He graduated MA at Edinburgh in 1694 and then spent some time at Episcopalian Oxford and perhaps had been abroad as well. At some time before 1699, he had proposed to teach Greek at Edinburgh as an unsalaried professor teaching for the fees of his students. This offer was ignored or rejected but it showed that Pringle, like Erskine, sought a career teaching in a university and that he wanted to teach Greek. Before his appointment at St Leonard's, he had been a tutor and in that capacity went to St Andrews probably in

1699. He would have been well known to those who elected him to the living. His qualities and antecedents were right and at St Andrews he found friends among Episcopalians and Jacobites, among whom he was counted by some.[83] His personal views did not reflect those of his Whiggish family. The masters would have found him a cultured man who later advised others on literary matters and was able to play the flute and compose music.[84] What they may not have realised was that this rather aristocratic young man was perfectly willing to sue his colleagues to get what he thought to be his due. In 1702, Pringle secured the post of professor of Greek. This was partly only a change in title since all the regents had hitherto been teaching Greek, but now the subject was given to him as a specialist professor.

When Greek professorships were mandated by the University Commission in 1700, the intention was to make Greek the required first-year college subject after a preliminary year of Latin if the student's Latin was not good enough. Readings in Greek would be required in the students' subsequent university courses leading to the MA degree.[85] Few of the masters in Scotland welcomed either of these requirements. They knew that Greek was not popular with students or their parents, who regarded a year spent on Greek as largely a waste of time and money. They also did not think that learning philosophy required a knowledge of Greek. Were it to be required, the boys' parents might choose to send them to attend foreign colleges, which might not require Greek, rather than a Scottish one which did. In that case, the masters would all receive lower incomes as enrolments shrank and fees declined with them. Fixing the chair also seemed to be determining to pay one regent at a rate lower than the others unless the course was made a requirement. The Visitors solved that problem by requiring all the colleges in Scotland to make their students take Greek in the year after the entry-level year of Latin for those who needed it. The colleges resisted implementing this decree. St Leonard's appointed Pringle to teach the subject only in 1702. He may have had some independent means, such as a pension from his tutoring, which allowed him to assume a burden that others would evade. Perhaps he just loved the language and culture of the Greeks.

St Andrews complied with this rule but the other colleges did not. So, St Andrews revoked its rule and did not require its students to take Greek in their first year as it had said they should when Pringle was appointed. Seeing his income going down, and all the colleges in violation of a clear rule, Pringle appealed for justice. He sought it first in 1704 from the rector, Thomas Forrester, the principal of St Mary's

College. He sent the matter to the University Senatus. Pringle argued that the University was guilty of ignoring a clearly stated and binding rule given to it by the Visitation Commission which was empowered to regulate University affairs. The rector and a majority of the University men believed that until all the colleges enforced the rule, St Andrews was under no obligation to do so. When the meeting found against him, Pringle sued the rector and those who adhered to him in the Court of Session where his relatives would have ensured that he got a fair hearing. The St Andrews principals circulated a letter to the other universities in Scotland asking them for whatever aid they could give to defeat Pringle's case.[86] The Court of Session found for Pringle and established the Greek requirement in the colleges of Scotland. The judges were not able to enforce the rules that students should study Greek in classes taken after a preliminary year of Latin, if needed, or that boys could not skip the year of Greek altogether. Indeed, the Visitation Commission's rule was widely ignored but not at St Andrews. At St Salvator's, the creation of a Greek chair came only in 1705, in the wake of the Court's decision.

In 1707, James Preston died and a new humanist had to be appointed by the Scot family. They gave the place to Ninian Young (c. 1681–7 June 1752), almost certainly a younger relative of William Young, the St Salvator's regent. Ninian Young remained in the University until he died. He too may have been a man who leaned toward Jacobitism and episcopacy. Young, Pringle, Vilant, Craigie and his cousin, Scrymgeour, were the ones usually cited as being the disaffected men in the University c. 1715. The Scots had appointed three of them and two of these men had voted to advance the other two.

About the same time that this appointment was made, regent Thomas Tailzour was replaced by Henry Rymer (1684–13 June 1758) after a long struggle between the principal and the masters. This fight involved local ministers who had concluded that the St Leonard's men were not overly committed to the Kirk as then established. When the vacancy occurred, probably in late 1707, Principal Drew was not yet settled. This seemed to leave the disposition of the chair to Ninian Young, Pringle, Craigie and Vilant – the very men thought unsound by the ministers. The fear of the local clerics was almost certainly well-founded.

Pringle and Vilant were masters favoured by at least one family with Episcopal leanings, one which had a Jacobite son whose estate was forfeited after the '15. Pringle had been the tutor of Lord Aboyne, the grandson of a cadet of the still Catholic family of the Duke of Gordon. The regent was said to attend Episcopalian services and his dissatisfaction with the Kirk was perhaps shared by Vilant.[87] If these were not their views on appointment, they had very likely set in during the debates over the Union with England and with the enactment of new oaths required by the General Assembly in 1706 – requirements which Pringle carefully noted in his collection of College Papers.[88] Their unease could only have been enhanced by the uncertainty of the succession after Queen Anne ran out of children to inherit the Crown.[89] It must also have been felt by the other masters since they unanimously chose to fill the vacancy with a Dr Lindsay, brother of Lindsay of Wormiston.[90] Dr Lindsay had the backing of known Jacobites and Episcopalians such as Archibald Pitcairne, MD. When he came to office, Drew would not have Lindsay. He said he had not been consulted, as he should have been, and that the man was backed by Episcopalians. Drew's choice was Henry Rymer, a pious Whig whom he had 'tried' in some fashion.[91]

The commotion over this appointment was intensified by the ongoing difficulties over the appointment of Charles Gregory (c. 1682–15 September 1754) as professor of mathematics in 1707/8. The St Andrews Presbytery did not want to see appointed this younger half-brother of David and James Gregory, both of whom had been harassed because of their religious and political views in 1690–1. The professors had another candidate. The town's ministers refused to allow Gregory to subscribe the Confession of Faith. Without subscription, the University could not and would not admit him even though he had the Queen's warrant.[92] Gregory was presented on 13 July 1707 but not admitted until 11 December 1708, and then only on an order of the Court of Session. These events very much affected the contest over the regency.

Lindsay and Rymer were not the only ones thought of for this regency. In 1707, or early January 1708, a Mr Napier of Buchquhnaple was disappointed when he attempted to secure it.[93] A little over a month later, William Carstares wrote to Mar summing up the situation from the point of view of one who wanted only an orthodox man in the place:

> As for the vacant Regencies in St Leonards College, I doe indeed pitie Mr Drew who through your Losp and the Earl of Loudouns favour which I with all thankfulness & doe remember is now principal [illegible] for the matter My Lord is plainlie thus; that Universitie hath been unhappie by the divisions and the Ministers of the Presbiterie of St Andrews doe look

upon many of the Masters, particularly of the College of St Leonard to be not well affected to the constitution of our Church; and the Regents of that College did propose and to Mr Drew before he was installed in his office, but he telling them that he did not think it fitt for him to concern himselfe in that business till he was settled in his post they did afterwards conclude amongst themselves without adviseing with their Principal that they would all Join in proposing Dr Lindsay and they have spoken to Mr Drew about him and told him if he will give his consent to this gentleman they hope that there shall never any thing occurr again where they shall differ from him; he upon the other hand takes it amiss that they should have come to a positive determination as to a particular person without adviseing with him, but My Lord his reall strait is that if he should go in with the Regents as to Dr Lindsay[,] he disgusts severall Ministers of that Presbyterie and many Presbyterians, and if he does not agree to them, then he involves himself with the Regents, but if they will pass from Mr Lindsay he will not insist upon one that he had in his eye to supplie the vacancie and I believe would fall in with the person whom some of them mentioned to him before he was installed, but this is not like to doe.[94]

Carstares concluded, a bit disingenuously, that he could 'give no judgment' on Lindsay. It would be very surprising if he had not known that Lindsay was being recommended to Mar by the Earl's physician, Dr Pitcairne, a Jacobite, a defamer of the orthodox and an Episcopalian-deist (if that is not too oxymoronic).[95] Throughout his life, Pitcairne supported men who were Jacobites and Episcopalians. In 1707/8 he was trying very hard to get Charles Gregory accepted as the professor of mathematics at St Andrews and was also supporting the candidacy of Lindsay for the St Leonard's regency. On 9 December 1708, Pitcairne wrote to the Earl of Mar asking his help for Lyndsay, the brother of 'a considerable gentleman (Wormiston near St Andrews)'. He went on:

> The Principal and Regents are Ye electors. The Regents are for Lyndsay justlie, but ye principal is for an ignorant and incendiary Rymer, the priviledges to the major part, but the principal says he's got a patent for Rymer over there bellies. The like case was advocated last year by the Lords in favour of the regents of the old Colledge there – against that principal, with much contempt.[96] Lyndsay will be assisted by [David Melville] my Lord Levin &c and is an excellent schollar & good man.[97]

Mar's response, if any, to this plea is not known.

The regents came close to winning. They took the case to court where it dragged on until 1710, when the principal got his 'enthusiast'. He had, in fact, ignored the regents' wishes and got his man by securing an extraordinary royal mandate for Rymer's placement.[98] He too had political friends able to get favours from the Court. But the masters also got something. They secured signed 'Articles of Agreement betwixt the Principal & Regents of St Leonards College'. Although these stipulated that they were only to bind the present incumbents, they gave considerable power to the regents and the humanist. The humanist got a vote in the College meeting. The College funds and lands were to be administered jointly by the principal and regents with a simple majority prevailing in the meeting. Principal Drew got one of two keys to the charter chest; the regents held the other. Discipline was to be jointly administered and the College bursars were to be chosen by a plurality of votes. All future regencies were to be filled by well-recommended MA's after a trial in which the regents were to concur about the outcome. The victory was made slightly hollow by the fact that between 1708 and 1747 only one more regent was chosen, David Young (?–16 May 1759) in 1716. He was the son of the St Salvator's provost, a graduate of that College and a man who, after the '15, when he served as a volunteer with the Hanoverians, was beyond suspicion when it came to loyalties. With that placement, which involved no trial, the College went on unchanged until the union of 1747.

6. THE MATHEMATICS PROFESSORSHIP, 1690–1708

The regius chair of mathematics at St Andrews began auspiciously in 1668 when James Gregory I was appointed to it as a professor belonging to neither of the arts colleges but to the University.[99] He was followed by William Sanders (1674–88) and James Fenton (1689–90). James Gregory II taught briefly as a regent at St Salvator's College in 1689–90 but he did not hold his uncle's mathematics chair.[100] From 1690 to 1708, the chair was vacant because it was funded only by extraordinary grants from the Crown which were not paid or regularly paid.[101] Mathematics was taught by regents and from 1706 on, either extramurally or in the University, by William Bethune [Beaton or Beton].[102] With the windup of the Scottish state, efforts were renewed to preserve and fund the chair. In early July 1707, Robert Ramsay, the provost of St Salvator's and rector, recommended Bethune to the Earl of Mar, the Secretary of State. Mar later in the month wrote to the Scottish Chancellor, the Earl of Seafield, that Bethune had been willing to serve without a salary drawn from the University funds. The masters wanted him to obtain the appointment.[103] In the following month,

James Hadow approached William Carstares about the appointment of Bethune. Hadow's interest in Bethune perhaps stemmed from the fact that the competitor for the post, Charles Gregory, looked less orthodox and less politically reliable. The views of his half-brothers, James and David, were almost certainly presumed, falsely as it happened, to be his. Hadow thought Bethune ought 'to be professor of Mathematics in ys University' and noted further that 'He was recommended by all our Masters to my Lord Commissioner [James Douglas, 2nd Duke of Queensberry] & both Secretaries [John Erskine, Earl of Mar and Hugh Campbell, Earl of Loudoun] while they were here.'[104] On the following day, the rector, Robert Ramsay, wrote to Mar begging again for the appointment of Bethune:

> . . . 'tis really of importance to all of us that he be settled before the meeting of our Colleges at the first of November, least the want of him may make the number of our students yet fewer, and so our decaying society may not be more and more discouraged by the entire want of that profession. We are fully satisfied of this Gentleman's merit for that office, and we hope Your Lordship will accept of our testimony and do us the kindness to procure him a presentation, which would be a very good office and a lasting obligation upon all the Members of this University by whose appointment this is subscribed . . .[105]

Hadow's and Ramsay's letters would have reached Carstares and Mar after the matter had in fact been settled by men not much interested in the fate of the University.

Carstares and the politicians would have seen these letters in the context of others dealing with the Crown's appointments of John Syme and Patrick Haldane at St Mary's, and of Principal Drew at St Leonard's. They were being pressed by others for jobs at the other colleges and in Scotland generally. Funding was being sought for all manner of good causes by those who believed that they would never have as good a chance again to secure grants for themselves and their friends. It is doubtful that the ministers put much effort into helping Bethune. Charles Gregory was better recommended and came from a family of mathematicians long associated with Episcopalians and Jacobites and to which the government had an obligation.

Gregory's half-brother, David, now the professor of astronomy at Oxford, had recently been in Edinburgh helping with the mathematical problems encountered by those calculating the Equivalent Fund, the money which was to be paid to Scots as part of the settlement at the Union of the two kingdoms.[106] These calculations had engaged him, his brother, James, the Edinburgh professor of mathematics, and Thomas Bower, MD, who had got the mathematics chair at King's College, Aberdeen in 1703. Dr Bower, like David Gregory, was a Newtonian iatro-mechanist and a protégé and friend of Archibald Pitcairne. Pitcairne had played a role in Bower's appointment at King's College, a place which Charles Gregory probably had sought.[107] Bower had been aided by the Earl of Erroll. Bower expected some compensation for the work done on the Equivalent Fund calculations in 1707. He sought a salary for his chair. The Gregories would have found their satisfaction in a job for half-brother Charles. Dr Pitcairne campaigned for Charles Gregory and enlisted Bower's help.

Bower wrote to Mar on 21 May 1707 to say, '. . . upon my own knowledge I can recommend Mr Charles Gregory (the Doctors Brother) as a Good Man and Good Scholar and fitter for a Mathematical Profession, than any Candidate I now know in the Kingdom'. He also told him that Pitcairne had the form of the warrant and could give it to him should he need it to expedite the matter.[108] Five days later, Pitcairne wrote to Mar saying that he had sent to him a letter from Bower asking that Gregory be appointed so that 'Your Lordship, as patron of Mathematics here' may 'perpetuate your name amongst the lovers of true learning, that is Mathematics and civil law; for Medicine belongs to Mathematics, and Divinity to South-britain.'[109] The doctor, an iatro-mechanist, must have thought religion best practised in England in a different establishment with a different theology. The patent was granted to Charles Gregory by Seafield on or before 13 July 1707. The debt to the Gregories had been paid but Bower never got a proper salary and soon stopped teaching in Aberdeen. Gregory's case signals at St Andrews University a heightening of political and religious tensions but it also demonstrates the ways in which outside interference could bring in good men when local interests were lined up for a local nobody.

Once Gregory was named to the chair, a very different game began as resentful men in St Andrews tried to prevent him from taking his place. This was a difficult business since Gregory held a royal patent valid in a kingdom where Christ was not King despite what some presbyters might think. The local Presbytery was exercised about the new regent at St Leonard's, by appointments at St Mary's, and now by the new mathematician who looked suspect to them as well as to some in the colleges.

The St Andrews Presbytery sometime in July or August refused to allow Gregory to sign the Confession of Faith, which he then signed elsewhere.[110] The Presbytery wanted him to produce testificates of good morals but he argued that he needed only to present his royal patent which said, or implied, he was sound in religion and politics.[111] The masters continued to be unhappy with his appointment and obstructed his installation. Because of that, they were summoned to Edinburgh to consult with Chancellor Seafield in early September 1707.[112] Being told to admit Gregory did not go down well. At the beginning of the school year, the masters ordered the boys to boycott Gregory's classes. Pitcairne wrote to Mar on 6 January 1708 asking for protection of Gregory because the masters, 'under penalties discharged all their schollars to goe to him, tho the gentrie are verie desirous to have their son's with him'. The doctor also noted that the masters had ignored letters from the Lord Advocate. 'No body is more wicked than Mr Pringle the litle Greek professor, tho' he promised otherways to me.'[113] A month later (10 February 1708), there had been no change for the better; Gregory had still not been admitted to office: 'That Colledge will not receive him, and laughs at her Majesties patent.'[114] Not long after, the rector, Robert Ramsay, refused again to admit him. Finally, Gregory produced 'testificates' from the Fellows of Balliol College and was ordered to be admitted and was admitted by Principal Hadow on 11 February 1708.[115] Nine months later, Gregory was still being boycotted. Pitcairne again wrote to Mar that 'her majesties patent is not regarded' and Gregory is 'ill us'd'.[116] The case was settled and he then disappeared from Pitcairne's record of complaints, which now switched to the appointment of Henry Rymer and the tyranny of Principal Drew.

7. So?

What can one make of these early years? The initial appointments were of men academically qualified if not brilliant. Principals Pitcairne, Forrester and Vilant wrote things of importance to their time and were seen as men of courage and conviction. Alexander Pitcairne figures in the ODNB because of his political activities and his books but he finds no place in the DSCHT; James Hadow receives an entry.[117] The record was spotty and got worse. William Tullideph and Robert Ramsay published nothing of note and none of the St Salvator's College regents made a name as authors save for Gershom Carmichael who hardly counts as a St Andrews man. Alexander Scrymgeour, a bright and talented man, brought only trouble to the University where for years he was harassed and prevented from functioning as professor of divinity by the local ministers. Patrick Haldane, after a time as the sinecure professor of ecclesiastical history, became a lawyer and made a legal and political career of some notoriety.[118] Other regents appointed after 1700 were ordinary in the extreme. This was also true at St Leonard's College. Francis Pringle and perhaps a couple of others were distinguished teachers. St Andrews had no men the equals of the enterprising principals at Glasgow University, William Dunlop and John Stirling, or regents like 'Blind Jameson', Robert Simson, the mathematician, or innovative teachers like Andrew Ross or Robert Dick I. It could not keep Rowe, Carmichael and Loudoun.

St Andrews was less nepotistic than King's College but the seeds of future inbreeding had been planted. The patronage of the arts chairs at St Andrews already shows a higher degree of nepotism than did those in Edinburgh and it would not have been far from what the Glasgow record would have been had Principal Stirling always had his way. There would be descendants of the Tullidephs, Youngs and Vilants in the University until the end of the period considered here. This closed the institutions to new men and ideas and sapped the vitality of the colleges.

Most of the St Andrews men were well connected enough to secure livings but they do not seem to have been very cosmopolitan in outlook. The masters seem to have seen less of the world than those appointed elsewhere. Some of the older men had been abroad as exiles but few of the regents are definitely known to have themselves studied abroad by the time of their appointment. None are certainly known to have been travelling tutors who had been abroad with their charges. They taught at the University where they themselves had been educated and were often the sons of lairds and ministers, some of whom had also been teachers at St Andrews. They were recruited from the same small area from which the students came and were not the sort of men Glasgow could point to after 1688.

Local men with influence and power seem largely responsible for the placing of these masters. The most important of the local notables – the Earls of Crawford, Rothes, Leven and Cassillis and Lord Raith – were all men from Fifeshire families. They counted locally but for less in the country at large, where their estates collectively would not have matched those of the Dukes of Hamilton or Argyll. Few counted in London. For long periods of time, none among them seems to have mattered much anywhere but locally. The noblemen of this region were not like their Whiggish Glasgow counterparts either in the influence they could command or in their commitment to their University.

The local patrons were neither concerned enough nor powerful enough to shape the University as such men did elsewhere. No principal here was backed by a Duke who led an important political faction, as was Glasgow's Stirling. Principal Drew could sometimes count on the backing of the Duke of Atholl, but the Duke was no paragon of political loyalty and had little impact on Scottish affairs when compared with Montrose or Argyll. William Carstares and Mar sometimes aided Principals Hadow and Drew but only when it suited the Edinburgh men to aid them. They knew the value of aiding St Andrews was not great and seem not to have exerted themselves so much as they did at Glasgow.

Because the St Andrews men were also long-lived, relatively few men were added to the teaching staffs between 1700 and 1747 – to the detriment of the colleges. New appointments, which might have brought in new ideas, could not be made. The place stagnated as the undistinguished lived into the mid-century.

The claim that St Salvator's had been infested with Jacobites or Episcopalians does not quite ring true. The first masters appointed were neither. By 1715 that had changed somewhat. The genteel families of Fife were Episcopalian and Jacobite in outlook, as the '15 was to prove. That was partly shown by the ease with which the Jacobites in 1715 recruited in the area from which St Andrews drew its students and teachers. The Scots, if not the Kennedys, seem to have chosen as humanists for St Leonard's men who were 'soft' on episcopacy and wavering in their political loyalties – as was the Scot family itself. Because of this, the story of the St Andrews arts colleges in these years is also the story of the transformation of institutions from orthodox and Whiggish beginnings into institutions where sympathies for episcopacy were dominant in one college and present in the other. The addition of Francis Pringle to the staff at St Leonard's created a majority for the election of new regents like themselves – men leaning to episcopacy and perhaps Jacobitism. It also helped to perpetuate the mediocrity of those appointed.

St Andrews, like the other Scottish colleges, had tensions and problems engendered by the religious and political tensions in Scotland as a whole and others rooted in the autocratic attitudes of heads of colleges or in the headstrong actions of regents who were as litigious as their principals. St Andrews was not a happy place in the years leading up to 1715. In that respect it was like King's College, where there were also fierce fights over power and appointments, fights in which men divided along religious and political lines. Glasgow's similar problems tended to be within the Presbyterian and Whig fold and involved somewhat personal disputes within the University and colleges. Edinburgh and Marischal College to some extent escaped these because the masters there could not make appointments. Anger over missed jobs in Edinburgh was directed at politicians and not other masters. What may have mattered more in Fife was the fact that the St Andrews men in general could not aspire to places worth much more than the equivalent of an ensigncy. Men of little distinction fought for crumbs.

Notes

1 Dates for matriculations, college attendance and years of appointment given below come either from that source, from manuscripts or Smart's *Register*. I am indebted to Mr Smart for his generosity and good will over many years. Without his assistance, this portion of the book would not have been possible.
2 Lang, *St Andrews*, 1893, p. 313. This is a generally worthless, pot-boiling book but this information is quoted from a contemporary source.
3 For these, see Devine and Jackson, *Glasgow*, 3 vols, vol. I, *Beginnings to 1830*, 1995; Dingwall, *Late Seventeenth-century Edinburgh*, 1994; Houston, *Social Change in the Age of Enlightenment: Edinburgh 1660–1760*, 1994; and *Aberdeen Before 1800*, 2 vols, ed. Dennison, Ditchburn and Lynch, 2002.
4 According to one source, the population of the burgh shrank from 4,913 in 1755 to 4,205 in 1801; Alexander Millar, *Fife: Pictorial and Historical*, 1895, I:105.
5 Professors John Adamson and Joseph M'Cormick, 'PARISHES of St ANDREW'S and St LEONARD'S', *The Statistical Account of Scotland*, ed. Withrington and Grant, 1983, X:702–35. This describes the burgh constitution set in 1740 by Ilay's friends; see *Constitution of the Royal Burghs . . .*, 1793, p. 171f.
6 Lee, 'Copies of papers relative to a projected translation of the University of St Andrews to the city of Perth, in the years 1697 and 1698', *Transactions of the Literary and Antiquarian Society of Perth*, 1827, I:1, pp. 25–9; Cant, *The University of St Andrews*, 2002, pp. 95–7.
7 Smart, 'Some observations on the provinces of the Scottish Universities, 1560–1850', in *The Scottish Tradition*, ed. Barrow, 1974, pp. 91–106.
8 See Appendix 1.
9 After 1747, the Kennedys' chair was converted to a chair in civil history.

10 Mr R. N. Smart assures me that the records show a number of medical students and the burgh records list at least one who became a burgess.

11 Blair, *History of Medicine in the University of St Andrews*, 1987, p. 30.

12 I thank R. N. Smart for the information that has allowed me to make this deduction.

13 These feudal rights included the right to vote in elections.

14 I thank R. N. Smart for this information.

15 St Andrews University Minutes [hereafter Minutes], 6 January 1698, 16 August 1697, SAUL, UYUY 452/1; Lyon, *History of St Andrews*, 2 vols, 1843, II:118; Lee, 'Copies of Papers relative to a projected translation', *Transactions of the Literary and Antiquarian Society of Perth*, 1827, I:1, pp. 25–9.

16 A University Minute (15 June 1799) says that 'During the greatest part of this Century, there has been no Vice Chancellor; and the Rector or the Person chosen Praeses in absence of the Rector is styled Promoter, because he in name of the University confers degrees, promovet ad honorei . . .'; SAUL, UYUY 454/10.

17 Cant, *University*, 2002, pp. 79, 124f, 134.

18 Ibid., pp. 99, 134.

19 Ibid., p. 134f.

20 Its original members included the Earls of Crawford, Morton, Cassillis and Kintore; David Melville, Lord Balgonie and later Earl of Leven; Robert Balfour, the Master of Burley [Burleigh]; Sir Thomas Burnet, Sir Francis Montgomery, James Melville, and the lairds of Newington and Meggins [?Drummond of Megginch]; and the ministers Henry Rymer, William Tullideph, David Blair, James McGill and James Rymer; see Monro, *Presbyterian Inquisition*, 1691, p. 22f. The Visitors were mostly from the areas in which the University recruited students but included a laird from the West and one from the Lothians.

21 Cant, *University*, 2002, p. 92f.

22 *An Account of the Proceedings of the Estates . . . 1689–1690*, ed. Balfour-Melville, 1955, II:271; other entries also deal with this visitation; II:246, 261, 267, 280, 281–2.

23 Hannay, 'The Visitation of St Andrews University in 1690', *Scottish Historical Review*, 1915, pp. 1–15, 15.

24 *An Account of the Proceedings of the Estates*, ed. Balfour-Melville, 1955, II:281. This account does not square with the accounts of the Visitors as vindictive, zealous men with outmoded ideas.

25 David Gregorie Papers, EUL, Dk.1.2².26. Gregorie added, 'except Mr Menzies, my brother & Mr Mullican'. His brother, James Gregory, refused to take the oaths and was sacked for 'contumacy' two days later, on 27 September, along with Menzies and Mullican. The date given by David Gregorie is two days earlier than that set out in the *Account of the Proceedings*. A version of events appears in a letter of Thomas Reid,

their nephew, who wrote: 'I asked him [James] once, How he came to give up his place at St Andrews on the change of Government, & afterwards to take the Mathematical Chair at Edinburgh. Faith, Nephew, said he, I never minded Politicks much but my dearest Companions in the College were going out, & I did not like those that were to keep their places; & I thought it better to go out in good Company than to stay behind with ill.' Thomas Reid to James Gregory, 24 August 1787, *The Correspondence of Thomas Reid*, ed. Wood, 2002, p. 188. James Gregory succeeded his brother at Edinburgh two years later. Perhaps politics meant little to him and orthodoxy less to those of the time than we are used to thinking.

26 David Gregorie Papers, EUL Dk.1.2^2.26.

27 *An Account of the Proceedings of the Estates*, ed. Balfour-Melville, 1955, II:281.

28 Extracted 'Act made by the Commissioners . . .', AUL, K 257/23/15/2.

29 '. . . the members of the Commission were judges in the tryals of the professors and the last King did by patent supply those that were recommended by the Visitors.' Carstares to Mar, 23 December 1708, Mar and Kellie Papers, NAS, GD124/15/765/4.

30 A copy of the Commission as it stood on 15 December 1690 says the Commissioners had 'Ratified and Approven' the men tried and lists the Commissioners as including Crawford and the ministers Mr Robert Learmont, Peter Hay of Naughton, Alexander Pitcairne, Mr James Rymer, Mr Edward Jamieson and Mr Tullideph. '[A]ny four of them' could try and admit regents. NAS, SP54/16/118. Pitcairne, Tullideph and Rymer all had later ties to the universities.

31 Robert Dalgleish, 'Parish of Ferry-Port-on Craig', in *Statistical Account*, ed. Withrington and Grant, 1983, X:365–80; Scott, *Fasti Ecclesiae Scoticanae*, 1928, VII:421; Robert Wodrow, *Analecta*, ed. Leishman, 1853, II:332, III:58, 438f.

32 Wodrow, *Analecta*, ed. Leishman, 1853, II:150, 332.

33 For a brief discussion of his politics, see Jackson, *Restoration Scotland*, 2003, pp. 124f, 128, 129, 163.

34 Marshall, *The Days of Duchess Anne*, 1962, p. 107f.

35 His biographer in the ODNB says that he had been invited to accept this post by William III; 'Alexander Pitcairne', Pearce, ODNB, 44:422. He and most of the St Andrews professors appear in the Minutes of the St Andrew Presbytery, a source not used for this study.

36 Scott, *Fasti*, IV:202; 'A Catalogue of Books belonging [tear] Library of ye University of St Andrews', SAUL, UYLY 105/3/27.

37 'Alexander Pitcairne', Pearce, ODNB, 44:422.

38 *Compendiaria et perfacilis Physiologiae idea Aristotlinae una cum Anatome cartesianismi* (London, 1676). His *Harmonia Evangelica Apostolorum Pauli et Jacobi in doctrina de Justificatione* (1685) was

dedicated to James Dalrymple, 1st Viscount Stair, a fellow exile noted for his virtuoso interests, his charity and his great book on Scots law. Scott, *Fasti*, 4:202, 7:421.

39 Scott, *Fasti*, V:156; the patrons are listed there.

40 On 22 and 23 May 1691, Tarbat, not a good Presbyterian, had supported 'Mr H. Anderson' for this place, citing his 'prudence and charity'. He sought aid for Anderson from the Earl of Melville and Lord Raith, both members of the Visitation Commission, whom he believed would be among those who filled this post. George Mackenzie, 1st Viscount Tarbat, to George Melville, 1st Earl of Melville, 22 and 23 May 1691, in *Leven and Melville Papers*, ed. Melville, 1843, pp. 614–16.

41 Ibid. Both of these lords had been supporters of the Stuarts until shortly before the Revolution and neither could be described as either a thoroughly convinced Whig or Calvinist.

42 Cassillis had been outlawed in the 1680s but was made a Privy Councillor and Lord of Treasury by William III.

43 Anne Skoczylas has recently argued for Scrymgeour's Calvinist orthodoxy and Whiggism in 'The Regulation of Academic Society in Early Eighteenth-Century Scotland', *Scottish Historical Review*, 2004, pp. 171–95.

44 Cant, *University*, 2002, pp. 93, 97. The men involved with the logic and metaphysics texts included John Arrot, Thomas Tailzour, John Craigie and Alexander Scrymgeour, who jointly submitted a bill for £2,824 12s 0d [Scots] for their expenses; 'Scroll accompt for ye expenses . . .', AUL, M 387/11/3/13; Minutes, 20 December 1698, SAUL, UYUY 452/2.

45 I thank R. N. Smart for this information.

46 Minutes, 3 January 1707, 24 March 1727, SAUL, UYUY 452/4.

47 There is no record of him being a Writer to the Signet, which suggests that he had been content to work in areas where he would not have to appear for the state or sign and notarize documents which would have required him to qualify by taking oaths. Writers were often factors or worked as solicitors who did no court business. This was a profession which he must have followed for some time if he is the man of the same name who matriculated at St Andrews in 1666.

48 Minutes, 6 January 1698, SAUL, UYUY 452/1.

49 Scott, *Fasti*, V:110; VII:411.

50 'The Diary of the Rev. George Turnbull', ed. R. Paul, 1893, I:442; Turnbull, *Memoirs of the Life of Hogg*, ed. Paul, 1893, p. 312.

51 *Memoirs of the Life of the Rev. Thomas Halyburton*, ed. Watson, n.d. (cited from an undated Edinburgh and London edition), p. 58; Scott, *Fasti*, VII:429.

52 University Minutes, 5 February, 19 June and 5 December 1705, SAUL, UY 542/2/120u, 122/5 and 123.

53 Minutes, 17 February 1707, SAUL, UYLY 542/2/132.

54 Scott, *Fasti*, 5:131. The principal heritor of the parish was the Earl of Crawford.

55 Margaret the Countess of Rothes married Charles Hamilton, 5th Earl of Haddington, and their oldest sons became respectively the 9th Earl of Rothes and 6th Earl of Haddington.

56 Scott, *Fasti*, V:131.

57 *The Faculty of Advocates of Scotland*, compiled by Grant, 1944, p. 44.

58 One of William II's sons, Alexander, would later be the College factor; another held the living of Kingsbarns which was in the gift of the Earl of Crawford. Scott, *Fasti*, III:240, V:201, VII:420.

59 Principal Forrester had been deprived of his living and became a field preacher. He was a learned man who was a protégé of the Earl of Argyll and had been out in the rising of 1685. His biographers in the DNB and ODNB describe this ex-curate as 'one of the ablest advocates of presbyterianism of his day'. W. G. Blaikie and Stephen Wright, ODNB, 20:392f.

60 M. A. Stewart, 'The Origins of the Scottish Greek Chairs', in '*Owls to Athens*', ed. Craik, 1990, pp. 391–400.

61 Lord Hyndford to Principal John Stirling, 23 May 1704, Stirling Letters, GUL, Murray MS 650/1.

62 Scrymgeour was recorded as being chosen for the chair of Greek on 27 February 1707, but this was probably only the designation of a sitting regent to do the duty of the chair on a temporary basis. No date of resignation has been found for him, but if he had a real appointment he vacated it before the appointment of James Haldane on 21 August 1707.

63 By c. 1770 this family had disappeared from the parish and Gallary was held by George Dempster, MP; *A Directory of Landownership in Scotland c. 1770*, compiled by Timperley, 1976, p. 267.

64 There was a conflict between Provost Robert Ramsay and the masters over this appointment since Dr Archibald Pitcairne wrote c. 1708 that the Court of Session decided a St Salvator's case between the provost and the masters in favour of the masters who had chosen a regent in spite of the provost's desires. '*The best of of our owne*', ed. Johnston, 1979, p. 55.

65 *Two Students at St Andrews 1711–1716*, ed. Croft Dickinson, 1952, p. 30.

66 Hyndford wrote to Principal Stirling at Glasgow that Rothes had been pushing Duncan for the professorship of Greek. Earl of Hyndford to Stirling, 31 March 1720, Stirling Letters, GUL Gen 204/1.

67 Scott, *Fasti*, I:60; V:228; VII:413.

68 Minutes, 5 April 1708, SAUL, UY 452/2.

69 Drew in 1739 was described to a supporter of Lord Ilay as 'a man of steady Conduct moderate Principals and a submissive regard to the

proper Authority of the nation of which he gave a proof at his last [Drew had died in 1738], for only he and I in our Presbytery continued to read Porteous Act til the year elapsed.' John McCormick to Charles Erskine, 1 May 1739, Erskine-Murray Papers, NLS, 5074. The Porteous Act called for the delation of the lynchers of Captain Porteous who had been hanged by an Edinburgh mob. The author of the letter was the father of the future principal, Joseph McCormick.

70 Carstares to Mar, 23 December 1708, Mar and Kellie Papers, NAS, GD124/796/4.

71 Francis Pringle, 'Collection of College Papers', SAUL, UYSL 156, p. 243.

72 This David Erskine was almost certainly David Erskine of Dun, MP and later SCJ. He is remembered for the fine house he built in the 1720s. The house, partly designed by Lord Mar and partly by William Adam, has a saloon which 'made a grandiloquent stucco exhibition of Jacobite iconography', Gifford, *William Adam 1689–1748*, 1989, pp. 127–33, 133. Erskine wrote to Mar on 8 November 1707 to say that Principal Anderson was dying and again on 19 February 1708 to recommend Vilant: 'favouring Mr Vilant is your interest, will oblige very many, and his friends will not be unmindful of the favour.' Mar and Kellie Papers, NAS, GD124/513/40 and GD124/756/7. Vilant was later to be accused of being a Jacobite.

73 Pringle, 'College Papers', SAUL, UYSL 156, p. 245. Lords Leslie and Haddington were brothers who inherited two earldoms, one from each side of the family.

74 Carstares to Mar, 23 December 1708, NAS, GD12/15/765/4. Carstares was wrong about there being no comparative trial when Pringle was appointed. 'Mr Pringles Book', SAUL, FL1111:P8C99/136.

75 Ronald Cant thought this development came later; *University History*, 2002, p. 94.

76 Preston could have been a brother of the Edinburgh botanists, Charles and George Preston; Cowan, 'The History of the Royal Botanic Garden, Edinburgh – The Prestons', *Notes of the Royal Botanic Garden, Edinburgh*, 1935, p. 103. If he was the youngest brother of those men, he was born on 7 July 1674 and would have been a student somewhat older than most when he took his MA at St Andrews in 1694. Sometimes a late MA was taken to qualify for a teaching post.

77 *Phil. Trans.* No. 272 (November and December 1701). This anonymous note was written by Sir Robert Sibbald or some member of his circle in Edinburgh. It mentions works by Sir Andrew Balfour, George Sibbald, MD, James Scougal of Whitehill, SCJ (brother of Henry Scougal), John Adair and Sibbald himself. Being in this company suggests that Preston shared their interests and was part of that circle as Charles Preston certainly was. For an account of these men, see

Simpson, 'Sir Robert Sibbald', in *Proceedings of the Royal College of Physicians of Edinburgh Tercentenary Congress*, 1982, pp. 59–91; Emerson, 'Sir Robert Sibbald', *Annals of Science*, 1988, pp. 41–72; the material on Adair and Sir Robert Sibbald in Withers, *Geography, Science and National Identity*, 2001, pp. 74, 93f, 242f, 258f and 260; and Mendyk, 'Scottish Regional Natural Historians and the *Britannia* Project', *Scottish Geographical Magazine*, 1985, pp. 165–73.

78 'Mr Pringles Book', SAUL, FL1111:P8C99/136.

79 I thank John Cairns for this information; see Cairns, *Legal Education in Edinburgh*, forthcoming.

80 Ibid.

81 Minutes, 17 May 1699, SAUL, UYUY 452/2.

82 'Mr Pringles Book', SAUL LF1111:P8C99.

83 Croft Dickinson, *Two Students*, 1952, p. xlvii.

84 The William Aikman portrait of him at the University shows a poised and confident gentleman. Aikman, a gentleman about Pringle's age, was an artist then much in vogue in Scotland and London. The portrait is reproduced in Cant, *University*, p. 101.

85 What follows relies on the account given of the founding of the Greek chairs by Stewart, 'The Origins of the Scottish Greek Chairs', in *'Owls to Athens'*, ed. Craik, 1990, p. 393.

86 Thomas Forrester, Robert Ramsay and John Anderson to Principal John Stirling, Stirling Letters, GUL, Gen 204/2/37.

87 Croft Dickinson, *Two Students*, 1952, pp. xii, xix, xlvi–li. Vilant was the candidate for the principalship pushed by the Jacobite, David Erskine in 1707/8; see note 72.

88 Pringle, 'Collection of College Papers', SAUL, UYSL 156, entry for 1706.

89 I thank Anne Skoczylas for pointing this out to me.

90 He may have been the William Lindsay who received a St Andrews MD in 1707.

91 The Scottish antiquary, David Doig, claimed that 'Mr Henry Rymer . . . had more piety than parts, and was better acquainted with the Stagirite [Aristotle] than with the philosophers of modern times.' The ethics he taught was scholastic, a Christianised Aristotelianism. He seems to have used the compendia of DeVries as his text in pneumatics until the end of his teaching in 1756. Doig concluded: '. . . if our professor's lectures were somewhat cumbered with the rubbish of the schools, we might surely have learned a great deal from them which it imported us to know. If his class was no school of rhetoric and taste, it had the merit of being scientific and orthodox.' Ramsay of Ochtertyre, *Scotland and Scotsmen*, ed. Allardyce, 1888, I:269f; see also St Andrews Presbytery Minutes, CH2/1132/1/10. I thank Dr Anne Skoczylas for this reference.

92 Pitcairne, *The best of our owne*, ed. Johnston, 1979, pp. 45–55.

93 Regent William Scott of Edinburgh to the Earl of Mar, 15 January 1708. NAS, GD124/15/765/1. Napier seems to have been a relative of Scott; in disappointment, Napier now sought an ensigncy seen as a better and more honourable post than a St Andrews regency, one which offered more prospects if one survived.

94 Carstares to Mar, 23 December 1708, NAS, GD124/796/4.

95 Pitcairne had ridiculed the Kirk and its clergy in a satirical poem, 'Babel', and in a witty play, 'The Assembly', both published in 1692. He was locked up for a short time in 1700 for writing scandalous things about the government.

96 This would have been the appointment of one of the Haldanes.

97 Pitcairne to Mar, 9 December 1708, NAS, GD124/755/4. The Earl of Leven was not like the other supporters. He was a strong Whig deprived of offices by the Tory government after 1710, but his family lived in the neighbourhood of Wormiston which lay in the parish of Crail. He was presumably looking after a neighbour.

98 Pringle, 'College Papers', SAUL, UYSL 156, p. 243.

99 He had some connection with St Salvator's College.

100 A. G. Stewart, *The Academic Gregories*, 1901, p. 84. The set of theses defended by his students were dedicated to Viscount Tarbat. Tarbat gave legal advice to David Gregorie and is said to have helped James Gregory obtain his Edinburgh chair in 1692.

101 There were disputes with the Crown over funds mortified by Charles II. These were not made available to the University either for this chair or for the chair of Hebrew; Minutes, 16 March 1696, SAUL, UYUY 452/1.

102 'There is a Young man come hither to teach Mathematics, one Mr Bethune, but I know not his character'; Francis Pringle to John Mackenzie, 6 December 1706, Delvine Papers, NLS, 1423/64.

103 Minutes, 17 February 1707; Ramsay to Mar, 2 July 1707; Mar to the Earl of Seafield, 17 July 1707, NAS, GD124/15/633/1; GD124/15/635/4. Bethune did not expect pay from the same funds as had paid the salary of Fenton. He seems to have had £50 from the colleges and nothing from whatever fund the Crown had once set up for the chair. Ramsay to Mar, 21 August 1707, NAS, GD124/15/633/1.

104 Hadow to Carstares, 20 August 1707, EUL, DK1.1.²

105 Ramsay to Mar, 21 August 1707, NAS, GD125/15/633/1.

106 David Nairne to M[y] Lord [Mar?], 26 October 1706, NAS, GD124/15/449/45.

107 Emerson, *Professors, Patronage and Politics*, 1991, p. 112, n.46.

108 Bower to Mar, 21 May 1707, NAS, GD124/15/573.

109 This comment was probably meant as a compliment to Episcopalians. Pitcairne, *The best of our owne*, ed. Johnston, 1979, p. 45f.

110 Minutes, 5 September 1707, SAUL, UYUY 452/2.

111 Minutes, 5 September, 10 and 26 December 1707, 3 and 6 February 1708, SAUL UYUY 452/2. In 1758, William Brown was given the ecclesiastical history chair and pleaded that his patent was itself a testimonial to his character – one far more dubious than Gregory's. Gregory's son David made available to him papers concerned with this point.

112 Minutes, 5 September 1707, SAUL UYUY 452/2.

113 Pitcairne to Mar, 6 January 1708, *The best of our owne*, ed. Johnston, 1979, p. 52.

114 Pitcairne to Mar, 10 February 1708, ibid., p. 53.

115 Minutes, 4 and 6 February 1708, SAUL UYUY 452/4.

116 Pitcairne to Mar, 4 November 1708, ibid., p. 55.

117 'Alexander Pitcairne', Pearce, ODNB, 44:422; Lachman, 'Hadow', in DSCHT p. 384; D. F. Wright, 'James Hadow', ODNB, 24:434f.

118 See below, p. 421.

14

ST MARY'S COLLEGE AND OTHER
APPOINTMENTS, 1713–1747

ↄ

1. ST MARY'S APPOINTMENTS, 1693–1713

Positions at St Mary's College were filled by politicians with one eye fixed on the religious views of the men appointed and the other on political advantage. It is not surprising that the initial appointment of 1690 should have been of a man who had suffered, and who had been chaplain to the Earl of Cassillis who himself had suffered even more.[1] What is surprising is that there were no other appointments to fill other chairs in the College until 1695 and 1699. The divinity school must have been nearly non-functional for much of the 1690s because William Vilant, its first principal and *primarius* professor of divinity, was a relatively old man when he was appointed, and his replacement in 1693, Alexander Pitcairne, was about seventy-one. They are unlikely to have been active teachers, but Pitcairne at least must have been lecturing in those years and doing the other work of a professor of divinity.

The first addition to the faculty came on 28 December 1695 when John Syme (?–19 November 1718) was appointed to the fourth mastership or chair of Hebrew. Syme was perhaps the son of George Sym, a cooper in Aberdeen.[2] His Crown appointment to teach Hebrew carried with it a nominal salary of £50 a year. However, it was not a post included in the original foundation but one which had been created only in 1668 and filled only for two years. Syme was not initially admitted to the College or University because his colleagues did not recognise him as a founded member. He had to wait until 2 January 1696. The masters' obstruction almost certainly signified their dislike not of him but of the circumstances of his appointment. They were unwilling to pay him out of College funds, believing that he should have been paid from funds from King Charles' Mortification. Like the professor of mathematics, he had trouble collecting. His situation could not have been pleasant but at least the masters made no moves to replace him. Instead, they made him

Oeconomus on 29 January 1697. By 1698 he was using his title and sitting in the Senatus, which implies admission to office.[3] Still, things continued in an unsatisfactory state until Syme's grant of the professorship was ratified by the Crown on 20 November 1707. His situation was regularised before the Treaty of Union took effect. He taught until c. 1718, when he left St Andrews because he could not account for, or pay, the amounts owing on his accounts. He was probably also ill since he died a short time later.

Following Syme's departure, the chair was vacant again until 1722. There seems to be no record of anyone teaching Hebrew in these years, although it must have been taught by someone. The Presbytery may have been overly orthodox but, like zealots elsewhere, they were not too concerned about the teaching of the language in which their God chose first to speak. The curious indifference to language study which we have noticed at Glasgow and Edinburgh was present here too and seems of equally little concern.

The third principal of St Mary's, Thomas Forrester (c. 1635–? November 1706), was chosen in November 1697 and installed on 26 January 1698. He was the son of a minor laird who disinherited him because he became a Whig. Forrester had been outed and imprisoned for field preaching and became a fugitive in May 1684. He eventually made his way to Holland and was involved with the rising of the Earl of Argyll in 1685. He returned with other exiles in 1688 and was then called to the living of Killearn in Stirlingshire, a parish where many of the heritors were Grahams and a place made memorable to men like Forrester for containing the birthplace of George Buchanan. From there he was translated to St Andrews in 1690 and eight years later to the principalship.[4] A convert from episcopacy, he wrote learnedly against it. He was a man needed in Fife and at St Mary's.[5] About sixty-three when he was appointed, he had not gone to sleep intellectually if his purchases for the University library are an indication of his personal interests. He bought several works of theological controversy: 'Melvil's Memoirs' (a classic account of the Marian period), the philosophical writings of Dr Henry Monro, Malebranche's *De la recherche de la verité* (1674–5), and Locke on government (1690).[6] These were not the selections of a narrow-minded Calvinist.

Only in 1699 did St Mary's College get an active younger man who could teach and make St Andrews count again in the world of clerical politics. He was James Hadow (13 August 1667–4 May 1747), who was appointed second master or professor of divinity on 5 April 1699. He came from Douglas in Lanarkshire and had studied at

Utrecht, then a more orthodox seminary than Leiden or the other Dutch universities.[7] Ordained at Cupar, Fife in 1694, he would have been well known to clerics in the area. Although he was later to be a leader in the prosecutions of John Simson of Glasgow and of the 'Marrow Men', he was no stiff-necked bigot, as is made clear in the account given of him by one who disliked his clerical politics and his theology:

> Hadow, while not by any means like the later Moderates, was of the compromising, mediating tendency, which, while it professed a high regard for sound doctrine, was yet not at all prepared to put up a fight for the rights of the Christian people for which the old Reformed divines stood. A man in his position was naturally in touch with the 'ecclesiastical machine,' or as it came in after times to be called, 'the circumtabular oligarchy,' which virtually held the reins of government in the Church's annual Parliament.[8]

It is not known who sponsored Hadow for his chair of divinity (probably Carstares) but they picked a man who liked order, who could compromise and would not protest too much against patronage by heritors and interference in church affairs by men in government. Like Forrester, he opposed episcopacy in more than one work issued between 1703 and 1705. His sponsors probably saw a need for that in Fife. Hadow was close to Forrester in another way too; his second wife was probably the former principal's daughter. Hadow's first wife had been the daughter of another principal, William Tullideph of St Leonard's. When Hadow was hired, the University made room for an outsider who had become one of the family. Hadow succeeded Forrester as principal in September 1707, but he had for some time been performing many of the duties of that office, including handling the College's monies. His succession opened the chair of divinity to a hot contest between Thomas Black and others.[9] The place finally went, in 1710, to Thomas Halyburton (25 December 1674–23 September 1712), who seems not to have sought it.[10]

Hadow was asked by the Presbytery of St Andrews in February 1707 to recommend a successor to his chair.[11] He named Black, a friend who agreed with him on theological and ecclesiological issues and who served a parish in Perth.[12] Black was favoured for the divinity chair by other leading clerics, such as Principal Carstares. Black's support from the Presbytery would not and did not make him a popular choice in the University. By 1707, there was a cabal at the University to defeat Black's candidacy but there was also opposition elsewhere and he himself may not have been eager for the post.

The situation was further complicated because this was not the only chair in play. Syme wanted to secure the better-paying and more prestigious chair of ecclesiastical history which had remained unfunded and vacant since the purge of 1690. Patrick Haldane was also seeking this chair. If Syme got it, a new man to teach Hebrew would have to be appointed. Three chairs – divinity, Hebrew and ecclesiastical history – might be filled and the tensions arising in such a circumstance were great. What was at issue was the control of the seminary. If Black were elected, then he, with the principal giving a casting vote, could control the institution. If John Syme or Patrick Haldane were chosen for the history chair and masters unfavourable to Hadow's views were chosen in Hebrew and divinity, then the control of the seminary might well go out of the hands of the ortho- dox and vest in men indifferent to what the zealous thought import- ant. That would have been of only political interest to men like Lord Mar but Carstares and his friends would have seen the matter in a very different light. Tensions rose at St Andrews.

How things stood on Lady Day 1707 is recounted in a letter by Hadow to Carstares, the government's principal advisor on church patronage. Hadow's letter is one of a series, the previous one of which had been 'refreshing on account of good hopes it gives of desirable success in our affair'. He now said:

I am also glad you did not find it needful to deliver the addresses of the principal masters [who presumably did not support Hadow]. These same regents who oppose us in Mr Black's affair have also entered in concert that I may not be chosen to represent the University in the ensuing Assembly, though at present they have not another capable of being a member who is also able to travel[13] . . . Mr John Sym is gone for Edinburgh, perhaps to further the affair of his own patent to be third Master in this College [Hadow hoped Mar would not grant Syme's wish to be made the professor of ecclesiastical history] . . . Mr Patrick Haldane did fully discourse my Lord Grange [Mar's brother James Erskine] upon the memorial I left with you about that affair. The Foundation of our [?] Mary College alloweth three professors of divinity, viz the principal, Licentiatus, & Bacchalaurenis, and a professor of [the] popes Canon Law . . . Mr Syms profession of Hebrew is by Gift & Mortification of K. Ch. 2^d . . . but was never owned as a foundation person of our Society . . . If Mr Patrick Haldane's project succeed, I wish rather he were made third master seeing he would bring alongst a salarie without any burden on the present rents of the society: and indeed Mr Sym is so unworthy of advancement that he is scarce deserving of his present post, the students universally complaining of him that they cannot profit by his obscure teaching and designedly keeping them in the dark as to what he should make plain and easie to them . . . So soon as the presentation of the profession of divinity is filled up to our satisfaction I shall order the taking of it out and the advancing the money for that effect . . .[14]

A month later Carstares thought he had solved the problem of the divinity professorship. He wrote to Mar to thank him and Lord Loudoun for the patent issued by the Crown: 'I have now the Gift in my hand and only want to hear from the Earle of Rothes that the name may be filled up.'[15] Why Rothes should have been involved is unknown. Was deference being shown to the most prominent politician in Fife, one who was then supporting the Union, or had Rothes all along had a candidate?

When the royal warrant for Black's chair came down in May 1707, some of the local ministers went to Perth to request that Presbytery to loose Black from his church so that he might be translated to St Andrews. By August this request had been rejected and the matter taken to the Commission of the General Assembly, often the place of next resort in the clerical courts. In March 1708, the Commission decided to leave Black in Perth and the search for a new professor resumed.[16]

The next man considered was William Hamilton of Cramond, a man who would soon hold the Edinburgh divinity chair and act there as an innovator in much the same way as did John Simson in Glasgow. Nothing came of this overture made in April 1708. To complicate matters even more, there now went to the politicians a request to make Joseph Drew the principal of St Leonard's.[17] Drew got his chair but the divinity chair went unfilled until April 1710. Hadow continued to teach the students of theology and remained something of a one-man faculty.

Syme's original patent was confirmed by the Queen on 20 November 1707, but in December 1708 he was still seeking to get from the Crown either his salary or an augmentation to it. Failing that, he wanted the University to grant him the stipends of two bursars in divinity.[18] He presumably continued to teach Hebrew in the same unsatisfactory manner until he left St Andrews in November 1718.

Edinburgh University got a law chair in 1707; St Andrews got a chair of ecclesiastical history, for that is what the new endowment made the third master of St Mary's College. Like the post in Edinburgh, this too was a political job to pay off a Squadrone family for its support of the Union.[19] On 23 November 1708, Patrick Haldane was appointed to the chair which meant that a layman might now serve as rector since this professor was one of those allowed to hold that post. 'Discoursing' Mar and Lord Grange had done Haldane some good but his father's vote for the Union almost certainly mattered more.[20]

Haldane from the beginning treated his new post as a virtual sinecure. In 1711, he went to Leiden to study law. Passing advocate in 1715, he was also elected to the House of Commons. A year later he became Provost of St Andrews (1716–20) and Commissioner of Forfeitures. He resigned his University place only in 1718 and, after a three-year hiatus, it was given by the Squadrone politicians to his cousin, James Haldane. In 1722, Patrick Haldane, although he was appointed to the Court of Session, failed to become a judge. His work as a commissioner had made him very unpopular and his future court colleagues, backed by the Argathelians, found him unfit and refused to seat him.

In 1708, the chair of divinity was still empty and a crisis loomed in the College, indeed, in the University. Too many were now disaffected to the establishments, both political and religious. The control of St Leonard's had been wrested from the righteous and the impious and the inefficient had a grip on St Mary's. Even St Salvator's had a dodgy regent in the person of Alexander Scrymgeour. Hadow was dejected and thought of leaving. In March 1708, he wrote to Principal Stirling at Glasgow, saying he would happily accept the divinity chair there if they were unanimous in wanting him: 'I am wearied wrestling in ys place, and some other in my room might be capable of doing more service here than I.'[21] Carstares would have found that a blow to his management of the universities and was likely to have opposed the move. The on-going wrangling over the appointments induced Carstares to consider a Royal Visitation of the University. By November 1708, Carstares had decided that a Royal Visitation was in order. On 30 November, he wrote to Mar, '. . . as I told [Lord Grange] so I presume humblie to represent it to your Lo. that I cannot but acknowledge that it is expedient if not necessarie considering the debates at law that have been about their rights and their other divisions too.' He went on to say that the Visitors must be men without exception to those in both church and state. He clearly did not want the Visitors to include Fife gentlemen who favoured episcopacy or who leaned toward the repeal of the Union, which may already have turned the minds of some of the masters. He suggested that Grange get a list of Visitors from the Lord Advocate, Sir James Steuart of Goodtrees. Any list from this orthodox Presbyterian and Whig would

certainly have answered.[22] Several days later, Lord Grange wrote to
his brother Mar saying:

> Mr Carstairs thinks it will not be improper to appoint a visitation for St
> Andrew's Colledge, providing the visitors be men who are friendly to the
> present settlement of our church, for that University has these several years
> been full of factions and divisions. Sim is a poor silly body, tho' I do think
> that Haddo has been much in the wrong to him. I was surprised to hear
> he was at London, which I never knew till you wrote it to me.[23]

One suspects that Mar was less taken with the idea of a visitation
which might undercut the positions of men whose views he probably
shared.

The divinity chair was finally filled by an orthodox man who
posthumously would be recognised as a notable one, Thomas
Halyburton. He was said to have been appointed at the request of
the Synod of Fife.[24] The account, given in Halyburton's *Memoirs*, of
the process by which he got the chair is almost unbelievable given the
eagerness with which most men sought such places, but it was in
keeping with Halyburton's unworldly character. His biographer tells
us that Halyburton ignored the first offer of the chair. When it was
renewed, 'he gave no encouragement to it, resolving to be no way the
disposer of his lot.'[25] When a patent was issued in December 1709,
he said, 'Lord, crush it, if it is not for thy glory. Herein I have peace,
that I had no hand in it.' But the Lord so moved the hearts of the Earl
of Mar and others that His ways were accomplished in St Andrews.
The agent of the Lord may well have been the reverend James Hog,
who prayed movingly before the vote was taken to loose Halyburton
from his parish which was reluctant to see him leave. Professor
Halyburton died in the Lord on 23 September 1712, by which time
the Tory ministers in London would have no truck with men like him.
This was sad because their choice of Alexander Scrymgeour plunged
the University into years of useless strife and constituted one of the
most unfortunate interventions by politicians in the period here surveyed. It shows how well off the Scots generally were *not* to have had
their academic patronage handled by Englishmen, Anglicans, and by
mere politicians acting without religious principle or even concern for
character, learning or utility.

The politicians chose the next professor from four contenders,
three of them orthodox and one who was said not to be. The Glasgow
area diarist Robert Wodrow reported that the post was sought by
Thomas Black of Perth, George Chalmers of Kilwinning, and Henry

Forrester, Principal Hadow's brother-in-law.[26] Black seems not to have tried hard for the post and nothing more was heard of the others, although one or more of them must have had support to the very end since Wodrow thought that Alexander Scrymgeour was able to succeed because there was a divided interest in the University.[27] A unanimous recommendation from the masters might have succeeded but Scrymgeour apparently had the favour of Robert Ramsay, provost of St Salvator's, and very likely the approval of the regents suspected of episcopal leanings with whom he had long taught. Scrymgeour was supported by those whom Wodrow called the Episcopalians, Arminians and Jacobites. They would have been a majority or near majority of the masters in 1713 and that would have been known by Robert Harley and Lord Bolingbroke in London. As disposers of Crown patronage, these politicians had the gift of the place in their hands and used it to shore up their own interest in a corporation of importance in the management of the Kirk. The Jacobite or Episcopalian masters' recommendations resonated with the London politicians, who arranged for the patent to be given to Scrymgeour although he was not even a clergyman. They were asking for trouble but cared not about the consequences.[28]

Scrymgeour was made a Doctor of Divinity on 19 October 1713 by King's College, Aberdeen, which qualified him for the post, to which he had been appointed on 23 April 1713. The majority of the Aberdeen masters were Jacobites and certainly sympathetic to episcopalianism.[29] This grant of a DD was extraordinary because Scrymgeour was not only a layman but seems not to have had much, if any, formal theological training. At the same time, he does not seem a man likely to have undertaken to teach theology unless he were prepared to do so. He knew Hebrew well enough to offer to teach it when Syme left St Andrews in 1718.[30] He was conscientious enough to be diffident about taking the chair of ecclesiastical history in 1727, confessing his 'unfitness for this office'.[31] In 1713, he seems to have felt he was fit for his new post. When he tried to take the oaths that would qualify him to teach in St Andrews, he was put off and then proceeded against by the Presbytery and Synod of Fife[32] in cases which lasted in one form or another for nearly twenty years.[33] He qualified elsewhere and did teach.

Those who disliked him spread stories about his Jacobitism, his lack of qualifications and his unorthodoxy – stories that seem to have fit his wife but not him.[34] During the years in which he taught, students never found objectionable any political or religious matters in his lectures. This is significant in an age in which the 'errors' made by professor Simson at Glasgow were reported to ministers hostile to him and when other professors were closely watched. Surely, not all of Scrymgeour's students were Jacobite Episcopalians or Presbyterians incapable of delating a professor. The local clerics did not like him but they were unable to make a plausible case for his being theologically unsound. They did manage to prevent his teaching after 1718 when he was suspended. He did not suffer financially from this since he continued to receive his salary and enjoyed the other emoluments of his office.[35] With Scrymgeour's appointment, the College had a principal who had opposed all the members of his staff, a professor of divinity regarded as unsound, an Hebraist who was a poor teacher and a sinecure professor of ecclesiastical history attending law school in Holland. It must have lost students and certainly prestige at a time when the University as a whole was in a decline which these appointments did nothing to arrest. There were no other appointments at St Mary's until after the '15, by which time St Andrews' political and religious deviations had been well noted. It appeared to have been and probably was the nursery for some of the Jacobitism of the rebels from Fife.

2. THE '15 AND AFTER

Unlike the loyal gentlemen of the Glasgow area, the Fife gentry – but not always their tenants – were among the Scots most supportive of the uprising of 1715. The rebellious Earl of Mar landed in Fife when he arrived in Scotland from England. There he found willing adherents, many of whom would have been St Andrews alumni or the parents of sons at the University. The same gentlemen protected ministers with Episcopalian leanings. Some of the latter even made an open profession of these heresies. Fife's Jacobites in 1715 were numerous enough to allow the rebels to seize and occupy many Fifeshire burghs and to levy taxes on their inhabitants. Professor Scrymgeour was later faulted for paying taxes to the Jacobite collector of the cess.[36] During the rising, many soldiers were recruited from Fife and the adjoining counties and there were successful military actions by rebels in the region.[37]

What was true of the rural areas of Fife was also true of its chief town, where Jacobites were noticeable even before the uprising in 1715. Riots having the support of masters had occurred in 1688–90 – as the Visitors of 1690 remarked. Although the burgh fathers had changed in 1689 from Jacobites to Whigs, tensions persisted through the 1690s and contributed to the University's willingness to move to Perth in 1697–8. Some of these strains continued throughout the century as they did in every university town where they often centred on conflicts over jurisdiction in cases involving the misdeeds of university members and over property disputes. It was tempting for those who disliked the local burgh officials to link them with a future ruler and church they also increasingly disliked. These irritants accumulated in the years before the rising in 1715 but other tensions were evident. In 1703, the rector and principal of St Mary's College, Thomas Forrester, complained that masters were frequenting the Episcopal meeting house, which he described as 'seditious' as well as illegal.[38] The efforts of Dr Archibald Pitcairne c. 1707 to install his friends in the University were political in purpose as well as in the interest of good mathematics and learning. By 1712, Episcopalian meeting houses were legal and well attended. Among the communicants in St Andrews was Mrs Alexander Scrymgeour, the wife of the professor of divinity.[39] Robert Wodrow noted that the students celebrated the wrong occasions with bonfires and noise, if not with worse. His friend, William Dunlop, found this unchanged in 1713, as did others.[40]

> The gentlemen in this country are generally poisoned with ill principles, which too much appears from their sons attending the Episcopal meeting-house in this place [St Andrews], . . . for I believe the large half of the students in both colledges go there, and though the old colledge [St Salvator's] masters are pretty right, and all the regents here attend the established Church, yet severals of the St Leonardine masters incline that way, and I believe, instead of discouraging their scholars they influence them to separate from the church, and great many people in the town are tainted with jacobitish principles, and the students fired guns throughout all the pretender's birthday, and I believe that impostor's health was generally drank on that occasion, and though both the town and colledge churches are pretty throng, yet the archdeacon [the most reverend Richard Waddell] has by far the gentilest congregation in town.[41]

Then in 1715 came open support for the Old Pretender who was 'proclaimed King at St Andrews' by some of the students, including George Martine who was later denied an Edinburgh chair of medicine. Martine and his friends rang the bells of St Salvator's and threatened some of the locals with pistols. Another of the boys took a proclamation from the post man.[42] The masters, late in the summer of 1715, sent protestations of loyalty to King George.[43] When the rebellion was over, the masters, perhaps as a way of saving their skins, petitioned the Crown for a visitation. They considered doing this in 1716 but waited until 27 August 1717.[44]

In 1718, they were duly visited by a Royal Commission. The Visitors sorted out the finances of the University and the colleges and insisted on loyalty (to be manifested by orderly and regular attendance at the Kirk by law established). They did not extrude anyone but in 1718 Scrymgeour was suspended pending further meetings of the Commission. Because the Earl of Rothes, *praeses* of the Commission, died in May 1722 and was not replaced, the Visitors never met again to dispose of Scrymgeour's case.[45] The Commission never completed its work and the professor remained suspended, but enjoying his full pay and other privileges, until his death in 1732.[46]

Despite its seeming ineffectiveness, the Visitation had been upsetting from the beginning. Francis Pringle wrote to the Episcopalian and Jacobite-leaning lawyer, John Mackenzie of Delvine, on 3 February 1718 complaining that Principal Drew (he was also rector) was trying to rule despotically and that Pringle and his friends 'are calling in the Assistance of all our friends to stem that tide of Malice and Calumny wherein the principal would overwhelm us.'[47] This meant they were lobbying the local notables, some of whom were Visitors. Part of the 'calumny' was the charge of disloyalty – a charge countered in the masters' address to the King in 1719 after the most recent Jacobite scare. This proclaimed their allegiance to King and Church.[48] St Andrews had not been notably loyal but it escaped the purges which denuded King's and Marischal Colleges in 1716–17.

While St Andrews was concerned with Jacobites, it was also planning and then inaugurating a chair of medicine. The Chandos chair of medicine was founded in 1720–1 but like medical chairs elsewhere it did not come out of the blue as is sometimes supposed. In 1705, the year a professorship of anatomy was created by the Edinburgh surgeons, St Andrews University indicated in correspondence with the Royal College of Physicians of Edinburgh that it intended someday to teach medicine.[49] In 1715, two years after Edinburgh appointed a professor of chemistry and medicine and one year after Glasgow hired a professor of medicine, Dr Robert Wood asked the University if it would create a medical chair for him. This was probably not a whimsical request because Dr Wood was almost certainly a member of a notable family of medical men who worked in Perth throughout much of the century.[50] The family trained many apprentices.[51] Making Dr Wood a professor (he himself practised in St Andrews in the 1690s) would have given the University a bit of prestige and the convenience of a promoter of degree recipients whose numbers were increasing. The University did not turn Wood down flat but 'unanimously voted that no man should be recommended at this present time'.[52] Not long after, the masters approached the Scottish Secretary, the Duke of Montrose (he had arranged the funding of the Glasgow chair), about more money from King Charles' Mortification. They may have had a candidate other than Wood in mind because a little over a month after giving Wood a qualified 'no', the University Minutes note that 'Dr Hay has gone to London to procure a patent for being professor of Medicine in this University'. The University itself wrote to Montrose and his political rivals, the 2nd Duke of Argyll and his brother, the Earl of Ilay, asking for their help in this matter.[53] Nothing came of these requests. It was not a very good time for a university said to be sheltering political and religious dissidents to apply for a regius chair. Success came in 1720 through the generosity of James Brydges, 1st Duke of Chandos.

The Duke of Chandos' son and his tutor, Dr Charles Stuart, had visited St Andrews and Glasgow in 1719.[54] They had been well treated. The Duke was grateful to the masters of colleges in both places and signified his gratitude by making benefactions to the universities. Glasgow got £500 which was eventually spent on the erection of a new library.[55] St Andrews was given a £1,000 for the creation of a new chair.[56] The Duke had hoped that this might be laid out on a chair of rhetoric and *belles lettres* for Francis Pringle, who had impressed him, or perhaps for Thomas Ruddiman, the Librarian of the Advocates' Library in Edinburgh. After much discussion, the St Andrews masters decided to fund a chair of medicine which was to bear the name to the donor.

Their decision has often been seen as a foolish one which established a useless post in a place unsuited to the teaching of medicine and where the medical professors seldom lectured. There were other things at issue. Without a medical faculty, which required at least one professor, it was difficult to grant medical degrees that looked at all plausible. Local MDs, who lacked prestige, had to be brought in to go through the motions of an examination and to promote the candidates. Between 1696 and 1721, the University granted at least seventeen medical degrees and during the whole period from 1696 to 1806 it probably granted at least 1,015 degrees.[57] They needed a respectable promoter.

Most of the MDs were medics who had trained as surgeons or surgeon-apothecaries and now wished to practise as physicians.

Others had apprenticed themselves to physicians and now wished to be recognised as physicians of a higher class, real doctors with an MD. Many had made careers in the services and had retired or been put on half pay; they now wanted jobs in civilian life, increasingly as hospital physicians. Others were English dissenters who were precluded from taking medical degrees at Oxford and Cambridge because they could not comply with their religious tests. Men of those sorts showed up with, or sent in, certificates testifying to their abilities and to their character. If they presented themselves, they were examined with more or less seriousness by the Chandos professor. If they were absent, they would be granted degrees if their referees were well known and respected. Sometimes, if the referees were unknown or were known as referees who had recommended unsatisfactory men in the past, the applicant was refused or the candidate was told to appear for an examination. Once they had been examined and found fit, the Senatus conferred the degree and they paid their fees (£4–10) and were 'doctored'. The fees were split between the professor, the library, the man who engrossed the diploma and the rest of the teaching staff. This was not a useless chair, but one necessary to a peculiar kind of fund-raising helpful to a poor university. The chair's first incumbent was Thomas Simson (1696–30 March 1764), a diligent physician who did some teaching and had a reputation as a learned author.

Simson had studied at Glasgow and Leyden. He was a younger brother of Robert Simson, the Glasgow professor of mathematics. Simson had testimonials from Edinburgh and Glasgow physicians and seems to have impressed his St Andrews examiners when he defended the two theses he had been assigned to uphold against the questions of his impugners.[58] Among his several examiners were Drs Wood and Hay.[59] In the late 1720s and 1730s, Simson published a number of medical and anatomical studies. By then he moved in the circles of the Edinburgh medical professors and by the late 1730s he was a member of the Philosophical Society of Edinburgh. The University had chosen a capable man in a competitive examination.

The men Simson bested were also estimable and both seem to have been related to sitting members of the University.[60] Both had gone to considerable expense to secure this chair. James Stewart (or Stuart) of Chrystwell, whose father was the Edinburgh advocate of the same name, was, like Simson, a Leiden-trained MD who had become a licentiate of the RCPE in November 1721 so he could make a better appearance in St Andrews.[61] Dr John Rutherford, another Leiden man who held a Reims MD, was probably then teaching chemistry in Edinburgh either extramurally or for Professor James Crawford. Rutherford had taken an MA at King's College, Aberdeen on 12 October 1721 in order to meet one of the degree requirements for the post.[62] He had solicited political support since there exists a letter from Colonel[?] Erskine to a prominent minister, Allan Logan of Culross, asking the latter to lobby Principal Hadow on Rutherford's behalf. The phrasing of his letter suggests that Erskine did not know the young physician very well. He wrote, 'If he [Hadow] be not engaged & the doctor be a fit person[,] It is possible he may have Mr Haddows assistance.'[63] Rutherford did not get this chair, for which he may have been thankful. In 1726, he was appointed at Edinburgh where he went on to be one of the most distinguished medical professors of the century, not only in Scotland but in Europe too.

3. APPOINTMENTS IN THE ARTS COLLEGES, 1714–1739

Between 1714 and 1739, there were only five appointments made in the arts colleges. The colleges stagnated and became more inbred, partly because their livings were too meagre to interest good men.

William Petrie (c. 1696–August 1729) became professor of Greek at St Salvator's in 1716 and is notable only for being the first of the professors educated after 1700; little else is known of him save that he graduated MA from St Leonard's in 1710. He resigned in June 1729 and was replaced in August 1729 by James Kemp (c. 1698–17 April 1748). Kemp, the son of the minister of Carnbee, Fifeshire, had studied at Leiden and seems to have had connections good enough to get himself recommended to the Crown for appointment to the chair of ecclesiastical history in 1721, a chair he failed to get.[64] He had sought this with the support of the chancellor, the Duke of Atholl, but the Duke was probably acting as a spokesman for the masters as chancellors often did.

In 1733, regent William Young became provost of St Salvator's on the death of Robert Ramsay. Young had been unanimously recommended by the men of his College and by his other University colleagues to the chancellor, now the Duke of Chandos. Other letters went to Lord Ilay (now effectively the Secretary for Scotland) and to the Duke of Newcastle, the Secretary of State, whose office handled appointments such as this. In their letters, the masters noted that Young was the senior regent and had for some years been carrying on the work of the provost because of Ramsay's incapacity in old age.

After Ilay had checked to see that he was not objectionable, Young was appointed and installed on 20 April 1733.[65] Ilay was willing to satisfy the masters if there was not much at stake. As he prepared for the election of 1734, this may have seemed to Ilay the prudent thing to do. Young's son, John Young (c. 1706–1772), replaced him as regent on 8 June 1733.

At St Leonard's things were equally dull. Provost William Young's son, David (?c. 1695–16 May 1759), was appointed a regent on 8 November 1716. He was a more diligent teacher than many but his claims to fame now rest on his purchasing of some scientific instruments, his sponsorship of Benjamin Franklin for an LLD in 1759, and his role in what has become the Royal and Ancient Golf Club.[66] With his appointment, both colleges incorporated sons of Provost Young.

The one other teacher of an arts subject was the professor of mathematics, whose post was outwith the arts colleges. David Gregory (1712–13 April 1765) succeeded his father Charles as mathematics professor in 1739. Charles Gregory, unlike some other members of his family, was a Whig, which must have been a disappointment to those who had backed his application for the post they secured for him. He had been active politically in the burgh since at least 1714. Then he had aided the Leslie family in the elections to the Perth burghs, acts which led students to avoid his classes with the support of some of his colleagues.[67] His Whiggery was again displayed when, in the '15, he took part as a volunteer for King George in the Battle of Dunblane.[68] About 1727, his affairs became embarrassed because he had stood surety for a friend who had not been able to meet his debts. Gregory then, to the consternation of his colleagues, tried to sell his chair to a Mr Arnot. James Hadow, the rector, protested to 'his Grace' (probably the Duke of Chandos) and also to Newcastle.[69] Nothing came of Gregory's offer of sale, nor did the 9th Earl of Rothes get his wish that Gregory and his son David, then fifteen years old, be made joint professors with the right of survivorship vested in him who lived longest.[70] Gregory's financial woes seem to have been solved, in part, by his being awarded the clerkship of the St Andrews Commissary Court, an office which he held until his resignation of his chair in favour of his son in 1739. By then, his son had impeccable political backers. The Earl of Rothes would have felt some obligation to help the younger Gregory. So too would both the Laird of Leuchars (probably Lindsay of Balcarres) and the Duke of Gordon. Gregory had tutored the sons of both. Seeing him appointed would have shifted their burdens of looking after a former tutor to the University.[71]

Former employers were usually eager to write letters of recommendation for men who cost them money. The University men also backed Gregory's son's succession and recommended him to Lord Ilay.[72] After 1734 things began to change at St Andrews because of appointments made at St Mary's.

4. ST MARY'S COLLEGE, 1720–1747

For seven years after 1713, there were no changes in St Mary's College. James Hadow remained its principal and the teacher of its divinity courses. Alexander Scrymgeour was professor of divinity, although he could not and did not teach for most of the period between his suspension in 1718 and his death in 1732.[73] Patrick Haldane may have taught a bit when he was first installed but he soon became a sinecurist and absentee before resigning in 1718 to pursue his political and legal career. The chair of ecclesiastical history was vacant for long periods. From 1718 until 1721, the College had really only one effective member, James Hadow. Someone else may have been teaching some Hebrew, but whoever he was he was not a professor. The College was in disarray and the Visitation of 1718 had done nothing to remedy matters. This may have been in part because the chairman of the Visitation Commission was the Earl of Rothes. A Representative Peer and HM High Commissioner to the General Assembly, he had the power to protect the masters and might have been reluctant to embarrass professors at his alma mater from whom he could expect favours. He was also a member of the Squadrone political faction which for the next decade looked after affairs at the College.

The story of the filling of the regius chairs at St Mary's College in this period divides into two stories: one about the giving of jobs to quite young men who had political friends who could secure for them the chairs of ecclesiastical history and Hebrew, and another about the appointing of responsible and sensible men to the principalship and the chair of divinity where orthodoxy and political astuteness mattered to those who made the appointments. The two kinds of appointments were treated differently even when they were secured from the same politicians.

Scots may have prided themselves on their orthodoxy but they were increasingly ill-prepared by their divinity school training to defend the historical accounts of their faith or to read the languages in which their God had revealed Himself to His fallen and wayward creatures.[74] For much of the period, the study of Hebrew and other oriental languages was slighted here as at Edinburgh and Glasgow; so too was that of ecclesiastical history. Appointments to the chairs of Hebrew and ecclesiastical history went to young dependants of Squadrone families such as James Haldane, who got the ecclesiastical history chair in 1721.

James Haldane followed his cousin, Patrick, in the Old College chair of Greek in 1707 and, fourteen years later, into the ecclesiastical history chair. In 1707, the family was being paid off for its support for the Union. In 1721, Stirlingshire was represented in Parliament by Mungo Haldane, a cousin of James. Both were distantly related to the Duke of Montrose, an important Squadrone politician. The Perth Burghs, in which St Andrews was included, were represented by Patrick Haldane, who also served from 1716 to 1720 as Provost of St Andrews and as Commissioner for the Sale of the Forfeited Estates in Scotland (1716–25).[75] The tight election of 1721 was a time in which many families found it possible to extract something for their loyalty to party leaders. James was another Haldane who could be and was put on the gravy train.

The chair of Hebrew, worth £80 a year, had been vacant for some time, although there had been attempts to fill it. In 1718, it was seen as a place where Alexander Scrymgeour might be put were he willing to resign his chair of divinity. That scheme came to nothing. William Dunlop wrote to his brother in an undated letter almost certainly from 1718, 'the Court have positively refused to present Mr Scrymgeour to the Hebrew Profession and the D. of Roxburghe is positive that the King can never give a commission to one charged with disloyalty so that his prosecution must go on.'[76] Another impediment to such a scheme was the fact that Scrymgeour's chair paid him £120 for doing nothing. The next notice of efforts to fill the place comes in 1720 when Robert Ramsay, the rector, asked the University to recommend a professor 'as has been the use'. Nothing came of this.[77] Ramsay may well have had in mind either Gershom Carmichael's son, Frederick, or James Duncan, the St Salvator's regent. Both were mentioned for this post around this time. Duncan's sponsor was the Earl of Rothes, who was not only active on the Commission to visit the University but was also interfering at Glasgow at this time.[78] Things dragged on until 7 June 1721, when Gabriel Johnstoun (1698–17 July 1752), the son of a Dundee minister, secured the professorship of Hebrew.

Johnstoun was a great-grandson of a Marquis of Annandale. The family had ties to the Squadrone Lords. He was also a polite scholar who had studied divinity at St Andrews and had spent some time at

Leiden in the early 1720s. There he matriculated in the faculty of medicine, in which he may or may not have studied.[79] Johnstoun treated his chair as something of a sinecure and left St Andrews for London well before he resigned on 26 February 1728. In London, he wrote for the opposition paper, *The Craftsman*. He emigrated to Carolina, where he became the second royal governor of the province in March 1733. As governor he was distinguished by his efforts to improve the administration of the province so it would be more profitable to the Crown. He also introduced a printer, codified the laws and made educational reforms which largely failed.[80]

When Johnstoun resigned, the University worried that he would be replaced by an unqualified person. Principal Hadow wrote to someone (the Dukes of Newcastle or Chandos were the most likely recipients of his letter) saying that Johnstoun was going to Holland that spring and that the University hoped that, should he resign, he would not give his resignation into the hands of one who could use it to secure the chair for himself. That may have been the means by which his successor was really chosen.[81] Johnstoun was shortly thereafter replaced by a man with impeccable Squadrone ties, Hugh Warrender (c. 1714–8 May 1754).

Warrender was the son of Sir George Warrender, MP, who had defeated the Argathelian candidate for the provostship of Edinburgh in 1715. This lord provost had been active for Montrose and the government in the '15 and had incurred financial losses as a result of his service. He died in 1721 with claims on the government still outstanding. His friends seem to have made it up to his son, who had graduated MA at Edinburgh on 20 June 1728 and was appointed to the St Andrews living eight days later.[82] He was certainly not a profound Hebrew scholar but Lord Ilay, who had been consulted, thought him a fitter man than his predecessor.[83]

Warrender functioned in some fashion for about ten years and then became restive and was sometimes absent without leave. On 3 April 1738, he was given extended leave by the University and provided a substitute while he was in London studying civil and canon law and doing business for the University.[84] He had effectively left his post and finally resigned in 1741. He became first a barrister and, later, rector of Aston in Yorkshire.[85] St Andrews remembered him with some fondness (or at least gratified his patrons) by giving him an LLD on 22 February 1743.

These appointments at St Mary's were all granted while Squadrone men controlled most of the Crown patronage in Scotland. After

c. 1724, the Squadrone men were more or less excluded from dispensing patronage in Scotland. The change was soon evident at the
University. James Haldane's death in a College fire in 1727 set off a
scurry for his chair of ecclesiastical history now worth over £100 a
year.[86] First in the field seems to have been Alexander Scrymgeour,
who was pushed by others to accept this chair and thus solve the
problem he long had presented to the Kirk and to politicians.

Scrymgeour wanted to resume teaching divinity in 1726 and had
sought to have his suspension found void because of the long lapse of
time (eight years) since the last meeting of the Visitation Commission
which had ordered it. His lawyer and cousin, Lawrence Craigie of
Kilgraston, told him he might teach. The St Andrews Presbytery
quickly responded with renewed legal actions to bar an unordained
man from teaching theology. His problems again became ones for
lawyers. Those consulted found the Presbytery's position unwarranted, as did another of Scrymgeour's relatives, Robert Craigie, a
lawyer who later served the Squadrone party.[87] This matter went to
the Commission of the General Assembly in March 1727, but before
then the lawyers revived an old suggestion for a way out of the difficulties. Scrymgeour might take the chair of ecclesiastical history and
once legally admitted he might teach usefully in the room of the dead
Haldane.[88]

This suggestion was welcomed by the Argathelians who had
ousted the Squadrone men from doing the King's business in Scotland.
Ilay and his assistants, Andrew Fletcher of Saltoun, Lord Milton,
SCJ, and Charles Erskine, Solicitor General for Scotland, discouraged others from applying for the post for which they recommended Scrymgeour.[89] Robert Wodrow reported in March 1727 that
Scrymgeour was being urged to take up this post.[90] Erskine asked
Scrymgeour for a resignation to be presented when the new post was
secured, but Scrymgeour demurred. He said, 'Hadow has got promises
from court of a young scholar of the profession of history' and 'to help
repair the losses by the burning' the appointment would be put off for
a year so the money saved could be spent on the repairs. That 'will
oblige to a years delay in the admission to that office'. Scrymgeour
seems also to have thought he was too old and unprepared to lecture
on history. Taking up the new position would also risk the loss of his
University house, which was allocated only to the professor of divinity. He suggested that his third son, David, who had left college only
two years earlier, should be given the history chair in exchange for his
resigning his own.[91] That project turned out not to be feasible. The

younger Scrymgeour was hardly of age and was likely studying to be an advocate; he would not have been thought by many to have been a particularly fit person for the chair.[92] That meant that the only person left in the running was Hadow's man.

It is uncertain who Hadow intended for this post, but he was likely to have been William Dalgleish, minister of Carnbee in Fife, whom the University voted to recommend to the chancellor on 26 January 1727, even before Scrymgeour's candidacy had run its course.[93] Nothing came of this nomination, perhaps because Dalgleish came from a parish where the principal heritors were members of the Anstruther family. The Anstruthers belonged to the Squadrone faction and an appointment to one of their dependants would have been opposed by Ilay, who in 1727 was trying to secure his hold on all the colleges. He would not have appointed a Squadrone-backed man to any college living. It is not known when Dalgleish was refused the position, but by March the masters were worried about someone inappropriate being appointed – someone like David Scrymgeour. Hadow proposed and the masters voted for a resolution that 'every succeeding professor of Church History that shall be admitted to the said office, be obliged, besides praelections, to teach a Compend of Church History, for the greater profit and benefit of the Students, that shall attend the Said profession.'[94] This signalled their willingness to cause problems for any unqualified professor who might be appointed or any who meant to continue the chair as a sinecure office. Those who came to the post after this time could be taken to at least the rector's court for non-feasance. In 1727, this may also have been an act directed at Ilay.

Another known applicant was David Verner (or Warner), a Marischal College regent. He had gone to Aberdeen as a stranger in 1717 to bolster the orthodox and the Whigs but he was now eager to return south or to have something better in Aberdeen.[95] He had approached the reverend Alexander Innes, an Argathelian church manager, who then wrote to Lord Milton on 26 February 1728 asking that Verner be given either the principality at Aberdeen or the St Andrews ecclesiastical history chair. In a further letter, written in March, Innes cited one of this applicant's most important qualifications: 'Zeal for the Duke of Argyll's interest.' During the summer, Verner was in London on Marischal College business. He sought to get augmentations to the salaries paid at his College and more money for the 'repair of buildings'. He also 'endeavoured to do some things for my self but wtout any further success in either than some few

Court promises'.[96] Despite his 'Zeal', his application went nowhere. Later men thought him a very heavy drinker.

Verner was not the only Aberdeen applicant. George Turnbull, another Marischal College regent, had resigned his place there in the spring of 1727 and applied for this one. In a letter to Charles Mackie, he asked for his old friend's support. Turnbull promised that he would not make the place a sinecure. He had sent similar letters to professor Colin Maclaurin and Charles Erskine, the Solicitor General, and to the Lord Provost of Edinburgh, George Drummond – all of them Argathelians. Turnbull and Verner were surely among the men whom Erskine had been putting off.[97] By the end of that year, Turnbull had become a travelling tutor to the son of Wauchope of Niddry. In the end he took Anglican orders and lived in England.

By March 1728, James Kemp, the man appointed to the St Salvator's professorship of Greek in 1729, had almost certainly been recommended for the chair, which was not to include a commission as professor of divinity. Chandos sent a letter on to the Duke of Newcastle who then passed on his name to the King.[98] Nothing came of this because Ilay intervened to prevent Kemp's appointment as he clearly had done in the other cases. Writing the day after Newcastle had sent his letter to Chandos, Ilay said that the appointment had been handled in a slapdash manner which showed an ignorance of the realities of Scottish politics:

> I don't at all know this Kemp, whether he is a Minister, or even a Presbeterian, if he is not a Minister of the Church of Scotland, & that the exchange [with Scrymgeour] cannot be made, it may do more harm than the value of tenn such offices are worth, which makes it very well worthy of the consideration of the Kings Ministers: the having a professor of Divinity there agreeable to the Clergy I thought of that moment that I have not yet been able to recommend one against whom I could be sure there would be no objection, so that it is not any partiality of mine to any particular person which makes me offer these considerations, but since as I am informed to day the Duke of Chandos goes to morrow to Cambridg I should think it might be delayed till his return & by that time I shall be able to inform you who this Mr Kemp is.[99]

This was not a very clear letter, but the rebuke to those who had not consulted the Earl was clear enough. Ilay may not have had a partiality to a particular nominee at that time but he would have found that Kemp's father was a minister at Carnbee put in by heritors who were mostly Squadrone supporters if they voted with the chief heritors who all belonged to that party.

Another man named as a possible teacher for this chair was Glasgow's professor John Simson, whose friends claimed he had been offered the position but had turned it down. This would at least have got two problem clerics into one institution but the story is inherently implausible – which is not to say it is incorrect.[100] At least one other man was recommended in 1727. Someone named Johnson (?Johnston, Johnstoun) was nominated by the chancellor, the Duke of Chandos, perhaps acting for the masters. This nomination was rejected probably through Ilay's influence.[101] In the end, the chair went to the reverend Mr Archibald Campbell (24 July 1691–24 April 1756) on 17 December 1730. The University had had a decent interval to save for the rebuilding after the fire but little of the money saved seems to have gone for that end.

Campbell was the first of a better sort of appointee in the College. The son of an Edinburgh merchant who was a cadet of Campbell of Succoth, one of the principal tacksmen to the Dukes of Argyll, he was himself the minister of Larbert in Stirlingshire. This was a living to which the Crown appointed, which suggests that he was well connected before 1730.[102] He was offered the St Mary's post partly because he had written a book published by a man he presumed a friend until the book appeared under the friend's name and not anonymously or under his.[103] The 'friend' accepted a Church of England living bestowed on him by Peter King, the Lord Chancellor, who had admired Campbell's work. Those who had taken care of the friend, Alexander Innes, now sought to help the real author, Archibald Campbell. His candidacy was backed at Court by the Bishop of London, the Lord Chancellor, Sir Robert Walpole and others, including Lord Ilay, who said he had not met him as soon as the others named.[104] When Ilay did meet him, it seems to have been through an introduction from Dr Charles Stuart, the mutual friend of Ilay and the Duke of Chandos. Campbell fulsomely dedicated the second edition of his book to Ilay.[105] This and a sermon against enthusiasts (which Ilay would have applauded) ultimately got its author into trouble in 1735–6. His first book argued that self love is a motive for virtuous action, a position held in ancient philosophy by Epicureans and then currently supported by Bernard Mandeville.[106] The book seemed heretical. Campbell's sermon annoyed the local zealots.[107] Litigation over his views dragged on until 1738.

Campbell's appointment had not been quite so straightforward as it might seem. On 20 June 1730, Ilay wrote to an unnamed correspondent that Campbell ought to be given

> . . . an additional clause in the Commission constituting him also profes-
> sor of Divinity in the said University: The reason of this I mentioned in the
> Paper I left in Your Office, viz. Either to make the present lay professor
> accept of an exchange, or to serve as an expedient for the evil my Church
> complains of.[108]

This was done but it resulted neither in Scrymgeour's resignation nor
in Campbell's lecturing on divinity. In the very short run it likely
helped Ilay politically with those in the evangelical wing of the Kirk
who had been made suspicious by his defence of professor Simson
over the previous few years. In the long run it would have confirmed
their suspicions of both the Earl and the professor. Campbell lectured
twice a week, but not on theology, and in the end left a course of lectures in which history was used in the defence of Christianity. These
were posthumously published as *The Authenticity of the Gospel-
History Justified* (1759).

Campbell brought to St Andrews a more modern spirit which was,
like his politics, not relished by all his colleagues. John Ramsay of
Ochtertyre, himself something of an evangelical, summed up the professor's contribution to the life of the College by saying that he was a
kindly, popular and eloquent defender of orthodoxy and revelation
and that '. . . this gentleman was doubtless the first who gave a new
turn to taste and studies of the young men bred at St Andrews'.[109] By
that he meant that Campbell had them reading Shaftesbury, thinking
more critically and trying to reconcile their religious beliefs with
modern ideas as his own professor and friend, John Simson, had
taught him to do. Campbell was a Moderate in the Church and sat
for some years in the General Assembly, but his unpopularity with his
colleagues is shown by the fact that only once, in 1733, was he chosen
to be rector. He then beat professor Tullideph. The occasion was
marked by the burning of Calvin's works before the College gates, a
sure sign of Campbell's theological tastes and of those who sought to
keep him out of office.[110]

When Alexander Scrymgeour died in November 1732, the search
for a new professor of divinity began again. How the search proceeded
has not been found if any record now exists. Thomas Tullideph, the
minister of Markinch (the principal heritor there was the Earl of
Leven), was chosen as his replacement and installed on 17 October
1734. He would almost certainly have been approved by Ilay but the
delay between the former incumbent's death and Tullideph's appointment suggests that there had been others in the field and that this was
a complex business. Tullideph had been given the chair of divinity

almost certainly through the influence of the Squadrone faction, for whom he later served as a manager of ecclesiastical patronage, a role he shared with the reverend Mr Robert Wallace of Edinburgh.[111] This man too brought new ideas to the University. John Ramsay records that his preaching

> was rather of a philosophical than of a pathetic cast and [was] addressed more to the understanding than to the imagination. He indeed excelled in close reasoning, and in reconciling dark passages of Scripture; and that he was one of the best lecturers of his time.

Ramsay counted him among the Calvinists, among the Moderates, and among those who could not keep their temper – a fact which made him less popular with students and his colleagues than his learning and accomplishments deserved.[112] When he was elevated to the principality of St Leonard's in 1739, the College thanked Ilay for the appointment for which it had asked.[113] Ilay's help may have been given because the Earl was under attack by the Squadrone and needed to trim to stay in power. His brother, the 2nd Duke of Argyll, had gone into opposition to the government and Ilay sometimes had to placate opponents. This is likely to be a case in which he did so. So too was the appointment of Tullideph's replacement.

Andrew Shaw (?–27 November 1779), the minister of St Madois in the Carse of Gowrie and a former tutor to the Laird of Balmanno, was picked as the new professor of divinity. One of the three heritors in his parish was Craigie of Kilgraston.[114] Since Shaw sat in the General Assembly only for the years in which the Squadrone were in power in the 1740s (1742–5) – and not again for fifteen years, by which time Ilay was near the end of his career – he was undoubtedly sympathetic to the Squadrone interest and not to Ilay's. The appointment was quickly made. Tullideph resigned on 2 August and Shaw was appointed on 29 August 1739. That meant that, exclusive of the posting time, it took less than two weeks to get all the papers drawn and sealed in London and Edinburgh. This points to prior arrangements meant to cut out other applicants and leading to a quick warrant with a minimum of fuss. Shaw resembled his recently appointed colleagues although he was no match for them intellectually or in the mark he made on his College.[115]

Only two other appointments were made at St Mary's before the end of 1747. One went to Thomas Craigie (c. 1707–27 November 1751), who in 1741 became professor of Hebrew in succession to Hugh Warrender, a little over three years after Warrender resigned in

1738. Craigie's family had long supplied masters to St Andrews. Thomas Craigie was the son of the minister of St Monans, a nearby parish, and the grandson of Thomas Forrester, formerly principal of St Leonard's. Craigie was also a nephew of Robert Craigie, who served the Squadrone politicians as Lord Advocate from 1742 to 1746. Robert Craigie would have been able to secure a Crown appointment for a relative in the declining days of Robert Walpole's administration when it seemed inevitable that the end of 'Robinocracy' would also spell the end of Lord Ilay's power. Craigie was considered for an Edinburgh chair in 1746 and was later that year translated to Glasgow with the support of the Squadrone politicians and very likely that of Lord Cathcart.[116] Cathcart's patron, the Duke of Cumberland, in that year was denied nothing by Scots. In the first case, he was thought of as a mathematician, in the second as a philosopher; there is no indication that he was a good Hebraist.

The second appointment put James Murison (c. 1707–3 July 1779) into the principal's chair at St Mary's. Murison was from Kincardineshire and had worked his way south serving country parishes in Kincardine and Forfarshire. Ramsay of Ochtertyre described him as one whose

> learning, which had never been very great, was barely sufficient for the discharge of his duty. The lads, therefore sometimes made themselves merry with his slips in Latinity. But though he did not superabound in classical lore, he had an ample share of mother-wit and discretion, which made him be respected, if not admired.[117]

Murison would have had outside backing because the masters would not have recommended such a man, but who his sponsors were is unknown.

By the mid-1740s, St Mary's College had been considerably changed. Principal Hadow still remained but he was now old and Tullideph and Shaw had been doing his work since c. 1740, the last year in which Hadow served as rector. Tullideph and Campbell had reputations as modern preachers whose sermons displayed modern learning and politeness. Shaw seems little different in outlook. Their views were far from the Calvinism preached in Fife and taught in the College when Hadow came to office in 1699. The College also now had three functioning teachers – a relative novelty. All that had an impact on the arts colleges too. Again Tullideph was at the centre of changes.

Thomas Tullideph (1700–14 November 1777) became the principal of St Leonard's on 2 August 1739. His appointment brought into the College an active man quite unlike his predecessors. Indeed, when the appointment was being considered, professor Francis Pringle wrote about him and the College to Dr Charles Stuart, the aide of the Duke of Chandos and the friend of Lord Ilay:

> . . . Our Principal [Drew] is dead. It imports us greatly to have a Man of good Sence & Discretion for our Head, One that we know is capable to Support the office with Dignity, & is accustomed to live in a Social way.
>
> Such a One is our professor of Divinitie, Mr Thomas Tullideph, who I am glad to hear is not unknown to you. Him I would have you to promote Velis Remesqe, with Lord Ilay, Duke of Chandos, &c. And to employ all your gain'ly talents to make us for once happy.
>
> We have had a long and dreary trial (God forgive the Court) of one Countrie Minister after another at the head of our Affairs: and So has come on't. We have for the most part lived under a Cloud, or in Confusion.
>
> I would fain See better days, and before I quit the Stage, have the pleasure to behold us in a prosperous way.
>
> The man I have named is recommended by the Universitie to his Grace of Newcastle, to the Earl of Ilay, and to our beloved Chancellor the Duke of Chandos. And I, as a private man, recommend him to my own private, but publick-Spirited friend, whom god long preserve.[118]

Pringle and others who wrote to Ilay noted that they had 'been graciously heard on like occasions', a remark which implies more correspondence with Lord Ilay than now survives.[119] In the end, Pringle thanked Ilay for the appointment while complaining about Drew's 'Imbezzlement' of University and College funds.[120] Others were not so approving. George Logan, an Edinburgh minister, sent a memorial to Lord Milton which expressed his and very likely professor Archibald Campbell's opposition to the appointment.[121] They were two Argathelians slanging a man whose friends were in the Squadrone camp.[122]

Tullideph had had a varied career and had seen a bit of the world. The grandson of the earlier Principal Tullideph, he had attended Edinburgh c. 1715 and then possibly served as a mercenary soldier in Sweden. He may also have been in business in Edinburgh for a short time.[123] He qualified as a minister in 1726/7.[124] By marriage he was related to the family of the Earls of Rothes and to several lots of ministers in Fife and the Lothians. While not a notable scholar, he was a worthy and welcome successor to Joseph Drew who, compared with him, seems like a man from another age. Tullideph was an active administrator who got things done. In his first year at St Leonard's he refloored part of the building, repaired stairs, had windows and sashes replaced and the building harled. Within a year he had issued new rules for the bursars and given new feus to some tenants who found themselves paying a bit more.[125] He tried to collect old debts and searched the records for sources of money. His long tenure in office continued in this way. By 1769 he had raised College revenues by £340 per annum since the Union of 1747; they were even higher by the time of his death in 1777.[126] But, like others before him, he became autocratic and ill-tempered and was, in the end, not well liked by either his colleagues or the students.

Notes

1 Wodrow, *Analecta*, ed. Leishman, 1853, II:58, 332, 421f, 438f.
2 If this is the right Syme, then his birth date would likely have been c. 1660. If this is the case, then he likely attended Marischal College where in 1677 a 'Joannes Sim' appears in a list of students paying chamber mails. Syme, like many others, might have put off preparing for the ministry until after 1689 and the restoration of Presbyterianism. His matriculation at St Mary's College in 1693 need not be the date on which he first entered upon his studies. Indeed, he might well have stayed on in Aberdeen where there was a respected teacher of Hebrew, Patrick Gordon of King's College. Had he entered on the seven-year course in c. 1689, he would have been just finishing when he was appointed to the Hebrew chair. That would make sense of the fact that in 1696 Syme seems still to have been studying divinity. Scott, *Fasti*, VII:425; *Records of the Marischal College and University of Aberdeen*, ed. Anderson, 1893, II:247.
3 His work was increased about a month later when he was made collector of the College's rents and charged to prepare a state of affairs for the Visitation of the College which occurred that year. Minutes, 11 February 1697, 27 December 1698, SAUL, UYUY 452/2.
4 Tullibardine, the chancellor, was asked to expedite the granting of his patent on 16 August 1697 and was told that the 'University are thinking seriously on one to be Second Master'. Minutes, 16 August 1697, SAUL, UYUY 452/1.
5 He is mentioned with approval by Wodrow, *Analecta*, ed. Leishman, 1853, II:284; see also Scott, *Fasti*, VII:421; Wright, 'James Hadow', ODNB, 24:434f.
6 'A Catalogue of Books', SAUL, UYLY 105/3/29–30. James Hadow's known purchases ran to controversial divinity, books on ancient languages and Dr Christopher Irvine's book on Scottish place names.
7 Scott, *Fasti*, VII:421; Hadow, 'Hadow Pedigree', SAUL, 37862/10; Wright, 'James Hadow', ODNB, 24:434f.

8 MacLeod, *Scottish Theology Edinburgh*, 1974, p. 144. An account of his theology can be found in Lachman, *The Marrow Controversy*, 1988, pp. 170–7, 207–35. There is additional information on Hadow's appointments in the St Andrews Presbytery Minutes, Ch2/1132/1. I thank Dr Anne Skoczylas for this information.

9 Black became Moderator of the General Assembly in 1721. The best indicator of Black's theological interests is his editing of Halyburton's *Ten Sermons* (1723). He himself was the author of *A Meditation or Sililoquy on the Soul* (Glasgow, 1743), a work which formed part of the 'Awakening' of that time.

10 The principal land-owner in Halyburton's parish was the Earl of Crawford, who had been involved in other appointments.

11 Minutes, 27 February 1707, SAUL, UY 452/2. I thank Anne Skoczylas for this reference.

12 Scott, *Fasti*, IV:231.

13 Despite this gloomy prediction, Hadow was chosen and did sit.

14 Hadow to Carstares, 26 March 1707, in *HMC Report of the Laing MSS*, ed. Paton, 1925, II:141; the original of this letter is at the NAS and differs slightly from the printed version in spelling, capitalisations and added italics.

15 Carstares to Mar, 19 April 1707, Mar and Kellie Papers, NAS, GD124/15/532/1.

16 There is more on the politics of Black's failed appointment in the St Andrews Presbytery Minutes for 14 May 1707, 30 July 1707, 19 November 1707 to March 1708, Ch2/1132/1. These exist at St Andrews and on microfilm at the NAS. I thank Anne Skoczylas for these references.

17 Minutes, 5 April 1708, SAUL, UY452/2. In 1707, several bursaries at St Andrews were converted to the support of the ecclesiastical history chair with the support of William Carstares; see Principal Hadow to Carstares, 2 June 1707, EUL, Dk.1.1.[2]. I thank John Cairns for this reference.

18 William Carstares to Mar, 23 December 1708, NAS, GD124/15/796/4.

19 Colonel Alexander Monypenny, when asking Henry Dundas for this place for a friend on 28 November 1790, said that the professorship 'was instituted about the time of the union to make a pension for Mr Patk. Haldane'. SAUL, Melville MS 4440.

20 John Haldane, MP, was a prominent member of the Squadrone faction in the last Scottish Parliament and was present and voted Yes to the First Article and for the ratification of the Treaty, as did almost all members of this faction. Riley, *The Union of England and Scotland*, 1978, p. 334.

21 Hadow to Principal Stirling, 16 March 1708, Stirling Letters, GUL, Gen 204/1/95.

22 The date roughly coincides with the appointment of Haldane to the ecclesiastical history chair and of Syme's visit to London.

23 Grange to Mar, 4 December 1708, in HMC Manuscripts of the Earl of Mar and Kellie, ed. Paton, 1904, I:477.

24 M. A. Stewart, 'Thomas Halyburton', ODNB, 24:732f. Halyburton had been a classmate of Thomas Aikenhead and in his Memoirs tells how attractive he too had once found sceptical and heretical ideas.

25 Memoirs of Halyburton, ed. Watson, Edinburgh and London, n.d., p. 223.

26 Wodrow, [?] May 1713. Analecta, ed. Leishman, 1853, II:197f. Margaret Forrester was almost certainly related to a previous principal of St Mary's. Chalmers' wife was the daughter of George Campbell, the Edinburgh divinity professor. The orthodox intended to keep control of the seminaries 'in the family', which also ensured that the colleges would generally speak with one voice. Scrymgeour's appointment was an affront to more than local men.

27 Ibid., II:197f. Principal Ramsay and other masters who had supported him for this post in 1707 were likely to be still in his corner. See Skoczylas, 'The Regulation of Academic Society', Scottish Historical Review, 2004, pp. 171–95.

28 There were no formal requirements for the chair of divinity save that of being proficient in the subject. Proficiency could be inferred from ordination, which involved trials, or from having a degree in the subject. The Presbytery's objections to Scrymgeour did not cite any requirement but quarrelled with his degree, which they held to be irregularly granted and not granted by men sincerely members of the Kirk. I thank Dr Anne Skoczylas for this information.

29 Officers and Graduates of University and King's College Aberdeen, ed. Anderson, 1893, p. 99.

30 William Dunlop to Andrew Dunlop, n.d. [autumn 1718], GUL, Gen 83. There is with these a disordered typescript of the letters: 'Transcripts of Thirty Six Letters Passing Between Professor William Dunlop and Professor Alexander Dunlop, Glasgow, 1715–1720.'

31 Alexander Scrymgeour to Charles Erskine, [?] April 1727, Scrymgeour MSS, NAS, GD137/1105. Scrymgeour may only have been seeking to enhance his son's chance of gaining this living.

32 Wodrow left scattered accounts of this case beginning in Analecta, II:197f.

33 HMS Report on the Laing Manuscripts, ed. Paton, 1914, II:17f; Skoczylas, 'The Regulation of Academic Society', Scottish Historical Review, 2004, passim.

34 Skocyzlas, 'The Regulation of Academic Society', Scottish Historical Review, 2004, pp. 171–95, passim.

35 Cant, University, 2002, p. 100.

36 Skoczylas, 'The Regulation of Academic Society', *Scottish Historical Review*, 2004, p. 181.

37 Lenman, *The Jacobite Risings in Britain*, 1980, pp. 150–2.

38 Croft Dickinson, *Two Students*, 1952, pp. xlv–xlvi.

39 Her husband is not known to have attended. I thank Anne Skoczylas for this information.

40 Croft Dickinson, *Two Students*, 1952, p. xlv.

41 Professor William Dunlop of Edinburgh to Robert Wodrow, 1713; cited in Croft Dickinson, *Two Students*, 1952, p. xlivf. See also, *Edinburgh Christian Instructor*, 25 (1840), p. 740, and Wodrow, *Analecta*, ed. Leishman, 1853, III:50.

42 Mackenzie, 'George Martine, M.D., F.R.S. (1700–1741)', *Journal of Thermal Analysis*, 1989, pp. 1823–36, 1823f; Croft Dickinson, *Two Students*, 1952, pp. xlix–li.

43 The St Andrews statement can be found in NAS, SP54/7/99.

44 Minutes, 12 May 1716, 27 August 1717, SAUL, UYUY 452/2.

45 The Commission, like those at Aberdeen and Glasgow, was packed with Squadrone men. It included Atholl, Montrose, Rothes, Haddington, Leven, Lord Haddo, Lord James Murray, Lord Edward Murray, Adam Cockburn, Andrew Hume of Kimmerghame, Sir Francis Grant of Cullen, Sir Alexander Ogilvie of fforglen, Sir Walter Pringle of Newhall, Sir David Dalrymple, Sir John Anstruther, Sir William Hope of Balcomie, Sir Peter Hacket [Halket] of Pitferran, Sir John Weems of Bogie, Sir Robert Anstruther of Balcaskie, Solicitor General Robert Dundas, Mr Robert Hay of Naughton, John Haldane of Gleneagles, Mungo Haldane of Gleneagles, Patrick Haldane of Gleneagles, Alexander Duncan of Lundie, John Drummond of Megginch, Dr Douglas of Kinglassie, Major Archibald —— of Tarrit, Principal John Stirling of Glasgow, William Hamilton, professor of divinity at Edinburgh, and the ministers James Ramsay, Patrick Clow, Adam Ferguson of Logierait, James Henry, William Mitchell and James Smith, any seven of whom were to form a quorum.

46 Croft Dickinson, *Two Students*, 1952, p. li. At Aberdeen, where the involvement in the Rebellion of masters at both colleges had been flagrant, men were deposed and the colleges filled with Whigs from the south.

47 Pringle to John Mackenzie of Delvine, NLS, 1423/46.

48 Minutes, 24 January 1719, SAUL, UYUY 452/3.

49 Minutes, 19 June 1705, SAUL, UYUY 452/2.

50 He was one of the examiners for Dr John Arbuthnot in 1696; Minutes, 3 August 1696, SAUL, UYUY 452/1.

51 Many of them and their students are recorded in *Eighteenth Century Medics*, compiled by Wallis and Wallis, 1988.

52 Minutes, 10 March 1715, SAUL, UYUY 452/2.

53 Minutes, 6 April 1715, SAUL, UYUY 452/2. The Dr Hay in question
    was likely to have been John Hay, MD of King's College, Aberdeen
    (1701) and FRCPE (1702), who, according to the Wallises, had prob-
    ably been practising in Letham, Fife. *Eighteenth Century Medics*, com-
    piled by Wallis and Wallis, 1988, p. 275.

54 Dr Charles Stuart was a sort of in-house intellectual for the Duke and
    later in his career was much with Lord Ilay, an age-mate, who found
    him good company. They may have been students together in Holland.
    As Chandos's assistant, Stuart was involved in the varied activities
    which concerned the Duke as a businessman. For a glimpse of the range
    of his interests, see Stewart, *The Rise of Public Science*, 1992, pp. 361–
    81.

55 Coutts, *History*, 1909, pp. 214, 253ff.

56 What is known of the foundation of this chair is told in Anderson, 'The
    Princely Chandos and the University of St Andrews', *Scottish Historical
    Review*, 1895, pp. 41–70, and in the surviving University Minutes for
    1720–1.

57 I thank R. N. Smart for providing me with a partial list of the known
    degree recipients 1696–1747 and for tallies by year for the period 1748
    to 1810. The list of degree recipients recorded by Peter and Ruth Wallis
    is certainly incomplete but lists well over 200 recipients for the eigh-
    teenth century and has miscellaneous information about many of them.
    The Wallises' valuable volume probably records less than half of the
    Scottish medics of the time.

58 Anderson, 'Princely Chandos', *Scottish Historical Review*, 1895,
    p. 60f.

59 Minutes, 5 December 1721, SAUL, UYUY 452/3.

60 A minute of 1764 notes that Simson was 'elected by the Rectors <u>Casting
    Vote</u>' and that his opponents were related by blood to unnamed pro-
    fessors. Minutes, 18 July 1764, SAUL, UYUY 452/27.

61 Transcript Minutes of the RCPE, Library of the RCPE. I thank Dr
    Andrew Cunningham for this information. See also Underwood,
    Boerhaave's Men, 1977, p. 140.

62 *Officers and Graduates of University and King's College Aberdeen*, ed.
    Anderson, 1893, p. 225.

63 Col. —— Erskine to Allan Logan, Minister in Culross, 11 October
    1721, NAS, GD124/15/1214/14.

64 For details of this appointment, see below, p. 426.

65 Archibald Campbell to [?], 29 January 1733, NAS, SP54/22/1A; Ilay to
    [?Charles Delafaye], 19 February 1733, NAS, SP54/22/17; Minutes, 29
    January 1733, 20 April 1733, SAUL, UYUY 452/4.

66 Young, *St Andrews*, 1969, p. 208.

67 Croft Dickinson, *Two Students*, 1952, pp. xlv, 58. The election of 1715
    saw Patrick Haldane returned unopposed in a contest in which the

Jacobite and Tories had been more or less forced from the field. In 1715, Dundee, Perth and St Andrews, three of the five burghs, were centres of Jacobite strength, which more accurately gauged the political sentiments of the area; *The House of Commons 1690–1715*, ed. Cruickshanks, Handley and Hayton, 2002, II:930f, and *The House of Commons 1715–1754*, ed. Sedgwick, 1970, I:403f.

68 Earl of Rothes to [?], n.d. [1727], PRO, SP54/18/84. Rothes was his former student. I thank Andrew Cunningham for a copy of this letter.

69 Hadow to [?], 5 December 1727, PRO SP54/18/53/a–b. 53b is a 'Memorial' addressed to Newcastle saying that Gregory was willing to sell his post to John Arnot, son to Dr Hugh Arnot, 'a Physician in our Neighbourhood, who is neither yet of standing or Character for the Office'.

70 If Rothes knew the age of the boy, this is an extraordinary act and without parallel in the whole period covered by this survey. Rothes to [?], n.d. [1727], PRO, SP54/18/84. I thank Andrew Cunningham for a transcript of this letter.

71 A. G. Stewart, *Academic Gregories*, 1901, pp. 88–91.

72 Minutes, 1 August 1738, SAUL, UYUY 452/4.

73 An attempt was made by the Argathelians to allow him to resume teaching in 1726 but it came to nothing. 'Memorial for Doctor Alexander Scrymgeour', Scrymgeour Wedderburn Muniments, NAS, GD137/2160, GD137/3301, GD137/1102–6.

74 Scots lived too long with the assurances of a faith felt but not defended on rational or historical grounds. By mid-century it showed in the shallowness of Moderate theology. This tended to ignore the claims of historical Christianity and preferred a glib, but inadequate, philosophy which was wholly destroyed by David Hume, whose historical critiques were in the long run equally devastating.

75 The foregoing relies on the entries for Mungo and Patrick Haldane contained in *The House of Commons 1715–1754*, ed. Sedgwick, II:94–6. See also Scott, *Fasti*, VII:431. In 1763, Haldane was still in receipt of a 'Scotch pension' of £400; 'State of the Scottish Revenues, 1763', uncatalogued manuscript in the Stuart Mackenzie Papers at Mount Stuart House.

76 Letters of William and Andrew Dunlop, GUL, Gen 83, letter 2.

77 Minutes, 7 December 1720, SAUL, UYUY 452/3.

78 'I have endeavour'd to speak in favour of [Carmichael's] other son, but I find Earle rothes engadged for Mr duncan professor of philosophy in St Andrews to be professor of Languages there.' Only this chair was then on offer. Earl of Hyndford to Principal John Stirling, 31 March 1720, Stirling Letters in Murray, GUL, Gen 650.II.

79 Some matriculants wished only to be members of the University and were not students in the faculties they joined. For a divinity student to

study medicine generally meant he expected to have a parish. This seems a bit remote from Johnstoun's likely expectation of a career.

80 Scott, *Fasti*, VII:426; Brock, *Scotus Americanus*, 1982, p. 182; Max R. Williams, 'Gabriel Johnston', DAB, 12:149–51.

81 James Hadow to [?], 11 March 1728, PRO, SP54/19/15. I thank Andrew Cunningham for a copy of this letter.

82 Warrender was a friend and classmate of Sir Andrew Mitchell, the Squadrone MP and secretary to the Marquis of Tweeddale, the leader of that faction in the late 1730s and 1740s. Warrender throughout his life enjoyed the favour and protection of Mitchell and his employers: Patrick Murdock to John Forbes of Culloden, 16 May 1754, *Culloden Papers*, ed. R. H. Duff, 1815, p. 311.

83 Ilay to Newcastle, NAS, SP54/19/28.

84 Minutes, 3 April 1738, SAUL, UYUY 452/24.

85 Scott, *Fasti*, VII:426.

86 The fire of 17 January 1727 burned the Public Schools, Refectory, Haldane's quarters and some student chambers, resulting in damage assessed at £505 15s 8d. The University hoped that the salary from Haldane's post could be used for a year to partly defray the costs of repair; other funds they hoped to obtain from the Crown out of the Bishop's rents and the Royal Bounty. The buildings were never fully repaired. 'Petition of the Principal and professors of St Mary's College', 4 October 1731, Lee Papers, NLS, 3431; James Hadow to Lord Townshend, 20 January 1727, NAS, SP54/18/4.

87 'Memorial for Doctor Alexander Scrymgeour Professor of Divinity in the New College of St Andrews' [by Duncan Forbes and Charles Erskine], 14 July 1726, Scrymgeour Papers, NAS, GD137/2160.

88 Francis Gray's 'Memorial for the Presberty of St Andrews', 26 October 1726, Lee Papers, NLS, 3431/5; Lawrence Craigie to Alexander Scrymgeour, 10 November 1726, Scrymgeour MSS, SRO, GD137/1102; Robert Craigie to Scrymgeour, 26 January 1727, NAS, GD137/1106; Lawrence Craigie to Scrymgeour, 2 December 1726, NAS, GD137/1103.

89 Charles Erskine to Scrymgeour, 28 April 1727, NAS, GD137/1104, 1106.

90 Wodrow, *Analecta*, ed. Leishman, 1815, IV:409.

91 Scrymgeour to Erskine, [?] April 1727, NAS, GD137/1105.

92 David Scrymgeour passed advocate on 7 July 1731.

93 Minutes, 26 January 1727, SAUL, UYUY 452/4; James Hadow to [?Ilay], 26 January 1727, NAS, SP54/18/4.

94 Minutes, 24 March 1727, SAUL, UYUY 452/4.

95 See the section on the appointment to the chair of moral philosophy at Glasgow in 1729–30, p. 96.

96 —— Verner to Robert Wodrow, 5 November 1728, NLS, Wodrow Quarto Letters, XVIII/181.

97 George Turnbull to Mackie, 23 January 1727; [?] March 1728, EUL, MS La.II 91.

98 Newcastle to Chandos, 27 June 1728, PRO, SP54/19/35.

99 PRO, SP54/19/36. I thank Dr Andrew Cunningham for a copy of this letter.

100 Skoczylas, *Mr Simson's Knotty Case*, 2001, p. 328.

101 Ilay to [?] 28 June 1728, PRO SP5419/36. I thank Andrew Cunningham for a copy of this and other PRO letters cited below.

102 Scott, *Fasti*, VII:432; ODNB, 9:733f.

103 Wodrow, *Analecta*, ed. Leishman, 1853, IV:182; Alexander Innes was a dodgy fellow who had been in scrapes before. See Skoczylas, 'The Regulation of Academic Society in Early Eighteenth-Century Scotland', *Scottish Historical Review*, 2004, pp. 171–95.

104 Ilay to Milton, 25 July 1730, NLS, 16542/55.

105 Archibald Campbell, *Enquiry into the Original of Moral Virtue*, 2nd rev. edn, Edinburgh, 1733.

106 Francis Hutcheson, also an admirer of Shaftesbury, thought of Campbell as an Epicurean. McCosh, *The Scottish Philosophy*, 1875, p. 90.

107 McCosh, *The Scottish Philosophy*, 1980, p. 89f; Skoczylas, *Mr Simson's Knotty Case*, 2001, p. 336; J. V. Price, 'Archibald Campbell' in the *Dictionary of Eighteenth-Century British Philosophers*, I:171–4. In 1739, after his case had ended, Campbell again recognised his debt to the Argathelians by dedicating to the 2nd Duke of Argyll *The Necessity of Revelation or an Enquiry into the Human Powers with respect to Matters of Religion especially those two fundamental Articles The Being of God and the Immortality of the Soul* (London, 1739). The Duke was described as having 'a Character universally confess'd Illustrious'.

108 Ilay to [?], probably the Under Secretary of State, Charles Delafaye, who served the Duke of Newcastle], 20 June 1730, PRO, SP54/20/22.

109 Ramsay, *Scotland and Scotsmen*, ed. Allardyce, 1888, I:268.

110 John Ramsay of Ochtertyre, 'Manuscript Memoirs', NLS, 1635/635.

111 Robert Wallace to Tweeddale, 5 June 1744; Thomas Tullideph to Tweeddale, 9 June 1744, Yester Papers, NLS 7062/75, 89. Both letters thank the Marquis for their chaplaincies.

112 Ramsay, *Scotland and Scotsmen*, ed. Allardyce, 1888, I:265f. Ramsay's comment about his philosophising should be read as meaning that he, like Campbell, stressed morality in his preaching.

113 Minutes, 16 October 1738, 6 June 1739, SAUL, UYUY 452/4.

114 Scott, *Fasti*, VII:429; *The Statistical Account*, ed. Witherington and Grant, 1983, XI:551.

115 Ramsay, *Scotland and Scotsmen*, ed. Allardyce, 1888, I:269.

116 They had been behind his Edinburgh nomination. D. B. Horn Papers, EUL, Gen. 1824, 'History of the Chair of Mathematics'.

117 Ramsay, *Scotland and Scotsmen*, ed. Allardyce, 1888, I:269.

118 'Commonplace Book of Francis Pringle,' SAUL, LF1111.P81C99, p. 148.
119 Ibid.; Minutes, 16 October 1738, SAUL, UYUY 452/4.
120 'Commonplace Book of Francis Pringle', pp. 148, 155f.
121 Campbell himself had probably sought the post, since he is named as the likely successor to it in a letter of Robert Laurie to Charles Erskine, 29 May 1739, Erskine-Murray Papers, NLS, 5074.
122 George Logan to Milton, 16 November 1738, NLS, 16574/208. Tullideph was said to have been opposed by one member of St Mary's; that would be Campbell, the likely source of Logan's information. Minutes, 16 October 1738.
123 One of Tullideph's commonplace books survives at St Andrews with entries from 1717 to 9 September 1727. It shows him to have been reading Locke, Samuel Clarke, Bishop Wilkins, Jean LeClerc, some of the Boyle Lecturers, Antony Collins and a number of Scottish historians and poets. He belonged to a 'Society for collecting Scots poems'. That almost certainly put him in the circle of the principal collector of those years, Allan Ramsay, who in turn was associated with both James Thomson and David Mallet. 'Commonplace Book of Thomas Tullideph 1717', SAUL, LF1109.T8C6. An Edinburgh burgess ticket for a Thomas Tullideph was issued on 14 February 1724.
124 Scott, *Fasti*, VII:413f; IV:204f; see also the character of him given by John Ramsay of Ochtertyre, *Scotland and Scotsmen*, ed. Allardyce, 1888, I:265f.
125 Minutes of St Leonard's College, 2 August, 10 September, 12 October, 9 November, 21 December 1739; 4 January, 8 February 1740, SAUL, UYUYSL 400.
126 United College Minutes, 12 May 1769 and 12 May 1779, SAUL, UYUC 400/3. One reason for the increases was the sale of property. The College also realised £54 1s 6d from the sale of old silver in Edinburgh; United College Minute, 20 July 1754. It sold superiorities and property in 1763, 1765, 1779 and 1789 amounting to £1,409, and another £400 was realised from the sale of the buildings of St Leonard's College to Robert Watson, who turned them into a boarding house. United College Minutes, 30 March 1763, 16 December 1765, 3 June 1769, 24 December 1771, 17 February 1772, 13 December 1779, [?] July 1781, 5 August 1789, 1 October 1789, 26 December 1789, SAUL UYUC 400/1–6. These sales yielded over £1,863 and some annual feu duties to increase the annual revenues by at least £85.

15

THE UNTOLD STORY

෭

1. ASPIRATIONS AND DISAPPOINTMENTS

The impression of the University given in the story of its appointments so far does not do justice to its accomplishments during this period. St Andrews was not so lively a place as expanding and changing Glasgow or Edinburgh but it was not altogether dull and lifeless. It aspired to keeping up with its competitors though it failed to do so.

William Vilant and James Preston, its humanists in 1699, 'offered to the University ane overture, That the University by their act would be pleased to Warrant and allow them to teach Lessons of history and Romi antiquity to all the Students in the several societies Hoping that it may tend to the splendour and flourishing of their University and advancement of Learning therin And for that effect to recommend it to the several professors of philosophie to encourage their student to attend s^d Lessons.' After a day to think it over, the University approved.[1] This was not an unprecedented initiative; classicists had been teaching history as background to the Latin and Greek courses since the 1500s. It was also not an initiative about which more is heard, but Preston, the St Leonard's humanist, did publish a *History of the World from the Creation to the Birth of Abraham* (1701) which may have been a partial by-product of this aspiration. The effort to establish history teaching should also be seen in the context of what other colleges were doing. In Holland and elsewhere on the continent, aspiring lawyers and polite gentlemen took such courses. Glasgow had employed William Jameson in a lectureship in civil and ecclesiastical history by 1692 and in Edinburgh the humanist had the right to give such lectures. Extramural teachers of history were associated with John Spottiswoode's teaching of law at about the same time.[2] The St Andrews humanists were making a bid to be fashionable and to keep up with the competition. How long their efforts lasted is unknown but two students from around 1712–16 were reading some classical history, although not in many modern compends.[3]

St Andrews was the first of the Scottish colleges to require Greek and to teach it with a specialist professor as the Kirk and Visitation Commission had mandated.[4] Its first Grecian, Francis Pringle, was not a publishing scholar.[5] Unlike the other university towns, St Andrews had no printers in his day. The University, aware of trends in humanity and a leader in the teaching of Greek, was as quick as other colleges to teach French. While no lecturer was appointed until the 1790s, there was a room assigned to a French teacher at St Leonard's College in 1695. Someone was teaching French in 1708, and 1727. In 1728 a M. Buerd gave lessons. This is earlier than the appearance of similar men in other universities where such teachers could find a market in the towns and not just in the colleges. If the St Andrews teachers taught townies, they were likely to have done so in college rooms.[6] It is unclear if this continued without interruption until the 1790s.

Similar signs of interest in modern learning can be found in most other subjects. St Andrews had shown concerns with science from at least 1668, when James Gregory I was appointed to the newly founded chair of mathematics. His teaching had been continued by his successor, William Sanders, who earlier had assisted Gregory in experiments related to polemics against George Sinclair.[7] James Gregory II, for a brief while, sustained the introduction of the 'new science', which in his case meant not Copernican and Galilean theories but Newtonianism, as can be seen from still-extant St Andrews theses of 1690.[8] Thomas Reid was acquainted with this older relative with whom he talked about the 1690s. He thought James Gregory II had introduced Newtonianism to the Scottish universities but that seems more based on family pride than on the reality.[9]

James Gregory's half-brother, Charles, taught practical mathematics and Newtonian physics after 1708. His courses, like those of James Gregory II at Edinburgh, included modern mixed mathematics and algebra to a higher level than seems to have been taught earlier. Charles is likely to have used Whiston's text based on the Cambridge lectures of Sir Isaac Newton.[10] In geometry, the texts he used considered problems in gunnery and fortification which would have been of interest to boys heading toward military careers. Charles Gregory's physics, like that of the regents of his time, came from the books standard in the Scottish colleges – John Keill's *Introductio ad verum physicam* (1718) and Samuel Clarke's edition of Rohault's *Physics* (1697), famous for its footnote refutations of Cartesianism.[11] This Newtonian curriculum was taught at least from the time of Gregory's appointment in 1708 and was supplemented by the teaching of regents like Alexander Scrymgeour. The introduction of Newtonianism at St Andrews was probably earlier than at Glasgow and Marischal College, contemporary with its introduction at King's College, and may have been antedated only at Edinburgh where another Gregory was among the first to teach Newton's ideas in mathematics and physics.

To support the teaching of the new science, instruments were essential, especially those for an astronomer or a regent teaching natural philosophy using experiments. Like the other universities in Scotland, St Andrews expanded its instrument collection and did so earlier than Glasgow, Edinburgh or King's College, Aberdeen, but not as early as Marischal College. James Gregory I, in 1673, raised money for the purchase of instruments by begging at Kirk doors after the Sunday services.[12] Judging by what he bought in 1673, he was quite successful.[13]

James Gregory I had a twelve-foot-long refracting telescope taking a three-inch lens. It was probably bought in 1673 along with other smaller ones. He used these in an observatory which was completed in 1677 but which became derelict and was razed in 1736.[14] Gregory had three clocks, including one which beat thirds of seconds. These were fine astronomical clocks that would have been used to time observations yielding data which could then be compared with that gathered elsewhere. They would have been set to local time using the sundials he also possessed. He had astrolabes which would probably have been used to teach navigation, just as his circumferentor would have enabled the boys to survey land with accuracy. An armillary sphere would have allowed the boys to visualise the reasons why the seasons changed and to understand the motions of the earth, moon and sun. Also likely to have been bought by James Gregory I was 'ye Machina Boiliana' which needed repairs in 1697. This was likely used in the experiments which Gregory and William Sanders conducted in the 1670s. Their experiments would also have required thermometers and barometers. Another item held with these things in the Library was a complicated glass thermometer which was broken by the students of Mr Arrot. They had gone to the Library to witness experiments performed by him. Since Arrot had resigned by 1705, experimental teaching by regents had begun before that date. At that time the Library contained a 'brass horizontal Dyal' which may have also been Gregory's.

The eighteenth-century minutes books contain numerous references to the clocks, the air pump and other instruments and scientific specimens held in the Library. The clocks were regularly repaired. To the collection kept in the Library were added, by 1714, globes, a quadrant, and other devices to measure angles. Interest in different aspects of Newtonianism is shown by the prisms, magnets and capillary tubes. There was now a microscope. The surveying instruments included surveyors' staffs and chains. The skeleton of the University's former carrier, who had died a suicide in 1707, also graced the hall. The man had been publicly anatomised for the boys by Mr Arnot, a local surgeon. He was then boiled and his cleaned bones were articulated and displayed in a glass case.[15]

In 1714, the University issued an appeal for funds which were to be spent partly on 'an annual Course of Experimental Philosophy in the University'.[16] The 'Proposals' show the masters' awareness of the need to catch up with the other colleges, which about this time had begun similar collections and courses.[17] Unfortunately, this seems not to have resulted in much improvement in the instrument collection. A similar proposal was issued c. 1725 when the colleges again sought to improve their collection of instruments and to use them in an annual course.[18] Courses of experiments are not heard of after 1714 or 1727, which probably means the University never raised enough money to mount courses or courses of any sophistication. One thing that probably came from the effort to raise funds was the fixing of the teaching of natural philosophy to one regent in each college by 1727.[19] This would have made sense since one master would then have been in constant charge of the instruments. Both arts colleges had instrument rooms, although we do not know what they contained. The contents of both probably went to the University Library on the creation of the United College. The things in St Leonard's are known to have done so.[20]

The old observatory might have been in ruins in 1736, but in that year the University decided to buy a new reflecting telescope from James Short of Edinburgh at a cost of £25.[21] St Andrews men were probably preparing to observe the annular eclipse of the sun which occurred on 18 February 1737 and which Scots were well positioned to track. Colin Maclaurin, who observed the event and organised others to do so, is likely to have recommended Short. Charles Gregory and David Young used the University's telescopes and clocks to observe the eclipse and sent a report of their observations to Maclaurin, who forwarded pertinent details from it to the Royal Society of London.[22] The new telescope joined older instruments mounted in or on the Library.[23] Maclaurin also had a hand in the improvement of the University's equipment.[24] In 1741, Short offered, and the University accepted, a free upgrade for the newest telescope. The addition was 'a contrivance for finding the planets & some of the fixt Stars in day-light'.[25] Later, the long gallery of the Library had a meridian line inscribed on its floor and a trident was set at a distance on Scoonie Hill where there was another meridan marker.[26]

The new science included much more than mathematics, astronomy and physics and instruments devoted to the study of these fields. As early as the 1680s, local virtuosi, including some who taught at the University, were in contact with men in the Oxford Philosophical Society and the Royal Society of London.[27] Here, as elsewhere in Scotland, the virtuosi thought about a range of things included in natural and civil history.[28] There may even have been an ephemeral virtuoso club in St Andrews, since an effort had been made to establish groups in provincial centres and put them in contact with the Royal Society of London.[29] Men like the Gregorys already knew many in London. On his trip to Paris (probably in the 1690s), James Gregory II was to see the naturalist Joseph Pitton de Tournefort and the King's physician, Guy Crescent Fagon.[30] In Patrick Blair, a Dundee man, the region had a medical man who hoped to carry out a natural history survey of the area. Surveys were everywhere in Europe, one of the first signs of an interest in improvements and science as the means leading to them. Blair was in touch with London naturalists like Sir Hans Sloane and James Petiver. He contributed things to their collections; they patronised him and promoted his work.[31] The University, on 23 January 1714, gave Blair a general 'Recommendation' which, it hoped, would facilitate his work. Unfortunately, he was a Jacobite who became involved in '15. He was lucky not to have been executed or exiled in its aftermath.

The University Library held curiosities and natural historical objects related to the interests of men like Blair. Indeed, it probably looked a bit like a virtuoso's cabinet. In 1700 the principal of St Leonard's showed the members of the Senate some 'lopes Asbestos[,] A petrified Shell and some of the liny incombustibill and some fragments of petrified shells which he had received from My Lord pittmeddan.' These were ordered to be listed in 'the Catalouges' by the Bibliothecar.[32] What else was in the catalogues, one can only guess, but contemporary cabinets such as that of Robert Wodrow may offer clues.[33] The dream of doing more in natural history and the sciences and of keeping up with competitors must at least partly have motivated the effort to create a medical chair in 1715 and the determination to do so a few years later.

In civil and ecclesiastical history, St Andrews was not much behind other places. The most notable St Andrews antiquary of the late seventeenth century was George Martine of Cleremont (1635–1712). Martine was a Jacobite and Episcopalian, but that did not prevent him from dealing with more Whiggish antiquaries like Robert Wodrow, who had the perusal of Martine's *Reliquiæ divi Andreæ, or the State of the Venerable See of St Andrews* (1683). Copies of this royalist Jacobite work circulated in manuscript until its publication in 1797.[34] Martine was not unique. Sir Robert Sibbald of Kipps wrote a good chorography of Fife. He was a man whose many other historical projects, like the projects he urged friends to undertake, were useful to later scholars throughout the Scottish Enlightenment. His chief Edinburgh rival, Dr Archibald Pitcairne, also from a Fifeshire family, was interested in history and antiquities. So too were David and James Gregory II. Martine, Sibbald, Pitcairne and others in various ways connected the University and the burgh to the world of the virtuosi. This did not change until c. 1740, when the virtuosi themselves were becoming less international and less generalist in their outlooks.

The philosophy taught at St Andrews up to c. 1730 does not seem more archaic than that dictated to students elsewhere. Indeed, there were signs besides James Gregory's theses of 1690 that some masters believed the scholasticism still being taught was outmoded and inadequate.[35] By 1735 that was even clear to some students. A student named James Playfair protested against the futility of the philosophy courses, which he described as 'useless' and scholastic. He recommended to his fellow students not pneumatics and natural theology, but 'onely the Study of Mathematicks, Moral and Natural Philosophy'. Had this happened a bit later, one might think he had read Hume. He was extruded despite the objections of three professors – Thomas Tullideph, Archibald Campbell and Francis Pringle. They argued that his expulsion was an act which would prevent free thought about logic and metaphysics within the University. It would stifle criticism in those fields. They claimed that the form and manner of the expulsion violated the charter rights of students. Playfair was expelled, became contrite, apologised and was allowed to return after some time at home.[36] Those who had supported him knew well the costs of free thinking. Campbell was a friend of the Glasgow professor of divinity John Simson, and had himself been decried as an heretic. All of them knew about the persecutions of Calvinist dissidents, old Whigs and deists. Pringle, a very independent man, was one who resisted restraints unless he imposed them. Interesting as the case was, the real sign of a change in the philosophical outlook of the place can best be found in the appointments of Campbell and Tullideph and in the granting of honorary degrees to two Glasgow professors in 1746: an LLD to Francis Hutcheson and an honorary MD to Robert Simson.[37] The student might be said to have won, since the masters were honouring Scotland's leading Newtonian mathematician (Colin Maclaurin had just died) and a philosopher who would rest morals on sense experience and not, in the first instance, on the will of God expressed in the Bible.

The divinity school had had fewer aspirations to modernity and had changed little until the 1730s, when new appointments brought new conflicts. Arguments about staffing, clashes over the views of professors and the lack of a sense of obligation to teach caused a decline which went on until the mid-century. St Andrews may have produced only about 1,000 clerics in the course of the century, about 50–60 per cent of the production of Glasgow in the same period.[38] The majority were trained after this period. But even at St Mary's, Archibald Campbell and Thomas Tullideph were teaching, if not a new theology, novel attitudes to the study of divinity.

There were also notable changes in the libraries. Neither arts college had a modern collection. The library at St Salvator's was small. In 1744 it was said to have about 1,100 volumes, but only seven published after 1700.[39] It had the better collection of natural philosophy books, perhaps because James Gregory I had had a connection of some sort at St Salvator's. St Leonard's had more books. It was said to have had about 5,000 books in 1700, some of which may have been lost in a 1702 fire.[40] In 1744 there were about 1,700 titles, which would translate into many more volumes.[41] Divinity students seem to have depended on the University library and not principally on that in St Mary's College. Undergraduates and theologues would have found the college libraries clearly oriented to the classics and to the divinity of the seventeenth century. Still, there were books on such moderns as Bacon, Kepler, Descartes, Mersenne, Gassendi, Malebranche, Hobbes, Boyle, James Gregory I, Ole Worme and Walter Charleton, although the ones on or by Aristotle were more numerous than those of any modern author.

The University library in 1695 had about 2,000 titles.[42] After the passage of the Copyright Act in 1709, the University was entitled to receive copies of all books published but it had to pay the freight from London which was a considerable expense and limited what was in fact acquired. Despite this, the collection grew and changed in character.[43] The shelf list of c. 1717 catalogues about 2,500 titles, of which perhaps a quarter were folio volumes often containing more than one work. The collection might have had over 5,000 works. A press catalogue for the period 1734–57 lists 3,135 titles. This describes a collection about the same size as Glasgow's, which in 1760 totalled about 5,634 volumes. By 1757 the St Andrews library contained the books from the three college libraries, so it probably had many duplicate copies. What was more serious was that its rate of growth was about half of Glasgow's. There the University's collection had been growing since 1709 at about thirty-four books a year from all sources including the copyright grant.[44] The St Andrews growth rate seems to have been about half that. Despite the free books available from Stationer's Hall, many books were not ordered up because of the costs of carriage. Still, by 1757 the University Library, unlike the former college libraries, had a distinctly modern collection with books in every field.

The pre-1747 career of the arts colleges and the university chairs was one which showed institutions struggling to keep up and failing – but not as badly as is sometimes thought. The University and its Colleges had lacked the resources to realise aspirations. Poverty restricted not only purchases and repairs but the recruitment of good men from outside the University's normal recruitment area. Half of the outstanding men at the University between 1700 and 1747 had come from outside that region and had not all been appointed by the locals. The Fife gentry – particularly the Leslies, Kennedys and Scots – had not promoted men of much distinction. The colleges declined as men aged, facilities deteriorated or were not kept up to date. The decline had become obvious to all as early as 1720.

2. Signs of Crisis

After 1690, the University had neither the Archbishopric nor a populous town with a powerful town council and wealthy merchants to sustain it. It lacked the support which Edinburgh and Glasgow Universities received from those who wanted political control of the burghs. Even the Aberdeen colleges did better, perhaps because they were more needed than was St Andrews. All this was exacerbated by dreadful fires. That of 1702 damaged or destroyed much of St Leonard's, which was still being rebuilt in 1723.[45] Another, in 1727, burned down the south building of the St Mary's quadrangle.[46] That loss was not made good. Daniel Defoe in the late teens or early 1720s described a University in decline for lack of funds. St Salvator's, he thought, would be as good as most colleges in England 'were sufficient funds appointed to repair and keep up the buildings', but for 'want of this, and other encouragements . . . the whole building . . . seem[s] as if it was in its declining state, and looking into its grave.' St Leonard's he knew to be better endowed but its buildings were 'old enough to be falling down', even though 'they are now repairing them and adding a great pile of building to complete the square and join that side to the north where the chapel stands.' That construction had been going on very slowly since 1718 and was never finished. Defoe claimed to find no scholars at all in St Mary's, about which he clearly knew little.[47] John Macky, another tourist whose 1723 account contains observations made at about the same time as Defoe's, found St Salvator's 'unaccountably out of Repair, they being hardly at Pains of keeping out the Rain or mending the Windows.'[48] Others reported similar dilapidation in 1728 and 1732.[49] Destruction and disrepair cut into housing for students, made the place less attractive than it had been and imposed costs which poor institutions could not meet. St Leonard's was never completely built or rebuilt and St Mary's did without a professor for some time to find the means to restore some of what the flames had consumed and then did not spend the money on that project.[50]

The political upsets of the time hurt St Andrews. After the Revolution, the Crown had never made the University or its colleges adequate allowances out of the Bishops' Rents and other funds. Before 1715, the University had been divided by personal animosities and political and religious conflicts which may have gone deeper than did the fights between the supporters of different factions elsewhere. The University livings were filled principally with men from families that tended to be Jacobite or allied to the Squadrone faction of Whigs. Neither faction was influential after c. 1720; neither could aid the University as effectively as did the Argathelians who, before 1742, were in power for about twenty years, as opposed to the Squadrone's ten. Moreover, the University was of little interest to most Scots or to the government in London. The local gentry were unable to do much for the colleges. After 1715, some probably found it difficult to send their boys to university at all. St Andrews educated no professional men other than clerics, although education provided by it did enable boys to pursue legal and medical studies elsewhere. Lacking lawyers trained there meant that it also lacked the vocal alumni working in Edinburgh or London which Glasgow and Edinburgh produced and who often proved useful. St Andrews had many medical graduates but they were not men likely to be loyal benefactors of the colleges or University. Its clerical graduates, in a period of relatively declining clerical incomes, were not men who could help much with funding. For years after the '15, St Andrews was politically suspect and not likely to be aided by the Crown. The Kirk worried about the orthodoxy of those in its seminary, which seldom ran efficiently. Politicians wanted its teachers to be loyal but few cared deeply about what happened to the St Andrews colleges and fewer of that number gave them money. St Andrews suffered neglect because its professors and alumni had little to offer politicians in a venal world.

That distress was reflected in enrolments, which shrank and drastically reduced the fees paid to professors. The decline in morale must have been equally dreadful. By 1747, there was scarcely enough money to pay salaries and little to keep up or repair the properties. If the University were to survive, it had to have additional grants or a rationalisation of costs. Consolidation to rationalise costs was the option chosen. This meant the union of at least the arts colleges.

3. The Union of the Arts Colleges in 1747

Union schemes for Scottish colleges were not new. The Aberdeen colleges had been united in the Caroline University for part of the seventeenth century, but that arrangement had been rescinded (as much by accident as policy) in the Act Resissory passed in 1661. Proposals for the union of King's and Marischal College were made from time to time, with serious ones coming around the years 1754, 1770, 1774 and 1786. At St Andrews there seems to have been no eagerness for a union of the arts colleges until they experienced extreme financial hardships after the Revolution of 1690. Even then it took a generation to come to a determination to unite the arts colleges.

The answer to the problems of the institutions had been found by 26 December 1738, when the University Minutes first mention the possibility of joining the arts colleges in a union which St Mary's would not join. Its principal was not only an administrative figure but a teaching member of the foundation. Unity with the other colleges might have meant the reduction of their teaching staff by one position. St Mary's was unwilling to lose its head or to see a teaching post abolished. By November 1741, there was enough agreement on the terms for the masters at St Leonard's to vote to spend £60 out of the College funds if the other college would find an equivalent amount to secure the parliamentary Act which would establish a new United College of St Salvator and St Leonard.[51] Discussions continued among all of the masters until December 1744, by which time the terms were 'unanimously agreed upon among ourselves' and the leaders of the Squadrone faction were approached.[52] The unity bill was apparently drafted by Charles Erskine, a wavering Argathelian about to become a Lord of Session. Squadrone politicians saw the Act through Parliament, a process slowed by the uprising in 1745 during which St Andrews was loyal to the Crown. It came into effect on 24 June 1747.

The preamble to the act uniting the arts colleges starkly sum-marised their problems and the need for finding more funds for the maintenance of properties and the augmentation of salaries.[53] It pro-vided for these things by ending the duplication of functions at St Andrews, both among the professors and eventually in the build-ings. There was to be only one set of arts professors and they were all to be fixed to particular subjects. While the divines remained outside the proposed United College, the professors of mathematics and med-icine, David Gregory and Thomas Simson, were incorporated into it. The sitting members of both colleges retained their positions and pay until they died, or they were retired on their present pay. Conveniently, Provost William Young of St Salvator's died shortly before the Union, leaving Thomas Tullideph to became the first prin-cipal of the United College of St Salvator's and St Leonard's. Ninian Young of St Leonard's was also the sole surviving humanist. Some buildings were sold and costs reduced by the boarding of fewer stu-dents. Students, somewhat later, continued to live in the buildings of St Leonard's because they had been bought and turned into a board-ing house run by professor Robert Watson.

The right to appoint to the chair of humanity remained vested in the family of the Scots of Scotstarvit, but the other humanist's post, still filled by the Kennedys of Cassilis, was turned into a chair of civil history.[54] In making this provision, the negotiators of the Union were thinking along lines similar to those which led the men at Marischal College a few years later (1753) to create a chair of civil and natural history when chairs at that university were fixed. Both Marischal and the United College were paying a decent regard to the Baconian notion that the study of facts, natural and civil, should antedate the consideration of the generalisations based on those facts made by natural philosophers or moralists. The decision to have a chair of civil history honoured a Baconian aspiration and a principle of empiricism. It also gave the University a history chair similar to ones at Glasgow and Edinburgh. It was not just a move to accommodate a superfluous man, William Vilant, who seemed unwilling to retire.[55]

Retirements helped in the settlement. Francis Pringle retired from the St Leonard's Greek chair, leaving James Kemp as the sole professor of Greek until he died in April 1748. Henry Rymer hung on until 1756 as the new professor of logic, rhetoric and metaphysics.[56] By then he had taught his version of scholastic philosophy for forty-seven years. His colleagues as professors of moral and natural philosophy were John Young from St Salvator's and David Young from St Leonard's. John Craigie of St Leonard's retired after having taught for fifty-six years and Henry Ramsay of St Salvator's left after a career of forty years. Death removed James Duncan from the Old College on 5 May 1746, just before the Act came into effect. The old men had mostly gone by 1750. The United College could now expect to attract better men, since it could pay them more than the old teachers were paid.

Militating against the appointment of the best men was the decision made by the masters not to fill new vacancies by comparative trial but by positive trials only. This meant that positions did not need to be advertised, that no written or oral competitions would be held and that men could be chosen on grounds other than demonstrated merit. In short, the old system of recruitment was continued because the masters found that comparative trials were 'inconvenient, and that they had been disused in both this and the other Universities in Scotland.' Principal Tullideph objected to this decision, saying that it would limit the pool of applicants and was contrary to the intention of the Act of Parliament.[57] He was prescient. This decision allowed nepotism to overtake the institution toward the end of the century. In this, St Andrews was little different from King's College (or even Glasgow) but quite unlike Marischal College and Edinburgh, where outsiders were very involved in appointment processes and economic constraints forced the institutions to have more regard for merit and less for birth.

When one looks for reasons why the Union had been possible, one ends with Principal Tullideph. The St Mary's appointments of the 1730s and 1740s brought the University into contact with a political world in which a few of the college men became actors and not just passive agents. During the period of Squadrone ascendency in the early 1740s, Tullideph acted with Robert Wallace, an Edinburgh minister, as a manager of church patronage for the Squadrone. This happened partly because Edinburgh and Glasgow were too full of men owing too much to Ilay. Tullideph's politicking gave St Andrews men a measure of power and importance that had been denied them in most years since the Revolution. In that long period, only James Hadow, because of his political activity in the Kirk, had counted in Scotland as a whole but he had never counted enough to serve as Moderator of the General Assembly. Tullideph became Moderator in 1742 and was followed by Wallace in 1743. Both were active in the 1740s promoting the 'Widows and Orphans Scheme' under which ministers and university professors could take out life insurance at cost. In 1744, both thanked the Squadrone leader, the Marquis of Tweeddale, for Royal Chaplaincies.[58] Tullideph's prominence and abilities facilitated working out the details of the union of the arts colleges. He proved of much more use than the University's new chancellor, the Duke of Cumberland.[59]

The Act uniting the colleges created an arts college with livings worth about 50 per cent more than the old ones (see Appendix 1). It now concerned politicians to actively promote the candidacy of men and to place them not just to decide on the fitness of men recommended by others. The interference of important politicians in the University's affairs increased and worked to the advantage of the Moderate Party in the Kirk. By the 1770s a number of the Moderate leaders in the Kirk were St Andrews men who had been protégés of Principal Robertson and later of Henry Dundas. St Andrews kept its new-found political prominence into the nineteenth century. Its divines were most useful to the politicians who interfered in university affairs.

Notes

1 Minutes, 13 and 14 November 1699, SAUL, UYUY 452/2.
2 John Cairns, 'John Spotswood', *Miscellany Three*, Stair Society, Edinburgh, 1992, pp. 131–59, p. 145f.
3 Among the history texts seemingly purchased for the Mackenzie boys of Delvine were: Marcus Junianus Justinus, *Historiae Phillippicae*, Helvicius's *Chronological Tables in English*, 'the 12 book of Buchanane's Chronicles', and works by Livy, Herodian, Xenophon; Croft Dickinson, *Two Students at St Andrews*, 1952, 'Appendix I', pp. lv–lxv.
4 King's and Marischal College had assigned regents to teach it earlier (1700, 1701) but they had not really specialised the chair by the appointment of a fixed professor.
5 Pringle was good enough for his relatives to get him nominated to hold the Edinburgh chair of humanity; see p. 253.
6 I owe this information to R. N. Smart.

454 ACADEMIC PATRONAGE IN THE SCOTTISH ENLIGHTENMENT

7 This was probably the William Sanders who in 1673 was Clerk to the University and later a regent of philosophy. See *James Gregory: Tercentenary Volume*, ed. Turnbull, 1939, pp. 510–13; A. G. Stewart, *The Academic Gregories*, 1901, p. 47.

8 The theses were published in Edinburgh by the Society of Stationers as *Specimina . . . sub praesidio J Gregorii* (Aldis No. 3097.5). They consisted of 'twenty-five propositions, most of which are related to Newton's *Principia*. Three relate to Logic, and the abuse of it in the Aristotelian and Cartesian Philosophy'; A. G. Stewart, *The Academic Gregories*, 1901, p. 85. Christina Eagles' description of the theses notes that two dealt with light and one with sound. She finds in the logic theses 'the logical basis of Newton's method'. There are copies of the theses in the Bodleian Library, Oxford and at Clare College, Cambridge. What Gregory was doing in St Andrews may well have been of interest to others and shows the University to have possessed in him a man at the forefront of the Newtonian revolution. Eagles, 'David Gregory and Newtonian Science', *British Journal for the History of Science*, 1977, pp. 216–25, 217.

9 In a letter to his much younger cousin, James Gregory IV, the Edinburgh medical professor, Reid wrote: 'I believe he was the first Professor of Philosophy that taught the doctrines of Newton in a scotch University. For the Cartesian was the orthodox System at that time and continued to be so till 1715.' Thomas Reid to James Gregory, 24 August 1787, *The Correspondence of Thomas Reid*, ed. Wood, 2002, p. 188. Reid's judgement is shared by Paul Wood, and by Eagles. The priority is given to David Gregory and his Edinburgh colleagues by John Russell and Christine Shepherd: Russell, 'Cosmological Teaching', *Journal of the History of Astronomy*, 1974, p. 129; Shepherd, 'Newtonianism in the Scottish Universities', in *Origins and Nature of the Scottish Enlightenment*, ed. Campbell and Skinner, 1982, pp. 67–75.

10 This information is drawn from Croft Dickinson's *Two Students*, 1952, pp. lv–lxv, and assumes that the books the tutor reported bought for the sons of John Mackenzie of Delvine were used in classes or recommended there and were not texts bought and used only by the tutor so that he could help the boys with their studies.

11 Both books are listed among the books purchased for the Mackenzie boys. Croft Dickinson, ibid., pp. lviii, lxiv.

12 A. G. Stewart, *The Academic Gregories*, 1901, p. 48f.

13 See the forthcoming catalogue of those by Helen Rawson.

14 Cant says it was razed in 1736 (*University*, 2002, p. 89) but the University Minutes for 17 October 1761 refer to 'the South part of the observatory [being] in danger of falling' because rents in its walls were widening.

15 Minutes, 3 January 1707, SAUL, UYUY 452/2.

16 Minutes, 23 October 1714, SAUL, UY 452/2. For the range of things which might be referred to by this term, see Bryden, 'A 1701 Dictionary of Mathematical Instruments', in *Making Instruments Count*, ed. Anderson, Bennet and Ryan, 1993, pp. 365–82.

17 The first 'Proposals' can be found in the Minutes for 23 October 1714, SAUL, UY 452/2.

18 Cant, *University*, 2002, p. 97.

19 Ibid., p. 97. Cant dated the fixing of the teaching of natural philosophy to 1724–6. This followed the trend in other places, although all of the chairs were not formally converted to specialist professorships until 1747. Humanity had been fixed before the beginning of the period. Greek had had separate professors since 1702 and 1705; natural philosophy was fixed in each college by 1726, which left logic and moral philosophy to alternate between the two professors at St Salvator's until 1742 and at St Leonard's until 1744, when they too were assigned to permanent instructors. See, Cant, ibid., p. 109. It seems clear that natural philosophy was integrated with mathematics to some extent since Principal Hadow noted in a memorial of 1727 that mathematics was 'particularly Subservient to the two new professions we have lately fixed and established amongst us for advanceing Natural & Experimental Philosophy.' NAS, SP54/18/53.

20 Ibid. p. 97.

21 Minutes, 22 November 1736, 18 December 1736, 3 June 1737, SAUL, UYUY 452/4.

22 *Philosophical Transactions*, No. 447.6, 40:175–95; Mills, *Collected Letters*, 1982, p. 282. This gives the letter sent to the *Phil. Trans.* and defines the community of mathematicians and astronomers in which Gregory should be placed.

23 Minutes, 30 December 1737, SAUL, UYUY 452/4.

24 Minutes, 13 April 1741, SAUL, UYUY 452/4. David Young in a later factional fight was held responsible for incurring costs for this change which were said to be unwarranted. He was probably the principal user of the telescopes. Minutes, 28 September 1750, SAUL, UYUY 452/6.

25 Minutes, 20 February 1751, SAUL, UYUY 452/6.

26 Cant, *University*, 2002, p. 89; Turnbull, *James Gregory*, p. 514f; Minutes, 2 May 1705, SAUL, UY 452/2.

27 Emerson, 'Natural philosophy and the problem of the Scottish Enlightenment', *Studies on Voltaire and the Eighteenth Century*, 1986, pp. 243–91, 268f. The greatest of the Scottish virtuosi of this period, Sir Robert Sibbald, MD, was from Fife. For Sibbald and his interests see: Simpson, 'Sir Robert Sibbald – The Founder of the College', in *Proceedings of the Royal College of Physicians of Edinburgh Tercentenary Congress*, 1982, pp. 59–91; Emerson, 'Sir Robert Sibbald', *Annals of Science*, 1988; pp. 41–72; C. W. J. Withers, 'Geography,

Science and National Identity in Early Modern Britain', *Annals of Science*, 1996, pp. 29–73.

28 Cant, *University*, 2002, p. 87; Emerson, 'Natural philosophy and the problem of the Scottish Enlightenment', *Studies on Voltaire and the Eighteenth Century*, 1986, pp. 243–91, 257.

29 Ibid., p. 268f.

30 EUL, DK1.2.1./90 (see the memorandum on the back of those miscellaneous notes).

31 Minutes, 23 January 1714, SAUL, UY 452/2; see also Lord Colville to [?], 24 January 1714, NAS GD124/15/1113. John, 6th Baron Colville, was a local man who made a career in the army but was later a founding member of the Edinburgh Philosophical Society.

32 Minutes, 26 November 1700, SAUL, UY 452/1.

33 An inventory of Wodrow's cabinet is held at the Library of the University of Strathclyde, Anderson MSS, 11. Wodrow collected natural and civil history objects and some which it is difficult to classify.

34 Martine (1635–26 August 1712) had been secretary to Archbishop Sharp and Commissary Clerk of St Andrews. His work belongs to the cultural flourish of the 1680s. See Ouston, 'Cultural Life from the Restoration to the Union', in *The History of Scottish Literature*, Gen. Ed. Cairns Craig, vol. II, '. . . 1660–1800', ed. Andrew Hook, 1989, II:11–30; Emerson, 'Scottish Cultural Change 1660–1710 and the Union of 1707', in *A Union for Empire*, ed. John Robertson, 1995, pp. 121–44.

35 Gregory defined logic as 'the art of making proper use of things granted in order to find what is sought' – a definition that restricted it to formal matters but not to Aristotelian logic. A. G. Stewart, *The Academic Gregories*, 1901, p. 85.

36 Playfair apologised by saying that he had drawn his oration very hurriedly and only meant to criticise the abuses of logic and metaphysics and that he really enjoyed the study of pneumatics and natural theology. Minutes, 22 and 23 April 1735, 10 and 13 June 1735, SAUL, UYUY 452/4.

37 See Moore and Silverthorne, 'Hutcheson's LL.D', *Eighteenth-Century Scotland*, 20 (2006), pp. 10–12.

38 I thank R. N. Smart for the estimate of the St Andrews clerics; the other is my own rough estimate of those educated at Glasgow. It is based on sampling the published matriculation lists.

39 *Votiva Tabella*, no ed., 1911, pp. 96–103. See also 'A Catalogue of the Books belonging to the Old College taken in the Year 1744', SAUL, UYLY 106/5. Whether this lists volumes or titles is unclear.

40 It is not certain that they were in the burned portions; Cant, *University*, p. 103, n.2.

41 'St Leonard's College Library', SAUL, UYLY 106/2, 106/4.

42 *Votiva Tabella*, no ed., 1911, p. 103.

43 'Catalogue of Books belonging [tear] Library of ye University of St Andrews', SAUL, UYLY 105/3.

44 Black and Gaskell, 'Special Collections in Glasgow University Library', *The Book Collector*, 1967, pp. 161–8, 162.

45 Cant, *University*, 2002, p. 106; Cant lists other accounts of St Andrews in these years, notably William Douglass, *Some Historical Remarks* (1728) and John Loveday, *Diary of a Tour* (1732). A sense of what at St Leonard's was destroyed and ruinous and when, may be gained from the plate giving the ground plan of the College in the eighteenth century which is printed with a commentary in Croft Dickinson, *Two Students*, 1952, pp. lxxiii–lxxvii. Cant's *History*, 2002, contains drawings of the three colleges in the eighteenth century (pp. 203–9).

46 '. . . a dreadful fire broke out in St Marys College wherein Mr James Haldane professor of Church History was lost, and wherby the Public Schools, the Refectory, the Apartment of the Professor of Church history, and some Scholars Chambers were consumed.' 'Petition of the Principals and professors of St Mary's College 4 October 1731', Lee MSS, NLS, 3431.

47 Daniel Defoe, *A Tour Through the Whole Island*, 1979, p. 641f. Defoe's remark is surprising given the number of divinity students at the College. I thank R. N. Smart for this observation.

48 Cited in Cant, *University*, 2002, p. 106; see also Cant, *St Salvator's*, 1950, p. 209ff. There Cant quotes Macky's account and excerpts from two others. He also says that broken windows may have been a temporary thing. The boys had to pay 'caution money' which was never refunded so they always broke the windows at the end session. Had Macky visited then, he would have seen broken windows.

49 Cant, *University*, 2002, p. 106, n.1.

50 Ibid., p. 103.

51 Minutes of St Leonard's College, 18 November 1741, SAUL, UYSL 400.

52 Principals William Young and Thomas Tullideph to Tweeddale, 22 December 1744, Yester Papers, NLS, 7064/132. William Young, Tullideph and David Young seem to have been those to whom fell the burden of working out the terms of settlement.

53 It is printed in Cant, *St Salvator's*, 1950, p. 188.

54 Those private patrons had to consent to the new arrangements; Minutes of St Leonard's College, 18 November 1741, SAUL, UYSL 400.

55 Cant, *University*, 2002, p. 109. I know of no discussions about this chair at St Andrews but the idea was a commonplace among empiricists and the arguments for the Marischal College changes were set out anonymously by Alexander Gerrard in 'Plan of Education in the Marischal College' (1755). A shortened statement of this appeared in the *Scots Magazine*, XIV:606 (December 1752). William Vilant was presented to this post only on 11 October 1748, probably because the private patron

had delayed exercising his right to present for the first time under the new regime.

56 This is close to the title adopted by the Marischal College men for the chair they created in 1753: 'Moral Philosophy and Logic.' Their chair taught pneumatics, natural theology, some logic and rhetoric. James Beattie's *Moral Science* (1790–3) is a publication of the lectures he gave while in this chair for about thirty years after 1760. At Aberdeen, the professor of 'Civil and Natural History' taught both natural and civil history but in time it became mainly a natural history chair; at St Andrews the chair was a history chair sometimes held by men with political-economic interests. It resembled the Glasgow chair of ecclesiastical and civil history as it was filled by William Wight.

57 Minutes of St Leonard's College, 8 June 1748, SAUL, UYSL 400.

58 Robert Wallace to Tweeddale, 5 June 1744; Thomas Tullideph to Tweeddale, 9 June 1744, Yester Papers, NLS, 7062/75, 89.

59 When Chancellor Chandos died in 1744, he was replaced in early 1746 by the Duke of Cumberland whom the masters expected to protect their interests. The Duke turned out to be neither a good patron nor a protector. He was uninterested, busy and often not in London but on the continent with his troops, about whom he did care. The College's new tie to a powerful man turned out to be worse than useless.

16

THOMAS TULLIDEPH'S ST ANDREWS, 1747–1777

⌒

1. The Making of a 'Usurping Tyrant'

Principal Tullideph became the dominant figure at St Andrews after his appointment as principal at St Leonard's in 1739. During his tenure at St Leonard's and then as principal of the United College, the level of government involvement with the University steadily increased. After 1747, valuable places ensured the attention of political managers such as Ilay, his nephews, John Stuart, 3rd Earl of Bute, and James Stuart Mackenzie, and William Mure of Caldwell, Baron of Exchequer. These four men were all more interested in seeing university positions go to those best qualified to serve in them than had been the Squadrone politicians. They also generally had men to push. Local men, but not Tullideph, were more content to see the level of nepotism rise. It did so as professorial families proved able to bargain effectively with the politicians, particularly with Henry Dundas in the late 1770s and early 1780s. Bargaining created tensions between political managers and sitting professors who were eager to secure good things for their junior relatives. On more than one occasion, this would be complicated by party infighting at the University. Tullideph was an eager warrior and had many fights as the University's staff was renewed during his admin-istration. His own party ties ran to Squadrone politicians and then to the Moderate Party in the Kirk. Here as elsewhere, the Moderates filled a power vacuum between c. 1765 and c. 1780. Tullideph much improved the University but at a cost. When Ramsay of Ochtertyre wrote his character, which he based on the recollections of others since he was too young to have known the principal, he recalled a man who

> . . . with all his parts and accomplishments . . . was far from being a very popular principal; for though a number of young men were warmly attached to him; a great proportion of the Students looked on him as proud, and selfish, and unlucky in his favourites who were supposed to have gained his favour by flattery. For a good many years he lived very retired being very infirm.[1]

Tullideph's first big battle came in 1748.

In 1748, United College made two appointments. Walter Wilson (c. 1705–2 February 1769) got the chair of Greek and Dr George Hadow was picked to be professor of Hebrew. Both appointments were family affairs. Wilson was the son-in-law of Thomas Simson, professor of medicine. He was also the son of a local minister and the grandson of Alexander Pitcairne, a former principal of St Leonard's. It was just this sort of appointment which Tullideph had argued should not be made and against which he remonstrated and voted. Had the place been advertised and a trial held, he thought, they might well have hired a better man. After all, the Greek chair was now worth more than it had been and might attract a scholar rather than just another son of a local minister to whom at least two of the electors were related. Wilson was given a 'positive trial' on 13 June 1748, about eight weeks after Kemp had died. To this the principal objected, saying the election was null and void without his concurrence. He then left the meeting. After he departed, the masters chose Henry Rymer to preside while they worked out a way to choose Wilson. They advertised the job and on 28 June held a pro forma comparative trial to which no one came but the man destined for the position.[2] Tullideph gave over his protests but the affair rankled and was to play a part in the fight involving all the masters a short while later. This appointment should be seen as one which set the College on a course of nepotistic appointments culminating in the University becoming divided by two family factions by 1806.[3]

George Hadow (1712–11 September 1780), who got the regius chair of Hebrew, was also the grandson of a principal of St Leonard's, William Tullideph, and a relative of Thomas Tullideph. His father was James Hadow, who had died in the previous year. Many probably believed James Hadow deserved better than he got from the government, especially for his pursuit of enthusiasts in the Kirk. The younger Hadow's appointment looks very like a pay-off to a dead man who had never been made Moderator despite his more than twenty-five years of diligent service in the General Assembly. Who in government secured his warrant is not known, but there is one hint. Hadow was admitted to office on 8 November 1748; two weeks later the College resigned the 'Lands of Balgouner [Balgonar], in favour of the present Duke of Argyle'. This may well tell us who managed the transaction for university men eager to see an old colleague's son well placed. If Ilay, now the Duke of Argyll, was to manage the politics of this burgh, as he hoped to do, it would be good to have a local holding, however small, and to gratify men in the College. The Perth Burghs seat had been regained by a Squadrone politician in the elections of 1743 and 1747, after having been previously held by a friend of the Argathelians since 1722. The granting of land to Argyll was surely a sign of his hope to return to the management of public affairs at St Andrews after being more or less out of power during the early 1740s. If it was that, it did not work; the Rothes interest dominated the town until 1760. The lawyer for the United College also remained a Squadrone man, John Craigie of Kilgraston.[4]

George Hadow was a somewhat unlikely appointee. Like his brother James, who taught Hebrew at Aberdeen, he had learned Hebrew while a divinity student with his father, but then studied medicine at Edinburgh and took a St Andrews MD in 1740. It is unlikely that he could have taught other Oriental languages, especially useful modern ones, such as Persian and Arabic, as did Charles Morthland at Glasgow and James Robertson in Edinburgh. Dr Hadow maintained a St Andrews practice throughout his professorship, which lasted until 1780.[5] Placing Hadow added a vote to Tullideph's faction in the University but must have caused a bit of laughter from those whom Tullideph had opposed over the appointment of Wilson. In such circumstances, laughter and bad blood were not far apart, as soon became clear.

Following these appointments, the masters settled down to a rancorous fight which began with the rectorial election in the autumn of 1749.[6] One suspects that the recent appointments and tensions engendered by the union and restructuring of the colleges and University played a role in that quarrel. Given the intensity and duration of its pursuit, there must have been more at issue than the legalities of that election. It also followed the return to power of Argyll and the loss of power and status by Tullideph's Squadrone friends. Whatever the underlying causes for their animosity, the professorial quarrel was fierce and lasted actively until at least the spring of 1753. Tullideph bullied the masters, particularly David Young, whom he tried to suspend, and some of the masters called the principal usurping and tyrannical.

At the rectorial election of 1749, the proper presiding officer should have been the outgoing rector, professor Murison of St Mary's College, but a majority of the masters chose Henry Rymer, dean of the faculty. This led to legal wrangles about whether or not the masters could choose the dean for this task and, thus, to the issue of the legality of an election which was not liked by the losers – principals

Tullideph and Murison and professors Shaw (divinity) and Gregory (mathematics), and Hadow (Hebrew). The first three were among the four men eligible to be rector; they were defending their rights. Hadow was a relative. The masters who had voted for Rymer were all men from the United College, with the exception of professor Archibald Campbell (divinity and ecclesiastical history).[7] Ninian Young (humanist) and William Vilant (civil history) seem to have been *hors de combat*, probably because of age or illness. At this point, the conflict looks like a grudge match between men qualified to be rector, most of whom were long associated with St Mary's, and others in the United College, but the substantive legal point was not a small matter. If the United College men were right, then a majority of the masters could, in effect, choose a new head of the Senatus when and if they wished to do so. It was an assertion of professorial wilfulness which pitted the men who could wield authority as rectors and principals against the rest.

Matters quickly got out of hand. The faction which questioned Rymer's right to preside in the meeting ignored the proceedings and continued Murison in office. David Young possessed himself of the College seal for Rymer's party and would not give it back. His faction – Rymer (logic), John and David Young (moral and natural philosophy), Walter Wilson (Greek) and Thomas Simson (medicine) – refused to attend senate meetings which they held to be illegal. Their antagonists prosecuted Young in the rectorial court held by the old rector, who found Young guilty and fined him. The latter appealed his sentence to the Court of Session. Shortly thereafter, he was prosecuted in a magistrate's court for hunting on someone's land. That case the rector removed to his own court since Young was triable only there for an offence such as this. Young was next hassled over his management of the quaestor's accounts which he refused to produce until a legal rector was elected. He was replaced as quaestor by George Hadow and was suspended from his teaching duties but continued to teach. Wilson was also suspended for preventing the matriculation of students and for dismissing a student servant. He and his faction protested the election of the dean on 3 March 1750 but later acknowledged the choice of Shaw as rector.

On 23 March 1750, Rymer and his friends returned to the senate meetings and offered a memorandum which was meant to clear the air. They recognised the election of Shaw as rector but not that of his 1749 predecessor, Tullideph. He, they said, had been chosen *in absentia*, had never given his consent, had been privately and illegally admitted to that office by Murison and did not act as rector. They asked that Young's suspension be lifted and Wilson assoiled of contempt. In all this they were vehemently opposed by Murison, Gregory and Hadow, who wanted Young and Wilson removed from the meeting. Motions made by Shaw's faction evoked a counter-response: '. . . these five Gentlemen [of Young's faction] did in the most turbulent Manner oppose the Consideration of them.' They argued that they were legally called to the elections, had a right to sit and vote and that they now formed a majority and would not see 'Mr Da. Young to be removed'. His removal would have deprived them of a majority.[8] The rector then did a sensible thing. He asked if this was the way to make peace, offered to adjourn the meeting and talk things over 'in an amicable way, & concert proper Measures for an Accommodation'. Rymer's faction would now have none of it and demanded that their memorandum be recorded. The rector then adjourned the meeting 'with prayer'.[9] The fight continued.

By April, the Court of Session, in the minds of Rymer's friends, had lifted Young's suspension. In the mind of the rector's lawyer, it had only stopped his trial in the rector's court but had not reponed him. On 9 April, the Senate voted that he be removed from the meeting, against which his friends protested and then protested against earlier minutes and other things. Then they agreed to talk. The first thing to talk about was whether the rector could grant degrees to boys taught by Young while suspended. He was authorised to do so but said he would do so under protest. Talking it out would work only if done in good faith.

The committee appointed to enquire into the conduct of Young and his friends did not get on well. Those being investigated did not cooperate. On 8 May 1750, Tullideph, Murison, Vilant and Gregory demanded cooperation 'forthwith'. They were told that 'considering the present Circumstances of the university, & that they are divided into two parties, no good can be expected from such a Measure; but that Strife & Animosity would thereby be encreased' by continuing the enquiry. Rymer argued that they should wait for a further decision of the Court of Session.[10] Nothing had been gained except by the lawyers who received more fees.

These events made St Andrews a most unpleasant place for teachers and students, because the disputes affected the administration of everything. Degrees were not the only things threatened. Murison, rector in 1751, announced that he would matriculate all the students who had not been formally admitted because their teachers would not or might not legally admit them. Young replied to this by linking the issue to his accounts, which had not yet been passed. Should he vote, then the accounts would be passed and he would be cleared of the charge of incurring unauthorised expenditures connected with the telescope purchased in 1741 or the instruments of 1748. When he was found by the meeting unable to vote, he 'took instruments' to which his party adhered. Things went back to square one.[11] On 29 March 1751, his opponents tried to prevent him from sitting in the General Assembly by reciting his errors and sins to other interested parties. He was, they said, not a frequenter of communion, had played golf on a fast day, sat in taverns, had caused 'confusion' in the University and had altered the Minutes of St Leonard's College. He was clearly unfit to sit in the General Assembly, as they were willing to prove to the Presbytery of St Andrews or to the General Assembly itself. This evoked more protests. Young said it was not so. Rymer claimed that the 'confusions' had come from the other side, notably Murison. Wilson added that his library accounts should have been accepted and that the masters' characters had been traduced. He called the enquiry committee a 'Committee of Inquisition' and clearly implied that they would all seek further justice in courts fairer than that of the rector and his partisan assessors. So the stew simmered until the Senate met on 9 December 1751.

By then William Vilant had resigned and been replaced by Alexander Morton (admitted 13 June 1751). Morton would vote with and for Young. His appointment, and the likely debility of others on Tullideph's side, meant that the majority in the Senatus had shifted in Young's favour. Young's accounts were passed; the rector's protest of this was rejected as unfounded. Young was nominated as the member from the Presbytery of St Andrews to the General Assembly, which did not bar him despite the accusations of his enemies. Morton was chosen quaestor and a long memorandum of explanation was accepted from Young's friends. This tended to blame their opponents but it also addressed their charges. Young was not bound to fast on days not set as fast days in the parish where he was a communicant. He denied altering minutes but admitted that in transcription there may have been little word changes of no substantial importance. He admitted to doing business in taverns. There was no comment on his golfing. His side had won – for the moment.

On 27 February 1752, Tullideph was again elected to the rectorship and had the decency to name two assessors from the other side, Morton and Ninian Young. Young by then was too old to do much and the majority of the assessors were the principal's men. Tullideph seemed still determined to dominate. By March his old friend Murison was again objecting to David Young being named on the General Assembly leet for all the reasons previously given and answered. A riposte was predictable. Young and his friends threatened to sue for the money the University had spent on the cases against David Young and they refused to clear Hadow's accounts. When Young was chosen for the General Assembly on 2 April 1753, Tullideph, Murison, Shaw, Hadow and Gregory dissented, but they lacked the numbers to make up a majority and their protest died. The affair finally ended, perhaps out of weariness, perhaps out of fear of the financial cost to the five should a suit against them be won, perhaps because the prayers of March 1750 had finally been answered.

The man whose appointment did much to end the conflict among the professors, Alexander Morton, was a nominee of Argyll's supporters, the Kennedys of Cassillis. On 27 November 1749, professor David Young presented to his colleagues a letter from professor William Vilant which contained a 'presentation of Survivance to the Said Mr Morton [?–19 January 1781] of the professorship of History Sign'd by the Earl of Cassillis Augt 5th 1749, and desiring that the Said Presentation Should be read and marked in the Minutes which was accordingly done.'[12] Vilant had reached an agreement with Morton by which Vilant kept the salary but surrendered the other benefits of the chair.[13] Exactly how Morton secured his presentation from the Kennedy family is not known, but there is a clue in records dealing with the man whom he defeated in the competition for the office. The Earl of Morton had written to Argyll on 18 July 1753 asking that the place be given to his son's tutor, John Leslie, later a master at the Dalkeith Grammar School and then a professor at King's College, Aberdeen.[14] Argyll was asked to intercede with the Kennedy family, which had had a long association with the 2nd and 3rd Dukes of Argyll to whom its members owed places and favours.[15] It made very good sense for anyone seeking a place for a protégé to approach the Kennedys through Argyll. But Morton about 1745 also had been the travelling tutor to the son of Archibald Campbell of Stonefield, Sheriff Depute and Chamberlain of Argyll – the Duke of Argyll's man in Inveraray. When the latter weighed what he owed to Lord Morton and to long-time supporters and friends in his own clan, he is likely to have chosen to do as his better friends wished and to have recommended Mr Morton to Kennedy who was under obligations to the Duke.

Given the growing rancour in the University, Tullideph objected to Morton on the grounds that the letter from Cassillis was addressed 'to no body' and should therefore not be entered. The only colleague who agreed with him was David Gregory. The principal's objection was likely rooted in a desire to obstruct his enemies and the presumed politics of the new man. A Squadrone man like Tullideph would have found it worth his while to object to a man such as Morton who had Argathelian support. Nevertheless, the appointment stood and brought into the College a man who owed nothing to Tullideph or his friends. He voted against the principal with some consistency. Morton was also a more worldly man than most of his colleagues. He had spent time at Leiden in the company of men such as Charles Townshend, John Wilkes, William Dowdeswell and Scots like Alexander Carlyle.[16] Unfortunately, he seems to have had little interest in the subjects he was to teach. Alexander Morton kept this place until 20 September 1753, when he swapped it for the better-paying chair of humanity,[17] and that for the Greek chair in 1769.

2. THE TULLIDEPH REGIME

In 1756, the University appointed Robert Watson (c. 1730–31 February 1781) to the chair of logic, rhetoric and metaphysics.[18] Watson was from a St Andrews family (his father had been Provost of St Andrews)[19] and he had attended the University before going on to the universities of Glasgow and Edinburgh to study divinity. In Edinburgh, he had lectured extramurally on rhetoric between 1752 and 1756, a task for which he seems to have been recruited by Lord Kames and which he undertook while finishing his training as a minister.[20] His lecturing on a polite interest, like being a cousin of William Robertson, put him in the circle of the Moderates then coming to power in Edinburgh. In 1756, Watson applied for a minister's post in St Andrews, where he had been licensed by the Presbytery. That application failed but he was installed as a professor on 18 June 1756. It was not a bad berth for a man who had just finished divinity school. Who helped him to his job is not known. The arrangements are likely to have been made in face-to-face negotiations among the Edinburgh men who were Watson's friends. What is known is that Watson bought out the sitting professor, Henry Rymer, who got a lump sum and the salary for the two years he had to live. About a year after his appointment, Watson married Margaret Shaw, the daughter of the professor of divinity. A local boy had come home and would distinguish himself as a lecturer, historian and principal.

In the same month Watson was appointed, the reverend Mr William Brown (27 February 1719–10 January 1791) was appointed to the regius chair of ecclesiastical history without the University's knowledge and without its approval. Indeed, the University strenuously opposed his appointment because Brown had a dubious reputation.[21] During the '45, Brown had led a raid on Glamis Castle and had elsewhere forced the release of captured Whigs. In other places, he and the men he led took Jacobite prisoners. This may not have endeared him to some of his parishioners but they soon found another reason to dislike him. They, like his future colleagues, thought him to have been guilty of fornication with the wife of a parishioner. The husband blackened his name and threatened him with bodily harm. Brown was run out of Cortachy in Forfarshire, his parish, by the 'odium of the disaffected, the prejudices of the people, and his life [was threatened with] being attacked by a ruffian.'[22] Had he stayed, he would have faced trials in church courts and would, if the allegations were proven, have been deposed. He left the parish to become private secretary to Sir Everard Faulkner, who was himself secretary and aide to the Duke of Cumberland. At some point, Brown served as a regimental chaplain in Flanders but by 1749 he was settled in Utrecht as minister to the English Congregation. He remained in Holland until 1757.[23]

Faced with this unwelcome appointment, the University's rector, Andrew Shaw, its professors and the Presbytery of St Andrews wrote to the Secretary of State, Lord Holderness, and to the University's chancellor, the Duke of Cumberland, to ask that the appointment be quashed.[24] This was not done. Cumberland's secretary wrote Brown a letter, which the latter gave to the St Andrews ministers. It said that the King was 'satisfied with my abilities & Endowments for holding the office to which I am now presented by his Majesty.' The Presbytery of St Andrews still demanded that he clear himself of the charge of 'Fornication and other Misdemeanors', saying that he was not admissible until 'assoiled'. Brown was cited to appear before them and did so. He argued that he had never been charged with anything and that he had certificates from the Presbytery of Forfar and Utrecht testifying to his good behaviour and 'Character as a Clergyman'. The ministers were not impressed. The certificate he gave them from his old Presbytery of Forfar was not the same as one issued by that body in 1748.[25] When Brown demanded the right to qualify himself for office by signing the Confession, he was denied. He took instruments and appealed to the Court of Session.[26] Professor Gregory, whose father had had to resort to a similar process to be installed, aided in his appeal. The judges of the Court of Session ordered his admission and awarded him costs.[27] By the end of 1757, he was regularly attending senate meetings but he was not happy.

Not all the reasons for contesting this appointment concerned the character of the minister. Some of the Argathelians, particularly the Edinburgh Moderates and Lord Milton, supported the candidacy of the reverend Mr John Home, the controversial minister of Athelstaneford, who wanted the chair. Home belonged to the Moderate Party in the Scottish church, which had been gaining in confidence and whose members had been doing ever more daring things. Home had written a play, *Agis* (1749), which he had tried to get David Garrick to produce in London. This was widely known. In 1752, he and his friends had been attacked by conservatives in the Kirk during the General Assembly of that year and had counter-attacked by asserting the need to obey the laws concerning church patronage. The high-flyers wanted 'hotter' gospel preaching, fewer sermons on morals and less interference from the government and from heritors in the affairs of the Kirk, particularly in the choosing and placing of ministers. Their view of the character of a minister was different from that of the Moderate men who prized politeness over piety.[28] David Hume and Henry Home, Lord Kames, John Home's friends, were then set upon by the high flyers after 1753. John Home himself became the object of more criticism in 1755 when it became known that he had written another play. *Douglas* was read by his friends and first performed in Edinburgh in December 1756. That a minister had the temerity to write a play, aid in its rehearsal and then attend its performance created a scandal. Home and others, like the reverend Mr Alexander Carlyle, who also had been involved in this business, were harried in clerical courts. It was clear by 1756 that Home would leave his parish; he needed somewhere to go. The St Andrews chair of ecclesiastical history looked good to him and his friends.

John Home wrote to Lord Milton before the end of February 1756 expressing his interest in the ecclesiastical history chair. He told Milton that he would not oppose any man Argyll might support or set up but that he hoped for aid in his effort to obtain the vacancy: 'there is no place that I can as yet pretend to which would be so proper for a Poet.' He went on to say that if he had this place 'your Lordship would be freed from the trouble of defending the Maces against these Goths and Vandals who think themselves obliged to persecute an Ecclesiastical Bard.'[29] By April, Home was trying to get Bute to intervene.[30] Home's supporters, thought one Aberdeen commentator, blackened Brown's reputation to make Home more acceptable.[31] This was almost certainly true. Those at St Andrews who wanted him knew what he represented and the risks they ran in taking him in. Lord Milton may have supported Home's application and given hope to the men in St Andrews, but Argyll shied away from causes such as this. The Duke was well disposed to John Home and helped to promote *Douglas* when it came on the London stage in 1757.[32] However, there was no point in spending political capital on a case likely to bring no rewards outside the University. There could be no merit in a case which pitted the professors against their sovereign, who had the right to appoint to regius chairs and had appointed a man having the support of one of his sons.

Home had genuine interests in history. All his plays had historical settings and he later wrote a *History of the Rebellion of 1745* (1802). He would likely have made the chair notable in some fashion. Had he been appointed, he probably would have taught ecclesiastical history as included in general history, as was becoming the fashion. He would have brought some eminence, as well as scandal, to the College; Brown brought only scandal and had an undistinguished career. He left only one posthumous publication, a pamphlet on St Rule's Chapel.[33] He also turned out to be a cantankerous and litigious colleague neither respected nor liked by his colleagues. No sooner had he arrived in unwelcoming St Andrews than he felt aggrieved because he had not received diet money. It had been used to repair his house and to pay the window tax for which he was liable. When he was refused this sum, about £12, he horned his colleagues at St Mary's, that is he had them declared outlaws until they paid up. His chair allowed him to become rector but he was chosen for that office only once (1766) in a long career.[34]

It was not until near the end of 1759 that another appointment was made at St Andrews, one occasioned by the death of David Young. His chair of natural philosophy was sought by his brother, John Young, then the professor of moral philosophy, but it went to William ('Potato') Wilkie (5 October 1721–10 October 1772), the minister of Ratho. This parish he had received through the influence of the Earl of Lauderdale, a principal heritor in Ratho.[35] A bright virtuoso, Wilkie in 1757 had published the *Epigoniad*, an epic poem in heroic couplets, but he also interested himself in natural philosophy and in science of a practical sort, particularly improved farming.[36] He was a wit, a member of the Select Society of Edinburgh and probably of the Philosophical Society as well since he had been offered admission, refused it, and then sought it again once he had been appointed to the chair of natural philosophy at St Andrews.[37] Adam Smith, whose first academic interest was in science and mathematics, described Wilkie as 'undoubtedly the first Poet as well as one of the most eminent Philosophers of the present Age'. He went on to say that men in both Edinburgh and Glasgow were concerned to do something for him. Smith was referring to his fellow club-men, most of whom were Argathelians and Moderates.[38] Leading members of both groups had been trying for some time to place Wilkie in a university. As we have seen (see above, p. 137), Glasgow professors in 1757 asked that he should become their professor of Hebrew.[39] At St Andrews, his supporters likely included Principal Tullideph and Robert Watson. In May 1757, Wilkie applied to Lord Milton asking for the St Andrews chair, a request Milton willingly supported. Within a few days, Wilkie had changed his mind and preferred the professorship of divinity at Marischal College if Argyll could help him there.[40] He had got his old patron and parishioner, the Earl of Lauderdale, to approach Argyll directly.[41] All this dealing was complicated by the concomitant search for university posts for others, as is made clear in an undated letter from Wilkie to Milton received sometime in July 1759:

> My affair at St Andrews will certainly be lost[.] I have only Three against four[.] the Party which opposes the Principal has stuck together inspite of all our attempts to divide them. John Young is to have the Vacant Place[.] Mr Morton is to have Mr Youngs so that the Latine Class becomes vacant which is in Scotstarvets Gift and is already promised to Ld Deskford for one Mr Ross. The only Chance that Remains is Mr Ruats [ecclesiastical history chair] at Glasgow which Mr Fletcher mentioned to my Ld Lauderdale at London & has writen something about since. I am told that Mr [James] Russel is attempting to perswade Adam Ferguson to stand for Ruats place in hopes of succeeding him [in the natural philosophy chair] at Edinr I imagine that Ferguson will not relish this proposal and that he will not Choose to interfere with me in a matter where my interest is concerned.[42]

In the end, Young, Morton and Ferguson stayed put; Ross was made professor of Oriental languages at King's College, Aberdeen, and Rouet's place went to William Wight after a long delay caused by legal **difficulties** (see above, p. 155f.). To balance such competing claims and to minimise the friction they caused was what Milton and Argyll were good at doing. How they bought off the St Andrews men who opposed Wilkie is not known but they must have done so. Wilkie was admitted to office on 12 November 1759. By 1761 he was politicking with pro-fessors Wilson, Morton and Young (they had been against his appoint-ment) to oppose the election to the Perth Burghs of George Dempster. This involved slanging Alexander Vilant (?–?) whom Wilkie and others had temporarily outed from his places in the United College.

When William Vilant died in 1759, his son, Alexander, believed he held a reversion to the place given by the patron, so he tried to become professor of civil history even though, as George Dempster reported, 'he never discovered any turn for Letters'.[43] The masters decided to try him for the post expecting to find him unfit to hold it. He objected, saying it was 'neither usual nor necessary'. He took the masters to court and the case ended up before the Court of Session. A compro-mise was reached. Vilant would give over teaching and resign; the masters would again make him their factor and ask that the next incumbent pay him something.[44] Vilant resigned his commission but, because the earldom of Cassillis was in dispute, his resignation could not be accepted because the person to accept it was in doubt.[45] He continued as a nominal professor and as factor. When the general par-liamentary election of 1761 neared, he supported Dempster in the burgh, to the annoyance of five of the masters who backed Thomas Leslie, the candidate of the Earl of Rothes whose family had long con-trolled the town and the seat. Loyalty to a family which had been a benefactor to the University and long had dominated the politics of the burgh was expected of the professors.[46] There was also a legal issue involved here. Vilant held a municipal office which university men at St Andrews were prohibited from holding.[47] The masters told Vilant that he had to 'either renounce his office & quit my [Dempster's] party or he shall resign his Factory.' As further justifica-tion for their actions they cited a number of trivial offences, as well as his backing of Dempster, who was said to be 'engaged in a Jacobite faction to subvert the interest of the family of Rothes.' This was com-plete nonsense which they knew to be such. Vilant, without other prospects in the world (or so he said), resigned his factory, for which Dempster hoped to get him some recompense.[48] He could not quite resign his chair for the reason given above. The inheritance to the earldom of Cassillis was not settled until 27 January 1762, when Sir Thomas Kennedy was acknowledged to be 9th Earl of Cassillis and heir to the patronage rights. Vilant's resignation could then take effect and the place could be declared vacant and filled. By then Dempster had ousted Thomas Leslie as the dominant local politician. Vilant was allowed to continue as factor but 'sold' his chair to Richard Dick (?–15 February 1764) through the intercession of George Dempster. This transaction was part of Dempster's electioneering in St Andrews to become the MP for the Perth Burghs.

Dick had been the master of the St Andrews Grammar School since about 1740 and before that 'doctor' at the one in Haddington. He was brother-in-law to a St Andrews bailie named Morison who belonged to 'T. Lesly's party'. Demptster seems to have secured the place for Dick by getting his old friend Sir Thomas Kennedy, now the 9th Earl of Cassillis, to promise Dick the chair if Bailie Morison voted for Dempster when the burgh cast its votes for the MP to represent the district.[49] This happened and Dick was allowed to 'buy' the civil history chair from Alexander Vilant for £160. This represented two years' purchase but there may have been other sweeteners for Vilant. Dick was nominated by Cassillis on 10 April, tried on 10 May and admitted on 13 May 1762. He held the post until February 1764 when he died. His money was probably well spent. If he had a surviving wife, she would have qualified for a widow's pension.

In 1762, Dr Thomas Simson died and the Chandos chair of medicine, which he had held for over forty years, had to be filled. There were four applicants for this post. One, Robert Menzies, practised in Cupar, Fife and is but a name. He may initially have practised as a surgeon-apothecary but by 1770 he had an MD degree. He had had apprentices, which indicates that he was thought a capable man.[50] Another physician who applied was Alexander (later Sir Alexander) Douglas, the only son of Sir Robert Douglas, the author of the well-known *Scottish Peerage*.[51] Alexander Douglas had studied at Leiden but held a St Andrews MD. He was FRCPE and FRCPL but had made a career in the Army. A third applicant also had aristocratic ties which would have done him good. This was James Walker, who had apprenticed with William Wood and Robert Walker in Edinburgh and who in 1752 took a St Andrews MD. Four years later he became 'Surgeon and Agent to the Navy in North Britain' and the lessee of the Edinburgh baths. Both posts point to good connections. He entered the Edinburgh Surgeons' Company in 1757 but later became a licentiate of the RCPE so that he might compete for the position in St Andrews. Walker was a learned medic who by 1756 belonged to the Philosophical Society of Edinburgh. In 1762, he married Lady Mary Leslie, daughter of Alexander, 5th Earl of Leven.

The man who won the place was Thomas Simson's son, James (29 November 1729–30 August 1770), a well-trained man who had studied at Edinburgh and who was then Physician at the County Hospital in Wolverhampton. Simson was a respectable man but not the equal of his father and is not known to have had apprentices. He had left St Andrews hurriedly in 1747 after a body-snatching incident, which shows that he had been a keen anatomist. Professors Brown and Gregory did not vote for him and Principal Tullideph voted 'no' as he sometimes did when family members sought to succeed one another.[52] Simson converted the post, in which his father had sometimes taught, into a degree-granting sinecure attached to a local practice.

A new University chancellor had to be elected in 1765 owing to the death of the Duke of Cumberland. The Duke had not been an active chancellor and most of the University's correspondence concerning appointments seems to have been sent not to him but to Argyll, Newcastle or to some other politician. When he died in 1765, the University sought a more useful political protector. The University's choice lay between professor Wilkie's patron, Charles Maitland, 6th Earl of Lauderdale, and Thomas Hay, 8th Earl of Kinnoull, both of whom were put on the leet of 22 November 1765.[53] Lauderdale was also a good Whig who had had a political career as an old Argathelian, but by then the political machine of the 3rd Duke was no longer active. He was a modest improver but he had no particular claims to piety. Kinnoull came from a more Tory family and was more an Englishman than a Scot. His brother was Archbishop of York and he himself was Recorder of Cambridge. He had sat in Parliament for English constituencies (Scarborough and Cambridge) but never as a Representative Peer. Sir Robert Walpole, Henry Pelham and Lord Bute made use of Kinnoull's considerable expertise in elections and in financial matters. He was one of Bute's pious friends and became President of the Scottish Society for the Propagation of Christian Knowledge. Kinnoull retired from politics in 1762. He spent the rest of his life in Scotland residing mostly at Dupplin Castle, his estate in southwest Perthshire. There he busied himself with improvements in agriculture and in the economic and social infrastructure that sustained it. Highly thought of by the Moderates, he worked well with their leader, William Robertson. Kinnoull was the man chosen. He became an active chancellor and, because of his friendship with Principal William Robertson, much increased the purchase that the Moderate Party had at the University.

In the same year, two other men were appointed, Dr George Forrest of Gimmersmills (by 1735–5 October 1795) and Nicholas Vilant (c. 1738–25 May 1807). Forrest was presented to the chair of civil history by the Kennedy family on 10 January 1765 and held the place until his resignation on 12 November 1772. He came from Haddington where the estate, which he inherited later in life, was situated. He had attended Edinburgh University and held an MD granted there in 1755. About thirty years old when he brought the chair, he had some expertise in natural science but he was not notable as a civil historian. Dr Forrest practised in St Andrews and the chair would have substantially increased his income and helped him to obtain the natural philosophy chair at which he was likely aiming. He was sufficiently interested in intellectual matters to show up on book subscription lists[54] but little else is known about him except that some students found him a dull lecturer. In 1767, he spent much of the year in France, where he seems to have travelled as a tutor to the son of Charteris of Amisfield, a neighbour from the Haddington area.[55] This jaunt set a precedent which Hugh Cleghorn would later remember when he too took a boy to Europe in the late 1780s. How Dr Forrest came by this job is unknown.

The other appointee of 1765, Nicholas Vilant, received the regius chair of mathematics for which he competed with four other men. Vilant had attended St Andrews University, to which his family had already supplied four men since 1690.[56] He had more than family ties to recommend him. Letters sent by the College to the Lords Privy Seal, James Stuart Mackenzie, MP and Lord Frederick Campbell, MP, and to the Secretary of State, Lord Sandwich, noted that Vilant had been a teacher in Watt's Academy in London. This was an important training centre for men interested in the practical uses of mathematics.[57] Stuart Mackenzie also received letters of recommendation from Matthew Stewart, professor of mathematics at Edinburgh, and Robert Simson in Glasgow and one from the Earl of Glasgow, the High Commissioner to the General Assembly. The last letter suggests that Vilant had the patronage of the Moderates as well as the best mathematicians in Scotland.[58] Since his appointment involved patronage managers in London and Edinburgh who had a high regard for merit, it is likely that Vilant was chosen principally for his abilities rather than because of his family connections. He later published a textbook in his field, *Elements of Mathematical Analysis* (1798). Sometime in the late 1770s or early 1780s he became disabled and thereafter taught by deputies. Some of his deputies became distinguished men and included, among others, James Brown, John (later Sir John) Leslie, John Playfair, Thomas Chalmers and James (later Sir James) Ivory. All had clerical training but only Chalmers ultimately made his career as a minister. All served later as professors – at Glasgow, Edinburgh and the Royal Military College. All were men of distinction but Leslie and Brown were prevented from shining in St Andrews by their political beliefs which were too Whiggish to be borne.

The next appointments came four years later in 1769, when the College made two. The first translated Alexander Morton from the humanist's chair to the professorship of Greek, which he held for only three years and then sold to George Hill (22 May 1750–19 December 1819). Such promotions and transfers would become more common, as would members of the Hill family. The second selection involved John Cook (1739–1 July 1815), minister of Kilmany. The patrons of his parish were the principal and professors of the United College. They persuaded the Scots of Scotstarvit to choose Cook as the new humanist. It is unlikely that these positions involved interference by politicians since there was no politician who dominated Scottish politics at this time.[59] John was the first of many Cooks who would teach at St Andrews.

In 1770, James Simson died and a new Chandos professor of medicine had to be chosen. Dr Robert Menzies, who had sought it earlier, sought it again with no better luck. Another from farther away, who wished to hold this post and may even have entertained thoughts of teaching, was Peter or Patrick Wright, a physician member of the Glasgow Faculty of Physicians and Surgeons who was son to the Laird of Foodie (near Cupar, Fife) and had taken a St Andrews MD five years earlier. Wright served as president of his guild for ten years and was active in the establishment of the Glasgow Lunatic Asylum. He was a learned man and friendly with professor John Anderson of Glasgow, whose physician he was. Anderson picked him to be an executor of his will and the prospective professor of 'the Institutes or Theory of Medicine, and Dean of this Faculty' at the university he hoped to found.[60] Wright, like Anderson, had antiquarian interests and in the 1790s would be a passionate Whig. He would have had letters of recommendation from Glasgow but they would have palled in comparison with the credentials of another local boy who wanted to return, Andrew Duncan, MD.

Dr Duncan was the son of a Crail skipper and a grandson of regent William Vilant. He was also a St Andrews graduate who also had recently taken a St Andrews MD. His local connections were impeccable. He was also just back from a voyage to China on an East India Company ship and needed a settlement. He applied with 'flattering testimonials from all the members of the medical faculty of Edinburgh, and from other eminent members of the profession.'[61] Among his referees was William Cullen, then the foremost professor of medicine in Scotland and possibly in Europe. We may guess at what Cullen wrote since we have his letter to Baron Mure whom he expected to influence the appointment even though the chair was not one officially controlled by the Crown:

> . . . I venture to trouble you with this, to give you my word, so far as it will go, that you cannot employ your interests for a more worthy man than Mr Duncan. He was my pupil, and I have known him long and well, and I will pawn my credit upon it that he will make an ingenious Professor, and an able practitioner of physic. Dr [John] Gregory and I have given an opinion to this purpose to Lord Kinnoul, the Chancellor of St Andrews, and I am fond to give it whenever I can.[62]

The University was probably not looking for an 'ingenious professor' as active and ambitious as Duncan. They hired the fourth candidate, James Flint (1733–16 December 1810), an unremarkable physician practising in Dumbarton who had served as Surgeon to the Fencible Men of Argyllshire in the early 1760s. Why this Glasgow graduate and member of the Glasgow Faculty of Physicians and Surgeons should have been chosen is unclear. It might have been given to him because of his service background, limited though this was.[63] This would have been helpful since his principal task as professor was judging the merits of men recommended for degrees, men who in many instances had military or naval backgrounds. His army experience also suggests that he was not without political connections; surgeoncies in fencible regiments were patronage positions. Perhaps he was appointed owing to the sort of government influence which Cullen had hoped to gain for Duncan. If that were the case, then he would have had the good opinion of some Campbell (perhaps Lord Frederick Campbell, MP, Lord Clerk Register and the political manager for the Campbells of Inveraray) since the Fencible Men were effectively a clan regiment. Whatever the reason, his appointment was not one applauded by respectable men interested in the University.[64] Flint continued the post as a non-teaching one and was followed in it by his son. Neither of them seems to have taught even apprentices.[65]

In 1772–3, as if to exhibit the forces now dominant in St Andrews patronage – the Moderates in the Kirk, family connections in the

College and local gentlemen – the College hired a man associated with the Moderates, promoted a man from within and took a young gentleman with impressive family supporters.

The Moderates' man was George Hill, the son of a minister of St Andrews. Hill was a St Andrews graduate with theological training taken at Edinburgh and a man who had early impressed many.[66] Hill had been recommended by Principal Robertson as a tutor to the sons of Pryse Campbell, MP. Hill's later career owed much to Robertson, Kinnoull and to Henry Dundas. He was patronised by Kinnoull and allowed to 'buy' the Greek chair from Alexander Morton who then retired.[67] Hill was opposed by others for this job but his backers prevailed and he was admitted a conjoint professor with the right of survivancy on 21 May 1772. Three years later he was licensed to preach and was then employed as Principal Tullideph's deputy at St Leonard's church. George Hill was the first of many Hills who, with their relatives in the Cook family, would dominate the University by 1800.

The internal appointee was Dr George Forrest, who in 1772 was promoted to be professor of natural philosophy in succession to William Wilkie who had died. Forrest was opposed for this post by a far better man, John Playfair, who had deputised for Wilkie. Despite his relative youth (he was twenty-four years old), Playfair was a serious candidate.[68] He was given the living of Liff by Lord Gray after losing this place.[69]

In 1773, gentlemen in Edinburgh almost certainly placed the third professor at St Andrews. This was Hugh Cleghorn (21 March 1752–18 February 1836), a member of the extended family which included Edinburgh's professors Hamilton, Balfour and Whytt and Principal William Leechman in Glasgow. Their families had provided Scotland with at least seven professors in the previous two generations.[70] Cleghorn would have had many Edinburgh supporters. Indeed, he was presented to the chair of civil history by the Earl of Cassillis in December 1772 before he had graduated at Edinburgh. He was installed at the beginning of 1773, just before he attained the legal age for appointees.[71] Cleghorn used his chair to give lectures on political economy, politics and the progress of nations. His were up-to-date lectures which showed him interested in current problems. His lectures somewhat resembled parts of those given by John Millar, William Wight, Adam Ferguson, and Adam Smith. Like James Beattie at Marischal College, he lectured on the evils of slavery and the value of a balanced constitution which protected British liberties.

The interests of the Hill family were strengthened at St Andrews in the following year, by the appointment of John Hill (27 April 1747–7 December 1805) to the chair of humanity. What induced David Scot of Scotstarvit to make the presentation is unknown. John Hill was a somewhat older half-brother of George Hill and the grandson of Principal John Gowdie of Edinburgh, the clerical politician whom William Robertson had succeeded. John Hill was also brother-in-law of John Cook, whom he succeeded in this chair when Cook was translated by his colleagues to the chair of moral philosophy. By 1773 there were two Hills and one Cook in the College, the core of a family faction which was to increase in later years even though John Hill left two years later to take up the Edinburgh chair of humanity. To secure this post, Hill did a deal with George Stewart, the incumbent, which had the approval of Henry Dundas. It was one of the first appointments in which Dundas is known to have had a hand.[72] Dundas would do much for the Hills and they for him.

When John Hill left for Edinburgh in 1775, he was replaced by John Hunter (9 September 1745–18 January 1837), a former secretary to Lord Monboddo, who vouched for his good Latin. Hunter also enlisted the support of James Beattie, to whom he wrote, 'My Ld Monboddo desired you would take the Trouble to wait on Mr Scott and give him what Information concerning me he might desire.' Monboddo's request was unwelcome since the eccentric Scot was living incognito. Beattie was then asked 'to write him on the Subject & lay before him, as shortly as you please such a Character of me as you think just, both as a Man and a scholar.' Hunter then gave a sort of resumé saying that he had been educated for the church and had read classics with Monboddo – a curious but impressive qualification. He added, 'Mr Scott himself is a Scholar and, as is supposed, desires to bestow the office on the properest man he can find.'[73] Chancellor Kinnoull and others are said to have asked for his appointment.[74] Hunter became a fine scholar and editor, an agricultural improver and one of the men responsible for piping water into the town of St Andrews. He served as principal of the United College after 1804, the year in which one of his sons was installed in the chair of logic. Even the good outsiders (he was from Dumfriesshire) became nepotists at St Andrews.

The era of Principal Tullideph effectively ended in 1775 with his growing incapacity and near retirement. Here it will be convenient to look at the placement of a few more men before Henry Dundas began to exercise his full power at St Andrews.

In 1778, appointments were made which gave full control of the University to the Moderates. Robert Watson was picked to succeed Tullideph as principal by the chancellor, Lord Kinnoull, and William Robertson. The latter wrote to someone on 8 March 1774 to tell them to forget about seeking to make William Brown Tullideph's successor. Robertson said that Kinnoull had a man and that he approved of the choice.[75] With Kinnoull's contacts in London, it should have been no difficult thing for him to secure this regius chair for Watson.

Watson taught out the year as professor of logic but his elevation created a vacancy which was filled by William Barron (1735–28 December 1803). He was a protégé of Lord Kames but had also been patronised by Lord Provost George Drummond, the Earl of Hopetoun and Cunningham of Livingston. The last two had helped or tried to help him to church livings.[76] By the 1770s, he was known to some as the editor of John Bell of Antermony's *A Journey from St Petersburg to Pekin* (1763), a job he may well have got through his connection with William Robertson. Barron was a member of the Philosophical Society of Edinburgh and wrote an *Essay on the Mechanical Principles of the Plough* (1774). This topic was of much current interest, particularly to Lord Kames whose own discussion of ploughs appeared two years later in *The Gentleman Farmer*. Barron told Kames he wrote a later book, *History of the Colonization of the Free States of Antiquity* (1777), 'to convince the public I was not altogether unworthy of the partiality my friends have shown for me, and to procure if possible access to those books of which your Lordship thinks I deserve to have the perusal.'[77] His writings may well have done him good since he is said, somewhat implausibly, to have been 'nominated at St Andrews without his knowledge' and owed his appointment to Lord Suffolk, Secretary of the Northern Department.[78] Barron eventually was given a pension worth £100 a year for writings in defence of the government. He was also the author of a widely read book on *belles lettres* which contained the substance of his St Andrews lectures on that topic.[79]

Two more appointments were made by the Moderates before Henry Dundas gathered the national appointing power into his own hands. The principality of St Mary's went to James Gilliespie (1722–2 June 1791) in 1779. He had been given the St Andrews second charge in 1757 and was well known to the masters who in 1768 made him a DD, often a step toward a divinity chair.[80] He had earlier been chaplain to Lord Melville and was well enough connected to be chosen as Moderator in 1779. He had the support of Principal Robertson and Henry Dundas. Ramsay of Ochtertyre said the warrant for his appointment had been secured on the recommendation of Kinnoull.[81]

The other man was Harry Spens (c. 1714–27 November 1787), the minister of Wemyss and first translator into English of Plato's *Republic*. He became professor of divinity in 1779. His campaign to secure the chair had begun by 1778, when Spens asked Sir James Grant of Grant to solicit the chair from Kinnoull.[82] Spens said he stood well with the Earl and that the Moderates were eager for this appointment. Kinnoull recommended him; William Robertson seconded the nomination, writing to friends in London that Spens was needed 'at a time when a spirit of fanaticism and disorder is spreading among our Order.'[83] This was his way of referring to the resistance to the repeal of Catholic disabilities in Scotland which had occasioned riots and threats upon his own life by bigots opposed to this change. Spens would have lent his voice and authority to the opposition to the high-flying clerics who had supported the rioters in 1779. Robertson's recommendation may even have speeded the warrant which was received in Edinburgh about six weeks later. Spens became Moderator in 1780.

Moderate rule was now assured at St Andrews but, as in Glasgow, the Moderate men who came into office were not outstanding figures, although some of them were then notable ones. Wilkie's reputation has long vanished and few now read Watson's histories which in their day were widely read and often translated, although they were not as popular as were the works of Watson's cousin, William Robertson.[84] The theological writings of George Hill maintained their place in American divinity schools well into the nineteenth century but this only shows the backwardness of these Calvinist seminaries. John Hunter was a notable classical scholar but German scholarship was already making obsolete the critical editorial work he did. Barron, too, has long been forgotten. The greater, more interesting men of the Moderate Party appointed at Edinburgh and Glasgow were themselves the appointees of secular figures who prized them for reasons additional to their party-political and religious views. In hindsight, most of the men the Moderate clerics and their friends placed in the universities had little but Moderatism, politeness and conviviality to recommend them.

By the time Tullideph died in 1778, St Andrews seemed transformed. The changes which had come to the University were evident in the new philosophy which came late to St Andrews but did come. Archibald Campbell, Thomas Tullideph, Robert Watson and William

Barron changed the teaching of epistemology, logic and rhetoric between the mid-1730s and the 1770s. Their philosophy had a literary tinge which moved it further away from the formal logic and rhetoric of the early period. There was, however, less concern with the philosophical underpinning of the sciences such as one finds in the work of the Common Sense philosophers like Thomas Reid or among more Humean thinkers like William Cullen and Joseph Black or even John Robison. In moral philosophy, the transition may have come with John Young who was appointed in 1733, and who seems to have been eager to teach moral philosophy after 1747. With Cleghorn's appointment, moral philosophy was supplemented with a political-economics as modern but less original than that taught at Glasgow or Edinburgh – from which, indeed, it derived.

United College showed some interest in the sciences. It bought from James Short of Edinburgh a number of new instruments.[85] Short fixed meridian lines in St Andrews in 1748, one of which was in 1757 marked by a stone column.[86] All this looked forward to more observations to be made from the Library.[87] There the College installed 'supporters to the transit Telescope in the North Window of the Library . . . [and] a new Apparatus & Improvements of ye Reflecting Telescope' which also had been repaired in London and given a new stand.[88] This equipment was used by both David Young and William Wilkie. The astronomical clocks would still have been there, as was an orrery bought by Young. So were globes and maps which illustrated the discoveries reported in travellers' accounts and histories, about which professors like Cleghorn talked and which could be found on the library shelves. By the 1780s the library hall housed a growing collection of natural history objects. The old skeleton was joined by a mummy in 1781. Around them were botanical, animal and mineral specimens along with 'Eastern Curiosities', which almost certainly included arms, clothing and other ethnographic objects.[89] More pictures and prints were on the walls or in drawers. A separate instrument room had been created by 1756. It probably held the electrical generator and some of the model machines, optical equipment and surveying devices listed in the inventory of 1796.[90] There one might have found the new air pump that Dr Forrest was allowed to buy in 1777.[91] But no other substantial instrument purchases are listed in the minutes until the 1790s.

St Andrews science teaching had been at least competent and probably better than that. If we can believe the poet Robert Fergusson, the mathematics professor, David Gregory, was teaching, until 1765, not only elementary geometry and algebra but the useful applications of their theorems:

> Weel vers'd was he in architecture,
> And kent the nature o' the sector:
> Upo'baith globes he weel could lecture,
>   And gar's tak heed:
> O' geometry he was the Hector;
>   But now he's dead.[92]

His student, with considerable irony, mourned a man who was teaching maths as they were everywhere taught in Scotland – with reference metaphysics, civil and military architecture (fortification) and gunnery, surveying, astronomy and navigation. William Wilkie not only wrote verses but was said to be an interesting lecturer who made many astronomical observations. Forrest's dull course was likely to have been not very different, although one can infer from the state of neglect in which he left the instruments that he made few experiments or demonstrations and was not active as an observer.

Another sign that the University kept abreast of modern developments can be found in those to whom it gave honorary degrees. James Short received an honorary MA in 1753. Three years later, Lionel Chalmers, a distinguished Scottish émigré physician in Charles Town, South Carolina, received an honorary MD Three years after that, Benjamin Franklin received an honorary LLD.

In the divinity school there had probably been fewer changes. Principal Gillespie, who would have been teaching theology in 1781, advised someone to read during the vacation

> An approved System of Divinity. Pictet, Turretini, Mark, or some other, can be got in any Corner. Some one of these must be gone over and over with the Strictest attention; This labour will be tedious and less entertaining but is most improving, and indispensably necessary. [A]nd it will be Compensated by the Accuracy and facility in your Compositions, which this will enable you to teach, and which without it will be found unattainable.
>
> Good English Sermons may be got easily, and there is much advantage to be had from Reading them, they not only furnish Materials for the Pulpit, but will help to form a Style proper for it.[93]

The theologians he mentions were all read in the 1720s when John Simson recommended them to his students. Some of them would probably still have to be read in Latin or French. Men like Isaac Barrow, John Tillotson and Edward Stillingfleet were the English preachers whom Gillespie is likely to have had in mind. The English sermons dearest to George Hill (he was a generation younger than Gillespie) were those of the latitudinarian divines of late seventeenth and early eighteenth-century England.[94] Despite Gillespie's emphasis on English style and moralising, this was a distinctly old-fashioned course – but one which would have appalled James Hadow or Thomas Halyburton. It was still Calvinist, but Calvinism rationalised in Holland and Switzerland and insecurely tied to the Westminster Confession. It was Tillotson's Calvinism – which seemed to many Scots not captive to the Word of God or much concerned with 'Christ and Him crucified' – which had been the concerns of Halyburton. It also lacked the sort of critical thinking about the Christian message which Archibald Campbell, following John Simson, had apparently introduced to St Andrews and which was being encouraged in Aberdeen by George Campbell. There is no sign that William Brown taught a modern ecclesiastical history course and there is equally no sign that critical doctrines affected here the study of Hebrew sources as they had begun to do in France, Germany, England and in nearby Aberdeen.[95] Still, history and Hebrew were being regularly taught by the 1740s, which was an improvement over the early years of the century.

Among the honorary DDs awarded was one given in 1757 to Hugh Blair, an Edinburgh Moderate; another in 1769 went to John Witherspoon, the recently appointed President of the College of New Jersey (later Princeton University), who had written the classic send-up of the Moderates in *Ecclesiastical Characteristics* (1753). These men were opposite in their ecclesiastical politics but both were bright, learned and, in their differing ways, enlightened men honoured as such. That Witherspoon should have been given a degree shows some awareness among the divines of developments across the Atlantic, one perhaps not equal to that held by their colleagues in the sciences.[96] Few St Andrews men would have approved Witherspoon's later career as an American revolutionary.

The University Library also improved. A steady trickle of new books filled its shelves as the University benefited from the Copyright Act of 1709.[97] The College could also afford to buy or pay the freight on more than it had done in the past when acquisitions had been very meagre. By the end of Tullideph's reign, there was a plentiful store of new materials. In fact, the new additions had forced the repair and expansion of the library in 1764–7 at a cost of £778 6s 3d. What is more impressive is the range of the new acquisitions. There was no field of modern learning which was missing, although the collection tended to have a literary slant.[98]

More valuable chairs now drew the attention of patrons and applicants from outside the region. The 3rd Duke of Argyll and the government managers who followed him were more active in the distributing of those places and those who got them were on the whole a better class of academic than had been recruited earlier. Alexander Morton, William Wilkie, George Forrest, Hugh Cleghorn, William Barron and Henry Spens were all outsiders, recruited and more or less imposed on the place by men who would probably not have hired Gabriel Johnston, Hugh Warrender or William Brown because they prized merit more highly than had those who had helped that trio into office. Even the locals for a time improved with the appointments of Thomas Craigie, Robert Watson, Nicholas Vilant and George and John Hill. What had not happened was the establishment of a mechanism to ensure that good men would continue to find a place in the University. That the masters did not choose to employ competitive examinations was one blow to such a hope. Others came with the dominance of the Moderate Party and of Henry Dundas. For Moderates and Dundas Tories, party loyalty came to be the test of merit. The Moderates accepted that their control of the Kirk was tied to Dundas. He in turn was willing to allow them the nepotism for which the Hills and Cooks became infamous. As it progressed, so too did mediocrity.

Notes

1 Ochtertyre MSS, NLS, 16351/1/357.
2 6 and 23 May, 8 and 29 June 1748, SAUL, UYSL 400.
3 United College Minutes, 13 and 28 June 1748, SAUL, UYSL 400.
4 United College Minutes, 25 November 1748, SAUL, UYSL 400.
5 Scott, *Fasti*, VII:426; *St Andrews University Register*, compiled by Smart, 2004, p. 372.
6 This battle has even left a mark in the Edinburgh University MSS. See the minutes of several meetings of the St Andrews Senatus in 1720 and 1750 preserved in EUL, La.II. 677.
7 Shaw named Campbell, along with Tullideph, as one of his assessors when he was chosen as rector in 1750. Vilant was recorded as voting with Tullideph's faction in April 1750, but in 1749 he had been relying on David Young to represent him in the University meeting; Minutes, 27 November 1749, SAUL, UYUY 452/6.
8 Minutes, 23 March 1750, SAUL, UYUY 452/6.

9 Minutes, 23 March 1750, SAUL, UYUY 452/6.

10 Minutes, 8 May 1750, SAUL, UYUY 452/6.

11 Minutes, 20 February 1751, SAUL, UYUY 452/6.

12 United College Minutes, 27 November 1749, SAUL, UYSL400.

13 United College Minutes, 12 June 1751, SAUL, UYUC 400/1.

14 Morton to Argyll, 18 July 1753, NLS, 16682/164.

15 See the entry on Thomas Kennedy of Denure by J. M. Simpson in *The House of Commons 1715–1754*, ed. Sedgwick, 1970, II:411f.

16 Alexander Carlyle, *The Autobiography of . . .*, ed. Burton, 1910, p. 176. There is a bit more about Morton in Carlyle's MS notes for the book which are preserved in GUL, Murray MS 4. Stonefield is noticed in many places in Lindsay and Cosh, *Inveraray and the Dukes of Argyll*, 1973.

17 William Vilant under a conjoint appointment seems to have repossessed the former chair of humanity (then civil history) in 1753. He seems to have held it conjointly with his son, Alexander, until 1759 when William died. The Act creating the United College explicitly provided for Alexander Vilant's succession to the now-abolished chair of humanity. Alexander Vilant had been factor to the United College since 26 October 1747 and clerk for nearly as long. From his father's death until October 1761, Alexander claimed the chair, giving up his pretensions to it only in the autumn of 1761 when he was given a new appointment as College factor. The Vilant affair finally ended on 21 October 1761. It is not clear that any lectures were given between 1753 and 1762. United College Minutes, 26, 27, 30 October 1747, 2 November 1749, 12 June 1751, 20 September 1753, 22 December 1758, 8 January 1759, SAUL, UYUC400/1.

18 Chambers, *Biographical Dictionary of Eminent Scotsmen*, 1856, IV:420; Bator, 'The Unpublished Rhetoric Lectures of Robert Watson', *Rhetorica*, 1994, pp. 67–113. Bator's article begins with a short sketch of Watson's life. Henry Rymer kept the salary; United College Minutes, 17 June 1756, SAUL, UYUC400/1.

19 At Provost Watson's funeral on 6 March 1779, the University men marched in procession.

20 Ross, *Lord Kames*, 1972, p. 94; Howell, *British Logic and Rhetoric*, 1971, p. 544.

21 Professor Gregory, whose father had been opposed by the University, dissented from this decision and worked for Brown's admission. United College Minutes, 15 November 1756, SAUL, UYUC400/1.

22 Scott, *Fasti*, VII:432; Minutes, 16 June 1756, 20 July 1756, SAUL, UYUY 452/7.

23 Brown could return to Scotland only because the woman and her child were now both dead. I thank Mr R. N. Smart for this information.

24 Minutes, 15 June 1756, SAUL, UYUY 452/7; Ramsay of Ochtertyre, NLS, 1635/2/1399.

25 Minutes, 23 August 1756, SAUL, UYUY 452/7.

26 Ibid.

27 Minutes, 10 May 1756, 10 August 1756, 25 December 1756, 5, 28 February 1757, SAUL, UYUY 452/7.

28 It is against this background that one should read the many sermons and pamphlets on the character of ministers written around the mid-point of the century.

29 Home to Milton, n.d. [? February 1756], NLS, 16696/73 and 71.

30 John Home to Bute, 27 April 1756, Uncatalogued Bute MSS at Mount Stuart House. I thank R. B. Sher for this information.

31 'The appointment disappointed a party in the University who wished to see the chair given to a friend of their own and they revived an old scandal which they endeavoured to support in the Ecclesiastical Courts but they were completely defeated . . . [and forced] to pay from their private funds' the costs of the litigation in the clerical and civil courts. AUL, 2400, Box V.

32 John Home to Milton, 9 April 1757, NLS, 16700/196f.

33 'The History and Antiquities of St Rule's Chapel . . . with Remarks by Professor Brown' 1787 in *Bibliotheca Topographica*, ed. Nichols, 1787, vol. 5, part 4, 195–208.

34 St Mary's College Minutes, 4 September 1758, SAUL, UYSM 400/1. Brown was later an agitator in a long dispute between professor Hadow and the principal over a room which the principal thought belonged to the College and which Hadow claimed for his chair and for himself. This dispute ran from March 1773 until 1779, when Principal Morrison died. After this Brown feuded with the new principal, James Gillespie, over the building of a dovecote and other alleged extravagances.

35 Wilkie and his friends had appealed to Lord Milton for aid as early as 1751. Patrick Wilkie thanked Milton for favouring William at Ratho in 1751. This was two years before Wilkie actually became assistant and successor there. Other Wilkies had had aid from the Argathelians. William Wilkie to Alexander Lind, [?February 1751]; Alexander Lind to Lord Milton, 26 February 1751; Patrick Wilkie to Lord Milton, 11 March 1751, NLS, 16676/205.

36 Wilkie left 'many manuscripts . . . both scientific and miscellaneous, that have never been published' and which now seem lost. See the brief character of him given by the reverend Mr James Robertson in the account of Ratho in the *Statistical Account of Scotland*, ed. Withrington and Grant, 1975, II:421f. Another remark about him from a good mathematician and scientist is less flattering: 'Mr Bryce of Kirknewton . . . used to say, that Mr Wilkie was a man of tolerable abilities but knew little of mathematicks as his turn lay rather for poetry, moral philosophy & whimsical things of that kind. Mr Robertson his successor was little acquainted with the abstruser branches, but tolerably versant in the science of practical geometry.' Robert Hamilton's Commonplace Book, AUL, 451.

37 'I have now made trial of my new profession and find it a very agreeable one. Two circumstances make it easier than it would otherwise be – You know I am a piece of a poet and the same faculty which invents similes and metaphors in the one art helps to illustrations in the other. The second is that I remember Mr McLaurins way perfectly and endeavour to copy it as near as I can. He was master of a species of oratory the most perfectly adapted to philosophical subjects that can be imagined . . . Dr Whytt once proposed making me a member of your Philosophical Society – I refused that honour imagining that I should not be able to furnish anything in my way worthy of the Society. I hope better of myself at this time and would be glad to be admitted.' Wilkie to William Cullen, n.d. [1759], Thomson/Cullen MSS, GUL, 2255/192. Because there are very few surviving records of the Philosophical Society, it is not known if he was admitted, but it would be extraordinary had he not been. His description of his style of lecturing is interesting and suggests that Maclaurin gave many examples and analogies, something perhaps essential to the religious apologetic function which his teaching had. Secondly, it shows that, from the beginning of his tenure, Wilkie intended to do experimental or observational work which would yield novelties to report. He is not known to have succeeded but he did make astronomical observations.

38 Smith to Lord Milton, [?October 1757], NLS, 17702/83 and in *Correspondence of Adam Smith*, ed. Mossner and Ross, 1987, p. 22.

39 John Home to Milton, [?September 1757], NLS, 16700/198; James Moor and others to Lord Milton, 4 October 1757, 16698/104; Wilkie to Milton, 10 October 1757, 16702/223.

40 It went to George Campbell.

41 Wilkie to Milton, 15 May 1759 and [?May 1759], NLS, 16712/213 and 214.

42 Wilkie to Milton, July 1759, NLS, 16712/216.

43 George Dempster to Lord Milton, 3 January 1761, NLS.

44 His salary as factor was £33 6s 8d per year. As factor he dealt with George Dempster, merchant at Dundee and grandfather to the MP of the same name who in 1784 was given an honorary LLD. United College Minutes, 8 and 22 January, 8 November 1759, 21 October 1761, SAUL, UYUC400/1.

45 One contender for the earldom had appointed a Mr Monypenny to the chair when Morton vacated it. The patron said his only interest was that the chair should not become a sinecure and that the College should act as it saw fit. United College Minutes, 22 January 1759, SAUL, UYUC400/1.

46 Two letters from 1760 describe the canvassing prior to the election and Rothes' dominance of the town of St Andrews. *Letters of George Dempster*, ed. Fergusson, 1934, pp. 50–7; United College Minutes, 29 December 1760, 13, 16, 21 January 1761, SAUL, UYUC 400/1. Dempster

was a promoter of and partner in the Dundee Bank, which sometimes acted for St Mary's College during these years. Boase, *A Century of Banking in Dundee*, 1864, unpaginated.

47 University Minutes, 18 August 1724, SAUL, UYUY 452/3.

48 Dempster to Milton, 3 January 1760 [1761], NLS, 16719/185. The principal in the end wrote to the patron of the chair asking that Vilant be given something; NLS, Copy of Minutes of Mr Vilant's election (1761), NLS, 17603/49.

49 Dempster to Sir Adam Fergusson, 14 September 1760, *Letters of George Dempster*, ed. Fergusson, 1934, p. 52f.

50 *Eighteenth Century Medics*, compiled by Wallis and Wallis, 1988, p. 405.

51 *The Roll of the Royal College of Physicians of London*, compiled by Munk, 1878, II:461.

52 University Minutes, 9 May 1765, SAUL, UYUY 452/7.

53 University Minutes, 22 November 1765, SAUL, UYUY 452/7.

54 *Eighteenth Century Medics*, compiled by Wallis and Wallis, 1988, p. 206.

55 Minutes, 18 April 1767, SAUL, UYUY 452/8. The Charteris family was related to the Earl of Wemyss, a wealthy Fifeshire nobleman.

56 He was a grandson of Colin Vilant, regent at St Leonard's, and the third son of the second or third wife of the reverend William Vilant who was given his parish by the Earl of Crawford. Scott, *Fasti*, V:201. The others were Principal William, his son William and his son Alexander. Nicholas' brother served as University librarian.

57 United College Minutes, 13 and 23 May 1765, SAUL, UYUC400/1; Alonso D. Roberts, 'St Andrews Mathematics Teaching 1765–1858', unpublished MA thesis, pp. 13–22. See also Hans, *New Trends in Education*, 1951, pp. 82–7.

58 James Stuart Mackenzie to Baron William Mure of Caldwell, 22 April 1765, *Mure of Caldwell Papers*, 1885, Part 2, II:33f.

59 Scott, *Fasti*, VII:422.

60 James Muir, *John Anderson*, 1950, pp. 130, 133, 140. Anderson favoured evangelicals, which may help to explain Wright's failure to get a post at St Andrews.

61 Chambers, *Biographical Dictionary*, 1856, II:170.

62 Cullen to Baron Mure, 19 September 1770, *Mure of Caldwell Papers*, 1885, Part 2, II:176f.

63 Peter and Ruth Wallis' *Medics* list him as an army surgeon but his service seems to have been only in the Fencible Men of Argyllshire, a regiment which ceased to exist after 1763. *Roll of Commissioned Officers in the Medical Service of the British Army*, ed. Peterkin and Johnston, 1968, I:39.

64 Dr Sir John Pringle described him to William Cullen as 'a young physician of no distinction by Works or Academical courses'. Having seen his

own protégé fail, Cullen would have agreed. Pringle to Cullen, 19 August 1774, Thomson/Cullen MSS, GUL, 2255/31.

65 *Medics*, compiled by Wallis and Wallis, 1988, p. 204.

66 Chambers, *Biographical Dictionary*, 1856, III:93; McCallum, 'George Hill', ODNB, 27:132–4.

67 Marischal College Minutes, 29 April 1782, AUL, 41.

68 Scott, *Fasti*, V:349; Grant, *Story*, 1884, II:302.

69 Jack Morrell, 'John Playfair', ODNB, 44:555f.

70 Clark, *An Enlightened Scot: Hugh Cleghorn*, 1992, pp. 3–8; Cleghorn was distantly related to Adam Smith but that connection may have come later through his wife. Ross, *The Life of Adam Smith*, 1995, p. 407.

71 Clark, *Hugh Cleghorn*, 1992, p. 15.

72 D. B. Horn MSS, EUL, Gen 1824/1, 'Humanity'; Grant, *Story of the University*, 1884, II:319; Marischal College Minutes, 29 April 1782, AUL, 41.

73 John Hunter to James Beattie, 4 July 1775, AUL, 30/2/1–776.

74 *Biographical Dictionary of Eminent Men of Fife*, compiled by M. F. Conolly, 1866.

75 Robertson to [?] New College Library, EUL.136/615/Box 1; Ramsay of Ochtertyre, 'Memoirs', NLS, 1635/2/1397; see also David Allan's entry on him in ODNB, 4:91f.

76 Drummond had tried to secure for him the living at North Leith; Baron Mure to James Stuart Mackenzie, 26 February 1765, *Mure of Caldwell Papers*, 1885, Part 2, II:17f; Scott, *Fasti*, I:235f.

77 Barron to Henry Home, Lord Kames, Abercairnie MSS, SRO, GD24/1/585.

78 Printed obituary loose in the William Barron Papers, SAUL, UC 400, Box 1. If Suffolk really did get him the post, it would probably have been for political services, namely pamphleteering.

79 These are mentioned in Howell, *Eighteenth-Century British Logic and Rhetoric*, 1971.

80 His sponsors were said to be a Mr Wemyss, Lord Northesk, Lord Leven and Oliphant of Lossie, who had recommended him to James Stuart Mackenzie. Scott, *Fasti*, VII:422.

81 Ramsay of Ochtertyre, 'Memoirs', NLS, 1635/2/1406.

82 Spens to Sir James Grant of Grant, 31 August 1778, Seafield Papers, NAS, GD248/496/10; Scott, *Fasti*, VII:429. The Grant family had ties to St Andrews where it had founded a bursary but Spens was also a voter on Grant's interest.

83 Robertson to [?] 15 November 1779, PRO, SP54/47/364f. I thank Andrew Cunningham for the transcript of this letter.

84 I thank R. N. Smart for pointing this out to me. He also thinks that Watson hurt his chances with posterity by writing about a fading, not a rising, empire.

85 The orrery was made by Benjamin Cole (c. 1748–60). I thank Helen Rawson for this information.

86 Cant, *St Andrews*, 2002, p. 89, n.275; Minutes, 14 September 1748, SAUL, UYUY 452/5.

87 The Minutes for 27 October 1761 also recorded that 'the South part of the Observatory is in danger of falling'. It had been unroofed earlier and had long been a ruin but now the rents in the walls had widened. It had to be taken down. SAUL, UYUY 452/7.

88 Minutes, 28 September 1750, SAUL, UYUY 452/6.

89 Matthew Simpson, 'St Andrews University library in the Eighteenth Century', Unpublished St Andrews PhD dissertation, 1999, pp. 1, 11–13; ____, ' "You Have Not Such A One In England" ', *Library History*, 2001, pp. 41–56.

90 It existed by 1756 when it was broken into; United College Minutes, 15 November 1756, SAUL, UYUC400/1.

91 United College Minutes, 14 May 1777, SAUL, UYUC400/3.

92 'On the Death of Mr David Gregory', *The Works of Robert Fergusson*, ed.[?], 1970 (reprint of the London edn of 1807; the Edinburgh edition of the same year was edited by James Bannington), pp. 232–4. For a reading of the verses as less sympathetic to Gregory, see Freeman, *Robert Fergusson*, 1984, p. 142ff.

93 James Gillespie to [?], April 1781, SAUL, 37511(a).

94 These men were the ones whom George Hill cited in his *Lectures in Divinity* and the ones taught by George Campbell in Aberdeen. The great Anglicans from Chillingworth to Tillotson and Butler were much prized and read because they had sought to find the line between faith and reason. Suderman, *Orthodoxy and Enlightenment*, 2001, p. 71; Skoczylas, *Mr Simson's Knotty Case*, 2001, pp. 70–99.

95 Suderman, *Orthodoxy and Enlightenment*, 2001, pp. 46–8. George Campbell, the Marischal College professor of divinity, learned German to read Luther's translation of the Bible. He had some knowledge of the work of Johann David Michaelis and of French scholars like Jean Astruc whose work on the Pentateuch Campbell would have known as by an anonymous author.

96 R. N. Smart has informed me that this was reciprocated since Carter Braxton, one of the signers of the United States Constitution, sent two of his sons to be educated at St Andrews which much earlier had trained James Wilson, another signer and an important early American judge.

97 Fleming, *Hand-Book to St Andrews*, 1894, p. 35.

98 See the catalogues SAUL, UYLY 106/5 [1744], UYLY 105/4 [Press Catalogue, 1734–57]; other books are listed in various Minutes and in other sources.

17

THE DUNDAS ERA AT ST ANDREWS, 1780–1806

❧

1. GAINING CONTROL

By 1780, Scotland, indeed Britain, differed greatly from what they had been at mid-century. The economy had done well. Scots were noticed in the intellectual world but the American war was not going well and had begun to drain the country's energies and income and was focusing the attention of some on political dissidents. The anti-Catholic riots of 1779 in Scotland and continuing agitation in London and elsewhere in the south also pointed to the limits of enlightenment reforms and made the government conscious of the need for greater order and control. In Scotland, Henry Dundas' political machine would be the means of effecting that. In 1780, his machine was ready for the task of making Scotland orderly, which came to mean increasingly, 'as Tories would have it'. The control of the Kirk was essential because order and discipline was still preserved throughout much of the country by the church sessions and opinion directed by the preaching of reliable men. Dundas had to have a great interest in clerical affairs if he was to function effectively for the ministries he served. Clerical politicking had always been closely tied to patronage matters in the universities, where about half the appointees were still clerics or had trained as clerics. Dundas needed more influence in the Kirk than politicians had recently exercised. His opportunity to seize it came with the retirement of William Robertson from active management of the Kirk.

Robertson, for reasons which he refused to give, resigned as leader of the Moderate Party in 1780. His health had not been good. His life had been threatened in the struggle to repeal the anti-Catholic laws in Scotland in 1779, when he had been bested by his enemies. He saw other problems looming in the Church which would tax anyone.[1] With Robertson's departure and the death of Sir Lawrence Dundas, Henry Dundas was without a rival and free to put his stamp on Scotland. No place was stamped more surely than St Andrews, where he succeeded Kinnoull as chancellor in 1788. Dundas claimed to have appointed or approved every professor placed there from 1781 to 1801. Had he made the claim later, the time would have been longer.

The first appointment of the 1780s went to Charles Wilson (1736–5 September 1801), who was given the chair of Hebrew. Wilson had been the parish minister of David Murray, 6th Viscount Stormont, who was nephew of Lord Chief Justice William Murray, Lord Mansfield. It is not known how Wilson got his appointment – Dundas did not claim that one – but the Murrays had enough influence to secure a regius chair if they sought to use it. Wilson was later known for editing a Hebrew grammar, to which he added 'a dissertation on the two modes of reading, with or without points', a problem which had engaged the attention of Thomas Boston in the 1720s and one which among Scottish Calvinists went back to the controversy between Louis Cappel and Johann Buxtorf the younger in the 1620s and after.[2] Wilson said nothing notable about this problem but argued for reading the Hebrew text without the vowel points, which he thought were relatively modern additions. Charles Wilson, William Barron and John Hunter were eventually to be joined by family ties, ties which had an importance in some later appointments because they created an interest group opposed to the Cooks and Hills.

In 1781, Joseph McCormick (22 June 1733–17 June 1799), then an urbane minister in Prestonpans who had been an active member of the Moderate Party for many years, was recommended to Kinnoull by William Robertson as a man fit to become the new principal of the United College.[3] The chancellor presumably passed this nomination on to Dundas who then arranged for his appointment.[4] McCormick, this 'laughing philosopher' as Alexander Carlyle called him,[5] was the grandson of Principal Drew and the grand-nephew of William Carstares. By marriage, he was related to George Hill and John Cook. He was installed as principal in 1781 and was elected Moderator of the General Assembly, with Dundas' help, in 1782. In 1788 he was made Dean of the Chapel Royal.[6] His inclinations did not run to theology; his politicking was more important than his preaching. McCormick's scholarly accomplishment was his edition (with a brief life) of the *State Papers and Letters of William Carstares* (1774).

There were no further placements until January 1788, when George Hill was elevated by the efforts of the now-dead Kinnoull and the very much alive Henry Dundas to the chair of divinity. This he held for three years before becoming principal of St Mary's.[7] The

Greek chair then paid more than divinity so Hill was also given the Deanery of the Thistle to make up the difference.[8] When he vacated the Greek chair, it was filled by his brother, Henry David Hill, but his election was postponed because of the need to choose a new chancellor to replace Kinnoull.

Dundas was elected chancellor on 2 February 1788 and gained a place from which he could be sure of knowing all that went on within the University. He was, however, not the candidate of all the masters. Professors Flint, Vilant, Gillespie, Brown [he later changed his mind], Hunter and Cleghorn did not want him and they seem also to have delayed the appointment of Henry Hill to the chair of Greek so that he could not vote for Dundas. They had in mind the election of the 5th Duke of Argyll or his younger brother, Lord Frederick Campbell, MP and Lord Clerk Register, or of David Kennedy, 10th Earl of Cassillis. They had not decided on a candidate when Kinnoull died late in 1787. By early 1788, Dundas had got wind of what was going on. 'He instantly did the very thing you suggested in yours to me – He declined our Offer untill he should learn from the Duke [of Argyll] how far It would be acceptable to him for if it was, He would recommend him to his Friends.' Argyll declined. Dundas was then unanimously elected chancellor.[9] The University now had a chancellor who had the power to improve it greatly and claimed to have an interest in doing so.

The first thing the new chancellor did was to strengthen his own party in the University to ensure that it had an absolute majority. This could be done by filling the Greek chair with Henry David Hill (21 April 1762–14 February 1820), who was then in Europe. Dundas in this way repaid George Hill for the support he had given Dundas in his election as chancellor.[10] Others disliked this scheme but there was no agreement on who should have the chair. John Hunter wished to move from humanity to Greek. McCormick was a Hunterite because he 'felt it rather an unpleasant Circumstance to have so many Relations in one College'. Nicholas Vilant was for Hunter because he opposed the principal having an evenly divided College which would give him a casting vote, one which, if used, would lead to litigation to decide if it were valid.[11] Opposed to Hunter were not only the men for Hill (George Hill, John Cook, James Gillespie) but others who had different personal reasons. Professor Forrest is said to have thought that Hunter was a better Latinist than a Grecian. Cleghorn had 'a personal Grudge against' Hunter. Professor Flint wanted the post for one of his sons. William Barron seems not to have wished to see 'the family Compact' strengthened by the appointment of another Hill and joined that motive to a political difference since he and professor Forrest were 'tainted a little with the patriotic Leaven'.[12] They 'were not fond that Mr D——ss should have any more friends in the University'. Brown and Hunter seem to have voted against Dundas' man.[13] Dundas' election had not brought peace to the College but had brought to the surface tensions and animosities which characterised such institutions. These persisted.

Once all candidates had been named, negotiations became earnest. By 28 July 1788, Hunter had secured a bill of suspension to stop proceedings, a move which prompted his opponents to go to law as well. The Dundas faction, fearing to put their claim to a casting vote to a legal test, proposed to Hunter that 'if he would give up his own Pretensions they would agree to any Man he would recommend providing he was a Man no ways related to himself or to anyone of the Parties'. What happened next was that 'Barron gave up Charles Wilson, Flint his [own] son' but Hunter seems to have not quite accepted the terms. He named two men: one was his cousin, the second the son of his friend, professor Brown. That was William Lawrence Brown, who was later to become principal of Marischal College[14] but was then a minister in Utrecht, from which he would soon be driven by revolution. Under Hunter's scheme, the Scots of Scotstarvit would have been pressed to make Henry Hill the humanist, not the professor of Greek. Henry Dundas wrote to Mrs Scot of Scotstarvit asking her to make this possible. Principal McCormick noted that '. . . as it was his first interference with her patronage he did not doubt of success'.[15] Most of the professors were 'satisfied with his Recommendation of Dr William Brown of Utrecht excepting Cleghorn' and perhaps Flint.[16] McCormick was pleased with Brown's nomination because he believed that Brown was likely to attract students to the College. When Brown rejected this offer, he used the occasion to ask Dundas for the £100 pension, once granted to his uncle, to be the British Agent at Utrecht.[17] Brown's refusal rankled with the masters. They would not have him in 1791 when he very much needed a job.[18] Hunter took the matter to court again on the grounds that there had been no comparative trial.[19] By the late winter of 1788, they had got nowhere with this appointment. What happened next is unclear but Henry Hill won and was installed by 21 October 1789. What was clear was that appointments had become more clearly politicised and the University split into factions, with the faction supporting Dundas now dominant.

2. DUNDAS AS PATRON

The next three St Andrews livings on offer were in the divinity school and allowed Dundas to easily dominate that corporation since all those livings were in the gift of the Crown. Already George Hill was professor of divinity. When William Brown died in January 1791, his place went to Charles Wilson in 1793. This then allowed Dundas to fill the Hebrew chair, which was given to John Trotter.

In the first case, the interests of the University and the Dundas party were not quite the same. In December, 1790, William Lawrence Brown had told Dundas that he would happily succeed to his father's place. When his father died in January 1791, his hopes were supported by a disreputable dependant of the Earl of Wemyss, which did him no good.[20] Dundas did, however, tender an offer of the elder Brown's chair to William, who wrote from Utrecht on 27 June 1791 saying that he was grateful for the offer but that he could not accept it. Brown said he knew the Hills and other ungrateful men at St Andrews had cast aspersions on his reputation and that of his father despite the friendly offices done them in the past by his father.[21] They acted as they had because, should he be hired, he would board students in a house where French was spoken. This they knew would be 'prejudicial to the boarding house of Mr Cook married to Dr Hill's sister and to Dr McCormick's niece.' The lapsing of the student residences in St Andrews was not unrelated to the appearance of boarding houses run by masters and their relatives. Brown went on to tell Dundas that William Brown had engineered Dundas' appointment as chancellor. He added that the Hills, 'like the Supreme Councils in the Swiss Cantons . . . must exclude from the Academical Senate, every man who is not connected by blood or by affinity with the Ruling Powers of the University.'[22] This claim was disputed by Principal McCormick, who also denied that Brown had been eager to have Dundas as chancellor. According to him, Hunter and Brown had wanted Lord Stormont and had voted reluctantly for the Duke of Argyll. His letter, after pointing out the disagreeable and litigious nature of the elder Brown, said that his son was 'obnoxious' to most of the University men. Later McCormick wrote that Dundas had 'paid extraordinary Attentions to the [University men] particularly in choping Dr Brown'.[23]

Trotter's case was even more interesting. The day after professor Brown had died, Captain Alexander Duncan, on behalf of Lord Crawford, recommended Mr Arnot, minister of Ceres, for the ecclesiastical history chair. This was a serious nomination since Robert

Arnot (1745–2 July 1808) would later get a chair and become Moderator in 1795. In 1791, he was pronounced politically sound. The Earl of Crawford, who presented to the living at Ceres, wrote three days later to support Arnot's candidacy and again in May to ask that Arnot be given the Hebrew chair and Charles Wilson that of divinity.[24] Duncan hoped that a Mr Thomson might take over the Ceres kirk. All this anticipated the translation of George Hill to the principalship of St Mary's College, which the illness of Principal Gillespie signified was soon to be vacant. The consideration of these deals, and the fact that Gillespie was not dead, kept everything on hold. By April 1791, McCormick was pushing for Charles Wilson to be translated from the Hebrew to the ecclesiastical history chair. On 3 June, the day after Principal Gillespie's death, McCormick's plan became more elaborate. He wanted George Hill to be principal, Arnot to get Hill's divinity chair, Wilson the Hebrew chair, with the right of survivancy to vest in Robert Trotter. His claim was supported by the Lord Advocate, Robert Dundas, Henry's nephew and Edinburgh agent.[25] By 28 April 1791, McCormick and professor Hill had agreed that Wilson should take the ecclesiastical history chair without a chaplaincy, that Arnot would replace him in Hebrew and that Hill should get the chaplaincy, which paid more than his deanery. Complexities had multiplied.

Ilay Campbell, another Dundas friend who had recently been made Lord President of the Court of Session, asked late in May that Brown's replacement be Dr Laurie, minister of New Mills in Ayrshire. This was seconded by McCormick, who described the traits needed by a St Andrews professor of divinity in these years:

> Dr Laurie is a Man of real Worth and a very respectable Clergyman, with a moderate Portion of Learning and a great Share of good Temper and Conviviality. If you do not serve him in this Instance, We must keep his Application a dead Secret, otherwise all our female Academicians captivated by his eminent Talents will be upon you.[26]

A Moderate professor of theology did not need much learning but he had to be polite and social. Such standards, supplemented by a political test, determined much of the patronage of the Moderates and really defined what they meant by a polite ministry. It is easy to see why others who prized learning and despised worldliness should find them wanting.

Sometime in 1791, Colonel Alexander Monypenny inquired of Dundas about the chair of ecclesiastical history, probably for Charles

Wilson in whom he was interested.[27] George Dempster, now retired, nominated a Mr Small but was unheeded.[28]

By the middle of June, the situation in St Andrews had become tense. The appointment of George Hill as principal of St Mary's College had been decided on some time earlier. He took office on 28 June, less than a month after Gillespie had died.[29] Robert Dundas, Henry's Edinburgh manager, went to St Andrews to attend Principal Hill's installation and to sort things out. He was eager for Robert Trotter to obtain the Hebrew chair succession to Wilson, who would then get the ecclesiastical history chair. Arnot would be professor of divinity. All of the St Mary's masters would then be in debt to the Dundases. Robert Dundas thought Robert Trotter would make a good professor but he also noted 'I am really under an obligation to put him in a comfortable situation.'[30] In the end Arnot was promoted to the divinity chair and, eventually, Wilson and Trotter took over the chairs of ecclesiastical history and Hebrew. These arrangements disappointed John Adamson, who in 1790 had also sought the history chair. In a letter to Henry Dundas, he said that he had been promised Gillespie's post which others were then soliciting but he was also willing to take the ecclesiastical history chair. He prefaced a long description of his financial troubles with 'I throw myself on your favour.'[31] As far as is known he was not considered for any of these posts, but he did get professor Cleghorn's chair in 1793.

Arnot, who was no scholar, was the first served. He was installed in October 1791, after which he continued to be a person of interest to the Moderate Party leaders. In December 1793, George Hill thought of him as a possible Moderator and wrote to Alexander Carlyle praising him: 'There is not a more staunch friend to the true principles of moderation, or a man more firmly attached to the Constitution, in the whole Church than Dr Arnot.'[32] He was made Moderator in 1795.

Wilson was a greater problem and his affair dragged on for reasons which have not been found. Initially it was probably because William Lawrence Brown was, in Henry Dundas' mind, still in the running as revolutionaries in Europe threatened his life as a professor at Utrecht.[33] By June 1792, George Hill referred to Wilson as the 'expectant of the vacant office'.[34] The problem may have been in London, since on 6 November 1793 Robert Dundas (Henry's nephew) wrote to Lord Advocate Robert Dundas of Arniston, MP, imploring him to send the warrant for Wilson's appointment as professor of ecclesiastical history. He wrote again the next day to say that the Hebrew chair was not to be filled until he had made a nomination.[35] Wilson was installed in the ecclesiastical history chair on 19 November 1793, which then opened the Hebrew chair to the reverend Mr Trotter who was admitted to it on 30 April 1794. The delay in this appointment was almost certainly to make arrangements for the Dundases to use the University to pay political debts.

Edinburgh, Glasgow and Aberdeen were towns large enough to keep one or more teachers of French in custom. At Edinburgh, a teacher had moved into the College precincts by the 1730s. At Glasgow by the 1750s or early 1760s a faculty member was teaching French and later Italian; the town had had language teachers much earlier. In Aberdeen, no lecturer in the universities during this period is known but the town had sometimes had one. St Leonard's College had had a French teacher as early as 1695 and others show up after the union in 1755, 1756, 1775 and 1782, but not until 1794 did the position become relatively permanent with the appointment by the United College of Fr Pierre Lagrandierre.[36] Thereafter, one seems to have been more or less continually present.[37]

Lagrandierre was a French émigré priest who filled a peculiar bill. The minute setting out the qualifications for this office required the teacher to be of good character, able to speak good English and Parisian French and capable of teaching drawing.[38] For this the teacher was to be paid £24 a year and fees from his students. This would have given Fr Lagrandierre quite a nice income, since his fees were likely to come to more than £30 a year. Lagrandierre taught until 1802 when he left, giving the University thanks for 'the marks of attention which [he] had received'. His good wishes were reciprocated. The rector was instructed to 'express the sense which they entertain of the propriety of his conduct & the elegance of his manners, and their earnest wishes for his health and happiness in his native country', to which we was returning now that peace seemed to have come.[39] He went away with a handsome gratuity. His tenure helped St Andrews compete with the other Scottish universities which could rely on teachers in the towns in which they were situated as well as on men occasionally paid to teach languages in the colleges (as at Glasgow) or given a space to do so for fees (as seems to have happened sometimes at Edinburgh). Fr Lagrandierre's replacement in 1802 was the reverend James Hunter, minister of St Monans, who was paid 24 guineas a year and collected fees of one half-guinea a quarter for teaching each student an hour a day five days a week.[40]

Seventeen ninety-five was also the year in which the College had to choose a new professor of natural philosophy because of the resignation of Dr Forrest. He had long been willing to 'sell' his chair and retire. The man who 'bought' it was Dr John Rotherham (c. 1750–1804), the only Englishman appointed at St Andrews in the period here reviewed. He had been passed over at Edinburgh when Thomas Charles Hope was picked to succeed Joseph Black in the chair of chemistry (see above, p. 301f.), and he might well have been passed over at St Andrews, where there were strong local candidates, had the government not lobbied for him. What decided the issue was Rotherham's politics. He was sounder than the locals.

The contest for the chair had clearly begun by May 1792, when John Leslie, later professor of natural philosophy at Edinburgh, wrote to James Brown, minister of Dunino and assistant to Nicholas Vilant and later the professor of natural philosophy at Glasgow, telling him how important it was that the Hills not place another of their relatives in this chair:

> I entreat you to oppose their insatiable ambition. If the place is to be purchased cannot you make a greater offer than they? If ready money is demanded, I will chearfully supply you with it. The other professors must be conscious that they [should] behave to give you their support, to deliver them from an oppressive monopolizing spirit. At any rate you may foil the attempts of the Hills for the present; and more auspicious times may come, to confirm your election.[41]

Two years later, Brown was still interested in the job. He had probably been asked to teach for Dr Forrest, since Leslie wrote:

> I wish you would take some suitable opportunity of sounding the dispositions of the other professors, and of representing to them that now is the time to save the College by resisting the monopolizing spirit of a family junto. I would undertake to teach the class on no consideration unless the succession were secured to me, in which case I might be induced to give a small premium . . .

If he was willing to give a premium, the place was for sale in some fashion. He went on to say that, were he to succeed Brown as lecturer in mathematics, he would not welcome the task wholeheartedly:

> At St Andrews I could have very little society and I might perhaps catch the drowsy torpor which generally prevails there. The temper of the ruling powers in Scotland is such as well might wean one's affection to his native country. Not to mention that if the spirit of innovation should at last burst forth in this island those monkish institutions, the universities, would be in a ticklish situation.

Were he to go there to teach, he would try to 'rouse a spirit of discussion and kindle an ardour for science'.[42] His known sympathy for
the cause of reform cost Leslie any hope of a job at St Andrews and
put paid to any chance of one at Glasgow, where he later stood for a
post which went to his more circumspect friend Brown (see above,
p. 190). Leslie remained without a university post until the Foxite
Whigs and others who disliked Dundas and the Moderates helped
him to find one in Edinburgh in 1805 (see above, pp. 328–34).

Although Brown had been teaching mathematics classes for the
disabled professor Vilant since c. 1784, he was tarred with the radical
brush and could not figure as a serious candidate.[43] Principal
McCormick, writing to Henry Dundas on 27 October 1795, noted
that Brown would have the support of Vilant and probably professor
Hunter, who would then want the University men to give Brown's
church at Dunino to Hunter's son, 'a very deserving young Man'. He
went on:

> Mr Brown himself has great Merit as a Teacher, and we are all disposed
> to serve him; but there is an [?unsupportable] Objection to some perhaps
> the most of us: From his declining to subscribe a Paper that was handed
> about upwards of twelve-month ago as a Test of our Loyalty to the King
> and Constitution, Suspicions have arisen amongst the Gentlemen of the
> Country; that He is tainted with, Principles which I should be sorry to see
> countenanced by any Profr in this University.

He then made sure that in a time of loyalty oaths and subscriptions
to Toryism, Dundas understood that Leslie was equally suspect:

> Another Candidate is one Mr Leslie, an Eleve of our own, and a Protegé
> of Lord Kinnoull's, who educated him at his own Expense: He has an
> extraordinary Genius for Mathematicks and is warmly recommended to
> Me by Dr [Charles] Hutton of the royal [Military] Academy as Woolich,
> but he labours under the same Reputation with the former, and whilst that
> is the Case were he Sir Isaac Newton He can have no support from Me.

A third contender for Forrest's professorship was Dr John Flint
whose father, James, was the professor of medicine. About him
McCormick wrote, 'I do not find He will have any great Support'
other than from his father.[44] Professor Flint wrote to Dundas a few
days later saying that Leslie and Brown were acceptable candidates,
as was his son, whom the old chancellor, Kinnoull, would have
backed.[45] This, like other of Flint's projects, seems to have resulted in
nothing. As did the hopes of Dr Robert Small, a minister in Dundee.
He was a distinguished amateur natural philosopher who published

on mathematics and astronomy and had been Moderator in 1791. His political credentials were impeccable but he was sixty-three.

This left John Rotherham as the most viable candidate. Since he had been disappointed at Edinburgh and could not be appointed at Glasgow, St Andrews would have to do. This meant a considerable reduction in his prospects.[46] He was, however, a very desirable candidate. Rotherham's father had been physician to the Newcastle Infirmary and Dispensary so he had grown up with medicine. He himself had attended Edinburgh University and then studied botany and other subjects at Uppsala, where he took his MD. There he had been befriended by Linnaeus, in whose house he had lived and whose deathbed he attended.[47] He had been a travelling tutor, a medical editor for William Creech, the Edinburgh publisher and printer, and had been given the chance to teach for John Robison, the ailing professor of natural philosophy at Edinburgh. For several years he was Joseph Black's assistant and, for a time, his presumed successor. The College could not have hoped for a politically reliable man with better all-round science training or more experience as a teacher.[48]

Rotherham was recommended to the Dundases by the Edinburgh Lord Provost, Sir James Stirling. He pointed out that T. C. Hope's appointment had disappointed many town councilors, who had wanted Rotherham to succeed Joseph Black. Rotherham's placement at St Andrews would somewhat make up for this. Stirling also wrote to the United College; so did others. Principal McCormick came to the conclusion that Rotherham would be the man and believed that professors Adamson, John Cook and Henry Hill would join in voting for him. Only Barron was 'uncertain but I know he is not engaged'.[49] The other electors divided between Flint, Brown and Leslie. The problem was to swing Barron's vote for Rotherham. The Dundases now made a concerted attempt to secure this post for Rotherham, one which shows how much pressure they could bring to bear upon professorial electors.

Robert Dundas wrote to William Barron asking him to join the party for Rotherham, which he saw as headed by Principal McCormick.[50] Letters were sent to St Andrews by a number of Edinburgh professors. Professor John Hill, the Edinburgh humanist, wrote to the Lord Provost of Edinburgh asking him to write to Barron.[51] A letter was solicited from Dugald Stewart, who refused to write it. He was too good a Whig and too honest to give a testimonial for John Rotherham when Whigs and better scientists were in contention.[52] Professor Greenfield, Hugh Blair's replacement who became Moderator in 1796, sent a letter to Principal Hill. So too did professor James Gregory and 'others'. Hill noted that these letters had convinced his friends. They had thought Rotherham a bit vulgar but 'we consider him very far from being a Republican'.[53] Barron, who had republican leanings, voted for Rotherham. He wrote servilely to Robert Dundas:

> I have been so much flattered by marks of attention, and so much obliged by real favours, generously conferred by Mr Secretary [Henry] Dundas on a man, who had nothing but his industry to recommend him, that there is not a wish of his, the knowledge of which would not induce me to do every thing in my power to gratify it.

The alacrity with which Barron responded suggests that he had recalled that he was a pensioner. He went on in a way which says something about how the professors saw Dundas' behaviour to them.

> Mr Dundas s conduct as a Chancellour has been uncommonly delicate and condescending, as he has not disposed of any of our offices in the gift of the Crown without consulting us. I think in return, when the gift is our own, after we are satisfied about the man, the knowledge of his wishes should be decisive to us.[54]

Dundas had abetted the professors' nepotistic ways; they now toed his political line. Rotherham was elected and admitted on 23 and 24 November 1795.

The appointment created resentments which surfaced when the masters tried to deprive Vilant of the privilege of naming his deputy after Brown had been elected to the Glasgow chair of natural philosophy. Vilant or a friend (Hunter?) now took Instruments protesting Rotherham's election and demanded minutes of the proceedings so that Vilant could launch a lawsuit, which he did. The Lord Ordinary, Lord Craig, forced Vilant's colleagues to comply with his wishes and there the matter seems to have ended.[55]

While Dr Forrest was disposing of his natural philosophy chair, the Kennedy family had to find a new incumbent for the chair of civil history which had been held since 1773 by Hugh Cleghorn. Cleghorn had itchy feet and set off for Europe in May 1788 as a travelling tutor to one of his students, the 10th Earl of Home. They were gone for two years, during which they saw much of France, Switzerland and Italy at a very exciting time.[56] This experience whetted Cleghorn's appetite for a more active life. By 1791, he was trying to advise Dundas and the government on a range of political and diplomatic issues. This he thought justified further leave from the College. Principal McCormick did not think so; the College required him to return by 3 January 1792. This he would not do. Instead, he got Henry Dundas to request that he be given further leave, which was granted. During this time he may have been engaged in Secret Service work which took him to Switzerland in 1793. By then the College had lost all patience and told him to return. He effectively resigned on 2 February 1793, saying,

> . . . the gentlemen of the College may give themselves no further trouble respecting my absence. Lord Cassilis, who is in London, has fixed upon a gentleman of talents to be my successor and I shall resign into his Lordship's hands the office which I hold in St Andrews.[57]

He then embarked on a more colourful, exciting and much more rewarding career, one which would see him engineer the acquisition of Ceylon for Britain.

The man whom Cassillis appointed in his place was John Adamson (1742–20 August 1808), a local man whose published works amount to two political sermons, which inculcated political loyalty and celebrated British liberty and good sense, and the entry for St Andrews in the *Statistical Account of Scotland*. Adamson, a DD from St Andrews in 1777, had held a parish in the town since 1779. He was another stalwart of the Moderate Party.[58] He had sought a St Andrews posting in 1791, when he asked Dundas to make him the replacement for someone unnamed whom he believed would be translated to a divinity chair. He said in his letter that he thought he had been promised the principality of St Mary's College.[59] In Cleghorn's absence, he had been his substitute lecturer.

Adamson was not alone in seeking the chair. The reverend Stevenson MacGill is said to have turned it down after the place had been secured for him by David Erskine, the 11th Earl of Buchan.[60] This is not altogether implausible. MacGill had been a tutor in Buchan's family and he shared Cleghorn's and Adamson's interests in political economy.[61] Buchan might have been able to persuade a private patron to appoint his protégé, who seems to have been not unlike Cleghorn in some respects. MacGill's published works included some with historical materials, although most were sermons, exegetical pieces and pieces that addressed current issues centred on the character and education of ministers – a lively topic in Scotland after David Hume's attack on the character of clerics in the essay 'Of National Characters' (1748).[62] If MacGill did turn down this post, he was wise since he, like his patron, was a Foxite Whig, something of an evangelical, and involved with reforms which at St Andrews interested few of the masters.

One other applicant is also known. James Gartshorne asked the chair of Henry Dundas in the autumn of 1792, even though it was in the gift of the Kennedy family. He noted that he had 'the prospect of having my application seconded by the first political interest in Scotland'. Political soundness seemed to be all he offered. Gartshorne seems to have been a student at Glasgow, where he claimed to be studying 'some branches of science under the patronage of an uncle[,] Mr Stirling of Craiglarnet in Stirlingshire'.[63]

In 1799, after eighteen years in office, Principal McCormick was dying and the United College had to choose a new principal. George Hill turned the place down, although he clearly intended to continue to dominate the University from his less well-paid but more congenial seat. Hill recommended that John Cook, William Barron and Nicholas Vilant *not* be given the place although they were the senior professors. He also did *not* recommend John Hunter, who by then had considerable seniority but was not in Hill's faction. He suggested instead that Dundas

> . . . give the office to some respectable Clergyman, who would keep clear of all family parties. If he were principally attached to your family, he and I would coalesce upon all general points, and he would never find me disposed to fetter him in any Matter of private concern.[64]

A few days later, a John Hope wrote to Henry Dundas saying that professor Arnot wanted the principality and the living of St Leonard's. Moreover, he deserved them because he was a loyal and true Dundas man who had served well as Moderator in 1795. Three days later, Hope wrote again to say that gentlemen in the area wanted Arnot to have this post and that he was acting for them.[65]

Dundas mulled this over for a considerable time and then asked the masters for a unanimous nomination on which he would then act.[66] By then only two candidates remained: Arnot – backed by Wilson, Rotherham and Adamson – and Trotter – backed by the Hill faction plus Barron and Hunter. No one would yield. On 17 August 1799, Robert Dundas told the professors that Henry Dundas 'finds himself therefore obliged to look for some Gentleman not a member of the University, whom on public grounds, and exclusive of all personal regard and partiality, he may with propriety recommend to the honourable situation of Principal'.[67]

Dundas' first pick seems to have been Alexander Carlyle, who by 19 October 1795 had declined the place. Carlyle's only real claim to the honour rested on years of service to the Moderate cause; he had no academic credentials other than an honorary DD. His publications were limited to sermons and a few political pamphlets. George Hill then recommended James Playfair to the consideration of Lord Advocate Robert Dundas. He made enquiries about Playfair's suitability and concluded that he would be acceptable.[68] The place went to Playfair (7 December 1736–26 May 1819), a scholarly Moderate who was then minister of Meigle, a royal living whose vacancy would have given Dundas the chance to gratify another man. Playfair held a St Andrews DD (1779), which was almost certainly a sign that he had earlier aspired to a university post and that the masters had thought him fit for one. This appointment displeased many but it did bring a working scholar into the College, one who was eventually honoured by being made Historiographer to the Prince of Wales. Only eight of the St Andrews professors went to his installation on 12 December and no entertainment was given for him.[69] Writing of his promotion to his brother, Lyon, he thanked Dundas for the appointment which 'is not the effect of Sollicitations, or interest, or personal acquaintances – but has, I apprehend, been owing to some favourable representation of my poor talents and literary attainments, which I fear have been too well spoken of.'[70]

The next few appointments consolidated family interests at the University, ensuring their persistence into the nineteenth century. When John Trotter left the Hebrew chair in 1802, to become professor of ecclesiastical history, he was succeeded by John Cook's son, John (24 November 1771–28 November 1824).[71] John Cook was the grandson of John Hill, the Edinburgh humanist. He married in the following year the daughter of George Hill, John's half-brother. Like his grandfather, this younger John Cook was much later a Moderator, but modern and principled enough to have become by then a follower of Thomas Chalmers.

Three appointments were made in the College in 1803–4. One went to James McDonald (1752–30 September 1843), who was admitted to the natural philosophy chair on 2 February 1805. He had married a daughter of professor John Hill of Edinburgh in 1799. McDonald's distinctive qualification as a natural philosopher seems to have been the natural history prize he received as an undergraduate and a parish account in the *Statistical Account of Scotland*.

The eight other applicants for this post included much better men, such as Thomas Chalmers, later a notable reformer in Glasgow; Thomas Thomson, who was to hold a medical chair at Edinburgh University; John Leslie, soon to be a professor at Edinburgh; and

Thomas Jackson, who presented testimonials from two earls, several lairds, the magistrates of Ayr, the directors of Ayr Academy and six professors at Edinburgh and Glasgow. There were four other men of lesser note. Among them was the rector of Dundee Academy, the rector of the Academy at Perth, and a Dr Mackay for whom the place was solicited by a William Glen. Glen's letter said that Dr Charles Hutton of the Royal Military Academy at Woolwich and Neville Maskelyne, the Astronomer Royal, would be sending letters on his behalf.[72] The last man, named —— Campbell, had the recommendation of John Playfair. All were clearly more accomplished men than McDonald but Dundas ignored them, choosing to favour the candidate of the Hills and Cooks.[73] In the end, this was an evenly contested election in which Principal Playfair finally gave a casting vote for a man whom George Hill thought it necessary to appoint. This was doubtless an attempt to show the opposition in the College that they could not challenge George Hill's and Dundas' domination of the College and University.[74] In the past it had been feared that the casting vote would not be sustained in the courts. It had not been used. Now it was used and it was challenged. The case ended in the House of Lords, where the principal's casting vote was found not good. McDonald finally lost on 26 May 1809. After that, Thomas Jackson was chosen to fill this chair. Many years before, he had sought the Glasgow chair of natural philosophy but had not been allowed to take it for political reasons (see below, p. 507).

A second appointment also went to the House of Lords, which again voided the placement of a relative backed by the Hill faction and Dundas.[75] About 1802, James Flint began to think of resigning his medical chair in favour of his son John. On 28 April 1804, he did so and they were appointed conjoint professors. The Flints feed an attorney named Cook and were backed by the Hill-Cook faction throughout the proceedings raised against them. The Flints were admitted on 16 July 1804 by George Hill, vice rector, acting with Henry David Hill, both of the John Cooks and Dr Rotherham. There were protests and Principal Playfair, joined by professors Arnot, Hunter and Adamson, would not attend the installation ceremony. Arnot and the others, on 1 May 1804, presented 'a bill of suspension and interdict' prohibiting the University from engaging in 'all proceedings relating to the elections and inductions of Dr Jas. & Dr John Flint'.[76] This was appealed to the Court of Session, which allowed the election and installation.[77] The litigation cost money which the Hill faction now expected the University to repay. Those who had objected to the appointment objected to that too. Principal Playfair and professors Adamson and Hunter were quite unwilling to pay the bills presented by Walter Cook, WS. Playfair protested the admission of the Flints and a committee composed of John Cook, John Rotherham and George Hill was created to answer the protests lodged by Playfair and others. James Flint claimed his adversaries said they were not 'activated by animosity against me or my son', but he lamented that 'Playfair, Trotter, and Hunter &c' had imported discord into the University after thirty years of peace. One wonders where he had been for that length of time.[78] The committee's report was protested and the whole thing went back to the courts, where it was eventually settled on 26 May 1809 by a House of Lords decision which voided the election and quashed the appointment. James Flint was then re-elected on 29 July 1809 and died on 16 December 1810. By 1804, wits were remarking that the Hills endure forever.

Having had two successes that ensured their majority in the Senatus, the dominant faction failed to prevent the next appointment going to one of their usual opponents. It went to James Hunter (1772–25 February 1845), the son of John Hunter, the humanist. James Hunter was made professor of logic on 15 May 1804. An attempt to block his admission was foiled.[79]

There were no more appointments made in the period covered by this survey, but a third place seems to have been on the line in 1804 – Nicholas Vilant's mathematics chair. Vilant had long been unable to lecture and had taught by deputy. In 1804 his place was sought by Robert Haldane, who solicited Henry Dundas, Sir Peter Murray and the Lord Justice Clerk, Charles Hope. His was an effort that bore no immediate fruit, but in 1807, after the Whig ministry had been turfed out and Vilant had died, Haldane received the chair. He is another professor who does not make it into modern directories of the able and accomplished.[80]

3. A Summing Up

After 1780, St Andrews continued to build on earlier foundations. The instrument collection was continually used[81] and it grew remarkably under John Rotherham, who may have brought with him some chemical apparatus since no purchases for such items are reported in the Minutes.[82] The library grew. The masters hoped as early as 1748 to expand the library space and were more or less assured by the 3rd Duke of Argyll that the money to do so would be made available, but it was withheld by the Barons of Exchequer.[83] It was not until after Argyll died in 1761 that space was added to accommodate the books that came principally because of the copyright law of 1709. Among them were a surprising number of medical texts. The medical professor might not lecture but he was keeping up. During the long years of confrontation with America, the University bought books on that, even ordering from London pamphlets and maps to keep abreast of the arguments and then of the war. In the 1790s, many deistical and controversial books were purchased, presumably making up for earlier losses or adding what Calvinists would not buy when the books first came out. The library also got treasures such as the books on Herculaneum published by the King of Naples and procured for this library, as for the others in Scotland, by Alexander Menzies of Culdares.[84] Rarities of a different sort also graced the library in greater numbers. Sir John Pringle gave it a medal of Maria Theresa and her husband and later a bust of George III.[85] Many more natural history and ethnographical items were added to the collection.[86] The books, instruments and facilities were better in 1806, but it is doubtful that the attention given to hiring by the Dundases and the Hills had much improved teaching outside science. George Hill and Henry Dundas bear a heavy responsibility for what happened to the University at the end of this period. Perhaps the greater share belonged to Hill.

George Hill's political conservatism led him throughout his life to support the political and social status quo, for which he argued in the General Assemblies and in his published sermons and pamphlets. He exerted himself to keep the Kirk immune from change and his and other universities isolated from social concerns which might lead to reform. Indicative of his attitudes were the 1782–3 votes by the Moderates to support patronage in the Kirk. It was Hill's motion in 1784 which said, anent patronage, 'that there is no reason for any innovation being made in the mode of settling vacant parishes'. This motion was followed shortly thereafter by another rescinding the directive which instructed the Commission to protest each year 'the grievance of patronage'.[87] This had been followed since about 1710. Hill and his like made the 'Church little more than a pendicle of the life of the State, a department which in its courts was allowed to have the shadow of self-government so long as it took no step to which the civil rulers might take exception as out of keeping with their line of State policy.'[88] Hill's generation of Moderates tended, even before the French Revolution, to forget the liberal views which had once led the Party to support Catholic Relief, greater freedom of speech and thought, and to concern itself with the raising of ministers' stipends. Even in 1807, when Dundas was for the last of these measures, as he had been since 1793, Hill opposed any increase in pay for ministers. That would mean higher rates imposed on heritors.[89] Not raising the stipends did not make clergymen more genteel and better educated, but worked to reduce their social standing, educational level and their effectiveness. Dundas was a more generous man. He continued to support the increases until modest gains were finally conceded in 1810. Dundas even gave some countenance to the evangelicals by making some of them Royal Chaplains after Robertson's death in 1793.[90] Hill's attitudes, when backed by Dundas' patronage, led to the University being dominated by one family and to the appointments of men who were, at best, mediocre. Both Hill and Dundas were repressive within the University and Kirk and found it in their interest to stifle rather than adapt. All this may have rubbed off on the St Andrews undergraduates, whose Philosophical Society debated a large number of political topics.[91] One would like to know if those who won the debates supported Principal Hill's policies.

Hill's religious outlook was that of a fairly orthodox Calvinist in theology but his divinity was practical and oriented to works, which in this case meant being moral and accepting things as they were or were dictated by those above. His *Lectures in Divinity* (posthumously published in 1821) became a much-used text for some years, but they did not rest on anything which would keep them alive for long. They seem to have had little impact save in Calvinist America, which tended, outside of New England, to change more slowly than other Calvinist milieux.[92] Just as his Erastianism was a far cry from the views of those appointed to the colleges in 1690, his theology was distant from the enthusiastic divinity of Thomas Halyburton, who is still read, while Hill and his like are dead without the hope of resurrection. Hill had no time for the spirit working in the souls of men. Such enthusiasm he deeply distrusted. Scottish evangelicalism arose in part from the reactions of godly men to attitudes such as his.[93] George Hill was so unevangelical and so opposed to change that he would not even support missionary activity furth of the kingdom.[94] His legacy, like that of his party, was an ossified church which had lost interest in anything innovative and enlightened.

Moderatism had been a cultural force which had made for tolerance, improvement and politeness during the years from the 1750s to c. 1780, but it was not a movement which produced any great ideas or left a legacy of original and lasting work.[95] It contributed to the

Scottish Enlightenment principally by creating an ambiance in which secular activities and intellectual concerns could flourish without criticism from the religious establishment, which was even willing to espouse and further many enlightened projects. Moderates did little or nothing for religion per se. Their contributions were to make the establishment more filled with hypocrites[96] and to help convert the Church of Scotland into a more Erastian church less willing to demand treatment by the government as an equal. Moderates strengthened the state. This forced them into confrontations with an older Calvinism, which saw Christ as the only King in the Kirk, and with the new evangelicalism, which sought the conversion and redemption of men whom Moderates seemed only to want to make law-abiding and morally better in this world. These attitudes had driven thousands from the Established Church by the end of the century. The tensions set up in Scotland between the sects and the Kirk, between the Moderates and the High Flyers, would lead to the explosion of 1843 in which the Kirk bitterly split in two. St Andrews, from the time George Hill was appointed in 1778, was a forcing point for all that which the colleges in Aberdeen and Glasgow tended not to be. Men like George Campbell and William Lawrence Brown in Aberdeen or Robert Findlay in Glasgow were far more open to reconciliation and compromise with evangelicals than were the St Andrews men.[97] The latter, like those Moderates who drove the Leslie affair at Edinburgh, were determined to see Moderatism prevail at almost any cost. After the 1780s, this meant a determination to support reactionary goals and policies and a determination to make no concessions to the other side. All this fitted well with the political views of the Dundas Tories as those were transformed under the pressures of war and revolution. The Moderatism of George Hill entrenched family interests but narrowed the outlook of his seminary and of the Scottish universities where men were appointed whom he had approved.[98]

Dundas was a better man and, one senses, better liked at St Andrews than elsewhere, even though he was at all times a likeable man of considerable charm. He was the only chancellor in the period who is noted to have addressed the students and then to have gone to church with them preceded by the maces; that same afternoon he attended a service in the town.[99] In 1806, the University congratulated him on his acquittal on the charges for which he had been impeached and found in the outcome of the trial 'the full vindication of an illustrious character'. This was a widely shared sentiment, but most Scots knew that the mere fact he had been impeached on plausible grounds meant an end to his ministerial career and having to live with a tarnished reputation. They should also have considered what he had done at St Andrews. The Dundas years changed it by supporting the outlook and wishes of Principal Hill and his relatives.

As is noted above (p. 178), Dundas he began his career in the 1770s looking like an enlightened man. Even when he was picked as chancellor at St Andrews, Principal McCormick described him as 'One . . . who has ever been forward to exert that powerful Influence which he hath acquire'd for the Encouragement of Literature & Learned Men in his Native Country.'[100] It was a view which others held and was truer in 1788 than it became in later years. The chumminess behind Principal McCormick's comment resulted in Dundas being given patronage in the colleges which other men had to solicit or work harder to secure. Writing later to Dundas about bursaries supposedly given to the needy and meritorious, McCormick said, 'When you happen to have a young Man on your hands whom you wish to provide in that Line you have only to write me & I will let you know what Bursaries are vacant & in the Case of the best You should apply a Year before As they are often bespoke early.'[101] Dundas gave power to men like McCormick and Hill because he needed them to control the Kirk. Many of those whom he most trusted were in St Andrews. It became, for a short time, the centre of the Moderates' management of the Established Church. Principals McCormick and Hill were from the mid-1780s as powerful as any men in the Moderate Party. They used their power to further the ends of the Dundas party in the Kirk and they filled the University with relatives and loyal local clerics of little or no reputation and worth while passing over other better-qualified men. During the last twenty-five years covered by this survey, only George Hill, James Playfair and John Rotherham were notable men, but only one of them came from beyond Fife. By 1807, St Andrews had no good scientist, John Rotherham having died in 1804. It had in George Hill a distinguished theologian but no professor other than John Hunter who was noticed outside Scotland. It was divided by faction and its appointments were more governed by nepotism than ever before.

Elsewhere Dundas made appointments in a similar manner. By 1811 these trends had gone so far that they angered even Robert Dundas, who had for so long been one prop (perhaps an unwilling one) to the Hill-Cook connection. Writing in 1811 to Henry Dundas' son, the 2nd Viscount Melville, Robert Dundas, now Lord Chief Baron Dundas, described the Hill regime in words which sum up its devastation of the University:

The whole System of the University of St Andrews, has been, sence the Hills obtained their Influence there, to make it an asylum for their Family & Dependents, without regard to Merit of any sort. I prevailed on your Father some years ago to give a principality to Playfair, certainly one of the most learned Men in the Church, & then of the highest Character, – The Family were desirous of naming a friend of theirs viz. A Dr Arnot, I think; but he was for good reasons rejected. Your Father most justly, & with the approbation of every Man in Scotland, preferred last year, a Mr Briggs to the Medicine Class, the most meritorious Person in the medical Line in the Field: He incurred the mortal Hatred & Antipathy of Messr Cook, Hill &c because he would not lend himself to their Job of naming another Man whom they befriended, and whom they thought fit to propose: but though a good gentlemanly Person, of no pretensions whatever to such a Situation. – These Professors ought to be taught the Lesson, that in the filling up the vacant professorships, they have as little title to interfere, by canvassing of any Sort, as it is understood the Judges of the Courts of law have a Right to interfere with the filling up Vacancies on the Bench. And if HRH the Duke of Cambridge [he had succeeded Henry Dundas as chancellor] adheres to that System, and forms in recommending to the King the Gentlemen whose talents & Qualifications, apart from all College Jobbing, – appear from respectable Testimonies obtained from impartial Persons, to be best entitled to a Chair in the University, His R. Highness will be the means of restoring the degraded Character & Usefulness of this almost desolate University, and do to himself infinite Honour. – this professor Cook [John sr] is a weak silly sort of Body: and owes I believe his Situation to his being married to the Sister of the Hills. It is as you justly observe a Job to get his Son into the Family Junto, & strengthen their Influence in the College, & at the same time to obtain a Presentation to the Kirk to be vacated by the young Gentleman: Unless what may be the Case also, after getting the professorship, Mr Cook shall discover that his Son may hold both Church & Chair, which assuredly would be the Case, if you gave the Chair before he resign the Living.[102] The Report is that George Hill means the Chair for his own Son, a young Man[,] Tutor in the Family of Sir D. Carneigie. Whether they have adopted Cook, or that the Father is stealing a March on his Friends by recommending his Son without the Knowledge & Privity of George Hill, I really cannot pretend to say . . . If it is [HRH the duke's] Desire to look out for a Man of Character & Worth, utterly unconnected with all the College Politics of every Kind, and who will go into the University independent in his Mind, & to do Justice to the Choice of those who may appoint him, I shall be glad with the aid of the Advocate, President & Heads of the church and Literary People of good and loyal Character in Scotland, to select a List of Names out of which the vacant Professorship, may be filled up: And you may depend on it, so far as I am consulted, my Voice shall go in behalf of the most worthy . . . So let me hear whether these Ideas are agreable to those who must decide, as otherwise it would be useless for me to put myself or others to any Trouble on the Subject.[103]

All this was true but rings a bit hollow when one remembers that the professors and not the Crown and its officers had the right to appoint to most St Andrews livings. They had a right to canvass and it had long been the custom to ask for particular appointees in the chairs not controlled by the University men. The Lord Chief Baron could now see the faults of others, but the politicians in his own family and faction, including himself, were equally to blame. When John Lee, and not the young Mr Cook, was admitted in 1812 to the chair of ecclesiastical history, he came into a University in which he was the only man at St Mary's unrelated to either a Hill or Cook. Of the eight other men in the University, at least three were Cooks, Hills or their dependants, and another had just been outed by the House of Lords. The core of the group which opposed them was also a father and son pair, John and James Hunter. Things had begun to change but they would not be fully rectified until the religious and political tests, which Robert Dundas supported and which in the second case the law allowed, were abolished.

St Andrews had had a curious century. The place had been harshly treated by the politicians of the early eighteenth century whose neglect had not been compensated for by the attentions of local notables. They had been most concerned to place in its chairs their own dependants. These men had quarrelled among themselves and the colleges, ever poorer, had declined until the mid-century. Only the interventions of political outsiders introduced good men such as Archibald Campbell and Thomas Tullideph. After the formation of the United College in 1747, the livings were of more interest to men outside the area. As the salaries went up so, for a while, did the quality of the appointees. Unfortunately, that situation did not last. The intellectual and moral decline of the Moderate Party and the politics of Dundas in a period of revolutionary hysteria showed that outside interference was no panacea for the things which plagued this University. By the end of the century, the place had become a bastion of reaction and mediocrity emblematic of what Moderatism had also become.

Notes

1 Brown, 'William Robertson and the Scottish Enlightenment', in *William Robertson and the Expansion of Empire*, 1997, pp. 7–35, 31f.

2 For a discussion of the general context of this matter, see Manuel, *The Broken Staff*, 1992, chapters 2, 3 and 4. It was a topic also associated with the Amyraut heresy, for which see Armstrong, *Calvinism and the Amyraut Heresy*, 1969. Capel taught at Saumur, a seminary well known to Scots. The works of the Buxtorfs were used by all Hebraists.
3 Loose miscellaneous notes in D. B. Horn MSS, EUL, Gen 1824.
4 *View of the Political State of Scotland in the Last Century*, ed. Adam, 1887, p. 140.
5 Carlyle, *Autobiography*, ed. Burton, 1910, p. 232.
6 Scott, *Fasti*, V:235; VII:415.
7 'G. Hill some time ago pledged himself to K – [innoul] L and through him to Mr D – [unda]ss that he would accept of the Divinity Chair.' Joseph McCormick to Alexander Carlyle, n.d. [1787 or very early 1788], EUL, Dc.4.41. John Adamson to Dundas, 26 November 1790, SAUL, Melville MS 4439.
8 Joseph McCormick to Dundas, 28 April 1791, SAUL, Melville MS 4451.
9 Joseph McCormick to Alexander Carlyle, 2 February 1788, EUL, Dc.4.41.
10 Joseph McCormick to Carlyle, n.d. [1788], EUL, Dc.4.41.
11 It had been decided by Principal Watson that the principal was not entitled to a casting vote, but he had died before he subscribed the memorandum which contained his finding. United College Minutes, 20 July 1781, SAUL, UYUC 400/5.
12 Even before the Revolution in France had really started, extreme Whig views, Foxite views, were an issue.
13 Joseph McCormick to Alexander Carlyle, n.d. [perhaps February or March 1788], EUL, Dc.4.41.
14 Ibid. The syntax of this letter is somewhat uncertain but it seems to mean that he named two men.
15 Ibid.
16 McCormick to Carlyle, n.d. [but later than the last letter cited above] EUL, Dc.4.41. Flint about two years later asked a favour of Dundas, namely that he be made a 'Physician to an Expedition' and that his son supply his professorship while he was away. He was unlikely to have asked such indulgence unless he had incurred a debt. James Flint to Dundas, 25 October 1790, SAUL, Melville MS 4438.
17 William Lawrence Brown to Henry Dundas, 22 February and 17 May 1788, Melville Castle Muniments, NAS, GD51/6/817.
18 George Hill to Dundas, 9 January 1791, SAUL, Melville MS 4760.
19 Baxter, 'St Andrews and Scottish Latin', St Andrews MEd thesis, 1972, SAUL, MS 36700, p. 26f.
20 David Carsuel to Henry Dundas, 29 May 1791, SAUL, Melville MS 4454.

21 W. L. Brown to Henry Dundas, 28 December 1790, SAUL, Melville MS 4443; George Hill to Henry Dundas, 9 January 1791, SAUL, Melville MS 4760; W. L. Brown to Dundas, 27 June 1791, Dundas Papers, NLS, 6524.

22 Brown to Dundas, 27 June 1791, Dundas Papers, NLS, 6524.

23 Joseph McCormick to Henry Dundas, 11 January 1791 and June 1791, SAUL, Melville MSS 4446, 4460.

24 Captain Alexander Duncan to Dundas, 12 January 1791, Lord Crawford to Dundas, 15 January and 23 May 1791, SAUL, Melville MSS 4447, 4448, 4452. Arnot's candidacy was being pushed by the Earl of Crawford.

25 McCormick to Henry Dundas, 28 April and 3 June 1791, SAUL, Melville MSS 4451, 4457.

26 Ilay Campbell to Henry Dundas, 28 May 1791; McCormick to Henry Dundas, 7 June 1791, SAUL, Melville MSS 4453, 4460.

27 Colonel Alexander Monypenny to Henry Dundas, n.d. [1791]; 3 April 1791, SAUL, Melville MSS 4440, 4450.

28 George Dempster to Henry Dundas, 19 January 1791, SAUL, Melville MS 4449. This was almost certainly Robert Small, a Dundee minister since 1759 and a St Andrews DD in 1778. Small, Moderator in 1791, was known for his interests in natural philosophy, mathematics and astronomy. As an improver, he helped to found the Dundee Royal Infirmary.

29 George Hill had sent Robert Dundas nominations for this place in 1790 but it is not known if he also solicited it for himself. George Hill to Robert Dundas, 28 May 1790, SAUL, Melville MS 4757; George Hill to [?Henry Dundas] 2 June 1790, SAUL, Melville MS 4760.

30 Robert to Henry Dundas, 18 June 1791, NLS, 6.

31 Adamson to Henry Dundas, 26 November 1790, SAUL, Melville MS 4439.

32 Hill to Carlyle, 3 December 1793, EUL, Dc.4.41.

33 William Lawrence Brown to Henry Dundas, 27 June 1791, NLS, 6524.

34 George Hill to Henry Dundas, 13 June 1792, EUL, La.II. 500.

35 Robert Dundas to Lord Advocate Robert Dundas of Arniston, 6 and 7 November 1793, NLS, 6.

36 I am indebted to R. N. Smart for much of this information.

37 C. T. Carr, 'Early Teachers of French at St Andrews', *Alumnus Chronicle*, 1948, pp. 14–20; Cant, *St Andrews*, 2002, p. 119.

38 Minutes, 4 January 1794, SAUL, UYUY 452/9.

39 Minutes, 29 April 1802, SAUL, UYUY 452/109.

40 Minutes, 6 August 1802, SAUL UYUY 452/10.

41 John Leslie to James Brown, 12 May 1792, 'Letters Relating to Edinburgh and the University Life of the Time', EUL, Dc.2.57.

42 John Leslie to James Brown, 24 April 1794, EUL, Dc.2.57.

43 United College Minutes, 2 May 1796, SAUL, UYUC 400/7.

44 McCormick to Henry Dundas, 29 October 1795, Dundas Papers, NAS, GD51/5/643.

45 James Flint to Henry Dundas, 4 November 1795, Melville Papers, NLS, 4467.

46 Thomas Charles Hope's income rose to about £1,000 by c. 1800; the lecturer in chemistry at Glasgow probably made at least £300; Rotherham at St Andrews would have realised at best £200. All three of them would have done consulting for businessmen but in St Andrews there was little of that to do.

47 I thank R. N. Smart for this information.

48 This was not the view of John Leslie, who thought Rotherham an 'arrant sycophant'. He said even Black had tired of him in the end and that his knowledge of chemistry was only practical and that he had never made a chemical discovery. Furthermore, he was not a good mathematician. 'His father was an itinerant lecturer or showsman & Jackie turned the electrical wheel This was R[otherham's] school.' It was an amusing attack but by another arrogant man who had been bested in the race. John Leslie to James Brown, n.d. [1795], EUL, Dc.2.57/130.

49 McCormick to Henry Dundas, 29 October 1795, Dundas Papers, NAS, GD51/5/643.

50 Robert to Henry Dundas, 5 November 1795, NLS, 6; this contains the letter from Lord Provost Stirling.

51 John Hill to the Lord Provost of Edinburgh, n.d. [but certainly in November 1795], NLS, 7.

52 One of the numerous Hills at St Andrews wrote to Robert Dundas in November 1795, saying Stewart 'shows a keenness that I do not like'. But then, equally keenly, he retaliated: 'Leslie whom Stuart supports is a philosopher Sceptical and in political matters what no good man shou'd be. I cannot bear the thoughts of such a man getting to St Ands. & I am astonished at Stuart & Playfair who always go together giving him their Countenance.' Stewart, often seen as a somewhat passive Whig sufferer during these years, was as capable of acting on political judgements about men applying for posts as those who found faults with his own politics. He was also too much a gentleman to welch on a commitment that had been given. John Hill to Robert Dundas, n.d. [November 1795], NLS, 7.

53 George Hill to Alexander Carlyle, 24 November 1795, EUL, Dc.4.41.

54 Barron to Robert Dundas, Lord Advocate, 7 November 1795, NLS, 7.

55 United College Minutes, 23 November 1795, 12 May 1796. SAUL, UC 400/6.

56 Clark, *An Enlightened Scot*, 1992, pp. 40–90.

57 Ibid., p. 100; the rest of the paragraph above relies upon Clark's chapter 6, pp. 92–103. The United College Minutes of these transactions are

dated 19 November 1791, 28 January 1792, 25 February 1792, 24 November 1792, 28 December 1792, 19 January 1793, 2 and 28 February 1793, 2 March 1793, SAUL, UC 400/6.

58 Scott, *Fasti*, V:161, 235f.
59 John Adamson to Henry Dundas, 2 June 1791, SAUL, 4456.
60 Reid, *The Divinity Professors in the University of Glasgow*, 1923, p. 286.
61 All this is borne out by MacGill's entry for Eastwood, the parish he served; *The Statistical Account of Scotland*, ed. Withrington and Grant, 1983, VII:644–58.
62 Hume was having a go at a well-known sermon by his sometime friend, William Leechman, entitled 'On the Character of a Minister' (1741). This sermon was a popular work which saw several editions during the century. The topic was one taken up by literary clubs, notably by the Glasgow Literary Society, where it was several times the topic of meetings and the subject of published works by members other than Leechman.
63 James Gartshorne to Henry Dundas, 10 December 1792, SAUL, Melville MS 4462. Dundas' personal secretary was a William Gartshorne, Fry, *Dundas*, 1992, p. 203.
64 Hill to Dundas, 1 March 1799, SAUL, Melville MS 4782.
65 John Hope to Henry Dundas, 16 and 19 April 1999, EUL, La. II:500/2230, 2232f.
66 Henry Dundas to Principal McCormick, Minutes, 5 July 1799, SAUL, UYUY 452/10.
67 Robert Dundas to the Senate Minutes, 17 August 1799, SAUL, UYUY 452/10.
68 EUL, George Hill to Lord Advocate Robert Dundas, 19 October 1799, EUL, La. II:500/2357.
69 Minutes, 9 and 13 November 1799, 12 December 1799, SAUL, UY 452/10. Among those who did not attend were Hunter, Trotter and the disabled professor Vilant.
70 James to Lyon Playfair, 18 November 1799, NLS, 4471.
71 Charles Wilson had tried to name his successor to this chair. He asked Henry Dundas on 19 February 1800 to appoint his son-in-law, James Hunter, later professor of logic, as his assistant and successor. James Playfair to Henry Dundas, SAUL, Melville MS 4474.
72 William Glen to Henry Dundas, 20 November 1704, SAUL, Melville MS 4481.
73 James McDonald to Henry Dundas, 14 February 1805, SAUL, Melville MS 4486.
74 Fry, *Dundas*, 1992, p. 296.
75 United College Minutes, 30 November 1804, SAUL, UYUC 400/7; James Flint to Henry Dundas, 16 August 1804, SAUL, Melville MS

4479. This letter suggests that Lord Frederick Campbell may also have played some role in this appointment.

76 Minutes, 28 April 1804, 1 and 14 May 1804, SAUL, UYUY 452/11.

77 Minutes, 3 and 16 July 1804, SAUL, UYUY 452/11.

78 James Flint to Henry Dundas, 18 January 1805, SAUL, Melville MS 4485.

79 United College Minutes, 15 May 1804, SAUL, UYUC 400/7.

80 James Flint to Henry Dundas, 18 January 1803, SAUL, Melville MS 4484.

81 Minutes, 23 June 1770; 23 June 1772, SAUL, UYUY 452/8.

82 United College Minutes, 4 March 1797; 8 May 1799; 21 and 29 October 1802, SAUL, UYUC 400/7. See the forthcoming work by Helen Rawson on the instrument collections held by the University during this period. It will list Rotherham's purchases.

83 Minutes, 22 August, 19 and 26 October, 28 November 1748, SAUL, UYUY 452/6. The letters went to Ilay and to his henchman, Alexander Lind, Sheriff of Midlothian, who did chemical experiments with and for Ilay.

84 Minutes, 1 January 1763, SAUL, UYUY 452/7.

85 Minutes, 23 March 1770 and 6 June 1774, SAUL, UYUY 452/8. The first gift makes one suspect they had a numismatic collection, as did Glasgow University after it received the Hunterian Collection.

86 Matthew Simpson, ' "You have not such a one in England" ', *Library History*, 2001, pp. 41–56. Simpson gives a partial list of the objects held in the Library which now somewhat resembled a museum.

87 McIntosh, *Church and Theology*, 1998, p. 148.

88 Macleod, *Scottish Theology*, 1974, p. 209.

89 Fry, *Dundas*, 1992, p. 298.

90 Ibid., p. 182.

91 'Minutes of the Philosophical Society, 4 July 1787 to 25 March 1795', SAUL, UYUY 911; see also Cant, *History*, 2002, p. 116. The years for which the minutes exist may have made this inevitable but there are early papers given in 1787–8 on topics such as 'Ought the Civil Magistrate to interpose on matters of religion?', 'What are the Disadvantages of a Democratical form of Government?', can impressment be justified?, is capital punishment to be allowed? – all topics which among St Andrews professors were unlikely to attract much support for one side. It is worth noting that before 1760, when a Theology Club was instituted, there seems to have been no student groups meeting as they did elsewhere. Perhaps the Moderates should be credited with introducing these; they certainly supported them elsewhere.

92 Hill's works are not even mentioned by two religious scholars usually sensitive to such influences: Lefferts Loetscher in *Facing the*

Enlightenment and Pietism (1983) and Henry May's *The Enlightenment in America* (1976).

93 This was noted long ago by MacLeod, *Scottish Theology*, 1974, p. 208.

94 Calvinists had long held that work among fallen-away Christians was more important than winning souls in foreign mission fields. This was changing c. 1800, but not for George Hill.

95 Here I differ with the common opinion which has a rather more favourable view of the Moderates. Ian D. L. Clark, in a brilliant and nuanced 1970 essay ['From Protest to Reaction: The Moderate Regime in the Church of Scotland, 1752–1805', in *Scotland in the Age of Improvement*, eds Phillipson and Mitchison, 1970], saw the Moderate Party more or less equalling the enlightened in Scotland, but it is difficult to place in it men like Adam Smith, who despite his friendship for many Moderates was not much interested in church affairs, or men like Thomas Reid and George Campbell, who were too independent to count in those circles and sometimes voted against them in the General Assembly, or a man like Hume, who had Moderate friends but would not talk religion with the likes of Hugh Blair and showed in his writings the inadequacy of every argument upon which Moderate theology relied. Even Beattie, whom Clark mentions, was closer to some strains of tepid Anglican evangelicalism than to the sort of religion William Robertson preached and practised. Clark has been followed in his views by others less careful to make his reservations. Among them are Nicholas Phillipson and most of those whose training has included attendance at Phillipson's seminar at Edinburgh, especially Richard Sher whose account of the Moderates is in so many other ways commendable.

96 Many of them clearly did not believe the doctrines they were to preach, but hesitated to resign when their own personal beliefs were no longer those of the body in which they worked and whose Confession of Faith they had signed.

97 That is a claim which Donald McCallum has questioned, arguing that Hill's theology, if not his politics, was acceptable to evangelicals and that Hill's *Lectures in Divinity* were even used as a text by Thomas Chalmers. See Donald McCallum, 'George Hill, DD: Moderate or Evangelical Erastian?', unpublished MA thesis, 1989, p. 52. For Campbell's Moderatism, see Suderman, *Orthodoxy and Enlightenment*, 2001, pp. 238–53.

98 The best recent study of him is by McCallum, 'George Hill, DD: Moderate or Evangelical Erastian?', unpublished MA thesis, 1989.

99 Minutes, 27 November 1802, SAUL, UYUY 452/10.

100 Principal McCormick to[?], [?October 1788], SAUL, Melville MS 4433.

101 Principal McCormick to Henry Dundas, 19 September 1790, SAUL, Melville MS 4436.

102 This is a covert reference to the Arnot case which came before the General Assembly in 1799–1801, at which time George Hill managed to have the pluralism allowed. McCallum, 'George Hill', unpublished MA thesis, 1989, pp. 106–8.

103 Robert Dundas to 2nd Viscount Melville, 18 November 1811, SAUL, Melville MS 4513.

Part V

Conclusions

18

SUMMARIES AND RESULTS

℮

1. APPOINTMENTS: POLITICS, PROCESSES AND CONSTRAINTS

The processes of university patronage discussed above can be reduced to a scheme. When a vacancy was in the offing or had occurred, nominations and recommendations made their way to those who might aid a candidate. The men to whom the initial appeals went were generally local figures – professors, gentlemen, clerics, officials of the burghs or of the government. Names, vetted locally in Aberdeen by men like Brigadier John Middleton or Patrick Duff of Premnay, or in Glasgow by Mungo Graham of Gorthy or John Maxwell of Pollock, were then passed on to a manager in Edinburgh such as the reverend Patrick Cuming or Lord Milton. The latter would compare this candidate with others of whom he knew. His list would then be sent with comments to the ministry's man in London – the Duke of Montrose, Lord Ilay or Henry Dundas. They might or might not consult with others before making a decision to recommend a man to the legal patron. That patron might be the Crown, a corporation, an ad hoc committee or an individual. In most cases, at each stage there was some consultation with others and some negotiating with those who could appoint or with those who could twist their arms.

The process was from beginning to end political. The government's managers were interested in maintaining or building a party in Scottish institutions and in showing their power. They needed to aid or punish those whom they wanted to do their bidding. If the legal patron chose not to do as it was suggested he should do, there was sure to be trouble of some kind. Some cases went to court. Others were remembered and favours later asked were denied to the recalcitrant legal patron or to his dependants. If the patron were compliant, he could expect to be in some way rewarded. Business would come his way; his dependants would get commissions or hospital posts; his brother's widow would be put on a pension, whatever.

There were constraints on this politics. Managers were not free to do just as they pleased. Their freedom to get their way depended on several things. The most obvious ones were general ideological constraints dictated by being tied to governments which were Whiggish or Tory and burdened by all that may have meant. These pressures were most clearly shown when colleges were visited and purged, but they worked continually to exclude men thought to be subversive of orthodoxy – Jacobites, High Flyers, Jacobins. The next most important determinant of a manager's freedom was his power and standing with his ministry. Strong men could do more than weak ones. Strength was affected by the length of time a manager had been in power and his expectation of continuing to administer patronage for a government which fully supported him. A man like Lord Ilay, who had been giving out jobs a long time, often owed less to those who clamoured for appointments than one who was new to the game. Someone who had been in power for as long as Henry Dundas in 1800 could easily beg off in particular cases. These two were thus quite unlike the Marquis of Tweeddale in 1745. Because managers picked from leets of several men, whose own patrons were of about equal importance, they could often choose the man whom they thought to be best. Sometimes they lacked this freedom. There might be compelling political reasons to make or allow a particular choice. Ilay let the lawyers choose law professors in Edinburgh and he could not prevent opponents from naming John Stewart to the Marischal College mathematics chair in 1727 or Dr John Pringle to the Edinburgh chair of moral philosophy in 1734. Such reasons might involve political or ideological exigencies, earlier promises, the favouring of a family member, or some other clear obligation such as humouring the Duke of Cumberland, which seems to have secured the ecclesiastical history chair at St Mary's College for William Brown. And, in the end, managers could only recommend to a patron who might or might not act on their recommendation. At Glasgow the politicians did not quite force their choice for a professor of natural philosophy on the masters in 1757 or 1796.

It was important that the processes of appointment were from beginning to end almost public ones. Those who wanted the job were usually known. How much it paid and who was likely to secure it for a candidate were clear. Most appointments at all the colleges except Edinburgh involved chancellors, rectors and principals, but also professors and private patrons. They were often of equal concern to men outside the institution. Medical men at Edinburgh and Glasgow, clerics everywhere, lawyers in the capital and at Aberdeen, other candidates and political figures had interests in making known who was being considered and why. Appointments were a constant gauge of the power of individuals, factions and regimes. Even those excluded from the process could not be totally ignored because they commonly had friends in the colleges who could resort to legal action if they felt sufficiently aggrieved, wished to cause trouble and could afford to do so. As we have seen, this could happen while candidates were being considered or after an appointment had been made. It might involve masters or outsiders because many men had clear and enforceable interests in chairs or could pretend to them. The actions and ambitions of interested parties were thus checked and limited by the fact that, if managers and parties went too far, they would face litigation in either the clerical or civil courts or could expect to pay a political price. Such risks forced the views of opponents to be at least considered when places were awarded.

Public importance and the value of a post tended to increase the scrutiny of candidates and to force up the qualifications of would-be professors. This was notably the case with the teaching chairs of medicine and law and in the chairs of divinity, but not of Hebrew and ecclesiastical history. If clerics, professors, medical or legal corporations, town councillors and others could legitimately oppose an appointment they disliked, then patrons had to make sure there would be few grounds to take appointments to court. The more obvious the qualification of the candidate the better the chances that his appointment would not be challenged. Edinburgh, despite having more men appointed, seems to have had fewer suits than did the other colleges. St Andrews, King's College and Glasgow University had many court battles over appointments and other matters. In Edinburgh, the strength of parties on the Town Council had been publicly established in the autumn elections. There was generally no point to litigation about appointments. This may also have been true at Marischal College, where the Crown and the burgh had great influence.

While the processes of appointment were everywhere the same, there were variations in the recruitment patterns of the colleges. These depended mostly, but not exclusively, on the value of the livings. The number of applicants was also affected by the known inclinations of the patrons who had the disposal of the place, the qualifications needed to hold it and the likelihood that the competition would really be an open one. At Edinburgh, the high value of the livings drew many well-recommended candidates and the appointment process was relatively open. There were 124 men appointed or confirmed to 143 chairs from the time of the Visitation Commission in 1690 until the end of 1806.[1] Exclusive of the lawyers whose names went forward on leets but who never intended to serve, at least 124 other men, plus the unnamed 'numberless others', sought these posts.[2] At least 248 men are known to have tried for Edinburgh posts. The total number of competitors was certainly much greater. Some who initially failed were eventually successful elsewhere. As Table 2 shows, the patterns at the four other universities were not quite the same. At Edinburgh 43 per cent of the positions were contested, but at Glasgow 50 per cent of the positions were. Edinburgh's jobs were a bit more tightly controlled by politicians. Only at Marischal College were those figures bettered with 52 per cent, with the applicants mostly local men not drawn from a national recruitment pool. At Glasgow, the recruitment pool was larger and merit seems to have played a larger role, perhaps because of the interference of Lord Ilay and Bute. St Andrews and King's were more closed corporations, with 35 per cent and 21 per cent of the posts contested. These lower rates reflected the relatively meagre value of the livings and the fact that sitting professors could and did favour relatives and friends. The higher St Andrews rate was owing to the union of the colleges in 1747 and the subsequent interference of outsiders. The numbers competing for posts outside New Aberdeen, Edinburgh and Glasgow were smaller and the known failures more often went into teaching in grammar schools and academies rather than in other colleges in Scotland or elsewhere. Most of those known to have failed seem about equally well qualified – not equally fit or brilliant – about equal in accomplishment and equally well recommended when they sought a teaching post. They were also mostly men from the areas from which the colleges recruited their students.

Another constraint on the politicians came from the Kirk, which traditionally had some jurisdiction over the colleges. In the 1680s it had supplied chancellors to three of the universities and principals to all the colleges. The role of the church diminished throughout this period in almost every respect, even while the Moderates were politically powerful.

Until the 1850s, all professors were thought to be Presbyterians in good standing as the law required. The Established Church of Scotland retained its legal rights to determine the orthodoxy and morals of candidates for chairs but its position was weakened. The *avisamentum* fell into something like desuetude at Edinburgh while Gowdie and Robertson were principals (1754–93). The attempt to

Table 2. Professorial Appointments 1690–1806[3]

	Glasgow	Edinburgh	St Andrews	King's	Marischal	Total
Left in place by Visitors	3	4	1	9	7	24
Appointments to 1806	100	139	106	67	58	470
Total number of Appointments	103	143	107	76	65	494
Places known to have been contested (No./%)	51/50%	61/43%	36/34%	15/22%	30/52%	193/39%
Number of men who held Appointments	85	124	83	57	55	388
Failed to get a place applied for in the university	117	149	84	25	64	–
Failed ever to get a place in the universities						c. 100
Total known professors and failed applicants						496+

revive this power and to strengthen the Moderates' control of the Kirk made the Leslie case (1805) of importance. It concluded with a court ruling that the *avisamentum* of the Edinburgh ministers was advisory only and not binding. This decision was a blow against clerical influence in university education, but it did not end it. A presbytery's right to influence appointments was still being asserted in 1839.[4] The obligation to subscribe the Confession of Faith as one's own personal belief still remained and did not lapse with that decision, however much it was ignored by appointees in reality. This issue figured in the support for the Disruption of the Established Church in 1843.[5]

Clerical interventions extended beyond the initial trial and judgement of a man's orthodoxy and character. Those who tried to displace popular but errant divinity professors, such as Patrick Sibbald at Marischal (1690–97)[6] or James Garden at King's (1697–1714),[7] showed that local clerics could be troublesome over long periods of time when they liked an incumbent and did not want a new appointee.

These men were Jacobite Episcopalians. Jacobite clerics in Aberdeen and the surrounding countryside were still willing and able to make problems over the election to the King's College chair of divinity into the 1730s.[8] They could not win but they could delay appointments. Clerical influences, exerted for political as well as religious reasons, were exerted in the cases of the Glasgow professors John Simson, Francis Hutcheson and William Leechman. Edinburgh's William Hamilton was lucky not to have been subjected to similar treatment. Later, Edinburgh's principal, William Wishart II, was harassed by local ministers,[9] who also prevented the appointments of David Hume at Edinburgh (1745) and Glasgow (1751) and perhaps Gilbert Stuart at Edinburgh (1771, 1778).[10] At St Andrews, the local Presbytery and Synod of Fife set upon Alexander Scrimgeour and Archibald Campbell, men already in office.[11] This sort of interference more or less stopped around 1755. The Kirk, which had opposed the appointments and interfered with the careers of about 6 per cent of the professors placed up to 1755, did so in about 1 per cent after that time and did so less effectively.

The Kirk always had to be considered, if not always accommodated, and it had to be managed. This was done by judiciously selecting men who would vote the right way and could get others to join them when difficult cases came before church courts, especially the Kirk's court of final appeal, the General Assembly. Finding such men imposed another limitation on the appointments made in divinity faculties and to the principalships of colleges. Divines had to be orthodox but some also needed to possess political skills and to be willing to accept the lead of politicians who did not always have the Kirk's interest in the forefront of their minds. By 1805, the ability to play this kind of politics had been somewhat diminished by the divisions among Presbyterians and by the decline in public estimation of the Moderate Party. Still, the old regime in the Kirk and universities did not finally end until the reform of the universities in 1858.[12]

An increased secularity of outlook in the colleges reflected the outlook of patrons, indeed of Scottish society generally. At all the colleges, there was an absolute decline in the religious life in the institutions. There was everywhere less collective church going, catechising and praying. There was also less teaching of traditional religious subjects. Scottish moral philosophy ceased to be so closely tied to religion and became more based in sentiment or perceptions of rightness. Morals also broadened into politics and something resembling modern social sciences. Former ministers, such as Adam Ferguson, inculcated more Roman than Christian values in their students and gradually the religious component of science courses diminished, making way for more positive science and less speculative metaphysics. The time devoted to showing the relevance of natural philosophy to the existence of God diminished as physics progressed and demanded more mathematics. Partly the result of progress in the science, this also reflected the acceptance of a more stringent empirical methodology which did not lend itself to religious apology. More secular than religious chairs were created and somewhat diluted a clerical presence, although the number of teachers who were clerics or who had trained as clerics remained about the same – about half. The numbers who had been ordained decreased and the number of those who had left the clergy increased.

Theology remained Calvinist but was modernised to focus more on morals and works, on grace and mercy and not on 'the heart prepared' and predestination. 'Reason' somewhat replaced a sense of the primacy of the self-validating Word and being called by God's grace as the basic sources of belief. Hebrew did not flourish and the biblical roots of theology were neglected. For much of the century, Hebrew was taught not by notable scholars but by men who seem hardly competent. Only one of the teachers, James Robertson of Edinburgh, ever established a reputation as an Hebraist, but his renown was mainly local and rested principally on his teaching and the production of a grammar used in his classes. By the 1790s, at Glasgow, Edinburgh and Marischal College, some of the attention professors once gave to Hebrew was now spent on Persian and Arabic.

Among the ecclesiastical historians only two were of any distinction. William Dunlop made a promising beginning but his tenure was cut short by an early death.[13] 'Blind Jameson', an acerbic polemicist, knew his history but he was no writer of the sort of history which came to be preferred. This was better exemplified by Archibald Campbell's somewhat facile *The Gospel History Justified* (1759) and George Campbell's posthumously published *Lectures on Ecclesiastical History* (1815). These, and some writing by Robert Findlay, show that the ecclesiastical historians were not all idle, but they also show that they were not teaching an historical defence of their faith in its reformed and Calvinist version. This was hardly compatible with George Campbell's expressed admiration for Edward Gibbon's infamous Chapter 16. Campbell and others tended to see Christian history in the context of a world history which was not biblically centred.

Ecclesiastical history professors might insist that all events are providential and ultimately related to a grand scheme of salvation, but the history they wrote was not rooted in revelation and did not work to establish that thesis which required a different treatment of world history. That would have to wait until the Germans from Herder to Hegel had made that lesson clear. So too would a learned defence of the particularities of Calvinism which related them to apostolic times and showed them to be true to the essentials of Christianity. At Glasgow, the ecclesiastical historians William Rouet and William Wight may not always have given courses on church history. Rouet did not treat church history in isolation from secular history and even pioneered in lecturing on such topics as the history of art.

Managers were not unhappy with such trends because they strengthened the state as it diminished the importance of the Kirk. After c. 1720 that was every politician's objective. The schools reflected the increasingly practical and secular values of the patrons. The Moderates challenged little of this, however much they might protest their orthodoxy. They wanted harmony and order in a society in which the Kirk was an equal of the state, but their political behaviour shows them unwilling to assert that equality on a regular basis. They were better Erastians than defenders of an independent Kirk; this lessened religious influence in the colleges. At the same time, no manager could push this agenda too hard without risking an upset in the Kirk.

If the Kirk increasingly expected the divinity teachers to be orthodox but moderate, polite and accomplished, medical men and lawyers were equally concerned to have installed in chairs only those who could teach their subjects with distinction. Both medics and lawyers were tenacious about making their demands known to politicians who usually took their advice. Both groups offered a model of how good appointments should be made.

The doctors had no legal rights to appoint anywhere but they were the most effective group influencing appointments, because appointments in the two medical schools involved economic considerations. From the beginning of medical appointments in Edinburgh University, the physicians of the Royal College of Physicians in Edinburgh were consulted about appointments. Sitting medical professors enjoyed the same privilege. When they were only nominally consulted in the mid-1770s, there was a public ruckus and the man who made it, Andrew Duncan, was eventually appointed to a chair which he and others thought rightfully belonged to him. In Glasgow, the men consulted were the physicians at the Royal College of Physicians of Edinburgh and, by the 1750s, those in the Glasgow Faculty of Physicians and Surgeons. Even at St Andrews, where the medical chair was a non-teaching post, applicants with the countenance of the Edinburgh medical community would grant degrees worth more than a man who lacked that support.[14] Surgeons too had to be heard. In Edinburgh and Glasgow they could prevent their apprentices from taking anatomy and pharmacy courses with men of whom they disapproved. After c. 1775, the Edinburgh surgeons sponsored a second medical school operating in the Surgeons' Hall. From 1799, there was another at the Andersonian Institution in Glasgow. The universities had to appoint the best men they could find or lose custom to the men across the street – or to those in London and Paris.

The lawyers controlled the appointments to two of the three law chairs at Edinburgh and made up the leets for the chairs of humanity and history. They could not be ignored. In Glasgow, the University consulted lawyers in Edinburgh about the appointments of all the men who held the law chair in this period – William Forbes, William Cross, Hercules Lindsay, John Millar and Robert Davidson. In Aberdeen, the civilist's chair at King's was seen as a local perquisite for an Aberdeen advocate. When it went to a member of the Edinburgh Faculty of Advocates, who was promoted by the Argathelians and had no Aberdeen practice, there were protests and a suit which reached the House of Lords. This turned on whether or not Marischal College and University had the right to grant law degrees, but the real issue was whether or not the post should be awarded by those out of the burgh to one who did not practice in it. The Aberdeen advocates erected a monument to their victory.[15]

Professors tended to be what one professor called another, 'a political little body'.[16] They came from the political classes and knew how to play politics. They too had to be considered for a variety of reasons. Edinburgh professors put an end to James Beattie's hopes for a chair in their university by making it clear that he would be spurned even though he had the countenance of many of the great and the good. Other men felt the pressures which could be brought to bear on professors who were not welcome or who had overstayed their time. Masters had rights to discipline a colleague and could make life unpleasant for an appointee by assigning him teaching hours which would not draw students to pay the fees on which a major portion of most professorial incomes depended. At St Andrews, Charles Gregory found his students discouraged from taking his course at three different times in his career – once after his unpopular appointment and twice when his Whiggish politics offended his colleagues. They might even bring suits against a man in rectorial, clerical or civil courts.

Professors also looked after their families. By 1780, even in Edinburgh, there were five related men on the staff (19 per cent), and seven Edinburgh professors (26 per cent) could find relatives in other colleges.[17] Elsewhere, family ties among the faculty were proportionately more numerous, especially at King's College and at St Andrews. The more entrenched a family was, the less purchase outsiders had if the masters also had the right to elect new colleagues. Politicians could not continually antagonise professors or appoint the inefficient and slow-witted. All professorial incomes from fees would suffer in the long run if too many poor choices were made. Professors had to be consulted and jollied along, which is just what the best managers, Ilay and Dundas, consistently did.

The towns and their businessmen also asserted interests. Most at some time relied on the college staffs for expertise and were interested in having men who could and were willing to give it. It was not a major factor in appointments but it was not without some interest both to them and to patrons. Among those who taught artisans in the town of Glasgow were Robert Dick, I and II, and John Anderson. So too did Patrick Copland in Aberdeen. The latter received a government grant to buy model machines to be used in instruction.[18] Robert Stewart, William Cullen, Joseph Black, Francis Home, John Walker, William Irvine, Robert Cleghorn, T. C. Hope and Patrick Copland were among those who provided consulting services to farmers, businessmen or to the burghs of Edinburgh, Glasgow and Aberdeen. In Edinburgh, Colin Maclaurin did actuarial work for the Widows' Scheme which provided insurance for ministers and University men. Robert Hamilton aided in setting up Aberdeen's first insurance companies. Even St Andrews got help with its water supply from professor John Hunter. Such interests sometimes prompted interference in appointments and made indwellers interested in the talents of those seeking jobs.

That universities might economically benefit their towns had been clearly appreciated by 1700.[19] Some saw this as saving the costs of foreign study, but by 1710 it also meant educating English boys from dissenting families. After 1740, it was medical education that became a business in Scotland. The towns derived a lot of money from university students and were concerned with the reputation of their colleges and the quality of the men appointed to teach. At Marischal College, enrolments by 1800 had nearly doubled in a generation to about 500 and medical instruction had begun. That burgh had an interest in the success of its college and saw it as depending on good teaching.[20] The town councillors of Edinburgh had even more at stake. Edinburgh students probably contributed over £1,000,000 to the burgh's economy between 1700 and 1806.[21] The Town Council of Edinburgh, like the College in Glasgow, made sure that regius appointees came under its discipline and it asserted its right to create chairs which might duplicate the functions of those created by the Crown or private patrons. The value of the chairs depended very much on there being only one lecturer for a field. By reminding politicians and incumbents of their power, they ensured that their economic concerns were considered. They did sometimes set new rules to make teachers efficient or to discipline them when they were unsatisfactory. Despite its interests in appointments, the Edinburgh Town Council picked few of the professors which it commissioned. The realities of the processes of appointment were ones which seldom allowed legal patrons to act alone. Councillors in most cases saw their obligations as being to aid those who aided them. Once those people and their interests had been made clear, the legal patrons acted in ways which satisfied the outsiders but maintained the Council's rights and secured economic benefits for the city. The city's economy somewhat depended upon the reputation of the University and the brilliance of its staff. Political necessity required councillors to ensure that, for at least some chairs, the best men were found and appointed.

The politicians to whom recommendations for appointments ultimately went needed and sought expert advice when they made university appointments. In the entourages of the men of power were followers who must often have been asked about the qualifications of applicants. We know this happened. The Earl of Mar took advice from Carstares and Dr Archibald Pitcairne. William Rouet's letters show that Ilay's choices for chairs had been discussed around the Earl's dining table by men who had expertise in various academic subjects. Lord Milton, an almost independent figure by the end of his career, was advised by Edinburgh doctors and the young Moderates friendly with John Home and Adam Ferguson. Both had served him. Bute and Stuart Mackenzie sounded similar men; so too did Henry Dundas. When the politicians got advice from experts, it came from men whom they had employed in other contexts and to whom they had usually given something. Patrons had interests but much of their work was brokering offices and nudging ahead those whom they favoured.

There was another group which believed it had a right to interfere in appointments – the gentlemen of Scotland whose sons went to colleges which they had shaped to serve their interests. Their families had endowed bursaries and left monies to the foundations. Members of their families often ran the colleges. Families like the Mures of Caldwell with long connections to Glasgow College expected their needs to be looked after and their old tutors placed. There were good reasons to appoint their protégés. The wealthier and more powerful gentlemen picked able men to educate their boys. Their tutors were polite, accomplished men with some experience of the world. They had usually travelled abroad and were generally speakers of French. The advice and recommendations given by those who had employed them was often very good. No political manager worth his salt ignored the wishes of the gentlemen in his queue. They had, or thought they had, a stake just as clear as those asserted by the alumni of American Ivy League schools today; they were just as assertive. Politicians had to serve them too.

Other things also acted as constraints on the effectiveness of patrons and over these they had little control. At King's, Lord Ilay's influence was minimised not only by the closed nature of the corporation but also by the fact that the Squadrone men had virtually restaffed the place with young men in 1717–18. The new professors quickly assumed control of the institution. All the chairs were filled during Ilay's time in power but he affected only three placements. Local men looked after themselves. At Marischal College, his position was virtually that of chancellor, which some took him to be although he had no such office. He was the chief patron there for over thirty years. Deaths and the fact that most of the livings were in the gift of the Crown allowed Ilay more impact on this institution. Lord Bute, his successor as patron there, benefited less from deaths. Dundas during his period in power filled every chair there. The Squadrone men were lucky in the times when men died and Dundas was luckiest of all. The number of years during which patrons exercised power also mattered. Ilay held power for nearly forty years and by his death in April 1761 he had created a dominant interest in most Scottish institutions, but not at King's or St Andrews. At those places he managed the regius chairs but not much else. In Edinburgh, he got his way because the Town Council was usually in his grip. His power was perhaps greatest at Glasgow where, from 1726 until his death thirty-five years later, he brokered most of the professorial appointments and had a kinsman sitting as principal. His power left marks because of his long possession of it. Dundas was in office for nearly as long (about twenty-five years) but the political constraints of his last fifteen years were more severe than those under which Ilay usually worked. Dundas did not think he could weigh merit so heavily and he did not. Appointments during his early years were better than those made later, but the achievements of his appointees were generally not as great as those of Ilay's men.

Finally, politicians had responsibilities to those in London which limited what they could do. At no time could the political managers, or most other patrons, appoint men whose outlook was very different from the beliefs and values of the London ministers. The 1688 Revolution gave power to men who gave lip-service to notions of limited government and who expected Whiggism of some sort to be inculcated in the young. Jacobites and those preaching Jacobitism were proscribed in the 1690s, just as were Jacobins in the 1790s. The Tory governments under Anne did not allow Scots openly to show or support what many of them really believed. What Tories and Jacobites were given was the right to worship in Episcopalian meeting houses. It is doubtful if Scots, left to themselves c. 1710–20, would have been willing to appoint men as tolerant as the ones who came into office after English and Anglican politicians had forced on the Scots a measure of toleration (1710–12) and restored Kirk patronage to heritors or rate-payers (1712). The latter decision made the country more aristocratic in its management and more aligned with an England in which the franchise was increasingly exercised by relatively fewer people.[22] The Union forced Scots to be more tolerant and the failure to break it in 1712 or 1715 preserved that gain. Leading Scottish political figures had to defend these positions just as they had to accept a new treason law and the appellate jurisdiction of the House of Lords. Later, London governments made clear their intention to impose national taxes on the Scots. In the 1740s, it became equally clear that the government was willing to impose order on the Highlands even if it meant destroying a way of life – something about which Lowlanders had had few qualms since at least the reign of James VI, but which they had been unable to achieve. Professorial appointees had generally to be in agreement with such policies or at least willing to be quiet about their dissent from them. The many constraints on patrons did not change until after the Reform Bill of 1832, and some not until the Universities Act of 1858.

2. THE MANAGERS

The patronage system worked as well as it did and had the results it produced, partly because of the men who gave out jobs and acted as brokers. Generally the patrons and managers were not bigots but men of some culture and even learning. They often knew a good deal and cared about what was taught and who got to teach it. The educations and interests of the chief managers had often been acquired in Scotland. They had usually attended a Scottish university and knew its strengths and deficiencies and those of others. Most of them also knew England and Europe – which for them usually meant Holland, parts of France and Italy and the intervening bits through which they may have travelled while they studied abroad or toured. They often returned to Scotland with standards and attitudes that were neither altogether English nor continental. They tended to think of their country as backward, as it was when compared to much of the Europe they had seen, but not when compared to equally resource-poor regions which few tourists visited. They recognised the need to improve Scotland and felt less compunction about changing things than did those who had little or no experiences of other places. They were men who were, in a way, outsiders. Mar, Montrose, Ilay, Bute, the Earl of Kinnoull and even Henry Dundas spent much of their lives outside Scotland. Sometimes the greater Scottish patrons have been dismissed as but Englishmen in disguise. This seems unfair. Ilay, for example, may have been born in England, educated at Eton and Utrecht (as well as Glasgow) and spent most of his life in London, but anyone who thinks he was not a Scot does not know the man and has not read the lists of his Whitton dinner guests. He and the others tended to appoint forward-looking men much like themselves. While they did this partly as anglicised Scots with foreign examples to guide them, they also did it as Scots seeking to better the country from which they came and in which their estates chiefly lay. Their interests in improvements were first of all personal, but they recognised that a rising tide lifts all boats. Collectively they shaped a Scottish culture whose distinctive achievements even nationalists applaud without discerning their origins. To do so they had to make their management efficient and informed.

The patrons recognised that well-administered patronage could keep stable a turbulent political world in which the government lacked many means for keeping order. This was, in part, why they were willing to fight for the control of every office, every institution, every corporation. These fights were not driven solely by desires for increased power and spoils but to preserve order and to ensure that the future would not be unpredictable or worse than the present. All the managers recognised that organisation promoted effectiveness. Without a system, even a 'machine', there was uncertainty about who was really in charge of patronage throughout the country and about how one might seek it. Uncertainty bred turmoil and ill will among contending parties. It led to lawsuits and hard feelings. Management was not an evil so long as the patrons kept the processes open and favoured the better candidates. A greater evil was the disorder that came in its absence. University patronage fitted into larger schemes.

Mar, Ilay, Bute, Dundas and the rest certainly looked at candidates for any office with political ends in mind, but they also had personal interests that were not disregarded. Lord Mar, who helped William Adam design and decorate the House of Dun, may be presumed to have cared at least a bit about the men who were going to teach the rudiments of fortification or military architecture. Mar heard Dr Pitcairne's appeals for good mathematicians and appointed one who taught some architecture and not the Fifeshire nonentity wanted by the masters. Mar trusted the recommendations of William Carstares, who was more than his equal as a politician of the possible. Several of the Earl's appointments are hallmarked by expediency but also by personal interest. What Mar lacked was an organisation and a set way of making appointments. He lacked rules and probably could not have made them and acted on them given the factionalised world in which he operated. 'Machines' and rules mattered but Mar was never in a position to build one or set the others.

The Squadrone men, who succeeded Mar, invented a system of management which Ilay improved. They and he tried to find and place agents in all the corporations and burghs, in the Kirk and in the parliamentary districts. These men were to watch things and keep the politicians abreast of anything interesting so they would not be caught off guard. They were reporters and agents to whom managers could turn. In the long run, this made them natural centralisers of power in Edinburgh and in London, since these were the places where the chief managers were to be found. This accustomed Scots to decisions made there and helped to knit the two kingdoms together. It may also have made for convergence in law, manners, language and standards of living, indeed, in most ways – as most of the enlightened North Britons thought it should. Even Ilay was not always opposed to that. Most of them knew that the ways in which they acted generally strengthened the state vis à vis the Kirk and tended to rob Scots of independence. Despite their Scottishness, they weakened Scottish independence.

The Squadrone men tended to have rules about who could get jobs of differing kinds. Montrose and Roxburghe favoured men from the moderate wing of the Kirk and men who were loyal to the Squadrone connection centred on the clans of the Kers, Hays, Johnstons, Leslies, Crawfords, Sinclairs, Hopes, Grahams and the minor families which formed their queues. If they had an ideological test, it was one which involved the assertion of a modicum of independence for Scotland and its Kirk and something like a 'Country Party' line in oratory. No one man in this connection put his definitive stamp on their adminis-tration of patronage but the 1st Duke of Montrose and 1st Duke of Roxburghe do seem to have negotiated more positions than others. Roxburghe was something of an intellectual but that left little or no Scottish imprint. Montrose's men at Glasgow seem a bit less parochial than those whom they replaced. Both Roxburghe and Montrose aided in expanding the universities and promoting the teaching of law, med-icine and history.

Much more evidence exists about how Ilay ran his system. One can infer from his appointments and from casual remarks in letters about them that he had different tests for different jobs. He always wanted to appoint men loyal to himself and his masters but they had to have other qualities. Lawyers needed to be bright and honest but he did not care if they drank too much or discretely wenched. That would not do for clerics, who did not have to be bright but needed to be moral and at least seem pious. The Earl wanted customs and excise men to be rea-sonably honest and to possess some mathematics. If they lacked those traits, he would not willingly appoint them, just as he did not defend them if they were found to be peculators. Only with great reluctance would he give jobs to the protégés of those who, in the past, had rec-ommended the dishonest and incompetent. The men recommended to him for professorships he hoped would be moral and religious exam-ples for the boys, but fitness came first.[23] He seemed to favour those who were like himself – classicists and mathematicians with some modern learning. If they were polite, so much the better. If they stut-tered he might not give them the nod, despite their having all the other requirements for office. Matthew Stewart nearly lost his professorship for this reason. Ilay expected professors to have some additional use-fulness – such as being able to help manage the Kirk or do chemical analyses for miners or dyers. Better to have men who could do two things than those with only one speciality. His own valet was also a surveyor and map-maker. Ilay disliked giving the members of a single family more than one post in any college and he was against having sons follow their fathers in chairs. *Dislike* did not mean that he did not make such appointments, only that he had to be persuaded to do so. He tended to prefer the worldly and secular-minded to the 'Levites'. He may even have favoured Leiden graduates over those who studied elsewhere. He wanted to know the families from which men came and, occasionally, he asked how they voted. All this was noted by those who recommended men to him. Because Ilay knew a great deal about many areas – law and history, medicine, chemistry, botany, natural philosophy, even theology – he depended more on his own judgements than did any other chief manager in the period. Bute and his brother, James Stuart Mackenzie, could not match their uncle's knowledge of law and other erudite matters, but Bute was his equal or better in botany, chemistry and astronomy and James Stuart Mackenzie was almost equally learned in chemistry and agriculture. All these men took advice but they weighed it by themselves.

Bute and Stuart Mackenzie accepted much the same standards for appointees as had their uncle, but they looked more to the qualities which made a man meritorious than to the political value which their appointments might have. Lord Kinnoull and William Robertson, so important in the 1770s, judged men more according to religious, moral and utilitarian tests. They valued men who were polite and pleasant but expected to find them among the Moderates. They sought to place their friends, not lesser lights from the locality of a college. They wanted earnestness in the cause of Moderation. They seem not to have cared much if some appointees had specialised knowledge. These men could be moved to chairs in which their recognised skills would be valuable. Some learning was requisite but concern to improve Scotland and social skills were needed by the men they backed.

Henry Dundas also had his rules. He was more obviously political in his choices and his correspondence suggests that he took less advice from experts. He favoured his own supporters but sometimes picked evangelicals when there was political advantage to be had from doing so. After 1790, he was a resolute reactionary in his selection of men, passing over men of great merit to pick (and thus encouraging others to nominate) politically correct hacks from his party. Earlier, merit had counted for more with him. He could ignore recommendations and pick to suit himself if he thought this would prevent factional fights in St Andrews or give his party a decisive edge in some corporation. At the end of his career he cared as little about merit as had anyone since Mar's time.

The achievements of the managers varied with their tenures, personal proclivities and characters. Archibald Campbell, Earl of Ilay and 3rd Duke of Argyll, made the greatest impact of any of the patrons. He did much to make the Scottish enlightenment possible and brilliant. In the universities, Ilay's patronage can be measured in several ways. Of 494 appointments[24] made during the period 1690–1806, he approved about 68 (14 per cent).[25] That is, he or his immediate aids agreed to one man rather than another when he had the power to block an appointment. He often made final choices himself. If we count the men introduced into the universities while he administered patronage, then about 65 of the 386 men who taught in this period (17 per cent) were his appointees. Between 1 January 1724 and 1 January 1762,[26] about 150 appointments were made. Ilay probably played a decisive personal role in 62 of them (41 per cent), not a small number when one realises that most of the others were divided between private patrons, the college masters and local men of influence. These patrons, often without his interference, appointed men he would have favoured because the legal patrons were his friends and followers. His influence on the dynamic sectors of the universities was great. For about thirty-five years he and his friends appointed almost all of the principals[27] and divinity professors, most of the regius professors and almost all those put into the medical chairs in which men taught. He presided over the Glasgow Visitation of 1726, which mandated the fixing of chairs and the introduction of experimental classes in natural philosophy and a notable turn to more practical science in the colleges. He approved appointments made in the medical schools in Edinburgh and Glasgow, and most of those given to the clerics who established Moderatism as the prevailing theological outlook in the seminaries. In this way, and through his other ecclesiastical patronage, he gave the Moderates control of the Kirk. Where Ilay did not have a chance to make many appointments, where the turnover of staff was small and men stayed in office the longest – at St Andrews and at King's College – the colleges were poor in two senses of the word. Ilay's secularism, his interest in science and medicine and his delight in what was new and modern, helped to make the country of 1800 different from the one which he had known as a young student at Glasgow in the 1690s or as a fledgling politician in Edinburgh in 1705. His selections of professors (and sometimes of clerics and judges) were often of men not so different from himself. They helped to transform the country.

Only Henry Dundas and his friends came close to matching Ilay's figures. Dundas accounted for about 54 appointments between about 1778 and 1806, but for only 44 different men.[28] The Squadrone men made perhaps 32 appointments. Principals Carstares and Stirling named 14 and 8 men respectively. Bute and his brother weighed in with 11.

3. The People Appointed by the Patrons and What They Did

The Scottish universities were staffed in the period 1690–1806 by about sixty brilliant or notable men, by many more who were in some way distinguished at the time and by others who would be, at best, only average academics in any time. Not all the brightest and the best were appointed, but there were few incompetents and misfits.[29] Few professors left the profession or were extruded and not many others were found deserving of censure for dereliction of duty or incompetence. The relative scarcity of deviants is one of the best things that can be said about the system of appointment which was driven by influence and which today would be regarded as very corrupt.

Among the appointees was a high percentage of men who seem to have wanted to teach and who had experience doing so. About seventy men (18 per cent) before they were appointed are known to have served as tutors, while thirty-four had taught in grammar schools and academies or in some other setting. At least a quarter of the professors had served as professorial deputies and sixteen were translated from one college to another. Among the men teaching in the early years were some who had acted as regents much earlier in their careers. Quite a few of the physicians and surgeons had had apprentices. Those who sought places in the colleges seem often to have been men seeking a teaching career and eager to have university posts and not something else. Many of the rejects were not very different. A surprising number of men – about fifty (13 per cent) – had applied for one or more posts before getting the one in which they made a career. Those who recruited such men clearly paid attention to their backgrounds. It is probably too much to claim that one can see here the birth of a specialised teaching profession, but by the mid-century something like a career path seems discernible. Tutoring was followed by a time as a teacher in some school or as a professorial deputy; one then became a conjoint professor and then a professor – a sequence which had become almost regular at Glasgow by 1800.

Of course, not all who went into teaching stuck with it. Charles Erskine and Patrick Haldane prepared to teach, sought teaching posts, taught and then abandoned academic careers for the law. Some, like Adam Smith and George Forrest, left teaching to become tutors to the sons of noblemen. John Bruce, a friend of Dundas, took up a civil post, became an MP and held sinecure positions. Others, like Hugh Cleghorn, served as functionaries of some sort. But, in the latter half of the period, probably more men abandoned other careers to become college teachers than left teaching to follow other vocations. What made teaching attractive was the fact that parishes, the alternative for many, paid less and often required more work from the conscientious. At the same time, there were few other places to which a would-be teacher might go.

The recruitment of active, innovative professors begun in the 1690s did not stop. It reflected the pressures on the colleges to provide useful educations.[30] The men who pressed were principally the gentry, seconded by the lawyers, medical men and clerics. Men in these ranks had sons who had to make their way in the world and needed modern educations and professional training to do so. This was best available abroad until c. 1740, as both the fathers and sons knew. Of professors appointed before 1730, at least fifty-six of them (38 per cent) are known to have been abroad, mostly to Holland but with a few sojourning in England and Ireland, some as students, others as exiles. There were doubtless more who were abroad about whom we know nothing. The Netherlands were a hothouse for new ideas of all sorts. Men did not come back unchanged. Such men laid the foundations for the culture of enlightened Scotland. Men like principals William Carstares or William Dunlop were determined to make the Scottish universities better and more like the Dutch ones, then the world's best. They wanted to see curricula modernised, although the most efficient means of doing this in the late 1690s was not the one they chose – fixed professors teaching from a standard set of textbooks used in all the colleges.[31]

Carstares and Dunlop were not alone. We should stop thinking of the academics appointed in the generation after 1690 as the Calvinist mossbacks earlier historians sometimes found. This is belied by men in every college. Some did have interests in modern learning, politics and curriculum reform.[32] They were often men who had suffered but also men who had travelled and who sometimes worked with politique statesmen before their appointments, even with Episcopalian patrons or colleagues. Men appointed in the 1690s interested themselves in history, medicine and science like other virtuosi of their day. They were also not unmoved by the prospect of changes to bring Scottish universities into conformity with the Dutch and continental patterns of specialised chairs from which both polite and vocational subjects were taught. Their colleges fostered the teaching of Latin and Greek by fixed professors who, after 1690, probably taught to a somewhat higher standard than had earlier regents. Accompanying this development at Glasgow, by c. 1708, was some attention to the niceties of English composition and the work of English men of letters such as Dryden, Addison, Steele and Shaftesbury. History, both civil and natural, had been introduced into the arts faculties at Glasgow and Edinburgh, where the museum dated from 1696. The first generation noticed here included the first man to teach Newton in any arts course anywhere and modern mathematicians teaching higher algebra at Glasgow, St Andrews and, perhaps, for a while at King's College. By c. 1710 these men (James Gregory II, Thomas Bower, Robert Simson and Charles Gregory) and other regents in arts (including Charles Erskine, Robert Steuart, Robert Dick I and Alexander Scrymgeour) were eager to teach Newtonian sciences and the mathematics associated with them. By then, the colleges employed divinity professors like William Hamilton and John Simson whose theologies had been touched by the more liberal ideas of Swiss and Dutch Calvinists. Between 1697 and 1730, medical and legal education began in a significant way at the two largest colleges. This turned more attention onto the curricula of the arts students, which needed changes to better train men to study medicine and understand the world furth of the kingdom in which so many boys would find careers. These developments all served the interests of the gentry and the country's professional men. In sending their sons abroad for higher education, Scots had created in the Netherlands what was in effect a sixth Scottish university college attended yearly by several hundred young men and their tutors. By 1740, that university was no longer necessary. The costs of professional educations for Scots fell, as did Dutch enrolments.[33] The men who made much of this possible were the managers and political patrons.

The successors of the men of 1690–1710 continued to exercise a beneficent influence in the country. Divinity professors John Simson, William Hamilton, William Wishart II and Thomas Tullideph, or their students, including Archibald Campbell and George Campbell, somewhat later, were committed to teaching students to think for themselves and to consider modern views.[34] One reason this could happen was that doctrines justifying political resistance and conscientious decisions about religious beliefs were part and parcel of the Calvinist heritage of earlier generations and underpinned the beliefs of men like Francis Hutcheson and the divines named above. Such men produced students who were more enlightened than their teachers and lent their authority, sometimes their impassioned voices, to the defence of freedom and modern novelties.[35] Few went so far as David Hume, who left Edinburgh University in 1724, but other men resembled him – men like Lord Kames, William Leechman, Adam Smith, the early Edinburgh Moderates, the members of the Aberdeen Wise Club, and even some who preached every Sunday or practised in the courts but did not go to literary clubs. It is easy to deride the earnest God-fearing men of the early century, or even those of 1720, but their students became the politicians and the professors who formed the new generation in an Israel not yet the Athens of the North.

By the 1740s, appointments in the Kirk had made it more moderate; indeed, after that date evangelicals were generally frozen out of the divinity chairs. Principals like William Wishart II, William Leechman and Thomas Tullideph lent their prestige to improving innovations and tended to keep the enlightened from being harassed by the 'un'co guid'. Later Moderates modified the attitudes, values and ideas of the early period but they did not altogether forsake them. In the period c. 1755–80, William Robertson and his friends exercised power, backed by politicians who, like them, were willing to see the country changed but who did not think the Kirk would be fractured in the process – as later it was. The Kirk now sponsored enlightened activities such as the insurance scheme for ministers and professors, various civic improvements, the reverend John Walker's surveys of the Highlands and Islands (1764, 1771) and the production of Sir John Sinclair's *Statistical Account of Scotland* in the 1790s.[36] It was the moderate leadership of the Kirk, much of it composed of University men, which tried to commit Scots to more tolerant attitudes in c. 1712, in the 1740s and in 1779, when it supported the repeal of Catholic disabilities. In doing such things, ministers were pursuing what they took to be moral and religious duties, ones aimed at the betterment of their fellow men but also at the glory of God. After 1790, they continued to see their, now reactionary, policies as marking no real departure from earlier principles.

The same patrons and teachers involved in these changes were intimately associated with the new philosophy taught during the same time. Crucial to its development in Scotland was the work of the seventeenth-century experimental natural philosophers, particularly Boyle and Newton, but also a host of experimenters in London and on the continent. The findings of such men, said the Visitors of the 1690s, were to be taught by the regents. Boyle showed men how to reason tentatively from the data of experiments and accustomed them to think more critically but not irreligiously. Newton supplied more rigorous canons of methodology and produced a deductively ordered, contingent system which offered a model to be followed by others. It had great predictive power in many areas. Locke followed a bit later to give Scots not only other inducements to pursue novelties but a greater concern with the data of consciousness as this related to epistemology and to moral, social and political issues. Trying to emulate these thinkers produced in Scotland two differing philosophies, one which looked to the works of Hutcheson, Hume and Smith and was phenomenalist in outlook, and a second which led to the Common Sense realism found in the works of Thomas Reid, George Campbell and Dugald Stewart. Both sets of thinkers put a high value on empirical work and both were concerned to develop systems which would embrace the moral as well as the natural world. They extended the range of secular thought into areas which earlier had been far more tied to religion. As this happened, the college libraries began to resemble those of secular virtuosi.

The Scottish universities were not only among the first in Europe to teach Newtonian mathematics and science but they continued to be welcoming to these disciplines. In mathematics Robert Simson did important work in the reconstruction of ancient mathematics and the history of geometry. Colin Maclaurin became the most important Newtonian mathematician in Britain during the century and his work was carried forward in slight ways by Marischal College's John Stewart. In astronomy the country could point to observers who had been trained in the colleges where several professors advanced this science. Alexander Wilson made changes to the sighting mechanisms of telescopes which made them easier to use. He used his own telescopes to observe sunspots on which he lectured. His work was honoured with a gold medal by the Danish Academy of Science. Edinburgh's Matthew Stewart worked out a good approximation of the value of the astronomical unit. In optics the country could point to Thomas Melville, a divinity student at Glasgow who at mid-century had criticised and amended Newton's theories about light and colour.

In chemistry Scots were more notable. Study of the nature of latent and specific heats, how they were to be measured and the determination of absolute zero were all pioneered in Scotland by men who either taught or wished to teach in the universities. So too were the rudiments of quantitative chemistry and the problems associated with combustion. Joseph Black shared his friend James Hutton's interests in geology and mining, practical work meant to improve industry.

In botany, thanks to Edinburgh's academic botanists, the University, by 1690, served as a collection and exchange point of botanical information from the British colonies and others in Europe and Asia. This led to work in taxonomy, plant physiology and the medical and industrial uses of new plant materials. James Sutherland, Charles Alston, John Hope and Daniel Rutherford formed a chain of teachers whose students took their skills and interests into the Empire where they surveyed the flora and sometimes set up important gardens.[37] Scots were intensely interested in the systems of Tournefort, Linnaeus and Buffon and followed the debates over the lines to be drawn between plants and animals, debates that had flourished partly because of the works of Abraham Trembley and Charles Bonnet. Thomas Reid and his friends in the Aberdeen Philosophical Society, and other men in the Edinburgh Philosophical Society or the Glasgow Literary Society all followed the debates on life science and sometimes contributed to the fields. Such academic club-men knew this branch of scientific literature well and some of it found its way into their classes and from there into student societies. All this interested Scots scientists and amateurs whose important science clubs were based in the universities. Reid's friend David Skene corresponded with Linnaeus and sent papers on corallines to the Royal Society of London by way of John Ellis.[38] Scottish university men contributed to all the fields of science during the period surveyed, far more than might have been expected given the size of the educated population in Scotland.

Everywhere in enlightened Europe, men sought knowledge which was useful and would better their condition. Scots were no exceptions to this rule. It drove much of the technological development in the period. An improved theoretical mechanics ought to result in better machines – ploughs, ventilation systems for mines, winches, guns, canals and canal locks, and improved engines turning straight into rotative motion. Those who worried about these particular items included professors like William Cullen and William Barron, Colin Maclaurin, John Anderson, Alexander and Patrick Wilson, and Patrick Copland. This was also true of the men who made or invented new instruments and devices for measuring one thing or another. Among them was professor Alexander Wilson who made thermometers, barometers, hygrometers and micrometers. Several other instrument-makers in Glasgow and Edinburgh were associated with the colleges where they served as demonstrators in experimental courses in natural philosophy.[39] The connections with those who improved processes needed for the chemical industry and the trades it supplied were as numerous and tighter.[40]

Scots, like the Dutch and Swiss, used their schools and universities to make themselves more prosperous and exportable. Patrons like James Graham, 1st Duke of Montrose, or John Hay, 4th Marquis of Tweeddale, or their rival, the Earl of Ilay and 3rd Duke of Argyll, promoted this knowingly. They were eager to make the colleges and universities serve such goals – which were also theirs. Over the many years in which these men made appointments, the colleges came to be increasingly committed to utilitarian ends and to the education of boys who could thrive both in and out of Scotland. This achievement was very much a Scottish one and little concerned men in London or Oxbridge who tended to measure education by different standards. It made the Scottish Enlightenment an intensely practical one, less defined by literary calls for freedom than for the improvement of everything. This constituted an important difference in emphasis between the British and the continental Enlightenment which however formed parts of a common movement of ideas and practices.

4. SCOTLAND AND EUROPE

The culture of the Scots in the eighteenth century continued for a long time to be oriented to the continent in many ways.[41] Scots and the English might share the same court of last resort, but Scots continued to look to Europe for their legal principles and Scotland found lawyers trained in Holland to teach those principles to students who would be employed in a system different from England's.[42] To appoint men who were interested in systematising Scots law, such as John Erskine and David Hume the younger, was to work at the preservation of national distinctiveness. Scots' ideas about society owed more to continental humanists and civilians than to English lawyers, historians or social theorists. The moral and social philosophy developed by Scots as they modernised derived mainly from continental natural lawyers. When the first anonymous English translation of *L'esprit des lois* (1748) was made in 1750, it was done in Scotland, not in London;

and it was probably done by a Scot who, like Montesquieu, had trained as a civilian. Like the Persian and Arabic learned by some at Glasgow, Edinburgh and Marischal College, the Scottish social theory taught at these schools fitted men to go out to govern an empire. When Scots looked for medical professors, they did not want English-trained men (unless they were surgeons) but insisted on those trained on the continent, preferably at Leiden. Those dispensing patronage in the eighteenth-century universities gave the country its medical schools and good science training based on Dutch models. They might send their boys to Eton to learn English, Latin and Greek but they seldom educated them at Oxbridge. Even the recognition Scots wanted still often came from abroad. Colin Maclaurin was a great Newtonian but his recognition as a world-class mathematician came not with his FRS in 1719 but with his prize from the French Academy of Sciences in 1724. This tended to be true of the medical men as well. Even as late as the 1760s, Scots such as David Hume felt more at home in Paris than in London, where they also did not quite speak the language. The accumulated effects of decisions about cultural orientation, the acceptable sources of influence and patronage all helped to preserve Scottish identity in a United Kingdom where differences were being erased. Scots might be politically joined to the English but so long as they controlled their Kirk, courts and educational system, and used them for purposes they defined, they would be not Britons but North Britons or Scots. University appointments constituted an important species of cultural politics. Only slowly after c. 1740 were the foreign ties weakened. Their vestiges remained well into the nineteenth century as every reader of Henry Cockburn knows. Provinciality perhaps came late in the eighteenth century but it was the railways and the emergence of a truly national market economy in the nineteenth century that made for real integration.

This study began with a call for the study of patrons and patronage in enlightenments generally. It offers an example of the political life that was still possible in provincial regions which were largely independent in their internal affairs of the large countries into which they were being integrated. This was Scotland's situation after the Union with England in 1707. In an eighteenth-century world still fundamentally local in its organisation and functioning, this example cannot be irrelevant to other milieux. Scottish university appointments, like many made by the same patrons in the civil administration and the Kirk, constituted one aspect of local politics, worked out by and for the inhabitants of Scotland with little interference from metropolitan politicians who were not Scots. That politics had, of course, some relation to parliamentary politics of the United Kingdom but it primarily affected and concerned local interests. It concerned the furthering of Scottish ends and the preservation of cultural distinctiveness. In the nineteenth century, English interference in the Scottish universities showed what the 'Sassenachs' thought of that university system and the cultural distinctiveness it nourished. During the eighteenth century, London's only effective educational intervention came in the creation, at small cost and at the request of Scots, of a few regius chairs and the giving of small grants which increased funds for instructional and other purposes, and in setting restrictions on the political and religious views professors were to express. Scots chose to see their universities become, not the somnolent places which graced the banks of the Isis, Cherwell and Cam, but bustling schools which had many notable and often polite men teaching at them. This was a necessity for a people poorer than the English.

The patronage of the universities was one of the ways in which Scots both before and after 1707 decided what they would become. The greater patrons were among those who insisted that the colleges and Scotland be modern, tolerant, forward-looking and able to make the kingdom shine in a Europe becoming more enlightened. There were many other areas in Europe in which such integration was the rule not the exception. What was true of Scotland is likely to have analogues in Europe. Not every landed aristocracy spent so much time on its estates, was so patriotic, so effective, or, for that matter, so small and dominated by well-educated leaders for so much of the period. Still, important patronage of the enlightened elsewhere was also exercised by knowing political managers and bureaucrats. One thinks of the men placed by Turgot and his protégés who have been so well described by Charles C. Gillispie.[43] Patronage of some kind was the means of running that world, an omnipresent reality in the period and ignored only by those who chose to treat intellectual matters in a vacuum. If we would be historians of the Enlightenments of Europe, then we must look to see who initiated, promoted, shaped and ended them by giving men jobs, power and status.[44] It is my hope that this work contributes to that effort.

Notes

1 This excludes Joseph Gibson, the first Edinburgh city professor of midwifery, but counts all the conjoint professors who were joined to those

already holding a chair even though the conjoints may have died before the man they were to succeed.

2 This is the number who competed but who were not placed at Edinburgh (149) minus those who eventually were placed somewhere (25).

3 As noted in the text, the number of appointments made is not the number of men seeking them. From the latter number one has to subtract the 16 men who held posts in two places (494 – 16 = 478). From that must be taken those who already held a place in a college and were seeking promotion (478 – c. 50 = c. 428). Another roughly 45 men eventually found positions in Scottish universities. This comes to 383, which is approximately the number known to have had jobs. This left roughly 100 men who failed altogether to find a Scottish university place. Of these, seven eventually took teaching posts which were more or less equivalent in England or at the extramural medical school in Edinburgh. Since we have no idea of the percentage of applicants who have been found and how many of the unnamed may have been hired, these are at best approximate figures. Where the evidence is good and the value of the chairs average or better, the applicants were often numerous. My guess is that there were between 300 and 500 men who hoped for places in Scottish colleges but did not find them. This would bring the total number of applicants to over 800 men.

4 Maclaren, 'Privilege, Patronage and the Professions', *Scottish Universities*, ed. Carter and Withrington, 1992, p. 98.

5 Ibid.

6 Scott, *Fasti*, VII:62; Aberdeen Town Council Letter Books, vol. 7, 8 September 1697, Aberdeen Town Council Archives.

7 Henderson, *Mystics of the North-East*, 1934, pp. 61–5.

8 See Henderson, 'Professor John Lumsden, 1694–1770', *Aberdeen University Review*, 1939–40, pp. 106–15.

9 M. A. Stewart, 'Principal Wishart', *Records of the Scottish Church History Society*, 2000, pp. 60–102.

10 For Hume see above, pp. 340f. and 128f. For Stuart's case, see Zachs, *Without Regard to Good Manners*, 1992, pp. 33, 106–8. See also Henderson, 'Professor John Lumsden, 1694–1770', *Aberdeen University Review*, 1939–40, pp. 106–15.

11 Skoczylas, *Mr Simson's Knotty Case*, 2001, and her 'The Regulation of Academic Society in Early Eighteenth-Century Scotland', *Scottish Historical Review*, 2004, pp. 171–95.

12 The way to that was marked by the Leslie decision of 1805, the destruction of the Dundas political machine after 1832 and by the Disruption of 1843, when most of the Popular Party left to establish the Free Church of Scotland.

13 Dunlop's defence of subscription to the creed of the Established Church, which the Moderates adopted, was one which made their increasing

heterodoxy clear to all their opponents. The Moderates looked, and were, hypocritical; they should have left a church in whose teachings they no longer believed. See Clark, 'From Protest to Reaction: The Moderate Regime in the Church of Scotland, 1752–1805', in *Scotland in the Age of Improvement*, eds Phillipson and Mitchison, 1970, p. 208f.

14 The post of mediciner at King's and that of the professor of medicine at Marischal were near sinecures reserved for local physicians related to professors in the colleges. Their competence mattered mostly because those physicians treated the boys and professors who became ill.

15 *Fasti Academiae Mariscallanae Aberdonensis*, ed. Anderson, 1889, p. 71f; *History of the Society of Advocates in Aberdeen*, ed. Henderson, 1912, p. 114.

16 Professor George Stewart to Gilbert Elliot of Minto, MP, 10 October 1761, Minto Papers, NLS, 11015/123.

17 For a partial list of those men and their close friends on the staff, see Richard B. Sher, *Church and University*, 1985, p. 1139–41.

18 His instruments and models were made by the Edinburgh instrument-maker John King. Bryden, *Scottish Scientific Instrument Makers*, 1972, p. 10.

19 Sir John Clerk of Penicuik, 'Some observations of mine as to the State of the nation in 1700', Penicuik Papers, NAS, GD18/3122.

20 Chitnis, *The Scottish Enlightenment*, 1986, pp. 134ff.

21 R. L. Emerson, 'Numbering the Medics', unpublished paper. The estimate is a conservative one from a range of between £660,000 and £1,240,000 for the period 1700–1800. Most of that came late in the period.

22 Plumb, *The Growth of Political Stability in England 1675–1725*, 1967, pp. 28f, 66–97.

23 Ilay did not hesitate to appoint some professorial sinecurists but those postings were to offices acknowledged to be sinecures and were usually given to compensate their holders for other works of value to patrons or the government. No one expected the mediciner at King's College to teach.

24 This is *not* the number of men appointed, which was 388. The figure of 494 includes all professorial appointments and lectureships whether or not they were taken up. It counts men who were initially denied appointments but restored to them by court action and includes several who actually functioned in office for some years before courts held them to have been illegally appointed. It counts as one appointment the annually renewed appointments to men such as the lecturers in French at Glasgow and St Andrews or the several lecturers in chemistry, *materia medica* and midwifery who taught for decades on this basis at Glasgow. Excluded are the appointments of men commissioned to teach in the burghs but not in the universities. It excludes all deputies and substitutes chosen by

the incumbent or by his college if they lacked conjoint appointments. It counts as having one appointment those who held regencies which were later converted into professorships when chairs were fixed. Usually these men technically still remained regents of philosophy so that their charter rights could be maintained. Regents designated early in the century as professors of Greek have been counted only as regents, but those appointed to Greek chairs have been counted.

25 The actual number is difficult to ascertain because of the fragmentary records at my disposal. He certainly approved fifty-nine men and seems to have personally chosen about ten of them. He and his political advisors are known to have failed to make a difference in six other cases where they tried to interfere but were unsuccessful.

26 He had made arrangements for one appointment which was actually made only in 1763.

27 Ilay appointed or approved the appointments of principals William Hamilton, John Gowdie, James Smith and William Wishart II at Edinburgh. William Robertson came in under the auspices of his nephew, Lord Bute, whose attitudes regarding appointments reflected those of his uncle. At Glasgow, Neil Campbell was the choice of his brother, John, 2nd Duke of Argyll, but was one to which Ilay agreed. He may have had a hand in the selection of Thomas Tullideph at St Andrews while, at Marischal College, John Osborn and George Campbell had his support. Like most outsiders, he was ineffective at King's College, which was run by family cliques throughout most of the century. The divinity professors he installed were not High Flyers and his appointees were among those who effectively killed serious Hebrew teaching in Scotland and the pursuit of ecclesiastical history. This was especially true at Glasgow, where he had the most influence. For Bute's appointments, see Emerson, 'Lord Bute and the Scottish Universities', in *Lord Bute: Essays in Reinterpretation*, ed. Schweizer, 1988, pp. 147–79.

28 I may have undercounted here since Dundas claimed in 1800 to have appointed all the professors installed at Edinburgh, Glasgow and St Andrews in the previous twenty years. We should believe him. Nothing changed between 1800 and 1805 when the Whig opposition to him had its way for a short time. The Dundas party machine went on controlling Scotland until c. 1832.

29 About 2 per cent are known to have committed suicide, become deranged, taken to drugs or absconded, a rate which must compare favourably with most modern institutions of higher learning such as my own. Among those distinguished men who applied but who never received Scottish university appointments, one finds thirty at Glasgow and Edinburgh: Abraham Gronovius, William Graeme, MD, George Martine, MD, John Maclaurin, DD, David Hume, Alexander Bryce, DD, (possibly Edmund Burke), James Stirling of Keir, John Stedman,

MD, the reverend John Jardine, Henry Home, SCJ, Thomas Melville, David Skene, MD, Hector Maclean, Surgeon, Sir Robert Liston, Patrick Clason, William Buchan, MD, William Small, MD, James Lind, MD, William Wright, MD, Alexander Keith, WS, the reverend John Logan, Gilbert Stuart, William Smellie, Sir James MacIntosh, John Barclay, MD, Thomas Chalmers, DD, James Carmichael Smith, MD, William Stark, MD, Alexander Carlyle, DD; and one at St Andrews: the reverend John Home. There were none of distinction known to have been passed over at the Aberdeen colleges, which probably shows how closed to outsiders those were.

30 How they variously defined this can be inferred from such writings as *Proposals for the reformation of Schools and Universities*, 1704, attributed to Andrew Fletcher of Saltoun. As good as any are Sir John Clerk's comments on his education in Glasgow and Holland. He found the first scholastic and useless. In Holland he followed a broad course of study recommended by men like Sir George Mackenzie and John Spottiswoode. This included some science and philosophy, mathematics, music, languages, history and law: *Memoirs of Sir John Clerk of Penicuik*, ed. Gray, 1892, pp. 14–17. There are many similar justifications of new chairs and innovations which mention the saving of money effected by local educations which will fit men for work in or out of Scotland.

31 These books were to include some modern, experimental science even if the philosophy was still mainly scholastic.

32 Clare Jackson's recent studies of the politics and political theory of Scots in the late seventeenth century mention several of the University men appointed after 1690: *Restoration Scotland*, 2003, and 'Revolution Principles, Ius Naturae and Ius Gentium in Early Enlightenment Scotland', in *Early Modern Natural Law Theories*, ed. Hochstrasser and Schroder, 2003, pp. 107–40.

33 See Mijers, 'Scotland and the United Provinces, c. 1680–1730', unpublished PhD dissertation, 2002.

34 The first four had spent time abroad; the Campbells had not.

35 See M. A. Stewart, 'Freethinking', forthcoming.

36 For Walker, see *The Rev. Dr John Walker's Report on the Hebrides*, ed. McKay, Edinburgh, 1980; the best account of Sinclair's *Account* is still Mitchison, *Agricultural Sir John*, 1962.

37 The best place to look for the impact of the earlier men is still Stearns, *Science in the British Colonies of America*, 1970; more recent works concerning this topic can be found in the bibliographies at the ends of the essays in *Cultures of Science*, eds Jardine, Secord and Spary, 1996.

38 *The Minutes of the Aberdeen Philosophical Society 1758–1773*, ed. Ulman, 1990. This topic occurs in papers delivered 1762–4; see also David Skene, Discourse 6, 'Discourses on Natural History', AUL 480.

For a view of the relations Aberdeen men had with the larger world of science in Skene's lifetime, see Lenman and Kenworthy, 'Dr David Skene', *Aberdeen University Review*, 1977, pp. 32–44, 231–7.

39 Bryden, *Scientific Instrument-Makers*, 1972, passim. Others are mentioned in Emerson and Wood, 'Science and Enlightenment', in *Science and Medicine*, ed. Withers and Wood, 2002, pp. 79–142.

40 The best discussion of this is still that of Clow and Clow, *The Chemical Revolution*, 1970 (1st printing 1950). Many of their topics are discussed with references to Scots in Musson and Robinson, *Science and Technology in the Industrial Revolution*, 1969. Jenny Uglow's *The Lunar Men*, 2002, deals with a dozen English industrialists, six of whom were partially educated at the Edinburgh Medical School and a seventh (William Small) who tried for a post there. It is reflective of the world which young Scots were being prepared to enter by professors like William Cullen, Joseph Black and John Hope, John Robison, John Playfair, Sir John Leslie, Patrick Copland, Robert Hamilton and even John Rotherham.

41 Emerson, 'Did the Scottish Enlightenment Emerge in an English Cultural Province?', *Lumen*, 1995, pp. 1–24.

42 See John Cairns, 'The influence of Smith's jurisprudence on legal education in Scotland', in *Adam Smith Reviewed*, ed. Peter Jones and Andrew Skinner, Edinburgh, 1992, pp. 168–89; ——, 'Legal Theory', in *The Cambridge Companion to the Scottish Enlightenment*, ed. Broadie, 2002, pp. 222–42.

43 Charles Coulston Gillispie, *Science and Polity in France at the End of the Old Regime*, 1980.

44 For more on the contexts of the Scots during this time, see Emerson, 'The contexts of the Scottish Enlightenment', in *The Cambridge Companion to the Scottish Enlightenment*, ed. Broadie, 2003, pp. 9–30.

BIBLIOGRAPHY

This bibliography contains only the books used or cited in for this study. It includes books with incidental information about professors but does not contain books devoted to other topics concerning the universities. The bibliography lists manuscripts first by location, then unpublished theses and books devoted to the universities. Collections are listed by their titles and correspondence by the person writing or by those to whom the letters were mainly addressed. All books beginning with 'the', such as 'The Dictionary . . .', are listed under 'Dictionary'. Where clarity requires a publisher to be noted I have done so. Anonymous works whose authors are known are listed under the authors.

I. MANUSCRIPTS SOURCES

Aberdeen

Town Council Archives

Council Register, vols 58–65 (1711–80).
Letter Books, vols 7–15 (1689–1800).
Out Letter Book, vols 1–10 (1729–95).

Aberdeen University Library

[Many more MS references can be found in R. L. Emerson, *Professors and Patronage* and P. B. Wood, *The Aberdeen Enlightenment* (cited below)].

Miscellaneous King's College MSS, K 255, Crown Tower,* Box 43.
John Stewart MSS, 3017/10/11–22.
King's College
　Minutes, KC 40–8.
　Papers of Thomas Gordon, K 3107.
　Papers Relating to William Thom, K 216.
Marischal College
　Minute Book 1729–90, M 41.

Marischal College Collections [made by William Knight], M108–16. [This contains transcripts of materials which pertain to Aberdeen taken from the Public Record Office, State Papers – Scotland Domestic, Bundles 6–46.]

James Beattie Manuscripts, M 30.

George French, Collection of Letters, M 52.

Robert Hamilton MSS, M 451–8.

David Skene MSS.

    Correspondence, M 38.

    Papers, 38, 471–8, 480, 482, 484, 540.

St Andrews

St Andrews University Library and Muniments Room

'A Catalogue of Books belonging [tear] Library of ye university of St Andrews, [to 1716], UYLY 105/3.

'A Catalogue . . .', UYLY 106/5 [1744].

'A Catalogue . . .', UYLY 105/4 [1734–57].

'St Leonard's College Library', UYLY 106/2.

Minutes of the University, UYUY 452 /1–11 [1696–1806].

Minutes of St Leonard's College, 7 July 1710–9 July 1747, UY SL400.

Minutes of United College, 8 July 1747–1806, UYUC 400/1–7.

Minutes of St Mary's College, UYSM 400/1–3 [1736–1823].

Minutes of the Philosophical Society, 4 July 1787–25 March 1795.

Regulations and Proceedings of the Theology Club, 1760–6.

[William] Barron MSS, Boxes 1–4, UYUC 400/7.

James Gillespie MSS, 37511.

Hadow, Arthur Lovel, 'Hadow Pedigree', 37862/10.

Mackie, Charles, 'Index funereus 1727–1736', 36987.

Melville Manuscripts, 4433–4783.

Francis Pringle's Commonplace book LF1111.P81C99.

    Collection of College Papers, Acc. 4796, Box 108;

    Acc. 638.

'Commonplace Book of Thomas Tullideph 1717', LF1109.T8C6.

Edinburgh

National Archives of Scotland

Abercairny MSS, GD24.

Clerk of Penicuik Papers, GD18.

Papers of Sir Alexander Cunningham Dick, GD331.

Papers of Sir William Fraser, GD397.

Hume of Wedderburn Papers, GD267.
Leven and Melville Papers, GD26.
Papers of Reverend Dr Archibald McLea, GD1.
Mar and Kellie Papers, GD24.
Melville Castle Muniments, GD51.
Morton Papers, GD50.
Scottish Papers, SP54 [these are photostatic copies of National Archive papers held by the National Archives of Scotland; some MS copies are held at Aberdeen University Library].
Seafield Papers, GD248.
Scrymgeour-Wedderburn Muniments, GD137.

National Library of Scotland

Advocates' MSS

Papers of James Anderson, WS, Adv. 29.1.2; 29.5.4(ii).
Chalmers MSS, Adv. MS 21-1-11.
Papers of John Spotswood [Spottiswoode], Adv. 29.3.30.5.
Wodrow Quarto Letters, I–XVIII.
Wodrow Correspondence, Adv MS.29.1.2.

National Library MSS

[Beattie, James] Fettercairn MSS, ACC 4796, Boxes 91–4.
'Memoirs of the Reverend John Brand', 1668.
Alexander Carlyle MSS, 152.
[Dalrymple of] New Hailes Papers, 7228.
Delvine Papers, 1423.
Dundas Papers, 5–7.
Dundas Papers, 3834; 6524.
Erskine-Murray MSS, 5074–88.
[Fletcher of Saltoun], Saltoun Papers
    Correspondence, 16505–733.
    Miscellaneous Papers, 16750–4.
    'Diary of Andrew Fletcher', 17745–50.
    Scientific Papers, SB80.
[Forbes of] Culloden Papers, 2968.
David Hume Papers (formerly held at the RSE), MSS, 23151–64.
Lee Papers, 3431.
Liston MSS, 5513–17.
Minto Papers, 11007–19.
Mure of Caldwell Papers, 4941–5006.
John Ramsay of Ochtertyre, 'Manuscript Memoirs', 1635.

Robertson-Macdonald Letters, 3942–4.
William Rouet Papers, 4990–2.
Scott Papers, 5072.
T. C. Smout, 'George Drummond', typescript lecture to the Edinburgh District Council, March 1978 (accessible through the book catalogue).
John Spottiswoode Papers, 658, 2933.
Watson Autographs, 582.
Yester MSS, 7044–9, 7051, 7054–7, 7059, 7063–6, 7070, 7074.

Library of the Royal College of Physicians, Edinburgh

Minutes 1682–1800.
Letters to Dr Cullen, 1755–90, 21 vols, MS 31.
Francis Home MSS:
    Case Book [n.d. but 1788–9], MS Home (F) 4.
    Dr Francis Home's Cash Book, MS Home (F) 5.

Library of the Royal College of Surgeons of Edinburgh

Minutes of the Royal College of Surgeons of Edinburgh vols 3–7 (1695–1810).

Library of the Royal Botanic Garden, Edinburgh

John Hope, Memoirs, Papers and Transcripts of MSS held in other places.
Charles Preston, Letters and Miscellaneous Papers.
Daniel Rutherford, Miscellaneous Papers and Correspondence.
James Sutherland, Biographical notes, etc. Boxes 1–3.
John Walker, Papers and Transcripts.

Library of the Royal Highland Society

Fragmentary Minutes of the Society for Improving in the Knowledge of Agriculture of Scotland, 1731–6 and typescript 'Transcript Minutes of the Society for Improving in the Knowledge of Agriculture of Scotland', 1731–6.

Edinburgh University Library

Papers Illustrative of the History and Constitution of the University of Edinburgh and Acts and Charters of the University, Dc.1.4.1[1–2].
College Minutes [Senate Minutes], 1733–1811.
Letters Relating to Edinburgh and the University Life of the Time 1790–1830, Dc.2.57.

[This includes many letters by John (later Sir John) Leslie, James Brown and John Robison.]

Typescript Matriculation Registers of the University of Edinburgh held in the Manuscripts Reading Room (1680–1800).

Correspondence of Joseph Black, Gen 873/1–3.

Miscellaneous Black Papers Gen 874.

Letters to Dr Alexander Carlyle, Dc.4.4.

William Carstairs [sic] MSS, Ms Dk1.1^2.

[Erskine, David, Earl of Buchan], Miscellaneous Correspondence, Gen 1736.

[Gregorie, David], David Gregorie Papers, Dk.1.2.2^1.

D. B. Horn Papers, Gen 1824.

Laing MSS (see also *HMC Report of the Laing MSS*, cited below)

La.III. 375, Correspondence and Miscellaneous Papers of Charles Alston.

La.III. 379, John Bethune to ? [on the curriculum at Aberdeen 1787].

La.II. 407, Letters to William Carstares.

La.II. 577, Twenty letters addressed to the Rev. Principal Carstairs [c. 1707].

La.II. 676/182, 'Memorandum to Montrose'.

La.II. 500, Dundas papers 1–2430 [items 1103–8 contain letters from and about John Robison].

La.II. 419, Letters of John Logan to Alexander Carlyle.

La.II. 63, Scott Papers.

La.II. 115.13.2, Professor John Stevenson to William Wishart, 23 June 1746.

La.III. 352^{21}, Miscellaneous Letters and Papers of John Walker.

La.II. 690, 'An essay to recover some account of the Life of the Reverend James Wodrow.

La.III. 375, Letters to Charles Alston, 'Tractatus Chronologicus' [with a geography], transcribed by Robert Stewart, 1682, Dc.6.23, 'Compendium Logicae' [by Colin Drummond], c. 1725. MS 2651.

Charles Mackie MSS

Correspondence, La.II. 90–1.

Miscellaneous Papers of Charles Mackie, La.II. 232–5.

Common Place Book and Obituary 1737–1749, La.III. 537.

Index Funereus, Dc.1.47.

Commonplace Book, Dc.5.24.

'Minutes of the Professors of Medicine and Partners of the Chemical Elaboratory in Edinburgh, dated 26 January 1731', Gen 1959.

John Walker, Miscellaneous Papers, Dc.2.39

Fossil Collection, Gen 1061.

[Wilson, Alexander and Patrick], 'Notices Concerning the letter Foundry by Wilsons at St Andrews and Glasgow' (unsigned but probably by Patrick Wilson), Gen 1087.

Lothian Medical Archive

Miscellaneous papers relating to the Edinburgh professors of anatomy and midwifery: Alexander Monro II, Thomas Young, and Alexander and James Hamilton and to their appointments, MS GD1/1/75.

New College Library, University of Edinburgh

The Ecclesiastical History Lectures of Patrick Cuming, x136/615.

GLASGOW

Glasgow University Archives

'Grievances Relating to proceedings in ffaculty and other Business relating to the University' signed by Gershom Carmichael, William Forbes, Alexander Dunlop, John Johnstoun, Robert Simson, Robert Dick, 1717, GUA 47414–25.

Minutes of the Deans of Faculties, 26626.

Minute Book of the Facultie, ?–1720, 26630.

Minute Book of the Facultie of the University of Glasgow from Decr 18 1702–1720, 26631.

Minutes of the University of Glasgow Facultie Meeting 1701–1717, 26632.

Minutes of the University of Glasgow Meeting 1717–1719, 26633.

Minutes of the University of Glasgow Meeting, 1720–1727, 26634.

Minutes of the University of Glasgow Meeting, 1727–1730, 26635.

Minutes of the University of Glasgow Meeting, [n.d.], 26636.

Minutes of the Faculty, 1730–1735, 26647.

Minutes of Meetings of Faculty, 1735–1745, 26648.

Minutes of Meetings of Faculty, 1745–1753, 26649.

Minutes of Meetings of Faculty, 1753–1755 and 1761–1770, 26650.

Minutes of the Meetings of the Faculties and Dean of Faculties, 1768–1771, 26646.

Minutes of the Meetings of the Faculties and Dean of Faculties, 26645.

Minutes of the Dean of Faculties Meeting, 1768–1772, 26646.

Minutes of the University Meeting, 1730–1749, 26639.

Minutes of the Meetings of the Faculties and Dean of Faculties, 1732–1768, 26645.

Minutes of the University of Glasgow Meeting, 1749–1759, 26640.

Minutes of the University of Glasgow Meeting, 1759–1760, 26641.

Minutes of the University of Glasgow Meeting, 1760–1763, 26642.

Minutes of the University of Glasgow Meeting, 1763–1768, 26643.

Minutes of the Rector and the University of Glasgow Meeting, 1768–1770, 26644.

Minutes of the Faculty 1794–1806, 26695.

'Principals Memorandum Book, [1685–1702]', 26630/10.

'State of the University when Mr Stirling came in Sepr 1701 . . .', 47410 [extracts from this memorandum by Principal Stirling appear in *Notices and Documents*, ed. W. J. Duncan, see below].

Visitation Records
    1690–1702: 47294–303, 47360.
    1717–18: 27149, [?]43228, 45248, 47328, 47339, 47341, 47348, 47408–10, 47411–13, 58443.

Miscellaneous College and University MSS: 2020, 5412, 26223, 27026, 27027–9, 27095, 28893–6, 30297, 30492, 30638, 30664, 43155, 43163, 45224–5, 45234–6, 45237, 45268–73, 45272–8, 46718, 46758–61, 58442, 58445.

Robert Craigie to [?Marquis of Tweeddale], undated [c. 1743], concerning the Crown's right to appoint to the chair of Oriental languages, 47462–3.

Robert Simson Letters, 2020, 5412, 17983–6, 26105, 26107, 26197, 26223, 26233, 26388, 30485, 30489, 30491–2, 30499, 30522, 30525.

Letters related to Alexander and Patrick Wilson, 58355, 58359.

'Reasons for Transportation' [of Alexander Wodrow] etc', 45234–6.

Glasgow University Library

'Catalogus Librorum Bibliothecae Universitatis Glasguenses anno 1691' [additions run to c. 1718], Gen 1312.

Notebooks of John Anderson, MS Farmer 333.

Bannerman MSS, 1035/135–77.

William Cullen MSS, Boxes 1–4;
    Thomson/Cullen MSS, 2255.

Dunlop Letters, 'Transcripts of Thirty-six [*sic*, there are thirty-eight] Letters Passing Between Professor William Dunlop, Edinburgh and Professor Alexander Dunlop, Glasgow, 1715–1720', Gen 83. The typescript was prepared in 1932 by J. G. Dunlop. The letters are not in chronological order and possibly not in their original order.

John C. Eaton MSS, Gen 1320, 4 boxes [transcripts of letters by and to Colin Maclaurin and notes for a biography; much of this material has been published in Stella Mills' edition of Maclaurin's correspondence, see below].

Twelve letters of the Earl of Buchan [Erskine, David, 11th Earl of Buchan], Gen 1429/16.

Transcripts of 78 letters made by Dr Louisa Hamilton of letters between William Hamilton and his father Thomas and others, 1771–1787, Gen 1356/1–78 [includes many letters from James Jeffrey].

Letters of Francis Hutcheson, Gen 1018.

Letters of George Jardine and Robert Hunter, Gen 505–7.
George Martine to Dr James Douglas, 4 August 1735, Gen 505 D 626/3.
Murray MSS
    Earl of Buchan MS, 502, Boxes 1–4.
    Alexander Carlyle, 'Notes for Autobiography', 41/3.
    Letters of Robert Simson, 660 [mostly letters of William Rouet to Robert Simson 17].
    Stirling Letters, 650–3.
    Letters from and to William Rouet, 660.
    Letters to Robert Simson, Murray MS 660.
[Robert] Simson Correspondence
    Mathematical Correspondence of Robert Simson, Gen 145, 146, 146A [1760–3]; Correspondence, Gen 196.
[Principal John] Stirling Letters, Gen 204.1–2 [plus typescript]; these are also contained in Murray MSS 650–3.

Strathclyde University

Strathclyde University Archives

Anderson MSS, 11.
Correspondence of John Anderson and Gilbert Lang, A2.

Strathclyde University Library

Miscellaneous Papers and Journals of John Anderson, MSS 9–46.

Mitchell Library

Campbell of Succoth Papers, MS TD 219.

Mount Stuart House, Isle of Bute

Uncatalogued papers of the Marquis of Bute.
Uncatalogued Papers of John Campbell, 4th Earl of Loudoun 1753–75.
Uncatalogued Papers of John Stuart, 3rd Earl of Bute.
Uncatalogued Papers of James Stuart Mackenzie.

LONDON

British Library

Althorp MSS, G.23.
Sloane Papers, ADD.37915 vol. 74.

Thomas Birch Papers, Add. MSS 4101–478.
Wyndham Papers, Add. MS 37915, vol. 74.

Doctor Williams Library

Correspondence of Samuel Kenrick . . . and Dr James Wodrow . . ., MS
24.157/1–287.

II. UNPUBLISHED DISSERTATIONS, BOOKS AND ARTICLES

Barfoot, Michael, 'James Gregory (1753–1821) And Scottish Scientific
Metaphysics, 1750–1800', PhD dissertation, Edinburgh University,
1983.

Baxter, Alexander R. F., 'St Andrews and Scottish Latin', M Ed thesis, St
Andrews University, 1972.

Berry, Christopher, 'James Dunbar 1742–1798: A study of his thought and
his place in and contribution to the Scottish Enlightenment', PhD dissertation, University of London, 1970.

Cairns, John, *Legal Education in Eighteenth Century Edinburgh*, forthcoming.

Clark, Ian D. L., 'Moderatism and the Moderate Party in the Church of
Scotland 1752–1805', PhD dissertation, Cambridge University, 1963.

Cater, Jeremy, 'James Robertson, 1720–1795: An Anti-Enlightenment
Professor in the University of Edinburgh', PhD dissertation, New York
University, New York, 1976.

McCallum, Donald P., 'George Hill, DD: Moderate or Evangelical
Erastian?', MA thesis, University of Western Ontario, 1989.

Mijers, Esther, 'Scotland and the United Provinces, c. 1680–1730: A Study
in Intellectual and Educational Relations', PhD dissertation, St Andrews
University, 2002.

Roberts, Alonso D., 'St Andrews Mathematics Teaching 1765–1858', MA
thesis, St Andrews University, 1970.

Scott, Richard, 'The Politics and administration of Scotland 1725–1748',
PhD dissertation, Edinburgh University, 1982.

Shepherd, Christine M. [King], 'Philosophy and Science in the Arts
Curriculum of the Scottish Universities in the 17th Century', PhD dissertation, Edinburgh University, 1974.

Sher, Richard, 'Church, University, Enlightenment: the Moderate Literati of
Edinburgh, 1720–93', PhD dissertation, University of Chicago, 1979.

Stott, Rosalie, 'The Incorporation of Surgeons and Medical Education and
Practice in Edinburgh, 1696–1755', PhD dissertation, Edinburgh
University, 1984.

Wehrli, Eric G. J., 'Scottish Politics in the Age of Walpole', PhD dissertation,
Edinburgh University, 1983.

III. OTHER SOURCES

Periodicals

Aberdeen University Review (various issues c. 1950–).
The Caledonian Mercury, 28 April 1720–1807.
The Guardian, ed. John Calhoun Stephens, Lexington, Kentucky, 1982.
Medical and Philosophical Commentaries, 1773–1804 when it became the *Annals of Medicine*, ed. Andrew Duncan and Andrew Duncan II. [These volumes contain many obituaries and biographical notices.]
Philosophical Transactions of the Royal Society of London (London, 1700–80; reprinted New York, 1963).
[St Andrews] *Alumnus Chronicle* (various issues c. 1930–).
Scots Magazine, 1739–1804 (various issues).
Transactions of the Royal Society of Edinburgh, I–IXX (Edinburgh, 1785–1810).
The University of Edinburgh Journal (various issues c. 1940–).

Books and Articles

Aberdeen and the Enlightenment, ed. Jennifer J. Carter and Joan H. Pittock (Aberdeen, 1987).
An Account of the Proceedings of the Estates of Scotland 1689–1690, 2 vols, ed. E. W. M. Balfour-Melville, *Scottish History Society*, 3rd Series, vols 46 and 47, 1954, 1955.
Adamson, John and Joseph M'Cormick, 'PARISHES of St ANDREW'S and St LEONARD'S', in *The Statistical Account of Scotland*, 1978 [see below], 10:702–35.
Aldis, H. G., *A List of Books printed in Scotland before 1700 . . . with additions* (Edinburgh Bibliographical Society, Edinburgh, 1970).
Allan, David, 'Prudence and Patronage: The Politics of Culture in Seventeenth-Century Scotland', *History of European Ideas*, 18 (1994), pp. 467–80.
——, 'John Ramsay of Ochtertyre', in *Oxford Dictionary of National Biography* [ODNB, see below], 4:91f.
Anderson, J. M., 'The Princely Chandos and the University of St Andrews', *Scottish Historical Review*, 15 (1895), pp. 41–70.
Anderson, Peter J., 'The Arts Curriculum', in *Records of the Arts Class, 1868–72*, Aberdeen, 1892, pp. 227–46.
Anderson, R. D., Michael Lynch and Nicholas Phillipson, *The University of Edinburgh: An Illustrated History* (Edinburgh, 2003).
Anderson, R. G. W., *The Playfair Collection and the Teaching of Chemistry at the University of Edinburgh 1713–1858* (Royal Scottish Museum, Edinburgh, 1978).
Andreapolis being writings in praise of St Andrews, ed. William Knight (Edinburgh, 1903).

Anglo-Scottish Tracts, 1701–1714: A Descriptive Checklist, compiled by W. R. and V. B. MacLeod (University of Kansas Publications, Library Series 44, Lawrence, 19790). [This contains biographical materials.]

Anonymous, 'An Account of the Rise and Establishment of the Infirmary, or hospital for Sick Poor, erected at Edinburgh' (Edinburgh [pamphlet], 1730).

——, *A Letter to the Author of the North Briton . . . with a Striking Character . . . of Archibald, late Duke of Argyll* (London,1763).

——, *Gentleman's Magazine*, 'Original Memoires of Dr Robertson of Wolverhampton', September 1783, pp. 745–50.

——, *'Proposals for the Reformation of Schools and Universities in order to better the Education of youth in Scotland* (London, 1704). [This is often attributed to Andrew Fletcher of Saltoun.]

The Argyll Papers, ed. Thomas G. Stevenson (Edinburgh, 1834).

Armstrong, Brian, *Calvinism and the Amyraut Heresy* (Madison,WI, 1969).

Arnot, Hugh, *The History of Edinburgh* (Edinburgh, 1779).

Atheism from the Reformation to the Enlightenment, ed. Michael Hunter and David Wooton (Oxford, 1992).

Baird, William, 'George Drummond, an Edinburgh Lord Provost of the Eighteenth Century', *Book of the Old Edinburgh Club*, 4 (1911), pp. 1–54.

Balfour, Sir Isaac Bayley, 'A Sketch of the Professors of Botany in Edinburgh from 1760 until 1887', in *Makers of British Botany*, ed. F. W. Oliver (London, 1913).

——, 'William Arthur, MD Botanist to the King in Scotland 1715–1716', *Transactions and Proceedings of the Botanical Society of Edinburgh*, 26 (1914–15), pp. 375–404.

Balfour-Melville, Barbara, *The Balfours of Pilrig: A History for the Family* (Edinburgh, 1907).

Barfoot, Michael, 'Hume and the Culture of Science in the Early Eighteenth Century', in *Studies in the Philosophy of the Scottish Enlightenment*, vol. I, *Oxford Studies in the History of Philosophy*, ed. M. A. Stewart (Oxford, 1990), pp. 151–90.

——, ' "To ask the Suffrages of the Patrons": Thomas Laycock and the Edinburgh Chair of medicine, 1855', *Medical History*, Supplement No. 15 (London, 1995).

Bator, Paul G., 'The Unpublished Rhetoric Lectures of Robert Watson, Professor of Logic, Rhetoric, and Metaphysics at the University of St Andrews, 1756–1778', *Rhetorica*, 12 (1994), pp. 67–112.

Beattie, James, *James Beattie's London Diary 1773*, ed. Ralph S. Walker (Aberdeen, 1946).

——, *Moral Science*, 3 vols (Philadelphia, 1790–93, 1st edn, 1790–3).

Bibliographia Aberdonensis . . . 1641–1700, 2 vols, compiled by James Fowler Kellas Johnstoun and Alexander Webster Robertson, *Third Spalding Club* (Aberdeen, 1929 and 1930).

Biographical Dictionary of Eminent Men of Fife, compiled by M. F. Conolly (Cupar and Edinburgh, 1866).

A Biographical Dictionary of Eminent Scotsmen, 4 vols, ed. Robert Chambers (Glasgow and Edinburgh, 1856).

Biographical Register of the University of St Andrews 1747–1897, compiled by Robert Smart (St Andrews University Library, St Andrews, 2004).

Black, Hester and Philip Gaskel, 'Special Collections in Glasgow University Library', *The Book Collector*, 16 (1967), pp. 161–8.

[Blackwell, Thomas I], 'Letters from Principal Blackwell and others . . .,' *Miscellany I, Spalding Club* (Aberdeen, 1841); 3:195–223.

Blair, John S. G., *History of Medicine in the University of St Andrews* (Edinburgh, 1987).

Boase, C. W., *A Century of Banking in Dundee . . .* (Dundee, 1864).

[Bonar], 'Letters from John Bonar to William Creech Concerning the formation of the Speculative Society', *Book of the Old Edinburgh Club*, 5 (1912), pp. 163–90.

Boney, A.D., *The Lost Gardens of Glasgow University*, London, 1988 [this has accounts of the Glasgow University botanists 1703–1806].

Book of Discipline
   The First Book of Discipline, ed. James K. Cameron (Edinburgh, 1972).
   The Second Book of Discipline, ed. James Kirk (Edinburgh, 1980).

[Boston, Thomas], *Memoirs of the Life, Time and Writings of the Reverend and Learned Thomas Boston*, ed. George Morrison (Edinburgh and London, 1899).

[Boswell], 'The Journal of John Boswell', ed. Joy Pitman, *Proceedings of the Royal College of Physicians Edinburgh*, 19 (1989), pp. 487–91 and 20 (1990), pp. 67–77, 205–12.

Bower, Alexander, *History of the University of Edinburgh*, 3 vols (Edinburgh, 1817, 1817, 1830).

Box, Mark A., David Harvey and Michael Silverthorne, 'A Diplomatic Transcription of Hume's "volunteer pamphlet" for Archibald Stewart: Political Whigs, Religious Whigs, and Jacobites', *Hume Studies*, 29 (2003), pp. 223–66.

Brock, C. Helen, 'The happiness of riches', in *William Hunter and the eighteenth-century medical world*, ed. W. F. Bynum and Roy Porter (Cambridge, 1985), pp. 35–54.

Brock, William and Helen, *Scotus Americanus* (Edinburgh, 1982).

Brockliss, Lawrence, 'Science, the Universities, and Other Public Spaces', in *The Cambridge History of Science*, 8 vols, Gen. Eds D. C. Lindberg and R. L. Numbers; vol. 4, ed. Roy Porter (Cambridge, 2003), pp. 44–86.

Brown, Isabel, 'A Short Account of the [Glasgow] Town's Hospital', *Bibliotheck*, 1 (1958), pp. 37–41.

Brown, Stewart J., 'William Robertson and the Scottish Enlightenment', in *William Robertson and the Expansion of Empire*, ed. Stewart J. Brown (Cambridge, 1997), p. 35.

Brown, William, *The History and Antiquities of St Rule's Chapel . . . with Remarks by Professor Brown*, in *Bibliotheca Topographica*, ed. John Nichols, 10 vols (London, 1780–1800); vol. 5, part 4, pp. 195–208.

Bruce, James, *Eminent Men of Aberdeen* (Aberdeen, 1841).

Bryden, David, *Scottish Scientific Instrument-Makers 1600–1900* (Royal Scottish Museum, Edinburgh, 1972).

——, 'The Edinburgh Observatory 1736–1811: A Story of Failure', *Annals of Science*, 47 (1990), pp. 445–74.

——, 'Dictionary of Mathematical Instruments', in *Making Instruments Count: Essays on Historical Scientific Instruments presented to Gerard L'Estrange Turner*, ed. R. G. W. Anderson, J. A. Bennet, W. F. Ryan (Aldershot, Hampshire and Brookfield, VT, 1993), pp. 365–82.

Bulloch, John Malcolm, *History of the University of Aberdeen 1495–1895* (London, 1895).

Bunch, Antonia J., *Hospital and Medical Libraries in Scotland: An historical and sociological study* (Glasgow, 1975).

The Burgesses and Guild Brethren of Glasgow, 1573–1750, compiled by James Anderson, *Scottish Record Society*, vols 56 and 66 (Edinburgh, 1925).

Burnett, J. G., 'An Aberdeen Professor of the Eighteenth Century', *Scottish Historical Review*, 16 (1915), pp. 1–16.

Burns, J. H., 'Twilight of the Enlightenment: James Headrick (1759–1841)', *Scottish Historical Review*, 81 (2002), pp. 186–211.

[Bute], *Lord Bute: Essays in Re-interpretation*, ed. Karl Schweizer (Leicester, 1988).

Butt, John, *John Anderson* (East Linton, 2000).

Cable, John, 'Early Scottish Science: The Vocational Provision', *Annals of Science*, 30 (1973), pp. 179–99.

Cairns, John, 'Sir George Mackenzie, The Faculty of Advocates & the Advocates' Library', in *Oratio Inauguralis in Aperienda Jurisconsultorum Bibliotheca Sir George Mackenzie*, ed. John Cairns and A. M. Cain (Edinburgh, 1989), pp. 19–35.

——, 'Rhetoric, Language and Roman Law: Legal Education and Improvement in Eighteenth-Century Scotland', *Law and History Review*, 9 (1991), pp. 31–58.

——, 'John Spotswood, Professor of Law: A preliminary Sketch', *Miscellany Three, Stair Society*, Edinburgh, 1992, pp. 131–59.

——, 'William Cross, Regius Professor of Civil Law in the University of Glasgow, 1746–1749: A Failure of Enlightened patronage', *History of Universities*, 12 (1993), pp. 159–96.

Cairns, John, 'The influence of Smith's jurisprudence on legal education in Scotland', in *Adam Smith Reviewed*, ed. Peter Jones and Andrew Skinner (Edinburgh, 1992), pp. 168–89.

——, 'The Origins of the Glasgow Law School: the Professors of Civil Law, 1714–61', in *The Life of the Law: Proceedings of the Tenth British Legal History Conference Oxford, 1991*, ed. Peter Birks (London and Rio Grande, 1993), pp. 151–94.

——, 'From "Speculative" to "Practical" Legal Education: The Decline of the Glasgow Law School, 1801–1830', *The Legal History Review*, 62 (1994), pp. 331–56.

——, 'Lawyers, Law Professors, and Localities: The Universities of Aberdeen, 1680–1750', *Northern Ireland Legal Quarterly*, 46 (1995), pp. 304–31.

——, 'Scottish law, Scottish Lawyers and the Status of the Union', in *A Union for Empire: Political Thought and the Union of 1707*, ed. John Robertson, (Cambridge, 1995), pp. 243–68.

——, 'Legal Study in Utrecht in the Late 1740's: The Education of Sir David Dalrymple, Lord Hailes', in *Summa Eloquentia: Essays in honour of Margaret Hewett*, ed. Rena van den Bergh (*Fundamina*, Editio specialis, University of South Africa, n.p., 2002), pp. 30–74.

——, 'Legal Theory', in *The Cambridge Companion to the Scottish Enlightenment*, ed. Alexander Broadie (Cambridge, 2003), pp. 222–42.

——, 'The First Edinburgh Chair of Law: Grotius and the Scottish Enlightenment', *Fundamina, Journal of the Legal History Society of Southern Africa* (2005), and at http//www.law.ed.ac.uk/Tercentenary/documents/(2006).

Calamy, Edmund, *An historical Account of My Own Life . . .*, 2 vols, ed. J. T. Rutt (London, 1829).

The Cambridge Companion to the Scottish Enlightenment, ed. Alexander Broadie (Cambridge, 2003).

Cant, Ronald Gordon, 'The St Andrews University Theses 1579–1747', *Edinburgh Bibliographical Society Transactions*, 2 (1946).

——, *The College of St Salvator: Its Foundation and Development, Including a Selection of Documents* (Edinburgh, 1950).

——, *The University of St Andrews: A Short History*, 4th edn (Dundee, 2002).

[Carlyle], *The Autobiography of Dr Alexander Carlyle of Inveresk 1722–1805*, ed. John Hill Burton (Edinburgh, 1910).

[Carmichael], *Natural Rights and the Threshold of the Scottish Enlightenment: the Writings of Gershom Carmichael*, trans. and ed. James Moore and Michael Silverthorne, (Indianapolis, IN, 2002).

Carr, C. T., 'Early Teachers of French at St Andrews', [St Andrews] *Alumnus Chronicle*, 29 (1948), pp. 14–20.

[Carstares], *State-Papers and Letters Addressed to William Carstares . . . with a Life*, ed. Joseph McCormick (Edinburgh, 1774).

A Catalogue of the Graduates in the Faculties of Arts, Divinity, and Law of the University of Edinburgh . . ., ed. David Laing (Edinburgh, 1858).

Cater, Jeremy, 'The Making of Principal Robertson in 1762: Politics and the University of Edinburgh in the Second Half of the Eighteenth Century', *Scottish Historical Review*, 49 (1970), pp. 60–84.

——, 'General Oughton *versus* Edinburgh's Enlightenment', in *History and Imagination: Essays in Honor of H. R. Trevor-Roper*, ed. Hugh Lloyd-Jones, Valerie Pearl and Blair Worden (New York, 1982), pp. 254–71.

Charters, Statutes, and Acts of the Town Council and the Senatus 1583–1858, ed. Alexander Morgan and Robert Kerr Hannay (Edinburgh, 1937).

Chitnis, Anand, *The Scottish Enlightenment: A Social History* (London, 1976).

——, 'Provost Drummond and the Origins of the Edinburgh Medicine', in *The Origins and Nature of the Scottish Enlightenment*, ed. R. C. Campbell and A. S. Skinner (Edinburgh, 1982), pp. 86–97.

——, *The Scottish Enlightenment & Early Victorian English Society* (London, 1986).

Christie, John R. R., 'The Origins and Development of the Scottish Scientific Community, 1680–1760', *History of Science*, 12 (1974), pp. 122–41.

——, 'The Culture of Science in Eighteenth-Century Scotland', in *The History of Scottish Literature*, Gen. Ed. Cairns Craig, 4 vols (Aberdeen, 1989); vol. 2, ed. Andrew Hook, II:291–305.

Clark, Aylwin, *An Enlightened Scot: Hugh Cleghorn 1752–1837* (Duns, 1992).

Clark, Ian D. L., 'The Leslie Controversy, 1805', *Records of the Scottish Church History Society*, 14 (1963), pp. 179–97.

——, 'From Protest to Reaction: The Moderate Regime in the Church of Scotland, 1752–1805', in *Scotland in the Age of Improvement*, ed. Nicholas T. Phillipson and Rosalind Mitchison (Edinburgh, 1970).

Clason, Patrick, *An Inquiry whether the study of the ancient languages be a necessary branch of modern education* (Glasgow, 1769).

[Cleghorn], *The Cleghorn Papers A Footnote to History being the Diary, 1795–1796 of Hugh Cleghorn of Strathvitie*, ed. William Neil (London, 1927).

Clerk, Sir John, *Memoirs of Sir John Clerk . . . 1676–1755*, ed. John M. Gray, *Scottish History Society*, 1st Series, 13 (Edinburgh, 1892).

Clow, Archibald and Nan, *The Chemical Revolution: A Contribution to Social Technology* (New York, 1970; 1st printing London, 1950).

[Cochrane, Andrew], *The Cochrane Correspondence Regarding the Affairs of Glasgow 1745–46*, ed. James Smith, *Maitland Club* (Glasgow, 1836).

[Cockburn, Henry], *Memorials of His Time*, ed. H. A. Cockburn (Edinburgh and London, 1909).

[Cockburn, Henry], 'Account of the Friday Club', in *Lord Cockburn: A Bicentenary Commemoration*, ed. Alan Bell (Edinburgh, 1979), pp. 181–97.

Colman, George, the Younger, *Random Records*, 2 vols (London, 1830), pp. 84–212.

A Complete Collection of the Papers Relating to the Union of the King's and Marischal Colleges of Aberdeen . . ., compiled by A. Leighton (Aberdeen, 1787).

Comrie, John, *History of Scottish Medicine*, 2 vols (London, 1932).

——, 'John and James Gregory [III]', *University of Edinburgh Journal*, 8 (1936–7), pp. 126–30.

Constitution of the Royal Burghs of Scotland . . . in the Report of the Committee to the House of Commons (Glasgow, 1818).

Courtney, C. P., 'An Eighteenth-century education: Benjamin Constant at Erlangen and Edinburgh (1782–1785)', in *Rousseau & the eighteenth century: essays in memory of R. A. Leigh* (Oxford, 1992), pp. 295–324.

Cowan, John Macqueen, 'The History of the Royal Botanic Garden, Edinburgh: The Prestons', *Notes of the Royal Botanic Garden, Edinburgh*, 92 (1935), pp. 63–131.

Coutts, James, *A History of the University of Glasgow* (Glasgow, 1909).

Craig, John, 'An Account of John Millar's Life and Writings', in *The Origin of the Distinction of Ranks*, 4th edn (Glasgow, 1806).

Craig, W. S., *History of the Royal College of Physicians of Edinburgh* (Oxford, 1976).

Creech, William, *Edinburgh Fugitive Pieces with Letters . . . to which are prefixed An Account of His Life* (Edinburgh, 1815).

[Creech, William] see Bonar.

[Crawford, James], *A Memorial Concerning Doctor Crawford, Edinburgh* (Edinburgh, 1719) [in NLS Pamphlet Series, No. 1.10.158].

Croft Dickinson, William, *Two Students at St Andrews 1711–1716* (Edinburgh, 1952).

Croft Dickinson, William and Gordon Donaldson, eds, *A Source Book of Scottish History*, 3 vols (Edinburgh, 1954).

Cunningham, Andrew, 'Sir Robert Sibbald and Medical Education, Edinburgh, 1706', *Clio Medica*, 13 (1979), pp. 135–61.

——, 'The Medical Professions and the Pattern of Medical Care: the Case of Edinburgh, c. 1670–c. 1700', in *Heilberufe und Kranke im 17. Und 18 Jahrhundert*, ed. Wolfgang Eckhart and Johanna Geyer-Kordesch (Munster, 1982), pp. 9–28.

——, 'Medicine to calm the mind: Boerhaave's medical system, and why it was adopted in Edinburgh', in *The Medical enlightenment of the eighteenth century*, ed. Andrew Cunningham and Roger French (Cambridge, 1990), pp. 40–66.

Cunningham, John, *The Church History of Scotland*, 2 vols (Aberdeen, 1859).

[Cullen], *William Cullen and the Eighteenth Century Medical World*, eds A. Doig, J .P. S. Ferguson, I. A. Milne and R. Passmore (Edinburgh, 1993).

Dalgleish, Robert, 'Parish of Ferry-Port-on Craig', in *Statistical Account* [see below], 10:365–80.

Dalzel, Andrew, *History of Edinburgh University From its Foundation*, ed. David Laing, 2 vols (Edinburgh, 1862).

Davie, George, *The Democratic Intellect: Scotland and Her Universities in the Nineteenth Century*, 2nd edn (Edinburgh, 1964).

Defoe, Daniel, *A Tour Through the Whole Island of Great Britain*, 3 vols, 1724–6; abridged and edited by Pat Rogers (Harmondsworth, 1979; Penguin Books reprint of London, 1971).

[Dempster], *Letters of George Dempster to Sir Adam Fergusson 1756–1813*, ed. James (later Sir James) Fergusson (London, 1934).

Dennison, Patricia E., David Ditchburn and Michael Lynch, eds, *Aberdeen Before 1800*, 2 vols (East Linton, 2002).

Dictionary of American National Biography, ed. John A. Garraty and Mark Carnes (New York and Oxford, 1999).

The Dictionary of Eighteenth-Century British Philosophers, eds John W. Yolton, John Valdimir Price and John Stephens, 2 vols (Bristol, 1999).

Dictionary of Scientific Biography, 18 vols, ed. C. C. Gillispie (New York, 1970–81).

Dictionary of Scottish Church History and Theology, ed. N. M. De S. Cameron et al. (Downers Grove, IL, 1993).

Dingwall, Helen, *Physicians, Surgeons and Apothecaries: Medical Practice in Seventeenth-Century Edinburgh* (*Scottish Historical Review Monograph*, Edinburgh, 1995).

——, *Late Seventeenth-century Edinburgh* (Aldershot and Brookfield, VT, 1994).

A Directory of Landownership in Scotland c. 1770, compiled by Loretta A. Timperley, *Scottish Record Society*, New Series, 5 (Edinburgh, 1976).

Donald, David, 'James Gregory and His time', *Aberdeen University Review*, 36 (1955–6), pp. 372–81.

Donovan, Arthur, *Philosophical Chemistry in the Scottish Enlightenment* (Edinburgh, 1975).

Dorn, 'John Robison', DSB [see above], 9:495–8.

Douglass, William, *Some Historical Remarks on the City of St Andrews* (London, 1728).

Dow, Derek and Michael Moss, 'Medical Curriculum at Glasgow', *History of Universities*, 7 (1988), pp. 227–57.

Doyle,W. P., 'James Crawford, M.D., 1682–1731' (Scotland's Cultural History, Edinburgh, 1981).

[Drummond, George], *Edinburgh's Infirmary: A Symposium*, no. ed. (Edinburgh, 1979).

Lord Provost George Drummond, 1687–1766, ed. Michael Hook et. al. (Scotland's Cultural History, Edinburgh, 1987).

Dunlop, A. Ian, *William Carstares and the Kirk by Law Established* (Edinburgh, 1964).

Durkan, John, 'The Early history of Glasgow University Library: 1475–1710', *Bibliotheck*, 8 (1976–7), pp. 102–26.

Dwyer, John, *Virtuous Discourses: Sensibility and Community in late Eighteenth-Century Scotland* (Edinburgh, 1987).

Eagles, Christina M., 'David Gregory and Newtonian Science', *British Journal for the History of Science*, 10 (1977), pp. 216–25.

The Early Years of the Edinburgh Medical School, ed. R. G. W. Anderson and A. D. C. Simpson, (Royal Scottish Museum, Edinburgh, 1976).

Edinburgh's Infirmary: A Symposium, no. ed. (Scottish Society of the History of Medicine, Edinburgh, 1979).

An Eighteenth Century Lectureship in Chemistry: Essays and Bicentenary Addresses relating to the Chemistry Department of Glasgow University, ed. Andrew Kent (Glasgow, 1950) [contains essays on William Cullen, Joseph Black, John Robison, Robert Cleghorn, William Irvine and T. C. Hope].

Eighteenth Century Medics, compiled by Peter and Ruth Wallis, 2nd rev. edn (Newcastle on Tyne, 1988).

Emerson, Roger L., 'The Scottish Universities in the 18th century', *Studies on Voltaire and the eighteenth century*, 162 (1977), pp. 453–74.

——, 'The Philosophical Society of Edinburgh 1737–1747', *British Journal for the History of Science*, 12 (1979), pp. 154–91.

——, 'The Philosophical Society of Edinburgh 1748–1768', *The British Journal for the History of Science*, 14 (1981), pp. 134–76.

——, 'The Edinburgh Society for the Importation of Foreign Seeds and Plants, 1764–1773', *Eighteenth-Century Life* (Special Issue), 7, New Series (1982), pp. 73–95.

——, 'The Philosophical Society of Edinburgh 1768–1783', *British Journal of the History of Science*, 18 (1985), pp. 255–303.

——, 'Natural philosophy and the problem of the Scottish Enlightenment', *Studies on Voltaire and the eighteenth century*, 242 (1986), pp. 243–91.

——, 'Aberdeen Professors 1690–1800: Two Structures, Two Professoriates, Two Careers', in *Aberdeen and the Enlightenment* [see above], pp. 155–67.

——, 'Lord Bute and the Scottish Universities, 1760–1792', in *Lord Bute Essays in Re-interpretation*, ed. Karl W. Schweizer (Leicester, 1988), pp. 147–79.

——, 'The Scottish Enlightenment and the End of the Philosophical Society of Edinburgh', *British Journal of the History of Science*, 21 (1988), pp. 33–66.

——, 'Sir Robert Sibblad, Kt., the Royal Society of Scotland and the Origins of the Scottish Enlightenment', *Annals of Science*, 45 (1988), pp. 41–72.

——, *Professors, Patronage and Politics: The Aberdeen Universities in the Eighteenth Century* (Aberdeen, 1991).

——, 'Medical Men, Politicians and the Medical Schools at Glasgow and Edinburgh 1685–1803', in *William Cullen and the Eighteenth Century Medical World*, ed. Andrew Doig, Joan P. S. Ferguson, Iain A. Milne and Reginald Passmore (Edinburgh, 1993), pp. 186–215.

——, 'The "affair" at Edinburgh and the "project" at Glasgow: the politics of Hume's attempts to become a professor', in *Hume and Hume's Connexions*, eds M. A. Stewart and John P. Wright, Edinburgh, 1994, pp. 1–22.

——, 'Politics and the Glasgow Professors, 1690–1800', in *Glasgow and the Enlightenment*, ed. Andrew Hook and Richard B. Sher (Edinburgh, 1995), pp. 21–39.

——, 'Did the Scottish Enlightenment Emerge in an English Cultural Province?', *Lumen*, 14 (1995), pp. 1–24.

——, 'Scottish Cultural Change 1660–1710 and the Union of 1707', in *A Union for Empire*, ed. John Robertson (Cambridge, 1995), pp. 121–44.

——, '*Catalogus Librorum A. C. D. A.*: The Library of the 3rd Duke of Argyll', in *The Culture of the Book in the Scottish Enlightenment*, ed. Philip Oldfield (Thomas Fisher Rare Book Library, University of Toronto, 2000), pp. 12–39.

——, 'The Scientific Interests of Archibald Campbell, 3rd Duke of Argyll (1682–1761)', *Annals of Science*, 59 (2002), pp. 21–56.

——, 'The Historical Context of the Scottish Enlightenment', in *The Cambridge Companion to the Scottish Enlightenment*, ed. Alexander Broadie (Cambridge, 2002), pp. 9–30.

——, 'Archibald Campbell, Terzo Duca di Argyll (1682–1761): Il Patronage e la Creazione dell'Illuminismo Scozze' [translated by Letizia Bonetti], in *Filosofia, Scienza e Politica nel Settecento Britannico*, ed. Luigi Turco (Padova, 2003), pp. 127–61.

——, 'The Founding of the Edinburgh Medical School: The Real Story', *Journal of the History of Medicine and Allied Sciences*, 59 (2004), pp. 183–218.

Emerson, R. L. and P. B. Wood, 'Science and Enlightenment in Glasgow, 1690–1802', in *Science and Medicine in the Scottish Enlightenment*, ed. C. W. J. Withers and P. B. Wood (East Linton, 2002), pp. 79–142.

Encyclopedia of the Enlightenment, ed. Michel Delon (Chicago and London, 2001), translated by Gwen Wells from *Dictionnaire européen des lumières* (Paris, 1997).

Evidence . . . taken and received by the Commissioners . . . for visiting the Universities of Scotland (London, 1837).

Extracts from the Council Register of the Burgh of Aberdeen 1643–1747, ed. William Chambers, *Burgh Record Society*, 8 (1872).

Extracts from the Records of the Burgh of Edinburgh 1701–1718, ed. Helen Armet (Edinburgh, 1967).

Extracts of the Records of the Burgh of Glasgow, A.D. 1691–1808, 9 vols, ed. R. Renwick et al. (Glasgow, 1908–14).

Eyles, Joan M., 'Robert Jameson', *Dictionary of Scientific Biography* [see above], 7:69–71.

The Faculty of Advocates of Scotland 1532–1943, compiled by Sir Francis Grant (Scottish Record Society, Edinburgh, 1944). [This omits some adevocates.]

Fasti Aberdonensis: Selections from the Records of the University and King's College of Aberdeen 1494–1854, ed. Cosmo Innes (*Spalding Club*, Aberdeen, 1854).

Records of Marischal College and University: Fasti Academiae Mariscallanae Aberdonensis. Selections from the records of the Marischal College and University of Aberdeen, MDXCIII-MDCCCLX, 2 vols, compiled by Peter John Anderson, (*New Spalding Club*, Aberdeen, vol. 1, 1889; vol. 2, 1893).

Fasti Ecclesaie Scoticanae, Hew Scott et al., 8 vols, revised edn (Edinburgh, 1915–30).

Fawcett, Arthur, *The Cambuslang Revival* (1st edn 1971; Edinburgh and Carlisle, PA, 1996).

[Ferguson, Adam], *The Correspondence of Adam Ferguson*, 2 vols, ed. Vincenzo Merolle et al., (London, 1995).

[Fergusson], *The Works of Robert Fergusson . . . with a Life*, ed ? (Edinburgh, 1970; reprint of the London edn of 1807 edited by ? (the Edinburgh edition of the same year was edited by James Bannington).

Findlay, Alexander, 'The Teaching of chemistry in the Universities of Aberdeen', *Aberdeen University Studies*, 112 (1935), pp. 4–15.

Finlayson, Charles P., 'Edinburgh University and the Darien Scheme', *Scottish Historical Review*, 34 (1955), pp. 97–102.

Fleming, D. Hay, *Hand-Book to St Andrews* (St Andrews, 1894).

Fleming, John, *Robert Adam and His Circle* (Cambridge, MA, 1962).

Fletcher, Harold R. and William H. Brown, *The Royal Botanic Garden Edinburgh 1670–1970* (Edinburgh, 1970).

[Forbes of Culloden], *Culloden Papers*, ed. R. H. Duff (London, 1815).

——, *More Culloden Papers*, ed. Duncan Warrand, 5 vols (Inverness, 1923–30).

Forbes, Eric G., 'Philosophy and Science Teaching in the Seventeenth Century', in *Four Centuries* [see below], pp. 28–37.

Forbes, Margaret, *Beattie and his Friends* (London, 1904; reprinted Bristol, 1990).

Forbes, Sir William, *An Account of the Life and Writings of James Beattie, LL.D.* (London, 1824).

Fortuna Domus, A Series of lectures . . . in commemoration of the Fifth Centenary . . . [of Glasgow University], ed. J. B. Neilson (Glasgow, 1952).

Four Centuries: Edinburgh University Life 1583–1983, ed. Gordon Donaldson (Edinburgh, 1983).

Freeman, F. W., *Robert Fergusson and the Scots Humanist Compromise* (Edinburgh, 1984).

French, R. K., *Robert Whytt, The Soul, and Medicine* (London, 1969).

Fry, Michael, *The Dundas Despotism* (Edinburgh, 1992).

[Garden, James], 'Professor James Garden's letters to John Aubrey 1692–1695', ed. Cosmo Gordon, *Miscellany of the Third Spalding Club*, 3 (1960), pp. 1–56.

[General Assembly], *The Principal Acts of the General Assembly of the Church of Scotland*, extracted by the clerks, 2 vols (Edinburgh, 1721–66). [The fascicles were printed yearly.]

——, *Index to the Acts and proceedings of the General Assembly of the Church of Scotland from the Revolution to the Present Time*, compiled by John Wilson (Edinburgh and London, 1863).

Gerard, Alexander, 'Plan of Education in the Marischal College and University of Aberdeen, with the reasons for it. Drawn up by the Order of the Faculty' (Aberdeen, 1755). [An abbreviated version appeared in the *Scots Magazine*, 14 (December 1752)].

Geyer-Kordesch, Johanna and Fiona Macdonald, *Physicians and Surgeons: The History of the Royal College of Physicians and Surgeons of Glasgow: 1599–1858* (Glasgow, 1999).

Gibson, A. J. S. and T. C. Smout, *Prices, food and wages in Scotland 1550–1780* (Cambridge, 1995).

Gibson-Wood, Carol, 'George Turnbull and Art History at Scottish Universities in the Eighteenth Century', *Revue d'art canadienne / Canadian Art Review*, 28 (2001–3), pp. 7–18.

Gifford, John, *William Adam 1689–1748* (Edinburgh, 1989).

Gillispie, Charles Coulston, *Science and Polity in France at the End of the Old Regime* (Princeton, 1980).

Glasgow, 3 vols, ed. Thomas M. Devine and Gordon Jackson; vol. 1, *Glasgow: Beginnings to 1830* (Manchester and New York, 1995).

The Glasgow Enlightenment, ed. Richard B. Sher and Andrew Hook (East Linton, 1995).

Gordon, Pryse Lockhart, *Personal Memoirs or Reminiscences of Men and Manners . . .* (London, 1830).

[Gordon, Thomas], 'University and King's College of Aberdeen', in *The Statistical Account of Scotland 1791–1799*, see below. 1:248–301.

Goslings, W. R. O., 'Leiden and Edinburgh: The Seeds, the Soil and the Climate', in *The Early Years of the Edinburgh Medical School*, ed. R. G. W. Anderson and A. D. C. Simpson (Royal Scottish Museum, Edinburgh, 1976), pp. 1–18.

Grabiner, Judith, *Life of Colin Maclaurin*, forthcoming.

Graeme, William, *An Essay on the Method of Acquiring Knowledge in Physick* (London, 1729).

——, 'A Proposal to teach the Theory and Practice of Physick, in a Course of lectures' (London, 1728).

Grant, Sir Alexander, *The Story of the University*, 2 vols (London, 1884).

Gray, James, *History of the Royal Medical Society* (Edinburgh, 1952).

Gray, W. Forbes, 'An Eighteenth-Century Riding School,' *Book of the Old Edinburgh Club*, 20 (1935), pp. 111–59.

Green, J. Reynolds, *A History of Botany in the United Kingdom from the earliest times to the end of the 19th century* (London and Toronto, 1914).

[Gregory], *David Gregory, Isaac Newton and Their Circle: Extracts from David Gregory's Memoranda 1677–1708*, ed. W. G. Hiscock (Oxford, 1937).

[Gregory], *James Gregory Tercentenary*, ed. G. H. Bushnell (St Andrews, 1939).

[Gregory], *James Gregory: Tercentenary Memorial Volume containing . . . His Correspondence . . .*, ed. Herbert Westren Turnbull (London, 1939).

Grierson, James, *Delineation of St Andrews*, 2nd edn (Cupar, 1833; 1st edn 1822).

Guerrini, Anita, *Obesity and Depression in the Enlightenment: The Life and Times of George Cheyne* (Norman, OK, 2000).

——, 'George Preston', ODNB [see below], 45:254f.

Guthrie, Douglas, *Extramural Medical Education in Edinburgh and the School of Medicine* (Edinburgh, 1965).

Haakonssen, Lisbeth, *Medicine and Morals in the Enlightenment: John Gregory, Thomas Percival and Benjamin Rush* (Amsterdam, 1997).

[Halyburton], *Memoirs of the Life of the Rev. Thomas Halyburton . . . 1674–1712 . . . with an Appendix*, ed. Janet Watson (Edinburgh and London, n.d.; 1st edn 1715).

Hamilton, David, *The Healers: A History of Medicine in Scotland* (Edinburgh, 1981).

Hannay, R. K., 'The Visitation of St Andrews university in 1690', *Scottish Historical Review*, 13 (1915), pp. 1–15.

Hans, Nicholas, *New Trends in Education in the Eighteenth Century* (London, 1951).

Hay, Denys, 'The Historiographers Royal in England and Scotland', *Scottish Historical Review*, 30 (1951), pp. 15–29.

Henderson, G. D., *Mystics of the North-East: Letters of James Keith, M.D. . . . (3rd Spalding Club*, Aberdeen, 1934).

——, 'Professor John Lumsden, 1694–1770', *Aberdeen University Review*, 27 (1939–40), pp. 106–15.

——, 'Professor James Garden', *Aberdeen University Review*, 28 (1940–1), pp. 202–9.

——, 'Professor David Anderson (1711–1737)', *Aberdeen University Review*, 35 (1948), pp. 27–31.

Herkless, John, and Robert K. Hannay, *The College of St Leonard* (Edinburgh and London, 1905).

The History of the University of Oxford, 8 vols, Gen. Ed. T. H. Ashton; vol. 5, ed. L. S. Sutherland and L. G. Mitchell (Oxford, 1986).

Historical Manuscript Commission Reports
  Fourth Report . . . Part I . . . Manuscripts of the Duke of Argyll, K.T., ed. William Fraser (London, 1874).
  Report of the Laing MSS Preserved in the University of Edinburgh, 2 vols, ed. Henry Paton (London, 1914 and 1925).
  Historical Manuscripts of the Earl of Mar and Kellie preserved at Alloa House Clackmannanshire, vol. 1, ed. H. Paton (London, 1904).
  Manuscripts of the Duke of Roxburghe . . ., no ed. (London, 1894).
The History of Scottish Literature, 4 vols, Gen. Ed. Cairns Craig, 2nd edn 1989; vol. II, ed. Hook (Aberdeen, 1989), pp. 11–32.
The History of Parliament
  The House of Commons 1690–1715, 5 vols, eds Eveline Cruickshanks, Stuart Handley and D. W. Hayton (Cambridge, 2002).
  The House of Commons 1715–1754, 2 vols, ed. Romney Sedgwick (New York, 1970).
  The House of Commons 1754–1790, 3 vols, ed. Sir Lewis Namier and John Brooke (London, 1964).
History of the Society of Advocates in Aberdeen, ed. John Alexander Henderson (*New Spalding Club*, Aberdeen, 1912).
Horn, D. B., *A Short History of the University of Edinburgh 1556–1889* (Edinburgh, 1967).
Howell, Wilbur S., *Eighteenth-Century British Logic and Rhetoric* (Princeton, 1971).
Houston, R. A., *Social Change in the Age of the Enlightenment: Edinburgh 1660–1760* (Oxford, 1994).
Hume and Hume's Connexions, ed. M. A. Stewart and John P. Wright, Edinburgh, 1994.
Letters of David Hume, 2 vols, ed. J. Y. T. Greig (Oxford, 1969; 1st edn, 1932).
New Hume Letters, ed. E. C. Mossner and Raymond Klibansky (Montreal, 1954).
Humphries, Walter Robson, 'William Ogilvie and the Projected Union of the Colleges 1786–1787', *Aberdeen University Studies*, 117 (1940).
Hunter, Michael, ' "Aikenhead the Atheist": The Context and Consequences of Articulate Irreligion in the Late Seventeenth Century', in *Atheism from the Reformation* [see above], pp. 221–54.
Ignatieff, Michael, 'John Millar and Individualism', in *Wealth And Virtue* [see below], pp. 317–43.
Jackson, Clare, *Restoration Scotland, 1660–1690: Royalist Politics, Religion and Ideas* (Woodbridge, 2003).
——, 'Revolution Principles, Ius Naturae and Ius Gentium in Early Enlightenment Scotland: The Contribution of Sr Francis Grant, Lord Cullen (c. 1660–1726)', in *Early Modern Natural Law Theories*, ed. T. J. Hochstrasser and P. Schroder (Dordrecht, 2003).

Jardine, Nicholas, J. A. Secord and E. C. Spary, eds, *Cultures of Science* (Cambridge, 1996).

Johnston, Dorothy B., 'The Papers of Professor Thomas Gordon Relating to the First Aberdeen Philosophical Society, AUL, MS 3107/1–3', *Northern Scotland*, 5 (1983), pp. 179–89.

Johnstoun, William, 'William Rouet', in *Enlightenment in France and Scotland* (a Compact Disk produced by Officina Educational Publications, Livingstoun, Scotland, 2003).

Jones, Peter, 'The Scottish professoriate and the polite academy, 1720–46', in *Wealth and Virtue* [see below], pp. 89–117.

Kaufman, Matthew H., *Medical Teaching during the 18th and 19th centuries* (Edinburgh, 2003).

Kay, John, *A Series of Original Portraits and Caricature Etchings by the Late John Kay with Biographical Sketches and Illustrative Anecdotes* [by Hugh Paton], 2 vols (Edinburgh, 1877).

Kelsall, Helen and Keith, *Scottish Lifestyle 300 Years Ago*, 2nd edn (Aberdeen, 1993).

Lachman, David, *The Marrow Controversy 1718–1723: An Historical and Theological Analysis* (Edinburgh, 1988).

Laird, Mark, *The Flowering of the Landscape Garden: English Pleasure Grounds 1720–1800* (Philadelphia, 1999).

Landsman, Ned, 'Presbyterians and Provincial Society: The Evangelical Enlightenment in the West of Scotland, 1740–1775', in *Sociability and Society in Eighteenth-Century Scotland*, ed. John Dwyer and Richard B. Sher, Special Issue of *Eighteenth Century Life*, 15 (1991) pp. 194–209.

Lang, Andrew, *St Andrews* (London, 1893).

Lawrence, Christopher, 'Early Edinburgh Medicine: Theory and Practice', in *The Early Years of the Edinburgh Medical School* [see above], pp. 81–94.

——, 'The Edinburgh Medical School and the End of the "Old Thing" 1790–1830', *History of Universities*, 7 (1988), pp. 259–86.

Lawrence, Paul, 'James Gregory', ODNB, 23:673–5.

Lee, John, 'Copies of papers relative to a projected translation of the University of St Andrews to the city of Perth, in the years 1697 and 1698', *Transactions of the Literary and Antiquarian Society of Perth*, 1 (1827), pp. 25–9.

Lenman, Bruce, *The Jacobite Risings in Britain 1689–1746* (London, 1980).

Lenman, Bruce P. and J. B. Kenworthy, 'Dr David Skene, Linnaeus, and the Applied Geology of the Scottish Enlightenment', *Aberdeen University Review*, 47 (1977), pp. 32–44, 231–7.

Leven and Melville Papers: Letters and State Papers Addressed to George Earl of Melville, Secretary of State for Scotland 1689–1691, ed. W. L. Mellville (*Bannatyne Club*, Edinburgh, 1843).

Levy-Mortera, Emanuelle, The Life and Intellectual History of Dugald Stewart, forthcoming.

Lindsay, Ian and Mary Cosh, *Inveraray and the Dukes of Argyll* (Edinburgh, 1973).

[Lockhart], *Letters of George Lockhart of Carnwath 1698–1732*, ed. Daniel Szechi, *Scottish History Society*, Fifth Series, 2, 1989.

——, *'Scotland's Ruine': Lockhart of Carnwath's Memoirs of the Union*, ed. Daniel Szechi (Aberdeen, 1995).

Loetscher, Lefferts, *Facing the Enlightenment and Pietism: Archibald Alexander and the Founding of the Princeton Theological Seminary* (Westport, CT, 1983).

Logan, George, *Logan's Sermons*, no ed. (n.p., n.d. [?1783]).

The Lord Provosts of Edinburgh 1296–1932, no ed. (Edinburgh, 1932).

Lorimer, George, *The Days of Neil M'Vicar: Minister of the West Kirk, Edinburgh, 1707–1747* (Edinburgh and London, 1926).

Lyon, C. J., *History of St Andrews*, 2 vols (Edinburgh, 1843).

McCallum, Donald, 'George Hill', ODNB, 27:132–4.

McCosh, James, *The Scottish Philosophy, Biographical, Expository, Critical From Hutcheson to Hamilton* (New York, 1980; reprint of New York, 1875).

Macdonald, Fiona, 'The Infirmary of the Glasgow Town's Hospital, 1733–1800: A Case for Voluntarism', *Bulletin of the History of Medicine*, 73 (1999), pp. 64–105.

——, 'Reading Cleghorn the Clinician: The Clinical Case Records of Robert Cleghorn, 1785–1818', in *Science and Medicine* [see below], pp. 255–79.

MacGregor, Arthur, *Sir Hans Sloane: Collector, Scientist, Antiquary* (London, 1994).

McIntosh, John R., *Church and Theology in Enlightenment Scotland: The Popular Party, 1740–1800* (East Linton, 1998).

Mackenzie, R. C., 'George Martine, M.D., F.R.S. (1700–1741): An Early Thermal Analyst', *Journal of Thermal Analysis*, 35 (1989), pp. 1823–36.

MacKillop, Andrew, *'More Fruitful than the Soil': Army, Empire and the Scottish Highlands 1715–1815* (East Linton, 2000).

Mackie, J. D., *The University of Glasgow 1451–1951* (Glasgow, 1954).

McLaren, Colin, 'Privilege, Patronage and the Professions: Aberdeen and its Universities, 1760–1860', in *Scottish Universities: Distinctiveness and Diversity*, eds Jennifer Carter and Donald J. Withrington (Edinburgh, 1992).

——, *Aberdeen Students 1600–1800* (Aberdeen, 2005).

Maclaurin, Colin, *An Account of Sir Isaac Newton's Philosophical Discoveries*, London, 1748 [with a life by Patrick Murdoch], ed. L. L. Laudan, for *The Sources of Science* (New York and London, 1968).

The Collected Letters of Colin Maclaurin, ed. Stella Mills (Nantwich, 1982). [There are many errors in the transcriptions and notes of this book.]

MacLeod, John, *Scottish Theology* (Edinburgh, 1974; 1st edn 1943).

Manuel, F. E., *The Broken Staff: Judaism Through Christian Eyes* (Cambridge, MA, 1992).

Marshall, Rosalind K., *The Days of Duchess Anne: Life in the Household of the Duchess of Hamilton 1656–1716* (New York, 1973).

Mathematical Practitioners of Hanoverian England, ed. E. G. R. Taylor (London, 1966).

'Matriculates in the Faculty of Medicine Prior to 1858', *University of Edinburgh Journal* (1936).

The Matriculation Albums of the University of Glasgow from 1728–1858, compiled by W. Innes Addison (Glasgow, 1913). [Earlier matriculants are listed in *Munimenta*, see below].

The Matriculation Rolls of the University of St Andrews, ed. James Maitland Anderson (Edinburgh, 1905).

May, Henry, *The Enlightenment in America* (Oxford, 1976).

Memorials of the Faculty of Physicians and Surgeons of Glasgow 1555–1850, compiled by Alexander Duncan (Glasgow, 1896).

Mendyk, Stan, 'Scottish Regional Natural Historians and the *Britannia* Project', *Scottish Geographical Magazine*, 101 (1985), pp. 165–73.

Michael, Emily, 'Francis Hutcheson's *Logicae compendium* and the Glasgow school of logic', in *Logic and the Workings of the Mind*, ed. P. Easton (Atascadero, CA, 1997), pp. 83–96.

Miège, Guy, *The Present State of Great Britain*, London. The nearly annual editions of this work have descriptions of the colleges which are interesting but often unreliable and out of date.

Mijers, Esther, *'News from the Republic of Letters': Charles Mackie, Scotland's First Professor of History* [forthcoming, Leiden, 2008].

Millar, Alexander, *Fife: Pictorial and Historical*, 2 vols (Edinburgh and Glasgow, 1895).

Millar, John, *The letters of Crito e Letters of Sidney*, ed. Vincenzo Merolle (Rome, 1984).

The Minute Book of the Faculty of Advocates, 1661–1712 and 1712–1750, 2 vols, ed. John Macpherson Pinkerton, *Stair Society*, 31 and 32 (Edinburgh, 1976 and 1980).

The Minutes of the Aberdeen Philosophical Society 1758–1773, ed. H. Lewis Ulman (Aberdeen, 1990).

Mitchison, Rosalind, *Agricultural Sir John: the life of Sir John Sinclair of Ulbster 1754–1835* (London, 1962).

Moderators of the Church of Scotland from 1690–1740, compiled by John Warrick (Edinburgh, 1913).

Monro, Alexander, *Presbyterian Inquisition, As it was lately Practised against the professors of the Colledge of Edinburgh August and September 1690* . . . (London, 1691).

[Monro, Alexander, anatomist],' Alexander Monro, *primus*,' ed. H. D. Erlam, *University of Edinburgh Journal*, 17 (1953–4), pp. 77–105.

——, *The Works of Alexander Monro, M.D.*, ed. Donald Monro (Edinburgh, 1781) [with a life by his son Donald Monro, MD].

Moore, James and Michael Silverthorne, 'Hutcheson's LL.D', *Eighteenth-Century Scotland*, 20 (2006), pp. 10–12.

Morgan, Alexander, *Scottish University Studies* (Oxford, 1933).

Morrell, Jack, 'The University of Edinburgh in the Late Eighteenth Century: Its Scientific Eminence and Academic Structure', *Isis*, 62 (1971), pp. 158–71.

——, 'The Edinburgh Town Council And Its University, 1717–1766', in *The Early Years of the Edinburgh Medical School* [see above], pp. 46–57.

——, 'Medicine and Science in the Eighteenth Century', in *Four Centuries of Edinburgh University Life* [see above], pp. 38–52.

——, 'John Leslie,' ODNB, 33:462–4.

——, 'John Playfair,' ODNB. 44:555f.

Morton, A. G., 'John Hope 1725–1786: Scottish Botanist' (pamphlet published by the Edinburgh Botanic Garden, Edinburgh, 1986).

Mossner, Ernest C., *The Life of David Hume* (Edinburgh and London, 1954; 1st edn corrected 1969).

Munimenta Alme Universatitis Glasguensis: Records of the University of Glasgow from its Foundation till 1727, 4 vols, ed. Cosmo Innes (Glasgow, 1854).

Munn, Charles W., *The Scottish Provincial Banking Companies, 1747–1864* (Edinburgh, 1981).

Muir, James, *John Anderson: Pioneer of Technical Education and the College He Founded* (Glasgow, 1950).

Murdoch, Alexander, *'The People Above': Politics and Administration in Mid-Eighteenth Century Scotland* (Edinburgh, 1980).

[Mure] *Selections from the Family Papers Preserved at Caldwell*, 3 vols, no editor listed (*Maitland Club*, 73; 2 parts in 3 vols, Glasgow, 1854; reprinted as *Selections* etc., 2 parts in 3 vols, Paisley, 1883–5).

Murray, David, *Memories of the Old College of Glasgow* (Glasgow, 1927).

Mackie, J. D., *The University of Glasgow 1451–1951* (Glasgow, 1954).

Musson, A. E. and Eric Robinson, *Science and Technology in the Industrial Revolution* (Manchester, 1969).

Nève, Paul, 'Disputation of Scots Students Attending Universities in the Northern Netherlands', *Legal History in the Making*, ed. W. M. Gordon and T. D. Fergus (London and Rio Grande, 1991).

New Perspectives on the Politics and Culture of Early Modern Scotland, eds John, Dwyer, Roger A. Mason and Alexander Murdoch (Edinburgh, n.d. [1982]).

[Newton], *The Correspondence of Sir Isaac Newton*, eds H. W. Turnbull, J. F. Scott, A. R. Hall and L. Tilling, 7 vols (Cambridge, 1959–77).

Nobbs, Douglas, 'The British Ideas of William Cleghorn, Hume's academic rival', *Journal of the History of Ideas*, 26 (1965), pp. 575–86.

North, J. D., 'Thomas Melvill', DSB [see above], 9:266–7.

Notices and Documents Illustrative of the Literary History of Glasgow during the greater part of the last century, ed. William J. Duncan (*Maitland Club*, 14, Glasgow, 1831).

Officers and Graduates of University and King's College Aberdeen, ed. Peter John Anderson, (*New Spalding Club*, Aberdeen, 1893).

O'Leary, Patrick, *Sir James Mackintosh: the Whig Cicero* (Aberdeen, 1989).

Olsen, Richard, *Scottish Philosophy and British Physics 1750–1880* (Princeton, 1975).

——, 'John Leslie', DSB [see above], 8:261f.

Orem, William, *History of Aberdeen . . .* (Aberdeen, 1728).

The Origins and Nature of the Scottish Enlightenment, ed. R. H. Campbell and Andrew S. Skinner (Edinburgh, 1982), pp. 65–85.

Ouston, Hugh, 'Cultural Life from the Restoration to the Union', in *The History of Scottish Literature* [see above], 2:11–30.

Outram, Dorinda, *The Enlightenment* (Cambridge, 1995).

The Oxford Dictionary of National Biography, 60 vols, ed. H. C. G. Matthew and Brian Harrison (Oxford, 2004) [there is an online, updated version].

Oxford Encyclopedia of the Enlightenment, 4 vols, ed. Alan Charles Kors (New York, 2002).

Peel Ritchie, Robert, *The Early Days of the Royall Colledge of Phisitians, Edinburgh* (Edinburgh, 1899).

Phillipson, Nicholas, 'Culture and Society in the 18th Century Province: The Case of Edinburgh and the Scottish Enlightenment', in *The University in Society*, 2 vols, ed. Lawrence Stone (Princeton, 1974), 2: 407–48.

——, 'Scottish Enlightenment', *Encyclopedia of the Enlightenment* [see above].

[Pitcairne], *'The best of our owne': Letters of Archibald Pitcairne 1652–1713*, ed. W. T. Johnstoun (Edinburgh, 1979).

Plumb, J. H., *Sir Robert Walpole: The King's Minister*, 2 vols (London, 1960).

——, *The Growth of Political Stability in England 1675–1725* (London, 1967).

Pocock, J. A. C., *Barbarism and Religion: narratives of civil Government* (Cambridge, 1999).

Ponting, Betty, 'Mathematics, Characters and Events, 1717–1860', *Aberdeen University Review*, No. 162 (1979), pp. 162–76.

Porter, Roy, *The Enlightenment* (Atlantic Highlands, NJ, 1990).

——, *The Creation of the Modern World: The Untold Story of the British Enlightenment* (London and New York, 2000). [This appeared in Britain under the title *Enlightenment: Britain and the Creation of the Modern World*, 2000.]

[Preston, Charles and George], [See above under John Macqueen Cowan].

Preston, James, *History of the World* (Edinburgh, 1701).

Price, J. V., 'Archibald Campbell', in *Dictionary of Eighteenth-Century British Philosophers* [see above], 1:171–4.

Ramsay, John of Ochtertyre, *Scotland and Scotsmen in the Eighteenth Century*, 2 vols, ed. Alexander Allardyce (Edinburgh and London, 1888).

——, *Letters of John Ramsay of Ochtertyre 1799-1812*, ed. Barbara L. H. Horn, Edinburgh, *Scottish Historical Society*, 4th Series 3 (1966).

Rait, R. S., *The Universities of Aberdeen: A History* (Aberdeen, 1895).

Raphael, D. D., D. R. Raynor and I. S. Ross, ' "This very awkward affair": an entanglement of Scottish professors with English lords', *Studies on Voltaire and the Eighteenth Century*, 278 (1990), pp. 419–63.

Records of Old Aberdeen MCLVII–MDCCCXCI, ed. Alexander MacDonald Munro (Aberdeen, 1899).

Records of the Aberdeen Universities Commission 1716–17, compiled by Peter J. Anderson (Aberdeen, 1900). [This is a rare publication which was limited to fifty copies.]

Register of the Episcopal Congregation in Leith 1733–1777, ed. Angus MacIntyre, *Scottish Record Society*, 81 (1949).

Reid, H. M. B., *The Divinity Professors in the University of Glasgow 1640–1903* (Glasgow, 1923).

Reid, John S., 'Patrick Copland 1748–1822: Aspects of His Life and Times at Marischal College', *Aberdeen University Review*, 172 (1984), pp. 359–79.

[Thomas Reid], 'Statistical Account of the Universities of Scotland: Number I. University of Glasgow', in *The Statistical Account of Scotland 1791–1799* [see below], 1:198–247 [this also appears in Reid's *Philosophical Works*, see below; 2:721–39].

——, *Philosophical Works*, 2 vols, ed. Sir William Hamilton and H. L. Mansell (Hildesheim, 1967 [reprint of the Edinburgh edition of 1895, 1st edn 1846–63]).

——, 'The Correspondence of Thomas Reid', in *The Edinburgh Edition of Thomas Reid*, Gen. Ed. Knud Haakonssen; vol. 4., ed. Paul B. Wood (Edinburgh, 2002).

[Rendall, Jane], *The Origins of the Scottish Enlightenment 1707–1776*, ed. Jane Rendall (New York, 1978).

Richards, Eric, 'Agriculture', in *Oxford Encyclopedia of the Enlightenment* [see above], 1:32–8.

[William Richardson], 'An Account of some of the Particulars of the life and character of the Rev. Mr. Archibald Arthur, late Professor of Moral Philosophy in the University of Glasgow', in *Discourses on Theological and Literary subjects, by the late Archibald Arthur*, ed. William Richardson (Glasgow, 1803).

Riley, P. W. J., *The English Ministers and Scotland* (London, 1964).

——, *King William and the Scottish Politicians* (Edinburgh, 1979).

——, *The Union of England and Scotland* (Manchester, 1978).

Risse, Guenther, *Hospital life in Enlightenment Scotland: Care and Teaching at the Royal Infirmary of Edinburgh* (Cambridge, 1986).

——, *New Medical Challenges during the Scottish Enlightenment* (Amsterdam and New York, 2005).

Robertson, Eric, *Old St Andrews* (London, 1923).

Robertson, Marjorie, 'Manuscript Sources in the library on the life of the University', in *Four Centuries: Edinburgh University Life* [see above], pp. 131–41.

[Robertson, of Wolverhampton], 'Original Memoirs of Dr. Robertson of Wolverhampton', *Gentlemen's Magazine*, September 1783, pp. 744–50.

[Robertson, Principal William] *Correspondence*, ed. Jeffrey Smitten, forthcoming.

William Robertson and the Expansion of Empire, ed. Stewart J. Brown (Cambridge, 1997).

Robertson, William [Keeper of the Records of Scotland], *Proceedings Relating to the Peerage* (Edinburgh, 1790).

Robison, John, *A System of Mechanical Philosophy*, ed. P. B. Wood (Bristol, 2004). [This has a biographical introduction.]

Roche, Daniel, *La France des Lumières* (1993), translated by Arthur Goldhammer as *France in the Enlightenment* (Cambridge, MA, 1998).

Roll of the Alumni: University and King's College 1596–1860 (Aberdeen, 1900).

Roll of Commissioned Officers in the Medical Service of the British Army, 2 vols, compiled by A. Peterkin and William Johnstoun (London, 1968).

The Roll of the College of Physicians of London, 4 vols, compiled by William Munk (London, 1878).

Roll of Graduates at the University of Glasgow . . . 1727 . . . 1897 compiled by W. Innes Addison (Glasgow, 1898).

Rosner, Lisa, 'Andrew Duncan, M.D., F.R.S.E.' (Edinburgh, a Scotland's Cultural Heritage pamphlet, 1981).

——, *Medical Education in the Age of Improvement* (Edinburgh, 1991).

——, 'Andrew Duncan' [revisor of the DNB article by G. T. Bettany], ODNB, 17:224–6.

Ross, Ian, *Lord Kames and the Scotland of His Day* (Oxford, 1972).

——, *The Life of Adam Smith* (Oxford, 1995).

[Royal Infirmary], *Edinburgh's Infirmary: A Symposium . . .*, no editor listed (Scottish Society for the History of Medicine, Edinburgh, 1979).

The Royal Society of Edinburgh [from1783 to 1882], 5 fascicles, ed. Sheila Devlin-Thorpe and others (Scotland's Cultural Heritage, Edinburgh, 1980–4. [Each fascicle has about 100 short biographies which should be used with caution since they contain many errors.]

John Russell, 'Cosmological Teaching in the Seventeenth-Century Scottish Universities', *Journal of the History of Astronomy*, 5 (1974), Part I, pp. 122–32; Part II, pp. 145–54.

Science and Medicine in the Scottish Enlightenment, eds C .W. J. Withers and P. B. Wood (East Linton, 2002).

Scotland in the Age of Improvement, ed. N. T. Phillipson and Rosalind Mitchison (Edinburgh, 1970).

Scott, William Robert, *Francis Hutcheson: His Life, Teaching and Position in the History of Philosophy* (New York, 1966; 1st edn, Cambridge, 1900).

The Scottish Enlightenment: Essays in Reinterpretation, ed. P. B. Wood (Rochester, NY, 2000).

Sefton, Henry, 'Lord Ilay and Patrick Cuming: A Study in Eighteenth-Century Ecclesiastical Management', *Records of the Church History Society of Scotland*, 16 (1969), pp. 203–16.

——, 'St Mary's College, St Andrews, in the Eighteenth Century', *Records of the Church History Society of Scotland*, 24 (1890–2), pp. 161–80.

——, William Hamilton', in DSCHT [see above], p. 391.

——, 'Patrick Cuming', in DSCHT, p. 227.

Sharp, L. W., 'Charles Mackie: the First Professor of History at Edinburgh University', *Scottish Historical Review*, 41 (1962), pp. 23–44.

Shaw, John Stuart, *The Management of Scottish Society 1707–1764* (Edinburgh, 1983).

——, *The Political History of Eighteenth-Century Scotland* (London, 1999).

Sheets-Pyenson, Susan, 'Horse Race: John William Dawson, Charles Lyell, and the Competition over the Edinburgh Natural History Chair in 1854–1855', *Annals of Science*, 49 (1992), pp. 461–77.

Shepherd, Christine M. [King], 'Newtonianism in the Scottish Universities in the Seventeenth Century', in *The Origins and Nature of the Scottish Enlightenment* [see above], pp. 65–85.

——, 'The Arts Curriculum at Aberdeen at the Beginning of the Eighteenth Century', in *Aberdeen and the Enlightenment* [see above], pp. 146–54.

Sher, Richard B., 'Moderates, Managers and Popular Politics in Mid-Eighteenth Century Edinburgh: The Drysdale "Bustle" of the 1760s', in *New Perspectives* [see above], pp. 179–209.

——, *Church and University in the Scottish Enlightenment: the Moderate Literati of Edinburgh*, Princeton, 1985. [This book and the previous entry contain large bibliographies which include titles not contained in this bibliography].

——, 'Professors of Virtue: The Social history of the Edinburgh Moral Philosophy Chair', in *Studies in the Philosophy of the Scottish Enlightenment*, ed. M. A. Stewart (Oxford, 1990), pp. 87–126.

——, 'Alexander Carlyle', ODNB, 10:139–42.

Sibbald, Sir Robert, *Memoria Balfouriana* (Edinburgh, 1699).

Simpson, A. D. C., 'Sir Robert Sibbald – The Founder of the College', in *Proceedings of the Royal College of Physicians of Edinburgh Tercentenary Congress*, ed. Reginald Passmore (Edinburgh, RCPE, 1982), pp. 59–91.

Simpson, Matthew, ' "O man do not scribble on the book": Print and Counter-print in a Scottish Enlightenment University', *Oral Tradition*, 15 (2000), pp. 74–95.

——, ' "You have not such a one in England": St Andrews University Library as an Eighteenth-Century Mission Statement', *Library History*, 17 (2001), pp. 41–57.

Sinclair, George, *Satan's Invisible World Discovered*, ed. Coleman O. Parsons (Gainseville, FL, 1969; 1st edn 1685).

Skoczylas, Anne, *Mr Simson's Knotty Case: Divinity, Politics and Due Process in Early Eighteenth-Century Scotland* (Montreal and Kingston, 2001).

——, 'The Regulation of Academic Society in Early Eighteenth-Century Scotland: The Tribulations of Two Divinity professors', *Scottish Historical Review*, 83 (2004), pp. 171–95.

Smart, Robert Noyes, 'Some observations on the provinces of the Scottish Universities, 1560–1850', in *The Scottish Tradition: Essays in Honour of Ronald Gordon Cant*, ed. W.S. Barrow (Edinburgh, 1974), pp. 91–106.

[Smellie], *Memoirs of the Life, Writings and Correspondence of William Smellie . . .*, ed. Robert Kerr (Edinburgh, 1811; reprinted New York, 1974).

[Smith], *Correspondence of Adam Smith*, ed. E. C. Mossner and I. S. Ross, vol. 6 in the *Glasgow Edition of the Works and Correspondence of Adam Smith*, Gen. Eds D. D. Raphael and A. S. Skinner, 2nd edn rev. (Oxford, 1987; facsimile reprint by Liberty Classics, Indianapolis, n.d.).

[Smollett], *The Letters of Tobias Smollett*, ed. Lewis M. Knapp (Oxford, 1970).

Sneddan, Ian, 'Robert Simson', DSB [see above], 12:445–7.

The Snell Exhibitioners from the University of Glasgow to Balliol College, Oxford, compiled by W. Innes Addison (Glasgow, 1901).

Somerville, Thomas, *My Own Life and Times 1741–1814* (Edinburgh, 1861).

The Statistical Account of Scotland 1791–1799, 20 vols, ed. Donald Witherington and Ian Grant (Ilkley, 1983; 1st edn 1791–9, ed. Sir John Sinclair).

Stearns, Raymond Phineas, *Science in the British Colonies of America* (Urbana, Chicago, London, 1970).

Stephens, James, *The Memoirs of James Stephens Written for the Use of His Children*, ed. Merle M. Bevington (London, 1954).

Stewart, Agnes Grainger, *The Academic Gregories* (London, 1901).

Stewart, Larry, *The Rise of Public Science: Rhetoric, Technology and Natural Philosophy in Newtonian Britain, 1660–1750* (Cambridge, 1992).

Stewart, M. A., 'Berkeley and the Rankenian Club', *Hermanthena: A Trinity College Dublin Review*, 139 (1985), pp. 25–45.

——, 'John Smith and the Molesworth Circle', *Eighteenth-Century Ireland*, 2 (1987), pp. 89–102. [This issue was devoted to articles on Francis Hutcheson and has others on his career in Glasgow.]

——, 'Origins of the Scottish Greek Chairs', in *Owls to Athens': Essays on Classical Subjects Presented to Sir Kenneth Dover*, ed. E. Craik (Oxford, 1990).

——, 'The Kirk and the Infidel: An Inaugural Lecture delivered at Lancaster University on 9 November 1994', privately published, 1994.

——, 'Abating bigotry and hot zeal', A Supplement to *Fortnight*, No. 308 (1998), ed. Damian Smith, pp. 4–6. [This supplement was devoted to essays on Hutcheson].

——, 'Principal Wishart (1692–1753) and the controversies of his day', *Records of the Scottish Church History Society*, 30 (2000), pp. 60–102.

——, 'Thomas Halyburton', ODNB [see above], 24:732f.

——, 'Hume's Intellectual Development, 1711–1752', in *Impressions of Hume*, ed. M. Frasca-Spada and P. J. E. Kail (Oxford, 2005).

Stewart, Marian M., 'Crime and Punishment in 17th and 18th Century Records of Dumfries', *Dumfriesshire and Galloway Natural History and Antiquarian Society*, 72 (1997), pp. 69–78.

Stone, Lawrence, ed., *The University in Society*, 2 vols (Princeton, 1974).

Story, Robert, *William Carstares: A Character and Career of the Revolutionary Epoch (1649–1715)* (London, 1874).

Strang, John, *Glasgow and Its Clubs*, 3rd edn (Glasgow, 1864).

Struthers, J., *Historical Sketch of the Edinburgh Anatomical School* (Edinburgh, 1867).

[Stuart] *Calendar of Stuart Papers belonging to His Majesty the King preserved at Windsor Castle*, 7 vols, various editors (London, 1902–23).

[Stuart, John], 'Historical Account and Present State of the Marischal College and University of Aberdeen', *Statistical Account of Scotland* [see above], 1:302–39.

Studies in the Philosophy of the Scottish Enlightenment, ed. M. A. Stewart (Oxford, 1990).

Sturdy, David J., *Science and Social Status: the Membership of the Académie des Sciences, 1666–1750* (Woodbridge, 1995).

Suderman, Jeffrey, *Orthodoxy and Enlightenment: George Campbell in the Eighteenth Century* (Montreal and Kingston, 2001).

Sunter, Ronald M., *Patronage and Politics in Scotland 1707–1832* (Edinburgh, 1986).

——, Review of R. L. Emerson, *Professors, Patronage and Politics*, in *Scottish Tradition*, 20 (1995), pp. 93–5.

Szechi, Daniel, *George Lockhart of Carnwath 1681–1731: A Study in Jacobitism* (East Linton, 2002).

——, *1715 The Great Jacobite Rebellion* (London and New Haven, CT, 2006).

Taylor, George, 'John Walker D.D.', *Transactions of the Botanic Society, Edinburgh*, 38 (1959), pp. 180–203.

Thomson, Alexander, *Biographical Sketch of David Skene, M.D. of Aberdeen* (Edinburgh, 1859).

Thomson, Duncan, et al., *Raeburn: The Art of Sir Henry Raeburn 1756–1823*, no ed. (Scottish National Portrait Gallery, Edinburgh, 1997).

Thomson, John, *An Account of the Life, and Writings of William Cullen, M.D.*, 2 vols (Vol. I, Edinburgh, 1832; I and II, Edinburgh, 1859).

Trail, William, *Life and Writings of Robert Simson* (Bath and London, 1812).

[Turnbull, George, the elder], 'The Diary of the Rev. George Turnbull', ed. Robert Paul, *Miscellany of the Scottish History Society* (Edinburgh, 1893).

Turnbull, George, the younger, *A Treatise of Ancient Painting 1740*, ed. Vincent M. Bevilacqua (Munich, 1971). [This has a biographical preface.]

Turnbull, H. W., 'Bi-Centenary of the Death of Colin Maclaurin (1698–1746)', *Aberdeen University Studies*, 127 (Aberdeen, 1951).

Twiss, Gregory, and Paul Chennell, *Famous Rectors of St Andrews* (St Andrews, 1982).

Uglow, Jenny, *The Lunar Men: Five Friends Who Changed the World* (New York, 2002).

Underwood, E. Ashworth, *Boerhaave's Men at Leyden and After* (Edinburgh, 1977).

The University [of Edinburgh] Portraits, compiled by D. Talbot Rice . . . with Biographies by Peter McIntyre, 2 vols (Edinburgh, 1957).

Veterum Laudes: A Tribute to the Achievements of the Members of St Salvator's College During Five Hundred Years, ed. James B. Salmond (Edinburgh, 1950).

View of the Political State of Scotland in the Last Century, ed. Sir Charles Elphinstone Adam (Edinburgh, 1887).

Votiva Tabella: A Memorial Volume of St Andrews University in Connection with the Quincentenary Festival, no ed. (Glasgow, 1911).

Walker, David M., *The Scottish Jurists* (Edinburgh, 1985).

Walker, John, *Lectures on Geology . . .*, ed. Harold W. Scott (Chicago, 1966). [This has a 'Biographical introduction'.]

The Rev. Dr John Walker's Report on the Hebrides of 1764 and 1771, ed. Margaret McKay (Edinburgh, 1980).

Wealth and Virtue: The Shaping of Political Economy in the Scottish Enlightenment, ed. Istvan Hont and Michael Ignatieff (Cambridge, 1985; 1st edn 1983).

Whetstone, Ann E., *Scottish County Government in the Eighteenth and Nineteenth Centuries*, (Edinburgh, 1981).

Whiteley, Lawrence, A. B., 'James Smith', *Oxford Dictionary of National Biography* [see above] 51:185.

——, Patrick Cuming, ODNB, 14:626f.

Wight, William, *Heads of a Course of Lectures on the Study of History Given Annually by William Wight D.D. Professor of History in the University of Glasgow* [Glasgow, n.d.; ?1767].

Williams, Max R., 'Gabriel Johnston', *Dictionary of American Biography* [see above], 12:149–51.

[Wilson, Alexander], 'Biographical Account of Alexander Wilson, M.D. . . .', *The Edinburgh Journal of Science*, 10 (1829), pp. 1–17.

Wilson, J. Gordon, 'The [John and James III] Gregorys and Andrew Duncan', *University of Edinburgh Journal*, 9 (1937–8), pp. 160–3.

C. W. J. Withers, 'Geography, Science and National Identity in Early Modern Britain: The Case of Scotland and the Work of Sir Robert Sibbald (1641–1722)', *Annals of Science*, 53 (1996), pp. 29–73.

——, *Geography, Science and National Identity: Scotland since 1520* (Cambridge, 2001).

Wodrow, Robert, *Analecta: or, Materials for a history of Remarkable Providences mostly relating to Scotch Ministers and Christians*, 4 vols, ed. Mathew Leishman, *Maitland Club*, Edinburgh, 1853).

——, *Early Letters of . . . 1698–1709*, ed. L. W. Sharp, Edinburgh, *Scottish History Society*, 3rd Series, 24 (1937).

——, *The Correspondence of . . .*, ed. Thomas M'Crie, 3 vols (*Wodrow Society*, Edinburgh, 1842–3).

Wood, Paul B., *The Aberdeen Enlightenment: The Arts Curriculum in the Eighteenth Century* (Aberdeen, 1993).

——, ' "The Fittest Man in the Kingdom": Thomas Reid and the Glasgow Chair of Moral Philosophy', *Hume Studies*, 23 (1997), pp. 277–313.

——, 'John Robison', in ODNB, 47:432–4.

The Life of Thomas Reid, vol. 11 of *The Works of Thomas Reid*, Gen. Ed. Knud Haakonssen (Edinburgh, forthcoming).

Wright, D. F., 'William Dunlop (d. 1720)', in DSCHT, p. 264f.

'James Hadow' by W. G. Blackie revised by Stephen Wright in ODNB, 20:393f.

Wright-St Clair, R. E., *Doctors Monro* (London, 1964).

John Wynne, *An Abridgement of Mr Locke's Essay concerning Human Understanding* (1st edn, London, 1696; the 1731 edn was reprinted in Bristol, 1990).

Young, Douglas, *St Andrews* (London, 1969).

Zachs, William, *Without Regard to Good Manners: A Biography of Gilbert Stuart 1743–1786* (Edinburgh, 1992).

APPENDICES

1. ESTIMATED VALUES OF THE CHAIRS IN THE SCOTTISH UNIVERSITIES FOR THE 1690s, 1725, 1760, 1795

The estimated values given below include the salaries, fees and, where they are known (or can be estimated with some accuracy), perquisites, offices and other income. Showing the latter shows something about the social levels from which the professors came and helps to define the expectations of those who took university chairs in preference to pursuing other careers. None of these figures are easily estimated. The income for Thomas Tullideph, the principal of St Leonard's College in 1739, derived from income from the parsonage of Kinkell, rents from the bishopric of St Andrews, money from the civil list, cess lands, 'diet money' (an allowance for the cost of keeping his house), garden rent and his stipends as principal and minister of St Leonard's parish.[1] All this came to about £101 3s 8d, to which should be added his share of minor fees such as came from graduations and other perquisites. Later he added to this more rents and the income from a Royal Chaplaincy and the Moderator's stipend for the year he served in that office. Other men could add money from pensions, offices and books.

Salaries, in the early period, are particularly difficult to calculate. Some regents and professors still had stipends which were dependent on the varying price of meal and bear or bere, a form of barley; others had had special favours which raised their wages. Salaries rose over time. This reflected increases in the value of government grants and at Glasgow the prosperity of the city, which brought higher rents to the College. At Edinburgh, the Town Council raised some salaries. At St Andrews, increases resulted from the union of the colleges in 1747. When a chair was jointly held by two men, this has been ignored and the value of the place has been given as if it were possessed by one person. Where two university chairs were held by one man, the value of each has been given separately and not added in the highest salary column.

Professorial incomes based on fees were variable and are harder to calculate. One cannot simply multiply the numbers of boys by a standard fee. The numbers of those paying fees is usually not accurately known. The number of matriculates in public courses exists in some printed or manuscript lists but these omit boys who did not matriculate. The matriculates, who took the public courses, are more easily ascertained than those who took the private or optional courses which professors taught but did not always teach every year. Other boys took these courses but are listed nowhere. To approximate student numbers in private courses, I have counted them as being equal to half those who matriculated and attended the public course. Where matriculation lists exist, I have used those; where other sources give the numbers in a course, I have used the figures they supply. The ordinary courses are probably undercounted but the private courses may be overestimated.

There are equal problems about fees. The masters received higher fees from well-born students than were paid by poorer boys. Like the sons of colleagues, the poor were often taught for nothing. We do not know how many students paid the standard fee or in some cases what it was. Aristocratic boys traditionally gave teachers more and poor ones less than the standard fee – 1 guinea for an arts course for much of the century. There are recorded instances of the sons of Earls giving 10 guineas for an arts course valued at 1 guinea, but for which others paid 10 shillings. I have given the salaries and then an *estimate* of what the fees equalled for those who received them. They have then been rated in the first two columns at 1 guinea each for arts courses, to yield a plausible estimate of income from fees. This overstates the early payments but these were also balanced in most cases by tips to the regents for looking after boys given into the master's care. At some time, that fee doubled and, in the case of a few courses, 3 guineas was the fee. The fee in the second two columns had been assumed to be 2 guineas. Where income figures from fees have been found, they have been used. Even less data exists about payments for extra tutoring which some professors provided, often to boys who boarded with them.

Divinity professors did not charge fees, although the Oriental languages teachers charged boys taking Arabic and Persian who were not going into the ministry. The ecclesiastical historians seem to have charged fees too if the student was not intending to be a minister. The fees for the legal and medical courses were higher and have been estimated at 2 guineas for each registrant. Those numbers I have calculated for the years given, when they are known, or when they are not, by taking an average of the enrolments for years around the stated year. I have added to the sum the remuneration from private courses when I know that. Where other income is known to have existed, but cannot be estimated, I have merely put a + sign after the sums given.

All professors got perquisites. These covered an array of things from kain hens at St Andrews to a percentage of graduation fees and sometimes a share of the proceeds of sales of college properties. Among the perquisites that mattered most were houses which at St Andrews were valued as £10–20 during the period. In Aberdeen, King's College provided manses to most of its regents and professors but Marischal does not seem to have done so. At Edinburgh, the principal and the professors of divinity, Hebrew and Greek had houses, as did some regents in the early part of the period. These were not purpose-built but converted from unused student rooms in the College. Some masters had houses belonging to the church livings held by them. In Glasgow, some men lived rent free; others got a rent allowance; some got nothing. In the last class were all lecturers and almost all of the conjoint professors whose older colleagues were still alive. Some College houses were rented and granted on the basis of seniority. The rents seem to have been somewhat lower than in the town generally. Those with houses often boarded students for substantial sums. Principal Campbell writing from Glasgow in 1737 noted that professor Dunlop had charged Sir John Anstruther £40 for the school year for room and board for his son, the boy's governor and a servant. Robert Dick got £10 a quarter, which was twice the going rate in the boarding houses of the town.[2] Elsewhere the costs ranged over the century from about £5 to the £200 which Colin Maclaurin is said to have charged to keep Hans Stanley in 1740–1. I have assumed that a man had the usual number of boarders which he was known to keep in years around the dates chosen to estimate incomes. Boarders usually paid for extra tuition, washing, food and some social activities. Other perquisites included a share in a miscellany of other funds. Graduation fees were often shared in some fashion and could amount to a good deal. Late in the period, the St Andrews professor of medicine made about £3 on each doctorate of medicine that was granted. In some years as many as thirty-two were awarded.[3] He did not teach but maintained a practice, as did most medical professors elsewhere. Everywhere professorships enhanced the values of medical practices and thus added considerably to professors' incomes. Having a professorship probably had the same effect for a few lawyers. Medical professors in Edinburgh shared in the fees from clinical lecturing at the Infirmary and, from the mid-1730s, some of them divided the £100 stipend of the King's Physician in Scotland. Later, Glasgow professors had the stipend of the physician in Scotland to the Prince of Wales. These like the church livings possessed by others gave them, in effect, higher salaries. If one were a Moderator, then one had a very handsome income, but only for a year. Publications could bring equally high bumps in incomes as the careers of Hugh Blair and William Robertson show. Other things enhancing incomes were windfalls arising from the management of college properties and other occasional sources such as income generated by the sale of property.

Many professors had sources of income not related to their teaching posts. Some men inherited (or married into) landed property which produced rents of varying size; others had valuable urban properties. Some were consultants, investors, or in receipt of pensions which came from having tutored the sons of affluent gentlemen or from services which were rewarded by the government. Where these incomes are known, they have been included in the estimates of total income. The figures given below are meant to be minimal estimates showing the value of what was sought and expected and the kinds of men who expected them. Estimates of total incomes have been set within brackets. Many incomes would have been higher but, I think, few were lower than the ones given in the dated columns. These values are generally higher than have been assumed by many who deplored the low salaries paid to Scottish teachers. Scottish professors did have to teach effectively to maximise their incomes but they were a well-off group making several times more than the run-of-the-mill cleric and often as much or more than their counterparts at Oxbridge.

The sources for all these figures are miscellaneous and too numerous to mention here. Some are well known. The Universities Commission 1826–30[4] provided data, as have politicians' calculations of the values of the chairs they were dispensing. They generally knew better than later Commissioners the value of what was on offer and they had reasons to be more accurate in their statements. The politicians' estimates were often of the salaries, likely fees and perquisites. Among other sources are Jack Morrell's fine article, 'The University of Edinburgh in the Late Eighteenth Century: Its Scientific Eminence and Academic Structure', *Isis*, 62 (1971), which has been used to give the 1795 figures for Edinburgh.[5] For Glasgow, there is a useful memorandum written by Principal Stirling in 1717 stating all the salaries

[GUA, MS 47410]. Robert Wallace listed the regius chairs c. 1743 [EUL, MS La.II. 620.29] and James Stuart Mackenzie's 'Accounts of the Values of Presbytery Livings, Pensions on the Scotch Establishment', c. 1763 [Bute MSS held at Mount Stuart House, Isle of Bute] notes the values of the chairs and many church livings. Charles Mackie, 'State of ye Principal & and St Andrews Regents of St Leonard's College', Commonplace book, EUL, MS La.III.537/74f, is also helpful, as are various editions of the *Edinburgh Almanack* and other such publications.

Finally, I have given the highest income which I know to have been received by a professor holding a given chair. This is interesting for what it shows about the men who held these posts and as a definer of backgrounds and expectations. Most of the figures come from the years after 1780 but some do not and reflect the presence of wealthy men like Principal Wishart II or Robert Hamilton, the divinity professor at Edinburgh whose income peaked in 1754 when he held the Moderatorship of the General Assembly.

1. Estimated Values of the Glasgow University Chairs (£ sterling)

Chair	1695	1725	1760	1795	Highest known total income from all sources, 1690–1807
Principality	147 + house + perqs + office = 40+ [187+]	100 + house + perqs + Chaplaincy = 67 [167+]	157 + house + perqs + Chaplaincy = 67 [224+]	219 + house + perqs + 50 for boarders + Deanery = 200 [469+]	469+
Divinity	102 + house + kirk = c. 100 + perqs [202+]	102 + house + perqs [102+]	150 + house + perqs + rents [150+]	130 + house + perqs + investments [130+]	238+
Ecclesiastical History	33 + fees +perqs [33+]	103 + fees + perqs [103+]	103 + fees + perqs [103+]	103 + fees + perqs + rents [103+]	164+
Oriental Languages	33 + fees + perqs [33+]	50 + fees + clerkship and factory = 10 + perqs [60+]	76 + fees + perqs + [76+]	100 + fees and from teaching French and Italian = 30 + perqs + boarders [130+]	158+
Humanity	20 + fees = 30 [50+]	58 + fees = 37 [95+]	33 + fees = 30 + Librarian's salary = 7 + editing [70+]	85 + fees = 83 + perqs + boarders = 80[6] + publishing [248+]	248+

Professorship					
Greek (founded 1704)	[1704] 25 + fees = 25 [50+]	64 + fees = 16 + perqs + pension = 25 + rents [105+]	44 + fees = 28 + perqs + editing [72+]	44 + fees = 40 + perqs = 2 + boarders = 160+ [246+]	255+
Regents	22 + fees = .40 + perqs [62+]	55 + fees = 65 + perqs [110+]	-Regenting ended in 1727	–	110+
Logic (chair was fixed in 1727)		[1727] 44 + fees = 25 + perqs [69+]	47 + fees = 12 + perqs + boarders [59+]	85 + fees = 130 + perqs + boarders = 160+ [375+]	415+
Moral Philosophy (chair was fixed in 1727)		[1727] 50 + fees = + 25 + house + perqs [75+]	44 + fees = 100 + perqs + boarders + [144+]	96 + fees = 60 + perqs + boarders + investments = 60 [216+]	216+
Natural Philosophy (chair was fixed in 1727)		[1727] 44 + fees = 25 + perqs [65+]	44 + fees = 40 + perqs + boarders [84+]	90 + fees = 60 + perqs + boarders = 50 [200+]	200+
(Lecturer in Natural History and Keeper of the Hunterian Museum, 1803)				?15 + Fees + [200+]	15+

Chair	1695	1725	1760	1795	Highest known total income from all sources, 1690–1807
Lecturer in Italian and French in most years after c. 1710			Fees	Fees	
Astronomy (founded 1761)			50 + fees + income from making instruments and type [50+]	50 + fees + clerkship to University + type foundry + sale of instruments + [50+]	200+
Law (founded 1713)		90 + fees + practice + perqs [90+]	90 + fees = c. 36 + perqs? + practice [126+]	90 + fees = 160 + perqs + boarders = 200 + practice + rents [450+]	450+
Anatomy & Botany (Lectureship founded 1704; Professorship 1720)		30 + fees = 30 + perqs + practice + rents [60+]	30 + fees = 60 + perqs + practice [90+]	30 + fees = 200 + perqs + practice + rents + pension = 10+ [240+]	340+

Medicine (founded 1713)		40 + fees + perqs = 8 + practice + [48+]	40 + fees = 60 + practice and consulting + investments + [100+]	40 + fees = c. 200 + perqs + practice + consulting [240+]	400+
Chemistry (Lectureship founded 1747)			50 + fees = 50 + practice + chemical consulting + rents [100+]	70 + fees = 150 + practice + chemical consulting [220+]	260+
Materia Medica (Lectureship founded 1767)				25 + fees = 90 + practice + chemical consulting [115+]	260+
Midwifery (Lectureship founded 1791)				25 + fees = 100 + practice [124+]	230+
Mathematics	33 + fees = 50 + perqs [83+]	40 + fees = 50 + perqs [90+]	60 + fees = 75 + perqs + rents + [135+]	70 + fees = 100 + perqs [170+]	185+

2. Estimated Values of the Edinburgh University Chairs (£ sterling)

Chair	1695	1725	1760	1795	Highest known total income from all sources, 1690–1807
Principality	111 + house + kirk = 88 + perqs [199+]	122 + house + kirk = 138 + perqs + rents and other income = 1,000 [1,260+]	111 + house + pension = 67 + perqs [178+]	111 + house + church = c. 139 + fees + perqs + pension = 200 + Historiographer Royal = 200 [c. 650+]	1,480+
Divinity	88 + house + church = c. 110 [198+]	110 + house + perqs + pensions = 67 and 41 [218+]	161 + house + perqs + kirk = 138 + Deanery = 67 + Moderator in 1760 = 300 [666+]	161 + house + perqs + kirk = 138 + rents [299+]	666+
Ecclesiastical History (founded c. 1702)		80 + fees but no teaching fees for public course + perqs [80+]	115 + ? fees + perqs + kirk = 138 + rents [253+]	200 + fees + perqs + kirk = 138 + Deanery = 67 + rents [405]	405+
Oriental Languages (founded 1692)	55 + house + perqs [55+]	55 + fees for non-Hebrew courses + medical practice + fees + house + perqs [55+]	80 + fees + house + perqs + stipend as Librarian = ?8 [c. 88+]	80 + fees + house + perqs + kirk = c. 100 [c. 180]	350+

Regent of Humanity	26 + fees = 45 + fees [71]	26 + fees = 60 + fees [86+]	52 + fees = 64 + rent [116+]	52 + fees = 344 + fees + rents [396+]	438+
Greek (founded 1708)		52 + fees = 41 + house + perqs [91+]	52 + fees = 98 + house + perqs [150+]	52 + fees = 386 + house + perqs + [438]	582+
Regents of Philosophy	22 + fees = 50 + perqs [72+]				130+
Logic (chair fixed in 1708)		52 + fees = 51 + fees + perqs [103+]	52 + fees = = 160 + perqs [212+]	52 + fees = 174 + perqs + kirk = +138 [364]	364+
Moral Philosophy (chair fixed in 1708)		52 + fees = 50 + perqs + rents [102+]	52 + fees = 182 + perqs + rents + practice [234+]	52 + fees = 348 + perqs [400+]	650 +
Natural Philosophy (chair fixed in 1708)		52 + fees = c. 50 + perqs [102+]	52 + fees = 170 + perqs [222+]	52 + fees = 279 + perqs + fees + boarders + consulting [331+][7]	440+
Mathematics	50 + fees = 30 + perqs [c. 80]	50 + fees = 50 + perqs + office = c. 40 [140+]	83 + fees = c. 125 + perqs + rents [208+]	113 + fees = 216 + perqs [329+]	450+
Astronomy (founded 1785)				120 + fees + office + [120+][8]	120+

Chair	1695	1725	1760	1795	Highest known total income from all sources, 1690–1807
Agriculture (founded 1790)				50 + fees = 27 + perqs + practice, consulting + rents [77+]	300+
Rhetoric (founded 1762)			[1763] 70 + fees = 64 + perqs + kirk = 139+	70 + fees = 45 + kirk = 139 + editing and writing + pension = 200 and Chaplaincy + perqs [454+]	500+
History (founded 1719)		100 + fees = 50 + perqs + interest + [150+]	100 + fees = 40 + Keeper of Advocates' Library = 40 + rents + practice [180+]	100 + fees = 72 + perqs + legal office = 60 + rents + practice [232+]	625+
Public Law (founded 1707)		150 [sinecure]+ perqs + legal office = 500 + rents + [650+]	c. 200 [sinecure][9] + perqs + practice + office = 40 + rents [240+]	280 [sinecure] + perqs + practice + legal office = c. 200 + rents + investments [480+]	1,405+
Civil Law (founded 1710)		100 + fees = 60 + practice [160+]	100 + fees = 70 + rents + practice [170+]	100 + fees = 63 + practice [163+]	c. 342+

Subject					Total
Scots Law (founded 1722)	20 + fees = 40 + perqs = ? [60+]	100 + fees = c. 100 + legal office = 40 + rents [240+]	100 + fees = 120 + perqs + practice + rents = 120 [340+]	100 + fees = 339 + perqs + practice [439+]	439+
Botany		20 + fees = 30 + perqs + stipend as Surgeon Major = ? + apothecary's business [50+]	20 + fees = 180 + perqs + office = 50 [250+]	128 + fees = 234 + perqs + office = 50 [412+]	568+
Chemistry (founded 1713)		0 + fees = ? + perqs + practice + [?]	0 + fees = 300 + practice + rents [300+]	0 + fees = 675 + practice + consulting + investments [675+]	886+
Anatomy (founded 1720)		15 + fees = 200 + perqs + practice + writing + [215+]	20 + fees = 600 + perqs + fees + practice + [620+]	50 + fees = 921 + perqs + practice + rents + [971+]	1,007+
Theory of Medicine (founded 1726)[10]		0 + fees + perqs + practice + pharmaceutical company [?]	0 + fees = 300 + perqs + practice + rent + office = 33 [333+]	0 + fees = 240 + perqs + practice + office = 33 [273+]	1,026+
Practice of Medicine (founded 1726)		0 + fees + perqs + practice + pharmaceutical company [?]	0 + fees = 340 + perqs + practice + office = 33 [373+]	0 + fees = 675 + perqs + practice + office = 33 [708+]	869+

Chair	1695	1725	1760	1795	Highest known total income from all sources, 1690–1807
Materia Medica (founded 1768)				33 + fees = 174 + perqs + practice + rents [207+]	377+
Midwifery (founded 1739)[11]			0 + fees = c. 80 + practice [80+]	0 + fees = 237 practice+ rents + investments [c. 425+]	500+
Natural History (1767)				100 + fees = c. 150 + kirk = 66 [316+]	400+
Surgery (founded 1777)		This chair existed in name only as an adjunct to the chair of anatomy.			
Clinical Surgery (founded 1803)				? + fees + practice + land + perqs [?]	[?]
Military Surgery (founded 1806)				? + fees + practice + perqs [?]	[?]

3. Estimated Values of the St Andrews University Chairs (£ sterling)

Chair	1695	1725	1760	1795	Highest known total income from all sources, 1690–1807
University Mathematics (1690–1747)	(The chair was vacant until 1708) 61 + fees = 10 + perqs [71?]	61 + fees = 10 + perqs [71+]			108+
Medicine (1720–47)		50 + fees + perqs + practice [50+]			90+
St Mary's Principal	116 + house + diet money = 10 + perqs [126+]	116 + house + diet money = 10 + perqs [126+]	147 + house + diet money = 25 + perqs + rents [183+]	173 + house + diet money = 25 + perqs + Deanery = 50 + Chaplaincy = 50 + rents [298+]	423+
Divinity	100 + house + diet money = 10 + perqs [110+]	121 + house + diet money = 10 + perqs [131+]	121 + house + diet money = 25 + perqs [146+]	121+ house + diet money = 25 + perqs Moderator's stipend = 300 [446+]	446+
Ecclesiastical History (1708)	105 + house + diet money =10 + perqs [115+]	105 + house + diet money = 10 [115+]	140 + house + diet money = 25 [165+]	200 + house + diet money = 25 + [225+]	283+

Chair	1695	1725	1760	1795	Highest known total income from all sources, 1690–1807
Hebrew	75 + house + diet money = 10 + perqs [85+]	85 + house + diet money = 10 + perqs [95+]	102 + house + diet money = 25 + perqs + medical practice [127+]	102 + house + diet money = 25 + perqs [127+]	201+
St Salvator's –1747					
Provost	83 + house + perqs [83+]	83 + house + perqs [83+]			140+
Humanist	28 + fees = c. 25 + fees + perqs [53+]	40 + fees = c. 20 + perqs [60+]			70+
Greek (1705)	[1706] 35 + fees = ? + perqs [35+]	46 + fees = c. 20 + fees + perqs [66+]			66+
Regents	35 + fees = c. 30 + fees + perqs [65+]	46 + fees = c. 20 + fees + [66+]			72+
St Leonard's – 1747					
Principal	112 + house + diet money = 10 [122+]	120 + house + diet money = 10 + church = 60 + [190+]			220+
Humanist	19 + fees = c. 20 + fees + perqs [39+]	19 + fees = c. 20 + perqs [49+]			78+

Greek (1702)	[1702] 28 + fees = 12 + perqs [40+]	28 + fees = 20+, + perqs [48+]			83+
Regents	28 + fees = 20 + [58+]	28 + fees = 20 + [58+]			c. 100
United College 1747 – Principal			160 + house + diet money[12] = 15 + perqs + kirk = 60 + chaplaincy = 50 [285+]	194 + house + diet money = 15+, + kirk = 60 + deanery = 67 [336+]	660+
Humanist			60 + house[13] + diet money = 15+, + fees = 40+, + diet money = 15+, + perqs [115+]	80 + house + diet money = 15+, + fees = 60 + perqs [155+]	155+
Greek			80 + house + diet money = 15+, + fees = 50 + perqs [145+]	106 + house + diet money = 15+, + fees = 54 + perqs + boarders [175+]	251+
Logic			80 + house + diet money = 15 + fees = 40 + perqs + boarders + [135+]	106 + house + diet money = 15 + fees = 50 + perqs + pension = 100+ [271+]	271+

Chair	1695	1725	1760	1795	Highest known total income from all sources, 1690–1807
Moral Philosophy			80 + house + diet money = 15 + fees = 40 + perqs [135+]	106 + house + diet money = 15 + fees = 50 + perqs [171+]	
Civil History			60 + house + diet money = 15 + fees = 20 + perqs [95+]	96 + house + diet money = 15+, + fees = 30 + perqs + kirk = 60 + [201+]	237+
Natural Philosophy			80 + house + diet money = 15 + fees = 40 + perqs [135+]	106 + house + diet money = 15 + fees = 50 + perqs + medical practice + rents [171+]	219+
Lectureship in French				24 + fees = ? [?]	235+
Mathematics			71 + house + diet money = 15 + fees = 90 + perqs [176]	92 + house + diet money = 15+, + fees = 120 + perqs [227+]	24+
					227+

Medicine

60 + house + diet
money = 15+, + fees
= 27 + perqs +
practice +
[102+]

76 + house + diet
money = 15+, + fees
= 27 + perqs +
practice
[118+]

191+

4. Estimated Values of the King's College and University Chairs (£ sterling)[14]

Chair	1695	1725	1760	1795	Highest known total income from all sources, 1690–1807
Principal	68 + house + perqs + rents [68+]	83 + house + perqs [83+]	144 + house + perqs + rents [144+]	150 + house + perqs + rents >10 [160+]	175+
Sub-Principal[15]	15+	25+	55+	55+	55+
Divinity	64 + house + perqs + rents [64+]	71 + house + perqs + [75+]	71 + house + perqs + pension = 67 [138+]	141 + house + perqs + Chaplaincy = 50 [191+]	481+
Oriental Languages[16]	67 + fees + house + perqs [67 + fees +]	67 + fees + perqs + Deputy Collectorship of Bishop's rents + [67+]	67 + fees + house + perqs [67+]	137 + fees + house + perqs + rents [137]	137
Greek[17]					
Humanist	20 + fees = 20 + house + perqs [40+]	20 + fees = 20 + house + perqs [40+]	35 + fees = 16 + house + perqs + boarders at 13 guineas each[18] [64+]	100 + fees = 32 + house + perqs + investments [97+]	175+

Regents	c. 25 + fees = 30 + house + perqs [55+]	25 + fees = 25 + [45 + fees +]	35 + fees = 24 + house + perqs [69 + fees +]	100 + fees = 32 house + perqs [142+]	[142 + rents = 100?]
Mathematics[19]					
Civilist	15 + fees[20] + practice + perqs + Town Clerk of Aberdeen [15+]	25 + fees + practice + [25+]	25 + fees + perqs + practice [25+]	35 + fees + perqs + practice + land [35+]	210+
Mediciner	15 + fees[21] + perqs practice as MD and embalmer [15+]	25 + fees = 0 + perqs + practice + investments [25+]	25 + fees + practice + rents [25+]	35 + fees + practice + land [35+]	350+

5. Estimated Values of the Marischal College and University Chairs (£ sterling)

Chair	1690s	1725	1760	1795	Highest known total income from all sources, 1690–1807
Principal	66 + house + perqs + Commissary of Aberdeen = 80 + Sheriff Substitute of Aberdeen = c. 30 + rents [176+]	74 + house + kirk = 20 + perqs + [Divinity Professor = 66] [94 + Divinity Professor = 70 +]	100 + house + kirk = 126 + perqs = [226+]	c. 100 + house + kirk = 20 + [Divinity Professor = 100 +] perqs = [120 + Divinity Professor +]	226+
Divinity	67 + house + church = c. 100 + perqs [167+]	70 + house + kirk = 20 + perqs + [principality = 91] [90 + Principality = 181 +]	180 (+ house + kirk = 20 + perqs)	100 + house + kirk = 20 + perqs + [principality = 100] [220+]	220+
Oriental Languages[22] (1732)			50 + fees = ? + perqs + practice as MD + [Professor of Medicine = 10] [60+]	50 + fees = ?60 + perqs + [?110+]	170+
Greek (1701)	[1701] 40 + fees = 25 + perqs [65+]	34 + fees = c. 40 + perqs [74+]	40 + fees = c. 50 + perqs [90+]	66 + fees = 90 + perqs + rents [156+][23]	290+

Regents[24]	25 + fees = 50 + perqs [75]	35 + fees = 45 + perqs [80+]	_[25]		130
Professor of Civil and Natural History			40 + fees = 88 + perqs [128+]	67 + fees = 80 + perqs [147+][26]	300+
Professor of Logic and Moral Philosophy			40 + fees = 88 + perqs + [128+]	67 + fees = 100 + perqs + pension = 200 + copy money + a boarder? [347+]	393+
Professor of Natural Philosophy			40 + fees = 88 + perqs [128+]	67 + fees = 100 + perqs + ? consulting [167+]	170+
Mathematics	44 + fees = c. 16 + perqs [60+]	52 + fees = c. 20 + perqs [72+][27]	50 + fees = c. 80 + perqs [130+]	67 + fees = 100 + perqs + consulting [167]	167+
Law[28]					

Chair	1690s	1725	1760	1795	Highest known total income from all sources, 1690–1807
Medicine	10 + fees + perqs + practice and rents	10 + fees + perqs + practice + rents	10 + fees + perqs + [Professor of Oriental Languages = 80] + practice + rents + Physician to Aberdeen Infirmary =	43 + fees + perqs + practice + Physician to Gordon's hospital + rents =	
	[10+]	[10+]	[10 + OL+]	[c. 150+]	210+
Chemistry (1793)				40 + fees = 15 + apothecary's shop and practice [60+]	127+
Lecturer in Anatomy (1802)					

2. AVERAGE TOTAL INCOMES OF THE PROFESSORS FROM ALL SOURCES BY FACULTY

	1695	1725	1760	1795	Largest known income
Glasgow					
Principal	187	167	224	469	469+[29]
Divinity	118	103	127	117	238+
Law		90	126	450	450+*
Medicine		53	83	188	400+*
Arts	50	90	92	226	415+
Edinburgh					
Principal	200	1,260	178	650	1,480+
Divinity	198	199	460	352	666+
Law		383	250	361	1,405+*
Medicine	60	133	324	530	1,026+*
Arts	74	121	183	292	650+
St Andrews					
Principal[30]	102	137	285	336	660+
Divinity	109	117	155	274	446+
Law					
Medicine			102	118	191+
Arts	51	60	133	204	271+
King's College					
Principal	68	83	144	160	175+
Divinity	64	75	138	191	481+
Law	15	25	25	35	210+*
Medicine	15	25	25	35	350+*
Arts	55	52	77	143	175+
Marischal College					
Principal	176	164	226	220	226+
Divinity	167	171	180	220	220+
Law					
Medicine	10	10	90	105	210+*
Arts	70	73	133	166	393+

Notes to Appendices 1 and 2

1 'Francis Pringle's Common Place Book', SAUL, LF1111.P81C99, p. 154.
2 Neil Campbell to [?], 19 August 1737, NLS, 16669/255.
3 I thank Robert Smart for this information.
4 *Report . . . by a Royal Commission into the State of the Universities of Scotland*, 36 vols (1831–7).
5 Morrell's enrolment and income figures are good indicators of the income of the professors but they may be on the low side. There exists a set of accounts by James Gregory listing his income from his professorship 1776–1818 which shows higher incomes than the figures given by Morrell. I take the variation to be due to the issuance of tickets to men whose names did not make it onto the enrolment lists used by Morrell. See James Gregory, 'Accounts Relating to my Professorship in the University of Edinburgh From 1776 to . . .' [1776–1818 with omissions], EUL, 2206/12.
6 In 1791, John Young noted that John Millar charged £100 for a boarder for a six-month session while he, George Jardine and William Richardson were paid £80 for 'Board, Lodging [and tuition in] The Classicks & Philosophy', i.e. the fees for the courses they gave and for extra help. He went on to say that another colleague charged £50 but levied separate charges for the tuition given. The other colleague is likely to have been Patrick Cuming who sometimes had a boarder. John Young to Charles Burney, 11 October 1791, NLS, 786.
7 In 1773, when James Beattie was trying to obtain this chair, his friend Sir William Forbes the Edinburgh banker estimated its annual value at £300. Sir William Forbes to Beattie, 19 October 1773, AUL, MS 30/2.
8 Robert Blair, the first professor, treated this as a sinecure post and was not usually resident in Edinburgh. He never taught but held government offices in London. See David Bryden, 'The Edinburgh Observatory', *Annals of Science*, 47 (1990), pp. 445–74. Bryden noted the Town Council's objection to the founding of a regius chair in its University, but that was a usual objection to such interventions and means little. Blair could not function because the town would not spend money on needed equipment; a competing observatory was being built. Leaving important functions to private enterprise undertaken for profit does little for learning and less for those who would be taught.
9 Lectures were given in 1763, when the fees probably came to about £20.
10 What existed in 1725 was like the Glasgow chair, one of the theory and practice of medicine.
11 A post was granted to a town professor of midwifery in 1726, perhaps because he was an Episcopalian who could not qualify for a university post by subscribing the Confession of Faith.

12 After the 1747 Union this seems to have become a variable sum, which in 1795 was worth £76 to each of the professors and probably a bit more to the principal.

13 What was given was not a house but rent money of something in excess of £10.

14 At King's, salaries were partially stated in bolls and chalders of meal. The prices of these were set by the Sheriff Courts and were meant to reflect the prevailing market price. Grain or its value accounted for a high pro-portion of the salaries. Daniel Bradfute, who was appointed as a regent in 1717, received £10 4s 0d in cash and about the same amount paid from the assessed value of his meal ration which provided the varying remainder of his salary. This was paid annually at Michaelmas for the preceeding crop. Lee MS, NLS, 3431/148. The white oatmeal and bear prices or fiars are given for Aberdeen by A. J. S. Gibson and T. C. Smout in *Prices, Food and Wages in Scotland 1550–1780*, 1995, pp. 96–8.

15 This post almost always went to the senior regent, whose salary was topped up by this amount and whose importance in the College was thus recognised. Total income figures have been entered for the regents but not here.

16 Hebrew and Oriental languages was a divinity chair only at St Andrews.

17 This chair was a regency until 1800 when the regenting system ended, but the fees collected were likely to have been less since there were fewer students enrolled in Greek.

18 This is taken from a notice published by Thomas Gordon in 1744 which also contains the most extensive account of what those who took board-ers did for them in the way of tutoring and extra instruction. The notice is reprinted in P. B. Wood, *The Aberdeen Enlightenment* (Aberdeen, 1993), p. 57.

19 The College tried twice to establish a chair of mathematics, once in 1703 when Thomas Bower was appointed but no salary was provided for him. He not surprisingly taught little and eventually left Aberdeen. It tried again in 1730 when several men vied for the chair which could not be funded. The masters in 1731 appointed Alexander Rait to teach for fees; he later became a regent. In 1800, when the chairs were fixed, William Jack became professor of Mathematics, a post he combined with being sub-principal.

20 The civilist got something for all the honorary law degrees granted, but these sums amounted to very little.

21 The mediciner got something for all medical law degrees granted by the University which were not strictly honorary. These sums also amounted to very little.

22 This chair was often held with other posts. James Donaldson, its first incumbent, was a busy physician, as was his son who followed him in office. James Kidd, who held the place at the end of the period, was an

inoculator and had a chapel of ease after 1796. Hebrew and Oriental languages was a divinity chair only at St Andrews.

23 John Leslie gave £125 as the year's 'Profits of my Office' in December 1784; his total income was £290, *Powis Papers 1507–1894*, ed. Burnett (*Third Spalding Club*, 1951), p. 304.

24 Regents were not paid at a uniform rate. The senior regent in c. 1725 had a salary of £36, while that of the fourth regent was only about £33. Since enrolments also differed, the class fees also varied with the year and the year in the programme they were teaching.

25 Regenting in the college ended in 1754 and fixed professorships were created in place of the regents.

26 The chair was sold in 1788 at five years' purchase for £500.

27 In 1725, Colin Maclaurin began teaching. The salary is given in the Town Council Register 58, entry for 11 November 1717, as £45 but in a College memorandum of about this time it is stated to be £52; AUL, MS M.361/10/8.

28 There was no law professor until the nineteenth century, but one regent or professor was designated as professor of law so that there would be a promoter for law degrees. The first was probably David Warner or Verner, who had trained in law and seems to have lectured on law in 1724. He functioned as promoter until his death in 1752. The next known to have held this designation was Francis Skene in 1766. Later it went to James Beattie in 1776. The fees for the degree, when it was not an honour, ranged from 9 guineas to £15. They would have been split by the faculty members and the University, with a larger share going to the 'professor of law'.

29 '+' denotes another known source of income for which the amount is lacking; * denotes an income from the practice of law or medicine or some other profession or calling whose precise sum is not knowable.

30 This in the first two columns is the average of the known incomes of the provost of St Salvator's College and the principal of St Leonard's College; in the latter two columns it is what is known of the income of the principal of the United College of St Salvator and St Leonard.

INDEX OF NAMES

Author's note: All notes indexed give the page on which the reference occurs and the number of the note, i.e, p.240n53; the note itself is on p.250. People whose surnames alone are known are listed first. Others follow alphabetically by names with the titled coming before commoners with the same name. The latter are then listed by what I take to be the order of their birth dates. Unless there is a reason to identify a person by more than a title and name, nothing else has been given. Where there are many of the same name descriptive identifiers are given. Where there is a questionable identification, that is noted by a question mark. A few names of those who could not be identified have been omitted.

Abercrombie, George, 26, 343
Abercromby,? George, 280
Aberdeen, Earls of *see* Gordon
Aboyne, Earl of *see* Gordon
Adair, John, 386n77
Adamson, John, 497, 501, 503, 504, 506
Aikenhead, Thomas, 237
Aitkin, John, 287
Alexander, Robert, 57
Alexander, William, 300
Allan or Allen,? John, MD, 191n47
Alston, Charles, 546, 276–7
Alston or Alstyon, James, 84, 91, 234, 276–7, 289, 291
Anderson, H, 378n40
Anderson, John, Principal of St Leonard's College, 384
Anderson, Provost John of Glasgow, 27
Anderson, Rev. John, 48, 130
Anderson, Professor John, 10, 129–31, 134–8, 139, 140, 163, 165, 166, 167, 189, 190, 299, 475, 532, 546
Anderson, William, 72, 88, 89, 92, 100, 107, 109, 110, 111, 114, 116, 117, 124
Anne, Queen, 231, 389
Anstruther, Sir John, d. 1753, 416n45
Anstruther, Sir Robert, 416n45
Arbuckle, James, 68
Areskine or Aerskine *see* Erskine
Argyll, Dukes, Marquis, Earls of *see* Campbell
Arnot, John, surgeon, 420, 444
Arnot, Robert, 495, 504, 506, 512
Arrot or Arnot, John, 379
Arthur, Archibald, 171, 193, 194
Arthur, William, 274, 276
Auckland, Baron *see* Eden
Austin, Adam, 300n133

Baillie, James, 168, 169
Baillie, William, 258

Baird, George Husband, 236, 245–6
Balfour, Sir Andrew, 325, 326
Balfour, James, Master of Burley or Burleigh, 222, 374n20
Balfour, Professor James, 262, 265, 302, 338, 342, 343, 344, 477
Balgony, Lord *see* Leslie, Earls of Leven
Balmanno, ___, Laird of, 429
Banks, Sir Joseph, 308, 347
Bannatyne, J., 36n55
Barclay, Harry of Colarnie, 235
Barclay, John, surgeon, 286
Barron, William, 479, 480, 481, 484, 493, 494, 501, 502, 504, 546
Barrow, Isaac, 482
Bartram or Bertram, ?William, 114n25
Bayne, Alexander, 264–5
Beaton, John, 337
Beaton or Bethune, William, 380, 391, 392
Beattie, James, poet, 345, 348, 477, 478, 531
Belhaven, Master of *see* Hamilton
Bell, Benjamin, 286
Bell, Charles, 287
Bell, John, 287
Bentinck, William Henry Cavendish, 3rd Duke of Portland, 195–6
Betham, Richard, 125
Bethune *see* Beaton
Bevis, John, 135
Black, Joseph, 10, 132–4, 138, 140, 157, 159–60, 163, 184, 201, 278, 296, 300, 302, 305, 348, 481, 499, 501, 532, 546
Black, Thomas, 408, 410, 412–13
Black, Professor William, 28n14
Black, William, tutor, 50
Blackwell, Thomas, I, 58, 60
Blackwell, Thomas, II, 253
Blair, David, 36n55, 374n20
Blair, Hugh, 10, 236, 258, 278, 344, 349, 350, 483, 594

Blair, James Hunter, 238, 334, 345
Blair, Patrick, surgeon, 445
Blair, Robert of St Andrews, 380
Blair, Professor Robert, 334
Blair, Robert, SCJ, 287
Blantyre, Lords of see Stuart
Bogle, George of Daldowie, 99, 111, 114
Bolingbroke, Viscount see St John
Bonnet, Charles, 546
Boston, Thomas, 492
Boswell, Alexander, 257, 264
Boswell, James, 264, 373
Bower, Thomas, 393
Boyd, John, 28, 35
Boyd, William, 4th Earl of Kilmarnock,
    115
Boyle, David of Kelbourne, 1st Earl of
    Glasgow, 29, 85, 288n74
Boyle, John, 3rd Earl of Glasgow, 130,
    474
Boyle, Patrick of Shewalton, SCJ, 137, 138
Boyle, Hon. Robert, 337, 377, 545
Bradley, James, 134
Breadalbane, Earl of see Campbell
Bridges see Brydges
Briggs, ? Dr or Mr___, 512
Brisbane, Thomas, 68, 72, 86, 89, 94, 95,
    100, 281, 290
Brown, Andrew, 350, 483
Brown, David, 50
Brown, Rev. James, 52
Brown, Professor James, 190–2, 194, 199,
    200, 329, 375, 499, 500, 501
Brown, John, 52
Brown, Thomas, 308n186
Brown, William, 467–9, 473, 479, 484, 493,
    494, 495, 524
Brown, William Laurence, 494, 495, 497,
    510
Bruce, John, 339, 542
Bruce, Robert, 262
Bryce, Alexander, 327
Brydges, John 1st Duke of Chandos, 93,
    372, 417, 419, 420, 426, 427, 431
Brydone or Bryden, Patrick, 183
Brydone, Robert, 182, 183
Buccleuch, Dukes of see Scott
Buchan, William, 303, 348
Buchan, Earls of see Erskine
Buchanan, James, 134, 136, 137, 138, 139,
    140, 153
Buerd, M., 442; see also French teachers at
    St Andrews
Burke, Edmund, 198
Burleigh or Burley see Balfour
Burman, Pieter, 256
Burnet, James, Lord Monboddo,192, 478
Burnet, Sir Thomas, 374n20
Burnet, Regent Thomas, 214n2, 216n11,
    218, 222
Bute, 3rd Earl see Stuart
Buxtorf, Johann, I, 492

Calderwood, Sir William of Polton, 57
Campbell, ___ ?, candidate for St Andrews
    professorship, 506
Campbell of Boquhan, 125
Campbell, of Shawfield, 84
Campbell of Succoth, 94
Campbell, Archibald, Marquis and 8th Earl
    of Argyll, 33
Campbell, Archibald, 9th Earl of Argyll, 407
Campbell, Archibald 10th Earl of Argyll and
    1st Duke of Argyll, 225
Campbell, Archibald, Earl of Ilay and 3rd
    Duke, of Argyll
  Biographical, 5n7, 7n11, 8, 48, 73, 87,
    115, 121, 124, 128–9, 131, 140, 237,
    240–2, 281, 293–4, 298n124,
    327n15, 349, 534, 536, 546
  Importance as a patron, 10–11, 140–1,
    351, 353, 534, 535, 540
  Interests in mathematics and science,
    9–10, 86–7, 121–4, 132–8, 140, 277,
    295, 320, 327, 538
  Politician and Argathelian Leader, 7–8, 10
    n19, 44–8, 60, 61, 67, 73, 87–107,
    115, 120–1, 128, 131n106, 179,
    212–13, 283, 293, 341, 428, 461,
    469, 471, 523, 524, 533
  Politically active at the Aberdeen
    universities, 369, 534; at Edinburgh
    and its University, General, 534–5
  1705–1716, 213, 233, 281
  1717–1721, 212–13, 276, 283
  1722–1742, 234, 235, 240, 245, 261,
    263, 265, 275, 289, 293–5, 327, 335
  1742–1747, 303, 327
  1747–1761, 238, 258, 278, 299, 301,
    344; at Glasgow and its University
    General, 534
  1705–1716, 60, 61
  1717–1721, 66–8
  1722–1742, 69–70, 70n123, 84–7, 89,
    90–9 passim, 126–7, 132–5, 293
  1742–1747, 107–8, 112, 115, 116–19,
    121
  1747–1761, 120–2, 123–5, 128–9,
    138–40, 152, 154, 155; Active at St
    Andrews University, General, 452,
    484, 534
  1705–1716, 417
  1717–1721
  1722–1742, 419–20, 421, 423, 424,
    427–8, 429, 431
  1742–1747
  1747–1761, 465, 468–9, 470, 507
  Reasons for appointments, 5, 133, 156,
    235, 245, 261, 296, 342, 344, 538–9
Campbell, Archibald of Stonefield, 465
Campbell, Archibald of Inveraray, 234
Campbell, Professor Archibald, 427–8, 431,
    446, 447, 462, 480, 483, 513, 528, 529
Campbell, Colin of Blytheswood, 183
Campbell, Daniel of Shawfield, 61, 84

Campbell, Lord Frederick, 163, 166, 182, 474, 476, 493
Campbell, Sir George, 27n9
Campbell, Professor George, 10, 223, 237, 244
Campbell, George, mathematician, 93n48, 326
Campbell, Rev. George, 27, 66
Campbell, Principal George, 483, 510, 529–30
Campbell, Hugh, 3rd Earl of Loudoun, 260, 315n74, 384, 389, 392, 410
Campbell, Sir Ilay of Succoth, 186, 192, 199–200, 242, 258, 265, 496
Campbell, Sir James of Ardkinglass, I, 113, 130, 167
Campbell,? Sir James of Ardkinglass, II, 344
Campbell, John, 2nd Duke of Argyll, 7n11, 44–5, 60–1, 70, 90, 97, 98, 100, 118, 212, 234, 235, 281, 283, 326, 327, 340, 417, 429
Campbell, John, 3rd Earl of Breadalbane, 306
Campbell, John, 4th Earl of Loudoun, 159, 257–8, 306, 347
Campbell, John of Mamore, 4th Duke of Argyll, 69, 70, 94, 163, 245
Campbell, John, 5th Duke of Argyll, 166, 181, 493, 495
Campbell, John, Lord Provost of Edinburgh, 233, 256, 281, 284, 289, 298
Campbell, Col John of Blytheswood, 183
Campbell, John, 84, 234
Campbell, Dr John of Paisley, 95
Campbell, Kenneth, 337
Campbell, Lachlan, 53
Campbell, Principal Neil, 23, 90–1, 94, 95, 98, 99, 100, 108, 109, 110, 111, 116, 123, 125, 127, 130, 132, 138, 139, 150, 151, 593
Campbell, Pryse, 477
Campbell, Robert of Stockholm, 97
Campbell, Colonel William, 69–70, 94
Campbell, William, 63n78
Cappel, Louis, 492
Carburi, Comte de *see* Lascary, 306
Cardross, Barons of *see* Erskine
Carlyle, Alexander, 152, 156, 181–2, 258, 466, 468, 492, 505–5
Carmichael, Alexander, 69, 95
Carmichael, Frederick, 69n113, 96, 97, 422
Carmichael, Gerschom, 29, 34–5, 36, 35n45, 60, 62, 66, 69, 72, 88, 92, 93, 95, 381–2, 394, 395
Carmichael, James, 2nd Earl of Hyndford, 65, 65 n 91, 67n104
Carmichael, John, Lord Carmichael and 2nd Baron Carmichael and 1st Earl of Hyndford, 21, 27, 28–9, 33, 36, 35n45, 50, 55, 60, 218, 381, 382
Carmichael, John, 3rd Earl of Hyndford, 122, 124, 125, 133
Carniegie, John of Boysack, 57

Connell, Matthew, 95
Carrick, Robert, 120, 140
Carstares, Principal William
  General, 30, 231–3, 492, 533, 537, 542
  Active at Edinburgh, 232, 238, 239, 244, 255, 256, 263, 283, 288, 337, 351
  Active at Glasgow, 29, 30, 32, 33, 36, 49, 50, 54, 60, 70, 232
  Active at St Andrews, 376, 384, 389, 408, 409, 411, 412
Carteret, John, 1st Earl Granville, 7, 73
Cassillis, Earls of *see* Kennedy
Catanach, James, 116
Cathcart, Barons of *see* Shaw
Chalmers, George, 412
Chalmers, John, 118
Chalmers, Lionel, 482
Chalmers, Thomas, 329, 331, 333, 376, 475, 505
Chandos, 1st Duke of *see* Brydges
Charteris, Francis, 474
Charters, Samuel, 157
Chesterfield, Earl of *see* Stanhope
Christison, Alexander, 97
Clarke, Alexander, 97
Clason, Patrick, 161–2, 167, 170n49
Clason, Robert, 161–2, 164, 165, 167
Cleghorn, Hugh, 474, 477, 481, 484, 493, 502–3, 542
Cleghorn, Robert, 184–5, 187, 188, 190, 532
Cleghorn, William, 302, 340, 341, 342
Clelland, Thomas, 125–6n88
Clelland, William, 125–6
Clerk, David, MD, 132n109
Clerk, Baron Sir John of Penicuik, 53, 253, 265, 276, 277
Clerk, Dr John, 108, 132n4
Clow, James, 127–8, 129, 136, 139, 166, 167, 168
Clow, Patrick, 383, 416n45
Cochrane, Archibald, 9th Earl of Dundonald, 183
Cochrane, William, Lord, 34
Cochrane, Andrew, 117, 118
Cochrane, Charles, 65n91, 67n104
Cockburn, Adam, 65n91, 67n104, 276, 293, 295, 116n45
Connell, Matthew, 95–6
Cook, John, I, 475, 478, 493, 501, 504, 505, 506, 512
Cook, John, II, 505, 506
Copland, Patrick, 532, 546
Couper, James, 200–1
Coutts, James, 278, 305
Coutts, John, 340
Coventry, Andrew, 309n186
Craig, James, 57, 263
Craig, Sir Thomas, 263
Craig, Rev. William, 110
Craig, William, SCJ, 502
Craigie John, 380–1, 388, 452
Craigie, Lawrence, 380, 424, 461

Craigie, Robert, 114, 119, 327, 424, 430
Craigie, Thomas, 119, 124, 127, 327, 380, 429–30, 484
Crawford, Earls of *see* Lindsay
Crawford, James, 58
Crawford, Lady, 214
Crawford, Matthew, 240, 244
Creech, William, 501
Crombie, James, 153
Cross, William, 116–18, 119, 531
Cullen, Henry, 308
Cullen, William
  Active at Glasgow, 10, 116, 119–20, 121, 122, 126, 127, 130, 132–3, 140, 154, 157, 171, 201
  At Edinburgh, 278, 296, 300, 301, 303, 304, 305, 308, 348, 481
  At St Andrews, 475
Cumberland, HRH, William Augustus Guelf, 1st Duke of, 118, 179, 372, 430, 453, 467, 525
Cuming, John, 239
Cuming, Patrick, I, 36n55
Cuming (or Cumming), Patrick, II, 119, 152, 235, 236, 327, 341, 344, 523
Cuming, Patrick III, 152, 153, 163, 166, 191, 193, 236, 240–2
Cuming, Robert, 152, 236, 242
Cunningham of Livingston, 479
Cunningham, Regent Alexander, 214, 217, 219, 221, 222, 223, 255
Cunningham, Alexander of Blok or Block, 214n6
Cunningham, Gabriel, 27
Cunningham, Gilbert, 381
Cunningham, William of Craigends, 27

D'Arcy, Robert, 4th Earl of Holderness, 467
Dalgleish, Robert, 114n25
Dalgleish William, 425
Dalrymple, Sir David of Hailes, 56, 65n91, 416n45
Dalrymple, Sir David, SCJ, 307, 345
Dalrymple, David of Westerhall, 116
Dalrymple Hugh of Drommore, SCJ, 67
Dalrymple, Hew or Hugh, 116
Dalrymple, James, 1st Viscount of Stair, 27, 224
Dalrymple, John, 1st Earl of Stair, 218n20, 223, 224
Dalrymple, John, Lord Provost of Edinburgh, 345
Dalzel, Andrew, 336
Dartmouth, Earl of *see* Legge
Davidson, Archibald, 183, 188, 191, 195–7, 184n13
Davidson, John, 183
Davidson, John, WS, 287
Davidson, Robert, 198–9, 531
Dawson, William, 245
Defoe, Daniel, 335n52, 449

Dempster, George, 331, 368, 369, 471, 472, 497
Dick, James, 62n74, 71–2
Dick, Richard, 472
Dick, Rev. Robert, 114, 126–7
Dick, Robert, I, 59, 64, 66, 72, 86, 92, 95, 97, 99, 110, 111, 117, 122, 123, 135, 140, 395, 532, 593
Dick, Robert, II, 123, 124, 127, 134, 135, 140, 532
Dick, Professor Robert, 264
Douglas, Dr ?Robert of Kinglassie, 416n 45
Douglas, Dukes of Douglas and Dukes of Queensberry *see* Douglas
Douglas, Sir Alexander MD, 472
Douglas, Alexander, 222
Douglas, Archibald James Stewart, 1st Baron Douglas, 162
Douglas, Charles, 3rd Duke of Queensberry, 157, 166, 178, 166, 178, 253, 260
Douglas, Dunbar, 4th Earl of Selkirk, 115
Douglas, James, 2nd Duke of Queensberry, 29, 44
Douglas, 12th Earl of Morton, 374n20
Douglas, James, 14th Earl of Morton, 277, 327, 328, 465
Dowdeswell, William, 466
Drew, Joseph, 60, 384, 388, 389, 391, 392, 394, 410, 416, 431, 492
Drummond, ? Adam, of Megginch, 374n20
Drummond, Adam, 280, 283, 284, 338
Drummond, Alexander Monro, 303
Drummond, Colin, 256, 335, 338
Drummond, George, 18th-century Lord Provost of Edinburgh, 235, 240, 244, 282, 284, 285, 292, 296, 297, 298n122, 302, 303, 305, 343–4, 426, 479
Drummond, James of Blair Drummond, 302
Drummond, John, 1st Earl of Melfort, 215n11
Drummond, John of Megginch, 416n45
Drummond, John, 222
Drysdale, John, 163
Duff, Patrick of Premnay, 523
Dunbar, George, 336
Duncan, Captain Alexander, 495
Duncan, Alexander of Lundie, 416n45
Duncan, Andrew, 303–4, 475
Duncan, James, 383, 422, 452
Dundas, Henry, 1st Viscount Melville
  Biographical, 178–81, 181, 182, 198, 329–30, 339, 509, 510–12, 536
  Politician and patron, 4, 6, 8, 11, 171–2, 180–1, 198, 308, 333, 334, 484, 494, 511, 523, 536, 539–40
  Politically active at Edinburgh
    Before 1780, 286, 307, 478
    1780–1790, 213, 242, 262n54, 279, 287, 334
    1791–1806, 236, 242, 243, 246, 262, 264, 279, 285, 287, 299, 301, 302, 328, 330, 336, 339, 346, 350

Glasgow and its university
  1780–1790, 181–2, 183, 187
  1791–1806, 188, 190–2, 194–6, 197, 198, 201
  Active at St Andrews
  General, 369, 372, 459
  Before 1780, 478, 479
  1780–1790, 491–513 *passim*
  1791–1806, 495–8, 500, 502, 504, 505, 506
  Results of his patronage, 198, 262, 351, 372, 511, 541, 453, 502, 512, 513, 534, 535, 536, 540–1
Dundas, Sir Laurence, 179, 238, 258, 262, 286, 304, 307, 328, 347, 491
Dundas, Laurence, humanist, 223, 225, 252–3, 255
Dundas, Robert of Arniston, 2nd Viscount of Melville, 180, 497
Dundas, Robert, SCJ, d. 1726, 416n45
Dundas, Robert, SCJ, d. 1753, 65n91, 67n104, 111, 116, 117
Dundas, Robert, Lord Advocate and Lord Chief Baron, 180, 188, 191, 199, 243, 262, 266, 286, 287, 301, 362, 496, 497, 504, 505, 511–13
Dundas, Thomas, 263
Dundee, Earls of *see* Scrymgeour
Dundonald, Earls of *see* Cochrane
Dunlop, ___, the informer,188
Dunlop, Alexander, I, 50, 56, 57, 64, 65, 66, 70, 71, 72, 85, 87, 88, 90–100, 109–13, 115, 593
Dunlop, Alexander, II, 113–14
Dunlop, Francis, 97, 98
Dunlop, Principal, William, 29–30, 32, 33, 232, 256, 395, 542; *see also* virtuosi
Dunlop, William, professor at Edinburgh, 65, 239, 415, 529
Dunmore, Earls of *see* Murray

Eaton, ___, Goldsmith and Keeper of the Blue Blanket, 294
Ebenezer, MacFait, 348
Eden, William, 1st Lord Auckland, 180, 369
Edmonstoune, Colonel James, 169n68
Eglinton, Earls of *see* Montgomery
Eglinton, Lady Eglinton, 240
Elder, Thomas, 236, 246
Elliot, Sir Gilbert, 1st Earl of Minto, 166
Elliot, Sir Gilbert of Minto, MP,150, 152, 161, 162, 167, 236, 259, 343
Sir Gilbert Elliot of Minto, SCJ, 254, 342
Elliot, Robert, 279–80
Ellis, John, 546
Erroll, Earls of *see* Hay
Erskine, ___, 280
Erskine, Colonel ___, 419
Erskine, Sir Charles of Alva, 386
Erskine [Arskine or Ærskine] Charles, SCJ, 84, 88, 92, 240, 260–1, 335, 337, 386, 424, 426, 451, 542

Erskine, David, SCJ, 384, 537
Erskine, David 11th Earl of Buchan, 136, 185, 306, 307, 308, 503
Erskine, Ebenezer, 235
Erskine, of George of Balgowny, 280
Erskine, Henry, 10th Earl of Buchan, 216
Erskine, Henry, 3rd Baron Cardross, 27n9, 30
Erskine, Henry, 4th Baron Cardross, 222
Erskine, Henry, Advocate, 308, 333
Erskine, James, Lord Grange, SCJ, 8n15, 84, 92, 99, 276, 280, 292, 326, 409, 411, 412
Erskine, ?James of Alva, SCJ, 116n36
Erskine, John, 11th Earl of Mar
  General, 6, 9, 7n14, 47, 533, 536
  Politically active at Glasgow, 49, 52, 58, 60
  Active at Edinburgh, 216, 237, 255, 260, 280, 326, 337
  Active at St Andrews, 384, 389, 390, 391, 392, 393, 409, 410, 411, 412, 414, 494
Erskine, Professor John, 265, 547
Erskine, ?John, student, 136
Erskine Robert, 386
Erskine, Thomas, 308
Euler, Leonard, 349

Fagon, Guy Crescent, 326n5, 445
Falconer, Anthony Adrian, 5th Earl of Kintore, 199
Falconer, David, 215n9
Falkener, Sir Everard, 467
Fall, Principal James, 28
Fenton, James, 391
Ferdinand IV, King of Naples, 303
Ferguson, Rev. Adam, 416n45
Ferguson, Adam, 10, 139, 164, 182, 242, 261, 262, 328, 342–5, 347, 349, 368, 470, 528, 533
Fergusson, Sir Adam, 153, 186
Ferguson, Harry or Henry, 215, 217n19
Fergusson, James, SCJ *see* Pitfour
Fergusson, Robert, poet, 481
Fettes, Sir William, 331, 336
Findlay, Robert, 166, 170, 181–3, 191, 510, 529
Finlayson, James, 243, 330, 339
Fitzroy, Lt Gen. Charles, 1st Baron Southampton, 170
Fleming, Alexander, 242
Fletcher, Andrew of Saltoun, Lord Milton; *see also* Archibald Campbell, 3rd Duke of Argyll and Argathelians
  General, 8, 10n18, 150, 471, 523, 533
  Active at Edinburgh, 234, 235, 236, 242, 245, 254, 258, 261, 264, 265, 278, 292, 301, 304–5, 338, 342, 343–4, 349
  Active at Glasgow, 84, 87, 88, 92, 97, 98, 100, 116, 121, 125, 126–7, 128, 130, 131, 137, 138, 139, 150, 152
  Active at St Andrews, 424, 468, 470

Fletcher, Andrew, MP, 128, 152, 470
Fletcher, John, 127
Flint, James, 476, 493, 494, 500, 506–7
Flint, John, 500, 501, 506
Forbes, Duncan of Culloden, 67, 84, 88,
    116, 117, 118, 261, 284
Forbes, John of Culloden, 337
Forbes, Thomas, 92
Forbes, Sir William, Banker, 345, 347, 349
Forbes, William, 57, 59, 62, 64, 65, 66, 72,
    88, 92, 100, 101n7, 109, 110, 111,
    116, 290, 336, 531
Forrest, George, 474, 477
Forrester, William, 4th Baron Forrester, 382
Forrester, Henry, 413
Forrester, Hon. Margaret, 382
Forrester, Thomas, I, 382, 383, 430
Forrester, Principal Thomas, II, 382, 387,
    394, 407, 415, 430
Foulis, Sir James, 254
Foulis, Sir John of Ravelstone, SCJ, 223
Foulis, Sir John of Colinton, 225
Fox, Charles James, 190
Franklin, Benjamin, 373,420, 482
Fraser, Sir James of Brea, 35, 381
Fraser, Alexander, 9th Baron Salton of
    Abernethy, 216
Fraser, Sir William, 266
Freer, Robert, 187–9, 195

Garden, James, 527
Garlies, Lord see Stewart
Garrick, David, 468
Gartshorne, James, 504
George I, 47, 48, 89
George III, 155, 345
George, HRH, Prince of Wales, 190n45
Gibson, Sir Alexander, 218
Gibson, Edmund, Bishop of London, 427
Gibson, Joseph, 298–9
Gibson, Thomas, 299
Gilchrist, James, 191n49
Gillespie, James, 479, 482–3, 493, 496
Gillis, John, 168
Gillis, 36n55
Gillon, Robert, 124, 125
Glasgow, Earls of see Boyle
Glassford, Henry of Dugalston, 162, 185
Glassford, John, 191n49
Glen, William, 506
Goodal, John, 244
Gordon, Alexander, 4th Duke of Gordon,
    180
Gordon, Alexander, 266
Gordon, George, 1st Duke of Gordon,
    216n11
Gordon, George, 3rd Earl of Aberdeen,
    161
Gordon, Cosmo George, 3rd Duke of
    Gordon, 1739, 420
Gordon, Charles Hamilton, 116, 118
Gordon, John, surgeon, 58, 73

Gordon, John of Buthlaw, 257, 259, 265
Gordon, Thomas, 28n13
Gowdie, John, 235, 236, 240, 478
Graeme or Graham, William, 291–3, 296,
    297–8
Graham, James,1st Duke of Montrose
    Biographical, 536, 547
    Politician, 10, 15n11, 44, 47–8, 49, 128,
        523
    Politically active at Edinburgh, 239, 263,
        288, 292, 298
        At Glasgow, 1708–21, 21–2, 47, 49, 53,
            56, 63–5, 68; 1722–42, 59, 60, 63,
            64, 65, 67, 68–71, 88–9, 90, 93, 94,
            99; Role in Visitations, 65–8, 65n91,
            85–6
        At St Andrews, 417, 422, 423, 416n45
Graham, James, 3rd Duke of Montrose
    Politician, 183, 192, 201
    Montrose and the French Revolution, 171,
        181, 186, 187, 188–93, 195–8,
        199–200
Graham, John of Douglaston, I, 65, 99,
    107
Graham, John of Dougalston, II, 299
Graham, Mungo of Gorthy, 63, 65n91,
    67n104, 68, 71, 100, 107, 111, 112,
    523
Graham, William, 2nd Duke of Montrose
    Politician, 10, 15n11, 44, 128
    Active at Glasgow, 1742–22, 107, 109,
        114, 116, 123, 127, 179
Grange, Lord see James Erskine
Grant, Gregory, 303
Grant, Sir Francis of Cullen, SCJ, 416n45
Grant, Sir James, 265, 480
Grant, Patrick, SCJ, 84
Granville, 1st Earl see Carteret
Gray, James, 65n91
Gray or Grey, John, 65n91
Greenfield, William, 349, 350, 501–2
Gregory, Charles, 389, 390, 392, 393, 394,
    420, 442, 444, 591
Gregorie or Gregory, David of Kinnairdie, I,
    222
Gregorie or Gregory, Professor David, II,
    213–25 passim, 255, 325, 378, 389,
    392, 446, 469
Gregory, Professor David at St Andrews,
    420, 451, 462, 463, 465, 466, 473,
    481–2
Gregory, James, I, 325–6, 391, 442, 443,
    447
Gregory, James, II, 222, 325, 389, 391, 392,
    393, 442, 445, 446
[Gregory, James, III, professor at Aberdeen]
Gregory, James, IV, 303–4, 305, 502
Gregory, John, 305, 345, 476
Grenville, Richard, Earl Temple, 179
Grieve, Henry, 169–70, 181–2, 183, 332,
    345, 346
Gusthart (or Gusthard), ?William, 91

Hacket or Halket, Sir Peter, 416n45
Haddington, Earls of in 1695 *see* Hamilton
Haddo, Lord *see* Gordon
Hadow, George, 460, 461, 462, 463, 465
Hadow, James, 53, 65n91, 67n104, 392, 407–8, 409, 411, 412, 413, 419, 420, 423, 424, 453, 460, 483
Hadow, James, II, 461
Haldane, James, 382–3, 394, 411, 422, 424
Haldane, John, 382, 416n45
Haldane, Mungo, 422, 416n45
Haldane, Patrick, 50, 382–3, 392, 395, 409, 410–11, 416n45, 422, 542
Haldane, Robert, 507
Halket, James, 223n32, 282
Hall, Sir John of Dunglass, 215, 218n20, 326
Halyburton, Thomas, 380, 381, 408, 412, 483, 509
Hamilton, Master of Belhaven, 59
Hamilton, Alexander, 299
Hamilton, Anne, 3rd Duchess of Hamilton, 276, 377
Hamilton, Gavin, 111, 108ns5 and 6, 238, 302, 341, 342, 348
Hamilton, George, 193, 383
Hamilton, James, 4th Duke, 27, 34, 35, 44, 381
Hamilton, James, 5th Duke of Hamilton, 119, 60n64
Hamilton, the Hon. James, 257
Hamilton, James of Presmennan, SCJ, 57
Hamilton, James of Aikenhead, 65n91, 88
Hamilton, James of Pencaitland, 57, 63, 67n104
Hamilton, Rev. James, 67
Hamilton, Professor James, 299
Hamilton, Rev. John, 65n91
Hamilton, Robert, Professor at Edinburgh, 238, 338, 477
Hamilton, Robert, SCJ, 218, 218n20, 262
Hamilton, Robert, Professor at Glasgow, 107, 108, 110, 111, 120, 127, 130, 132–4, 201, 328
Hamilton, Robert, Professor at Marischal College, 348, 532
Hamilton, Thomas, 6th Earl of Haddington, 35, 337, 380, 385, 416n45
Hamilton, Thomas, 218
Hamilton, Thomas, Professor at Glasgow, 132–4, 138, 139, 166, 170, 201
Hamilton, Walter, 307
Hamilton, Sir William, 216, 218n20
Hamilton, William of Whitelaw, 228
Hamilton, Principal William, 65n91, 67n104, 91, 233–4, 235, 237–8, 240, 244, 335, 410, 416n45, 528
Hamilton, William Professor at Glasgow, 134, 184, 186, 187, 201
Hamilton, William, II, 170, 171
Hamilton-Douglas, 6th Duke of Hamilton, 133, 155

Hardy, Thomas, 242, 258
Harley Robert, 1st Earl of Oxford, 45, 46, 60, 413
Hart, Rev. James, 91
Harvey (or Hervey), Thomas, 73, 86, 95
Hastings, Francis Rawdon, 2nd Earl of Moira, 331
Hatchett, Charles, 308
Hay, Charles, 3rd Marquis, Tweeddale, 239
Hay, Charles, 13th Earl of Erroll, 393
Hay, Lord George, 110, 111
Hay, James, 15th Earl of Erroll, 115, 153, 155
Hay, John 4th Marquis of Tweeddale, 10, 8ns11and 15, 44, 107, 108, 109, 110, 111, 112, 114, 115, 116, 118, 131, 256, 263, 453, 524, 547
Hay, Peter of Naughton, 376n30
Hay, Robert of Naughton, 416n45
Hay, Thomas 8th Earl of Kinnoull, 180, 345, 372, 473,476, 477, 478, 480, 492, 536
Hay Thomas, SCJ, 110
Hay, William, 337
Hay, ?William, MD, 417, 418
Hay Drummond, Hon. Robert, Archbishop of York, 345
Headrick, Rev. James, 189–92
Henry, James, 416n45
Hepburn, Henry, 295
Herman, Paulus, 275
Hill, George, 169, 475, 476, 478, 480, 483, 484, 493, 496, 502, 504, 505, 506, 508–10, 512
Hill, Henry David, 493, 494, 501, 506
Hill, John, 163, 254, 484, 501, 505
Hodges, James, 50n11, 54
Hog, James, 412
Hog, Thomas, 380
Holderness, Earl of *see* D'Arcy
Home, Alexander, 9th Earl of, 192
Home, Alexander 10th Earl of Home, 502
Home or Hume, David, Lord Crossrig, 221, 218n20
Home, Francis, 278–9, 301, 304, 532
Home, Henry, Lord Kames, 121, 155, 157, 258, 264, 278, 301, 302, 303, 304, 307, 348, 466, 469, 479
Home, James, 279
Home, John, 137, 242, 278, 342, 349, 395, 469, 533
Hope or Hope-Weir, Hon. Charles, 110, 186, 187
Hope, Charles, Lord Advocate, 199, 332, 507
Hope, James, 3rd Earl of Hopetoun, 242, 243, 307
Hope, John, 2nd Earl of Hopetoun, 110, 125, 139, 155, 157, 168, 343, 479
Hope John, 10, 184, 277–9, 546
Hope, John of Fife, 504
Hope, Thomas Charles, 184, 301, 302, 499, 501, 532
Hope, Sir William of Balcomie, 416n45
Hopetoun, Earls of *see* Hope

Horsburgh, Rev. Robert, 65n91, 67n104
Houston ___ of Clerkington, 110
Howard, Henry, 12th Earl of Suffolk, 307, 479
Hume, Sir Andrew of Kimmerghame, 57, 416n35
Hume, David, 113, 128–9, 153, 162, 163, 168, 169, 235, 242, 261, 326, 328, 330, 332–3, 340–1, 342, 343, 368, 481, 503, 528, 548
Hume, Professor David, 266, 547
Hume, Hugh, 3rd Earl of Marchmont, 278, 326
Hume, Sir Patrick, 1st Earl of Marchmont, 44, 218n20
Hunter, Andrew, 238
Hunter, James, 190
Hunter, Professor James, 498, 500, 507, 513
Hunter Blair, James, 238, 345
Hunter, Professor John, 190, 330, 478, 480, 492, 493, 495, 500, 502, 504, 506, 511, 513, 532
Hunter, Surgeon-General John, 169, 286, 287
Hunter, Robert, 336
Hunter, William, 169, 286, 301, 303
Hutcheson, Francis, 10, 66, 96–7, 100, 109, 110, 111, 112, 116, 119, 194, 201, 339, 447, 528, 544
Hutchison, ___, 191
Hutton, Charles, 500, 506
Hutton, James, 546
Hyndford, Earls of see Carmichael

Ilay, Earl of see Archibald Campbell
Inglis, Sir John, 107, 276, 381
Innes, Alexander, 425
Innes, Alexander, plagiarist, 427
Innes, Gilbert, 242
Innes, John, 290, 292, 300
Irvine, William, 159, 160, 532
Irving, Alexander, 264
Ivory, Sir James, 475

Jackson, Thomas, 194–7, 329, 506
Jeffrey or Jeffray, Francis, 198
Jeffrey, James, 187, 188, 191, 195, 309n186
Jameson, Robert, 308–9
Jameson, William 31, 32, 52, 60, 71, 72, 395, 529
Jamieson, Edward, 218n20, 376n30
Jardine, John, 235, 240, 261, 343
Jardine, George, 161, 162, 163, 164–7, 168, 169, 184, 188, 190–1, 193, 195, 197, 198, 199
Johnson or Johnston, ___, 427
Johnston, Thomas, 338
Johnstoun or Johnston, Gabriel, 422–3, 484
Johnstoun, John, 58, 59, 62, 64, 66, 72, 73, 92, 95, 97, 100, 101n7, 109, 110, 111, 120, 121, 289, 290

Kames, Lord see Henry Home
Keill or Kyle, James, 216, 442
Keir, ___, Deacon in Edinburgh, 294
Keith, Alexander of Ravelston, 348
Kemp, James, 419, 426, 452
Kennedy, Archibald, 12th Earl of Cassillis, 194
Kennedy, David, 10th Earl of Cassillis, 265, 493
Kennedy, Rev. Hew, 218n20
Kennedy, Regent Hew, Hugh or Hubert, 214n6, 217, 218, 219, 221, 222, 223, 255
Kennedy, John, 7th Earl of Cassillis, 35, 377, 378, 374n20, 406
Kennedy, John, 8th Earl of Cassillis, 465, 466
Kennedy, Sir Thomas, 9th Earl of Cassillis, 67, 471, 472, 477
Kennedy, Sir Thomas, Lord Provost of Edinburgh, 216, 222
Ker, ?Robert of Morriston, 55
Ker, John, 1st Duke of Roxburgh, 7n11, 48, 73, 293, 422
Ker, Professor John, 253–4
Kerr, Robert, 4th Earl and 1st Marquis of Lothian, 91, 218n20, 222
Kerr, William, 2nd Marquis of Lothian, 91
Kilmarnock, Lords and Earls of see Boyd
King, Peter, 427
Kinloch, Magdalen, 97
Kinnoull, Earls of see Hay
Kintore, Earl of see Falconer
Kirkpatrick, Sir Thomas, 136
Kirkpatrick, William, 261
Kirkton, Mr ___, 218
Knibloe, James, 29, 31, 32, 34

Lagrandierre, Fr Pierre, 498
LaGrange, M., 185
Lascary, J. B., Comte de Carburi, 306
Lauderdale, Earls of see Maitland
Laurie, George of New Milne [Loudoun, Ayrshire], 496
Law, Rev. J., 218n20
Law, John of Ballarnock, 31, 36, 218, 225, 226
Law, Robert, 336
Law, William, I, 223, 255, 336, 338, 339
Law, William, II, 336
Learmont, Robert, 376n30
Leechman, Principal William, 23,109–13, 124, 125, 127, 130, 133, 136, 139, 151, 152, 155, 156, 162, 164, 165, 166, 169, 182, 183, 201, 342, 477, 528, 544
Lees, John, 338
Legge, William, 2nd Earl of Dartmouth, 345
Leighton, Bishop Robert, 377
Leslie, David Melville, Lord Balgonie, 3rd Earl of Leven and 2nd Earl of Melville, 218, 374n20, 378, 390
Leslie, David, Lord Melville and 8th Earl of Leven, 479

Leslie, James, 197–8
Leslie, John 8th Earl Rothes, 35, 65, 256, 384, 385, 410, 416, 421, 422, 435
Leslie, John 9th Earl of Rothes, 383, 420
Leslie, John [later Sir John], 190–2, 329–33, 349, 475, 499, 500–1, 505
Leslie, John of King's College, 465
Leslie, Lady Mary, 472
Leslie, Thomas, 471, 472
Leuchars, Laird of *see* ? Lindsay of Balcarres, 27
Leven and Melville, Earls of *see* Melville
Lind, Alexander of Gorgie, 347
Lind, George, 344
Lind, James, Physician to George III, 303, 347
Lindsay, Alexander, 6th Earl, 495, 496
Lindsay, Dr ___, brother to Lindsay of Wormiston, 389, 390
Lindsay,___ of Balcarres, 420
Lindsay, Hercules, 111, 118, 119, 123, 127, 154, 531
Lindsay, Patrick, 235, 245, 253, 340
Lindsay, William, 18th Earl of Crawford Liston, 27n7, 215, 218n28, 220, 378
Linnaeus, Carolus, 374n20, 501, 546
Liston, Sir Robert, 161–2, 164, 167, 245
Littlejohn, Alexander, 191n49
Lockhart, James, 65n91, 67n104
Lockhart,George of Carnwath, 7n14
Logan, Allan, 419
Logan, George, 431
Logan, John, 258n34
Lothian, Marquis of *see* Kerr
Loudoun, Earls of *see* Campbell
Loudoun, John, 35, 40n45, 60, 66, 69, 85, 88, 92, 95, 100, 109, 111, 113, 114, 380, 385, 386, 395
Lumsden, John, 525n8
Lyon, Patrick, 1st Earl of Strathmore, 376, 381
Lyttleton, George, 1st Baron, Lyttleton, 345

Macclesfield, Earl of *see* Parker
M'Cormick, Joseph, 182, 492, 493, 495, 496, 500, 501, 502, 511
McDonald, James, 505–6
Macdowall, William of Garthland, 191, 192
MacFait, Ebenezer, 348
MacGill, Alexander, 281
McGill, James, 374n20
MacGill, John, 280, 281, 283, 284, 294
MacGill, Stevenson, 503
M'Ilham or McIlquham *see* Meikleham
Mackay, Dr___, 506
Mackenzie, George, 1st Viscount Tarbat, 215, 216, 218, 222, 224, 326, 378n40
Mackenzie, Henry, 178
Mackenzie, John of Delvine, 416
Mackenzie, Kenneth, 263
Mackie, Charles, 256–7, 328, 426

McKillop, Alexander, 191n49
McKillop, John, 191n49
MackIntosh, later Sir James, 346
Mackintosh or Macintosh, George, 185
Macknight, James, 242
MacKnight, Thomas, 329, 330, 331
Macky, John, 449
Maclaurin, Colin, 100, 110, 112, 211n1, 277, 326, 327, 426, 444, 532, 545, 546, 593
Maclaurin, Rev. John, 73, 100, 108–12
McLean, Hector, 107, 142n3
MacLeod, Hugh, 170, 191, 192, 197
Maconochie, Allan, 262, 336
MacQueen, Daniel, 236, 242, 344
MacTurk, William, 192–3, 197
MacVicar, Neil, 245, 342
Maitland,Charles, 6th Earl of, Lauderdale, 67n104
Maitland, James 7th Earl of Lauderdale, 9, 180, 469, 473
Maitland, James, 8th Earl of Lauderdale, 336
Maitland, John 1st Duke of Lauderdale, 379
Malebranche, Nicholas, 407
Mallet or Malloch, David, 431n123
Mansfield, Earls of *see* Murray
Mar, Earl of *see* Erskine
Marchmont, Earls of *see* Home
Marck [Markius] Jan [Joannes], 53, 482
Marshall, John 50, 60, 73
Martin, James 1690, 216n11
Martine, Arthur, 121, 296
Martine, George of Claremont, 446
Martine, George, MD, 291–3, 295–6, 415
Maskelyne, Neville, 194, 506
Massie Andrew, 214n2, 215, 216, 218, 222, 223n33, 226n2, 255
Maule, Baron John, 125, 301
Maxwell, Sir John of Pollock, I, 27, 31, 33, 36, 49, 55, 57, 60n64, 62, 63, 65n91, 66, 92
Maxwell, Sir John of Blawerthill and Pollock, II, 65, 99, 122, 125, 127, 128, 523
Meek, James, 195n71
Meikleham, William [earlier M'Ilham or McIlquham], 189, 192, 194–7, 200
Meiklejohn, Hugh, 242–3
Meiklejohn, ___, 189
Meldrum, George, 27n9, 31n28, 32
Melville, Viscounts *see* Dundas
Melville, Lord *see* David Melville Leslie
Melville, Alexander, Lord Raith, 215n10, 218n20, 222, 223
Melville, George, Lord Melville and 1st Earl of Melville, 214, 215n10, 216, 223, 378
Melville, James, 374n20
Melvil, or Melvill, Melville, Thomas, 125, 129, 545
Menzies, Alexander of Culdares, 508
Menzies, John, 375n25

Menzies, Robert, 472, 475
Menzies, William, Edinburgh rabble rouser, 215
Middleton, Brig. John of Seton, 245, 523
Millar, James, 185, 191, 193
Millar, Rev. John, 66–7
Millar, John, 10, 123, 154, 156, 157, 166, 170, 181, 185, 189, 190–1, 193, 201, 259, 262, 477, 531
Millar, Richard, 187, 190
Millar, Sir Thomas, SCJ, 125, 163, 344
Miller, Rev.William, 84, 85
Millar, William, 67, 94
Milton, Lord see Fletcher
Minto, Earls of see Elliot
Mitchell, Sir Andrew, 109, 110, 114
Mitchell, Rev. William,65, 67n104, 38, 416n45
Moira Earl of see Hastings
Molesworth, Robert, Baron Molesworth, 69n107
Monboddo see James Burnet
Moncrieff, ___ baillie, 222
Monro, Principal Alexander, 213, 214, 216–17, 220, 222
Monro, Provost Alexander, 379
Monro, Alexander I of Edinburgh, 277, 280, 281, 285, 290, 291
Monro, Alexander, II, 285, 286, 289
Monro, Alexander, III, 285–6
Monro, Donald, 285
Monro or Munro, Sir George, 218
Monro, Major George of Auchenbowie, 65n91, 67n104
Monro, Henry, 407
Monro or Monroe, John, regent, 223, 375, 379, 385
Monro, John, surgeon, 282, 284, 285, 290, 298
Montagu, John, 4th Earl of Sandwich, 474
Montgomerie, Sir Hugh of Hartfield, 65n91, 66, 67n104, 374n20
Montgomery, Alexander, 8th Earl of Eglinton, 31, 53
Montgomery, Alexander, 9th Earl of Eglinton, 53
Montgomery, Francis of Giffan, 65n91
Montgomery, George, MD, 120
Montgomery, Hugh, Lord Montgomery and 12th Earl of Eglinton, 199
Montgomery, James, 287, 334
Montgomery, Susanna, Lady Eglinton, 112, 240
Montrose, Dukes of see Graham
Monypenny, Col Alexander, 496
Moodie,William, 246
Moor, James, 115, 122, 138, 139, 140, 115n30, 164, 166, 167, 168
Moore, Dr John, 132
Morthland, Charles, 37n62, 55–6, 57, 60, 64, 66, 72, 87, 88, 89, 92, 94, 100, 109, 110, 111, 113

Morton, Alexander, 464, 465, 466, 470, 471, 475, 477, 484
Morton, Earl of see Douglas
Morrison, William, 68
Muirhead, George, 123, 126–7, 129, 130, 138, 157, 160, 162, 340
Muirhead, Lockhart, 193, 201
Mullican, Mr ___ of St Andrews, 375n25
Muray, Sir Peter, 507
Mure, ___ of Glanderston, 29
Mure, William of Caldwell, 63, 64
Mure, Baron William of Caldwell, 99, 109, 122, 150, 151,153, 159, 161, 163, 164, 165, 166, 169, 278, 301, 305, 459, 476
Murison, James, 430, 461, 462, 464, 465
Murray, Alexander of Murrayfield, 265
Murray, Alexander of Cringletie, 240
Murray, Archibald, 240, 265
Murray, David, 6th Viscount Stormont and 2nd Earl of Mansfield, 180, 492, 495
Murray, Lord Edward, 416n45
Murray, Lord James, later 3rd Duke of Atholl, 416n45
Murray, John, Marquis of Tullibardine and 1st Duke of Atholl, 371–2, 379, 382, 384, 396, 419, 416n45
Murray, John 4th Earl of Dunmore, 161
Murray, William, 1st Earl of Mansfield, 345, 492
Murray, William, 4th Duke of Atholl, 236, 339
Mylne, James, 193–4

Nairne, Sir David, 255
Napier, Francis, 6th Baron, 111
Napier, Mr ___ of Buchquhnaple, 389
Duke of Newcastle see Pelham-Holles
Newington, Laird of, 374n20
Newton, Sir Isaac, 325, 327, 337, 442, 443, 545
North, Francis, 7th Baron North, 1st Earl of Guildford, 161, 171, 179, 182

Oglethorpe, Fanny, 7n14
Ogilvie, Sir James, 3rd Earl Seafield, 153
Ogilvie, Sir James, 4th Earl of Findlatter and 1st Earl of Seafield, 84, 216, 237, 280
Ogilvie, James, Lord Deskford, 50, 139, 153, 154, 156, 157, 391, 394, 470
Ogilvie, Sir Alexander of Forglen, 416n45
Oliphant, John, 27
Ormiston, Lord see Cockburn
Orr, John of Barrowfield, 98, 99, 95n66
Orr, Rev. John, 65n91, 67n104
Oswald, George of Auchincruive, 196
Oswald, Rev. James, 151, 156, 237
Oswald, Richard, Lord Methven, 199
Oughton, General Sir James Augustus, 345

Paisley, John, Surgeon, 73, 94, 96
Parker, George, 2nd Earl of Macclesfield, 134

Parma, Prince of, 162
Paterson, Archbishop James, 27
Paton, Dr ?___, 94
Payten or Paton, Rev., 197
Pelham, Henry, 118, 131
Pelham-Holles, Thomas, 1st Duke of
    Newcastle under Lyme, 66, 70, 90,
    133, 139, 238, 293–5, 372, 419, 420,
    426, 431, 473
Petiver or Petifer, James, 275, 445
Petrie, William, 419
Petty, William, 2nd Earl of Shelburne, 1st
    Marquis of Lansdowne, 179
Pictet, Benedict, 482
Pitcairn, Alexander, 376n30, 377, 378, 382,
    394, 406, 460
Pitcairne, Archibald, 58n62, 216n15, 218,
    220, 222, 223n32, 280, 282, 288, 326,
    389, 390, 393, 394, 415, 446, 533
? Pitfour or Petifer [probably James
    Fergusson, Lord Pitfour], 218n20
Pitmeddan, Lord see Seton
Pitt, William, the younger, 180
Playfair, James, 446
Playfair, James Principal, 505, 506, 511, 512
Playfair, John, 190, 200, 330, 349, 475, 477,
    506
Plummer, Andrew, 290, 292, 300, 301
Plunket, Leonard, 275
Pollock, Sir Robert, 65
Porteous, William, 242
Porterfield, William, 289–90, 295
Portland, Duke of see Bentinck
Potter, Michael, 98–100, 108
Preston, Charles, 275
Preston, George, 275, 291
Preston, James, 385, 386n77, 388, 441
Preston, Sir Robert, 275
Pringle, Andrew, 309, 347
Pringle, Francis, 253, 264, 340, 385, 386–8,
    389, 395, 416, 417, 431, 442, 446, 452
Pringle, John, PRS, 307, 309, 340–1, 508, 525
Pringle, John, advocate, 258, 259
Pringle, Sir Walter, 253, 416n45
Pulteney, Sir William Johnstone, 309, 342
Pursell, John Warrock, 189n35

Queensberry, Dukes of see Douglas

Rae, Rev. James, 65n91
Rae, James, surgeon, 286, 287
Raith, Lord see Alexander Melville
Ramsay, Allan, poet, 264, 431n123
Ramsay, Andrew, 306
Ramsay, George, 383
Ramsay, Henry 379, 383, 452
Ramsay, Rev. James, 65, 65n91, 67n104
Ramsay, John of Ochtertyre, 238, 241–2
Ramsay, Professor Robert of Edinburgh, 306
Ramsay, Regent and Principal Robert, 373,
    379, 382, 391, 392, 394, 413, 419,
    422

Ray, John, 275
Reid, Thomas, 23, 151, 154, 156–8, 166,
    167, 191, 193, 194, 201, 339, 442,
    481, 546
Reland, Henri, 56
Richardson, William, 161, 163, 164, 165,
    166, 188, 191, 195, 198, 199, 201
Ritchie, David, 199–200, 331
Robertson, Dr ___, 350
Robertson, James, 245
Robertson William, student, 69–70, 85
Robertson, Principal William
    Biographical, 10, 113, 181, 235, 236, 344,
        372, 453, 466, 473, 491, 594
    Politically active at Edinburgh 258, 262,
        278, 301, 305, 307, 308, 332, 336,
        345, 348
    At Glasgow 168, 169, 343
    At St Andrews, 477, 479, 492
Robertson, William, advocate, 266
Robison, John, 159, 164, 168, 329, 348–9,
    481, 501
Rockingham see Watson-Wentworth
Ross, George, Master of Ross and 13th Baron,
    72, 84, 85, 87, 88, 89, 93, 95, 110
Ross, William 12th Baron, 52
Ross, Andrew, 52, 54, 60, 66, 67, 52n26,
    89, 92, 96, 97, 100, 109, 110, 111,
    112, 129, 395
Ross, Professor George, 97, 129
Ross, John, 470
Rossal, Michael, 256
Rotherham, John, 301, 329, 499–502, 506,
    507, 511
Rothes, Earls of see Leslie
Rouet, William, 122, 125, 127, 129, 130,
    133, 134, 135, 136, 139, 140, 151,
    152, 155, 163, 470, 530, 533
Rousseau, J.-J., 162n49
Rowe, John, 214, 336, 380, 395
Roxburghe, Duke of see Ker
Roy, Niel, 347
Roy, William, 347
Ruddiman, Thomas, 254, 417
Rule, Alexander, 244
Rule, Gilbert, 34, 215, 218n20, 220, 221,
    225, 244, 255
Rule, Bailie, 225
Russel or Russell, James, I, professor and
    surgeon, 262, 300, 342, 343, 344,
    345, 347, 470
Russell, James, II, 287
Rutherford, Dr ?Daniel, 303
Rutherford, Daniel, 279, 301,?303, 307, 546
Rutherford, John, 278, 280, 290, 292, 302,
    303, 305, 418–19
Ruthven, David, 2nd Baron Ruthven, 222,
    218n20
Rymer, Rev. Henry, 374n20, 376n30
Rymer, Henry,regent, 388, 389, 391, 394,
    452, 460, 462, 463, 464, 466
Rymer, Rev. James, 374n20

Sanders, William,391, 442n7, 443
Sandilands, Walter, 6th Earl of Torpichen, 65n91, 67n104
Sandwich, Earl of see Montagu
Scarborough, Sir Charles, 216
Scot, David of Scotstarvit, I, 253
Scot, David of Scotstarvit, II, 162, 475, 478
Scot, Mrs of Scotstarvit, 494
Scott, George, 335n52
Scott, Henry, 3rd Duke of Buccleuch and 5th Duke of Queensberry, 152, 178, 179, 198
Scott, James, 1st Duke, Buccleuch, 335
Scott, James, diplomat, 335n52
Scott, John, 67
Scott, Sir Walter, 350
Scott, Willliam, I, 254, 260, 335ns52 and 55, 336, 338, 339
Scott, William, II, 335
Scott or Scot, General William, 162
Scougal, Sir James, 216
Scrymgeor, Alexander, 370, 378, 381, 383, 388, 394, 412, 413–14, 416, 422, 424, 426, 428, 443, 528
Scrymgeour, David, 424–5
Selkirk, Earls of see Douglas
Seton, Sir Alexander, Lord Pitmedden, 216
Seton, George, 4th Earl of Winton, 28
Shaw, Andrew, 429, 462, 463, 466
Shaw, Charles, 9th Baron Cathcart, 160, 163, 166, 430
Shaw, Margaret, 466
Shelburne, Earl of see Petty
Short, James, 444, 481, 482
Sibbland, Patrick, 527
Sibbald, Sir Robert, 30, 32, 35, 223n32, 273, 275, 282, 325, 326, 446
Simson, James, 473
Simson, John, 33, 52–3, 60, 67, 68, 92, 95, 97, 98, 233, 234, 237, 239, 293, 408, 414, 427, 428, 446, 482, 483, 528
Simson, Patrick, 33
Simson, Robert, 56, 63, 66, 72, 92, 95, 97, 99, 100, 109, 110, 111, 115, 122, 123, 126, 127, 130, 135, 136, 137, 154, 201, 327, 395, 418, 447, 474, 545
Simson, Thomas, 418, 451, 460, 462
Sinclair or St Clair, Andrew, 290, 292, 302, 304
Sinclair, George, 28, 32, 33, 35, 442
Sinclair, Sir John, MP, 19
Sinclair, Rev. John, 65n91, 67n104
Sinclair, Patrick, 33, 53, 244
St Clare, Sir Robert, 110
Sir Robert Sinclair of Stevenson, 27n9, 110n15
Sinclair, Robert, 35–6, 51, 55, 60, 214n7, 283
Skene, David, 158, 278n30, 546
Sloane, Sir Hans, 211n1, 275, 445
Small, Rev. Dr Robert, 497n25, 500–1

Smellie, William, 307, 308
Smith, Adam, 10, 123, 130, 138, 140, 153, 155, 157, 178, 194, 198, 201, 258, 261, 339, 342, 349, 470, 477, 542
Smith, James, 65n91, 71, 91 95, 96, 416n45
Smith, Principal James, 234, 236, 238
Smith, John, 69
Smith, Robert, 299
Smith, William, 124
Smollett, James, 27
Smyth, James Carmichael, 158
Southampton, Barons of see Fitzroy
Spencer, Charles, 3rd Earl of Sunderland, 7, 48, 55, 73
Spencer, John George, 2nd Earl of, 287
Spens, Henry, 155, 480, 484
Spens or Spence, Robert, 155–6
Spittal, Alexander, 27
Spottiswoode, John, 255
St John, Henry, 1st Viscount Bolingbroke
Stair, Viscounts, Earls, and Master of see Dalrymple
Stanhope, Philip Dormer, 4th Earl of, 345, 347
Stark, Daniel, 386
Stark, William, 158
Stedman, Rev. John, 110, 111
Stedman, John, MD, 328
Steuart, Sir James of Goodtrees, 33, 36, 50, 60n64, 335, 337, 411
Steuart (Steuart-Denham) Sir James, 117, 242
Stewart, Alexander, 6th Earl of Galloway, 123, 127
Stevenson, Alexander, 158–9, 163, 166, 186
Stevenson, Archibald, MD, 216n15
Stevenson, Professor Archibald, MD, 158–9, 163, 166, 184, 186
Stevenson, John, 163, 338
Stewart, Dugald, 190, 328, 332, 339, 346, 501
Stewart, James, MD, 418
Stewart, James, Lord Provost of Edinburgh, 305
Stewart, Professor John at Marischal College, 524, 545
Stewart, Professor John at Edinburgh, 346–7
Stewart, Matthew, 136, 327, 328, 474, 538, 545
Stewart, Robert, 336, 337, 338, 346, 532
Stewart, Walter of Pardovan, 57, 65n91
Stirling, Sir James, Lord Provost of Edinburgh, 302, 501
Stirling, James of Keir, 328
Stirling, ?James, of Craiglarnet, 504
Stirling, Principal John, 32, 36–7, 49–73, 84, 85, 86, 88, 89, 94, 395, 416n45
Stoddart, James, 304, 339
Stormont, Viscounts of see Murray
Strahan, John, 220–1
Strahan, William, 168
Strathmore, Earl of see Lyon
Stuart, 3rd or 4th Baron Blantyre, 31

Stuart, Charles, 417, 427, 431
Stuart, George, 162, 254, 345, 478
Stuart, Gilbert, 258, 528
Stuart, James Francis Edward, The Old
    Pretender, 7n14, 48
Stuart, James MD, 418
Stuart, James, Lord Provost of Edinburgh,
    236, 242
Stuart, John, 3rd Earl of Bute
    Biographical and general, 8, 9, 10, 131,
        150, 180, 213, 351, 534, 536, 539
    Active at Edinburgh, 236, 242, 277, 303,
        305, 343, 344, 349
    Active at Glasgow, 151, 152, 154, 155,
        156, 161, 169, 180
    Active at St Andrews, 459, 533
Stuart Mackenzie, James
    Biographical and general, 8, 10, 150, 156,
        157, 169, 156n30, 539
    Active at Edinburgh, 213, 265, 278, 305,
        344, 533, 536
    At St Andrews, 459, 469, 474
Suffolk, Earl of *see* Howard
Sunderland, Earl of *see* Spencer
Sutherland, James, 214, 273–4, 275, 546
Swinton, Sir Alexander, 218n20
Syme, John, 392, 406, 409, 410, 412

Tailzour or Tailor and other variants, James,
    379
Tailzour or Tailor, Thomas, 379–80, 384, 388
Tarbat, Viscount of *see* Mackenzie
Tarrit, Major ____ of Tarrit, 416n45
Taylor, Helen, 378
Taylor, Rev. William, 183, 193, 199–200
Temple, Earl *see* Grenville
Thomas Hardy, 242
Thompson, Dr___, 329
Thomson, James, 431n123
Thomson (?Dr John), 287
Thomson, Thomas, 505
Torpichen, Earl of *see* Sandilands
Tournefort, Joseph Pitton de, 275, 326n5,
    445
Towers, James, 187
Townshend, Charles, 2nd Viscount
    Townshend, 7, 48
Townshend, Charles, MP, 152, 466
Trail, Robert, minister at London, 36n55
Trail, Robert, 153, 157, 166, 168
Tran, John, 28, 31, 32, 33, 35, 36n55,
    28n14, 223
Trembley, Abraham, 546
Trotter, John, 495–8, 504, 505
Tullibardine, Marquis of *see* Murray
Tullideph, Thomas, 428–32, 460–6 *passim*,
    470, 473, 474, 477, 478, 480, 513,
    544, 591
Tullideph, William, 374n20, 376n30, 377–8,
    380, 385, 394, 408
Turgot, Anne Marie Robert, Baron d'Aulne,
    162

Turnbull, Professor George, 335, 426
Tweeddale, Marquis of *see* Hay
Tytler, Alexander Fraser, 258, 259
Tytler, Patrick, 258
Tytler, William Fraser, 258, 259

Verner or Warner, David, 96, 425–6
Vilant, Alexander, 471, 472
Vilant, Colin, I, 370, 384–5, 388, 389
Vilant, Nicholas, 192, 328, 329, 330, 474,
    484, 493, 499, 502, 504, 507
Vilant or Violant, William, 27n9, 376–7,
    384, 394, 406
Vilant, William, II, 382, 384, 452, 462, 465,
    475

Waddell, Richard, 415
Walker, James, 472
Walker, John, 307, 308, 309, 532, 544
Walker, Rev. Robert, 242, 350
Walker, Robert, MD, 472
Wallace, Robert, 241, 265, 326, 341, 429,
    452, 453
Wallace, George, 265
Wallace, Sir Thomas, 162
Wallace, William, 257–8, 259, 265
Walpole, Sir Robert 1st Earl of Orford, 7,
    48, 86, 98, 108, 293, 341, 427, 430,
    473
Wark, David, 136
Warner, David *see* Verner
Warrender, Sir George, 423
Warrender, Hugh, 423, 429, 484
Watson, Robert, 10, 113, 349, 451, 466–7,
    470, 480, 484
Watson-Wentworth, Charles, 2nd Marquis
    of Rockingham, 179
Watt, Adam, Edinburgh Town Clerk,
    253
Watt, Adam, 253
Watt, James, 124, 134
Webster, Alexander, 341
Weems, Sir John of Bogie, 416n45
Weymss, David, 6th Earl of Wemyss, 378
Whytt, Robert, 302, 304, 342, 477
Wight, Alexander, 265
Wight, William, 156, 160 162, 164, 166,
    167, 168, 169, 170, 181, 345, 346,
    348, 470, 477, 530
Wightman, John, Lord Provost of
    Edinburgh, 285
Wilkie, William, 10, 137, 138, 469–71, 477,
    480, 481, 482, 484
William III, 29, 30, 33, 46, 231
Williamson, David, 36n55
Williamson, James, 136, 140, 154, 162, 163,
    164, 166, 185, 327, 328, 348
Wilson, Charles, 492, 494, 496–8, 504
Wilson, Alexander, 135–41, 165, 166, 168,
    183, 343, 507, 545, 546
Wilson, Patrick, 183, 190, 191, 194–7, 329,
    546

Wilson, Walter, 460, 461, 462, 463, 464, 471
Winton, Earl of see Seton
Wishart, George, 241, 344
Wishart, Principal William, I, 84, 233, 244
Wishart, Principal William, II, 68, 89, 95, 97, 235, 241, 254, 528, 544
Witherspoon, John, 483
Wodrow, Alexander, 51–2, 96
Wodrow, James, I, 30–1, 33, 36, 51, 96
Whiston, William, 442
Wodrow, James, II, 128
Wodrow, John, MD, 72n138, 108, 125, 134
Wodrow, Robert, 31, 32, 36, 69, 73, 85, 87, 91, 96, 97, 337, 415, 424, 446
Wood, Robert, 416–17, 418
Wood, William, 472

Wright, ___, Laird of Foodie, 475
Wright, Peter, 475
Wright, Willliam, 348
Wylde, Wyld or Wilde, John, 264
Wilie or Wylie, Robert, 36n55

Yeaman or Yeoman,___, 217, 219
Yeaman or Yeoman, John, 218
Young, David, 391, 420, 444, 452, 461, 462, 463, 464, 465, 481
Young, John of Edinburgh, 214
Young, John of St Andrews, 420, 452, 462, 469, 470, 471, 481
Young, John, of Glasgow 167, 190–1
Young, Ninian, 370, 388, 451, 462, 464
Young, Thomas of Edinburgh, 299
Young, Thomas of Glasgow, 157
Young, Provost William, 379, 388, 419, 420, 451

INDEX OF SUBJECTS

Author's note: Listings of the chairs have marked the regius chairs with an 'R' and those with private patrons with a 'P'. Those filled by the Town Council of Edinburgh from leets supplied by lawyers have been marked TCL. All others were legally in the gift of the universities, colleges or of the Town Council of Edinburgh including the civil history chair at its first foundation. Other places were sometimes held by teachers (T) who *seem* not to have been lecturers.

Aberdeen Universities
  General, 4, 223, 450, 531
  Kings College and University, 4, 6, 7, 11,
      15n9, 26, 92, 116, 118, 157, 180,
      253, 293, 369, 370, 371, 393, 396,
      413, 416, 443, 470, 526, 527, 531,
      532, 534, 593
  Marischal College and University, 4, 6n9, 7,
      93, 180, 237, 293, 369, 370, 416,
      425–6, 443, 451, 470, 477, 525,
      526, 527, 528, 533, 534, 593
  Union of the Universities and Colleges, 450
Académie royale des sciences (Paris), 275, 326,
      548
Académie Impériale des Sciences de Saint
      Pétersbourg, 349
Academies of fencing, riding, dancing, 185,
      236n24
Act of Union [1707] and the universities, 46,
      212, 255, 335, 389, 391, 392, 407,
      410
Andersonian Institution [now the University of
      Strathclyde], 200, 201, 475, 531
Agriculture, lectures on and chairs of, 8, 121
Arabic teaching, 56, 245, 246, 461, 529, 548,
      592
Archbishops' and Bishop's rights as
      chancellors at Glasgow, St
      Andrews and Aberdeen, 21, 27,
      89, 92–4, 93n48, 368, 371, 374
Argathelians
  General, 7, 7n11, 27, 45, 46–8, 52–4,
      70n123, 89, 100, 212, 233, 283,
      293; *see also* Andrew Fletcher,
      Lord Milton and Archibald
      Campbell, 3rd Duke of Argyll
  Active at Aberdeen, 525, 531
  Active at Edinburgh, 212, 233, 234–6, 238,
      240–2, 244, 245, 253, 256, 278,
      283, 284–5, 288, 292–8, 303, 326,
      327, 340, 344
  Active at Glasgow, 44, 46, 48, 49, 62, 64,
      66, 67, 68, 69, 73, 85, 88, 89, 92,

      93, 95, 98–100, 235
St Andrews, 369, 424, 426, 449, 451, 465,
      468, 469, 470, 473
Avisamentum, 332, 341, 526–7
Ayr Bank (Douglas, Heron and Co.), 178

Board of Trustees for Fisheries and
      Manufactures, 121n63, 278; *see
      also* William Cullen, Francis Home
      and Joseph Black
Botanical Gardens, 50, 273–4, 276, 277, 278,
      326; *see also* chairs of botany and
      John Wodrow

Cambuslang 'Wark' or revival, 91, 96, 109–10,
      112; *see also* High Flyers
Clubs and societies in Scotland
  Aberdeen Philosophical Society, 546
  Chemical Society of Glasgow, 191
  Edinburgh Musical Society, 132n109, 299
  Edinburgh Seed Society, 277
  The Edinburgh Society for Improving Arts
      and Sciences *see* Select Society
  Feast of the Tabernacles, 178
  Glasgow Literary Society, 129, 183, 546
  The Honourable the Improvers in the
      Knowledge of Agriculture in
      Scotland, 276
  Mirror and Lounger clubs, 166, 178
  Medical Society of Edinburgh, 299
  Philosophical Society of Edinburgh, 121,
      129, 132n109, 157, 277, 291,
      299, 300n133, 317n118, 328,
      347, 348, 418, 470, 472, 479, 546
  Rankenian Club, 69ns107 and 117
  Revolution Society of Edinburgh, 299
  Royal and Ancient Golf Course, 420
  Royal Company of Archers, 132n109
  Royal Medical Society, 132n109, 185
  Royal Society of Edinburgh, 308 [all
      professors were offered
      membership in this in 1783]
  St Andrews Philosophical Society, 509

Select Society of Edinburgh, 132n109, 470
Society for Collecting Scots poems
    [Edinburgh], 431n123
Scottish Society for the Propagation of
    Christian Knowledge, 473
Society of the Antiquaries of Scotland, 185,
    308
Sophocardian Club, 68
Speculative Society, 178, 339
Trianphorian Society, 68, 69
Wernerian Society of Edinburgh, 348
Comparative trials for appointing professors
Glasgow, 27, 50–1, 97
Edinburgh, 223, 226, 243, 244, 252, 253,
    254, 336–8, 339
St Andrews, 376, 383, 385, 386, 418, 452,
    460, 404, 494
Court Party, 44, 45
Court of Sessions and other civil courts
    involved with university patronage
General, 13, 24, 94, 116, 525, 531
Glasgow, 66–7, 88, 93–4, 111n19, 155,
    168, 189
St Andrews, 383n64, 388, 389, 462, 463,
    465, 469, 471, 494, 502, 506–7
Crown's roles in the universities, 6, 12,13,
    25n4, 29, 30, 32, 54, 56, 57, 59,
    71, 93, 94, 101n48, 114, 139, 155,
    186, 195–6, 260, 263, 274, 276,
    279, 370, 374; see also Visitations,
    Archbishops etc., and the regius
    chairs listed under the universities
Curriculum
Arts, 32, 34n43, 52, 63n96, 86, 93n73, 156,
    232, 338, 339, 378n44, 379, 387,
    388, 441n3, 442–3, 443, 446, 477,
    480–2, 542–3, 545, 547–8; see also
    Glasgow Visitations 1717 and
    1726
Divinity, 31n28, 56, 156, 482–3, 520–30
Law, 199, 255, 262
Medicine, 282n56, 296n116, 546, 548

Ecclesiastical history teaching, 131, 243, 421;
    see also the chairs of ecclesiastical
    history
Economic benefits from the Universities, 211,
    273, 285, 301, 302, 305, 349,
    352–3, 371, 532–3
Edinburgh Hospitals, 29, 282, 290, 287, 290,
    299
Edinburgh Town Council
General, 12n21, 13, 14, 226, 233, 246, 259,
    293, 341, 359–2, 591
Elections, 213, 293–5, 525
Activities 1690–1715, 212, 213–15, 216,
    218, 222, 223, 226, 233, 235, 237,
    238, 260, 263, 274, 275, 279,
    280, 281, 282, 283, 288, 325, 334,
    336, 337, 352,532, 533
1716–1722, 240, 256, 278, 281, 284
1722–1742, 234, 245, 254, 281, 285, 289,

293, 294, 295, 297, 340, 346–7,
    352
1743–1747, 263–4, 336n60, 341, 342,
    346–7
1747–1761, 277, 285, 301, 342, 343
1761–1779, 236, 238, 301, 303, 306, 307,
    339, 345, 348, 350
1780–1806, 301, 305, 328, 330–2, 334,
    501, 533
Edinburgh University
General, 32, 184
Chairs fixed, 232, 338
Chairs of
    Agriculture, P, 278, 309
    Anatomy, 279–86
    Astronomy, R, 197, 334
    Botany, R after 1768, 214, 273–9, 282,
        546
    Chemistry and Medicine, 278, 283,
        288–90, 291, 296–7, 298, 300–2
    Civil Law, TCL, 232, 263
    Clinical Surgery, R, 287
    Divinity, 211, 225, 234, 236–43
    Ecclesiastical History, R, 232, 239–43
    Greek, 260, 334–6, 386
    Hebrew and Oriental Languages, 243–6
    History, TCL, 232, 255–60
    Humanity, P, 162, 223, 252–5, 340
    Institutes [theory] of Medicine, 289–98,
        302–4
    Logic and Metaphysics, 39–40, 338
    Materia Medica, 277, 278
    Mathematics, 218, 223, 325–34
    Medicine [1724–26], 223n32, 282, 289,
        290
    Midwifery, 298
    Military Surgery, R, 287
    Moral Philosophy, 164, 182, 338, 339–46
    Natural History, R, 306–9
    Natural Philosophy, 159, 166, 329, 330,
        337, 338, 343, 344, 346–9
    Practice of Medicine, 278, 289–98, 303,
        304–6
    Principalship, 152, 223, 225, 231–6, 344
    Public Law or Law of Nature and
        Nations, R, 232, 260–3, 335, 342,
        344
    Regencies, 223, 232, 252, 336–8, 380
    Rhetoric, R, 342, 349–50, 466
    Scots Law, TCL, 232, 264–6
    Surgery, 286, 287
Faculty of Medicine, 297, 298, 303
Libraries, 337n70, 508
Professors, 244, 254, 274, 278, 288, 300,
    301, 305
Revolution Settlement, 213–25
Rivalry with Glasgow, 60n65, 281, 283,
    288–9, 288n74
Senatus, 298, 299, 339
Students, 245
Teachers of French, 498
Visitations of, 213–26

Enlightenments
  European, 3, 445, 546, 547
  French, 14n1
  Scottish, 3–4, 26, 140, 180, 201–2, 491,
    509n95, 510, 544, 547, 548, 535
Established Church of Scotland ['The Kirk']
  General, 6, 8, 25, 37, 45, 46, 48, 49, 53, 69,
    71, 87, 90, 92, 93, 97, 98, 113, 377,
    410, 424, 509–10, 526–30, 543
  General Assembly, 112, 231, 233, 235, 332,
    333, 381, 408, 429, 453, 460, 464,
    465, 469, 474, 492, 493, 528
  Managers of, 225, 233, 236, 237, 240–2,
    330, 383, 408, 491, 511; *see also*
    the Moderators involved with the
    universities. They include, in the
    order of their first holding the
    place; Hugh Kennedy (1690), John
    Law, Patrick Simson, George
    Meldrum, George Hamilton (1699,
    William Carstares, William
    Wishart, John Stirling, William
    Mitchell (1710), William Hamilton
    (1720), Thomas Black, James
    Smith (1731), James Alston, Neil
    Campbell, John Gowdie, James
    Ramsay, George Logan (1740),
    Thomas Tullideph, Robert Wallace,
    William Wishart, II, John Lumsden,
    George Wishart, Patrick Cuming
    (1749), Alexander Webster, Robert
    Hamilton (1760), William
    Leechman, John Hyndman, Robert
    Trail, William Robertson,
    Alexander Gerard, James Oswald,
    James Murison, James Macknight,
    Alexander Carlyle (1770), Robert
    Walker, John Drysdale, James
    Gillespie, Harry Spens (1780),
    Joseph M'Cormick, Henry Grieve,
    Archibald Davidson, George Hill,
    John Walker (1790), Robert Small,
    Andrew Hunter, Thomas Hardy,
    Robert Arnot, William Greenfield,
    John Adamson, William Taylor,
    William Moodie, George Husband
    Baird (1800), James Finlayson
    (1802); *see also* professors of
    divinity and ecclesiastical history
  Presbyteries and ministers
    Edinburgh, 218, 237, 243, 244, 245, 252,
      331, 332, 337
    Glasgow, 25, 54, 73, 98, 112, 128
    St Andrews, 368, 384, 388, 389, 393, 407,
      408, 413, 424, 427, 464, 467, 468
    Others, 112, 410, 467
  Synods, 119, 332, 412, 413
Evangelicals *see* 'High Flyers'

Faculty of Advocates, 13, 253, 257, 258, 259,
    264; *see also* the law chairs at
    Edinburgh and Glasgow

Faculty of Physicians and Surgeons, Glasgow
  [later the Royal College of
  Physicians and Surgeons,
  Glasgow], 289, 475, 476, 531
Fifteen ['The '15'], 7, 414–16, 420, 450
Foulis Brothers' [James and Robert]
  Academy, 162
  Press, 56, 115, 135, 166
Forty-Five ['The '45'], 115, 117, 118
French Revolution, 171, 188, 189, 193, 201,
    236, 242, 243, 246, 264, 330

Glasgow Hospitals
  Royal Asylum, 185, 475
  Town Hospital and Infirmary and the Royal
    infirmary, 120, 185, 187, 475
Glasgow Town Council and Burgh, 117, 125,
    151
  Elections, 61, 66, 73, 83n143, 98, 101n29,
    107
Glasgow University, 7, 21, 23, 24, 27, 32
  Chancellor, 21, 22, 24, 26, 27, 29, 60, 66,
    195–6; *see also* Archbishop's rights
  Dean of Faculties, 22–3, 24, 25, 26, 62, 66
  Library, 37, 93, 95n66, 169, 417, 448, 508
  Rector, 21, 22, 24, 26, 62–9, 85, 87–9,
    92–5, 99, 180
  Rector's Assessors, 22, 66
  Revolution Settlement, 27
  Senatus, 23, 24
  Snell Exhibitioners, 86
  Vice Chancellor, 21, 88, 93
  Vice Rector, 23, 99
  Visitations and Visitors, 17, 22, 64–7, 70,
    200, 237
Glasgow College, 24, 51
  College Meeting, 23, 24
  Chairs fixed, 66n96, 86
  Chairs of
    Anatomy, T, 58, 94, 96
    Astronomy *see* Practical Astronomy
    Botany, L\T, 120, 307n186
    Botany and Anatomy, R, 49–50, 72–3, 86,
      94, 107, 120, 132–4, 170–1, 184,
      186–7, 281, 309n186
    Chemistry, L, 120, 132, 157, 159, 184,
      187
    Civil History, L, 32, 49, 156
    Divinity, 23, 24, 28, 30–1, 51, 52, 53, 98,
      99, 100, 108–13, 153, 168–70,
      181–3
    Ecclesiastical history, R, 70–2, 113, 124,
      125, 155–6, 164, 170, 176n68,
      192–3, 343
    French and Italian, T, 154, 193, 197, 498
    Greek, 32, 49, 50, 115, 164, 167–8
    Humanity, 31, 32, 52, 129–30, 162–6
    Law, R, 25, 49, 57, 86, 116–19, 123,
      154–5, 198–9
    Lectureships, 23
    Logic and Metaphysics, 127, 168, 341
    Materia Medica, L, 160, 184, 187

Glasgow College (*cont.*)
    Mathematics, 32, 56, 154, 185, 288
    Medicine, R, 35, 49, 58–9, 86, 119, 121,
        132–4, 157–9, 186, 187–9
    Midwifery, L, 187
    Moral Philosophy, 96–7, 119, 127,
        156–7, 171, 193–4
    Natural History, L\R (1806), 24, 201
    Natural Philosophy, 86, 134–8, 189–92,
        200
    Oriental Languages, 28, 29, 31, 32, 49,
        51, 54–5, 113–14, 122, 125,
        129–31,134, 137, 152–4
    Practical Astronomy, R, 138–40, 194–8,
        200–1, 334
    Principal, R, 21–3, 28–30, 36–7, 66, 90,
        151–3, 172n4, 183–4, 199–200,
        227
    Regents, 23, 28, 31–2, 37, 57, 59, 86

Hebrew instruction in 18th-century Scotland,
        131, 421, 492; *see also* chairs of
        oriental languages and Hebrew
High-flyers and Evangelicals, 48n5, 49, 66n92,
        97, 100n92, 109, 110, 112, 113,
        115, 181, 234, 235, 239, 246, 329,
        331, 332, 333, 424, 468, 480, 509,
        510, 524, 540n27, 544
Highlands, 7, 47, 115, 535, 544

Incomes of professors, 13–14, 257, 254n10,
        453, 525, 591–618
Incorporation of Surgeons *see* Royal College
        of Surgeons, Edinburgh
Inveraray Castle, 108, 121

Jacobites and Episcopalians, 7n14, 30, 43,
        44, 45, 47, 48, 118, 292, 413,
        535
    At Aberdeen, 256, 528
    At Edinburgh, 214, 219, 220, 223, 276,
        326
    At St Andrews, 256, 369, 370, 374, 386,
        387, 388, 389, 392, 396, 413, 414,
        415, 416, 445, 449

Lying-in Hospitals
    Edinburgh, 299
    Glasgow, 187

Malt Tax Riots, 7, 70, 73, 86; *see also* 3rd
        Duke of Argyll (1725)
Masters, 12n21, 21, 22, 66
Medical School at Surgeons' Hall, Edinburgh
        see Royal College of Surgeons
Minister of Glasgow, 23, 26
Moderatism and the Moderate Party
    General, 8, 9, 11, 150n2, 421n74, 496,
        508–10, 528, 530, 543–4
    At Edinburgh 213, 234, 235, 238, 240, 242,
        243, 246, 308, 334, 350, 408,
        466, 483

At Glasgow 109, 112, 113, 115, 150–1,
        155, 156, 161–3, 168, 169, 150n2,
        181, 182, 184
At St Andrews, 372, 408, 428, 429, 453,
        466,473, 474, 477, 479, 480, 491,
        492, 496, 497, 500, 503, 508–10
Montgomery Plot, 30
Museums
    Edinburgh's Balfourian, 279, 306, 325n2
    Glasgow's Hunterian, 169
    St Andrews, 445; *see also* St Andrews
        Library

Nepotism
    General, 532
    Edinburgh, 239, 262, 336
    Glasgow, 52, 53, 56, 58, 59, 70, 71–2
    King's College, 6
    Marischal College, 477
    St Andrews, 6, 395, 452, 459, 460, 477,
        492, 493, 498, 502, 505, 507
Newtonianism, 325, 442, 443, 444, 543, 545
The Netherlands, 225n35, 29–30, 32, 35, 36,
        53n30, 56, 57, 58, 225n35, 231–2,
        342, 518, 542, 543, 547, 548

Oxbridge, 549
Observatories
    Edinburgh, 328, 334
    Glasgow, 134, 135, 200, 201
    St Andrews, 443, 444, 481

Parisian *philosophes* and the professors, 161,
        162; *see also* J.-J. Rousseau and
        Baron Turgot
Parliaments
    Scottish, 215
    British: House of Lords, 93, 94, 116; House
        of Commons, 69
Patronage
    Kinds of: *De facto*, 12, 13; legal, 12, 13,
        6n9, 523, 524; private, 12, 25; *see*
        chair of agriculture and Kennedy
        and Scot families at St Andrews
    Importance of, 528–30, 548
    Patrons and Managers of patronage, 5–11,
        43–9, 536–41; *see also* Carstares
        (c.1700), Earl of Mar, 3rd Duke of
        Argyll, 1st Duke of Montrose,
        Duke of Roxburghe, Charles
        Erskine, Marquis of Tweeddale,
        Lord Milton, Patrick Cuming, Earl
        of Bute, James Stuart Mackenzie,
        William Mure of Caldwell,
        William Robertson, Henry
        Dundas, George Hill c.1800); *see*
        also Established Church-
        Moderators
    Processes of, 523–35
    Professional men involved with
        Clerics *see* Established Church of
            Scotland – managers and

moderators, professors of divinity
and ecclesiastical history, and
avisamentum
Lawyers, 212, 524, 525, 539
Medics, 212, 524–5, 530–1
Professors, 531–2
Regimes of 537–41
Persian teaching, 56, 245, 246, 461, 529, 548,
592
Political activities of professors; *see also*
patronage
General, 533
Edinburgh, 30, 231, 261, 274, 299, 531, 542
Glasgow, 29, 30, 37n62, 42n62, 49, 56, 72,
88n20, 90, 91, 99, 100, 118
St Andrews, 411, 420, 471–2
Politics and appointments, 4–11, 43–9, 353,
548–9
Professors; *see also* virtuosi
characteristics of appointees, 541–4
consultants and improvers, 30, 121, 135,
141, 158, 185, 187,189n36, 278,
279, 282–3, 296n116, 300, 304–5,
306n172, 307, 309, 329, 337,
349, 470, 473, 478, 479 524, 532,
546
recruitment of, 525, 541n29
remuneration of, 13–14, 51, 243, 94,
591–618 *passim*

Revolution Settlement in the universities, 26,
27, 213–26, 449, 534, 542, 544,
545
Royal College of Physicians, Edinburgh, 13,
281, 282, 288, 289, 293, 297, 299,
380, 416, 418, 530–1
Royal College of Surgeons, Edinburgh, 13,
159, 274, 275, 277, 279–80, 281,
282, 283, 286, 293; Surgeons' Hall
Medical Teachers, 41, 280,
282n56, 279–81, 286, 287, 291,
531
Royal Infirmary and other Edinburgh
hospitals, 282, 287, 290
Royal Military College, 475, 500, 506; *see also*
Charles Hutton

St Andrews
Archbishops of, 368, 371, 372; *see also*
Archbishops' rights
Burgh, 368–70, 450
Colleges, 26
Fixed chairs, 444n19
Private patrons
Kennedys of Cassilis, 8, 370, 381, 451,
465, 471, 474, 502, 503
Scots of Scotstarvit, 370, 381, 384,
388, 451, 470, 494
St Leonard's College to 1747, 11, 370,
374, 376, 415, 432, 448–9, 451
French teachers, 442, 498
Professor of Greek, 387–8, 442

Humanist, P, 374, 381, 384–5, 385–6,
388, 441
Principal, R, 372, 373, 377, 379, 383,
384, 391, 410, 429, 430, 459, 479
Regents, 379–81, 384–5, 386, 388–91,
420
St Mary's College, 11, 370, 372, 374,
406–14, 421–32, 449, 450–1
Principal, R, 372, 373, 376, 382, 406,
407, 408, 421, 430, 462
Professor of Divinity, R, 11, 233, 372,
383, 407–13, 421, 428, 429, 480,
482–3, 492, 493, 497
Professor of Hebrew and Oriental
languages, R, 11, 244, 370–1,
406–8, 409, 413, 421–2, 429, 460,
483, 492, 495–8, 505
Professor of Ecclesiastical History, R,
11, 370–1, 372, 409, 410, 411,
413, 419, 421–2, 424–7, 467–70,
483, 495–8, 505
Clerics trained, 447
St Salvator's College, 11, 370, 372, 374,
376, 415, 448–9
Humanist, P, 374, 381, 382, 441, 475,
493
Professor of Greek, 382, 388, 419, 442,
475
Provost, R, 372, 373, 377, 379, 382,
419, 479
Regents, 378–9, 381, 382, 383, 419,
420
United College of St Salvator and St
Leonard in the University of St
Andrews [1747–], 451
Instruments, 481
Professors and Lecturers (L), 452,
466n19
Civil History, 374, 451, 464, 466,
466n19, 471–2, 474, 477, 497,
502–4
French, L, 498
Greek, 460, 466, 477, 492–4
Humanity, P, 162, 163, 374, 451,
466, 475, 478, 494
Logic, Rhetoric and Metaphysics,
452, 466, 479, 481, 507
Ethics and Pneumaticks, 452, 478, 481
Mathematics, R, 451, 474–5, 482
Medicine, 371, 374, 451, 472–3,
475, 476, 506–7
Natural and Experimental
Philosophy, 138, 194, 197, 329,
330, 452, 469–71, 474, 477,
498–502, 505–6
Principal, R, 372, 373, 451, 462,
492, 504–5
Natural and civil history at St Andrews
before 1747, 445–6
University of
General, 6, 8, 367–70, 371, 395–7,
449–50, 480–513

University of (cont.)
    Crisis years, 448–51
    Chancellor, 93, 94, 180, 371–2, 373, 419,
        448–9, 453, 467, 473, 476, 479,
        492–3, 494, 495, 510; see also
        Archbishops' rights
    Deans of Faculties, 373, 379, 461, 462
    Degrees
        honorary, 452, 483
        medical, 417–18
    Enrolments, 370, 447
    Factor, 471–2
    French teachers in, 442, 498
    Instrument collections at, 443, 445, 464,
        481, 507n82; Meridian line fixed,
        481
    Libraries, 373, 443–6, 447–8, 481,
        483–4, 507–8
    Observatory see Observatories
    Professors
        General, 370, 373–4, 388, 389, 391–4,
            395, 419, 420, 467
        of Mathematics (to 1747), R, 389,
            391–4, 420
        of Medicine (to 1747), 373, 374,
            416–18
    Rector, 372–3, 379, 388, 415, 416, 420,
        428, 461, 462, 463, 464, 466, 469,
        498
    Rector's Assessors, 464
    Revolution settlement, 374–6
    Senatus, 371, 373, 388, 407, 462, 463,
        464
    Students, 368, 370, 414, 415, 450, 495
    Union of the Colleges, 373, 450–3
    Vice Chancellor, 371, 373, 379, 382,
        384
    Visitations of
        1690, 374–6, 377, 378, 379, 382, 388;
            1718, 414–16
Sales of university and college chairs, 29n17,
    96, 162, 167, 254, 262, 263, 264,
    307, 326, 342, 420, 452, 466, 472,
    475, 477, 478, 499
Scholasticism and its rejection, 32, 37,
    389n91, 446, 481–2, 545; see also
    Newtonianism and the
    universities' libraries
Society of Writers to the Signet, 13; see
    also chair of humanity at
    Edinburgh
The Squadrone; see also the Dukes of
    Montrose and Roxburghe, the
    Marquis of Tweeddale, Earl of
    Rothes, Robert Dundas, Andrew
    Mitchell, Thomas Hay
    General, 7n11, 8n15, 31, 73n143, 283, 341,
        424, 449, 537, 538
    Active at the Aberdeen Universities, 534
    Active at Edinburgh, 212, 233, 238, 239,
        240, 253, 256, 263, 264, 288, 292,
        293, 326, 327, 340, 351, 326

Active at Glasgow, 37, 44, 45, 47, 48, 49,
    53, 57, 60–1, 62, 63, 65, 66, 68,
    70, 72, 73, 84, 85, 88, 90, 92,
    93–4, 95, 98–100, 107–14, 115,
    116, 117, 118, 131, 178, 179
Active at St Andrews, 369, 380–1, 411, 421,
    422, 423, 424, 425, 429, 430, 431,
    451, 452, 459, 461, 466
Students
    Edinburgh, 245
    Glasgow, 85
    Student petitions to Parliament, 68–9, 96;
        Student riots and disturbances, 61,
        62, 63, 68
    St Andrews, 448, 450
    Student Fees and costs, 305n167, 352n144,
        592–4
    Numbers of, 211, 352n142, 533

Tories
    and Episcopalians, 44, 46–7, 231, 233, 473,
        524
    Tories c.1780–1806, 185, 193, 198, 242,
        287, 308, 333, 412, 499, 500, 501,
        508–13, 535

Universities and Scottish identity, 548

Virtuosi, 543; see also Sir Robert Sibbald,
    Archibald Pitcairne, James
    Sutherland, David Gregorie;
    William Dunlop, George Sinclair,
    George Martine of Claremont
    At Edinburgh, 224, 274, 275, 288, 325,
        337, 342
    At Glasgow, 28, 32, 36, 30 n22, 58, 224
    At St Andrews, 386n77, 445, 446
University Visitation Commissions, 27, 34
    Aberdeen, 7, 223, 534
    Edinburgh
        Royal and Parliamentary, 213–25, 237
        Town council, 215
    Glasgow, 24, 26–31, 34n44, 64–8, 70, 84–9,
        93
    St Andrews, 325, 374–7, 378, 387, 394,
        411–12, 416, 421, 424

Westminster Confession of Faith, 112, 221,
    222, 239, 298, 330, 332, 375, 389,
    483
Whigs
    General, 375, 535
    1688–1720, 33, 44, 382, 415, 420, 535
    Walpolean, 212, 341, 430, 524; see also
        Argathelians
    Foxite Whigs, 185, 188, 189, 190, 193,
        194, 198, 201, 304, 308, 330,
        332, 333, 475, 494, 499, 500, 501;
        see also Argathelians and
        Squadrone
Widows and Orphans Insurance Scheme,
    453